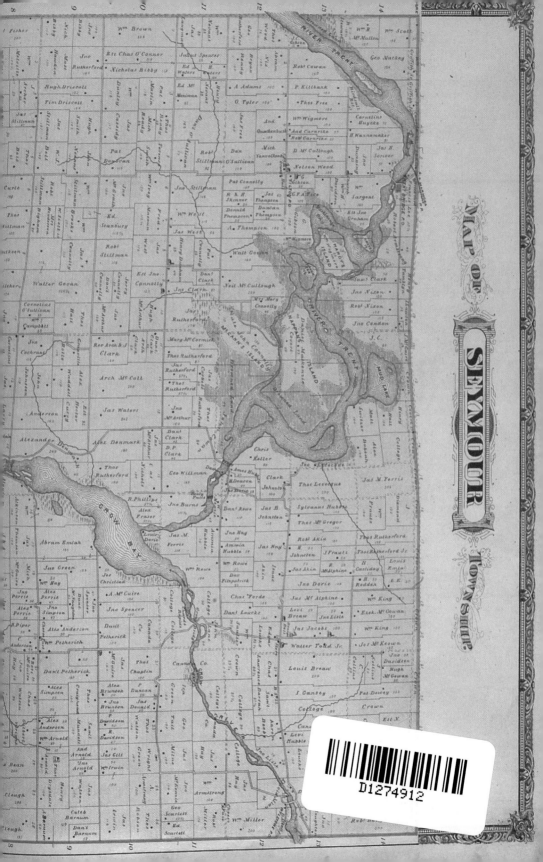

MAP OF SEYMOUR TOWNSHIP

GLEANINGS

A HISTORY OF

Campbellford/Seymour

MARGARET CROTHERS
ANN ROWE
BARBARA SAMSON-WILLIS

EDITORS

Campbellford/Seymour Heritage Society

MUNICIPALITY OF CAMPBELLFORD/SEYMOUR
2000

ISBN 0-9687566-0-3

Canadian Cataloguing in Publication Data

Main entry under title:
    Gleanings: a history of Campbellford/Seymour

Includes bibliographical references and index.
ISBN 0-9687566-0-3

1. Campbellford (Ont.) – History.   2. Seymour (Ont.) – History.
I. Crothers, Margaret, 1926-   .   II. Rowe, Ann.   III. Samson-Willis, Barbara, 1944-
IV. Campbellford/Seymour Heritage Society.

FC3099.C36G53 2000   971.3'57   C00-931893-3
F1059.5.C323G53 2000

DESIGN: David Murphy, Sarah Coviello/ArtPlus Limited
ELECTRONIC PAGEMAKE-UP: Heather Brunton, Ruth Nicholson/ArtPlus Limited

Printed and bound in Canada

Table of Contents

To Doris and Frank Potts
For believing that this book was possible

Frank and Doris Potts, 1986.

Photos courtesy of Frank and Doris Potts.

Preface and Acknowledgments

In 1983, largely as a result of the efforts of Margaret and Hector Macmillan, the Heritage Society was established by a group of interested citizens from Campbellford and Seymour. Until 1989, the Society had no permanent location. Through the generosity the Campbellford Town Council, the former PUC building at 113 Front Street North was given to the new society as a facility to house artifacts and archival materials. In 1996, a separate Archives Committee was formed within the Heritage Society to catalogue the collection of archival materials and to expand acquisitions. As requests for historical information about the area grew, it became apparent that the written accounts of the development of the area were somewhat scarce and fragmented, and that local lore had perpetuated many myths and inaccuracies. What was needed was a written history of the area using as many primary sources as possible.

In 1997, we formed a Book Committee and undertook the huge task of collecting and verifying information. Many calls went out in the local newspapers, to organizations, and at meetings for material relevant to the history of the area. Letters were sent to as many groups as we could identify and follow-up telephone calls were made. Volunteers from the Society interviewed some of the senior members of the community. We regret any over-sights or omissions, but adequate notice was given to any and all interested parties. Data was collected from oral histories, diaries, photographs, family histories, and the citizens and organizations of Campbellford/Seymour. Several members of the Heritage Society took this raw material and wrote accounts of the people, places, and events that shaped the history of the community. All this information was stored in computer files which were subsequently organized into chapters and sub-sections. The editorial team then worked to condense this material into a cohesive whole and added supporting documentation, maps, and photographs. Verification of information involved many trips to the Archives of Ontario in Toronto, the Northumberland Land Registry Office in Cobourg, the public libraries in Belleville, Cobourg, and Peterborough, and the library and archives of the University of Toronto. It should be emphasized that all of this work was undertaken by volunteers working countless hours and often covering expenses from their own pockets. It was a labour of love, and sometimes just plain labour.

Early in the project, the Book committee made a conscious decision not to make the book a collection of family histories, but rather a general history of the community. A collection of family histories would make an excellent companion volume to this text, but that is a project for the future.

The title of the book, *Gleanings: A History of Campbellford Seymour*, was suggested by the current president, Ann Rowe. The various definitions of the word *glean* seem to collect the essence of what the book is about and how it came to be written. One such definition is "To collect facts by patient efforts." This definition applies to the work of the Book Committee and all those who have diligently gathered information. Another definition of *glean* is "To gather the leavings from a field after the crop has been reaped." This definition suggests that this book, like any historical work, can only reflect what is left in the collective memory of the community, and cannot include the entire record of the past. The rustic symbolism of the word *glean* also pays tribute to the hard-working pioneers who laid the foundations for this community.

In compiling this manuscript, we have tried not to repeat to any great extent the material already published in the books listed in the *General Reference* section at the end. We have tried to add new facts, to clarify obscure material, and to correct what was clearly in error. All written and graphic materials pertaining to the individual chapters are included in the *Chapter References* section, which also acknowledges all those who contributed written or oral materials. We sincerely hope that we have not overlooked anyone. In identifying individuals throughout the book, we have omitted titles of address such as 'Mr' or 'Miss" unless we were unable to determine first names or initials. We tried to use first names and maiden names wherever possible and appropriate. We also preserved names as they were printed in the resource materials, recognizing that, in some cases, they were variations or incorrect. In some instances, the information is current to 1998, or 1999, and in some rare cases, to 2000; this reflects the length of time that compilation and editing actually took.

The Campbellford/Seymour Heritage Society would like to formally acknowledge the contribution of some of the individuals and organizations who were involved with the production of this book. Book Committee members, Gwen Dubay, Jean Tilney, Peter Wilson, Doris and Frank Potts, and Bob and Marilyn Scott, provided material, support, and guidance to the project from the beginning. The three editors, Margaret Crothers, Ann Rowe, and Barbara Samson-Willis, were a cohesive team who spent countless hours organizing, condensing, verifying, and polishing the material so that it would be enjoyable reading as well as good history.

Several of our contributors deserve special mention for their efforts, both in quantity and quality. They are Bob Eley, John Lisle, Ann Rowe, Gladys Petherick, Margaret Macmillan, Marilyn Scott, Neil Smith, John Campbell, and Doris and Frank Potts. In particular, we would like to pay recognition to the late Don Pollock, historian and cheesemaker, who gave us the first article for this book, a history of cheesemaking in Seymour Township. We regret that he did not live to see this publication. Groups such as the Lower Trent Conservation Authority in Trenton, the Trent-Severn Waterway, and the local Women's Institutes were especially helpful. Special recognition is extended to the late Ken Kingston for his column, Days of Yore, in the Campbellford Herald. His selection of events and people to remember over the years was of great assistance in writing this book. The Society also gratefully acknowledges the contribution by Jack Connor of his collection of Campbellford Herald newspapers covering the period between 1972 and 1996.

Our volunteer proofreader was Keith Howell, who made sure that we did not seriously abuse the Queen's English. Special thanks is due to the Rotary Club of Campbellford who provided us with the initial $500 toward the purchase of the computer which we have used to prepare this manuscript.

We would also like to thank the Town of Campbellford/Seymour for all the support and assistance which we received. The staff, in particular Jim Peters, Shirley Preston, and Susan Gordon, answered many questions and helped solve many dilemmas. We are especially grateful to Mayor Cathy Redden and the members of Council for their concrete demonstration of support for the book in the form of an interest-free loan to assist in publication costs.

The local press, the Courier, the Community Press, and the Independent have given us generous coverage in their publications and have often been a good source of information as well.

We are grateful to our publisher, ArtPlus of Belleville, and especially to editorial representative, Stephanie Campbell, for their efforts in producing this book.

Special thanks also to Frank Potts and Bob Scott who look after our finances, bookkeeping, and inventory control, and Marilyn Scott, who is our marketing manager. Their support is critical to the success of this project.

In conclusion, we hope that our readers notify us of any errors and/or omissions in the text, and provide us with written corrections for verification and inclusion in our archives and in any future edition of this book. Our address is:

Campbellford/Seymour Heritage Society
113 Front Street N.
P. O. Box 1294
Campbellford, Ontario
K0L 1L0
705-653-2634

The Heritage Centre is open every Wednesday from 10–4 from September through June. Summer hours are usually 10–4 , Tuesday through Saturday.

The Book Committee
Campbellford/Seymour Heritage Society

About the Editors

Margaret Whytock Crothers

Margaret is a native of Hamilton, Ontario where she received her elementary education at Central Public School and her secondary education at Westdale Collegiate. After graduation from Grade 13, she attended Queen's University, where she obtained her Bachelor of Nursing Science, in conjunction with her RN at Kingston General Hospital.

She was employed by the VON in Hamilton and the Canadian Red Cross in Toronto before her marriage to Jim Crothers. Her husband's work took them to various regions in the Canadian North, such as Témiscaming, PQ, and Smooth Rock Falls, Ontario. In Témiscaming, Margaret was responsible for introducing and running a large Brownie pack for the Canadian Girl Guides. She also started the first Auxiliary to the Témiscaming Hospital and became the first President. In Smooth Rock Falls, Margaret was employed as a public health nurse by the Porcupine Health Unit. She was involved with pre-natal classes, well-baby clinics, school health programs, pre-school Denver Development Screening Tests, and home visits. During the last two years at the Porcupine Health Unit, she was responsible for the area from Hornepayne to Cochrane.

There was no public library in Smooth Rock Falls, so Margaret enlisted the help of the town council and the Northeastern Regional Library System to establish a library. She was active in the United Church and on the Board of Directors of the Kapuskasing Children's Aid Society.

In 1973, Margaret and her family took possession of the Free family homestead at Concession 7, Lots 3 and 4. Margaret's husband, Jim, was the nephew of Harry Free, and great grandson of Abraham Free, the original owner. Many documents related to the family were found at the farm, and Margaret began the task of researching the Free family history. She went on to document the Crothers family, and her own family, the Whytocks, from Madoc. For two years, Margaret also worked with the Haliburton Kawartha Pine Ridge District Health Unit as a public health nurse. When she retired, she became active in the Campbellford/Seymour Heritage Society. She was involved in starting an Archives Department within the Society, and was instrumental in producing a heritage cookbook, entitled Vintage Vittles and Vignettes, which was a major fund raiser for the Society. In recognition of her efforts with heritage activities, she was awarded the Ontario Heritage Foundation Award in 1997.

Margaret considers that her most important accomplishment has been helping her husband raise four wonderful children.

Ann Boyd Rowe

Ann is a native of Campbellford where she received her early education before graduating from Peterborough Teacher's College and Queen's University. She then taught for thirty-two years for the Hastings County Board of Education, having experience from Kindergarten to Grade 8, Music, Library and Resource and retiring in June 1997 as Vice-Principal. During that time, she was actively involved with the Women Teachers' Association and served two years as President and one term as Chief Negotiator for collective bargaining. In 1990, she received the County Award for Excellence in Education.

In 1980, she began in earnest to become involved in genealogy. She is Past Chair of Quinte Branch of the Ontario Genealogical Society, Region VII Director and Corporate Secretary for OGS. She also chaired for some time the Places of Worship Project and continues to work locally on this effort. Ann has also served as Director and Secretary of the Hastings County Historical Society. In addition, Ann has conducted both junior and senior choirs in both the school and church.

Currently, she is kept busy as Conference Archivist for the Bay of Quinte Conference of the United Church of Canada, a member of the Old Hay Bay Church Committee and President of the Campbellford/Seymour Heritage Society.

Ann has presented workshops to numerous other groups, including the Madoc Historical Foundation, the Tweed and Area Historical Society, Kawartha Branch OGS, Oshawa Branch OGS, Kingston Branch OGS, Ottawa Branch OGS, the Scarborough District Historical Society, York Region Genealogical Group, OGS Seminar, UEL Bay of Quinte Branch, Knights Templar and numerous Women's Institutes. In the 1990s, she was one of the team which produced the Nehemiah Hubble book with 17,000 entries. Ann has given workshops on Tracing British Emigrant Children, Beginning Genealogy, The Fun Side of Cemetery Transcribing, Music of Early Canada, Hardships of Loyalist Women, Heraldry and Genealogy and Land Records.

In 1999, Ann was made one of the first life members of the amalgamated Hastings Elementary Teachers' Association and received a fifteen-year Ontario Volunteer Service Award.

Barbara Samson-Willis

Barbara Samson-Willis spent her early life in the Waterloo area where she graduated from Waterloo Collegiate in 1963. She subsequently attended the University of Waterloo from which she completed a Bachelor of Arts degree in History in 1967. Barbara chose to enter the teaching profession after completing her training at the Ontario College of Education in 1968. Between 1967 and 1980, she taught History, English and Co-operative Education in several secondary schools in Welland, Kitchener and Guelph. During the 1969–70 school year, she served as

Residence Co-ordinator at Notre Dame College at the University of Waterloo, supervising one hundred women university students. In 1971, Barbara returned to the University of Toronto to complete a Master of Education degree in Guidance and Counselling. She returned to teaching until 1974 when she became the Registrar of St. Jerome's College, University of Waterloo, a position which she held for two years. In 1976, she returned to secondary school teaching.

In 1978, Barbara married Hank Willis and moved to Toronto where she accepted a position with the federal Department of Employment and Immigration, managing job-creation programs in the Metropolitan Toronto area. In 1985, she and Hank moved to Campbellford and Barbara became the trainer and accountant for a family-operated income tax, financial services and real estate business.

In 1994–96, Barbara's passion for History and Research led her back to school once again to the Faculty of Information Services at the University of Toronto. She graduated in 1996 with a Master of Library Science degree. At that time, she was a member of the Dean's Honour List and received the Ellen Sheaf Prize for the highest marks in Research Collections in Canadiana.

Since then, she has devoted her strong research and entrepreneurial skills to a small personal business enterprise, named Yore Origins, which specializes in genealogical and historical land records research. Her focus is on training both amateur and professional genealogists and on conducting research either on a fee basis or as part of her personal publishing activities. Barbara is a member of the Association of Professional Genealogists, the Ontario Genealogical Society and several related groups. She has taught successful evening courses for Loyalist College and the Campbellford/Seymour Heritage Society. In 1999, Barbara received a five-year Ontario Volunteer Service Award.

Introduction

Photo by M. Proulx

It is my honour and pleasure as Mayor to extend the gratitude of the entire Municipality to the Heritage Society members for the fine job they have done. While it is probable that few, if any, of the Book Committee members anticipated the amount of work and research that lay before them, the end result will be an ongoing testimony to their hard work and dedication.

With the municipal amalgamation of the Town of Campbellford and the Township of Seymour in 1998 and with more changes to the Community anticipated, the decision of the Heritage Society to provide an accurate written history was very timely. An increasing number of requests for historical information about the area were being received and it was apparent that there was a need to supplement and update existing accounts.

Gleanings: A History of Campbellford/Seymour is a thoroughly good book. It contains enough story quality to interest the casual reader and plenty of details for the historian. It describes characters that are lively, intriguing, romantic, pioneering and independent, but hardly ever dull. It tells of life and death, happiness and sorrow, success and failure. It gives insight into the lives of early pioneers and present day residents, in a manner that makes their accomplishments all the more significant. This is a book that should be read and treasured by anyone with a connection to our community.

As the Municipality of Campbellford/Seymour faces the many challenges that lie ahead, this book will enable it to have a better knowledge of its past and a greater pride in the accomplishments of the people who pioneered it.

Mayor Catherine C. Redden
March 6, 2000

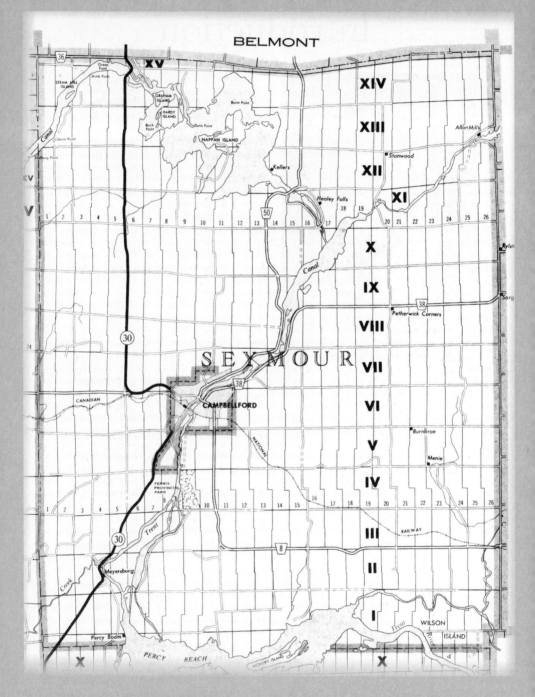

Map of Seymour County, copied and adapted from a 1975 map of Northumberland County, with the permission of the Ministry of Transportation, Province of Ontario.

Chapter One

Beginnings

In telling the story of any community, it is often wise to listen to the voice of someone who witnessed its beginnings. Henry Rowed was one of the early settlers in Seymour Township and was also the enumerator for the 1851 Canada West Census. The following is an unedited transcription of his observations about early life in the township.

～ 1851 Census of Seymour Township ～
Remarks of Henry Rowed, Enumerator

SCHOOLS

"I find that the schools in this Township cause general dissatisfaction. I am told in almost every house that the school houses are too distant or that the teachers are incompetent. And although I was aware that the attendance of children at school was small, I must confess my surprise at the small number returned. I could perceive no perceptible difference in the Free Schools and others. The only children to attend in either case are too young to assist their parents in their occupations. One great difficulty is not being able to find competent teachers. A large majority of them not being able to read and write."

LAND AND CROPS

"It is quite impossible to give any information of the value of separate farms at this season as we have between two and three feet of snow on the ground besides which the men belonging to the different farms are all in the woods working at lumber. The women and boys are ignorant on these subjects but the general price of land is from fifteen shillings to one pound fifteen shillings per acre, much above its real value in my estimation, but occasioned by the emigrants wishing to settle in the neighbourhood of their relatives already residing there.

I think among the industrious farmers where proper precautions are taken, winter wheat in this Township averages twenty bushels per acre but spring wheat does not succeed as well.

In almost every case in this Township, there are summer fallows and new land wheat and as both come under the heading of land under cultivation, I am forced to include it in the column for improved land and am therefore obliged to enter the new land and summer fallow under the heading of pasture to make the columns for land agree but it is undoubtedly wrong and I make no doubt in this Township I have entered as pasture more than double what is truly pasture. Also residing so far from the Commissioner, I could receive no instructions further than the printed directive. Mail is much too slow and uncertain to trust for information to that source.

I wish the Board to understand that orchards are very often under crops in some cases and that I had to deduct the quantity of orchards from the quantity under crop although to have come to a proper estimate such ought not to have been the case and I have to enter lands as under cultivation although laying waste because that land was once cleared. I also have to enter as pasture land that was fallow which in this Township is not less than one tenth of the whole improved land and nobody can tell the difficulty of getting answers to questions when it is necessary to be very accurate excepting those who have tried it.

Killed forty-two deer. Potatoes are almost all lost to rot, and, in most cases, they were very small before they rotted although they had arrived at maturity when the disease commenced.

Buck wheat also failed owing to the great heats we experienced in the month of September. At any rate, it is not cultivated to any extent with us. Turnips are not much cultivated although in the last two or three years we begin to attend more to root crops than formerly. This year, most of the turnips are left in the ground on account of the winter beginning a fortnight earlier than usual.

Many farmers who have been growing large quantities of wheat tell me and I know it from experience that they can no longer do so as the expense of raising, when it is done by hired labour, is greater than the return."

DIFFICULTIES OF ENUMERATION — DIVISION 1, PAGE 41

"I beg to call the attention of the Board to the great difficulties I have had to contend with in taking the census. Nine or ten lumber shanties in the most distant and wild parts of the Township have caused me much trouble as invariably the cook was the only person I could find to answer my questions and he could do little more than give me an idea of the names and ages of the men and I beg to assure the Board I did my best to give as accurate a return as laid in my power. Also not having forms sufficient delayed me several days as I was obliged to go to Cobourg, a distance of forty miles to procure more and when I returned a heavy snowstorm which lasted three days kept me from travelling. Then a severe cold caught by wading from house to house in two or three feet of snow confined me several days."

It is quite impossible to judge of the value of land more than the average price of wild land at twenty pounds, twenty-five shillings per acre.

For the religious census, I wish to impress on your minds that by Presbyterian is meant that church that is in connection with the Church of Scotland. I have not met with any other in this Township with the exception of some Free Church men whom I have entered such, namely, Free Church.

A mother informed me that child died of the Hives but I am not aware there is such a disease and the mother could not explain any further."

POPULATION

"I find the Scotch and English have succeeded best as agriculturists. The Roman Catholic Irish with very few exceptions have not become independent and seem satisfied to reside in small shanties surrounded by the cows and pigs. The English settlers appear to make their residences the most comfortable but the Scotch have cleared the most land. The old Canadians British do not get on as well here as old country people.

The last two hundred names consist almost entirely of squatters and shanty-men who are living on the northern boundary of the Township. It was with the greatest of difficulty they would tell what religion they professed. They consist mostly of British Canadians of American descent and have evidently lived for a generation or two in the back woods. They are without schools and I am afraid will remain without for some time longer and, indeed, if they get one, in that neighbourhood they are too much dispersed to reap much benefit from it. Moreover, if the school should be established, and conducted no better than the ones we already have in the Township, in my opinion, it could scarcely be a benefit."

LUMBERING AND MILLS

"This Township has been a very great favourite with the lumbermen who have completely gutted the woods of all the valuable timber and this year consider that the business is more considerable than it has been since that business was introduced into the country as it appears an inferior article is expected to find a ready sale at remunerating prices.

In the last few years, several saw mills have been erected on the Trent and Crow River and as the circular saws are used instead of the old fashioned upright saws, the amount of sawn lumber has increased very much and I make no doubt that branch of the business is only in its infancy as we have a country behind us with an inexhaustible supply of logs and splendid water power.

I think in all the above number there is not an individual with the exception of John Thos. Archer who has any right whatsoever to the land he lives on. It is a splendid country north of Crow River and the Trent, both possessing unequalled water power, and, if the contemplated rail road to Lake Huron should be constructed, it will pass directly through it.

One grist mill with two run of stones and one mill for sawing lumber (at Meyersburg). The grist mill is quite capable of grinding one hundred bushels of super fine flour every twenty-four hours.

The saw mill contains two upright saws and one large circular saw besides six smaller ones for the construction of shingles, lathing, etc. The saw mill will easily average from twelve to fifteen thousand feet per diem of fine lumber. Mr. Meyers being absent, I am not able to arrive at the costs of these mills but I have understood from himself that he exported four million feet in the past years.

Mr. Meyers has since informed me that the original cost of these mills was about fifteen thousand pounds each. Fifteen workers are employed in the saw mill.

William and Charles Ford have one saw mill capable of sawing nine thousand feet per diem. Cost of the mill, not including the dam, was about five hundred pounds. It produced about nine hundred thousand feet about one half of which was exported to the United States. Six people are employed.

Mr. (Gilbert) Hunter saws for the American Market. He exported eight hundred thousand feet. His mill has two upright saws valued at five hundred pounds.

Mr. (John) Gibb's Store contains stock to the amount of fifteen hundred pounds.

In Part 2, one grist mill with water power and one run of stones, valued at forty pounds per year. Also one saw mill with water power, producing 60,000 feet per year. (Charles Taylor or John Mitchell)

One other saw mill with water power cuts 45,000 per year. (Andrew Lowry or Hiram Munro)" [1]

These frank and often humourous observations touch on the main themes to be developed in looking at the beginnings of Campbellford/Seymour — the land, the people, the township, the village, and the districts and hamlets.

～ The Land ～

THE PLEISTOCENE ICE AGE

During the Pleistocene Ice Age, great glaciers covered the North American continent. Four times the continental ice cap retreated, thinned and melted away. Temperatures on northern latitudes began to rise and the great glaciers began to melt. At the end of the Pleistocene Age, some twelve thousand years ago, the glaciers, like huge bulldozers, gouged and molded the landscape into the Trent-Severn Waterway and Seymour Township. Sometimes, for some unknown reason, the ice "plastered" boulder clay into oval-shaped hills called drumlins. The name drumlin comes from a Celtic word meaning "little hill." These drumlins vary greatly in size but usually range in height from thirty to forty-five metres, and in length from eight hundred to sixteen hundred metres. They are often found in small groups resembling a herd of whales in the sea. The last advance of the glaciers also created the Peterborough drumlin field in which Campbellford and most of Seymour Township are situated, as well as the eskers, moraines, abandoned spillways, abandoned shorelines, and other glacial features for which the area is well known today.

The Peterborough drumlin field is one of the best examples of this glacial feature in the world and one of Ontario's main physiographic features. The drumlins in Campbellford/Seymour area are a part of the Peterborough drumlin field, which is unique since drumlins are seldom found in large groups or "swarms." Four drumlins may be observed clearly in Ferris Park in Seymour Township.

The lakes were formed by melting glaciers. One which covered this area was called Lake Iroquois, eventually becoming Lake Ontario. During the period when the Trent River was a large open bay of Lake Iroquois, many of the islands, which in actuality were immersed drumlins, were washed by wave action producing steeper sided slopes and boulder pavements. There are also stratified deposits of silt around Campbellford. The ancient 'islands' north of Campbellford had distinct bluffs and beaches on their eastern exposures. These interesting earth science features resulted after the large advances of water which covered this whole area receded. Of interest are the Campbellford Esker, the Campbellford Archipelago or raised shorelines, the Petherick Island raised shoreline complex and Rylstone Island.

THE CAMPBELLFORD ESKER

An esker is one of the most interesting of fluvio glacial or water washed deposits. It is a narrow, winding, steep-sided ridge, with something of the appearance of a railroad embankment. These ridges were formed by deposits on the beds of streams that flowed in tunnels near the edge of the ice sheet. They contain sand and gravel making them excellent sources of material for construction purposes.

The Campbellford Esker is about thirty-five kilometres long. It is not continuous south of Campbellford but crosses the Trent River about three kilometres north of Campbellford. Above Campbellford, it is fairly uniform and continuous. It disappears in the Squire Creek Valley about one and a half kilometres west of Springbrook and then reappears on its eastern side one and a half kilometres west of Bonarlaw, past which it continues to the Black River–Trenton escarpment. For practical purposes this esker runs from Concession 5, Lot 4, Seymour Township in a northeasterly direction to Concession 10, Lot 18 in Rawdon Township, Hastings County. This esker is composed of coarse gravel to sandy, fine and medium gravel. Numerous licensed and unlicensed pits have been established in the north-east portion of this esker. Some pits have been extracted and some have been covered by urban development in Campbellford. In Seymour Township there are eight licensed gravel pits and five abandoned pits and many of these are depleted and overgrown.

THE CAMPBELLFORD ARCHIPELAGO

This relatively narrow archipelago extends twelve kilometres from the Godolphin area to Healey Falls. It consists of three large 'islands' and numerous small neighbouring 'islands', most of which are joined together by bar-like formations. The gravel was derived from cliffs that were rapidly eroded along the south side of the archipelago. Excellent bars and terraces may be seen within short distances from Campbellford. The best formed boulder pavements occur to the northwest and northeast of Campbellford. The shore cliffs at these localities are very prominent. Beyond Healey Falls the glacial lake spreads west and north over the Kawartha Lakes Region.

PETHERICK 'ISLAND' RAISED SHORELINE COMPLEX

Concession 8, Part Lots 19, 20
Concession 9, Part Lots 19, 20
Concession 10, Part Lots 18, 19, 20, 21

Petherick 'Island' consists of several gravel bars radiating in a southwest direction onto a bedrock outcrop of Trenton limestone. These low relief bars or gravel beaches descend in altitude from 230 metres to 221 metres. The 'island', in conjunction with the regionally significant Rylstone 'Island', represents the shallow Trent Embayment environment of glacial Lake Iroquois and its successors. The significance of the Petherick 'Island' site is further increased by the presence of a section of the Campbellford esker to the southeast and the possible spillway feature.

RYLSTONE 'ISLAND'

Concession 10, Lots 24, 25, 26
Concession 11, Lots 24, 25, 26

Situated on the northerly edge of the Peterborough Drumlin field, Rylstone 'Island' is recognizable as a series of ridges which appear as minor undulations in the landscape. It is thought that these beach ridges were formed around an isolated island in Lake Iroquois. Below the beach ridges, a small vegetation choked lake, is trapped behind a gravel bar and may represent a remnant lagoon of glacial Lake Iroquois. Ringed by a young forest of trembling aspen, red ash and white cedar, is a marsh with great manna grass, marsh horse-tail and cat tail in three-tenths of a metre of standing water. Though the island and beach ridges are predominantly pasture, patches of forest spot the environs.

AREAS OF NATURAL INTEREST

The following areas in Seymour Township are environmentally sensitive and for many reasons should be left undisturbed.

Petherick's Corners Lowlands

Concession 7, Lots 16–19
Concession 8, Lots 19–21

The Petherick's Corners Lowland is a low-lying tract of land located in the Peterborough Drumlin Field directly southeast of a portion of the Campbellford Esker. The southwest section was bordered by the esker to the north and a drumlin partially covered with deciduous forest to the south. In the intervening area, a lowland mixed deciduous-coniferous forest has developed. It is dominated by cedar, mixed with balsam, fir, paper birch, white pine and sugar maple. The shrub layer is sparse and consisted of mountain maple and seedlings and saplings of black ash, white spruce, basswood and hemlock. The herb layer is luxurious and varied, including wild sarsaparilla, starflower, bishop's cap, stinging nettle, jack-in-the-pulpit, rough bedstraw, enchanter's nightshade, several violet species and yellow lady's slipper. A variety of ferns flourish on the moist forest floor, some of which are lady fern, cinnamon fern, bulblet fern, oak fern and sensitive fern. To the east, the cedar forest is mixed with sedge, grass meadows and alder thickets. Muck is the predominant soil type. The Petherick's Corners Lowland is considered to have high aesthetic value in the context of the surrounding landscape.

Slaughter Island

Concession 13, Part Lots 8, 9

Slaughter Island is one of several islands at a widening of the Trent River called Burnt Point Bay. It is situated between Hardy and Nappan Islands. On

Slaughter Island, sugar-maple-basswood forest merges with a cedar forest to the northeast. Marshland has developed along the more protected shoreline areas and patches of marsh vegetation dot the shallow off-shore reaches. The dense marsh vegetation is dominated by sedges, marsh cinquefoil and arrowhead with a sparse shrub cover of grey and red-osier dogwood. These marshes include several unusual species of plants, such as cotton grass species, water-willow and sweet gale.

Marshes, such as the pockets of marshland surrounding Slaughter Island, are important spawning and nursery areas for a number of fish species as well as a necessary environment for waterfowl, muskrat and a host of marsh birds. Several game fish species, notably maskinonge and largemouth bass – two of the most important game fish in the Kawarthas – are totally dependent on the marshes for reproduction. With the continued development along the Trent River System shoreline marshes are being reduced in number and in danger of being eliminated.

Nappan Island – Seymour Township
Concession 13, Part Lots 10–13

Nappan is an island in the Trent River with extensive marshland along the eastern side. A number of birds nest in the marsh and some rare plant species grow on the island and in the adjacent marshes. A small Pre-Cambrian inlier, which is an outcrop of older rock surrounded by later strata, has been mapped in the marshes on the east side of the island.

Wilson Island (western half)
Concession 1, Lots 18–26

Wilson Island lies in the Percy Reach section of the Trent River. Due to the island's size of nine hundred and sixty-three hectares, this section of the Trent River is restricted to a narrow channel between the mainland and the south shore of the island. A much narrower, meandering, marshy channel separates the northern shore from Seymour Township. Topographically, the island is very flat and thus subject to periodic flooding by the seasonally fluctuating water levels of the Trent Canal System. The highest point on the island is two hundred and fifteen metres on the western side and is some thirty metres above the level of the Trent River. It is surrounded by abandoned farmland, parts of which have been transformed into sedge and grass meadows.

Much of the western half of the island is covered by dense, low shrubs of two to three metres in height such as alder, red-osier dogwood and prickly ash. Trembling aspen, white birch, red and silver-maple trees form a very open canopy. A rare sedge, Gray's sedge, was observed in some places. Most of these sensitive areas have changed and are changing due to man's desire to alter the landscape to suit himself.

The marshy area forming part of Wilson Island is of high local importance as a waterfowl nesting area, particularly for wood ducks. It also supports a good population of fur-bearing animals. This marshy area is of regional significance as a spawning area for pike, pickerel, largemouth bass and maskinonge.

Birch Point Swamp
Concession 13, Part Lots 6, 7, 8

Birch Point Swamp is a low lying tract of land adjacent to the Trent River where it widens to become Burnt Point Bay. A lowland coniferous forest has developed in the low lying area which grades into upland coniferous forests of variable composition on the drier, outlying fringes of the area.

A dense, marsh vegetation rims the shoreline. Sweet gale, an unusual shrub for the region, is the dominant shrub and the herb dominants vary throughout and include: cat-tails, two-stamened sedge, sweet calamus, marsh spike rush, and rush-like aster, an unusual herb. The lowland coniferous forest, is dominated by cedar and balsam fir with scattered black spruce and paper birch.

The herb layer includes numerous plants of what is more typically a boreal or northern spruce forest such as Labrador tea, goldthread, bunchberry and several species of sphagnum moss. On the northwest fringes the lowland woods merges with a cedar balsam fir woods; and on the southeast with a dense cedar forest and a lowland mixed deciduous and coniferous forest dominated by balsam fir, trembling aspen, basswood and black ash.

The lowland cedar-balsam fir woods contains a number of unusual plants which are characteristic of more northern woods, such as: Labrador tea, twinflower, delicate sedge, star flower, goldthread, sweet blueberry, bishop's cap, clintonia, bunchberry, swamp fly-honeysuckle and several sphagnum moss species. Black spruce trees heavily covered with lichens measure twelve to seventeen centimetres in diameter. Other uncommon plants include the Queen's ladyslipper and royal fern and rush-like aster, a narrow leaved aster of bog and fen situations, very uncommon in southern Ontario.

Crowe Bridge Conservation Area
Concession 11, Part Lots 19–20

The geology of the Crowe Bridge Conservation Area is similar to that typical of the Canadian Shield. The area consists of granite outcrops covered in places with a thin layer of top soil. The area contains interesting geological features. It is a karst region, characterized by caves, sinkholes, and underground streams. There is a small crawl cave on the north side of the Crowe River in the bank of a secondary river channel. There are two Pre-Cambrian inliers within one kilometre southeast of Crowe Bridge.

Healey Falls
Concession 11, Part Lots 15, 16, 17
Trent-Severn Locks 15–17

Healey Falls offers a fine opportunity to see exposures of the Trenton and Black River limestones that were laid down about 470 million years ago. Two very different layers of rock are evident in the abandoned river channel below the dam. North of the falls, some of the limestones show giant ripple-marks which were formed by wave action when the rock was just soft sediment. Prairie vegetation, uncommon in Ontario, is found in the area.

～ The People ～

The Trent-Severn Waterway has played a significant role in the evolution and development of local culture over the past 11,000 years. As the glaciers retreated, nomadic tribes of Paleo-Indian hunters arrived using the river as a transportation route. Over the next 2,000 years, the Southern Woodland People, descendants of the Paleo-Indians began to form camps to take advantage of fish runs and wild rice. During the Middle Woodland Period, the lower Trent became a religious ceremonial centre with the building of burial mounds along the waterway. Remnants of one such mound have been found on the shores of Percy Reach near Bradley Bay, on land in the Gore and Concession 1 formerly belonging to the Levesconte family. In 1962, a team from the University of Toronto undertook an archaeological excavation of the site under the direction of Walter Kenyon. On completion of the dig, the site was marked with a rock cairn, which has since been levelled.

Around 1500 AD, with the establishment of Indian agriculture, villages grew larger. The use of tools allowed the native people to alter their environment and when soils, wildlife, and wood became depleted, villages were moved. When Champlain travelled the waterway in 1615, he found Huron Indians with a highly developed culture based on a mix of agriculture, hunting, and trade. With the arrival of European fur traders, the Indian population dropped off severely due to war and disease. By the end of the 1700s, the fur trade was flourishing and the population of fur-bearing animals was greatly reduced.

After the American Revolution, which ended in 1783 with the signing of the Treaty of Versailles, European settlement of the Trent Valley began in earnest from east to west with the Quinte region filling first, primarily with Loyalists and their descendants and British military claimants. In 1791, the Canada Act was passed by the British government, dividing Canada into two colonies – Lower Canada (Quebec and the Maritime Provinces) and Upper Canada (Ontario). The first

Lieutenant-Governor of Upper Canada, John Graves Simcoe, vigorously embarked on a campaign to attract settlers to populate and strengthen the new colony. He divided the District of Upper Canada into nineteen counties, laid the foundation for a network of roads and changed place names from French and native to English. Northumberland County was named for the county in England which contained similar geographic features with its rolling wooded hills and valleys. The Township of Seymour is thought to have been named for Lady Elizabeth Seymour, daughter of the Duke of Somerset and wife of the Duke of Northumberland.

Settlement began in Seymour Township in the early 1800s but it is difficult to document this activity accurately. There were problems with the early surveys which resulted in some renumbering of the lots. There was lack of compliance with patent and land registry obligations during the early settlement phase and there was a tendency for some settlers to occupy land without having clear title. The earliest settler is reputed to have been one Barnabas Bronson,[2] who is said to have arrived in 1806 and settled on 100 acres later described as Concession 3, Lot 2. A poignant reminder of the Bronson family was found in 1979 when a small rough stone grave marker[3] was recovered from the banks of the Trent Canal when water levels were lowered for maintenance. The words scratched on its uneven surface – 'BILLIE BRONSON 1781–1804; LOST IN RIVER' – are a reminder of the loss of a son of the Bronson family at age thirteen.

The Billy Bronson grave marker is preserved at the Campbellford/Seymour Heritage Centre.

Photo from the *Campbellford Herald*, Aug. 1, 1979.

Other early settlers and their locations are said to have been Richard Bamber at Concession 6, Lot 19, George W. Gibson at Concession 13, Lot 6, D'Arcy Boulton at the Gore Lot along the Trent River, and Adam Meyers at Concession 1, Lot 1.[4] In 1831, Samuel Dunk and his wife, Sarah Blackford, left the United States for Upper Canada, crossing Lake Ontario and travelling by stage and wagon to Cobourg and on to Seymour Township. They settled on Concession 2, Lot 15. A daughter, Sarah Jane Dunk, born in 1834, was said to be the first white child born in the township. Robert Stillman and Andrew Scott[5] are believed to have been the first to take up land in Seymour West[6] in 1831.[7]

The initial survey of Seymour Township was completed in 1819 by William Brown but was updated and corrected by Samuel S. Wilmot, Deputy Land Surveyor for the Commissioner of Crown Lands in 1832. In his inspection report of 1832, Wilmot lists the following occupants in the first five concessions of Seymour Township:

Occupant	Concession	Lot
A. H. Meyers	2	4
Samuel Dank(Dunk)	2	16
George Clute	2	25
Hezekiah Herd	2	26
A. H. Meyers	3	5
William Loake(Locke)	3	10
William Twick	3	24
Andrew Althouse	3	25
William Thrasher	3	26
James Hubble	4	23
Samuel Hubble	4	25
R. Baker & brother	5	6
R. C. Wilkins	5	8
Andrew Emery	5	25[8]

In the early 1830s, Lieutenant-Colonel Robert Campbell and his brother, Major David Campbell, began their association with the township. Crown Land documents[9] indicate that they received their land grants as military claimants or half-pay military officers[10] in 1831 and they probably arrived here shortly thereafter. The British government was anxious to settle Upper Canada and offered grants of land to retiring army and navy men. Soldiers and seamen received one hundred acres, captains, five hundred acres, majors, eight hundred acres, and lieutenant-colonels, one thousand acres – thus giving the Campbells eighteen hundred

*Memorial plaque in the public park
on Queen Street commemorating the
founding of Campbellford, erected
in 1966 by the Archaeological and
Historic Sites Board.*

Photo donated by Hank Willis

*David Campbell's grave marker in Lot 2204 in St. Peter's Anglican Cemetery, Elgin and
Ontario Street in Cobourg. It reads:*

In Memoriam

*Major David Campbell, late of Her Majesty's 63rd British Regiment.
He was born at Smiddygreen, County of Fife, Scotland,
Of the family of Ottar and Campbell, Jan 4, 1784.
Died at Sidbrooke, Cobourg, July 21, 1881, in his 97th year.
This monument erected as a tribute of affection
By his adopted daughter, Mary Angell Campbell, Wife of John Vance Gravely of Cobourg.*

*On the other side of the stone is a memoriam to Robert Campbell who is buried in
Campbellford. It reads:*

*Lt. Col. Robert Campbell of the 52nd British Regiment
Died Sept. 17, 1836, aged 52 years.*

Photo donated by Hank Willis

acres. They purchased another one thousand acres, for a total of twenty-eight hundred acres which then became the nucleus of the settlement of Seymour Township on both sides of the Trent River.

Much has already been written about the personal history of the Campbell brothers – some of it based on primary documents and some of it on local lore and tradition.[11] The Campbell brothers were born in Scotland,[12] and, according to British military records, were reputed to possibly be the sons of John Campbell of Achaladen, Blairgowrie, Perthshire. However, David Campbell's grave marker in St. Peter's Anglican Cemetery in Cobourg indicates that he was born in Smiddygreen, County Fife. According to that same marker, he was born on January 4, 1784;[13] however, British military records list his birth year as 1790. He apparently joined the 63rd Regiment of Foot in 1806 as an Ensign. He advanced through the ranks and purchased a commission as Major in 1826. He served with distinction in the Napoleonic Wars in France under the Duke of Wellington and went on half-pay retirement in 1832. The Major was made Crown Land Commissioner for Seymour, an office he held from 1832 until 1839. He used his influence in this position to encourage many retired British military men to settle in Seymour. In this capacity, he handled the dispersal of land to arriving families and also sold land for the Crown. He was known to be a kindly man, helping the inexperienced pioneers, many of whom were also retired half-pay army and navy officers, establish themselves in the harsh environment of the Canadian wilderness. David Campbell's original free grant was Concession 5, Lots 13 and 14 and Concession 6, Lots 11, 13 and 14. In 1834, he purchased from the Crown Concession 7, Part Lot 12 and Concession 6, Lot 10. In 1842, he purchased the rest of Concession 7, Lot 12.[14]

British military records appear to indicate that Lieutenant-Colonel Robert Campbell was born in 1779; however the memorial inscription for him on David Campbell's gravestone indicates that he was born in 1784. In any case, he entered military service in 1795 as a Lieutenant in the Royal Nova Scotia Regiment. In 1800, he entered the 52nd Regiment of Foot and was promoted to Captain in 1804. He served in the Napoleonic Wars and was wounded at the Battle of Coa in 1811, at Badajoz in 1812, and again during the storming of San Sebastian in 1813. For his great contribution in this charge, he was awarded a gold medal (one of only three issued) and a clasp,[15] and his rank as Major. On half-pay from 1818 onward as a result of his wounds, he was commissioned Lieutenant-Colonel of the 28th Regiment in 1830 and retired from the military in 1833. Robert Campbell's original free grant was located at Concession 4, Part Lot 8, Lot 9 and 10, Concession 6, Lot 17, 18, 19, and Concession 7, Lot 13, where he erected his house.[16] Robert Campbell died on April 17, 1836 at the age of fifty-two, never having fully recovered from his wounds, and was buried in an unmarked grave on his farm, currently owned by Arthur C. Nelson. On his death, his land was deeded to his brother, Major David Campbell.

In addition to the Campbell brothers, some retired military men who settled in Seymour Township as military claimants were:

Thomas MacIntosh	Thomas Allan
Matthew S. Cassan	Henry Levesconte
James Raines (Raynes)	Robert Cleugh
John Landon	V. Joseph Geary
Mungo Ponton	Robert Cock
Robert Butcher (Boucher)	Harris Hall
John Shea	James Davis
Benjamin Hayter	James Matchett
William Sherlock	James Masson

Other British military officers, such as Alexander Denmark and Henry Bonny-castle, purchased land from some of these early settlers or married into local families.

These newly-arriving families usually came overland from Cobourg, crossing on the ferry from Percy Landing. In the early 1830s, a steamboat ran from Rice Lake to Healey Falls as well. After clearing the land by cutting timber, and tilling the soil by the most primitive methods, the settlers planted and harvested their first crops. To grind their grain into flour, the Seymour East pioneers, carrying the grain on their backs, forded the Trent to reach the mills on the west side of the river at Meyersburg and Ranney Falls. This ford, at the calmest and shallowest stretch of the river at Major Campbell's property, became known as Campbell's Ford which eventually became Campbellford. They later crossed on a ferry which operated until 1840 when the first bridge was built connecting the small communities which had sprung up on both sides of the Trent. This wooden bridge was constantly in a state of disrepair, with spring flooding taking its toll. Roads were non-existent, with the exception of a trail or rough track built by the government along the Trent from Government Landing near Percy Boom to Shea's Bay — thought to have been near Island Park Marina, Concession 1, Lots 17 and 18. At Government Landing, the incoming settlers obtained supplies and secured overnight lodging as they journeyed to their allotted land. Provisions were brought from Belleville or Cobourg by oxen harnessed to sleighs in winter and primitive stone boats or rough wagons in the summer.

About 1834, a small settlement named "The Patch" was established in the vicinity of the old pulp mill near Ranney Falls. The first post office was located there and mail was delivered by coach travelling over rough forest trails from Colborne by way of Warkworth. St. John Keyes and then John Boland served as the first postmasters. A medical practice was set up by Dr. Patrick Fergus. In 1835, a small Anglican congregation existed there and a rough log school was built for about twenty students. Three miles south, the hamlet of Meyersburg grew around a saw mill and grist mill built by A. H. Meyers, who was an early Member of the Legislative Assembly. Meyersburg was a coach stop for mail and passengers.

County Road 35 from Hoard's Station to Campbellford is commonly known as the "English Line," so named for the English settlers who took up land along this route which was earlier known as "the Iroquois Trail." It was a well worn path used by migrant First Nations bands and families before the white settlers arrived. The retired half-pay officers of the British regulars had briefly settled along the Atlantic seaboard before moving to Upper Canada. The English from North Devonshire were in the majority, with many Scots and a few Irish making up the population of this community. Some families were the descendants of United Empire Loyalists. The names of some of these pioneers are Grills, Hopps, Stephens, Hoard, Smith, Peake, Muir, McAvilla, Dunk, Diamond, Cassan, Hall, Levesconte, Locke, Hoey, and Naylor. Descendants of some of these families are still to be found on their original properties.

Business and commerce began to develop in the vicinity of the bridge. Factories, mills, hotels and stores were erected on both sides of the river in the vicinity of Seymour Bridge. A community named Emilyville, located west of Grand Road and extending to Garry Street, joined with the burgeoning hamlet and the community's future seemed assured.

Just prior to 1846, plans were made for laying out the village streets and building lots. Major Campbell returned to Cobourg in 1852 and in 1856 he sold most of his east side property, including lots willed to him by his brother, to Robert Cockburn of Cobourg and Nesbitt Kirchoffer of Port Hope. However, he retained some interest in the property, forming a syndicate with Kirchoffer and Cockburn for the purpose of developing the future village of Campbellford which was now emerging on Concession 6, Lot 10.[17] Kirchoffer, a surveyor, laid out this section of Campbellford in lots, incorporating many improvements such as roads, streets, and a proposed plan for a railway line. At this time, a number of other large property owners were James and Adam Dinwoodie, J. M. Ferris, Daniel Kennedy, Alex Bonnycastle, Henry Rowed, William Ogilvie and William Oulton. On the west side of the Trent, William Ogilvie laid out the portion of his own property, Lot 9, in streets and lots bordering on Garry and Portage Streets. Henry Rowed who owned a large property, Lot 10 on both sides of Church Street and all of Queen Street, donated the land for the English Church glebe and laid out the remainder between Kent Street and Queen Street in lots and streets. Thus, with many revisions, additions and improvements, Campbellford assumed the appearance of a progressive and properly planned town.

～ The Township ～

The first meeting of council for the Township of Seymour was held at 11 AM on January 21, 1850. Dr. Robert Denmark was Reeve and Councillors were David Allan, John Mitchell, George Tunnah and Henry Rowed. George Ranney was Clerk. No official building was yet erected and meetings took place in homes and taverns. The office of Deputy-Reeve was added in 1854 with Charles French serving the first term. The population of the township was 2,117 residents.

Much of the business of early councils was taken up with day to day management of the meagre resources available. Roads were trails which were cared for by statute labour required of every resident. A pathmaster was appointed by council for each beat. The hours of labour required from residents was based upon the size of the farm they possessed. One man was equal to one day of work; a team and wagon was equal to two days. Gravel had to be spread by hand and the dusty roads often needed to be watered. Many by-laws were needed pertaining to the running at large of animals, appropriate fines and the appointment of pound keepers, as well as the licensing of taverns and inns. On May 25, 1850, a by-law was created to provide assessment of the township to erect a school house. In August 1850, an assessment of the township was required to meet the appropriation for the Provincial Lunatic Asylum. Regular appointments had to be made for pathmasters, auditors, tax collectors, fence viewers, overseers of highways, election of councillors, naming of returning officers, establishment of polling places and electoral divisions, issuance of debentures and appointments to the board of health. By 1865, the total taxes for the township were $5,478.77. By 1871, there were five electoral districts in the township and appropriations were set for each to improve the roads. Seymour formed part of the East Riding of Northumberland. J.M. Ferris was a member of the Ontario Legislature for several terms.

In the early 1870s, the Township of Seymour was considered to be very progressive in enacting a by-law prohibiting the outdoor exposure of food stuffs at store fronts. In 1872, it was the first municipality in Ontario to have a Fish and Game Protection Society. President of the Society was James Dinwoodie and the Secretary-Treasurer was Stewart Cock. In addition, the municipality was one of the first in the province to introduce a kindergarten in a public school.

In 1855, the township hall, currently the home of Campbellford/Seymour Heritage Society at 113 Front Street North, was built. It was used for many purposes, including a community centre, a jail, a school house, a market place and a council chamber. In 1894, Seymour Township relocated its offices to the Ferris Block at the southwest corner of Bridge and Front Streets. The offices remained in this second storey location until 1966 when they were moved to the Colin

The Seymour Township Hall, built in 1855, became the home of the Campbellford PUC in 1933, and became the home of the Campbellford/Seymour Heritage Society in 1989.

Photo from Campbellford/Seymour Heritage Society Archives.

Collins Block on Front Street North. In 1978, the township offices relocated once again to the stone house at 37 Saskatoon Avenue, back of the former Post Office. The final move came in 1989 when the offices moved to the present location of the Municipality of Campbellford/Seymour at 66 Front Street South.

~ The Village ~

By 1874, the area had grown sufficiently that, at a meeting held in the township hall, an application was made to create the Village of Campbellford as a separate municipality. On January 17, 1876, the necessary legislation for separation from Seymour was obtained. Harry E. Skinner became the first Village Clerk. John Clarke, Reeve of Seymour, became Warden of the United Counties of

Northumberland and Durham. The township sold the hall to the village for $600 but retained the right to hold meetings there. The village was responsible for the appointment of construction and tavern inspectors. In this capacity, Luke Horkins was paid $3 for a two month period. Fire protection, the erection of the fire hall, the creation of a new library and the installation of the first street lights in 1890 were important accomplishments. The new village, with a population of 1,092, was home to sixty-six businesses. In 1878, the council approved the extension of wooden sidewalks to all churches. Merchants paid for watering of the streets in 1884. In the same year, the village passed a by-law for the prevention of vice and immorality. It provided penalties for drunkenness on the street, giving liquor to a minor, putting up indecent placards, keeping houses of ill repute, swearing or using obscene language on the street, shouting or disturbing the peace at night, indecent exposure, exposing goods for sale, and "to do or exercise any worldly action of business or work on the Sabbath." [18] Also in 1884, the right to vote in municipal elections was extended to widows or unmarried ladies who were property own-ers. In 1888, J. M. Ferris was chosen Police Magistrate to hear and determine upon all acts in violation of the Temperance Act, which controlled the sale, distribution, and consumption of alcoholic beverages. In May 1889, Charles Nelson was named as engineer for the township under the Ditches and Water Courses Act at a salary of $3 per day for each day's work required.

～ Districts and Hamlets ～

ALLAN'S MILLS

This name was given to the land owned by David Allan and his descendants located at Concessions 12 and 13, Lot 25. On this site, during the 1840s, the Allan pioneers built a saw mill and a grist mill on the Crowe River. About the same time, David Allan also built the first bridge to span the Crowe in Seymour to replace the ford which had been previously used. It was a wooden structure that was replaced in 1891 by a 150 foot steel bridge that cost $3496. When it, too, was replaced in 1976, the cost was reported to be $300,000. For a short time, Allan's Store was also the site of the Post Office. Allan descendants operated the mill until it burned in 1952. The area reverted to a rural and tourist area. It was a popular swimming spot for local residents into the 1960s.

BURNBRAE

The mainly Scottish settlement of Burnbrae on Concessions 5 and 6, Lot 22 received its name from its location near a stream of water or "burn" and a hill or

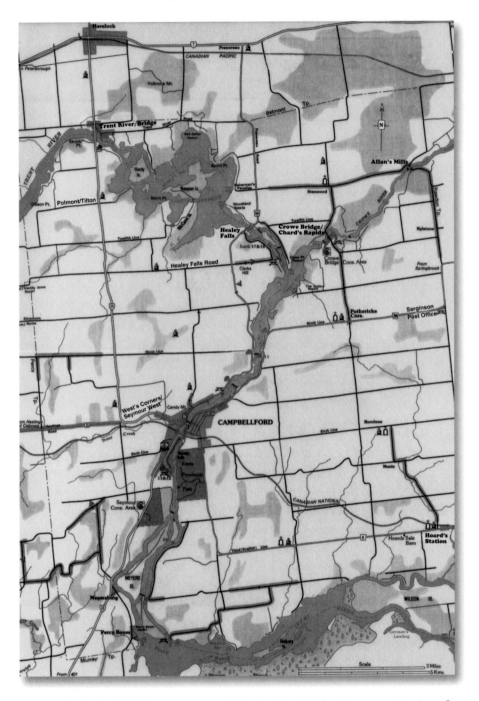

Map of Campbellford/Seymour, prepared for the Campbellford/Seymour Chamber of Commerce in the late 1970s by Ken McCartney and others; reproduced and adapted with the permission of the Chamber.

"brae." The post office was located on Concession 6 by about 1864 and Alex Donald was an early, if not its first, postmaster. In later years, Janet Donald operated the post office in the home of her brother, A. T. Donald on Concession 6, Lot 21. This post office served a wide area from Campbellford to Rylstone. There was also Orange Lodge # 1114 on Concession 6, Lot 20. St. Andrew's Presbyterian Church was established in 1836. In 1849, Mr. and Mrs. James Whitton moved to Seymour from Glenburnie, near Kingston, and opened Whitton's Inn on Concession 6. This was a stopping place for stage coach travellers and a gathering place for men of the community. Early settlers included the families of Little, Bedford, Buchanan, Watson, Whitton, Cleugh, Hay, and Rev. Robert Neill.

Tug-of-war was a popular sport brought from Scotland. In 1909, the Burnbrae team was organized with W. W. Little as the anchor man with pullers Bert Third, Alex Stewart, James A. Stewart, Lindsay Watson, A. G. Watson, G. V. Taylor, William Doxsee and Roy Walker. This team was very successful in competitions and won many cups and trophies. Although the sport declined during the war years, it was alive and well again in the 1920s with many members from the early team and several additional members achieving great success.

CHARD'S RAPIDS / CROWE RIVER BRIDGE

The Crowe River received its name from Chief Crowe of the Mississauga Indian tribe. One of the most popular spots on the Crowe River has always been the area on Concession 11, Lot 19, which received its name from the Chard family who had a log cabin nearby. About 1898, a bridge was built across the Crowe by Dickson Brothers, replacing the shallow, narrow ford. An item from the Campbellford Herald (November 4, 1959) describes replacement of the bridge floor by Spencer & Son, Campbellford. Specially treated 2 x 8 inch planks of B.C. fir were laid on edge and secured with 1500 pounds of spikes. Engineers, who inspected the job, estimated the planking should last forty years. However, the complete bridge was replaced only nine years later in 1968. It had capsized under the weight of a construction truck carrying a bulldozer. A Bailey bridge served, for a short time, as a temporary crossing. The existing concrete crossing is more familiarly known as "Crowe River Bridge."

In the 1920s and 1930s, this was a favoured picnic and swimming spot as well as a location where cars or trucks could be driven out onto the flat rock and washed. It was also used as a spot to fill milk cans with water during a dry spell. From 1929 to 1945, the property on the west side of the bridge, on both sides of the road, was owned by George O'Sullivan who provided picnic tables and ran a small snack bar where he sold ice cream and cold pop. An ice-house was essential, since there was no electricity. This was the site of many family and Sunday School picnics because the shallow water provided a safe swimming spot. It was quite common for pic-nickers to walk to this area along a cement wall to explore Blaker's Cave.

Much of the property on the east side of the bridge is the present site of the Crowe Bridge Family Fun Park owned and operated by the Crowe Valley Conservation Authority. The 26 acre parcel of land was purchased in 1965 from Ernest Petherick. It consists of a camping area upriver from the bridge, and an excellent swimming/picnic area downstream at the weir dam. Within the camp-ing area there is also a great swimming hole which was always the choice of expe-rienced swimmers in times past. Known only as "The Big Rock", it featured an enormous granite boulder that barely surfaced in about 8 feet of water. The great rock, so out of place in limestone country, was nevertheless in the right location to serve as a crude diving platform.

ENGLISH LINE

English Line is an area to the south and east of Campbellford encompassing property in Concessions 1, 2 and 3, Lots 9 to 18. The name of the community acknowledged the many English military men who received land grants in the area.

English Line had two brickyards, one on Concession 3, Lot 10, operated by John Haig and another on Concession 5, Lot 10, operated by William Cock. A blacksmith shop located on Concession 3, Lot 15 was owned by Alex Craighead. The general store was built in 1930 by George Godden who ran it for a short time. Subsequent proprietors were Jim Potts and Harry Sanders, Tom Little and Bert Heagle, Joe Boulton, Roy McGee, Clem Milne and Arden Haig. The cheese factory, the school, and the church were popular gathering places. The proximity to the Trent River made it a natural area for fishing camps and cottages to accommodate the many fishermen and boaters who came dur-ing the summer months.

The property of the pioneer Levesconte family on Concession 1 was the site of an archeological dig in 1962. At this location, there was a burial site for Point Peninsular Indians associated with the Serpent Mounds at Keene. Several skeletons and artifacts were discovered by a team led by Dr. Walter Kenyon from the Royal Ontario Museum.

HOARD'S STATION

This settlement on Concession 3, Lots 25 and 26 on the road from Campbellford to Stirling was first known as Allandale in recognition of a prominent early pioneer, Thomas Allan, a British naval officer who received 200 acres of land in 1834. He increased his holdings until he owned 1000 acres in the area. In 1836, he brought equipment from Scotland to open a mill which was used for threshing grain, making

bone meal, and sawing lumber. The later name of Hoard's Station was to acknowledge the Hoard family, United Empire Loyalists, who settled in Rawdon Township.

In about 1865, a hotel operated by Thomas Landon was reputed to be the best
of its kind in the area. It was a popular spot for salesmen to display their wares for
local merchants. By 1883, a post office was established with Jane Donald as postmistress. After she retired in 1900, subsequent postmasters were Stephen Hoard,
F. N. Haig, James Knight, Lucas M. Sharpe, G. W. Brady, D. A. Weaver and Thomas
Walker. From Thomas Walker's death in 1943 until 1946, his widow, Minnie, held
the post. At that time, the post office was closed and a line of rural boxes served
the community. Ken Sisley was the faithful mail carrier for forty-five years. There
was no school in the hamlet and children attended classes at Masson's School.

The railway station was a busy spot. In its peak year, four passenger trains arrived
daily plus numerous freight trains. Between Belleville and Peterborough, Hoard's
Station had the only pumping station where the steam engine took on its supply of
water. Station masters were John Catton and John Parks. In 1909, the first rural hydro
line was run to John Parks' Grist Mill. The proximity of the mill to the station made
it ideal for shipping. Stockyards were built by the railroad and maintained by railway employees. W. J. Snarr was the last to ship livestock from Hoard's Station by
rail. The mill was later sold to the Snarr family and is now operated by Flemings.

Other industries included two small general stores, a blacksmith shop, and
later, a cheese factory. One general store was operated to the east of the laneway
to the mill by George Brady and later by Harold Gunning. Another was run by
Fred Remington and later, in the same location, by Harold and Agnes Rowe. Jack
and Ella Brown ran a blacksmith shop and, in 1952, their son, Don and his wife,
Audrey, opened a general store and garage in the same location. When the store
burned in the late 1950s, a new building was erected. It has housed a farm machinery dealership, rental space, and now, once again, a small general store.

During the mid 1920s, the side boards and dressing rooms from an old open air
rink in Stirling were transported to Hoard's Station on two horse driven sleighs and
set up behind Jack Brown's blacksmith shop. A seasonal charge was made for skating. The dressing rooms were heated by a box stove placed between the two rooms
in the partition. The ice was cleaned by a horse drawn scraper. Hockey sticks could
be purchased for fifty or seventy-five cents and skates sharpened in the blacksmith
shop for fifteen cents a pair. Some of the avid hockey players were Harold Gunning,
Frank Heagle, Bill Jeffs, Oscar Rannie, Fred Jones, Ken Oddie, Mac Remington, Ab
Jones, with Charles Hoard and John Coggins in goal. After this rink was demolished,
skaters used the creek beside the cheese factory.

Other farm-related businesses were opened further to the west. The Hoard's
Livestock Sale Barn was opened by Ray Williams. In 1959, it was purchased by

Delbert Hickson whose descendants took over as owners of the business in 1977 and continue today. Sales were held on Monday night until more recently when the sale became a daytime event held on Tuesday. Women's groups have provided nutritious meals for many years. The sale barn is a gathering point for the community. In addition, Al and Blanche Foote opened a farm supply business operated in more recent years by their son, David, as Foote's Farm Supply.

M E N I E

The tiny hamlet of Menie on Concession 5, Lot 23 was named by John and Robert Turner after their home, Menie House, in Aberdeen, Scotland. The Turners owned a saw mill and grist mill on a swift stream just south of the fifth concession corner on the road to Hoard's Station. For some years, this area was known as Turner's Mills. The mills were destroyed by fire, but the Turners also built a general store managed by Mr. Edwards. Later, Charles Ross owned the store and in 1867, sold it to Edward Atkinson.

Below the fourth concession was a foundry and cooperage operated by an Englishman named Bunse, who made kettles and iron utensils as well as casting bells. The bell which he cast for Stephen's Church at Hoard's Station cracked in forging and never had a true clear sound. Nearby, John Massie operated a lime kiln. Home industries included a tailor shop run by Alexander Brunton who made men's and boy's clothing and a shop where William Duff made shoes and boots for men and prunella felt boots for women.

In 1858, James Mather, who had clerked for Charles Ross in 1848, built a combined general store and house which also housed the post office. Subsequent owners were Lindsay Meiklejohn, Charles Rannie, O.B. Johnston, and Alex Milne. Frank and Doris Potts operated the store from 1946 to 1966. The store was turned over to the Peterborough County Centennial Committee for removal to Lang Pioneer Village in exchange for funds to landscape and fence the vacated area. When the store was moved, it went by a circuitous route[19] because bridges on the direct route were too narrow. The store has been preserved as a typical general store of the early 1900s.

In 1870, William Lamb built a home and a large shop where he made sleighs, buggies and cutters and did repair work. Upstairs was a large room, known as Lamb's Hall, used for community events and elections. The staff included a painter and a blacksmith. Later owners were Bill McCrory and Vern Schram. The Menie Cheese and Butter Company was built in 1922.

Menie was also a cultural centre for the area. The Seymour Literary and Temperance Society was organized in 1887 with the aim of "mutual improvement of our members in a literary point of view, together with the promotion of temperance principles." On October 20, 1887, the following officers were elected: President, James Strachan; Vice President, Henry Cleugh; Critic, W. R. Mather; Secretary, Jennie Hume; Marshal, William Rannie. Menie was also home to what was probably the first Brass Band in Seymour, organized by Lindsay Meiklejohn. Members included H. Atkinson, Charles Stephens, G. Dunk, A. Stewart, G. Ingram, V. Taylor, A. Dunk, Alex Stewart, H. Barrie, Ivan Clancy and drummers, C.U. Clancy and Sam Dunk. Their first engagement was at Wellman's Corners for July 12th.

Children from the community attended school at Burnbrae and many of the settlers worshipped at St. Andrew's Presbyterian Church. The Seymour East Women's Institute met regularly in their hall at Concession 5, Lot 23, until it was sold in 1998.

MEYERSBURG

At one time, Meyersburg was a bustling small community, home to three hotels, two stores, a post office, a booming lumber mill, and a flour and stave mill. Two loads of flour in barrels were hauled by team twice a day to Campbellford. At first, church and community gatherings were held in the old frame school house. The first settler in this area was Adam Meyers after whom the settlement was named. He owned an island in the Trent River containing 570 acres of pasture, a portion of which eventually was sold to Hugh Ross, hence the name, Ross's Island. Meyers also owned a gang saw mill on Meyers Island and a grist mill in the hamlet.

In later years, John Sills owned the grist and flour mill and also the stave mill. He was the owner of much property, including the site of the Methodist Church built in 1890. During his ownership of the grist mill, a dam was built across the river to supply power. He was also part of an unsuccessful endeavour to build a bridge to English Line via Meyers Island. Later owners of the mill were Mr. Yourex and Peter Bound who moved it to his own property, a half mile north, to use as a saw mill.

The post office and store were operated by George Potts and then by Sarah Runciman. Opposite the post office and store, stood another store, first owned by Mat Doody. This building was later converted to a popular hotel. Another hotel located diagonally across the road on the corner between the lane leading to the river and the Percy Boom Road was operated by Jim O'Sullivan. The third hotel, operated first by Smith and Empey, then Ned Coveney and Nelson Simmons, was at the north end of the burg near the mill. This hotel was the site of a triple wedding of Nelson Simmons' daughters.

Other pioneer families of the area were Driscoll, Gynon, Clute, Scott, MacDonald, Turner, Ivey, Fraser, Dingman, Conlin, Poole and Bertrand.

At Percy Reach, located to the southeast of Meyersburg on the Trent River, the small community of Percy Boom has developed. In its early days, it was primarily a fishing resort and cottage community but it now has many permanent residents. The Meyersburg Flea Market, the home of McCrory's Barn Dance from 1956 to 1977, is a popular attraction on weekends for bargain hunters.

PETHERICK'S CORNERS

Petherick's Corners, located on Concession 9, Lot 20, received its name from several families of Pethericks, among them Daniel who arrived in 1849 and William who arrived about 1843. Pethericks owned the land where the church, the cemetery, the school, the cheese factory, and the Orange Hall were eventually located. This portion of Seymour did not have its own post office, so mail had to be collected once or twice a week from Burnbrae, Campbellford or Sarginson.

Other early settlers in this area were the Barnums, Alex Simpson, William Atkinson, and John Arnold. The Bruntons were also early arrivals. A descendant, Walter Brunton, opened a garage in 1947 which he operated until 1974. It was then rented as a garage for about ten years and is now rented for storage. This property has more recently been the site of a snack bar which is now also closed.

This area has always been a farming community where excellent herds of cattle are raised.

POLMONT / TILTON

The names Polmont and Tilton have both been used to refer to the area at the intersection of Concession 13 and Highway 30 just south of Trent River. Polmont Orange Lodge was originally located on the southwest corner of the intersection on Concession 12, Lot 5, but was moved in about 1908 to the northeast corner on Concession 13, Lot 6. A schoolhouse, which also served as a church, was built on the northwest corner on the property of Nelson Wood on Concession 13, Lot 5, and there was a cemetery adjacent to it. The schoolhouse was abandoned in about 1878 and relocated closer to Trent River on the east side of Highway 30. The Tilton Methodist Church, later known as Wesley Church and then as Centre Church, was located on the property of George Gibson on the northeast corner of the intersection on Concession 13, Lot 6. Centre Cemetery, sometimes known as Gibson's Cemetery, was located adjacent to it. An Episcopal Methodist Church was built on the Cook property on Concession 14, Lot 5, sometime before 1878. Two locations have been noted for the post office but it is not clear which is the earliest. One was situated on George Gibson's property and called Tilton Post Office, and the other was across the intersection in the home of Michael Van Volkenburg on Concession 12, Lot 5. A few tombstones in the old cemetery on the northwest corner and the lodge building which is now a residence are all that remains of the community today. Early settlers in the area were Nelson Wood, A. Quackenbush, D. McCullough, G. Tice, Michael Van Volkenburg, and George Gibson.

RYLSTONE

Rylstone is located on Concession 11, Lot 26, Seymour Township, but is generally considered to encompass the neighbouring portion of the Township of Rawdon which lies across the boundary road. There was settlement in the area from the late 1830s, mostly of British origin. Incorporation of the Townships of Seymour and Rawdon did not occur until 1848. The area was predominantly a farming area where maple sugaring, logging bees, and barn raisings formed an important part of social life.

The local school and the church were the centres for many activities. A cheese factory also operated in the area for many years. In 1913, the cheesemaker, W.H. Gibson, opened a small general store in the curing room of the cheese factory and expanded it to include Amos Barnum's coal oil business. A separate building was constructed in 1915 to accommodate the increase in business. In 1919, W. H. Gibson sold the business to his brother, George, who operated the store until his death in 1940. Harold Peters then took over and after three years sold the business to W.P. Moore. In March 1944, the Moores sold the store to Fred Fry who operated it until 1966 at which time it was taken over by Earl Trumble. Due to declining business, the store closed in 1970.

In August 1940, about thirty women gathered at the home of Mrs. Charles Stewart to form a Red Cross Group which met monthly in the homes of its members. Monthly offerings and the money from pot luck dinners supported the important work which the group had undertaken. The entire community became involved, with pupils from the 9th Line School and the girls of the Gospel Hall each making a quilt which was sold to raise money for the Red Cross. In total, about seventy-five quilts were made by the women as well as a great variety of homemade clothing, knitted articles and bandages for hospitals. The group closed in 1946.

The Women's Institute purchased the former school at Concession 11, Lot 26, and it is still used as a local meeting hall for this group as well as the centre for community activities. In 1967, the Women's Institute established the Barnum Centennial Community Park at the junction of the ninth line of Seymour and the Seymour-Rawdon boundary road in memory of the Barnum family who lived in the area. It has since been closed.

SARGINSON POST OFFICE

The first post office in the area was in Rawdon Township on the corner of the boundary road on the farm of Charles Finch. The postmaster was Thomas Sarginson, hence the name. Later, it moved to the home of James Finch and many elderly residents recalled walking three times a week to collect the mail which came from Burnbrae. After the death of James Finch in 1907, the post office moved to Fred Barnum's house. In July 1913, rural mail delivery began in the area known as R.R. 2, Campbellford with Mr. and Mrs. Fred McMullen covering a route of twenty-three miles. Later carriers were George Walkenshaw, Andrew Hay, George Grills and Charles Stephens.

STANWOOD

Stanwood is a tiny hamlet on Concession 13, Lots 18 to 20. The derivation of the name is uncertain but one elderly resident claims to have been told that it was named for a settler called Stanley Wood. John Mackenzie operated the first store and post office. It was located across from the present United Church but moved later to the north side of the intersection with Crowe River Road. This store also served as the post office until 1913 when rural mail delivery commenced. It was a typical country store with barter being an acceptable form of payment. Eggs were the most popular product used in exchange for store goods. Mrs. Amos Green picked wild gooseberries and exchanged them at the store for a set of knitting needles. As motor cars became more numerous, a gasoline pump was installed in front perilously close to the road. On at least two occasions, it was knocked over by errant drivers. Following Mackenzie's tenure, successive storekeepers were Garnet and Emma Redden, Jack and Maggie Rowe, and finally, Albert and Gladys Hay. The store was a popular stopping place for students from the Stanwood School with a few pennies to spend on sweets. Licorice pipes, jawbreakers, chocolate bars and other treats filled the glass-topped display case which sat on the counter. Flour, oatmeal and sugar were sold in bulk from large barrels. A few chairs circled the wood stove in the same area, a local version of the "Hot Stove League." It was a popular spot for local lads to relax and discuss the current gossip.

By 1895, a cheese factory was opened just east of the store and run by James Johnson. Evidently, the first cheesemaker also raised a few hogs as there are frequent notations in Miller Allan's journal for periodic sales of chop to feed the pigs.

By 1899, Dan Brown had built a blacksmith shop on the east side of the factory. For many years, the smithy would be busy as he employed his skills shoeing horses, shaping plough points and repairing tools. The journal[20] of the Allan family, who operated the mill and store, records payment to Brown for setting wagon and buggy tires and sleigh runners. Threatened by fire more than once, the frame building, insulated with wood shavings, contained all the right ingredients for a conflagration. In 1942, the building caught fire and burned to the ground.

The new Methodist Church was erected in 1903. Another popular gathering place was the Victoria Orange Lodge #1338, located on Concession 13, Lot 20, a short distance north on the sideroad. In addition to its function as a lodge hall, it was used for many community social functions. Newly married couples were frequently treated to wedding showers there. Square dances, a popular and inexpensive recreation during the depression years, drew crowds from the community and beyond. Local musicians sawed away on fiddle, stroked guitar or plunked on the piano. There was always a caller eager to guide the dancers through the square – in his own inimitable style. It was common practice to pass the hat before the evening ended to collect a token of appreciation for the entertainers. Among those who provided music or called off were Ed Anderson, Clark Haig, Annie Dutton, Nettie Simpson, Harold Brunton and Robert Lisle.

TRENT BRIDGE/RIVER

The hamlet of Trent River lies on Concession 14, Lot 6 on the northern boundary of Seymour Township. Francis Lee, an Englishman, who was the first settler in this area, arrived in a canoe from Peterborough and landed on the shore near the narrows where it was possible to cross the Trent River on foot. This small community was first called "The Narrows" and later, "Trent Bridge." The newcomers soon realized the importance of the narrow crossing and built a wooden scow to transport people, produce, materials and animals from the south shore to the island lying close to the north shore. A low narrow wooden bridge with "A" supports was built to allow passage over the north channel. Once settled in his new location, Francis Lee operated a brick yard and lime kiln. This was a thriving business with many sales in Campbellford and Havelock. The Lee family donated both the land on which the church was located and the bricks with which it was built.

Another of Francis Lee's duties was the planning of a survey of the village which was not quite complete when he passed away in 1883. His widow, Mary, along with Provincial Land Surveyor C.F. Caddy, completed the plan in accordance with the Provincial Land Act. As there was only a rough wagon track, the road was re-routed. The first post office, established as Trent Bridge on June 1, 1874, was also in the Lee home. Francis Lee was the postmaster from its inception until his death and his wife, Mary, acted as postmistress from January 1, 1884 until September 25, 1903. Later post masters were Mr. McFadden, George Chiles and Frank Pollock. A general store was first operated by the Lees and later by George Chiles and Mr. Inkster. The store passed through several hands until purchased by Ron Retallick.

The river was a sight to behold in the spring as huge booms of logs floated down from Rice Lake to the mills on the lower Trent. The Garneaus were experienced lumbermen who cut great masts for ships from the immense trees. During the winter months, ice cutting for refrigeration provided employment. Conners and Garratt operated one saw mill and another mill, run by the Boswell family, was located on the back channel near the site of Cedar Isle Lodge. A railway spur was built from the Blairton Iron Mine to the old dock located near the Cenotaph. The ore was then loaded onto boats for shipment to the United States. The first cargo departed on August 25, 1867. The boat was the "Isaac Butts" which took the ore to Harwood where it went by train to Cobourg and eventually to Sandusky, Ohio.

A harness shop, cheese factory and a store first operated by George Laidley and later by A.V. Fuller, Abe Waller, Henry Pollock, and Frank McLaughlin were busy places in the community. A.M. Mann built a hotel operated by Stewart Wannamaker and George T. Cumming before George Brown named it Brown's Hotel. Later it was known as Sedgewick House. During the 1920s and 1930s, two attractive dance pavilions, Coral Gables and Sedgewick's Riverside were opened. These sponsored excellent live band music for jitney dancing. Large crowds regularly enjoyed several nights of dancing each week during the summer months. Since the dance pavilions were located on opposite sides of the river, the participants would move back and forth over the iron bridge to enjoy the best of both. Trent River was also the location for a summer regatta which always drew a large gathering of boating enthusiasts.

A museum was constructed by Frank Knapp and later rebuilt as the Trent River Museum which officially opened on May 24, 1963. This has now become the Pine Cone Gift Shop and some of the small museum buildings have been sold and removed from the site.

The Cenotaph, erected in 1923 by Alfred H. McKeel to recognize Private Richard Cowan, has recently undergone extensive renovations with significant assistance from the local Women's Institute. Because the monument is on Federal land, it was not possible to designate it as a heritage site. An inscribed plaque refers to its value to the community.

WEST'S CORNERS / SEYMOUR WEST

The area near Concession 7, Lot 6 is locally known as West's Corners. At this junction, Highway 30 makes a long curve to head toward Havelock and the road to Hastings veers to the left. This corner has been the site of many accidents over the years. The community, the small cemetery on Lot 5 and the old school building were named for the West family. On the Clarke farm, later owned by Wests, was a brickyard where much of the red brick common to the area was produced.

The surrounding area is usually referred to as Seymour West. On Concession 8, west of the highway, a cheese factory was built about 1875 and an Orange Lodge existed for some years as well. There was a good sugar bush on the Free farm on the 7th Concession and on the Curle farm on Concession 8. To the south on Concession 6, a lime kiln operated on the McDonald farm.

During the 1940s, a flying field was created on Concession 9 by Ernie Ayrhart. William Pigden of Belleville acted as instructor for a flying school for some time. Local people bought shares to assist in the purchase of airplanes and the erection of hangars. J.A.C. Allen, a veteran pilot of World War I acted as manager of the airport. Interest in this small venture dwindled and the farm and airport were sold to Douglas Stapley as a private field.

ENDNOTES

1   *1851 Census, Canada West, Northumberland County, Seymour Township, Part 1* (Ottawa: National Archives of Canada, RG31, Statistics Canada), pp. 64, 75, 78, 80.

2   He was the grandson of Richard Bronson of Farmington, Vermont, who was among the first fifteen hundred Puritans to arrive in America from England in 1630. Mrs. Marjorie McMullen, a descendant of Danial Bronson, another grandson of Richard Bronson, lives near Foxboro, Ontario, and has provided information on 10 generations of the Bronson family history.

3   This stone is now housed at the Campbellford/Seymour Heritage Centre at 113 Front Street N. in Campbellford/Seymour.

4   F B. DeCarrol, ed. *Reflections: Campbellford Centennial Year – 1976*, (Campbellford: Np, [1976]), p. 9.

5   W. A. Kingston, *The Light of Other Days: A History of Campbellford and Seymour Prior to 1900* (Campbellford: W. A. Kingston, 1967), p. 71.

6   The descriptors Seymour West and Seymour East are terminology used to describe land east and west of the Trent River.

7   Lists of the names of some of the earliest settlers in Seymour Township and some of their locations can be found in the following publications:

F. G. B. DeCarrol, ed. *Reflections: Campbellford Centennial Year – 1976*, (Campbellford: Np, [1976]), pp. 9–13.

A Century of Footprints (Campbellford: Campbellford/Seymour Agricultural Society, [1967]), pp. 8–11.

Illustrated Historical Atlas of the Counties of Northumberland and Durham, Ont. (Toronto: H. Belden & Co., 1878), p. ix.

8   Edwin C. Guillet, *Valley of the Trent* (Toronto: Champlain Society for the Government of Ontario, 1957), p. 37–47. Names in brackets supplied by the editors.

9   *Return of Lands sold and located in the Township of Seymour in the Newcastle District from the year 1823 to the 1st March 1832*, Archives of Ontario, RG 1 – A – IV, Crown Land and Resources, Schedules and Land Rolls, Vol. 31, microfilm, MS400, reel 11, pp.1–18. Also, *Computerized Land Records Index, alphabetical listing by name of township*, Archives of Ontario Microfiche, #057

10 The British government purchased the military settlers' commissions at a commuted allowance for life at a rate that amounted to about one-half of their military pay. See the account of Major M. S. Cassan in *The Light of Other Days: A History of Campbellford and Seymour Prior to 1900*), pp. 7–8.

11 See the following accounts:

F. G. B. DeCarrol, ed. *Reflections: Campbellford Centennial Year – 1976*, (Campbellford: Np, [1976]), pp. 9–12.

A Century of Footprints (Campbellford: Campbellford/Seymour Agricultural Society, [1967]), p. 9.

W. A. Kingston, *The Light of Other Days: A History of Campbellford and Seymour Prior to 1900* (Campbellford: W. A. Kingston, 1967), pp. 63–4, 69–71

T. J. Wilson, *Campbellford's Story* (Warkworth: Warkworth Journal, 1956), pp. 6–8.

12 David Campbell's obituary in the Campbellford Herald on July 28, 1881, (Microfilm N120, reel # 3, Archives of Ontario) indicates that he was born in Nova Scotia. This confusion, no doubt, arises from the fact that the Campbell brothers and some of the other British military officers who settled in the area spent some time in Nova Scotia on first arriving in North America.

13 David Campbell's gravemarker in St. Peter's Anglican Cemetery was erected by his adopted daughter, Mary Angell Graveley, whose husband, John Vance Graveley, was one of the executors of David's Campbell estate. John Vance Graveley also officially reported Campbell's death to the Registrar of Ontario and that registration confirms that he was born in 1784.

14 *Computerized Land Records Index, alphabetical listing by name of township and by surname*, Archives of Ontario, Microfiche, #057 and # 008.

15 Officials at the Public Record Office in London, England, in searching their military records in 1966 at the request of the Department of Public Records and Archives in Toronto, found no record of the Campbell brothers serving in the Peninsular War and no trace of Robert Campbell being awarded the St. Sebastian Clasp. However, local newspaper accounts report that, after the death of Robert Campbell, four bullets were removed from his body and were preserved, along with the medal and clasp, and his sabre and epaulettes. The location of these artifacts is not known at present; it is possible that they were buried with him or deposited somewhere in Cobourg.

16 *Computerized Land Records Index, alphabetical listing by name of township and by surname*, Archives of Ontario, Microfiche, # 057 and #008.

17 David Campbell lived to the age of ninety-seven and died in 1881 at Sidbrooke, his Cobourg estate.

18 *Seymour Township By-Law*, May 31, 1875.

19 The building was transported from Menie, east to the town line, north to the 14th Concession of Rawdon, east to Highway 14, north to Marmora, west on Highway 7 to the old Keene Road, south to the Lang turn and east to the Pioneer Village.

20 *Allan Journal*, property of the McKeown family, handed down to Reg McKeown by his mother, Grace Allan.

Chapter Two

The
River Valley

— Developing the Trent River — and Trent Canal

Commercial development of the Trent River Valley began with the logging industry. Logging entrepreneurs were drawn to the land by large stands of red and white pine which were cut and shipped to Britain as masts and spars for the British Navy. Logging on the Trent did not last as long as on the Ottawa River, as by 1850, most of the square timber trade was almost over. However, this early logging industry created environmental problems such as soil erosion, topsoil loss, and flooding. The square timber trade was followed by a thriving lumber industry which was able to use the smaller remaining trees. Wooden dams with log slides and timber sluices were built by the Federal Government and private enterprise to encourage lumbering.

For many years, controversy had raged between proponents of a railway from Cobourg to Rice Lake and another group who favoured improvement of the Trent River to allow navigation. In 1836, the Act to Improve the Navigation of the Inland Waters of the Newcastle District was passed along with funds of $80,000. This Act was intended to improve access to agricultural, mineral and forest products. No mention was made of through navigation to Lake Huron. A dam at Healey Falls and a lock at Hastings were part of these improvements. Commissioners were named for the project and an engineer named Nichol Hugh Baird was hired as superintendent. The portion at Healey Falls was supervised by Thomas McNeil who had worked on the Welland Canal. The work at Healey Falls involved construction of a rock-filled wooden dam 488 feet long and 12 feet high to be erected across the river at the top of the falls. This dam would raise the level of the water back to Hastings to enable the lock there to operate. Despite much activity, the contractors failed and the dam was never built.

In 1837, the government set aside an amount of $387,537 to build the section of the canal from the mouth of the Trent to Percy Landing. Various routes were studied to extend beyond that point, including the Percy Portage[1] between Percy Boom and Rice Lake which would have bypassed the rapids and falls in the upper section of the river. Funding was not raised and a revised plan which would have seen completion of the lower part and the Glen Ross section was abandoned in 1839. The improvements to navigation were among the first public works scrapped following the departure of Lieutenant-Governor, Sir Francis Bond Head. A new Board of Works was established to oversee all construction. The newly elected parliament decided against spending money on the Trent as a national scheme, designating it as a local work. There was support for limited improvements by building timber slides to move timber through the rapids. No roads were planned for the lower Trent area. Baird's position as superintendent was terminated in 1843. He was succeeded by James Lyons, Thomas Wilson and, in 1847, by George Ranney who held the position for twenty-five years.

Before the construction of the timber slides, lumbermen ran the logs toll free down the river in individual pieces and no attempt was made to raft them until they arrived at the mouth of the river at Trenton. The timber slides were huge structures used in 1845 and finally completed in 1846. Unfortunately, few of the lumbermen or slide masters knew how to use them properly. These slides were a unique Canadian invention. The slides built on the Trent rested on massive timber foundations bolted securely to the bedrock. The bottoms and sides were lined with two inch planks. They were thirty-three feet in width but the length varied according to the height of the falls and length of the rapids. The slides built at Healey Falls and Ranney Falls were very long. The upper slide at Healey Falls was 713 feet long and the lower slide 360 feet. At Ranney Falls, the upper slide was 1,102 feet long and the lower one 390 feet. Booms were strung across the river at Crowe Bay and Percy Landing to collect the rafts for reassembly and counting for toll purposes. The costs of the construction of the slides on the Trent far exceeded the estimates which had been presented to the Board of Works.

In 1845, a huge log jam occurred at Middle Falls at Crowe Bay as the entire winter's timber surged down the river. The pressure created broke the boom below the dam and the whole mass headed downstream. Logs piled up everywhere on the shore, on shoals, islands and the bridge at Campbellford. Crews of men managed to break up the jam and save the bridge, but further down the river they piled up again at Ranney Falls and Chisholm's Rapids. All the wood eventually made it to Trenton but the owners then had to sort it out and reraft it. The owners were furious and refused to pay the tolls.

By October 1, 1850, an advertisement appeared in local papers offering for sale the locks, dams, slides, roads and water powers – all the improvements recently completed in the Newcastle District. This decision was reassessed to preserve the existing locks but the timber slides were to be handed over to the municipalities. These slides were extremely expensive to maintain without government support. The lumbermen were outraged and formed a committee to take over the slides at Healey Falls, Middle Falls, Ranney Falls and Glen Ross. None of the dams or locks were part of this transaction. There were major difficulties in collecting the tolls in the early years, but a new committee formed in 1859 was more successful and operated the slides for many years. Unfortunately, a severe spring flood in 1870 wiped out the slides. Some were reconstructed to allow only single sticks to go through. The reconstructed slides were in decreasing demand from that time until 1906 when the canal was built. When railways became the preferred method of transporting timber, the glorious years of the river drivers came to an end.

Mills had been built and towns, including Campbellford, grew up around them. During the winter months, timber was cut in the northern parts of the area and in the spring the huge logs were floated down to the saw mills. In 1857, John Drennan built a wooden dam at the foot of Crowe Bay above Middle Falls on the site of the present Campbellford Power House. He operated a sawmill there which was later run by Alonzo Dunk Sr. and Thomas Dunk. After their time, the Gilmour Lumber Company of Trenton sawed lumber by water power until 1898. Within the town limits, the Trent Valley Woollen Mill and the Rathbun Lumber Company were the largest industries. The Rathbun sawmill, established in 1886 under Joseph Clairmont, was on the east bank of the river near the junction of Front Street North and Ranney Street. Giant smokestacks sent sparks flying as the workers operated on ten hour shifts, six days a week. Cut lumber, hauled by a donkey engine over a spur rail line of the Grand Junction and later Grand Trunk Railway, was stacked on the present high school yard. The Rathbun Mill alone turned out almost 100,000 board feet of lumber, planks, studs, railway ties, square timber, shingles and lath each day.

In 1878, the Federal Liberal Government transferred all its interests in the Trent works to the Provincial Government with no requirement to maintain the existing structures. Following the federal election in October 1878, which reinstated the Conservatives, the transfer of the Trent works being rescinded. Pressure continued through the ensuing years, until finally in 1887, the Trent Valley Canal Association was created by order-in-council. Not until 1895 did survey work actually begin. In that year, contracts were given on the upper section of the canal but little was accomplished. Discussions continued as the federal parties changed, each paying lip service to the idea of a canal. An earlier proposal to build the canal from Port Hope to Rice Lake was revived and this prolonged the controversy.

The main factor which switched favour to the Trent was the realization of its tremendous potential for generating and transmitting the latest invention – hydro-electric power. The Town of Campbellford already owned the water privileges at Crowe Bay where a small power plant operated at the old government dam. The firm of Kerry, Smith and Chace, operators of the Northumberland Paper and Electric Company were anxious to develop sites at Ranney Falls and the Seymour Power and Electric Company at the falls above the town. By 1906, there was no decision as the federal Liberal Government favoured private development while the provincial Conservative Government wished to use its agency, the Hydro Electric Power Commission of Ontario. Finally, in February 1907, the Dominion Government approved the order-in-council authorizing the Trent Canal construction. Transportation was given as the public rationale but control of electric power was the real motive behind the order. By keeping the construction under Federal jurisdiction, power rights could be leased to private developers.

View of the west bank of the Trent River looking north from the old lift bridge before the canal was built, ca. 1900. Buildings from south to north include Cassan's Garage, the Keir Mill with the tall chimney, and the former Baptist Church.

Original photo donated to Campbellford/Seymour Heritage Society Archives by Jack Torrance.

Contracts were called for seven sections based upon their potential to generate electrical power. Section #5 was a short stretch from the railway bridge in Campbellford to Crowe Bay which involved the building of two locks and two dams. Locks on the lower Trent River are longer than those in the upper stretch of the Trent-Severn system and have more expensive valves on the sides of the lock walls. John George Kerry who owned the Northumberland Power and Electric Company at Ranney Falls convinced the government that he had monopoly rights to the water for generating power at this location which he had bought in 1907. He then proceeded with his partners Smith and Chace to acquire the Stephens Mill property at Crowe Bay to build a power plant. On December 31, 1908, the company received the first power lease on the Trent River. One year later, electricity was transmitted to the Deloro Mining Company, twenty-two miles to the northeast.

Section #4 stretched from just above Glen Ross to Campbellford. This contract was let in June 1910. Some controversy arose with regard to the Dickson dam located near the town bridge which provided power to five local mills and the municipal water system. Once again, Kerry's proposal for a high dam at Ranney Falls and the building of retaining walls through the town was the selected new route for the canal. The new portion ran behind the Northumberland Paper and Electric Company to Locks 11 and 12. Kerry eventually had five power plants under the Electric Power Company. He resigned in 1914 and in 1916, the company was sold to the Ontario Government who in turn made it part of the Hydro Electric Power Company in 1928. The government offered no compensation to the five mills who lost their source of power. On August 10, 1912, the old Dickson dam was blown up. A change of federal government finally led in 1914 to an agreement, with the greatest compensation going to the Trent Valley Woollen Mill which received a cash settlement in addition to a perpetual lease for 350 horsepower per year from the Seymour Power Plant owned by Kerry. Campbellford Cloth Company inherited the lease in 1923 and Barrymore Carpets in 1978. In 1976, the Federal Government offered the Campbellford Cloth Company $225,000 but the deal fell through when Ontario Hydro, which was to participate in the acquisition, backed out. When the mill was demolished, the town, as owner of the mill property, requested that the power become part of the town power grid. The following year, the government attempted to terminate the lease and the town sued. The court decision in 1981 ruled in favour of the perpetual lease and the agreement continues in force.

Section #6 involved construction of the widest concrete dam on the Trent at Healey Falls to replace the old wooden 1844 structure. Because of the absence of good roads, material came to Healey Falls via the Grand Trunk Railway at Blairton. Dynamite and barrels of concrete were then brought by teams of horses to the building site. Plenty of sand and gravel was available from Rowe's farm on Concession 12.

Many years passed before the canal was fully navigable. On July 26, 1918, the first boat from Lake Ontario reached Orillia. The Trent-Severn Waterway took almost ninety years to build at a cost of over $24 million. The system contains remarkable engineering feats, such as the height of the Healey Falls lift which required three locks. Although the system was planned as a commercial venture to move wheat from the prairies to Lake Ontario and Montreal, by the time it was completed, grain was being moved in other ways. The Trent Canal never developed into the commercial enterprise envisioned by its founders. The 240 mile waterway with forty-two locks is basically a tourist attraction used by pleasure craft.

Steam shovel excavating the tailrace at Lock 15, Healey Falls in 1913.

Photo from Campbellford/Seymour Heritage Society Archives.

Canal barge carrying timber being towed by motorboat, the Ada, tied up on the canal core-wall near the present day Cenotaph, ca. 1920.

Original photo donated by Roy Williams to Campbellford/Seymour Heritage Society Archives.

THE CROWE RIVER

Headwaters of the Crowe River rise north of Paudash and Limerick Lakes, not far from the southern boundary of Algonquin Park. As it winds its way southward, mostly through the semi-wilderness of the Precambrian Shield, it connects a string of lakes and drains a watershed area of 2,007 square kilometres. The Crowe is a river of many features – in places rugged and wild, plunging waterfalls, whitewater and deep gorges; in other sections, placid and plodding. The route has many picturesque scenes and is a delight to experienced canoeists.

Although the river travels approximately 100 kilometres from source, less than 10 kilometres of total length are contained within Seymour Township. From its entry point in the northeast corner of the township above Allan's Mills, the Crowe flows in a southwesterly direction to join the Trent near Healey Falls. A great variety of fossils are encased in the limestone riverbed and the rock shelves of the shoreline in the lower portion of the stream – a prehistoric record etched in stone. Geologists, who have examined these impressions of former life, have dated them up to 500 million years. They are marine creatures that lived in the vast sea that once covered much of the interior of this continent. In the warm waters of this shallow sea, they thrived in vast numbers, lived and died, and were preserved in the limey sands and muds which are now the limestone rock.

The Crowe River played a significant role in the pioneer settlement of this area. Early settlers, pushing northward through Seymour Township, followed the Trent River and continued their trek on up the Crowe. Vast tracts of timber bordered the watercourse – the first harvest to be reaped from this wilderness. From lumber camps upriver, logs moved down river to waiting sawmills in the Campbellford area. The two rivers served as the initial transportation route, by boat in summer, by sled in wintertime.

BRIDGES

In the early years of the township, no bridges existed on the Trent River. Crossing the river was accomplished by using a ford near the present cenotaph. In 1840, Robert Cockburn was given permission to construct a dam just below the ford to power his flour mill. The construction of this dam raised the water level and ruined the ford requiring the construction of a simple wooden bridge. The township must have felt a need to exercise control over bridges, as it passed a by-law on February 21, 1850 which stated that, "All persons driving or riding on any bridge over thirty feet in length faster than a walk shall forfeit and pay a fine of five shillings. Any persons maliciously injuring or destroying any bridge or rendering it impassible shall, upon conviction, pay a fine of not less than one pound and not more than five pounds, and in default of payment shall be sentenced to the Common Gaol for a term not exceeding twenty days."

In 1855, G. W. Ranney received £550 to build a wooden bridge to replace the Seymour bridge. This bridge was almost lost in March of 1870 when a seven day uninterrupted snowfall followed by several warm days made the river a raging torrent. All that saved the bridge was the courageous effort of citizens weighing it down with boulders. Several businesses at the Patch were destroyed, including the mills of R.C. Wilkins. In 1875, the Campbellford Herald advocated placing lamps on the bridge in the village after dark to help citizens safely cross the river. That year, after a fire damaged much of the decking, a new bridge was desperately needed.

In 1877, the third bridge was constructed of iron with a column arch built by the Wrought Iron Bridge Company of Canton, Ohio at a cost of $4900 not including the floor joists and flooring. One end of the bridge was still made of wood. Two additional arches were added in 1884 at a cost of $2500. County Council denied the funding for a sidewalk on the south side at a cost of $300 so the sidewalk was completed by volunteers.

Other bridges were also being added as settlement increased. A bridge was built over Trout Creek on the present Grand Road. In August of 1898, a bridge over the Crowe River was completed. Dickson Brothers built the Healey Falls Bridge in 1902 to replace the ferry service which operated there since 1862. This was used until 1966 when the present span was built.

By 1897, the village of Campbellford was in need of an improved bridge. The cost of this structure was $8500 for the substructure and $3500 for the superstructure. This time the cost of the sidewalk was shared between the County Council and the Village. Part of the old bridge was used at Trout Creek.

In 1885, a drawbridge existed at the Seymour-Belmont-Methuen boundary. This was replaced in 1893 by a new bridge at The Narrows.

On November 23, 1904, a new bridge was built in Campbellford by the Weddle Bridge Company. This was soon converted on the west end to a bascule type which could be lifted to accommodate boat traffic. Under the direction of the Department of Railways and Canals, the large counterweight and electric lift were designed to raise only the west end of the bridge.

In 1968, the present high level bridge was constructed. During the removal of the old structure and the building of the new, a very steep pedestrian bridge crossed the river. Vehicles were required to cross further south on Grand Road over the old low black railway bridge. A wooden platform replaced the railway ties to accommodate vehicles. The only other way to cross was by making a full circle of the canal using Trent Drive.

Main lift bridge over the Trent River built in 1904 by Weddle Bridge Company. Campbellford Cloth Company is in the background. Photo ca. 1921

Photo from postcard collection of Campbellford/Seymour Heritage Society Archives.

~ Business on the Rivers ~

THE ALLAN MILL

In the 1840s, David Allan began his plans to build a grist mill on the Crowe River on Concession 12, Lot 26, Seymour Township. This was an ideal location where upstream the river widened into the present day Rylstone Lake and downstream the channel narrowed and dropped down a rapids. First, he constructed a wooden bridge to permit traffic to cross the river as his plans for a dam downstream would ruin the ford which was used. The northwest end of the dam was anchored to a rock shelf. In the same area, he also located the control works for the dam. The stop logs were square timbers which could be inserted or removed as the level of the river dictated. On the opposite shore, the dam was attached to a ridge of rock. A heavy steel gate controlled the flow to the raceway and waterwheel. The grist mill opened between 1846 and 1848, followed by a saw mill completed between 1850 and 1854. The saw mill was attached to the grist mill with one end extending over the mill pond. This allowed logs to be winched directly from the water to the carriage. A general store was also opened on the premises. In 1854, the first entries occur in the Allan Journal, providing a daily record of business transactions with the local residents and the lumber shanties. The nearby Allan home also provided a boarding house for mill and farm workers. During these early years, the miller controlled water levels in the river and thus was able to protect his interests.

In the 1860s, John Lisle, an Englishman who had been employed at Canniff's Mill near Belleville, took over the operation of the Allan Mill. For twenty years, he served in this role until James Allan, David's son, succeeded him. The grist mill produced livestock feed, pastry and bread flour, bran and cornmeal while the saw mill cut lumber, planed boards and created tongue and groove lumber and cedar shingles. Stone boats were also made for local farmers.

In 1907, a second water wheel was installed to generate electricity for the neighbourhood. This primitive network used trees and fence posts as well as poles. The supply of power was often limited by the diversion of the water flow to the mill.

From 1888 until 1910, James Allan operated the mill. In 1915, James moved to Campbellford and sold the mill to his son, Will. The Allan Mill continued to serve the community and provided employment for many local men. However, the machinery was aging and parts were becoming difficult to replace. In October 1950, a disastrous fire destroyed the mill buildings. For some years after, Will Allan continued to operate a saw mill in one of his barn buildings using a tractor as a source of power. The mill was not rebuilt and the property was sold.

CAMPBELLFORD CLOTH COMPANY / TRENT VALLEY WOOLLEN MILL, 1879–1979

The first woollen mill on the site of Old Mill Park was operated by Samuel Mirfield. This firm was purchased by Trent Valley Woollen Mills, run by the Gaults of Montreal. When Hamilton Gault withdrew from the firm in 1921, the mill became the Campbellford Cloth Company, owned by a Toronto firm. For many years, this firm was the town's biggest employer. The sounding of the mill whistle, which was first heard on September 25, 1879, was a familiar event by which citizens could check the time of day. In busy times, the clatter of the looms could be heard for twenty-four hours a day.

During the first few years, fine flannels were made, which became famous throughout Canada. During both World Wars khaki was produced. At other times, overcoat fabrics, tweeds, and automobile upholstery fabrics were made. The manufacture of yarn, weaving of the cloth, dying and finishing were all done at the mill. When F. B. Hayes purchased the mill in 1921, he moved the dying and finishing out to his Toronto mill. In 1935, there were about three hundred employees and at one time there were four hundred. Sixty percent of the workers were female. In the late 1940s, the Textile Workers of America established a local at the Campbellford mill. In the early 1950s, a carpet manufacturing plant was started across the road from the Mill and was called the Barrymore Carpet Factory. It was the first place in Canada to manufacture tufted carpet. The mill also branched out into synthetics such as rayon and nylon in the 1950s.

The announcement in 1975 that the mill and carpet factory were closing came as quite a blow to the economy of the town. At that time, there were eighty employees. In 1979, the buildings were demolished and Old Mill Park was created on the site. A plaque in Old Mill Park reads:

History of Trent Valley Woollen and Campbellford Cloth Company

> Original five storey building was erected in the late 1870s and opened in 1882. Built by Gault Brothers of Montreal and built of brick kilned at West Brick Yards of West's Corners.
>
> Operated as Trent Valley Woollens and used own power generated from Trent River until canal built and government bought up power rights.
>
> Sold in 1921 to Toronto Company, Barrymore Cloth of Toronto owned by F.B. Hayes. From then known as Campbellford Cloth Company.
>
> The weave shed along Grand Road was built in 1913–14 as canal was being built. In 1922, Campbellford Cloth purchased Keller Hotel at the corner of Bridge and Grand Road and used as an office.[2]

CAMPBELLFORD PULP MILL

The Campbellford Pulp Mill was built in 1911 near Ranney Falls by the Northumberland Paper and Electric Company who operated it for four years. The manager was E. Brunelle. The mill used thirty cords of wood per day and employed forty-five men. It required thirty-three hundred horse power to run at full capacity. Four grinders were used to make mechanical ground wood pulp. Before shipping, this pulp was pressed in hydraulic presses. The resulting product was sold to paper mills, newsprint mills, and board mills. On April 23, 1932, the pulp mill was demolished by fire and subsequently rebuilt. The Campbellford Herald noted in November 1953, that several long-time employees of the Gair Company in Campbellford were the recipients of gold watches for twenty-five years of service. At a banquet at the Yellow Salon of the King Edward Hotel in Toronto, the local men honoured were Thomas McAvilla, Manley Grills, Charles Keir, and Wilbert Reid.

The Gair mill closed in 1957, putting the wage-earners for fifty families out of work. The Gair Company owned the site until it was purchased by Continental Can Company and the Ross Paper Machinery Company of Newark, New Jersey. On September 26, 1960, Daniel W. Holmes purchased the plant from the two owners. It was several months before the plant was operable, because the machinery which had been idle for so long needed much repair and rebuilding. The Campbellford PUC built a new sub-station to ensure an adequate power supply. Ground wood pulp produced at the mill was used in the manufacture of facial tissue, paper towels and the outer coating of cardboard. The new plant employed up to forty people. In 1970, the property passed to Morley Tanner who, in 1971, tore down the buildings and laid out the subdivision now known as Parkview Estates.

COCKBURN/CHARLES SMITH FLOUR MILL

The original flour mill owned by Robert and James Cockburn was a stone building erected in 1850 on Saskatoon Avenue, formerly Mill Street. This business was purchased in 1881 by Charles Smith who had operated a similar mill in Warkworth. This structure burned in 1883 and a new brick building with a mansard roof and gable windows on the upper floor was erected on the same site. The top three floors contained twelve silos which made it difficult to adapt the building to any other purpose. Smith was instrumental in introducing a new roller press perfected in Hungary for grinding the grain as well as traditional methods. The mill produced all kinds of flour and Charles Smith was not shy about praising his product. A circular advertising his wares spells out why Campbellford Flour should be used.

1st – Its Superior Quality cannot be surpassed anywhere in this wide world. It's the best.

2nd – It's a Home Manufacture, and the entire proceeds are distributed here and in England. Manitoba mills do not spend their money here.

3rd – When you buy Manitoba Flour your money goes to enrich the Mills and people of Manitoba at the expense of Campbellford.

4th – Every sack of Manitoba Flour you buy strikes a blow at the prosperity of your town and encourages others to do the same.

5th – Every dollar you spend on Flour made outside Campbellford, you make this town that much poorer.

6th – One great need of Campbellford is more Manufacturers. Loyal support of those that are here will encourage others to come.

7th – The Campbellford Flour Mills have saved you money – from 25 c. to 75 c. per barrel on your Flour, and $2.00 to $5.00 per ton on Mill Feed. If you want cheaper Bran, Shorts, etc., use Campbellford Flour and thus increase the supply.

8th – Tell your Grocer you must have Campbellford Flour, and if he sends you anything else, be loyal and send it back with your compliments, stating you patronize home manufacture.[3]

Later, his sons, William and Fred, were in charge of the business.

In 1918, the mill was taken over by the Peterborough Cereal Company operated by John Meyers. McKelvie and McCook purchased the Peterborough Cereal Company and took over the mill. In 1944, a frozen food locker business was established on the first floor by H.N. Carr. It is told that he smoked ham in the race-

View of Smith Mill from the river in 1908. Built in 1883, it was demolished in 1996.
Photos from Archives Collection of Campbellford/Seymour Heritage Society.
Original mill photo is of unknown origin; photo of demolition from donation by Scott MacLeod.

way under the street and the delicious odours wafted around town. In 1950, the locker business was purchased by Herbert J. Taylor who operated it as Frostee Lockers for several years. In 1954, the south part of the building was sold to the district co-operative. In 1973, James B. Cranfield restored the interior of the building to its original state. Hector Macmillan purchased the site in 1984 and reopened the locker business on the first floor. In 1988, the entire mill property was bought by Mr. and Mrs. Harry Cheung who sold it to Otto Feiden. This landmark was demolished in 1996.

DICKSON'S FOUNDRY

In 1860, John Dickson opened an iron foundry and machine shop on Saskatoon Avenue. Later, his sons James and George operated the business as Dickson Brothers. This firm was noteworthy for the making of bells for churches, steel for bridges, wagon wheels and many other items. In 1905, the business relocated to a building on Alma Street near the railway station. The building at the old location became Davidson's Garage. In 1915, the new location became the site of the shell factory which produced ammunition ranging from eighteen to ninety pounds in size. The firm was destroyed by a disastrous fire in 1917 but was rebuilt. After World War I, it was sold to A.W. Robertson and later to Walter and Edith Henson who ran a machine shop. In 1945, it was purchased by Wallace Stapley.

NORTHUMBERLAND PAPER AND ELECTRIC COMPANY / GAIR PAPER MILL / BREITHAUPT LEATHER

One of the oldest industries in the early years of the settlement was the Northumberland Paper and Electric Company, known locally as "The Paper Mill." The Campbellford Herald noted that a notice appeared in the Ontario Gazette in May 1883, that Edmund Grover Burk(e), Isabella Burk(e) and D. Burk(e) Simpson, of Bowmanville, Blanch Elizabeth Keeler of Seymour, and Charles Alexander Weller of Peterborough were going to apply for incorporation under the name of Northumberland Paper Co., the object being to manufacture all kinds of paper at the Campbellford Paper Mills. Buildings were erected on the two hundred acres of land at Ranney Falls owned by W. Keeler. In addition to the paper mill, he had a carding and weaving mill for a short time. He also erected some houses. There were no drying machines in the mill and the paper was laid to dry in a field. This mill was a very busy industry which operated both day and night, at its peak employing ninety men. In addition, a large number of drivers and horse teams were kept busy drawing loads of straw to the mill for the making of cardboard. At another time, rags would be run through the machines to make roofing felt. Cedar bark was run through the machines to manufacture carpet felt. After the sale of the mill to E.G. Burke, a machine was installed to dry the paper. While Burke operated the business, it produced tarpaper, boxboard, and egg crates made of pine with cardboard fillers. In 1886, a generator was installed at the mill which ran five arc and five incandescent lights.

By 1888, two new water turbines were installed to increase power. In 1891, business was booming at the mill and a new office building was constructed. On July 16, 1894, Edmund Burke died suddenly at age forty-eight. In 1895, the paper mill went bankrupt and was bought and improved by H.A. Mulholland. He used

The Campbellford Herald

Campbellford, Ontario, Friday, March 29th, 1946

EXTRA
Breithaupt Buys Old Paper Mill

The Breithaupt Leather Company of Kitchener, The Largest Leather Company in Canada, Completed Deal Thursday with Mayor J. E. Ayrhart. First of Flood of Outside Capital Invested in Campbellford

The good news broke on Thursday afternoon, when Mayor Ayrhart announced that he had decided to put the interest of Campbellford ahead of his personal desire and sell the building in which he had recently set up his cement block factory. At great inconvenience to himself and his organization, the Mayor will be forced to move from the commodious property his installations, put there at great cost. In addition Ayrhart Enterprises are obligated to completely remodel the premises, installing water, power and the rail siding.

These items, we are informed, will be accomplished at a cost which will not make the deal especially inviting from a money point of view, as the brick factory will have to be moved to the Ayrhart gravel pit, in addition to the above mentioned undertakings.

For the time being the saw mill will remain in its present location.

First New Capital in Years

The coming of this new company, The Breithaupt Leather Co. Limited, marks the first influx of outside capital in quite a number of years, but we do not expect it to be the last. We are informed that there are many manufacturers seeking to find out about our town and the possibilities, in view of present publicity spread far and wide by our Mayor.

The Breithaupt Company is a substantial and reliable firm, with branches at Kitchener, Hastings and Penetang. They are the makers, we are told, of shoe leathers, gloves, and other leather goods. It is our understanding that they will employ at the start as many as 75 hands, and perhaps up to 200.

Work on Airport Starts Next Week

Another development of the past few days is the announcement that work on the new airport is about to commence. We announced the purchase of the Stillman farm by Mayor Ayrhart and his associates in our last regular edition.

More Homes Needed

Now that we have a new industry in sight the next big step is to build homes for more workers, and our versatile Mayor says he is going to do that too. More power to him!

Mayor J. E. Ayrhart announces the purchase of the old paper mill by the Breithaupt Leather Company of Kitchener.

Broadsheet donated by Larry Healey to the Campbellford/Seymour Heritage Society Archives.

the old dryer for some time but eventually purchased a new dryer which was seventy-two inches in width. For a short time, W. Keir used part of the mill as a carding and weaving establishment which he later relocated to Queen Street near the cenotaph. In 1907, the mill was bought by Cecil Smith, John George Kerry and

W. G. Chace. When Smith died, Chace became the President of the company. In 1910, the mill burned, but, by 1916, was rebuilt with additions that included houses, a blacksmith shop and a pumping station. In 1916, the Hydro Electric Power Commission purchased the central Ontario system and, with it, the water rights. Competition from the Canadian Paper Board Company of Toronto reduced the production in the mill, which was eventually closed in 1939 and purchased by the Robert Gair Company. Most of the time, the plant was idle. For some of the time, J. E. Ayrhart used it as a cement block factory.

In 1946, the property was bought by Breithaupt Leather and renovated for a leather tannery and finishing factory. In 1983, Larry and Margaret Healey purchased the property on which they built a home in 1989. The outlying buildings were rented until 1994 when the Healeys opened a flea market which has since closed.

WESTON SHOE FACTORY

In 1902, Fred Weston opened a shoe factory in the old stone building which was built in 1876 beside the fire hall. This had previously housed a knitting mill owned by Mr. McMurchy and, later, a mill operated by John Routh that produced a coarse cloth. Dalgleish, Patterson and Barrett also used this building. The Weston Company made women's and children's shoes from 1902 until 1933 with a staff of sixty to seventy people. In June 1939, Russel J. Bale purchased the business which became known as Gravlin and Bale with a staff of forty-five. The product changed to men's boots for farmers, miners and prospectors and boy's school boots. They made as many as two thousand pair per week. Following this, Johnston Shoes and Sisman Shoes operated the plant.[4] In the early 1950s, the building housed Canadian Flight Equipment which, until 1964, made the first ejection seats for jet fighter aircraft. Later, Frank Towns operated his upholstery business from lower floor of the site. After many years of being idle, the building was dismantled in 1996.

⁓ Resorts ⁓

CATCHMORE FISHING /
CAMPING AND HOUSEKEEPING COTTAGES

This cottage resort features seven three bedroom cottages as well as camping and trailer sites both with and without hydro service, boat and motor rentals, a boat launch, docking facilities, horse shoe pit, picnic tables, swimming, great fishing and a camp store. It is located on Bradley Bay on Concession 1, Lot 16, Seymour Township. Many years ago, it was owned by the Hendricks family and the Grills family but now is hosted by Duncan and Rita Slater.

CEDAR ISLE LODGE

In November 1900, Cedar Isle Lodge at Trent River on Concession 14, Lot 6 became the home of the Wight family. They arrived by team and sleigh. Thomas Wight, born in 1840, had come to Canada from Selkirk, Scotland. He was the father of Andrew Noble Wight born in March 1871 and James born in 1873. Andrew and his wife, Anne Melville had operated a summer resort in Belmont Township before moving to Cedar Isle. Here they made their home, along with daughters, Mary and Annie, later parenting six more children. The lodge was situated on the first of three islands known as Wight Islands. The first two islands were joined by a short bridge. This eventually became unusable and the narrow channel between the two islands was filled in by the residents living beside it. The third island is joined to the mainland by a small bridge on the easterly side. This island also housed the former Jorgenson's Marina. The guest register used by the Wights showed the first entry as a Mr. H. Coxwell arriving from Toronto on June 15, 1901. Thomas Wight and his son Andrew along with a Mr. Croft operated a fishing tackle manufacturing business at the lodge, employing local people. The business was sold in 1923 due to the illness and death of Andrew Wight. The Canadian Needle and Fishing Tackle Company was relocated to Havelock. The lodge continued to operate under numerous owners, including John, Ev, and Ron Haylock, until recently when it was converted into rental apartments.

CEDARMERE

This resort consisted of 200 acres on Concession 11, Lot 14 owned by Margaret Dunham who was a widow with a young family. They resided in the big house and built six cottages on the Trent River. In 1946, the property was sold to Clyde Wallick of Dover, Ohio. He was a coal miner who had struck it rich, maintaining homes in Hollywood and Florida and he used the Cedarmere development as a free vacation resort for his employees. He eventually divided the property into three pieces, keeping the house and eight acres which were later sold to Ross Richardson. Dennis Little now owns one piece of this property. It is no longer a resort.

THE CEDARS

The Cedars was a popular resort on Concession 10, Lot 18 on the shores of Crowe Bay opened by Fred Smith. Housekeeping cottages, boats and motors, fishing tackle and a general store were located on the site. After Smith, the resort had several other owners, including Roy Southworth, who bought it in the spring of 1949. In recent years, the resort was operated by Joe and Sherry Michael and Roy Geis. By 1997, the resort was permanently closed.

COLE'S POINT RESORT/DORIE'S POINT

Cole's Point Resort, originally owned by R. H. Cole, is located at the junction of the Crowe and the Trent Rivers on Concession 12, Lot 15, originally owned by the Dorie family. This family resort has fully equipped two and three bedroom cottages as well as seasonal trailer sites. A recreation hall with pool table and arcade, boat, motor, canoe and paddle boat rentals, fishing, horseshoe pits, heated pool, hiking trails, a camp store, a children's playground and water sports are all available. Later operators of the site included Hans and Marie Jehle. In 1993, it was purchased by John Hoefman.

CROWE BAY CAMP

Crowe Bay Camp was established in 1959 on the east side of County Road 38 just opposite the generating station at the foot of Crowe Bay. The site was initially developed by Doug Burgis and consisted of 25 serviced camp sites, a shuffleboard court, and a pond. The facility was given some good publicity by Pierre Berton on his travels through the Trent-Severn Waterway in July 1961. Doug sold the property to Agnes and James Ross in the early 1960s and they operated it until it was taken over by Margaret and Fritz Wilms who added a small variety store. The camp was closed in the early 1990s and is a private residence today.

CROWE BRIDGE FAMILY FUN PARK

This relatively new attraction, owned and operated by the Crowe Valley Conservation Authority, is located on Concession 11, Lot 20. The Family Fun Park offers forty secluded campsites, swimming with tube rentals, golf at the Wild Woods Golf, and twenty-two acres along the Crowe River which can accommodate family gatherings, church picnics or birthday parties. The quiet surroundings, natural settings, fossils and scenic lookouts provide plenty of space to commune with nature.

FRIENDLY ACRES

Friendly Acres is located on a ten acre site on the Puffball Road just west of Trent River village. The resort has five cottages as well as two trailer site areas, recreation hall, shuffle board, heated pool, playground, boat rentals including jet ski and pontoon boats, boat slips, excellent fishing, horseshoe pits, a sandy beach and a camp store with video rentals and a lending library. In the 1950s, the resort was owned by the Jewell family; Gerry and Rip Van Ginkel operated it later. Presently, Gary and Mary Anne Barnett and family are the hosts at Friendly Acres.

HICKORY GROVE COTTAGES

This small resort is located on County Road 50 just outside the town limits. It was developed in the early 1940s by the Clements family. Bert and Minnie Budd were the second owners. George and Pat Banton have owned and operated the business for the past thirty years and live on the site. It consists of housekeeping cottages and campsites and has access to the Trent River from the waterfront portion of the property. It is one of the oldest resorts in the area and draws much of its clientele from the Toronto and Hamilton areas.

ISLAND PARK

Island Park is located on Wilson Island at the southeast end of Seymour Township. This resort, opened in the 1960s by Carleton and David Potts, is open year round. A recreation hall is available for dances, bingo and arts and crafts. The campground offers a safe, sandy beach, excellent fishing, boat rentals and a grocery store. Presently, Island Park is owned and operated by Carl and Patricia Cashin.

KELLER VACATION PROPERTIES: WOODLAND ESTATE, KELLER'S KAMP AND FISHERMAN'S PARADISE

When the first tourist homes were established in the Healey Falls area at the turn of the century, vacationers were primarily American. They travelled by train to Toronto and then on to Havelock where they were met by tourist operators and transported by horse and wagon to their final destination seven miles to the southeast. In the early days, cottages were not the usual accommodation. People stayed at tourist homes and were provided with food and lodging much like bed and breakfast places but, in the early years, three meals a day were included and guests stayed one or two weeks.

As a young man in the 1830s, Christopher Keller was given a grant of 100 acres of Crown Land on Concession 12, Lot 14 near Healey Falls. He travelled from the Kingston area to establish a homestead on that land and was required to build a cabin and clear a few acres of farm land. He later married Elizabeth Hubble of Hubble Hill in Rawdon Township. As a young married couple, Christopher and Elizabeth went to Missouri where they lived for eight years until the Civil War broke out in 1861. Two daughters had tragically died there of the black plague. Christopher and his sixteen year old son were taken into the Union Army along with a ten year old son, Roderick. After one of the fiercest battles of the Civil War took place in Missouri, Christopher decided it was time to leave for Canada and his farm at Healey Falls. Christopher's sympathies lay with the South. He picked up a cannonball from a battlefield as a memento of his life in the United States. In order to avoid the army, he and his two sons travelled by night while his wife and the rest of the family travelled in daylight by way of horse and wagon. They arrived at Healey Falls sometime during the 1860s and took up farming the 100 acres that Christopher had established as a young man.

First cottage built at Healey Falls as part of Woodland Estate/Rest-a-While Resort owned by the Keller family. It was constructed from the material from the old Roman Catholic chapel at Healey Falls which was used when the power house was being built at that location. The small peaked structure in the foreground is the belfry of the chapel.

Photo donated by Helen Abernethy to Campbellford/Seymour Heritage Society Archives.

Subsequently, Christopher divided his property into three parcels. One parcel of about twenty acres was given to Roderick Keller who later established the first tourist home in the Healey Falls area, now known as Woodland Estate. Roderick had met two men from Toronto who needed accommodation while duck hunting. He brought them home with him and thus began a lengthy love of the tourist industry. Roderick Keller's widow sold the resort but later her son Frederick bought it back and renamed it Rest-a-while. About 1946, Fred sold the resort to Ernest Ayrhart who renamed the resort Woodland Estate. It has changed hands several times since and is currently owned by a corporation. It has an active camping area, trailer park, swimming pool and cottages. It is still frequented by many long time clients who visit annually from the United States.

Another piece containing about ten acres was given to Christopher's son, Christopher Jr., who in time established a tourist home known as Fisherman's Paradise. Christopher Keller Jr. left his property to his son, Stanley and his wife Marguerite who operated the resort until 1961. It has since changed hands several times. Fisherman's Paradise is a busy summer area with a ten acre field for trailers to the south of the road allowance which gives river access at the public boat launch. Immediately adjacent to the north of Fisherman's Paradise resort is a subdivision of summer cottages which are part of the former Camp Eagle Eye.

The third parcel of sixty-seven acres was retained by Christopher, Sr., and, after his death, it was inherited by his youngest son, Charles. In 1931, Charles gave his farm to his son, Sanford, who established a tourist home known as Keller's Kamp in the 1940s. When Sanford Keller died in 1958, the property was bequeathed to his wife, Minnie. Their daughter, Marcia, moved from Campbellford to Keller's Kamp to live with her mother and for thirty years assisted with the operation of Keller's Kamp. After Minnie's death in 1986, it was left to her daughters, Betty Brown and Marcia Keller. The property was given by Betty Brown and Marcia Keller to Rick Brown, grandson of Sanford and Minnie Keller, in 1988. Keller's Kamp now consists of only sixty-two acres since Charles Keller gave his brother, Christopher, an additional five acres. Many faithful clients continue to spend their annual vacation at the Kamp.

MARINE TERRACE COTTAGES
Marine Terrace Cottages are just east of the bridge on the south shore of the Trent River on Concession 14, Lot 6. Both two and three bedroom, fully-equipped cottages are available as well as boat, motor and canoe rentals. Many improvements are in the works at this location under host Ken Rowe.

PARKSIDE COTTAGES
Parkside Cottages are located adjacent to Marine Terrace and consists of three cottages on the waterfront and a boat launch area. The resort is currently owned by Raymond and Jacqui Whyte who purchased it in 1998 from Doris Johnston.

PERCY BOOM HAVEN / JAKE'S COTTAGES
This resort on Concession 1, Lot 5, originally owned and operated by Pops Bailey, has a long history as an excellent holiday location. Now the site has seventeen cottages, both regular and deluxe. It is well known as a fishing haven with boat and motor rentals, beach and playground and a general store on site. Most of the clientele is American. Presently, Dan and Linda Heidt operate this resort.

PERCY BOOM LODGE
Another memorable fishing camp is Percy Boom Lodge, situated on the Trent River south of Campbellford. This area with its breath-taking view of the river has always been a favourite camping and fishing haven. In the early 1900s, Campbellford and Seymour residents often took their tents and canoes to this area in the summer as part of their vacation.

Percy Boom Lodge was established in 1937 by Mr. Tait, who had a hardware store in Toronto. The main building had been a cook house for the men who ran logs down the Trent to Percy Boom in the 1800s. They were paid "seed money", which was indeed used to buy seed for their farms when they returned home from the log drive. James Jackson owned the lodge until January 1999 when it was purchased by Henry Tremblay and his wife, Morag Gow.

Each summer there is a grand fishing derby and, in 1998, there were one hundred and fifty fishermen competing for the biggest catch. The fish are measured and put back in the river.

PUFFBALL INN

One of the former resorts with an interesting history is Puffball Inn. This lovely building, which would house as many as eighty people, was situated on Concession 13, Lots 10, 11, 12, and 13 on Nappan Island in the Trent River north of Campbellford. On June 7, 1926, Frank Dobscha of Rochester, N.Y. purchased the property from Richard McKelvie and erected the building. It was a fishing lodge catering to people from Ohio. The guests would come by train to Havelock and be met by horse and wagon and transported to the Inn for their fishing vacation. In 1947, the lodge was purchased by Mr. and Mrs. R.W. Umnitz and son from Cleveland, Ohio.

The building had a beautiful dining room and kitchen on the main floor where meals were served. There was an enormous cook stove in the kitchen where all meals were prepared. A local woman who worked there as a teenager remembers

Puffball Inn on the Trent River when Frank Dobscha was proprietor.
Photo courtesy of Ann Rowe.

spreading the bread out to toast on the stove and running back to where she started to turn the slices over. They were then buttered with a paint brush. In season, local puffballs fried in butter were served. There is a rumour that Al Capone stayed at the Inn during its heyday!

The guests were mostly male, but occasionally the family came along to fish or swim or sit on the huge verandah, which ran across the whole front of the building. In the 1950s, the cost was $48 per week all inclusive, even boat rental. During the 1960s, owners were Stanley Iwaschko, Eugene Kostyrko, and Alex Kociumbas. In 1962, it was sold to Nappan Island Development Ltd. Unfortunately, the building burned in the 1970s, but the local cottagers can identify the spot where the hotel used to sit. When Puffball Inn was built, there were no cottages at all on the island; now there are many.

RED SETTER RESORT

Red Setter Resort is located east of the village of Trent River on the north shore. The site boasts eight bright and airy modern cottages as well as numerous serviced or non-serviced trailer and camping sites, with picnic table and fire pit. Other activities are fishing, boating, hiking, swimming pool, horse shoes, children's playground, recreation hall and camp store. Boat and motor rentals are available as well as docking facilities and dumping stations for trailers. In the 1980s, the resort was owner by Nick and Kathy Pinto; current hosts are Brent and Mary Marchant.

SEDGEWICK'S HOTEL

The building was constructed in the 1870s by A. M. Mann. Stewart Wannamaker and George T. Cummings operated this hotel followed by George Brown. Brown's Hotel housed the first tourists to Trent River. It also provided a boarding arrangement for the workers who were building the Trent Canal. In 1884, the post office was in the front hall of the building. After George Brown passed away, his wife, Elizabeth, married John Boyd, who was a Scottish stone mason employed as a foreman on the canal project. Operation of the hotel passed to Mr. and Mrs. Jack Sedgewick who renamed the business, Sedgewick House. A 1932 advertisement promised "good accommodation and home cooking." Later, the site became McLaughlin Enterprises. The hotel was closed many years ago and has since been used for other business purposes.

SHADYNOOK

This was another popular resort operated by Mrs. W. J. Latta on a location near the Healey Falls bridge. A 1932 advertisement promised "good home-cooked meals, excellent fishing and good accommodation at reasonable rates."

TRENT HOUSE MOTEL

From a small beginning in 1942, the Trent House, situated on the river opposite the corner of Queen and Church Streets in Campbellford, has expanded from a home offering overnight accommodation for one or two guests to a full fledged modern motel. The Trent House was owned and operated for many years by Roy and Kay Smith who came to Campbellford in 1940 when they relocated their toy company from Toronto. In the early years, the only guests at the home were salesmen calling on the Monarch Toy Company. In 1945, the Smiths sold the toy company but decided to remain in Campbellford and operate the Trent House. Extensive renovations were made and the home became a full time operation.

The guest register is filled with signatures from all over the world, and includes guests who were engaged in a wide variety of occupations and professions. One page contains the names of a cattle buyer from Puerto Rico, businessmen from Chicago, New York and Mexico City, an entertainer and a government official. The names of salesmen selling everything from toothpaste to heavy construction equipment are also found within its pages. Before 1960, two motel units were added at the north end of the property overlooking the river. In 1963, several more motel units were added and the old ones completely remodelled. Each unit contained a four-piece bath, wall-to-wall broadloom, picture window and electric heating. All work was completed by local contractors and suppliers.

After Mr. Smith's death, Kay continued to operate the motel for many years until she left to reside with her daughter, Eva. She still has a great love for Campbellford and keeps in touch with the current owners of the property, who are Madeleine Montrose and Saleem Kahn.

VILLA TRENT

Villa Trent was located on Front Street North, across from the fair grounds, on the site of a former saw mill. Abram Rappaport had come to Campbellford in 1931 to open the Hollywood Theatre. He was delighted with the town but was disappointed to learn that the river captured many lives. He made a resolution to give every child a chance to learn to swim. For this reason, he bought the six acres of property. He cleaned up the shoreline, engaged an instructor, erected a diving board and invited the children of the town to come to the beach to learn how to swim.

The resort opened in 1933 when Rappaport built his first cabin. A second was added in the spring of 1934, and by 1936 he had begun building a hotel. This was a two storey structure, seventy feet in length with river frontage on the Trent. The ground floor was a dine and dance facility with three fireplaces, buffet counter and kitchen. Upstairs were nine bedrooms and two shower bathrooms as well as an enclosed veranda facing the river. An advertisement from July 13, 1939 relates the serving of breakfast, lunch and dinner daily as well as the opportunity to make reservations for bridge and dinner parties.

The small cottages, of which there were eventually about ten, were intended to accommodate two persons. Each cottage had a radio, electric stove, wood fireplace, ice box and other necessities. To beautify the camping grounds, Mr. Rappaport bought five hundred trees, both deciduous and coniferous, and planted them effectively around the cottages and along the entrance roads. This resort was considered to be one of the finest tourist camps in the area during its heyday.

Swimming instruction continued at Villa Trent up to the 1950s. Countless children learned the necessary skills through the generosity of this local entrepreneur. One of the later instructors was Dorothy Tremblay.

In 1963, Kees Vandegraff, the new owner, renamed the property the Riviera Inn. In about 1966, Kay and Art Kaye bought the business and operated it with the assistance of Kay's daughter, Kathy Herrold. Kay had been a resident of Campbellford for many years previously when she was the owner of Kay's Place, located on the present site of the Hydra Restaurant. She had left town and moved to Toronto where she lived for several years. Soon after purchasing the Riviera, a dining room was built facing the river. The business prospered and required the construction of two new banquet rooms. This was in addition to the nine rooms within the main building and the cottages which were rented during the summer. Weekends were a very busy time catering to weddings and other celebrations as well as offering a Prime Rib smorgasbord, with lobster and shrimp and an assortment of twenty salads featured on the menu. During the week, a soup and salad lunch bar was offered for $1.50. Kay was always a very gracious hostess.

In 1971, a section of the property was severed and Kathy's uncle and aunt, Ral and Irene Elia built the motel. All but one of the cottages were removed at that time. This property is now known as Campbellford River Inn. Present owners, Agnes and Peter Emmenegger offer an in-ground pool, picnic area, docking facilities, campfire pits, boat rentals, boat docking facilities and a playground. About 1974, the restaurant business was sold to the Kanellos family of Trenton. They operated it for a short time and then it was taken over by John Gaspic, who operated the business as the Riviera Inn. Presently the restaurant is not operating and is for sale.

Parks and Conservation Areas

FERRIS PROVINCIAL PARK

The park occupies approximately 500 acres in Concessions 4 and 5 of Seymour East. It is bounded by farmland on the south, the Trent River on the west, Campbellford on the north and County Road 8, known locally as the "English Line," on the east.

Entrance to Ferris Park from County Road 8 or English Line.

Original dry-stone fences built by Mr. Clarke in Ferris Park.
Photos courtesy of Margaret Crothers, taken in 1999.

Since the first cabin was built in 1836, surprisingly few people lived on the property, although a number of different people have owned parts of it. Lieutenant-Colonel Robert Campbell acquired Lots 9 and 10, Concession 4 from the Crown in 1834, and was the first owner of the southern section of the park. In 1856, when David Campbell sold all of his Seymour holdings, Nesbitt Kirchoffer and James Cockburn purchased the land. The simplest way to trace the ownership of the park land is to examine each lot individually.

Concession 4, Lot 9

Nathan Grills (1822–1891) and his wife, Elizabeth Saunders (1831–1918) bought this parcel next to the river from Nesbitt Kirchoffer in 1871. Nathan's property was split into two parcels of approximately one hundred acres each. Nathan retained the north half and Thomas Brachoney purchased the south half. In 1887, Nathan's son, Richard, acquired the original 200 acres. This family occupied the land until 1919 when the property was again split and the northern half was sold to their younger son, George Wesley Grills. The southern portion was not incorporated into Ferris Park. George and his family lived on this farm until Victor J. Hay bought it in 1926. The road allowance between Concessions 4 and 5 was the entrance to this property but it is possible that the family made use of an entry off Saskatoon Avenue or along the river. The buildings were situated southeast of the sheepwash at the bottom of a steep hill. Campsite #93 is the site of the former Grills' home. Now a few old apple trees, a clump of lilac bushes and a patch of rhubarb mark the place where the house stood; the outbuildings and barns were west of the house closer to the river. The two storey house burned in the spring of 1929 but no one was living in it at the time. In 1934, the farm was sold to Wm. F. Scott. At that time, the foundation of the burned house was still there, as was the barn. Later the lumber from the barn was moved to the Scott farm in Seymour West. Cattle were pastured on this land until the Province bought it in 1968.

Concession 4, Lot 10

Charles French bought this land from James Cockburn in 1862. The property extended from the park gates south to French's Hill at the 4th Line. The south half did not become part of the park. The north half, consisting of 100 acres, was split three ways.

1st Section

Richard Grills purchased 30 acres from the French family in 1893 and the property remained in the Grills family until George Grills sold it to Victor Hay in 1926. William Scott bought this 30 acre parcel in 1934 and used it, along with his other property on Lot 9, as pasture land until it was sold to the Province in 1968.

2nd Section

In 1899 John Miller bought 20 acres from Elizabeth French. The property remained in the Miller family until it was sold to Thomas Stephens in 1916. The Stephens family owned it until Arthur Stephens sold it to the Province in 1968.

3rd Section

In 1912 Gordon Anderson bought 50 acres from the French family and Joshua Anderson built a frame house just south of the park gates. This property remained in the Anderson family until Joshua sold it to Thomas Horkins in 1921. The house burned and one of the outbuildings was converted to a house and the property was leased. John Meier, one of the tenants, brought his family over from Switzerland and he and his family lived there for a time. A number of people remember the beautiful vegetable garden Mr. Meier had. Several people wanted to buy this land but no one could get a clear title. Hugh and Edith Gratton and their family rented this property for a number of years. Their granddaughter remembers Edith's well-stocked fruit cellar. She also recalls being sent to the spring-fed well where food was kept cool in the summer. Bruce Gratton, Hugh's son, eventually bought the 50 acres from a member of the Horkins family in 1969. When it was decided that a provincial park was to be created in the neighbourhood, this was one of the parcels of land the Province intended to purchase. Bruce sold his land to the Province in 1971 and part of it was leased back to him until shortly after his father's death in 1973. All the buildings on this property were bulldozed in 1973.

Concession 5, Lot 10

The northeastern section of the park, consisting of 200 acres, was Crown land until June 20, 1836 when it, along with other property, was granted to Robert Cock. He arrived in Seymour in 1834 from Scotland. In 1835, he returned to bring his wife and four children to their new home. Lieutenant John V. Geary, who settled on Lot 19, Concession 10, near Crow Bay in 1834, sheltered the family over the winter of 1835–36. A cabin was built on Robert's property in the spring of 1836 not far from the present park office. The remains of the foundation can still be seen. When Robert Sr. died in 1855, his property was left to his wife, Elizabeth who sold the homestead in 1859 to their eldest son, Robert, for the sum of five shillings. The brick house that Robert and his wife, Mary, built north of the present park office burned in 1924 and a smaller house was built on part of the old foundation. This house and the surrounding three acres did not become part of the park. Robert Jr. was a clerk, licence inspector, auctioneer and farmer. He opened a brickyard on his property on the outskirts of town in the spring of 1887. The old press in the brickyard was still in the field in 1928.

When a Game Protective Society was formed in Campbellford on August 29, 1878, Stewart Cock was the Secretary and his brother-in-law, James Dinwoodie, was the President. Apparently this was the first Fish and Game Society in Ontario.

When Robert Jr. died in 1888 the homestead, along with other property, was divided among the family. William (1865–1943) remained on the farm. He and his wife Jessie (McKelvie) had two daughters, Margaret (Mrs. Oscar Rannie) and Ella (Mrs. Allan Curle). After William died in 1943, the farm, left to his wife, Jessie, was sold to Oscar and Margaret Rannie in 1945.

Oscar Rannie, like his father-in-law before him, operated a mixed farm along with his son Robert (Bob). Eggs were sold in town, milk was sold to Anderson's Cheese Factory and later cream was sold to the Trent Valley Creamery in town. Firewood was supplied to a number of customers in and around Campbellford. In early spring sap was collected and made into maple syrup.

In the mid 1960s, when it was decided that Ferris Memorial Park was to be expanded, the Province offered to purchase the farm. After months of refusing to sell his property, Oscar finally gave in when he was threatened with expropriation. The property was sold in August 1969 but it was farmed until March 1970 when the stock and farm implements were sold at an auction sale. This ended the five-generation tenure of the Cock/Rannie families on this farm.

Concession 5, Lot 9

Lot 9, Concession 5, includes the northwestern section of the park, as well as land on the west side of the Trent River opposite the picnic area at Ranney Falls. This lot, consisting of 147 acres, was Crown Land until May 1839, when it, along with other property, was granted to the Hon. R. C. Wilkins. Wilkins sold his property in 1843 to the Rev. George Romanes. Subsequently the ownership of the land changed frequently until 1869 when Daniel Kennedy purchased the part of Lot 9, Con. 5 that lies east of the Trent River. Between 1873 and 1892, the property, known later as "Ferris' Woods," was owned by business partners, James Marshall Ferris, Daniel Kennedy and William B. Archer. By 1892 James Marshall Ferris was the sole owner. The unusual dry-stone fences on the Ferris property were built by Mr. Clarke, caretaker of the Ferris land. These fences were built to clear the land and to serve as divisions for fields. They are freestanding, 4 to 5 feet high in some places and skillfully built. Because J. M. and his associates were occupied with business affairs, the land was more a hobby than a necessity. Different schemes were attempted through the years and wood was cut and used as fuel at the house and store. When he died in 1893, the property passed to his son, John Berry Ferris.

When John Berry Ferris died in July 1920, his son, also called James Marshall Ferris, inherited the land and responsibility for the woodlot. He used it only for recreational purposes and people from the community, such as church groups, scouts, and guides, always felt free to use the land for picnics and hiking and were able to enjoy its natural beauty. When Jay died in July 1960, it was his wish that the property remain in its natural state and be available to the public. Family members donated Ferris' Woods to the Sportsmen's Club with a stipulation that another group or body would be named to look after the property if the arrangement with the club did not work out.

The Sportsmen's Club was a service club, made up of members from five different clubs – the Rifle Club, Pistol Club, Fishing Club, Skeet Club and Trap Club.

It was a well-established organization in Campbellford and was the catalyst for the creation of other clubs throughout Ontario who helped bring about the formation of the Ontario Department of Lands and Forests, now the Ministry of Natural Resources. The members of the Sportsmen's Club took the initial steps in developing Ferris' Woods by constructing an entry way to Ferris' Woods off Saskatoon Avenue. Stone gates were erected and the sign 'Ferris Memorial Park' was put in place. Trails were cleared and coniferous trees were planted in the fields, The club members wanted this property to be a community park where people could come and go as they pleased with no fees involved. They had other plans as well, which included the construction of a club house and rifle range, but their plans did not work out.

In 1962, Ferris' Woods was named a Provincial Park by Order-in-Council and the property was officially transferred to the Province of Ontario in 1963. The Campbellford Sportsmen's Club expressed an interest in the development and management of the area. The Sportsmen's Club members were informed that only activities approved by the Department of Lands and Forests would be allowed in the park. That meant no guns, of course. The club members were also told that a chain link fence would have to be installed all along the gorge, public liability insurance would have to be purchased, and rent would have to be paid on Crown property, all very expensive items. Because of the restrictions, fund raising activities were curtailed and special events that would have generated money for the club were not allowed. In the late summer of 1964, the members, with misgivings, decided that they would not take up the option of managing the park for another term.

The Department of Lands and Forests then agreed to fully establish Ferris Memorial Park as a provincial park and obtained permission to change the name to Ferris Provincial Park. Plans for the development of the property were drawn up by the Department of Lands and Forests in the fall of 1964. A meeting was arranged between local citizens, several Cabinet Ministers, including the Ministers of Natural Resources, Highways, and Forestry, as well as the local MP and MPP to discuss the proposals for the park. The local citizens were informed that in order to qualify for provincial funding, the park had to be bigger – at least 350 acres. This posed a problem as Ferris Memorial Park was bounded by the Trent River on the west, the Town of Campbellford on the north and privately-owned farm land on the east and south.

In 1965, the Province of Ontario granted financing to purchase the necessary acreage from four neighbouring property owners. Bill Scott and Art Stephens sold their properties in 1968, Oscar Rannie sold his farm in 1969 and Bruce Gratton sold his land in 1971. Concession 4, Lots 9 and 10, and Concession 5, Lots 9 and 10 were incorporated as Ferris Provincial Park and the official opening took place on June 24, 1975. With the exception of the barn on Oscar Rannie's place, all the buildings were levelled. The Saskatoon Avenue entrance became a pedestrian right-of-way only, granted to the Ministry over privately owned property and the new main entrance to the park was built on County Road 8. Roads were constructed, three comfort stations were built, one of which contains showers, and vault toilets were placed throughout the park. Water lines were connected to the town water supply. One hundred and sixty-three campsites were laid out, fireplaces were constructed and trails were made through the woods and along the river. Local people were hired for the stonework, blockwork and the construction of the washrooms and office buildings. The barn was used as a workshop and storage area for picnic tables and equipment. A new maintenance building was constructed near the park office and the Rannie barn was torn down in 1994.

The park was operated by the province until 1994 when the decision was made to close Ferris Provincial Park along with seven other parks. A group of concerned citizens from the town and township formed a group called "The Friends of Ferris" who were willing to operate the park. However, a partnership agreement was reached between Campbellford/Seymour and the Ministry of Natural Resources and the park was re-opened on June 25, 1994. At the present time (1999), Ferris Park is operated by the Municipality of Campbellford/Seymour through the Recreation Department but without provincial funding. This agreement will be re-assessed in 2001.

SEYMOUR CONSERVATION AREA

The Seymour Conservation Area consists of eighty-two hectares of woodland adjacent to Highway #30, just south of the Town of Campbellford. This area was purchased in 1973 for the purpose of preserving a natural setting in the face of urban development. It is supervised by the Lower Trent Conservation Authority.

Present recreation facilities include cross-country skiing, hiking, swimming and picnicking. Many varieties of wildflowers and animals can be spotted for viewing and photography. A great many fossils can be found in the area and used for study. The area is open daily from sunrise to sunset. No hunting, camping or motorized vehicles are permitted on the premises. The area offers a quarry that is a very popular swimming hole for many residents.

THE LOWER TRENT CONSERVATION AUTHORITY

The realization that natural resources were not inexhaustible unless managed and protected began to take hold in the late 1950s and early 1960s. Led by Branch 110 of the Royal Canadian Legion at Trenton, a conservation committee began the work of establishing a Conservation Authority to deal with concerns with industrial and sewage waste, weed control and garbage dumping along the Trent River. It took almost ten years of hard work and dedication by a local group of conservation-minded individuals to make progress. Finally, on April 30, 1968, with over one hundred people in attendance, and after a lively discussion, the majority of the municipalities voted in favour of the establishment of the Lower Trent Conservation Authority. The order-in-council from the Ontario Government was received on May 16, 1968.

Through the unique partnership with local municipalities, the Conservation authority has carried out community-based environmental protection programs for over thirty years. The area of jurisdiction covers 2121 square kilometres and includes all or portions of twelve municipalities in an area stretching from Lake Ontario to Rice Lake and from Grafton to Quinte West. The Conservation Authority was given the mandate to develop and implement a program for protecting the renewable natural resources of the region and includes a history packed with conservation achievements.

Through the early years, many properties were acquired to fulfill conservation objectives such as flood and erosion control, natural resource protection or cultural heritage protection. Today, the Lower Trent Conservation Authority owns approximately 3,500 acres of natural open space, including the Seymour Conservation Area. The lands serve as living examples of the natural ecosystems the Authority strives to protect.

Following flooding in March 1980, the next ten years focussed on constructing various flood protection projects, including a dam and diversion channels and berms, to help protect lives and property from future flood damages.

Tree planting and streambank erosion control programs were also initiated in the early years to assist private landowners with environmental problems on their properties. By 1991, one million trees had been planted in the region through this assistance program. With growing public awareness of environmental issues through the 1990s, the conservation program moved beyond dealing with immediate problems toward preventative planning and action. Environmental education, information management, watershed strategies and environmental land use planning have become the core of the Lower Trent Conservation services. Since 1968, the needs of local communities have changed as well, but the mandate remains the same – the natural environment must be protected now – children's futures depends on it.

TROUT CREEK FLOOD REDUCTION PROJECT

The Trout Creek watershed drains approximately 44 square kilometres of land and flows into the Trent River at Campbellford. Low lying areas in the Town and the surrounding region frequently experienced some flooding.

In the Spring of 1986, Trout Creek, swollen by heavy rainfall which could not penetrate frozen ground overflowed its banks and poured down Inkerman and

Flood waters from Trout Creek overflowed, causing basement flooding in the McKeel housing development on Inkerman Street.

Photo by F. C. Bonnycastle, ca. 1920, donated by Roy Williams to the Campbellford/Seymour Heritage Society Archives.

Pellisier Streets, tearing up pavement and flooding basements. Residents called the flooding the worst of its kind in more than a generation.

The Lower Trent Conservation responded the following year with the completion of flood plain mapping as a first step to protect residents along the creek. The construction of the Trout Creek Flood Reduction Project began in November 1986. This included the realigning and deepening of the creek between Simpson and Balaclava Streets to increase its capacity to handle floodwaters. Discovery of a sanitary sewer running beneath the creek delayed the completion of the project until 1988 as additional work was required including a pumping station and redirection of portions of the sanitary sewers. The use of rizi-stone, a type of interlocking block stabilized the banks and provided a more aesthetic appearance than gabion baskets. The project cost of over $400,000 provides protection from future flood damages to approximately forty properties which abut the creek.

CROWE VALLEY CONSERVATION AUTHORITY

On November 6, 1958, the Crowe Valley Conservation Authority was formally established under the Conservation Authorities Act of 1946. The CVCA is an autonomous corporation primarily responsible for watershed management, including: erosion control, the allocation of water resources, the co-ordination of water and related land management, and the management of habitat for fish and wildlife. The CVCA is directed and funded by its member municipalities and the Province of Ontario.

Fifteen dams and weirs control water levels and resultant flows within the Crowe River watershed. Nine of these are owned and operated by the CVCA; the others are owned by the Ministry of Natural Resources and regulated by the Crowe Valley Conservation Authority.

Towards the fulfillment of its mandate to allocate water resources and related management, the CVCA has acquired four parcels of property which also serve to provide recreational opportunities for the residents of the watershed and surrounding areas. Total land holdings of the authority include:

Crowe Bridge Conservation Area	(26 acres)
Callaghan's Rapids Conservation Area	(400 acres)
The "Gut" Conservation Area	(400 acres)
Agreement Forest	(200 acres)

ENDNOTES

1 Ferne Cristall et al., *The Percy Portage* (Peterborough: Trent University Press, 1973), pp. 100–102.
2 Plaque was installed by the town in 1988.
3 From an article by Lewis Zandbergen, prepared with assistance from the notes of Charles M. Smith, grandson of Charles Smith.
4 *Walking Tour* (Campbellford: Campbellford/Seymour Heritage Society, June 26, 1994), p. 2.

Chapter Three
Agriculture

Agriculture, the backbone of Seymour township, has changed drastically

over the centuries. In the early 1800's, the pioneer and his family built

a log shanty and cleared a few acres to grow some wheat and a few

vegetables. In his autobiography, John Macoun said of the Seymour settlers:

"... they were all willing to help each other and "Bees" were the regular way
of helping a farmer in distress, or who wanted help for a big undertaking.
We were just as ready to go out and cut a man's grain and plow his land
as we were to go and help him erect a home or a big frame barn. All
worked and all helped. The slogan of the country was "Root hog or die!"[1]

From the early pioneer colony, the future province of Ontario was emerging as
an economic power. By the 1850s, farmers began to produce a few items for sale —
wheat, potash, timber and livestock. Cash was needed to buy such items as sugar,
salt, clothes, tea, stoves and farm implements. A steady income meant better cattle
and larger farm buildings and homes. Improved methods of transportation increased
export of commodities to other countries. The Ontario Dairymen's Association was
formed in 1868 and Ontario products were becoming famous. Cheese factories
were established all over the province, including Seymour township. The growth
of urban Ontario provided a market for farm products. The interest in education
became apparent as schoolhouses were improved and new ones built. Increasing
literacy caused the spread of ideas and information by the written word.

In 1888, the Ministry of Agriculture became an independent ministry and by
1910 it contained many branches with responsibility for agriculture societies,
farmers groups, Women's Institutes, agricultural and veterinary colleges, and
research and production of livestock and crops. By 1919 every county had an agriculture representative to assist farmers and support rural organizations. The
arrival of the motor car changed rural communities drastically, as people could
travel outside the local community. During the 1930s, the great depression

J. I. Adams outfit threshing at R. S. Stephens farm, September 1930.

Photo from Campbellford/Seymour Heritage Society Archives.

occurred and farm community was reduced to a subsistence level of operation. Women were becoming increasingly active in trying to improve domestic and rural life through the Women's Institutes, agriculture societies and agricultural fairs. The two great wars did much to increase production of tools and food for Canada and starving Europe.

After 1950, farm production increased while farm populations decreased drastically. The number of farms also dropped from 204,000 in 1901 to 70,000 in 1991. Farm acreage declined from 1941–1961 as 3.8 million acres of farmland went out of production. Average farm size grew from 105 acres in 1901 to 154 acres in 1961. The decline in acreage did not have an impact on production; levels soared. From 1950 to 1980, corn production rose three and one half times, while apple production doubled. Potato production rose from 108 bushels per acre in 1940 to 201 bushels in 1950. These increases were due to many factors – breed organizations, commodity groups, improvement societies and government-sponsored research and development.[2]

Today, the small family-operated farm has been replaced by large business-like acreages which specialize in cattle, swine, poultry, milk, or food products. Farmers must use modern technology, current business practices, and educational expertise to succeed. In spite of this, many local farmer families still supplement agricultural income with off-farm employment.

~ Dairy Farming ~

HOLSTEINS

Holstein cattle originate in Holland where, according to legend, two central European tribes settled. Each tribe had its own cattle, one having white animals, the other black. The present black and white Holstein cow is the result of inter-breeding between the two strains. Since that time, careful selection and management have resulted in the highly specialized Holstein of today. In 1938, the first issue of the Holstein Journal was published and it soon became the Holstein breeders' "Bible." In 1942, the All-Canadian Contest was established.

In 1883, Michael Cook of Aultsville imported one hundred head directly from Holland, and placed them in quarantine at Port Lewis for six months. In September of that year, nineteen head were shown at the Toronto Industrial Exhibition. Interest in these cattle was very high and many were sold to Holstein enthusiasts all over Ontario. In 1884, the first Holstein breeders association was formed. Probably the first to own purebred stock in Northumberland was Edward Macklin of Fenella. This herd continued till 1974 and provided seed for Richard Honey of Warkworth to start his herd in 1892. The Honey farm is still in opera-tion at Warkworth. Some of the first Holstein breeders recorded in the Campbellford/Seymour area were Blythe Nelson, William Grills, James Eagleson, George Anderson, Fred Smith and Herb Tinney. In 1933, Aylmer Petherick received his first purebreds as a wedding present from his father-in-law, Herb Tinney. Art Nelson carried on the tradition in the next generation, as did Cliff Grills and Lindsay Anderson.

The Holstein, the largest of the dairy breeds, has the highest milk production of all dairy cattle and the milk also contains the lowest percentage of butter fat. The breed is also a source of good beef. In 1905, the Department of Agriculture established a Record of Performance to track and record milk production and since that time, Seymour farmers have made significant contributions to Holstein history. For example, in 1922, "Gertrude Jean Dekol," Registration 22601, bred by Ben Hopps of Seymour Township, on three daily milkings produced 26,554 pounds of milk, 841 pounds of fat with a 3.17% butterfat. In 1939, James Nelson's "Maude Triumph Dutchland" would top that, when in her eighth year she pro-duced 28,090 pounds of milk, 941 pound of fat with 3.35% butterfat. In 1958, "Opal Pasch (V.G.) 2 Star," belonging to Lindsay Anderson's Glenkindie herd was announced as a new lifetime milk champion on a twice daily milking; over fifteen years she produced 229,383 pounds of milk.

In 1961, use of prefix names was made compulsory for all Holstein breeders and names like Almerson, Ingholm, and Nelcam from this area became famous for reaching Master Breeder Status, the highest honour given by the Holstein Association of Canada. Aylmer Petherick was the first to receive the award in Seymour in 1966 with the Almerson prefix. He also served as National Holstein Director for several years. Clare and Harold Ingram were next to receive a Master Breeder award on their Ingholm herd, and Eldon Petherick was awarded the second for Almerson in 1977. Art Nelson's Nelcam herd won Master Breeder status in 1995. "Ingholm Rag Apple President EX5 Star" was the first cow in the world to make over a ton of butterfat in a year. Bred by Clare and Harold Ingram, she produced, as a seven-year-old, 3600 pounds of milk and 2098 pounds of butterfat in three hundred and sixty five days. Altogether she achieved thirteen national championship records.

Perhaps the greatest bull in Northumberland was bred by Aylmer Petherick. "Sovereign Supreme EX&EXTRA" had over twenty excellent daughters in Canada and many more in the United States. His two sisters made "All Canadian Produce of Dam" in 1956. One of them, "Almerson Rocket Supreme EX 2 Star" was the all-Canadian four year old. The same year another great cow was "Almerson Marquis Echo EX 6 Star," five time Grand Champion at the Northumberland County Show held at Campbellford Fair. In 1975, Carl Petherick and sons showed "Carlencrest Ned Dominion EX" to first place at the Royal Winter Fair, receiving all Canadian Honours. Many fine animals have been produced in the lush pastures and on the hills of Seymour Township.

Ingholm Rag Apple President EX5 Star.

Photo from Campbellford/Seymour Heritage Society Archives.

JERSEYS

The origin of these cattle was the English Channel Island of Jersey where breeders were able to keep the strain pure through strong import regulations. The smallest and most refined of the dairy breeds, these fawn-coloured animals are noted for their docile and gentle temperament. While their milk production is the lowest of the main dairy breeds, they are prized for having the highest percentage of butterfat. By 1868, Jerseys were being exported to Canada where demand was strong. By 1912, when the first volume of the Canadian Jersey Cattle Club Record was published, there were more Jerseys registered than any other breed. Local owners were James Atwell, James Carr, Robert Cochrane, John Fry, Minnie A. Locke, Josiah Tinney, and E. Wilson of the Campbellford area; Alexander Donald of Burnbrae; B. W. Herrington of Rylstone; and William Clarke of Meyersburg. Most of them had only one or two cows. Later owners included Thomas Varcoe, Thomas Petherick, Garnet Kerr, Valentine and Edith Chaplin, Abraham Free, David McCook, Henry Redden and James Sanders.

From 1940 to 1956, Garnet Kerr was the only registered Jersey farmer in the Campbellford area, but many farmers still had in their Holstein herds a Jersey cow bred at Kerr's farm and used as the house milk cow. Jerseys were quiet enough that even a child could milk them. Stan Kerr, at age four, learned to milk Spy who was a twenty-one year old.

Recently, Jerseys have gained in popularity in the area. In April 1999, John Kelleher received the Wm. Teasdale Memorial Award from Jersey Ontario. The award is presented to a young farmer, under thirty-five, for significant contributions to the Jersey breed.

AYRSHIRES

These dairy cattle are native to Ayrshire, Scotland, and were introduced into Canada by Scottish settlers in the mid-1800's. They were prized for their efficient foraging and grazing and at one time were the most populous of the dairy cows in Ontario. Ayrshires are medium-sized cattle, red and white in colour, although either colour may predominate. In temperament, they tend to be more excitable than either the Holstein or placid Jersey. Milk production, while less than the Holstein, is offset by a higher percentage of butterfat. The average is 10,000 pounds per year with 4% butterfat test.

Noted for their hardiness, Ayrshires will do better than other breeds on marginal land. The ability to thrive on inferior pasturage was probably the reason they were initially so popular on the smaller farms in the northern part of Seymour. However, large herds of registered stock gradually appeared throughout the township after the formation of the Dominion Ayrshire Breeders Association in 1872.

Early farmers who maintained registered herds were William Hume, John Locke, Tom Kerr, Jim Thompson, and Jim Stewart. They were followed by Bill Little, Charlie Keller, Archie McCook, Herb Hendy, and Ralph and Ross Kerr. Today, Duane Kerr still raises some Ayrshires, though he is moving more to Holsteins. This once predominant breed has largely been replaced by the Holsteins which have a much higher volume of production.

ONTARIO MILK MARKETING BOARD

One of the biggest changes in the entire dairy industry in the late 1960s was the formation of the Ontario Milk Marketing Board. This Board was given absolute power over all milk producers in Ontario. All milk had to be sold to the Milk Marketing Board who, in turn, resold it to the manufacturing plants. All milk producers and processors were allocated a quota with fluid milk plants getting first choice of the supply and manufacturing plants getting the balance, based upon the quota allotment. This removed any competition between the local cheese factories, and plants were encouraged to sell as much of their cheese as possible over the counter. Such retail sales were quota free and, therefore, the factories located on a main road had the best chance to take advantage of the situation. At first, there was no price on quota and when Hoard's Factory closed, two-thirds of their quota went to Menie Factory and one-third went to Empire Factory, as this reflected the ratio of patron distribution. In 1966, Empire Factory sold only about 5% of the cheese over the counter but, by 1974, nearly 25% was being sold over the counter with the balance being shipped to Black Diamond in Belleville. At the start of the 1970s, the factories which remained open became the subject of strong bidding as large plants sought to buy the quota which had now taken on value. By the early 1980s, all factories in Seymour Township had closed except Empire.

As the milk producers in Seymour changed to bulk shipping, some of them were directed to the fluid milk market and those continuing to ship in cans were sent to Empire. In 1977, the Milk Marketing Board decreed that all can shipping cease and all milk be shipped in bulk. This was a major change. Don Pollock was working at the Ontario Ministry of Agriculture and Food in Stirling at this time. Many of the shippers he remembers were small farmers or those nearing retirement age who did not want to make this transition because of the cost of building a milk house and installing a bulk tank, all of which had to meet Government and Milk Marketing Board Regulations. Don recalls being asked to visit one farmer who had shipped can milk to the local cheese factory all his life. As he was seventy years old, he had to decide whether to build a milk house and install a bulk tank or quit shipping milk. Surprisingly, he did install the necessary requirements and continued to ship milk for another several years. On Don's last visit to that farm, he found that the milk house was being neglected because the owner had installed a satellite TV dish. The gentleman admitted that he spent too much time watching television. At nearly eighty years of age, who can blame him!

Another of Don's visits was in the company of Bill Derry, his supervisor from Kemptville. They were paying a return visit to an area farmer to check improvements which Don had recommended two weeks previously. There had been some clean up but the farmer was explaining to Bill why the rest was not done. All the time he was talking, his son, who would have been about ten years of age, was standing beside him and occasionally tugging on his father's pant leg. Finally the farmer turned to him and said, "What do you want?" The son replied, "Excuses, excuses, excuses!" Bill could hardly contain himself until he got back to the car and he laughed all the way back to Stirling. On the last visit that Don made to this farm, some eight or nine years later, they were still arguing about how things should be done.

By 1986, when Don returned to Empire Factory, all cheese was sold through the store at the plant or directly to stores with some bulk sales to other plants. This trend continues today.

In the early 1990s, the Belleville Cheese Board, the last surviving one in Ontario, closed and the Cheese Producer's Warehouse which had been taken over by the Milk Marketing Board was sold.

MILK DELIVERY

In 1900, two milk delivery routes operated in village of Campbellford. Both of these had new owners that year. John Hall bought his business from James Cock, who, in turn, had purchased it from W. Whitton. George Osterhout bought his business from John Oliver and L. A. Denike.

RUTHERFORD'S DAIRY

Rutherford's Dairy was located on Cockburn Street on the present site of the Garshell apartment building. This business was operated by Walter Rutherford and subsequently his son, Wally, who was killed in a tragic accident on Highway #7 in March 1967. The dairy opened in about 1927 and continued until 1965 when it was sold to Anderson's Dairy. Ernie Wilks worked at Rutherford's for thirty-five years, for many years delivering milk door-to-door using a horse-drawn milk wagon.

TRENT VALLEY CREAMERY

Trent Valley Creamery started in business on the west side of town under the ownership of Stanley Southworth. Later, it relocated to a building on Doxsee Avenue which had previously been a wood working factory operated by Edward

Skitch. In 1925, Harold Carr took over the business and installed modern equipment for pasteurizing cream for butter making. His products won many prizes for their superior taste. Three of the butter makers over the years were Edison Wynn, Carl Stephens and Gerald Fitchett. During the depression years, farmers could not afford to buy buttermilk which they had been feeding to their hogs. Since disposal of large quantities of buttermilk was difficult, a machine was installed which dried the liquid to a powder which was bagged and sold as chicken feed. Trucks were sent out to pick up cream but many farmers chose to deliver their cream on their regular Saturday night trip to town. Stuart Carr managed the business from 1934 until 1943, while his father Harold acted as MPP for the area. Stuart eventually took over the family firm which he operated until the late 1950s when Art Moody purchased the business. This is now the site of Campbellford Office Supplies.

EGG GRADING STATIONS

Fresh eggs were graded and sold to stores and individuals from several egg grading stations. The farmers either brought crates of eggs to the store or the owner had a route for picking up the eggs weekly. The station owned by P. H. Macmillan was first located near the Aron Theatre and later in the back end of the IGA, now Giant Tiger. This business was sold to Don Petherick who eventually relocated it to his house on Raglan Street. Eldon Carlaw also had an egg business on Bridge Street near the Aron Theatre. Bun Crossen's business was on the site of the present Toronto-Dominion Bank.

CHEESE INDUSTRY

Harvey Farrington is credited with starting the first cheese factory in Ontario at Norwich in 1864. Prior to this, cheese was made at home, usually by the farmer's wife. There is some dispute as to the location of the first commercial cheese factory in Central Ontario. Both the Front of Sidney in Sidney Township and Plum Grove at Wellman's Corners on Concession 6 of Rawdon Township are reputed to have been started in 1866 or 1867. In the 1980s, a copy of an 1880 minute book of the Eastern Ontario Dairymen's Association held in Kingston was found in an attic in Thurlow Township. It contained a list of all the cheese plants which sent reports to the Association. A copy of this list is in the possession of Don Pollock, a retired veteran cheesemaker of the area. The list includes Brae, Crowe Bay, Menie, Royal, Seymour West and Woodlands Cheese Factories as well as the Plum Grove and Front of Sidney in Hastings County. Little is known about the Royal Factory, possibly located near Ranney Falls and torn down to make way for the Trent Canal. One of the things that was debated at the 1880 Kingston conference was the new invention called the cream separator and it was the opinion of most delegates that this was just a passing fancy and that nothing could take the place of skimming the cream off the top of the milk. How wrong they were, as the cream separator is still in use today and the traditional skimming stopped about one hundred years ago!

BRAE CHEESE AND BUTTER MANUFACTURING COMPANY

The Brae Factory, located on Concession 6, Lot 25 on the John Hay farm, is credited with being the first cheese factory in Seymour Township and in Northumberland County. Production started in 1873 with James Whitton as cheesemaker. He had previously been associated with the Plum Grove Factory at Wellman's Corners. Some of the later cheesemakers were Henry Johnston, F. D. Barton, George Pollard, Les Shillinglaw, Alex Stewart, John Lain, Harry Fry and Keith Brown. The Brae Factory closed in 1946.

CROWE BAY CHEESE AND BUTTER MANUFACTURING COMPANY

The Crowe Bay Cheese Factory was started in 1874 on the east half of Concession 9, Lot 20 at Petherick's Corners on land provided by William Petherick. The first directors and stockholders were John Fry, Harry Drysdale, Alex Anderson, Alex Innes and Michael McGuire. Later, Hector Arnold was President and also Chairman of the Ontario Cheese Producers Marketing Board for many years. He was inducted into the Agricultural Hall of Fame at the Agricultural Museum in Milton, Ontario. Some of the cheesemakers in later years were James Craighead, Cyril McKeown, Claude Reid, Don Pollock, Keith Stephens and Gary Rowe. In 1911 the factory was moved from the initial site to higher ground on the same lot on recommendation of the Department of Health. This factory closed in 1972 and the building is now a residence.

EMPIRE CHEESE AND BUTTER CO-OPERATIVE

The first Empire Cheese Factory was built in 1876 on Concession 3, Lot 10 on the farm of John Haig who was the first cheesemaker. The second factory was built around the corner on Concession 2, Lot 11, where the well that supplies the current factory is situated.

The present factory was built on land donated by Harry Stephens and was constructed by Wilfred Spencer Construction Company which built and designed many other cheese plants in Central Ontario. This building was partially funded by a government grant made available as a consequence of amalgamating with Kimberley Cheese Factory. It is now the only operating cheese plant in Seymour

Early photograph of Empire Cheese Factory, ca 1930.
Photo courtesy of Ann Rowe.

Township and Northumberland County. Some of the cheesemakers over the years have been Tom Naylor, Dave Wallace Jr., Charlie Stephens, Jack Kitchen, Bob Maybee, Les Shillinglaw, Don Pollock, Murray Heath, Glen Anderson, Brent Gray, and Mike Jackson. Keith Stephens is the present cheesemaker.

FOREST CHEESE FACTORY

This cheese factory was located beside the creek on Concession 4, Lot 24 and was built in the late 1870s. The builder and first cheesemaker was Will Doxsee. The first factory burned and Nelson Sexsmith rebuilt on the other side of the creek and became the cheesemaker. As there was no factory at Hoard's at the time, milk was brought to the plant from farms along the Stirling Road (Pump Street) by drivers, Mr. Emmons, Mr. Summers and John Huffman. Other makers in this factory were Abraham W. Free, George Ivey and Dave Wallace. Forest Factory closed in the 1920s.

HOARD'S CHEESE AND BUTTER MANUFACTURING COMPANY

In 1904, cheesemaking began on Concession 2, Lot 25, at Hoard's with William Donald as cheesemaker. The first directors were Fred Jeffs, Wallace Hoard, William Gunning, Lester Anderson, James Dunkley, James Haig and Archie Thompson. This factory stayed open at least part time during the winter months while many others were closed. Some of the cheesemakers over the years were Frank Little, George Jackman, Clayton Chambers, Ernest Sadler, Fred Remington, Mac Remington, and

Doug Rowe. Harold Rowe was cheesemaker for twenty-five years until the factory closed in 1970. The building has been converted to a very popular dining establishment initially called The Cheddar House and operating currently as Chubby's.

I X L   F A C T O R Y

The Ninth Line Factory was a frame building erected around 1876 on Concession 10, Lot 10 on the property of Archie Clarke. The first cheesemaker was Alex (Sandy) Anderson. It is said that this factory opened on May 5 and that the patrons had to draw their milk on sleighs because of a heavy snowfall. Amos Green was an early cheesemaker and Eli White was the last. When the factory closed in 1945, the building and its equipment were sold and the patrons generously donated all proceeds to the building fund for Campbellford Memorial Hospital.

K I M B E R L E Y   C H E E S E   F A C T O R Y

This factory was built in 1900 using some of the best material from the Valley Factory which had been closed. The name Kimberley came from all the newspaper accounts of the finding of the diamond mines at Kimberley, South Africa. The factory site was on the present location of Jack Dunk's house, Concession 2, Lot 15. It was built there because of the excellent well and adjacent creek. Some of the cheesemakers over the years were Robert Maybee, James Shillinglaw, Dave Wallace, and Frank Brough. Don Pollock was the last cheesemaker when the plant closed in 1952. After closing, Kimberley amalgamated with Empire and helped build the new plant there. The building has been torn down.

M E N I E   C H E E S E   F A C T O R Y

Menie Cheese Factory was built in 1922 and the building is still standing beside the creek on Concession 5, Lot 23 in the hamlet of Menie. Some of the patrons were from the Forest Factory and later from the Prince of Wales Factory which burned. Cheesemakers over the years were Walter Barker, Frank Little, Vernon Spencer, Art Reid, Bert Wallace, George Haggerty, and Glen Anderson. Robert Akins was the last cheesemaker in the mid 1970s. Some of the Presidents were William Rannie, Roy Walker and Harold Milne while Stewart Milne and Frank Potts acted as Secretaries.

M E Y E R S B U R G   C H E E S E   F A C T O R Y

Not too much is known of the Meyersburg Factory although the first one was built on the Walter Scott farm on Concession 3, Lot 2, Later, a flour and grist mill was converted to a factory. George Ivey and Thomas Dillworth were cheesemakers in this plant which closed in 1930.

PRINCE OF WALES CHEESE FACTORY

James Shillinglaw built this plant in 1889 and was the cheesemaker until 1909 when he sold it to John Murray. It was located on Concession 7, Lot 20 just west of the Burnbrae sideroad. In 1929, John Murray sold the plant to Grant Anderson who operated it until it burned in 1942. John Murray went on to become a cheese instructor. Don Pollock's uncle, Elvin Pollock, farmed on the corner of Concession 7 and the Burnbrae sideroad but happened to be away on the day the factory burned. That evening upon returning home, he asked Watson Murray if they got much out of the factory. Watson replied, "We got everything out but the fire!" The plant was not rebuilt.

RYLSTONE CHEESE FACTORY

The first Rylstone Factory was built in the late 1880s on the south side of Concession 12, Lot 26, Seymour Township, on the farm of Thomas Reid. It was later moved to the west side of the boundary road just north of Concession 10. Some of the cheesemakers in this plant were Thomas Fry, Mr. Taylor, Orrie Barton, W.P. Moore and Harold Henderson. This factory burned in 1945 and the new plant was built across the road in Rawdon Township. This was one of the first cheese factories built by the Wilfred Spencer Construction Company. Some of the makers in the new plant were Harold Henderson, Murray Heath, Doug Reid, Glen Anderson and Louie Keller. This factory closed in 1970 and has since been used as a workshop and residence.

STANWOOD CHEESE FACTORY

The first factory at Stanwood was on Concession 12, Lot 20, on the John Lain farm, just east of the house. In 1895, James Johnston built a new Stanwood Factory across the road on Concession 13 which he operated for a number of years. He sold to Mel McComb who operated it until it was sold to a group of shareholders. Some of the later cheesemakers were Howard Dafoe, Roy Brown, James Woodcock, Jim Gray and Gerald Thompson. This factory closed in 1952 and the building has been torn down.

SEYMOUR WEST CHEESE FACTORY

This factory was built in the mid 1870s on Concession 8, Lot 5, just west of Highway #30. Some of the cheesemakers were Abraham (Little Abe) Free, Bruce Hoard, Grant Anderson and Alex Green. This factory closed in 1934, but the building was carefully preserved and is now used as a storage area. The cheese-maker's house was located to the west of the factory and is still used as a residence today.

TRENT RIVER CHEESE FACTORY

The first Trent River Cheese Factory was located on the Belmont side of the Belmont-Seymour Boundary road at Highway #30 in Trent River. Steven Watson, his wife, and son, Claud, operated this factory. Archie Scott purchased the plant in 1924 and later sold it to Fred Scott. Fred's son-in-law, George Brooks, was the next owner and cheesemaker for many years. He sold it to William P. Moore, who, in partnership with a Toronto area dairy, built a new factory just south of Trent River on Highway #30. This building was later sold to Walter Joss who operated it as the Joss Swiss Cheese Factory until 1978. In recent years, it has housed a grocery store and it later became the Seahorse Banquet Hall.

TRENT VALLEY CHEESE FACTORY / ANDERSON'S DAIRY PRODUCTS

This factory was built in 1899 by James Whitton and T.J. Naylor on the site of an old tannery which was converted to a curing room. It was located on Saskatoon Avenue in the Town of Campbellford and operated until the early 1940s when it was purchased by Grant Anderson who changed the name to Anderson's Dairy Products. The factory closed in the late 1970s but a bulk milk transportation business continued to operate until the late 1980s. Some of the cheesemakers were Grant Anderson, Harold Petherick, Jim Gray, Don Pollock and Gerald Brunton. In 1957, Don Pollock came across cancelled cheque books from the Trent Valley Factory. These were found in the attic of a house which Don had purchased from Mel McKeown. The house had previously been owned by William Locke who had been Secretary-Treasurer of the factory in the early 1900s. At its peak, Anderson's produced cheese, butter, bottled milk and cream and cheese boxes. Bill Bertrand drove both the can and bulk milk pickup truck. Ellis Hoard was the cheese box maker.

VALLEY CHEESE FACTORY

This plant was built and operated in the early 1880s on the southwest corner of Concession 5, Lot 16 by Abraham (Little Abe) Free. At one time, two women from Rylstone, Maria Barton and Louise Stewart, were the cheesemakers. When the factory ceased operation in the early 1900s, the building was dismantled and material was salvaged to build the Kimberley Cheese Factory. The last cheesemaker was Dave Wallace under owner Albert Cassan.

WOODLANDS CHEESE FACTORY

The first Woodlands Cheese Factory was built on Concession 10, Lot 6 before 1880, and was a frame structure that burned in 1912. This plant was owned and operated by Neal Loucks. In 1895, the cheesemaker was J.W. Valleau. The second cement block factory was built on the same site and is still standing. This second plant was owned and operated by William Baker until purchased by Walter Joss who ran it as the Swiss Cheese Factory until 1960 when he purchased the Trent River Cheese Factory and moved operations there.

PROMINENT MEMBERS OF THE SEYMOUR CHEESE INDUSTRY

The Shillinglaw Family

In 1889, James Shillinglaw Sr. built the Prince of Wales Cheese Factory which he operated for many years. He also was the cheesemaker at Kimberley and Beaver Factories after selling Prince of Wales in 1909. His son, Leslie, was the cheese-maker at the Brae Factory until he moved to Empire Factory for thirty-six years, continuing as an assistant even after his retirement. Leslie's son, James Jr., also assisted at Empire Factory for many years. James Jr. left in 1982, ending the ninety year involvement of the Shillinglaw family in the Seymour cheese industry.

Grant Anderson and Family

Grant Anderson was born in Rawdon Township in 1900 and began working at Empire Cheese Factory at age thirteen as an apprentice. He was a cheesemaker at Seymour West before purchasing the Prince of Wales Factory in the 1930s. He operated this plant until it burned in 1942. Then he moved into town, purchasing the former Trent Valley Factory and renaming it Anderson's Dairy Products. He was the first businessman to deliver bottled milk to the residents of Campbellford by horse and wagon. He was also president of the Central Ontario Cheesemakers' Association for a term. Grant's son, Robert was also involved in the business for many years and his wife, Eva, worked in the retail outlet. Robert's son, Steve, is still involved in the dairy industry, driving a bulk milk pickup truck part time. Grant's half brother, Harold Petherick, worked in the factory for many years.

W.P. (Bill) Moore

Bill came to the Seymour area in the 1930s to make cheese at the Rylstone Factory. He later became a cheese instructor. Bill and Sara Moore lived on Doxsee Avenue in Campbellford. He purchased the old Trent River Factory and operated it until the new plant was built on Highway #30, south of the village. He super-vised many of the local factories, including Kimberley and Empire before his retire-ment in the mid 1970s. Bill was well known and respected in the community.

Don Pollock

Don Pollock came to the Kimberley Cheese Factory in 1948, after learning the trade at Plum Grove and Central Factories in neighbouring Rawdon Township and attending Dairy School at Guelph in 1945. He later moved on to Crowe Bay, Anderson's Dairy and the new Empire Factory as well as Evergreen and Foxboro in Hastings County. Don also tried his hand as plant foreman at Rutherford's Dairy in Campbellford in the 1950s before returning to cheesemaking. He moved to the Ministry of Agriculture and Food for nine years as a milk and cheese inspector before returning to Empire in 1986. In 1989, Don started Cheese on Wheels to promote cheese sales and also as a retirement hobby. After his retirement in 1992 from Empire, he carried on with demonstrations of cheesemaking with his portable vat. This hobby has taken him from Walkerton in the west of Ontario to Ottawa in the east with most demonstrations tied to fairs.

The Rowe Family

The Rowe family has long been associated with cheesemaking, beginning with Will Rowe and his wife, the former Millie Shore, who were married in 1906. They moved to Cold Springs Cheese Factory and later to Champion Cheese Factory in Madoc Township. When Will died in 1918, Millie had no choice but to use her cheese-making skills to raise their five children, the oldest being only five years old. For two years she remained at Champion and then, in 1920, the family moved to the Fourth Line Cheese Factory in Rawdon Township. When Will's younger brother Harold returned from active service in World War I, he joined Millie to help with the cheese-making which he had previously learned at the Empire Cheese Factory. He remained with the family when they moved to Central Cheese Factory in Rawdon Township, providing some much needed stability for the young family when Millie died in 1928.

Millie's son, Doug, who had worked at the Central Cheese Factory with Morris Rose in 1930, attended Dairy School in Kingston in 1931. He then worked at Central, Plum Grove, and Fourth Line Cheese Factories in Rawdon Township before returning to a position at Hoard's Cheese Factory in Seymour Township. In 1945, Doug bought the Warkworth Cheese Factory in Percy Township and became very successful in business and was an ardent community supporter. Both Doug's sons, Bob and John, completed Dairy School at Guelph in 1965, anticipating a long term position at the Warkworth Cheese Factory. Bob's son, Jeremy, had also completed his dairy certificate and was involved in the business.

In 1970, the Milk Marketing Board sounded the death knell for small cheese factories. By 1980 only 49% of the cheese quota was available for cheddar cheese, causing the Rowe family to reluctantly sell the business to Ault Foods. Positions were available at Ault's for any employees and John moved first to the Napanee plant and later to Winchester. Bob took up a sales position with Ault but later operated Dairy World and the Old Northumberland Cheese Factory in Campbellford. Doug Rowe retired and was made a member of the Central Ontario Cheesemaker's Honour Roll in 1992.

Delbert Rowe, the second of Millie's sons, began making cheese in 1931 and in 1936 he became head cheesemaker at Plum Grove in Rawdon Township. He moved to Zion Cheese Factory in Thurlow Township in 1940 and remained there until 1964 when he moved to the new Maple Dale Factory in Thurlow Township. He retired from there in 1983. Delbert's three sons, Gary, Gordon, and Rodney also went into the cheesemaking business. The eldest son, Gary, made cheese at the Crowe Bay Factory for ten years until it closed in 1972. He then purchased a buttermilk truck and operated under the name Groson. Gary's son, Bruce, also held a milkgrader's certificate. Gary's brothers, Gordon and Rodney, were also cheesemakers and worked at various factories in southern Ontario for several years before moving to the Grunthal Factory in Manitoba. Gordon's son, Troy, is also employed at Grunthal which has recently been sold to a large Italian firm called Parmalot.

Harold Rowe, Millie's youngest son, made cheese at several factories in Sidney Township before moving to Hoard's in 1945. He was head cheesemaker there for twenty-five years until its closure in 1970. He then worked for a short time at the Central Cheese Factory in Rawdon Township before going into real estate sales. He spent his remaining working years as a popular member of the housekeeping staff at the Campbellford Memorial Hospital. For a short time, his sons, Don and Lynn, worked at Hoards. Don left in 1961 to join Ontario Hydro. Lynn died in 1964 and Harold died in 1992, ending a long legacy of cheesemaking in Seymour Township.

CENTRAL ONTARIO CHEESEMAKERS ASSOCIATION

The Central Ontario Cheesemakers Association was started in 1928, and since that time, has sponsored the British Empire Dairy Show in Belleville. Several Seymour residents, namely Grant Anderson, Murray Heath, Doug Reid and Don Pollock, have served as President of this Association. In 1993–94, while Don was President, the Directors decided to start an Honour Roll of past cheesemakers for all Ontario. To gain entry, persons had to spend at least twenty years in the cheese industry. To date, Grant Anderson, Jim Gray and Don Pollock from Seymour have received this honour. Potential future candidates include Les Shillinglaw.

The Dutch Clock system which was used by the Belleville Cheese Board was donated to the Central Ontario Cheesemaker's Association to be placed in a local agricultural museum if possible. Recently it was announced that the system will be installed in the new agricultural museum in Stirling.

~ Other Types of Farming ~

BEEF CATTLE

In the 1960s, farmers in the area, including Harry Free, began to raise pure-bred beef cattle as a specialty. Prior to this, beef was raised by some farmers for their own and local consumption only. Currently there are seventy or more different types of beef cattle being raised in Ontario, such as Charolais, Simmental, Limousin, and Blonde d'Aquitaine.

Since 1985, Pat Quinn and his wife, Jean, have raised Simmental cattle full time on their farm at R.R. #4, Campbellford. Pat has been president of the Quinte Stockers Sales since its formation. In 1992, he became the first recipient of the Northumberland County Cattleman of the Year Award for his major contribution to the smooth operation of the Quinte Stockers Sales held at Hoard's Station sale barn. He has also been involved in a weigh-in program for calves.

Breeders of the Blonde D'Aquitaine include Darren and Donald Dunham, Laverne McGee, and Del Merrill. In 1993, a Blonde d'Aquitaine Beef Show took place at the Campbellford/Seymour Agricultural Fair and has since become a regular event. Wayne Mack and John and William Robinson raise Charolais, and a Charolais Beef Show took place in 1998. Elizabeth and Otto Feiden have a large herd of Limousin on their farm at Concession 5, Lot 5, Seymour Township, the original farm of pioneer Henry Bonnycastle.

HORSES

Although the days are gone when horses were a necessity for many chores, there will always exist a love affair between horses and people. In the 1912 Annual Exhibition catalogue of the Seymour Agricultural Society there were seven categories for horses: Heavy Draught, General Purpose, Agricultural Purposes, Roadster, Carriage Horses, Blood Horses – Thoroughbred, and Pure Bred Draught Horses. By 1975, the classes for horses at the Campbellford Fair included heavy horses such as Clyde, Percheron, Belgian, and Commercial, as well as Roadster and Carriage Horses, Hackney and Commercial Ponies. At that time, local citizens associated with the raising and showing of horses include Ken Parr, Murray Heath, Doug Sager, Alfred Parker, Les Glenn, Charles MacDonald, Alex Linn, Eugene Brahaney, Milton Haig, Gerald Stephens, Paul Sager, and John DeNure. There was also a western horse division and a draw match for teams.

In 1994, a Troika class, which involves horses hitched three abreast doing a special step, was added. By 1996, horses were still an important attraction at the fair and included classes for Heavy Horses, Commercial Horses, Light Horses, Roadster and Carriage Horses, Ponies, Fine Harness. There were shows for Open

Western and English, Western Gymkhana, and Drawing Matches. Local citizens associated with the Heavy Horse class were John McKelvie, Fred Thomson, Lloyd Anderson, Bonnie Stephens, Lyle Heath, Mark Curle, Harold Ingram, and Earl Little. Light Horse Committee members were Ron Isaac, Bill Linn, Morris Campbell, Kathy Galbraith, Carl Heath, Scott Campbell, and Mike Forestell. The Riding Horse Committee included Rochelle Rutherford, Wayne Mack, and Russ and Shelley Anderson. Drawing matches continue to be popular; names to watch are Lloyd Anderson, Colin Petherick, Bill Linn, Ron Isaac, Fred Darling, John McKelvie, Mark Curle, Morris Campbell, and Darren Dunham.

People breeding horses in this area travel far and wide to fairs to show and compete at horse events, often bringing home prizes for their efforts. Lloyd Anderson has been raising pure-bred heavy horses for twenty years for show and sale as a hobby. Recently he attended a large sale in the United States where he sold some of his prize-winning horses to some Amish buyers who use work horses on their farms.

FIELD CROPS

Seymour Township has many acres of beautiful farmland with a diversity of crops. The predominant field crops are hay, barley, oats, wheat, soybeans, alfalfa, corn and red clover . Some farmers today are installing drainage tiles in wet fields so that they have more acres to plant. Arable land is at a premium as herd sizes increase and more feed is needed. Some land is also being severed and purchased for building lots. Both farmers and small land owners produce wonderful kitchen gardens as evidenced at the Campbellford/Seymour Market and the Annual Fair. Asparagus, beans, onions, potatoes, cabbage, tomatoes, peppers, radishes, strawberries and raspberries are grown. Also for sale at the Market in season are zucchini, broccoli, cauliflower, cucumbers, squash, turnips, corn and pumpkins. In Fall, many varieties of apples are displayed, even some of the older species — Russet, Spy, McIntosh and Talman Sweets. There are bee keepers who produce their own honey for sale.

SWINE, SHEEP AND GOATS

Pigs have always been raised in the township. The early pioneers used their meat and skins. In 1912, at the Annual Exhibition of the Seymour Agricultural Society, the following classes of swine were judged — Tamworth, Yorkshire, Berkshire, Chester White and Poland White. In 1958, Don Heath took most of the Yorkshire pig class prizes, but by 1975 there were no classes at the fair for swine. Today Paul and Tracy Cocchio of R.R. #5, Campbellford raise pigs and, at present, have about 3,000 animals — a big operation.

In 1975, sheep classes were included at the fair and G. Curle and Son were winners for Suffolk sheep. The Directors for the sheep classes were John Lightle , William Curle and Joel Redden. In 1993, there were six classes of sheep, Suffolk, Polled Dorset, N.C. Cheviot, Oxford, Down, Leicester and Hampshire, judged under the committee which was composed of Bob Bennett, Bobbi Bennett, Marilyn Martin and Phil Martin.

At the 1975 Fair dairy goats, such as Nubian, Alpine, Togenburg and Saanen, were judged. Goat's milk has become popular again for human consumption. Today there are goats raised in the Township by breeders such as Dave and Melanie Brockwell of R.R. #5, who raise ponies and goats for sale. Ponies are in demand for birthday parties or weddings and may be rented for these events.

POULTRY

Poultry has always been important for rural people. Chickens, regular and bantam, ducks, geese and turkeys are valued for food, eggs and feathers. There are many breeds judged at the Campbellford/Seymour Fair. In the 1912 Fair, there were the following types of poultry – Brahma, Cochin, Plymouth Rock, Hamburg, Leghorn, Wyandotte, Spanish Minorca, Poland, Houdon and Bantam. For many years, poultry judging was dropped from the Fair but in 1987 it was introduced again. Six hundred birds were entered in the poultry show that year, now a permanent event every year. In 1996, twenty-three types of standard poultry, thirty-two of bantams, seven of ducks and eight of geese were judged. The committee for this event included Sharon Ireland, Gerald Fry and Frank Haig.

FLOWERS

There are the many beautiful flower gardens in Campbellford/Seymour. At the fair over the years, the flower exhibits have been spectacular. Some of the common types entered are begonia, pansy, fuschia, African violet, petunia, rose, geranium, coleus, dahlia, gladiolus, zinnia, aster, nasturtium, marigold, cosmos, sweet pea, impatiens, phlox, salvia, daisy, snapdragon and many others. A beautiful sight in Seymour during the spring, summer and early fall are the lilac bushes and the orange lilies, both of which were introduced by the early settlers and mark early homestead and cemetery sites.

— Maple Syrup and Sugar Industry —

There are many maple syrup producers in Seymour Township. For some it is a commercial project to augment income; for others a hobby. It is not unusual to see a home in country or town with syrup pails on a few sugar maples in the lane or on the lawn. Until 1875, maple syrup and maple sugar were the standard sweeteners in pioneer households. Today it is a truly Canadian product shipped to other parts of the world, and a treat to be enjoyed at home as it currently costs about fifteen dollars a litre. Diane and Marcus H. Curle tap a large sugar bush at Concession 8, Lot 6, in Seymour Township where sap has been collected for six generations, and processed into maple syrup, maple sugar and maple butter on the premises. The Curles tap twelve hundred trees using a plastic pipeline that carries the sap from the trees to the sugar house for boiling down. An additional eight hundred trees that are easily accessible are tapped by spigot and bucket and the sap is picked up by sleigh equipped with a tank and drawn by a magnificent team of Clydesdale horses. In a good year, one tap produces one litre of maple syrup. Diane makes the maple sugar and maple butter and these, along with the syrup, are sold at the sugar shack on their property which is open most of the year.

Shirley and Bill Little of Concession 6, Lot 4, in Seymour Township have been producing maple syrup for 50 years. Over the years, they have tapped between eight hundred and fifty to a thousand trees. They used to provide an educational program for local school children to learn about syrup production. Their syrup is sold in stores in Campbellford and area. Other producers include Carl Free, the Brouwers family, the Oddie family, the Fox family, Derek Jeffs, and Bernice and Stan Kerr.

⁓ Farm Associations ⁓

CAMPBELLFORD FARMERS' MARKET ASSOCIATION

There is no more beautiful sight than the Campbellford/Seymour Farmer's Market on a fine spring morning — with vivid plants, hanging baskets, and spring flowers, crates of strawberries, pungent herbs, and people celebrating the rebirth of another season. Along with summer, come the garden vegetables and flowers of the season, red and black currents, gooseberries, raspberries, and the tender young vegetables from the earth. Then there is autumn, with gourds and pumpkins, dried flowers, squash, mounds of carrots, beets, potatoes, and pickles and preserves. What a feast for the eyes and the belly!

There are cheeses, chickens, beef, pork, lamb, and fresh eggs, and many interesting craft items for sale. There is honey, spring maple syrup, cider in apple harvest time, and apples of every colour — even russets! Every week there are pies, bread, buns, and sweet desserts fresh from the oven. Some bakers are up most of the night preparing these delights for market the next day.

Debbie Fox of Foxview Farms selling her farm products to a local customer.
Photo courtesy of Margaret Crothers, taken 1999.

In 1989, the Campbellford Business Improvement Association realized that a market could be a dynamic economic development tool and would add social fabric to the community, so they invited the farmers to set up a market in town Saturday mornings. The first season there were six vendors who participated and now there are seventeen regular vendors with four of the original vendors still present. In 1990, Art Gater established the Campbellford Farmers' Market Association. A constitution of rules and regulations was written to ensure that at least 70% of the products brought to the market were home grown, raised, and harvested.

Over the years the quantity and quality of products has greatly increased to provide a higher level of consumer satisfaction. But folk come to the market for other reasons as well. It is a wonderful place to meet friends, seek advice, and be warmly welcomed. It is a link to the past; the foods are prepared using Grandma's methods. People come for the fresh products and stay for the fun!

The market runs from May to October, Saturdays, 8 am until noon and Wednesday afternoons, July and August, 3:30 PM until 6 PM.

NORTHUMBERLAND JUNIOR FARMERS

The first Junior Farmers club in Northumberland County was organized in Castleton in 1923. The Northumberland County Association became active in 1945. Wesley Down was the first County President and later became the fourth president of the Provincial Association. Over the years, the County Association members have been involved in leadership camps, field days, debating, conferences, dances, the annual banquet, travelling scholarships, exchanges and fund raising for charities. The motto, "Self Help and Community Betterment", helped members to become leaders in many walks of life. The Century Farm Sign Project, introduced in Centennial year 1967, designated Ontario farms that had been in the same family for one hundred years. This truly celebrated Canada's rural heritage. Junior Farmers has a well-earned reputation as a "marriage bureau", to which many Northumberland members can attest.

Presidents

1945	Wesley Down	1968	Duane Kerr
1946	Doug Deviney	1969	Clifford Grills
1947	Howard Evans	1970	Ron Ireland
1948	Sam Davidson	1971	Earl Pollock
1949	Earl Nelson	1972	Edna (Grills) Pearse
1950	Bruce Elmhirst	1973	Cathy (Down) Redden
1951	Helen Davidson	1974	Ralph Dunk
1952	Jack Dorland	1975	Don Watson
1953	Alfred Gooding	1976	David Dunham
1954	Don Carruthers	1977	David Dorland
1955	Bill Curle	1978	David Glover
1956	Ruth (Deviney) Haig	1979	Evelyn Waddell
1957	Paul McKinley	1980	Cathie Lowry
1958	Fern Tinney	1981	Bill Dorland
1959	Milton Haig	1982	Kelly Sharp
1960	Howard McCann	1983	Arlene Dorland
1961	Richard Usher (dec.)	1984	Alan Carruthers
	Peter Newton	1985	Terry Linton
1962	Mike Clitherow	1986	John Curle
1963	Bill Honey	1987	Van Darling
1964	Wayne Pollock	1988	Jim Curle
1965	Owen McCann	1989	Dan Darling
1966	Eugene Brahaney	1990	Doug Carr
1967	Don Honey	1991	Darcy McKague

Presidents (continued)

1992	Jennifer (McCann) Jeffs	1996	Rajean Meiklejohn
1993	Keven Haig	1997	Bev McCulloch
1994	Jennifer (Johnston) Petherick	1998	Matt Young
1995	Glenn Milne		

4-H CLUBS

4-H Clubs began in Manitoba in 1913 as Boys' and Girls' Clubs and first appeared in Seymour Township in 1930. In 1952, these clubs became known as 4-H Clubs, adopting the motto:

> I pledge my Head to clearer thinking, my Heart to greater loyalty, my Hands to larger service, and my Health to better living, for my Club, my Community, and my Country.

The stated purpose of these clubs was to provide rural young people the opportunity to learn farming and home-making skills. The local Women's Institutes sponsored the groups for girls. For many rural young people this was and continues to be a wonderful opportunity to meet others. Some were able to attend leadership training camps and take field trips to interesting places which broadened their horizons. One important event was participation in the Canadian National Exhibition competitions in Toronto. As one young women reports "4-H was the most important part of my teen years."

Girls' Leaders – Seymour East

Ina Thompson	Mildred Heagle	Lois Heagle
Hilda Hume	Elsie Rannie	Lorna Oddie
Aileen Airhart	Doris Thomson	June Hagerman
Norma Thompson	Shirley Twigg	Elaine Petherick
Thelma Parr	Carol Kerr	Tina Darling
Phyllis Johnston	Janice Shelley	Marilyn Lyn
Maudie Fry	Sharon Puddephatt	Cara Owens
Edna Grills	Eleanor Bennett	Susan Stevenson

Girls' Leaders – Seymour West

Stella Duran	Hazel Fisher	Arlene Brouwers
Isobel Hooper	Gladys Free	Doreen Westlake
May Campbell	Verna Fairman	Sandra Douglas
Catherine Brahaney	Gerane McConnell	Gayle Fox

Girls' Leaders – Seymour West (continued)

Maudie Clark	Grace Lewis	Marie Pearson
Eva Fraser	Helen McGee	Donna Brown
Elsie Rannie	Fleda Stillman	Pam Clarke
Marion Waddell	Lois Brown	Esther Watson
Verna Fairman	Ruby McCulloch	Belinda Fox
Iona Bright	Marilyn Beattie	Jean Curle
Gertrude McCulloch	Judy Fisher	Marion Curle
Phyllis McCulloch	Betty Thain	Brenda Townsend
Eileen McKelvie	Joan Brouwers	Marion Hay
Fern Rutherford	Marie Locke	Debbie Petherick
	Doreen Westlake	Jill Fisher

Today the club groups still focus on personal achievement. Now all young people, urban and rural from 10–21, are invited to attend. Clubs focus on veterinary work, calf-raising, goat and sheep raising, maple syrup production and other issues, all promoting agriculture and life skills.

The highlight of the 1999 Campbellford fair for youngsters belonging to 4-H clubs in the area has to be Achievement Day and the Dairy Inter-Club Show. Some eighty boys and girls aged ten to twenty-one, from the Campbellford, Colborne and Brighton areas, took nervous and proud turns in the arena to show their calves. These showmanship events are, as Judge John DeVries of Bowmanville observed, "what it's all about," and are consequently heavily contested. To qualify for an Achievement Award a boy or girl has to attend 4-H club meetings regularly during the year and prepare their calves for presentation. This means training them to walk with the halter, grooming, dressing and even powdering them so that they look clean and neat and then actually leading them into and around the ring, controlling their movement so that they show well for the judge and onlookers.

Campbellford/Seymour Agricultural Society/Fair

DEVELOPMENT OF THE FAIR

Ontario's first fair was organized in 1792 under the Agricultural Society of Upper Canada at Newark (Niagara on the Lake). Governor John Graves Simcoe was the first President. Unfortunately, this fair declined over the years and no longer exists.

Locally, the Campbellford/Seymour Agricultural Society, which sponsors the annual agricultural fair, has made a great contribution to the history and development of the area and its agricultural industry. One of the oldest organizations in the area, it was formed in 1854 with a total of 81 members who each paid a subscription of $1.25. The fair which usually took place during the month of October, had no real home. It was held in various locations throughout the town of Campbellford, the first being at the Town Hall. The admission price to this premier event was five cents and it was entitled "The East Riding Show." Among the displays were farm implements, stock, and crops. Prize money given for entries such as cattle, sheep, swine horses, butter, cheese, weaving and full cloth amounted to $75 and the Legislative Grant was $48. During this time, the prize money was paid in sterling and described in pounds, shillings and pence.

By the year 1878, attractions included horses, sheep, swine, grains, and seeds. Also displayed were dairy and kitchen products. The Riding Show continued to have success and became a popular event for the farmers in the area. By 1889, along with usual farm products, roots and fruit were also displayed. Campbellford and Hastings challenged each other to a friendly baseball game to start off the festivities. The midway consisted of three side shows, Canada's Little World, a Panorama of the Northwest Rebellion and some fakers. Often these fakers were shady characters who hoodwinked their customers by illegal means, making much money for themselves and their cronies during a season. The real attraction took place in the afternoon when the horse races drew a large crowd.

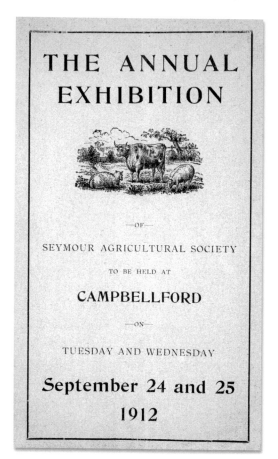

THE ANNUAL
EXHIBITION

—OF—

SEYMOUR AGRICULTURAL SOCIETY

TO BE HELD AT

CAMPBELLFORD

—ON—

TUESDAY AND WEDNESDAY

September 24 and 25
1912

Seymour Agricultural Society annual pamphlet, September 1912.

From Campbellford/Seymour Heritage Society Archives.

The Society purchased land on the present location of the Campbellford Fair Grounds on March 29, 1895. Eleven acres were bought at a cost of $1,086 and the first building was constructed. After ten years, four more acres were added, this time at a cost of $300. Eventually more buildings were erected including a cattle barn and a horse barn. As a result of volunteer labour, a grandstand and a track were also added. The General Exhibits Arena was built in 1922 to be used for the housing of poultry but, by the year 1937, was being used as an exhibition area for produce, cheese, school projects, and homemaking and flower displays. Finally, in the year 1946, an additional two acres was added for the price of $200. This brought the total acreage of the fair grounds to seventeen acres at a total cost of $1,586. A very memorable evening for all Fair Directors occurred in April of 1945 when a banquet was held and the mortgage was burned.

In 1937, a liaison from the women's group was appointed to the Fair Board. At the Provincial Convention in 1947, the Board was advised to formally organize the women's fair committees. A full slate of officers was elected and the secretary on the women's board was also made an associate of the secretary of the Fair Board. After this re-organization, improvements were made to the oldest building on the grounds which was renamed the Homemaker's Centre. All exhibits were re-arranged and spread out due to the growing interest and participation of the women.

During the years 1952–1967, several new buildings were added to the grounds. These included race horse barns, pig pens and a cattle barn which was partly made from old church sheds from St. Andrews Presbyterian Church in town. Refreshment stands dotted the grounds and the fences were upgraded with picket and wire. 1954 marked the Centennial year for the Campbellford Fair but, as the early records of the fair were lost, it was not until 1958 that the date was established and the centennial celebration held. In 1954, the Coronation Gates were erected close to the General Exhibits building, with the aid of a centennial grant from the Province. The inscription reads: "To honour the pioneers of this Community, and all those, who, during the past one hundred years have served the cause of agriculture." During this time period, the current baseball diamond was set up complete with bleachers and flood lights. Also constructed by the Society in conjunction with Seymour Township was a large building suitable for housing the township road equipment. At fair time, this structure is used as a cattle barn.

The major Centennial project for the town and township was the construction of the Campbellford/Seymour Community Arena which officially opened in May 1967. The arena is available to the Agricultural Society at fair time for various shows, displays and vendors. On July 19, 1967, as part of the Canadian Centennial year festivities, the Centennial Caravan was located at the fair grounds and proved to be a crowd pleaser.

Over the years, the Society has encouraged school children and 4-H boys and girls to become involved in the Fair and join as Junior Directors to make the Campbellford Fair more of a family affair. Another youth leadership activity is the Campbellford/Seymour Fair Ambassador Competition which provides a chance for the winner to advance to the Canadian National Exhibition Ambassador of the Fairs Pageant in Toronto. In 1991, Amy-Jo Lowe, was chosen the provincial Fair Ambassador at the Canadian National Exhibition pageant, competing against 105 contestants from throughout Ontario. As Ontario Ambassador she travelled extensively, promoting Ontario fairs, and participating in public speaking events, parades, charity activities, fair openings, and judging competitions.

Many things have changed over the past years. By 1992, membership in the Society had increased to 134 and the membership fee to $7. The provincial grant had increased to $4,500 and the total amount of prize money had grown to $21,910. In 1996, the highlight of the fair was the opening of the renovated 101-year old Red Barn. It is used as a meeting place, display centre, and auction barn. The proposed addition of washrooms and a kitchen will give it rental possibilities.

The Campbellford Fair today is a continuing success. It is held over a three day period on the second week in August each year. It is still an agriculturally dominated fair but has many other attractions, including a large midway with various rides, many novelty contests for the children and young at heart, Old Macdonald's Petting Zoo, school displays, and the biggest attraction – the demolition derby. The traditional homemaking displays and livestock shows still take place through the weekend. Horses, cattle, ponies, swine, and poultry are exhibited and judged. Other attractions are Western and English horse shows, a display of classic cars and motorcycles, a tractor-pull competition, and horse and pony drawing matches. In 1999, a Llama Show and Katahdin Sheep Show were introduced, sparking a great deal of interest. After 145 years, the Fair is still wonderful entertainment.

Past Presidents

Alex Donald	1873–76	C. S. Owens	1896
Donald Johnston	1877–79	E.C. West	1897–98
This. Hume	1880	T.J. Naylor	1899
Fred Macoun	1881–82	A.A. Mulholland	1900–07
John Morrison	1883–84, 1888–89	J.B. Ferris	1908–10
F. Bonnycastle	1885, 1890–91, 1895	Geo. Dunham	1911–13
Robert. Cock	1886	Chas. Bedford	1914–20
Jasper Locke	1887	John Locke	1924–25
Alex Hume	1892, 1921–23	W.A. Wynn	1926
Wm. Stillman	1893–94	Henry Waters	1927

Past Presidents (continued)

T.J. Horkins	1928	Allan Curle	1955–56
G. Vanvolkenburg	1929	Clare Ingram	1957–59
W.M. Stephens	1930	Leo Doherty	1960–63
Dr. S.L. O'Hara	1931	Alex Linn	1964–68
W.J. Abernethy	1932	Clayton Thompson	1969–70
Robt. Innes	1933	Donald W. Clarke	1971–72
W.S. Milne	1934	Everett Parr	1973–74
Wm. Ross	1935	Murray Heath	1975–77
W.J. Duncan	1936	Maurice Brunton	1978–79
A.D. Bennett	1937	Neil McCulloch	1980–81
E.A. McCook	1938	Eldon Petherick	1982–83
Jas. Waters	1939	Ronald Isaac	1984–85
Garnet Curle	1940	Jim Trotter	1986–87
Robt. McCulloch	1941	Lorne McKeown	1988
W.A. Hume	1942	Brian Redden	1989–90
W.W. Archer	1943–44	Eugene Brahaney	1991–92
John Murray	1945	Elvin Petherick	1993–94
Marcus Curle	1946–47	Art Nelson	1995–97
P.R. Oddie	1948–49	Lyle Heath	1997–98
R.P. Seymour	1950–54	Doug Brunton	1999

Past Secretary Treasurers

John Clarke	1879–97	Darlene Brown	1970
Dr. G.A. Hay	1898–1920	Tom & Norma Thompson	1971–76
Nelson Stone	1921–31	Carol Desoer	1977–78
G.A. Kingston	1932–35	Helen Brahaney	1979–85
G.G. Stephens	1936–53	Murray Heath	1996–8
Jesse Locke	1954–67	Ron Isaac	1990–91
Mel Wight	1968–69	Pamela Moran	1992–97
Marg Stapley	1997–98	Alison Wagner	1999

Past Homecraft Presidents

Hilda Hume	1947–48	Jennie Stephens	1955–56
Eva Locke	1949–50	Ruby McCulloch	1959–60
Lillian Irwin	1951–52	Thelma Parr	1961–62,
Mary Rannie	1953–54,		1970–71
	1957–58, 1967	Lorna Oddie	1963–64

Past Homecraft Presidents (continued)

Betty Thompson	1965–66	Carol Darling	1986–87
Bernice Kerr	1968–69, 1978–79	Leila Grills	1988–89
Olive Brunton	1972–73	Cathy Redden	1990–92
Dorothy Milne	1974–75	Helen Brahaney	1993–94
Joyce Parr	1976–77	Connie Sheppard	1995–96
Phyllis McCulloch	1980–81	Joy Petherick	1997–98
Grace Joss	1982–83	Janice Rutherford	1999
June Keating	1984–85		

Past Secretary-Treasurers: Ladies Division

Mary Rannie	1947–49	Betty Thompson	1971–77
Ruby McCulloch	1950–51, 1962–63	Evelyn Brunton	1977–81
Hilda Hume	1952–56, 1970–71	Connie Sheppard	1982–93
Mary Nelson	1957–61	Brenda Petherick	1994–95
Thelma Parr	1964–68	Suzanne Inglis	1996–99
Mel Wight	1969		

Past Fair Queens/Ambassadors

1971	Mary Ellen Thompson	1986	Marie Austin
1972	June Rutherford	1987	Heather Owens
1973	Kim Haley	1988	Jennifer Brahaney
1974	June Rutherford	1989	Kim Isaac
1975	Cindy Haley	1990	Lorelei Rowe
1976–7	NO FAIR QUEENS	1991	Amy-Jo Lowe
1978	Lynn Curle	1992	Shawna Allen
1979	Cheryl Stephens	1993	Lisa Curle
1980	Jennifer Graham	1994	Melissa Allen
1981	Sherry Snarr	1995	Michelle McFadden
1982	Sherrie Kerr	1996	Tara Marshall
1983	Diane Goacher	1997	NO CONTEST
1984	Karen Sparling	1998	Lisa Atkinson
1985	Crystal Nelson	1999	NO FAIR AMBASSADOR

THE HOLSTEIN SHOW —
CAMPBELLFORD FAIR

Northumberland County Holstein Show, held at the Campbellford Fair each year, is recognized as one of the best in Canada, both in numbers and quality and is a fine tribute to the participating breeders. The Campbellford/Seymour arena makes a perfect place to show cattle and has lots of seating capacity for onlookers. It is generally agreed that Blythe Nelson was instrumental in organizing Holstein classes and cattle judging in the early years of the fair. Craig Nelson as a teenager helped his uncle and soon became a leading breeder and showmen himself. In the 1940s many farmers' sons and daughters, under the guidance of leaders like Lindsay Anderson and Earle Nelson, became good show persons and judges. The Holstein show at Campbellford grew rapidly. Gerry Nelson, son of George Nelson, was also very active in the development of Holstein shows and served Holstein breeders of Northumberland and nine other counties for thirty-five years. Many battles for top honours took place between the Nelsons of Campbellford and the Honeys of Warkworth at these shows. In 1948, Bill Petherick showed his first calf and Almerson Farms gave Craig Nelson keen competition. Fifty consecutive show years later, in 1997, Almerson "Charles Silvia" was Grand Champion for Eldon and Evan Petherick.

Breeders in the Campbellford Area showing Grand Champions in recent years are:

Almerson Farms – Eldon and Evan Petherick

Kingsway Holsteins – Gordon McMillan

Carlencrest Farms – Carl Petherick and Sons

Nelcam Holsteins – Art Nelson

Grillsdale Holsteins – Cliff Grills

Sunnybrooke Farms – Ron Watson

Hailcroft Holsteins – Milton Haig

～ Hoard's Station Sale Barn ～

In 1949, Ray Williams established a livestock auction facility in his barn at Hoard's Station to serve the needs of local farmers. He and his sons, Roy and Stan, set up a sale ring in which he was known to spend up to fifteen hours a day auctioning livestock for customers from far and wide. Auctions were usually held on Monday evening. Ray's wife, Esther, helped with bookkeeping and organizing the operation of the concession stand operated by local women's groups. In 1951, Roy Williams formally joined the business after training as an auctioneer in Mason City, Iowa.

In 1959, the sale barn was sold to Delbert Hickson and his family continues to operate the facility to this day. In 1998, the original barn was enlarged to about double the original size. The sale barn now accommodates an average of 500 people per auction day. Daytime sales are held on Tuesdays and the average sale volume is $100,000 per sale day.

R. Williams Community Live Stock Exchange, initially held every Monday.
From postcard collection of Campbellford/Seymour Heritage Society Archives.

Status of Agriculture in Campbellford/ Seymour Today

According to a survey conducted recently by the Campbellford/Seymour Strategic Planning Team, the area has a total of 238 farms, of which 207 responded to the survey. Among the respondents, the type of farms are:

Dairy	76	Grain/Oilseed	9	Livestock/Combination	7
Beef	67	Field Crops	21	Vegetable	3
Hog	1	Fruit	2	Other	4
Wheat	1	Miscellanous/Specialty	16		

ENDNOTES

1 John Macoun, *Autobiography of John Macoun, Canadian Explorer and Naturalist*, 1831–1920 (Ottawa: Ottawa Field-Naturalists' Club, 1979), p. 27.

2 *A Fair Share: A History of Agricultural Societies and Fairs in Ontario, 1792–1992* (Toronto: Ontario Association of Agricultural Societies, 1992), p. 117.

Chapter Four

Business, Commerce and the Professions

Business and commerce in Campbellford/Seymour has changed over the years to meet the needs of the community. When the first settlers came to Seymour Township, they started business districts in different areas that were convenient to them at that time and within close proximity to their residences.

Two such areas "The Patch," now Ranney Falls, and Emilyville, which is now the residential area inclusive of Henson, Wallace, and Alma Streets. Eventually business concentrated on both sides of the river in the area of Seymour Bridge which became the village of Campbellford. This area became the centre of the retail business district as we know it today. When trains were the primary means for transporting products in the first half of the twentieth century, major businesses tended to concentrate along the railway line. With the decline of the railways and the emergence of the trucking industry over the past fifty years, industrial areas or parks have been developed in the periphery of the town and along the main traffic arteries.

～ A Stroll Down Memory Lane ～

Don Frederick, Murray Johnston, and Lawrence Craighead have combined their recollections of how the business community appeared in the 1930s. By 1940, some of the shops noted had relocated or disappeared – not an unusual occurrence through succeeding years.

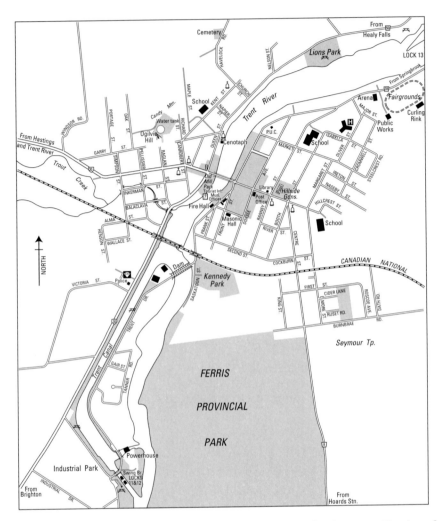

Map of the Town of Campbellford, prepared for the Campbellford/Seymour Chamber of Commerce in the late 1970s by Ken McCartney, reproduced and adapted with the permission of the Chamber.

The starting point for this Memory Lane stroll is the west side of the bridge. Then known as Tice Street as far west as the United Church, it will be referred to by the present name – Bridge Street. On the north side of the street going west were: Ackerman's Ice Cream Parlour, O'Connor's Pool Room, J. A. Frederick, Tailor, Tripp's General Store, Gay's Red and White Grocery, and at the corner of Bridge and Queen Streets – Anderson's Men's Wear. Continuing north on Queen on the east side were: Frederick's Fishing Tackle Works, Harris Flour and Feed, Cassan Bros. Garage, Turner's Garage and Keir's Mill. Crossing Queen Street to the west side, going south from Dr. Longmore's house and office were: Anderson's Hardware, Ernest Lee, Tailor, Atkinson's Grocery and on the corner, MacArthur's Butcher Shop. From the corner and to the west were: Sutherland's Shoe Repair, Ackerman's Barber Shop, McGregor's Cycle Shop and Fraser's Gas Station and Appliance Store. Across Bridge Street to the south side and to the east were: Henson's Harness Shop, Albert Rowe's Pool Room with Porrier's Barber Shop in back, J. Jacobs Tinsmith and Plumber, Clifton Tea Room, Doak Sisters Millinery, Sam Clegg, Grocer, Mrs. Wood's Grocery, and Ernie Birk's Drug Store on the corner. Across the street, the Campbellford Cloth Company took up the whole south side from the Grand Road intersection east to the bridge. This made up the main shopping area of the west side of the river, numerous small shops crowded together – all vying for a portion of the trade.

The next stage of the stroll involves crossing the bridge to the east side of town. Located on Bridge Street East on the south side was the Ferris Store and Block. Upstairs in the Block were the businesses of Alex MacColl, Lawyer, Dr. H. O. Richardson, Dentist, and the Town and Township offices. On the corner of Front and Bridge Streets was Fred Wood's Drug Store. South on the west side of Front Street were the following shops: Fred Lang, Barber Shop, Weston's Shoes, W. J. Armstrong Clothing, J. M. Bygott Express & Telegraph, G. Wing's Chinese Laundry, the Smith Grist Mill and Davidson's Garage.

On the corner of River Street and Front Street South was the Regent Theatre – now the Masonic Temple. Across River Street and going north were: J. W. Frederick and Son paint shop, Meyers Garage and Freight Office, Frederick's Shoe Repair, Campbellford Herald Office, Telephone Office, Jim Archer Insurance, A. D. Bennett Furniture and Undertaking, Locke Bros. Billiards and Tobacco, Vitalli's Fruit and Vegetables, Osterhout Express, Tom Lavell's Book Store, and Cooke's Restaurant.

To the east on Bridge Street, the following businesses occupied the south side: Davies' Fish and Chips, Tweedie Jewellers, Lipson's Furniture, Dunk's Grocery, Dolman's Clothing, T. J. Horkins' General Store, and Clark's Feed Store. The latter was on the corner of Bridge Street and Rear Street, now Doxsee Avenue. East of the Bridge and Rear Street intersection were Ackerman's Egg Grading and T. E. Hall's Garage on the south side and C. B. Williams Service Station and Neil Thompson Farm Implements on the north side. Harold Spencer's Welding, Alex MacDonald Blacksmith and Petherick's Garage clustered along Rear Street just south of the intersection. To the north of the intersection was Harry Meiklejohn's Garage on the west side and Harvey Donald's Farm Implements on the east.

West on the north side of Bridge Street between Rear and Front Streets were: Jack Phillips, Butcher, George O'Sullivan, Grocer, Bennett's Livery, P. H. Macmillan, Egg Grading, Dr. O'Hara, Veterinarian, Bell's Insurance, Fairman's Bakery, Frank DeCarrol Electric, and at the corner of Bridge and Front Streets, the Bank of Commerce. On

Front Street North on the east side were: the Royal Bank, Linton's Men's Wear, Cournyea's Barber Shop, Macoun's Billiards, the Dominion Store, Patterson's Jewellery, O'Keefe's Hotel, Denyes' Hardware, Simbrow's Ladies Wear, Vessey's Bakery, Dr. O. C. Watson, Dentist, Harry Denike's Grocery, Herb Leonard Men's Wear, George Pace Fruit and Vegetables, Tait's Hardware, Johnny Irwin's General Store, Baker's Egg Grading, and Rowe Brothers' Garage and Davidson's Arena.

The last stage of the stroll is the west side of Front Street south to Bridge Street again. Where the present Petro-Canada station is situated was the blacksmith shop, formerly owned by Clem Bayes and later operated by Barry Machine. Percy and Ken Morgan Car Sales was next with an old hand-cranked gas pump out front. Continuing on down the street was the Hollywood Theatre, the Police Station, Long's Confectionery, Benny Runnells Barber Shop, Sloggett Men's Wear, Hutchison's Harness Shop, Hay's Insurance, Riendeau Insurance and Music Store with Robertson's Barber Shop at the back, Les Diamond Real Estate, Charlie Lee's Royal Café, Menzies Hardware, Loucks Rexall Drugs, Glover Men's Wear, Bailey's Photo, Wiggins Five and Ten, Loftchy's Ladies Wear, Marsh's Confectionery, Eaton's Order Office, Selrite Store, Craighead's Book Store with the telegraph office in back, Abernethy's Barber Shop, Pulman's Clothing, and at the corner of Bridge and Front Streets, the Bank of Montreal. Above the bank were Bonnycastle's Photo Studio and Arthur Armour Stock Broker.

This covers the main business sections on both sides of the bridge and is representative of the businesses at about 1930. A similar survey taken ten years later would have found many of the shop owners in different locations. There were other notable businesses scattered around town, including H. M. Fowlds and A. C. Connor, fuel and lumber dealers. Charles Horsman manufactured and bottled soft drinks. Gibsons had a confectionery on Balaclava. There was Henson's Machine Shop, Vern Marks Planing Mill, J. Benor Sash & Door, Fox Oil & Gas, and Craighead Oil & Gas. Charles Palliser was a long-time florist, Andersons ran a dairy, as did Rutherfords and H. N. Carr operated a creamery. Ronald Young ran one of several firewood businesses.

It would appear remarkable that so many shops involved in similar business activities could eke out a living, but they did an active trade. Travel was more localized, shopping malls were still in the future and the community shopped at home.

～ Accounting ～

With the introduction of the new Income Tax Act in January 1, 1971, the need for professional accounting services by farmers and small business owners increased greatly. For the first time in Canadian tax law, capital gains became subject to income tax and the rules were very complex.

In April 1971 Carl E. Sherk, Chartered Accountant, opened an office in Campbellford on Front Street North above the former offices of Bowes & Cocks, realtors. The following year he moved the office to the old telephone building at 15 Front Street South. He continued his practice there until his death on April 15, 1995. Carl graduated as a Chartered Accountant in 1953. He practiced in Toronto until he moved to Campbellford with his wife Marie and three children in June 1971.

During the 1970s and 1980s the use of computers in accounting increased greatly until it became commonplace in most offices. Carl was very interested in computers and acquired one by the mid-1970s, using it to do bookkeeping and accounting for clients. Word processing programs made the typing of financial statements much easier. By the late 1980s tax returns were being prepared using computer programs.

In April 1972, Lilian M. Brode, Chartered Accountant, moved to Seymour Township from California with her husband, John, and infant daughter. Two boys were born in the 1970s. Lilian graduated as a Chartered Accountant in 1965 after having worked in public accounting in Toronto for five years. She then moved to San Francisco and worked in public accounting in the San Francisco area, qualifying as a C.P.A. in 1970. In the winter of 1972–73 she started preparing income tax returns for farmers out of her home in Campbellford. In October 1978 she opened an office at 80 Front Street North and expanded the accounting practice to include accounting for small businesses as well as the preparation of individual income tax returns and auditing. John Brode was the computer specialist and he was in charge of maintaining up-to-date equipment and programs as well as customizing computer programs. Estate planning and financial planning services were added in the 1990s.

In January 1986, the practice was merged with Welch & Company LLP, Chartered Accountants (formerly George A. Welch & Company, Levesque Marchand) a regional firm with eleven offices in eastern Ontario and western Quebec. Lilian became a partner in the firm at this time.

Charles (Charlie) J. Thompson, B.A., B.Comm., C.A., joined the firm of Welch & Company in September 1988 and became a partner with the firm in 1993. Charlie moved to Seymour Township with his wife Cathy and infant daughter in June 1987 from Toronto. They also have a son born in early 1990s. Charlie obtained his C.A. in 1979 in Toronto where he had been a partner with Clarke, Henning & Co., Chartered Accountants.

Cathy Thompson who is a Certified Management Accountant joined the staff on a full-time basis after the move. At present the full-time staff members are Anne Pope, CGA, Karen Wyse-Nicholas and Lynda Cartwright. They all joined the firm in 1989 or 1990. Two or three persons join the staff part-time during the peak season from January through April. The firm's offices remained at the Front Street North address until October 1999 when the practice moved to 57 Bridge Street East to allow for further expansion.

⟶ Banking ⟶

The Standard Bank opened in 1880 on the upper west side of Front Street North. Later it moved to the east side of the street beside Dr. Derumaux's present office with Mr. Gosling as manager. He was followed by E. A. Bog who was manager for fourteen years until his transfer to Picton in 1900. W.C. Boddy was appointed manager at that time. In 1920, the Standard Bank was taken over by the Bank of Commerce and moved to the northeast corner of Front and Bridge Street. A. G. Thompson was the manager in 1934. This bank ceased operation in the late 1940s, but returned for a short time in the 1970s at the old Bank of Montreal building.

Another early financial institution was the Union Bank which eventually became the Royal Bank. The manager of the Union Bank was Stanley Neale. The Royal Bank was located a few doors north of the corner of Front Street and Bridge Streets. When the Bank of Commerce ceased operations in Campbellford, its corner location at the northeast side of Front and Bridge became the site of the Royal Bank until it moved to the new building on Doxsee Avenue. In 1949, C. Austin Putnam was posted to the Campbellford Branch from Hastings. He was an active community supporter for many years.

In September 1904, the Bank of British North America opened a branch in Campbellford. This was located in the Sloggett Block under the management of H.F. Skey. By 1905, the bank had moved to the northwest corner of Front and Bridge Streets. In 1917, the building received extensive renovations and, while these were completed, the bank was temporarily housed in the O'Sullivan Block. In 1918, the Bank of British North America became the Bank of Montreal and business continued at the same location. Fire caused extensive damage in 1937 and, once again, temporary housing was needed. The branch was enlarged and renovated in 1948 and 1962 to meet the changing needs of its customers. The present new building at the corner of Bridge Street and Doxsee Avenue opened on August 30, 1975.

In January 1979, the Toronto–Dominion Bank was added at Front and River Streets. This building has been remodeled to better serve newer banking needs.

In earlier times, the bank teller handled all transactions personally. The advent of computerized banking, automatic teller machines and cash counters have resulted in many changes in the delivery of banking service in Campbellford/Seymour.

⁓ Lawyers ⁓

The Campbellford/Seymour area has had the benefit of the services of several fine lawyers over the years. Among the first is Arthur Lindhurst Colville who was born on March 16, 1845 in England. He practiced in an office in the Ferris Block above the former Burgis' Hardware and also in the Wallace Block. His home was at 87 Booth Street North and is currently the home of the William Baker family. The home was called 'Maplehurst.' Colville was a well-known amateur actor and a fervent Anglican, serving as a Christ Church warden for 20 years. His wife was Mary Frances Boucher, from one of Campbellford's pioneer families and a relative of Robert and David Campbell. Colville died on October 6, 1903 in Campbellford and is buried in Christ Church Cemetery. His wife died March 22, 1920 and is buried in the same plot.

Arthur Boucher Colville followed his father into the legal profession. He practiced law in Campbellford in partnership with Ira A. Humphries until February 1925. He also served in World War I as a lieutenant. Arthur B. Colville later became Vice-President and Solicitor for the Electric Power Company, which later became the Hydro Electric Power Commission. He subsequently became head of the legal department of Sun Life in Montreal.

George A. Payne, 1859–1932, was the Solicitor for the Town of Campbellford and for the Standard Bank of Canada. He was the Secretary-Treasurer of Campbellford Baseball Club in 1888. His wife was Ida A. Harris Payne and they lived in the Ibey house on 79 Frank Street.

Daniel Johnson Lynch was born in Uxbridge, Ontario, in 1861. He attended Osgoode Hall and was called to the Bar on February 6, 1882. He established a law practice in Campbellford in 1883 in an office in the Kennedy Block on Front Street where Stedman's is now located. He married Emily McKenna and had two daughters, Margaret and Emily, and a son, Charles. He was very active in the affairs of the Town, serving two terms on the Town Council, and as a member of the Public School Board for many years. He led a delegation to Ontario Department of Education in Toronto to persuade it to establish Campbellford High School. He was a member of the Board of Governors of the Mechanics' Institute, and was instrumental in bringing the Carnegie library to Campbellford. Lynch served two terms as the Town of Campbellford Solicitor and was appointed to the office of Police Magistrate in 1892. He retired in 1939 to Windsor, Ontario, and died May 5, 1944. His wife predeceased him a month earlier, and they are both buried in St. Mary's Cemetery, Campbellford.

Ira A. Humphries was born on August 10, 1885, in Warkworth, Ontario. He graduated from the University of Toronto in 1908, and from Osgoode Hall in

1911, when he was also called to the Bar. He was appointed a King's Counsel in 1928. He was a partner in a law practice with Arthur Boucher Colville until February 1925, and he subsequently became the Deputy Attorney General for the Province of Ontario. In 1920, he was also the Grand Superintendent of the Royal Arch Masons. He was married, had three children, and was an avid fisherman, football player and cricketer.

In the Herald, there are a few references to two other early lawyers, A. L. MacLellen, about 1876, and W. H. Harris, about 1900. In 1901, Harris left Campbellford and went to Port Perry.

Alex MacColl, 1895–1967, took over Ira Humphries practice in 1925. He was a graduate of Osgoode Hall Law School. His wife was R. Faye McCleary and they lived on Pellissier St. They are buried in Christ Church Cemetery.

J. F. Ross Douglas graduated from the University of Toronto in 1926 and from Osgoode Hall in 1929. He bought George A. Payne's practice in 1932. He also practiced from his home at 60 Front Street North in Campbellford. His wife was Eleanor Ferris. He died on September 2, 1977 and is buried in Mount Pleasant Cemetery.

Trevor Clarke was born in Barbados in 1925 and graduated from Osgoode Hall in the 1950s. He practiced litigation law in partnership with a Peterborough firm. He opened his practice in Campbellford in the 1960s on Front Street South where Wallace Brown is currently located. He died in 1978 and is buried in St. Mary's Cemetery.

Paul Smith graduated from Osgoode Hall Law School in 1966 and called to the Bar in 1968. He opened his practice in Campbellford in March 1968, and currently practices at 32 Pellissier Street South.

Wallace Brown graduated from the University of Toronto and from law school in 1970. He was called to the Bar in 1972. He opened his practice in Campbellford in 1978.

Wayne Buck graduated from the University of Western Ontario in 1972 and was called to the Bar in 1973. He opened his practice in Campbellford in 1973 and currently practices at 6 Queen Street.

William Baker graduated from the University of Western Ontario in 1972 and was called to the Bar in 1974. He opened his office in Campbellford in 1973 and currently practices at 79 Bridge Street East.

Two sons of Dr. David Burgess of Campbellford entered the law profession. Neil Burgess graduated from the University of Western Ontario in 1972, and was called to the Bar in March 1974. He opened his practice in Campbellford in 1974 and is currently located at 64 Front Street North. Paul Burgess graduated from the University of British Columbia in 1980 and was called to the British Columbia Bar in 1982, and the Ontario Bar in 1985. He opened his practice in Campbellford in 1990.

～ Business Organizations ～

CAMPBELLFORD/SEYMOUR
CHAMBER OF COMMERCE

The early history of the Campbellford/Seymour Chamber of Commerce is somewhat sketchy. There is some indication that there was a Chamber or Board of Trade as early as 1904, according to John E. King, the National Vice President of the Canadian Chamber of Commerce who addressed the local Chamber at the annual meeting at George's Restaurant in Campbellford in March 1973.[1] The earliest reference to a Board of Trade executive appeared in Herald in 1906. The officers were: President, E. C. West; Vice-President, J. A. Stewart; Treasurer, W. B. Archer; Secretary, H. F. Skey; Councillors, Messrs. Owen, Lynch, Scherk, Reesor, Ferris, Fowlds, Lowery, Mulholland, Colville, Macoun, and Golden. The Campbellford Herald reported that the Chamber of Commerce was formed in May of 1939 and the officers were: F. F. Long, Honorary President; H. J. Taylor, President; T. E. Hall, Vice-President; and W. A. Kingston, Secretary.[2] A later edition of the Herald indicates that in the autumn of 1950, a meeting was held in Edgewater Park Pavilion for the purpose of forming a Chamber of Commerce in Campbellford. Alex Fraser, president of the Marmora Chamber of Commerce addressed the gathering. Officers chosen were: President, Lynn Bradley; vice-President, R. D. McDonald; Secretary, Paul O'Sullivan; Treasurer, Austin Putnam.

Recent data obtained from the Chamber indicates that the current organization was formed in 1951 by a group of local businessmen and private citizens to promote tourism and commercial and industrial expansion The first Presidents were as follows:

Ernest C. McKeel	1951–1952	Donald H. Meyers	1959–1960
J.F.R. Douglas	1953–1956	George Nicholls	1961
Ralph J. Locke	1957	Robert B. Bennett	1962–1963
C.H. (Bud) Davidson	1958	Douglas R. Maybee	1964

In 1956, the executive of the Chamber was: President, J. F. R. Douglas; First Vice-President, C. H. Davidson; Secretary, Frank DeCarrol; and Treasurer, Austin Putnam. In 'Days of Yore' in the Campbellford Herald of February 17, 1960, it is reported that the annual dinner meeting of the Chamber was held on February 16 at the Parish Hall. Donald H. Meyers was re-elected President and the other officers were as follows: First Vice-President, George Nicholls; Second Vice-President, Gordon Oder; Treasurer, Austin Putnam; Directors, Ray Pettey, Mrs. Don Russell, and Robert B. Bennett. Committee chairs were: Retail Merchants, Harry Burgis; Tourist, Hugh McCarten; Industrial, C. H. Davidson; Membership, Colin Collins.

The Chamber was incorporated in 1979 and has continued to be a driving force within the community. It consists of a Board of Directors made up of eleven people. The 1999 Board of Directors is as follows:

James J. Rix	President
Rod Williams	Vice President
Paula Meier	Past President
Pat Watters	Treasurer
Sharon Hamilton	Director
Mario Milano	Director
Dr. Bruce Robertson	Director
Maisie Waters	Director
Steve McCarthy	Director
Gayle Crosmaz-Brown	Director
Harold Williams	Municipal Council representative

The Chamber of Commerce has been responsible for the Santa Claus parade for many years. Dolly Mills, George Bibby, Gene Dewey and Maisie Waters have been instrumental over the years in making the parade a success for the whole community. The Chamber also hosts the Chocolate and Cheese Festival and is involved in Canada Day celebrations and the Showcase of Lights. Other innovative changes included the Grouch of the Year Contest, a handbook for tourists, waterfront development in partnership with the town, the Main Street development project with the Business Improvement Area, and a history of Old Mill Park. The Chamber is responsible for the community Civic Awards that are presented at the Chamber's annual meeting every February. Several awards are presented by the Chamber, among them the most prestigious, the Citizen of the Year. The first Citizen of the Year was given to Mary Fotheringham who was the Director of ARC Industries in Campbellford in 1980. The second award was given to Maureen Dikun in 1981 for her extensive involvement in community service through Meals on Wheels, Blood Pressure Clinics, the Ontario Heart Foundation, St. Mary's Catholic Women's League, St. Mary's Parent-Teacher Association, the Campbellford Lioness Club, and Girl Guides. The awards were discontinued for several years until 1996 when the Chamber, under the direction of President Paula Meier decided it was time to start recognizing the contributions of local residents once again. Recent recipients of the awards were as follows:

1996

Citizen of the Year	Florence Headrick
Volunteer of the Year	Donald A. Thomson
Athlete of the Year	Cassandra Turner

Arts and Cultural Contribution	Dave Noble
Hero In Business	Janet Donald
Entrepreneur of the Year	Cathy Welsh

1997

Citizen of the Year	Lillian Turner
Volunteer of the Year	Jean Tilney
Athlete of the Year	Kyle Pettey
Arts and Cultural Contribution	Donna Bennett and Brian Finley
Heroes In Business	Steve Sharpe
	Nancy Coulter
Entrepreneur of the Year	Maria Cunningham

1998

Citizen of the Year	Angie Nestoruk
Volunteer of the Year	Pat Watters
Athlete of the Year	Angie Quinn
Arts and Cultural Contribution	Dave Noble and Eric Lorenzen
Heroes In Business	Paul Imperial
	Paula Meier
Entrepreneur of the Year	Sue Locke

A special award was also given in 1998 to Scott McKelvie, Andrew Towns and Adam Macmillan for their heroic efforts in saving a girl from drowning at Ranney Falls in 1997.

The Chamber has been responsible for managing the licensing bureau for the Ministry of Transportation for many years. The current manager at the License Bureau is Evelyn Martin who has been there since 1982.

The Chamber of Commerce moved to the Old Mill Park in the early 1980s and began registering boaters traveling down the Trent-Severn waterway. Showers and electrical outlets have been provided for the boaters since 1993 making the community a popular stop for visitors. The Chamber has been dedicated since it's inception to make this area a better place in which to live, work and play. In an effort to achieve this the Board of Directors decided in 1990 to hire a full time person to take care of the membership and tourism. The first full-time Chamber of Commerce Coordinator was Sharon Burgess, followed by Montse Pereira, Angela Risto, and Ann-Marie Kelleher. The present Coordinator is Lianne Wallace. The Chamber also hires students in the summer months to help during the peak season. It currently has a membership of 175 and works hard at promoting the area to achieve prosperity for its members and the community at large. The Chamber works closely with the Business Improvement Area, and the

Campbellford/Seymour Council to set and implement common goals. The Strategic Plan is the most recent document that the three organizations have been working on that sets the community's priorities until the year 2010.

Nineteenth Century Flashbacks

March 14/73

(From The Herald files, 1876)

OUR BUSINESS PROPORTIONS 1876

In the names which follow, we have endeavoured to present a correct list of all persons soliciting public favour. "Mutual dependence in the great law of the universe."

DRY GOODS, GROCERIES, LIQUORS
J. G. McKay & Company, Star House, dry goods, etc.; E. Nulty, Montreal House, dry goods and clothing; J. M. Ferris & Co., general merchants; J. & D. Waters, general merchants and merchant tailors; Donald & Mathieson, general merchants; B. M. & J. Frederick, general merchants and merchant tailors; Adam Dinwoodie, dry goods, groceries, and liquors; Morton & Chapman, general merchants; W. Shaw & Son, merchants and merchant tailors; B. S. Carnahan, groceries, boots and shoes; J. Martin & Co., dry goods and clothing; Brickley & Galvin, groceries and liquors.

HARDWARE
Gillespie Bros. and Martin & Cock.

DRUG STORES
Drs. R. J. Ough and I. D. Bogart.

WATCHMAKING AND JEWELRY
T. S. Porte

FACTORIES
D. Morris & Company's woollen factories; Jas. Benor, planing factory; Mott & Carter, carriage works.

MILLS
W. Dunk & Sons, saw mill; R. Cockburn's grist mill

HARNESS SHOPS
A. T. Green and G. A. Mitchell

CABINET MAKERS
R. J. Eley and W. H. Castiday

BLACKSMITHS
J. Flynn, R. Johnston, R. Linton and T. Johns

COOPER SHOPS
R. Cockburn's and Wm. Logan's

SHOEMAKERS
R. Harry, John Cogan, M. Morrison, Geo. Hazard, and J. McCarty.

BUTCHERS
Thorne & Upton and Jas. Gregor

HOTELS
T. Blute, St. Lawrence Hotel; D. Adams, Queen's Hotel; P. H. Brennan, Dominion Hotel; Smith & Sager Hotel; T. Johns, American Hotel.

LIVERY STABLES
Cadman Gibson, J. Kent, W. Phillips, and John Weese.

LAWYERS
A. K. Colville and A. L. Maclellan.

MILLINERS AND DRESSMAKERS
Miss D. E. Myles, Misses Alderdice & Carr, Miss Boland, Miss Ryan, Mrs. Doak, and Misses Hughes & Connelly.

MISCELLANEOUS
Jno. Dickson, Iron founder; Fitzgerald & Byrne, marble cutters; J. F. Taylor, dentist; C. Nancarrow, tanner; A. Dafoe, baker; J. Davidson, tailor; Geo. Bonter, photographer; D. Deacon, barber; Vosper Bros., Herald newspaper and printing establishment.

BIA — BUSINESS IMPROVEMENT AREA

In 1978, the Town of Campbellford designated an improvement area in the town of Campbellford, established a Board of Management for this area, and appointed members to the Board. On March 29, 1978, the Board of Management drew up a by-law regulating the activities of the BIA. The members appointed to the Board and signatories to the by-law were Brian Redden, Ted Kristensen, Bruce Sharpe, Jan Scheidt, Fred Tredree, Dave Smallwood, and Dan Derumaux. All persons or corporations assessed for business tax in the improvement area are entitled to vote at any annual or general meeting.

The main concern of the BIA is to bring shoppers to the downtown core of Campbellford, and to accomplish this, the organization focuses on improving roads, increasing accessibility to buildings, expanding parking facilities, and beautifying the area with seasonal plants, trees, benches, and Christmas decorations. One special event recently introduced by the BIA is the Cardboard Boat Races, held on the long weekend in mid-summer.

Nineteenth century flashbacks as printed in the Campbellford Herald, March 14, 1973.

～ Businesses ～

Over the years, Campbellford/Seymour has been well-served by many diverse business enterprises. Some have been randomly selected for detailed description.

ANDERSON HARDWARE

In 1918, James Cleatus (J.C.) Anderson came from Morganston to establish a hardware store on Queen Street. He was an astute businessman who chose to locate in a rural area where the demand for his products would be greater. This was a new business which he carefully built into a thriving, progressive hardware store. At first, he resided above the store but later purchased a home near the corner of Queen and Garry Streets.

In 1936, his son, Stuart A. assumed the management of the store. When World War II broke out, Stuart served in the Canadian Armed Forces and his wife, Helen, took over the store. After the end of the conflict, Stuart returned to the hardware business until his death in 1954. Helen once again operated the business until she turned the management over to Leith Crue who was in charge of both the hardware and the local motor licensing bureau. Samuel R. Wilson worked for the firm for twenty-five years. The Anderson Hardware Store served the community for fifty-eight years until its closure on March 31, 1976. This site now houses Redden's Cable TV Ltd.

BARBERS

1876	D. Deacon
1900	Thomas Oulton
1902–1951	Charles Ackerman
1911	John Wilson
1911	Hunt Cassan
1912	Ed Janeway
1912	Fred Lang
1927	John Abar – man's haircut – 25¢; shave – 10¢; ladies – 25¢; under age 18–15¢.
1937	Roland Jarvis presented a petition of behalf of the Campbellford barbers requesting earlier closing hours. Week nights they were open until 8 PM, on Tuesday and Thursday until 9:30 PM and on Saturday until 11 PM.
1940s	Ernie Abernethy, Jack Buchanan, Leo Doherty
1950s	Benny Runnells
1955	Jim Quinn
1964	Harold Douglas

BEATTIE MILLING COMPANY

In 1946, Craig Beattie erected a mill behind his home on Windsor Avenue. This building was totally destroyed by fire in 1951. The mill was rebuilt and in later years was operated by Dick and Marilyn Beattie. One specialty item produced by Craig Beattie was stone-ground flour. The mill was sold in January 1998 to Nicholson Brothers. The two large millstones were removed and are currently in the care of the Campbellford/Seymour Heritage Society.

CLEM BAYES, BLACKSMITH

This shop stood near the corner of Front Street North and Market Street. It was a tiny, white, run-down building whose owner lived just a bit further north on Front Street. In the blacksmith shop, Clem Bayes and Ernie Skitch also made wagons. In 1900, Clem Bayes moved his business to Whyte's Foundry where he leased the former planing mill from William Doxsee who had purchased it from John Whyte. This building was on Front Street South on the site of the Meyers Block. In 1901, Bayes moved again and rented the blacksmith shop from Ernie Skitch on the site of the Rear Street Carriage Works.

BENNETT'S FURNITURE STORE AND FUNERAL SERVICES

In 1926, Andrew Dwight Bennett arrived in Campbellford to purchase the furniture and funeral business from Allan Watson. This thriving Front Street business began in the early 1900s as a partnership between Ely and Irwin who had produced and retailed furniture as well as performing the services of local funeral directors. In 1921, Allan Watson had purchased the Ely and Irwin business and phased out the manufacturing portion of the enterprise. Five years later, the company became the A.D. Bennett Company. When A.D. Bennett purchased this business, he assumed the mortgage held by the former owner, Jim Irwin. This mortgage was finally paid off in the 1930s. A.D. Bennett, with his wife Flossie, and sons, Donald and James, made Campbellford their permanent home. The family grew with the addition of a daughter, Mary, and two sons, Robert and Paul.

Soon after the war began in 1939, shortages developed in furniture but especially in upholstered goods. A.D. Bennett made regular trips to Toronto to try to persuade chesterfield manufacturers to sell their scarce goods to him. This was a major effort as the roads were not paved all the way and cars were not too dependable.

Bennett's was a source of employment for many local people. Some of the early employees were Mr. Dalgleish, William Webber, Evelyn Bennett, Marshall Sills, Leitha Davidson Sisley and Stewart Nelson.

The store was the source of most of the home furnishings within the local area for many years. On the second floor was an area where caskets were displayed. Funeral notices were always displayed in the front window. The funeral home itself was first located in the Bennett home on Frank Street. In the late 1950s, the funeral home moved to the present site of the Weaver Funeral Home, known in the early years as Beaver Hall.

In July 1959, a disastrous fire destroyed the warehouse of Bennett's Furniture. A new complex of three thousand square feet for storage was erected on the south part of the property. In 1960, the pool room on the north side of the building was purchased and the store front thus doubled in size from twenty-four feet to forty-eight feet. Lorne Watson, son of Allan Watson, the previous owner, was the general contractor and designer. Many improvements were made during these renovations.

Bennett's needed an automotive fleet to serve their many enterprises. Usually there was a furniture van, a sedan for delivery, an ambulance, a hearse and several cars.

In 1961, Bill Seguire joined the staff and became General Manager. Don and Bob Bennett formed a limited company as partners in 1963. In 1965, the ambulance service was discontinued and the funeral business was sold to Weaver Funeral Home. For a short time, it carried the combined name of Bennett-Weaver Funeral Home.

Bennett's continued in the furniture business. Bob Bennett sold his shares of the company to Don and purchased the Canadian Tire Store in Sault Ste. Marie. He later moved to Sudbury. Don's sons, primarily Eric and, for a short time, Dwight, continued the tradition of providing quality products and service to the community. Team work provides the key to the secret of their success. Management and workers have pulled together for seventy-two years to provide excellent goods at competitive prices. In late March 1999, Bennett's Home Furnishings expanded with a new store in Peterborough in the Cherney's building at Clonsilla and Lansdowne Streets.

BERTRAND MOTORS

Six Bertrand families came to Meyersburg from Quebec in 1850. They were farmers, but some of the original families eventually moved away. Cecil Bertrand came to Campbellford in 1934 where he worked in the trucking business. On July 1, 1959, he opened his used car business on Bridge Street West. Art joined his father in 1961 and Wayne and Bill followed suit. Some of the mechanics working with them were Gar Irwin, Ron Wallace, Jim Post and Glen Brown. In 1996, leasing of cars was introduced but it is not an important facet of the business. Today Art states that people buy cars less frequently as they cost more, are built better and have little maintenance. This car lot is attractive as the cars are well polished and decorated to shine in the sun. Across the road are display models of older automobiles.

BURGIS PLUMBING, HEATING
AND TINSMITHING /
SPORTING GOODS / HARDWARE

Harry Burgis came to Campbellford in 1927 and worked for his brother, Alfred, in his plumbing, heating and tinsmithing business. In 1938, Harry bought the former F. Menzies Hardware on Front Street North. He relocated his business to 17 Front Street South on the present site of the Wallace Brown Law Office. A partnership was formed known as Burgis Brothers Hardware, Plumbing and Heating. In 1945, they purchased the Ferris Block at the corner of Front and Bridge Streets. In 1948, the partnership was dissolved and the plumbing business was sold to Burgis and Ford. Harry carried on the business known as T.H. Burgis Hardware, Electrical and Sporting Goods. In 1964, the store became Crest Hardware and, in 1978, Burgis' Pro Hardware. After Harry's retirement, his son Tom and wife Bev operated the business until 1996 when they sold the store to Ron and Virginia Brett who operated the business as Brett's Pro Hardware, until it closed in 1999.

CAMPBELLFORD WHOLESALE

Campbellford Wholesale, which has operated continuously since 1930, was purchased by Ralph and Percy Locke from Charles Nadeau. The firm originally operated both a retail and a wholesale outlet with Percy handling the retail portion. In 1940, the business was divided and Ralph Locke continued to operate the wholesale end of the business from an eight hundred square foot red brick building on his property at the corner of Front and River Streets. This building was demolished and became the site of the Bell Telephone dialing exchange.

The firm moved into its new location on Front Street South, seven times larger than the old site, in the summer of 1958 under the leadership of Ralph and his son, Murray. In more recent years, the business has relocated to the industrial park and the 1958 building has become first, the Seymour Township Office and, in 1998, the office for the amalgamated Municipality of Campbellford/Seymour. Campbellford Wholesale continues to provide excellent wholesale services to a large clientele.

CANADIAN FLIGHT EQUIPMENT

Between 1953 and 1964, Canadian Flight Equipment occupied the old stone building at 46 Saskatoon Avenue, next to the fire hall. This company was the sole manufacturer of ejection seats for the Royal Canadian Air Force's CF-100 fighter aircraft.

In the 1950s and into the early 1960s, through some of the stormiest Cold War years, the RCAF's thirteen CF-100 squadrons were the mainstay of our country's air defense against the USSR. Designed and built by AVRO Canada, and in its heyday the best of its breed, each CF-100 was equipped with two ejection seats – one for the pilot, one for the navigator. In an emergency, the lives of both crew members depended on the smooth working of this very complex piece of equipment. Bob Eley, a current Campbellford resident who researched the company, spent about 650 hours in the navigator's seat of various CF-100s, and in each of those hours his life was in the hands of an escape device manufactured right here in Campbellford!

Canadian Flight Equipment started in Cobourg in 1952, when Bob Murison came to Canada to set up the operation. Bob was offered the opportunity by James Baker, the inventor of what was considered to be the most advanced ejection seat in the world, to be both sales agent and licensed manufacturer of the seat. The original idea was to sub-contract the making of individual components and assemble them in the Cobourg plant, but Bob quickly decided that he could build a better product by using his knowledge to become his own sub-contractor. He formed a company called Campbellford Precision Products Limited, which set up shop in the former Weston Shoe Factory on Saskatoon Avenue. By the Spring of 1953 the entire operation had moved to Campbellford, and reverted to its original name: Canadian Flight Equipment.

Starting with three or four workers, the plant gradually built up to a trained work force of around seventy skilled men and women. In the basement of the tall building was the Tool Room; the first floor housed the Machine Shop; on the second floor was the Sheet Metal Shop; and on the floor above that were the sewing machines used to make the drogue chute, which held the seat upright as it fell. Completed seats went from Canadian Flight Equipment to the AVRO factory in Toronto, to be fitted into each of the 692 CF-100s built between 1952 and 1959.

With the cancellation of the CF-100's intended successor, the ill-fated AVRO Arrow, in February of 1959, the plant lost its main line of business. But by this time the skills of the team Bob Murison had assembled and trained were legendary. In Bob's words, "The whole manufacturing team was great." With the help of Canadian Government officials, who helped Bob to get a foothold in the U.S. market, the company was winning contracts from firms like Frankford Arsenal in Pennsylvania for the making of Cartridge Activator Devices. These intricate devices were used on the seat and cockpit canopy in the CF-100. The company also made passenger seats for civilian airliners and pleasure boats, and only missed out on a major bid to build aluminum boats for StarCraft because of a lack of plant space. They were unable to accommodate the large die needed to cast a complete aluminum hull. Canadian Flight Equipment continued operating in Campbellford until 1964, when the need for more room to expand the business forced a move to Trenton. During its latter years on Saskatoon Avenue, the plant was very ably managed by Lola Wallace Holmes, who still lives in Campbellford and was formerly in charge of the Sewing Machine Shop.

A further historic note: the RCAF's CF100's started being phased out of active squadron service in September 1961. By New Year's Eve of 1962 all thirteen squadrons had been either disbanded or were flying American built CF-101 Voodoos.

CANADIAN TIRE STORE

During the 1940s, Mason Brothers' Service Station, located on Market Street where Jumbo Joe's currently operates, sold Canadian Tire products. In 1951, the Canadian Tire Associate Store opened at the corner of Bridge Street and Doxsee Avenue under the ownership of Havelock Boulter and later William R. Dawson. It boasted a retail sales area with many products as well as a complete automotive service department. The business continued to expand, eventually taking over the former Masterson's Meat Market and the Northumberland Health Unit buildings. When Bill Dawson left Campbellford to take over the larger Sudbury store, Wayne Gunter, a former employee, purchased the business. In 1965, Wayne left for Elliot Lake to expand his horizons and the firm changed hands several times before Wayne returned in 1967. Wayne sold the business to John Gabriel in December 1990, and John Gabriel in turn sold it to Mark Caldwell. Steve McCarthy purchased the store from Mark in 1996. In the fall of 1998, a new store was opened on Grand Road. This location offers much expanded display space and plenty of parking.

CLARION BOATS

This business operated by Dwight Boyd opened in 1985 at 246 Front Street North in the former Seward Marine building. Dwight started the business in 1979, working out of the garage at his home near Warkworth. The firm specializes in antique and classic boat restoration on vessels dating back as early as 1918. He has expanded the business to include the design and building of new wooden boats. Some of these can take up to eighteen months to complete and are designed and executed using input from clients, leading boat architects, and the latest computer technology. The completed vessels have a deep, rich, high-gloss mirror finish achieved by careful hand work. Some of the fittings, such as steering wheels, windshield frames, and hinges, are custom designed and manufactured by the company because they are no longer available commercially. Dwight has succeeded in combining antique appearance with the latest in modern materials, such as epoxy resins and composites and single shell hull structures to eliminate the leaking, rot, and instability which plagues older boats.

Clarion's client base is world-wide and it has received international recognition. Among the awards won by the company are Antique Boat of the Year, several Best of Class and Craftsmanship awards, and the Walter B. Kincaid award from the Clayton New York Antique Boat Museum. At present the company has three employees – Richard Wall, Rick Pomeroy, and Keith Venables.

W. W. CLARK FLOUR MILL

For many years, the mill owned by the Clark family was on the site of the former Canadian Tire parking lot. It was a landmark in the central area of Campbellford, originally owned by John Meiklejohn and Will Russell until sold to W.W. Clark and Jack Stephens in 1925. When Mr. Stephens died in 1930, Jack Clark came into the business with his father and, on the death of W.W. Clark in 1956, Jack assumed full control and ownership of the business which he operated until 1971. At that time, Jack retired and the building was dismantled in June 1973.

CLIFTON TEA ROOM / CHATEAU RESTAURANT

Charlie Thompson started his career as a buttermaker in various factories, including H .N. Carr and Grant Anderson. In 1937, Charlie and his wife, Belle, decided to purchase the Clifton Tea Room on Bridge Street West which they operated until 1942. At this time, they sold the business and moved to Toronto where they bought a variety store. In 1946, they returned to Campbellford and purchased Cyril Sloggett's Men's Clothing Store on Front Street North which they operated until Charlie's death in 1959. Charlie was a popular local resident and served both as councillor and reeve. The Clifton Tea Room became the Chateau Restaurant which carried on the tradition of the Thompson's home cooked meals. A number of renovations were made including a phenomenal music system with an individual juke box in every booth. There also was a popular soda bar with stools. After changing hands several times, this location is presently vacant.

A.C. CONNOR AND SONS LUMBER AND FUEL

On October 3, 1922, A.C. (Anson) Connor and his son, Ray, purchased the lumber, coal and wood business on Grand Road from John O'Sullivan. The stock at that time consisted of about two cars of timber, lath and mouldings and some wood. The delivery equipment included a wagon, a sleigh, and a team of horses. Two of the first employees were Alf Hay, teamster, and P.J. (Pat) Sarginson who had formerly worked for O'Sullivans. Horses were used until well into the 1930s . The first truck purchased was a one-ton Ford with solid rubber tires. Among the first customers were Wellington Green and Walter Lowe who were buying pine lumber for $40 to $50 per thousand, cedar shingles at $5 a square and coal at $19 a ton. Some of the early carpenters who were customers included John Wallace and Harvey Donald, noted barn builders, as well as James Blue, John Nancarrow, Hugh Todd and William Runnells.

In the 1920s, changes in building materials began to appear with wood lath and shingles being replaced by gypsum lath and asphalt shingles. Framing lumber which had formerly been rough now became dressed. New types of wallboard such as gyproc and tentest, fire proof rock wool insulation, and plywood came onto the market. The 1930s were difficult times. During the war years, fuel was rationed. At this time, Jack and Bruce Connor, sons of Ray, came into the business. In the 1950s, coal was losing the battle with oil and the firm had to adjust. New fuel trucks were added to the fleet. By 1963, Connors had seven trucks, ten employees and a stock of building materials second to none in the area. Theodore Hardy and the Mechetuk brothers, Everett and Wesley, were long term employees. At this time, the firm also expanded to include the designing and erection of summer cottages in several subdivisions. In 1976, the firm was sold to the Campbellford Co-operative which, in turn, sold the property to the Baptist Church.

HARRY CUBITT SHOE REPAIR

Harry Cubitt established a shoe repair shop on Front Street South in the early 1950s. His business consisted of repairing and selling shoes and boots, sharpening skates, fixing leather goods and doing other odd jobs. He had customers from as far away as Madoc, Brighton, Colborne, and Roseneath. After thirty-three years of operation, he closed down in 1983.

DART CUP LTD.

Dart Cup Ltd. produces millions of polystyrene foam cups, bowls and containers each year. The plant has operated on Dart Drive, east of Burnbrae Road, since 1984. It is a subsidiary of Dart Container Corporation based in Michigan and is its only Canadian plant. In 1999, Dart Cup Ltd. employed sixty full-time employees, operating three shifts a day, five days per week. The products are sold to distributors who service all of Ontario and other regions within Canada. Many containers are custom printed to display company names and logos. The firm takes care to protect the manufacturing technology and feels that the quality of the product speaks for itself.

C.H. DAVIDSON MOTORS

In 1890, Charlie Davidson arrived in Campbellford with twenty-five cents in his pocket. He first worked at a bake shop and eventually became the owner of his own bake shop beside the river on the west side of the bridge. He was also one of the early fire chiefs. In 1910, he expanded his commercial ventures and opened a car business selling McLaughlin-Buick cars as well as continuing his confectionery business.

In 1913, he relocated to the old Dickson Foundry on Saskatoon Avenue and, in 1915, took on the Chevrolet agency. Two of his first customers were C.W. Turner who bought the first Buick in 1910 and Frank Long who bought the first Chevrolet Baby Grand in 1915. As the auto business expanded, new lines were added. Charlie's son, Bud, took over the business in 1936 after spending nine years with General Motors in Oshawa. The firm took on the entire General Motors line and became the largest dealer in the area. Davidson Motors is one of a very few dealerships which have remained directly in the family since GM Canada was formed in 1917. In 1961, Bud's son, Chuck, entered the firm. He assumed the position of Sales Manager as well as director and part owner. In 1963, the firm relocated to the corner of Front Street South and River Street, on the site of the present Toronto–Dominion Bank. Bud continued with the business until 1964.

Bud's son, John also worked for General Motors for several years before he relocated to Trenton in 1979, where he too took on the management of a General Motors dealership. Chuck continued to work with his father in Campbellford. The old building on Saskatoon Avenue was sold in 1960 to the Co-op, which in turn sold it to Hector Macmillan who operated it as a store until 1988. Hector then sold it to Mrs. Harry Cheung who continues to operate it as the Top Valu Store. In 1978, Davidson's erected a new building on Grand Road at Trent Drive which had a much expanded display area, both inside and out. This dealership continues to provide excellent service to the entire surrounding area under the leadership of Chuck Davidson, the third generation to be in charge of the firm. Chuck's son Charlie intends to become the first fourth generation family GM dealer. He is currently working toward this goal but has to wait to reach GM's minimum age rule.

DEPARTMENT STORES

C. J. Windrim operated the Selrite Store on Front Street North which he sold on May 20, 1935 to Morton Sayers of Havelock. The Sayers family remained in business for many years. Beamish Store was across the street in the present Bar and Grill. D. A. Sharpe was the source of specialized sewing and fabric needs for many years. A narrow store on the site of Harold Douglas' Barber Shop was the Barnes and Allan Store. Currently, Giant Tiger, which opened in 1972, Economy Fair, and O'Brien's V & S serve the community's needs.

W. A. DONALD PLUMBING, HEATING AND TINSMITHING

Bill Donald apprenticed in the plumbing trade with his uncle, James Jacobs. In 1939, Bill began his career working alone as a tinsmith, operating over the old Bibby blacksmith shop near the corner of Bridge and Queen Streets. After the war, he moved to a shop near the west end of the bridge where he had a number of employees including Angus, Jack and Stewart Donald, Jim Mackie, Art Tripp, and Bev Reycraft. The business had grown to include a fleet of several service trucks. When Bethlehem Steel built company houses in Marmora about 1950, the company was awarded the contract for plumbing and heating. This job required the hiring of two additional staff – Donald Rose and Bill Mechetuk. Bill's oldest son, Tom, joined the firm in the early 1960s and John and Bill also assisted during school holidays. In 1967, the firm moved to a new modern building on Bridge Street West beside the Donald family home. The new location was spacious and was conveniently located. At this time, Bev and Dennis Reycraft worked for the company. Uerlen Lloyd was the bookkeeper from 1949 until 1980, assisted by Bill's daughter, Jane, during holidays from high school. Ray Dunk was also added to the staff. When Bill retired, after forty-one years of service to the community, the shop was sold to the Campbellford Veterinary Services.

DOOHER'S BAKERY

Dooher's Bakery was started by Harry Dooher in February 1949 in Madoc, one block from the main downtown area. He took over the business which had a wood-fired oven and where everything had to be made by hand. Courage, determination and incredibly long hours made this venture a success.

In 1955, Harry and his wife Muriel purchased the former Fairman's Bakery in Campbellford. They were encouraged by the larger population, the downtown location, and the fact that this was Harry's hometown. They opened in November of that year and their first year in business outstripped their best years in Madoc. Their reputation grew as the bakery became the place to go for the best in fresh quality home baking.

The bakery eventually outgrew its limited floor space of nine hundred and sixty square feet. In June 1977, the Doohers, now with son Peter and wife, Christine, moved the shop across the street to its present location at 61 Bridge Street East. The new building offered almost three times the space, nearly two thousand, seven hundred square feet. The addition of new ovens and production equipment made baking quicker and easier and allowed for a more extensive line of products. Since the relocation, the front customer service area has been expanded twice in an effort to display an ever growing variety of fresh baked goods and to make serving customers more convenient and efficient. Dooher's continues to use all their own recipes for breads, buns, muffins, cookies, pastries and even pie fillings. This homemade quality has maintained Dooher's reputation as one of the finest home bakeries in southern Ontario.

DRUG STORES

In 1891, Fred Wood operated a drug store at the southwest corner of Front and Bridge Streets. This store had formerly been run by G. G. Eakins, who sold it to Dr. Thomas Brunskill. The store was later run by F. N. Brown who in turn sold to Roy Barnum in 1941. Further north on Front Street in 1909 was the drug store of J. A. Loucks, later sold to Arthur Loucks who sold it to Cleary's. Birks Drug Store operated on the southwest corner of Bridge and Queen Street for many years. Later, this store was run by Roy MacLaren who relocated to the east side of town following a disastrous fire. A pharmacy also operates in Economy Fair.

ELECTRICAL SALES AND SERVICE

As the demand for appliances increased, several local merchants offered electrical wares. Frank DeCarrol, Frank Garneau and Huck MacArthur provided both sales and service.

ELLIS DELIVERY SERVICE

In 1958, a delivery service was started by Clarence Ellis in Campbellford. Over the years, he delivered food for Gay's Grocery, Atkinson's Grocery, Pat Patrick's Meat Market, the Dominion Store, the IGA, Frank Root's Butcher Shop and McArthur's Meat Market. He also delivered for Brewer's Retail, Simpson's, Weldrest Cleaners and the T. Eaton Company. Clarence and his wife, Annabelle also delivered mail on the rural routes of Campbellford for twenty-seven years, beginning in 1965 and continuing with Canada Post until July 31, 1992. His pleasing personality made him well liked by all his customers.

FOLDAWAY FURNITURE LTD. / TIMBER STRUCTURES

Foldaway Furniture Ltd. on Second Street in Campbellford was established in 1948 on the site of the former alfalfa plant. This company turned out a wide variety of wood products, specializing in cabinets and mill work. The firm manufactured shelving, built-in units, folding tables and bunk beds which were shipped from coast to coast. The five thousand square foot plant employed fifteen workers.

In 1954, Foldaway Furniture Ltd. purchased the assets of Timber Structures of Peterborough which specialized in the manufacture of laminated structural timber. The Peterborough plant occupied forty thousand square feet with a staff of seventy-five, including its own engineering department. This firm was responsible for the construction of many large plants, community centres and churches from Winnipeg to St. John's, Newfoundland. David E. Ness of Campbellford was the President of both companies. This plant became the site of Cook's/World's Finest Chocolate.

R. E. FOX & SON / FOX FUELS

Jobs were scarce when Robert Edward (Bob) Fox was hired by Imperial Oil in 1930 to deliver fuels in Campbellford, Seymour and environs. It was physically demanding, requiring him to carry heavy cans of oil up steep stairs, haul and reel up long, heavy hoses, and drive miles of unpaved roads which often required tire chains in winter. Once, accompanied by his daughter Barbara (Pechkovsky), he drove down a trail through the bush to a core drilling site which became part of the iron ore mine at Marmora. By 1938, as a Farm Trade Commission Agent, he was equipped with only a White truck and a 500-gallon tank. Supplies were trucked from Cobourg or sent by railway car to the plant located at the dead end of Alma Street. The work day was long but Sundays and holidays such as Christmas and New Years were for family unless somebody was freezing.

As a control measure during wartime rationing, the gasoline used in farm vehicles was dyed. It was illegal to use dyed gas for any purpose other than the war effort. Robert's daughter recalls as a child being allowed to empty the packet of dye into this colourless gasoline and watch it turn purple. Nobody thought about toxic fumes. Undyed gasoline for personal use was rationed and controlled by means of gas coupons. Consequently, farmers often used horses instead of cars to get to town.

Business expanded as furnaces were converted from wood and coal to oil . When electricity was installed on more farms after World War II, there was less demand for coal oil and kerosene for lighting, but more farmers and businesses required gasoline for tractors and gas-powered machinery.

Following a work accident in the late 1940s, Robert Fox had to direct operations from his bed for many months. There was no Worker's Compensation. His wife, Lillian, and sixteen-year-old son, Tom, kept the business going. Tom maintained inventory and kept the trucks operating and made deliveries in an effort to continue to keep the customers satisfied.

This was always a family business. When Lillian Fox, nee Locke, a local teacher, married Robert, she took on some of the office jobs. She liked to pit her math skills against the hand-cranked adding machine of the company auditor and she usually won. The auditor stayed for meals over the two or three-day period of his visit. In summer he often tallied up the accounts in the comfort of the front porch at 51 Raglan Street.

When Robert retired in 1966, his son Thomas Edward and wife, Donna, took over the business. R. E. Fox and Son, located on Highway 30 South, became Fox Fuels. The Campbellford plant continued to service the northeastern portion of Northumberland County, Norwood, Havelock, Belmont and Methuen Townships. A sub-office in Madoc provided products to North Hastings. When Tom and Donna retired in 1994, Fergusson Fuels became the new owner.

The Fox family had pumped fuels under the Imperial Oil or Esso banner for sixty-four years. They had witnessed many improvements in equipment, products, automation, and computerization, but what was still most important was the service they tried to provide to retain the loyalty of their customers and their families.

GAY'S GROCERY

This was a family operated business, opened in 1906 by John Gay who operated the store in the former Elcome Grocery on Queen Street. In 1934, his son, Jim, took over. Much of the total sales volume of the store was on credit and the number of families who charged their purchases on a monthly charge account numbered in the scores. During the Depression, the number of charge accounts increased significantly. The store always remained on the west side of town, although it changed location three times. Jim Gay operated the business for 40 years until the business closed in November 1974. At that time, it held the record for being the only continuously operating business, other than the Campbellford Herald.

Invoice from Gay's Grocery, 1906.

Donated by the Pettifer family to the Campbellford/Seymour Heritage Society Archives.

GODDEN LUMBER COMPANY

This firm was originally established on Simpson Street as a coal and wood business by H.M. Fowlds who used horse drawn wagons and sleighs to deliver his products. He also built the grain elevator on the site. A few years later, the company was purchased by a Mr. Jenkins who sold the business back to Walter and Henry Fowlds in 1925. They continued until 1948, when Kenneth and Earl Godden became the new owners. Godden's continued to deliver fuel and expanded to include lumber and building supplies. They also began to design and build homes in the 1960s. This later became the site of O & R Lumber which has since closed.

GROCERY STORES

Before the advent of the supermarket in the 1950s, family operated grocery stores served the local community. The grocer or clerk served the customer personally as there were no shopping carts with aisles filled with goods. Simple shelves displayed the merchandise. Bills were handwritten and calculated, often without the aid of any cash register. Food was sold in bulk amounts from barrels or boxes and often had to be weighed. Since refrigeration in the home was very limited, blocks of ice being the usual source, meat was purchased in small quantities. Many merchants "ran a bill" for their customers and this account would be settled at regular intervals. Within the town, at various times, grocery stores were operated by the following individuals or families: Thomas, Gay, Osborne, Gillespie and Atkinson on the west side of the river and by Horkins, Shannon, Dunk and Hazell on the east side. Meat markets – butcher shops with sawdust on the floor – as separate operations were run by the following individuals or families: McArthur, Masterson and Root. The first chain store was a Dominion Store on Front Street North which operated until 1960.

HORSMAN'S BEVERAGES

In 1898, Charles L. Horsman started a soda and pop industry in a small building on Inkerman Street. In a few years, he moved to a better location on Pellissier Street. At first, he delivered his product with horse-drawn wagons, but in 1920, he purchased a truck. Everything was done by hand, including the washing and filling of the bottles. Eventually, machinery was purchased that not only did these tasks, but labeled them as well. The company made ginger beer, birch beer, cream soda, ginger ale, soda water, lemon sour, and in 1935, acquired a license to produce Pepsi Cola. The business was taken over by Charles' son, Morley in 1941. During World War II, while Morley Horsman was overseas, Morley Tanner ran the operation. Long-term employees included Laurie Nesbitt, Doug Seymour, and Ken Hazell. Horsman's Beverages closed in 1968 when it was purchased by Moira Beverages of Belleville. The building was sold and converted to apartments by David Donald and Jim Watters.

HOTELS IN CAMPBELLFORD

In the early lumbering days, lumberjacks arrived in town to follow the log drive. They had spent long months in the bush and were looking for some refreshment and enjoyment. Hotels sprang up along the river banks to accommodate these patrons.

The earliest hotel in the village was Miller's Hotel, originally operated by Peter and Nicholas Miller, and later known as the St. Lawrence Hotel, on the east side of Front Street North. It is one of two mentioned in an 1858 directory. Ironically, this is the only hotel which survived for many years and was the last to close. The original building was lost to fire in 1880, supposedly following a brawl between the proprietor and some drunken lumbermen, and a new brick structure was erected. This establishment was subsequently managed by D. Collins until sold to W. and Duncan Kerr. Later Duncan's son, James Kerr, was in charge until he sold to Neil O'Keefe in 1930.

On the west side of the river in present day Old Mill Park stood another hotel known over the years as Angel's Rest or Wellman's Hotel, when owned by Francis Wellman in 1858, and later as Smith and Sager's in 1873 and Goheen's Hotel. When purchased by the Gibson family, the building was moved to the south side of the street at the corner of Bridge and Queen Streets and became known as Gibson House. In 1909, the hotel was sold to Smith Abar, who operated it as a temperance house. This building eventually became the offices of Campbellford Cloth Company. It was demolished in 1979.

The Queen's Hotel, also known as the Campbellford Hotel, operated in 1876 by D. Adams, was located on the present site of V & S. Its stables were located on present Saskatoon Avenue near the fire hall. The stables were destroyed by fire in 1877.

Phoenix House, on the west side of Front Street, was operated in 1875 by Blute and Brickley. This building burned in the same year.

The Windsor Hotel, operated in 1878 by Tom Blute and his son, Jim, was situated next to the former Royal Bank building on the east side near the corner of Front and Bridge Streets.

The Dominion Hotel was on the southwest corner of Bridge and Doxsee. This was reported to be a boarding house and whiskey hole. In 1876, P.H. Brennan was the operator. Later owners were Olivers and D. Adams.

The Victoria Hotel on Front Street South burned in 1877 and its stables later the same year.

Cockburn's Hotel was run for many years by the McLaughlins. Reports say that it was a gambling den from the back porch of which more than one man fell into the river.

Mr. Church operated an oyster saloon on the west side of the river in a building just south of the Trent Block.

The Seymour Hotel at Meyersburg, at the north end of the village near the mill, was operated in 1873 by Nelson Simmons. Previous owners had been Smith and Empey, followed by Ned Coveney. This building was the site of the triple wedding of Simmons' three daughters.

JACK'S PLACE

Jack and Irene Torrance realized that there was a need for a take-out place in Campbellford where a person could get a hamburger or hot dog and a drink. Friends in Peterborough had a similar business and were pleased to provide advice, so the small building was erected on Bridge Street West. The dimensions were only twelve feet by twenty feet with room for only one chair for waiting customers. Because the business was strictly take-out, no space was provided to sit and eat. When it first opened, the men from the Legion came in for grilled hot dogs on toasted buns. Edgewater Park was in its heyday and about midnight on Saturday night both sides of the street were lined with cars and the small store was jammed with customers. Jack's Place was the only food outlet to stay open that late.

At first, the menu consisted of a hamburg with grilled cheese for 15 cents, a hot dog for 10 cents, a small drink for 5 cents with a 2 cent deposit on the bottle, ice cream with a choice of eight flavours. Ice cream was a specialty on Sundays as families came for an outing. Hamburgers were homemade from a special recipe which Irene still gets requests for today. The store sold a few groceries and milk from Anderson's and Rutherford's Dairy at a profit of 1 cent per quart. When the family wanted to buy something, it was a standing joke to calculate the cost in the value of quarts of milk to be sold. Large glass jars of penny candy and licorice pipes were popular with the children who often redeemed pop bottles for treats. The personal touch of this small enterprise delivered by the Torrances ended with the sale of Jack's Place in 1969.

JAMES JACOBS PLUMBING, HEATING AND TINSMITHING

In the early 1920s, the upper level of the Turner Block, on the corner of George and Tice Streets, was rented to James Jacobs and George Hawthorne who were partners in a plumbing, heating and tinsmithing business. A long set of stairs on the outside of the building led to the shop. A Mr. Scott worked for them. At this time, business was prosperous as people were beginning to have indoor plumbing and furnaces installed in their homes. In the autumn of 1931, James and George decided to dissolve their partnership and James Jacobs moved to a store on Tice Street formerly occupied by J. A. Anderson.

He purchased this property from Dr. E. V. Frederick. It was a two storey building with an apartment upstairs. The shop was heated by a pot-bellied stove. There were hand-operated crimping tools for making eavestrough and stove pipes. The tools for cutting the tin were giant scissors. A blow torch and soldering iron were required to fashion the articles.

Employees over the years included Bill Donald, Gordon Jacobs Sr., Percy Pierce, Jack Pierce, Chuck Newton, Jim Jacobs Jr., Tim Scriver, and Mr. Dunk. Some of these men took their apprenticeship and branched out on their own, after passing the examinations.

This building was not changed until 1970 when Jack Connor and Sons converted it into a two bedroom town house for Dorothy Jacobs. This property was sold in July 1978. Today it is the location of Creations Of Campbellford.

JEWELLRY STORES

Percy Tweedie operated a jewellry store on Bridge Street East during the 1930s. Rabethges came to Campbellford in 1934 and have operated a jewellry business at various sites since that time. They import diamonds directly from Antwerp and are skilled in jewellry appraisal and repair. Frank Rabethge was the original owner and the store is now operated by his son Karl and Karl's children. A small jewellry store operated on the east side of Front Street North for many years under the care of Miss Patterson. Unitts also operated a store for a short time in the 1950s, located on the west side of Front Street North. Colin Collins brought his many years of experience to Campbellford and when he retired in 1976, he had completed a fifty year career as a jeweller. His store was located on the east side of Front Street North.

ROBERT LINTON, BLACKSMITH AND CARRIAGE MAKER

Robert A. Linton was an early Scottish settler who operated a carriage shop and an adjacent blacksmith shop on Queen Street. The building, constructed in 1880, was used as the carriage factory with the carriages being built on the main floor and taken upstairs to be painted using a long outside ramp. In 1920, the building was sold to Frank Long who operated a candy factory. In 1923, the building was purchased by George A. Joyce and George Mason who established a business under the name of Harris Flour and Feed. This firm continued under Ronald Joyce until Neil Burgess purchased the property in 1985 and developed the upper level as an apartment.

Robert Linton Blacksmith Shop and Carriage Shop on Queen Street, ca. 1880.

Photo donated by Ruby McCulloch to Campbellford/Seymour Heritage Society Archives.

LONG'S RESTAURANT

Long's Restaurant is a legend in Campbellford. Many former high school students can tell tales of the time spent with friends in one of the booths at Long's, sharing secrets and sipping cherry cola from a glass. Frank Long, the original owner of the business, coined some catchy slogans to describe it:

"Long's – where you get the mostest of the bestest for the leastest."
"Satisfy that Long—-ing!"
"Long's Restaurant – the place to meet – good things to eat."

In 1920, Frank Long opened a candy factory on the west side of the river in the old Harris' Feed Mill building. He was a candy maker who operated stores in Stirling, Port Hope and Trenton. The Campbellford store was the most successful and the only one to survive.

In 1937, he started making ice cream with equipment from a novelty company called Country Freezer. He then expanded to home-made baked goods using his own recipes. Lucille LaBrash rolled out the cookies and Frank's wife, Violet, made the pies and tarts. A soda bar was also part of the restaurant and this was later purchased and displayed by Sharpe's Supermarket.

During the 1930s, ham and eggs, potatoes and soup along with a quarter of a nine-inch pie sold for 40 cents a plate. Boarders got the same meal for 25 cents. In the 1940s and1950s, chips were 25 cents, with gravy, 35 cents. A hot dog was 25 cents and a hamburg, 35 cents.

One of the most memorable of Long's products was the fair taffy which was made and wrapped in the store. Every fall local residents waited for their first taste of this delicious treat. It always remained soft and chewy, a true taste test! Long's always had a booth at the Campbellford Fair where the taffy was also sold. Many other small candies as well as sponge toffee were displayed in the glass cases to be purchased in bulk.

Another major activity was the school fairs and the firm had a monopoly on them. There were school fairs at eight country schools. Hot dogs were sold for 5 cents each and, at that price, generated a one hundred per cent profit. Twelve wieners cost 12 cents, buns were 12 cents a dozen and there was mustard and relish, so the cost was 35 cents a dozen!

On June 25, 1974, the business was sold to Laslo and Maria Jakob who operated it for a short time. After some renovations, the building was resold.

MACMILLAN'S IGA SUPERMARKET

This large independent store opened its doors at the corner of River Street and Doxsee Avenue in 1951 under the ownership of Hector Macmillan. Originally,

Front Street North, looking south, 1912.

Front Street North, looking south, 1930s.

From the postcard collection of the Campbellford/Seymour Heritage Society.

the floor space was only twelve hundred square feet but soon grew to thirteen thousand square feet with a permanent staff of twenty supplemented by additional summer help. In 1963, this business was the largest independent food store in eastern Ontario. In recent years, this has become the site of the Giant Tiger franchise.

MARKS CARPENTRY AND MACHINE SHOP

This business was located at the corner of Grand Road and Alma Street. Vernon Marks was a clever machinist and carpenter who made many of the tools and cutters for use in his business. His workshop was a rough wooden building and his rather ramshackle house stood to the south of the business. Vernon taught himself to read music and played the violin rather well. He was quite eccentric, gruff in manner and appearance, and did not allow customers behind the counter. His work was considered to be extremely well done. In later years, he left town to reside with his daughter. The property was sold to Frank Beaudoin who in turn sold to Kal Ojamae, the Ford dealer who erected a new building. Recently, this structure has been removed and the former location of Marks' is the site of the new Canadian Tire Store.

ALFRED FRED H. MCKEEL — BUILDER

Alfred H. McKeel was a builder of houses and yachts. Many of the houses built in Campbellford in the early years of this century were built by Alfred McKeel. Unfortunately, some were later demolished in order to build the Trent Canal through Campbellford. Fortunately many remain. Perhaps the best known are the six identical grey brick houses on the west end of Inkerman Street.

In addition to building houses, Alfred McKeel was responsible for the construction of the base and enclosure around the War Memorial in Campbellford. He also built the War Memorial located in the Ojibway Indian community of Alderville, near Rice Lake. The Memorial was erected in honour of the men in the community who served in World War I. The tall monument, with a square block perched on one corner above two columns has puzzled onlookers for many years. What holds the block in place? A length of iron railway track imbedded in the cement, joining the block to the columns.

ERNEST C. MCKEEL COMPANY

The Ernest C. McKeel Company, publisher of McKeel's Standard Freight Rate Guide, was unique to Campbellford and to Canada. The original idea for McKeel's freight rate guide was conceived by Ernest McKeel in 1929. Ernest McKeel had worked in Toronto, New York City and, at the age of twenty-one, was in Maracaibo, Venezuela, working for Shell Oil Company. Ernest McKeel observed that companies shipping large quantities of goods and products had no easy way of determining beforehand the cost of shipping their goods nor did they have any way to verify the accuracy of the bills from the shipping company. McKeel Freight Rate Guide provided this information.

Among McKeel's clients were the major manufacturers in Canada, including General Motors, General Electric, Westinghouse and major marketers such as

Eaton's, Simpson's, later Simpson-Sears, and Hudson's Bay. The Federal Government was also a client. The Guide originally listed every railway station in Canada. Mr. McKeel used to say "if it has a station, it's in the Guide." Later tariffs for Great Lakes Steamship Lines and Highway Transport Lines were added.

By 1934, Ernest McKeel, now married to Wava Wallace of Stirling, was running his publishing business from a bedroom in their home on Inkerman Street. The house was the first in a row of six identical houses on Inkerman Street built by Ernest's father, Alfred H. McKeel. Wava McKeel, who had been a librarian and telephone operator prior to her marriage, worked with her husband to develop the Ernest C. McKeel Company into a business with clients from coast to coast in Canada and in the United States.

In the mid 1940s, his company moved into a newly constructed office building beside his home on Inkerman Street. Ernest McKeel retired in 1966, selling the Company to new owners in Toronto, who insisted on retaining the name "McKeel's Freight Rate Guide."

MEYERS TRANSPORT

In early years, teams of horses hauled grain from district farms to the Peterborough Cereal Plant on Saskatoon Avenue in Campbellford. This business was owned by John Meyers and managed by his son, Archie J. Meyers, who was a civil engineer. During the 1919 to 1925 period, Model T's took the place of horse teams. These first vehicles presented many challenges for the drivers as they operated with very little horsepower. It was common for a driver to have to stop at the bottom of a hill, unload part of the load, drive up the hill, unload the rest of the load and then go back down, reload the first part, then go up the hill and reload the second part. This process would be repeated at each steep grade. Top speed was fifteen miles per hour and breakdowns were common. Many loads travelled on these trucks from the cereal plant to the CNR Station.

A 1921 four-wheel drive vehicle, nicknamed the "Colossus," which could haul up to six tons if the grade was not too steep, was purchased. This truck was the nemesis of Seymour Township roads and was looked upon with deep displeasure by Seymour Township officials because it broke through every single culvert in the Township, not once, but several times!

In 1927, A.J. Meyers purchased a Willys-Knight truck capable of carrying three tons to carry products of the Campbellford Cloth Company to Toronto. In 1931, a local freight carrier went out of business and Meyers started carrying package freight to and from Toronto as a regular service. Drivers, who made three trips a week, didn't just drive trucks. First the rounds were made of the Campbellford merchants who placed their orders for products to be picked up in

Toronto. This could involve as many as twenty stops in the city before the return trip. Goods were delivered around town the next day and the whole process repeated. Cost of this next day service was $1.50 per hundred pounds. This overnight delivery service was so superior to the mail and slow rail delivery that it expanded into the surrounding area. The company became wholly owned by D. H. Meyers in 1946 on A. J. Meyers retirement, and was incorporated as Meyers Transport Limited in 1953. In 1955–56, the freight terminal on Doxsee Avenue South was built and was the head office for the next twenty-four years. The daily delivery service was carried out in Campbellford and the surrounding villages by trucks of the Bonnie Bakery which was also owned by A. J. Meyers.

As the business expanded, and roads improved, new vehicles and routes were added. In 1940, the fleet added two semi-trailers. In 1941, a licence was granted to cover the area from Madoc to Hastings and Warkworth. By 1947, the bounds were extended to Tweed and Peterborough. By 1963, the fleet contained twenty-six motor vehicles and semi-trailers, some of which had a hauling capacity of twenty-six tons- twenty-six times the load which the originals could carry! Growth and development has continued over the more recent years. Donald H. Meyers took over the management in 1935, and became President in 1953. His sons, Larry, Evan, and Eric have since taken over the leadership of the greatly expanded company. Drivers who served the company for many years were Harold Petherick, Charles Cork, Ralph Stephens and Jack and Fred Rowe.

PACE'S FRUIT MARKET

This store on Front Street North was the only major source of fresh fruit and vegetables in the town during the 1940s and 1950s. A wide variety of common and exotic fruits were displayed both indoors and outside. George Pace was the owner for many years, assisted by his sons, Dante and Gino.

PALLISER'S MARKET GARDEN AND FLOWERS/GRAHAM'S

In 1862, the John Palliser family resided on the west side of Centre Street between First Street and Burnbrae Road. A large apple orchard was also located on the property. By 1918, Charles Palliser, son of John, and his family moved to Market Street where they had five acres of land. The property extended east from Margaret Street between Market and Naseby Streets. The area was planted with all kinds of vegetables and was popularly known as Palliser's Garden. Here Charles erected a small greenhouse on the present site of Graham's Florists. In the 1920s, a second larger greenhouse was added and, by 1946, Charles son, George, had taken over the business. Tomatoes, cabbage and celery were sold to local stores. In the spring, box plants were delivered by truck as far as Norwood. George grew all types of flowers outdoors for funeral arrangements, such as asters, carnations, snapdragons and roses. Orchids were always purchased from Dale's in Brampton. Palliser's were the only florist in the area. During the Christmas season, it was common to rent an empty store to sell cyclamens, which they grew themselves, and imported poinsettias. In 1968, George Palliser sold the business to Grahams and relocated to Stirling.

POOL HALLS

C.H. Nadoo opened a pool hall on December 1, 1903 which he sold in the fall of 1931 to Percy Locke. William J. Smith, Vilmas, and Bulls ran the west side pool hall which was later sold to George and Charlotte Crouchman. Ross Taylor bought Joe Smith's pool hall beside Bennett's Furniture Store in 1953 and relocated to the site of the former Hollywood Theatre in 1960.

Shaw's/K. C. Billiards on Front Street North was the last of the pool halls and has had a series of owners. Manse Shaw was a long-term proprietor who owned and operated the business from 1961 until it was sold in June of 1985 to Ken and Colleen Whitlock. Manse purchased the operation from Doug Maybee who had in turn bought it from Fred Macoun. At the time of the 1985 sale, it had the original five tables installed in 1936, each measuring five and a half by eleven and a half feet. Both snooker and billiards were played. The front area was a tobacco shop with cherry wood cabinets that stored tins of tobacco and smoking paraphernalia behind wood framed glass doors. The original ornate cash register was still in use in 1985. It is currently the location of the ReMax Real Estate Office.

Intersection of Bridge and Front Streets, looking north, ca. 1970s.

Photo from postcard collection of the Campbellford/Seymour Heritage Society Archives.

REPLICAR MOTOR CO. LTD./
CANADIAN PROTOTYPE RESEARCH
AND DEVELOPMENT LTD.

For most people a car is merely a form of transportation; for others, the auto-mobile is the ultimate freedom machine and a symbol of social stature. For these enthusiasts, the latest offerings from the Big Three auto manufacturers are not acceptable, nor are foreign $15,000 econo-boxes. They require an automobile that is simply unique.

Dave Carlaw's products met the needs of these car buffs. He manufactured fibreglass replicas of distinctive and rare automobiles. Beginning in 1980, Carlaw manufactured automobiles for clients from North America, and other parts of the world. He began with his first company, Canadian Replicar Motor Co. Ltd., cre-ating a replica of the 1935 Auburn 851 Boat Tail Speedster. After seeing a 1935 Auburn at a car show in Hershey, Pennsylvania, in 1972, he fell in love, but the $150,000 price tag was exorbitant. With permission from the Auburn Foundation, he obtained original blueprints and some original parts and thus began establishing his own automobile replica company. The start-up costs totaled around $300,000, and by 1984, total sales at Replicar topped $1million dollars. Replicar was originally located in a 1800 sq. ft. building on Industrial Drive and Carlaw also rented the 5,000 sq. ft. former Breithaupt Leather Factory building.

In 1987, Dave Carlaw sold Canadian Replicar Motor Co. Ltd. to Auto Group Inc. and continued as a shareholder, consultant and member of the board of direc-tors. During this time he kept busy with his second company, Prototype Research and Development Ltd., which was started in 1985. He continued to manufacture specialty replica automobiles, and amusement park rides. In 1988, Prototype Research and Development Ltd. moved from Industrial Drive to 230 Albert Street, its current home. Then in 1989, Dave Carlaw bought back Canadian Replicar from Auto Group Inc.

Every car was hand-built by a staff of highly skilled, and patient employees. The company manufactured replicas of cars such as: the 1937 Cord 812 Supercharged Phaeton, the 1934 Mercedes 500K, the 1929 Rolls-Royce, the 1952 MGTD, the 1955 Chevrolet BelAir Convertible, as well as the 1935 Auburn. Each car was custom-made to the purchaser's specifications. The Auburn required about 450 hours and the Mercedes about 400 hours for completion. The MGTD took only 50 hours before leaving the factory, thus making the MGTD substantially less expensive than the other two cars. Each car was made essentially from the same materials: fibreglass, steel, and aluminum. The fibreglass bodies are usually a half an inch thick reinforced by a steel skeleton. These materials ensure that the car is resistant to rust. The 1935 Auburn Speedster, and most other cars, use General

Motors equipment because of the inherent advantages in reliability and serviceability. The 1955 Chevrolet BelAir, for example, has a General Motors V-8 engine, power steering, and transmission. Owners could have opted for an original BelAir frame or the running gear and frame from a 1977-1990 Chevrolet Caprice. Most cars feature luxury options such as leather interiors, two-tone paint, air conditioning, wire wheels, and brass instrumentation.

Carlaw's products have been displayed at various special events. The 1952 MGTD replicas have been offered as prizes in several promotions by companies such as Shopper's Drug Mart and the Schweppes division of Cadbury Schweppes Powell Inc. One replica was on display at the Ontario Pavilion at Expo 86. The car, called the Trillium, was the Ontario government's representation of the provincial flower. Adorning the car was a custom-made ceramic emblem made by My Hideaway Ceramics of Campbellford. The four-inch emblem was done completely in mother of pearl, with a raised trillium on it. The car was the Ontario government's first prize to the victor of the CAN-AMX endurance car rally. Other cars have been leased or rented for use in commercials and television series.

In addition, the company constructed the exterior superstructure for SpaceProbe 2000, a large-size cylindrical video game in which the player sits in a large white ball and is propelled upward by air pressure. The interior of the ball is encircled by a large television screen, showing asteroids and other outer space oddities. The player moves closer to the top as more "aliens" are killed. This video game is installed at the West Edmonton Mall. Other Carlaw products on display at the Mall are a vintage-style train, that is used to shuttle weary shoppers about, and some old-fashioned biplanes, that are for display purposes only.

Dave Carlaw created his own niche in the automotive industry. His handmade, custom ordered automobiles have been a breath of fresh air in the dull world of copycat assembly line transportation. Numerous automotive magazines have featured Carlaw's vehicles and he has received letters, faxes and phone calls daily from all over the world. Dave Carlaw and his companies have proven that small towns don't necessarily breed small-town minds, and this is why he is one of many who make Campbellford proud.

SCHOOL BUS PARTS COMPANY

This unique industry is the only Canadian manufacturer of the stop arm for school buses. The company was launched in 1982 by Jim Reavell. It formerly operated from his home and a local warehouse on Saskatoon Avenue. More recently, the company has extended its production to include the manufacture of aluminum signs and is currently located on County Road 38 in the former Campbellford Silos building.

SERVICE STATIONS

As automobiles became more popular, several garages and service stations were available to meet the needs of motorists. At various times, the following individuals or families operated service stations: Davidson, Bell, Turner, Cassan, Clare Ames, Roy Canner, Jack Douglas, Bob Fox, Wes Sweet, Barton and Pearsall.

SHARPE'S MARKET /
SHARPE'S VALLEY FOODS /
SHARPE'S IGA

In 1963, Bruce Sharpe purchased the site of the old Davidson arena at the corner of Front and Market Streets to make way for a new supermarket. Cost of the property alone was $18,000. Edwin Little tore down the old arena for $500. Bruce Sharpe also promised an additional grant of $1800 to be used toward the building of a new community centre. The new store was one of the most modern of its type in the area. Bruce Sharpe had previously managed a successful grocery store in Toronto. When the family, including four small children, decided to locate to a smaller community, Campbellford was chosen because they had many relatives in nearby Rawdon Township.

For thirty-five years, the Sharpe family has been providing quality food and service. The store offers excellent produce, bakery and deli products. Because many employees have been on the team for a long time, they are familiar with the needs of the customers. The Sharpe family is very community-oriented and is involved with many local organizations.

In February 1996, Sharpe's became an IGA Store. Steve Sharpe, co-owner, stated that they decided to pursue the acquisition of the IGA franchise when the former holder went into receivership. Sharpe's had learned to respect the IGA chain over thirty-four years of competition. As a condition of its franchise with Oshawa Foods, Sharpe's added video sales and rental services carrying current top ranked movies. A small Kentucky Fried Chicken outlet has also been added. The changes resulting from the new franchise gave employment to additional staff.

SHOE STORES

In early times, shoes were handmade by a local shoemaker. The Maher's chain operated a store on Front Street North in the former Dominion Store for many years. It was purchased in 1959 by Monica Fralick, a former employee. Monica provided an excellent supply of footwear to the local community until 1989. Shirley Simpson, who had worked as a production line supervisor at the local Bata Shoe Plant, opened her own shop in the 1990s and continues to offer her services on Bridge Street East.

SIMPKIN MARINE MANUFACTURING COMPANY/SIMPKIN WOOD PRODUCTS

This firm was established in Campbellford in 1957 in a modern building on Trent Drive. The business was owned and operated by Paul and Ronald Simpkin. The Marine Manufacturing Company was a division of the Paul H. Simpkin Cabinet Company. The plant turned out many products but was probably best known for its popular line of wood and fibre glass boats. In addition, the trophy division made a wide variety of products for competitive sports. The cabinet division produced top quality television and stereo cabinets. The company ceased operation in Campbellford in 1998.

STAPLEY/LITTLE MACHINE SHOP

This business, which opened in 1945, was known as W.C. Stapley Machine and Supply Limited and operated at 185 Alma Street. Wally Stapley was widely known in the area as a talented machinist who could adjust, re-fit or create a variety of machine parts. In addition, Wally accumulated a wonderful collection of antique steam engines, cars and trucks, tractors, planers, drill presses and numerous other pieces of equipment and machinery. The old engines were popular at displays throughout the area. These items were all sold at auction in 1987 when the business was purchased by Dennis Little. Dennis moved the equipment from his former location at 143 Alma Street, which was torn down in 1998 to make way for the new Canadian Tire Store, to the Stapley site. The building gave him lots of room to build the giant snowblowers used to clear airport runways. His business today also caters to farmers who need a piece of equipment repaired, or to a handyman needing a piece of steel cut. He also fabricates specialized pieces of equipment, such as the railing at the river in Old Mill Park.

STATIONERY STORES

Tommy Craighead operated a stationery store on Front Street. Cliff Gibson's Store was the location for purchasing high school text books for many years. The store was first located at the site of the Top Drawer but relocated to larger quarters just to the north of the intersection of Front Street and Bridge Street following a disastrous fire in the 1950s.

TURNER BLOCK/TURNER'S SERVICE STATION

In about 1865, J.W. Turner, great grandfather of Wilfred Turner, came to the Campbellford/Seymour area from England. By 1888, his son, C.W. Turner, had removed a landmark on the northeast corner of Bridge and Queen Streets, known as the old tin shop built in 1859 by Milo A. Hawley, and erected the Turner Block.

At this site, he started a hardware business, which was later sold to E. T. Morton. C. E. Turner, Wilfred's father, worked for Morton and eventually bought the business back. In the early 1920s he sold it to Arthur Redden who later closed the hardware store. The subsequent occupants of the building were Johnny Anderson, who operated a clothing store, Frank Osborne, who ran a grocery store, and Frank DeCarrol who operated an electrical store. At the present time, it is occupied by a laundromat.

In 1925, C. E. Turner acquired the old warehouse on Queen Street from E. T. Morton. He converted this into a service station and an apartment. Erle ran the business until 1939 when he joined the army. Mrs. Turner and her daughter, Victoria, ran it until 1945. When Fred and Wilfred returned from the army they took over the operation. About 1964, Fred sold out to Wilfred's son, Adrian, who is currently running it along with his sons Steven and Kenneth. Originally the suppliers of gasoline were Imperial Oil (ESSO) and British American (BA). However, it was to Turner's advantage to go with British American alone. Many years later, BA sold out to Gulf who eventually sold out to Petro-Canada who already had a service station in town. As a result, in 1996, Petro-Canada decided to reduce their stations in the area and drop Turner's. When Imperial Esso heard of this plan, they immediately took over supplying Turner's with Esso products.

VALLEY VIEW TRANSPORT

Valley View Transport was started by W. D. Scott and his late father, W. F. Scott, in 1961. The trucking company did most of its business with the Ontario Pork Producers Association, transporting hogs from the assembly yard in Seymour Township to Toronto, Stouffville, Lindsay, Peterborough, Madoc, and Picton. When new slaughter-houses were built in Montreal and Quebec City most of the hogs were shipped there, and Valley View became the first livestock carrier in Ontario to purchase the new "possum belly" trailer which could carry 250 hogs, nearly twice as many as previously carried in a single load. These three deck trailers are now used extensively in the industry. Valley View also picked up cattle to be delivered to Toronto stockyards and carried stockers out of Quebec to western Ontario. The company delivered silo blocks for Superior Silo when it was in business in Campbellford. Valley View was a family-run business that started with two drivers. When the company was sold in 1988 to Harry Kloosterman, there were ten drivers that had been with the company between fourteen and twenty-five years, as well as two mechanics.

WEAVER FUNERAL HOME

In 1965, Al Weaver purchased the Bennett Funeral Home. He had previously worked with his brother in the funeral home business in Trenton from 1950 to 1965. During this time, home funerals were common. This presented some challenges when the temperatures rose and visitors came for an extended wake. The undertaker was expected to provide a heavy backdrop for better viewing, folding chairs, flower stands and other equipment. Narrow doorways caused the firm to seek alternate routes, even by removing windows.

When Weavers arrived in town, everyone was a complete stranger to them. The entire family helped with the business to reduce costs and pay off the mortgage. The first years presented many challenges as the methods of delivering service were changed. At first, embalming and viewing of caskets continued to be done in the second level of Bennett's store. Often the bereaved family ended up in the wrong place. In time, part of the garage and two upper bedrooms became the display area, but a winding oak stairs also presented difficulties for the establishment.

At this time, Paul Jolliffe applied to become an apprentice. The program was two years plus extra courses to complete an embalmer's licence. After that, the candidate could apply for a Funeral Director's Licence. In 1987, Al's son, Jeff took over the management after an apprenticeship and ten years of service with Armstrong's in Oshawa. A branch was opened in Trenton in 1995. Jeff's son, Tim, now assists in the business. The Weaver Funeral Home continues to provide excellent service to the community.

WELDREST / CLASSIC CLEANERS

This establishment was opened by Joe Smith on Bridge Street West and, in 1945, was purchased by the Ender family. The existing building was erected about 1950 by Joe Ender. The plant and two outlets in Peterborough provided employment for about fifteen people. There were also many pick-up and delivery sites established in the surrounding communities. Later a large addition across the back of the property was built. First a shirt laundry, then a hanger manufacturing business was established there, in addition to the dry cleaning plant. Machinery was brought in from Germany for the hanger business. This part of the business was later sold to Cobourg Wire and Cable, and Joe Ender was instrumental in getting that part of their business set up for them. In 1959, Bob Hughes and John Hay became the owner-operators of the cleaning plant. In the 1970s the original portion of the building burned and the remaining newer section was sold to William and Wayne Bertrand who reestablished the dry-cleaning business after the fire. In 1985, the Bertrands sold the business to Aris Marcus, the owner of Brighton Cleaners. He, in turn, sold it to his brother-in-law, Elzo Eisinga, the present owner, in 1991.

WILLIAMS' AUCTION SALES

The auctioning trade can be traced back to the early days when the Greeks and Romans auctioned slaves. Many famous auction houses can be found in Europe and the United States. Locally, on any given weekend, there will be an auction scheduled somewhere. This might be a farm auction, with cattle and machinery, a household sale or a consignment sale. Chances are that sales in the Campbellford area will have Rod Williams as the auctioneer. The Williams name has been associated with auction sales since Rod's grandfather began his trade in 1949. Ray Williams learned "the call" from J.R. Battisby. At that time, J.R. was selling real estate and thought that Ray would be a good student.

Because of his farming background, Ray believed that a community sale barn would help to serve local farmers. In 1949, the first sale was held on Ray's farm at Hoard's Station inside a small ring made of snow fence. Auctions were on Monday nights and, with the help of his sons, Roy and Stan, a ring was made and the sale barn was born. Buyers came from near and far to see Ray sell farm stock for fifteen hours straight. Apparently, he could sell four cows per minute as well as selling sixty pens of pigs in half an hour. Ray's wife, Esther, helped in the business, especially in the booking and management of the women's concession stand which served meals to the buyers.

In 1951, Roy Williams, Ray's son, joined the business after training at auctioneering school in Mason City, Iowa. Gradually, the firm began taking on farm and household auctions in addition to regular sales of farm animals. In 1959, the livestock sales barn was sold to Delbert Hickson while Ray and Roy continued public auctions. Roy went on his own while continuing to sell for Hickson's. Roy earned the reputation of closing sales rapidly while still acquiring best possible prices. Ray retired in 1965.

Rod, Roy's son, grew up around auction sales. By age sixteen, he was selling in partnership with his father. The father and son team took part in many charitable events, conducting sales for local churches, service clubs and organizations. They always made their services available for the Warkworth Donnybrook Auction. In 1988, Roy's health forced him to retire and Rod carried on. However, more recently Roy has once again been able to participate. Rod is a member of the Canadian Personal Property Appraisers Group of Canada which qualifies him to appraise and auction anything from precious antiques to farm equipment.

In 1998, Rod opened the new Auction Centre on Industrial Drive. This new building provides shelter from the elements for both customers and merchandise. Technology is also evident in the computerization of sales as well as the creation of an Internet site. Despite these improvements, the values displayed are those of the previous generations – hard work, honesty and integrity.

COOK CHOCOLATE COMPANY /
WORLD'S FINEST CHOCOLATE

After several visits to the Campbellford area in 1958, Ed Opler Sr. decided to locate his factory here.

Opler had begun selling cocoa products in New York City in 1910. After World War I, he and his brothers began their own cocoa packing business. In 1922, their operation was moved to Chicago and, in 1938, Cook Chocolate Company was formed. This was the start of chocolate manufacturing for the firm and the high quality line of World's Finest Chocolate bars were an instant success. Fund raising sales began in 1951 and the name World's Finest gained national recognition in the United States. In 1971, the corporate name was changed to World's Finest Chocolate. The Campbellford operation on Second Street manufactures and distributes chocolate products under the World's Finest trademark and cocoa under the Cook Chocolate Canada banner.

In 1971, the small operation in Campbellford was expanded to 55,600 square feet and, in 1989, a new warehouse was built. Additional changes in 1992, brought the local plant to 85,000 square feet. Products include chocolate covered biscuits, Caramel, Cappuccino and Mint Meltaways as well as the traditional milk chocolate bars and chocolate covered almonds which are distributed to all parts of Canada. The plant employs up to two hundred people during the busy season.

ENDNOTES

1 *Campbellford Herald*, March 14, 1973.
2 *Campbellford Herald*, May 11, 1939.

Chapter Five

Municipal Affairs and Services

Township / Village / Town and Municipal Councils

The first meeting of council for the Township of Seymour was held on January 21, 1850 at 11 AM Dr. Robert Denmark was Reeve and Councillors were David Allan, John Mitchell, George Tunnah and Henry Rowed. George Ranney was Clerk. No official building was as yet erected and meetings took place in homes and taverns. The office of Deputy-Reeve was added in 1854 with Charles French serving the first term. The population of the township was 2,117 residents.

Much of the business of early councils was taken up with day to day management of the meager resources available. Roads were trails which were cared for by statute labour required of every resident. A pathmaster was appointed by council for each beat. The hours of labour required from residents were based upon the size of the farm they possessed. One man was equal to one day of work; a team and wagon was equal to two days. Gravel had to be spread by hand and the dusty roads often needed to be watered. Many by-laws were needed pertaining to animals by-laws running at large, appropriate fines, and the appointment of pound keepers, as well as the licensing of taverns and inns. On May 25, 1850, a by-law was created to provide assessment of the township to erect a school house. In August 1850, an assessment of the township was required to meet the appropriation for the Provincial Lunatic Asylum. Regular appointments had to be made for pathmasters, auditors, tax collectors, fence viewers, overseers of highways, election of councillors, naming of returning officers, establishment of polling places and electoral divisions, issuance of debentures and appointments to the Board of Health.

By 1865, the total taxes for the township were $5,478.77. By 1871, there were five electoral districts in the township and appropriations were set for each to improve the roads in the township. Seymour formed part of the East Riding of Northumberland. J.M. Ferris was a member of the Ontario legislature for several terms.

The Township Council of Seymour was considered to be very progressive in enacting a by-law prohibiting the outdoor exposure of food stuffs at store fronts. They were also, in 1872, the first municipality in Ontario to have a Fish and Game Protection Society. President of the Society was James Dinwoodie and the Secretary Treasurer was Stewart Cock. In addition, the municipality was one of the first in the province to introduce a kindergarten in a public school.

The township hall, built in 1855, was used for many purposes, including, at various times, a community centre, a jail, a school house, a market place and a council chamber. In 1894, Seymour Township relocated their offices to the Ferris Block at the southwest corner of Bridge and Front Streets. They remained in this second storey location until 1966 when they moved to the Colin Collins Block on Front Street North. In 1978, the township offices relocated once again to the stone house at 37 Saskatoon Avenue. The final move came in 1989 when the offices moved to the present location at 66 Front Street South.

By 1874, the area had grown sufficiently that, at a meeting held in Crosby's Hall[1], an application was made to create the Village of Campbellford as a separate municipality. On January 17, 1876, the necessary legislation for separation from Seymour was obtained. Harry E. Skinner became the first Village Clerk. John Clarke, Reeve of Seymour, became Warden of the United Counties of Northumberland and Durham. The township sold the town hall to the village for six hundred dollars but retained the right to hold meetings there. The village was responsible for the appointment of construction and tavern inspectors. Luke Horkins was paid $3 for a two month period to serve as tavern inspector. Fire protection and the erection of the fire hall were important accomplishments. The creation of a new library and the first street lights in 1890 were also noteworthy. The new village, with a population of 1,092, was home to sixty-six businesses. In 1878, the council approved the extension of wooden sidewalks to all churches. Merchants paid for watering of the streets in 1884. In the same year, the village passed a by-law for the prevention of vice and immorality. It provided penalties for:

"drunkenness on the street, giving liquor to a minor, putting up indecent placards, keeping houses of ill repute, swearing or using obscene language on the street, shouting or disturbing the peace at night, indecent exposure, exposing goods for sale, to do or exercise any worldly action of business or work on the Sabbath."

Also in 1884, the right to vote in municipal elections was extended to widows or unmarried ladies who were property owners. In 1888, J. M. Ferris was chosen Police Magistrate to hear and determine upon all acts in violation of the Temperance Act. In May 1889, Charles Nelson was named as engineer for the township under the Ditches and Water Courses Act at a salary of $3 per day for each day's work required.

By 1906, the population of 2,251 was sufficient for Campbellford to be inaugurated as a town. In 1918, grants of fifty dollars were made to the Band and the Seymour Agricultural Society. In 1919, the number of councillors was increased to nine and the office of Deputy-Reeve was created. On January 24, 1920, John F. McGregor became Town Clerk and remained in that role for fifty-nine years. In 1927, citizens were complaining about the nuisance of dust from the streets and council agreed to study the use of oil or calcium chloride. Consideration was given to paving the main streets. In the same year, residents were asking for a brewery warehouse and council received a signed petition from one hundred and thirty-four businessmen in support of the proposal.

The Campbellford Town Hall was built in 1935 and served as the Post office until 1971. It was the seat of municipal government until the amalgamation of Campbellford and Seymour in 1997.

Photo from the postcard collection of Campbellford/Seymour Heritage Society Archives.

The 1960s and 1970s saw a flurry of changes and renovations. A new Community Centre was built, a municipal swimming pool was constructed, extensions were built on both the hospital and the high school, a new bridge spanned the river, the scout building was relocated to Kennedy Park, Senior Citizen's apartments were opened, the filtration plant and the sewage treatment plant were improved, and the Town Office was relocated to the former Post Office. Industries such as Bata Shoes and Cook Chocolate were attracted to the town. A new federal penitentiary was built near Warkworth.

The following lists identify the representatives elected to Seymour Township Council and Campbellford Council, as compiled from a variety of available sources.[2] It is unclear from these sources whether the year listed is the year of election or the year of installation in office.

REEVES OF SEYMOUR TOWNSHIP

1850 – Robert Denmark	1916 – John Currie
1851 – Henry Rowed	1918 – George Van Volkenburg
1854 – George Tice	1925 – William S. Grills
1857 – Henry Rowed	1929 – George Van Volkenburg
1867 – James Dinwoodie	1931 – Robert Innes
1871 – J. M. Ferris	1933 – W. J. Duncan
1872 – J. M. Ferris	1935 – John Currie
1876 – John Clark	1938 – Robert Innes
1878 – Gilbert Bedford	1940 – W. J. Ross
1883 – William Bell	1943 – William Rowe
1885 – Gilbert Bedford	1945 – Frank Lee
1887 – Fred Macoun	1946 – Mel Wight
1895 – Edward C. West	1948 – A. B. (Jack) Billen
1897 – R. D. Rutherford	1954 – Ward Archer
1899 – A. T. Donald	1955 – Samuel Diamond
1901 – John M. Arnold	1957 – Kenneth E. Parr
1903 – James H. Diamond	1960 – Alex Linn
1906 – Fred Peake	1961 – Carleton Rowe
1909 – J. H. Diamond	1962 – Morden McMillan
1910 – Alex Hume	1967 – Kenneth E. Parr
1915 – George A. Hay	1980 – William H. Petherick

DEPUTY-REEVES OF SEYMOUR TOWNSHIP

1867 – Gilbert Bedford

1876 – John Macoun

1882 – William J. Bell

1900 – John M. Arnold

1907 – Robert Rowed

1909 – George Third

1912 – John Currie

1925 – Russell Peake

1929 – Robert Innes

1943 – Frank Lee

1950 – Ward Archer

1952 – Samuel Diamond

1954 – Kenneth E. Parr

1956 – Alex Linn

1958 – Carleton Rowe

1960 – Morden McMillan

1962 – Kenneth E. Parr

1964 – Mel Wight

1968 – Alec Rutherford

1972 – Maurice R. Brunton

1974 – Donald W. Clarke

1976 – Doug K. Hagerman

1978 – William H. Petherick

1980 – Maurice R. Brunton

1985 – Donald W. Clarke

1994 – William J. Thompson

COUNCILLORS OF SEYMOUR

1875 – Bonnycastle, Kelleher, Macoun

1876 – R. H. Bonnycastle, Samuel Dunk, William Bell

1882 – Thomas Hume, Frederick Peake, Henry Dunham

1900 – John Currie, Thomas Rutherford, Robert Rowed

1906 – G. Third, E. Denmark, Thomas Rowe, G. Rutherford

1907 – Thomas Rutherford, John Currie, William Stewart

1909 – T. Varcoe, James A. Stewart Sr., George A. Hay

1912 – J. Stewart, T. Varcoe, G. A. Hay

1925 – W. T. Allan, Robert Innes, Robert A. Linn

1927 – W. T. Allan, Robert Innes, John Locke

1929 – W. J. Duncan, William S. Milne, Harold G. Rutherford

1934 – Frank Lee, William Rowe, Thomas Fry

1937 – Frank Lee, William Rowe, W. J. Ross

1943 – Duncan, Wight, Alfred Bennett

1954 – Ken Parr, Earl Brunton, George Elmhirst

1955 – Carleton Rowe, Alex Linn, George Elmhirst

1960 – Harry Stephens, Morden McMillan, Clifford M. Anderson

1965 – J. Goacher, Carleton Rowe, Maurice Brunton

1967 – Alec Rutherford, Neil McCulloch, J. Goacher

1969 – Carleton Rowe, Maurice Brunton, Neil McCulloch

1973 – Don Clarke, Doug Hagerman, Thornton Waters

1982 – Gordon Eady, Reginald J. L. Hay, Fred T. Fry

1985 – William J. Thompson, Harold A. Williams, Reginald J. L. Hay

1991 – Donald J. Pollock, Ruth Gater, Reginald J. L. Hay

1994 – Harold A. Williams, Betty Ellis, Donald J. Pollock

Seymour Township Council and Township Officials, 1922.

Front Row, left to right: C.N. Harris, Andrew Milne, W.Wynn, G.Van Volkenburg — Reeve, A. Cassan, P.B. Nelson. Back row, left to right:T. Rowe, G.A. Payne — Solicitor, G.P. Hay, J.A. Arnold, H. Dunham — Tax Collector, M.T. Stephen — Treasurer.

Photo from Campbellford/Seymour Heritage Society Archives.

COUNCILS OF CAMPBELLFORD

1876 — James Dinwoodie, Reeve; Dan Collins Jr., William S. Archer, Robert Linton, J. B. Morton, Councillors

1879 — James W. Dinwoodie, Reeve; Dan Collins, R. J. Ough, M. A. Hawley, Councillors

1882 — W .B. Archer, Reeve; Charles Gillespie, W. Hambly, Charles Nancarrow, John Shannon, Councillors

1893 — C. L. Owen, Reeve; R. B. Denike, Deputy Reeve; Dr. J. Macoun, George Horkins, A. E. Bailey, Councillors

1900 — Charles Smith, Reeve; J. N. Kent, Ed Nancarrow, James Shannon, Councillors

1904 — William J. Doxsee, Reeve

1906 — William Doxsee, Mayor ; J. A. Irwin, C. H. Cassan, A. H. McKeel, S. J. Abernethy, Councillors

1907 — William J. Doxsee, Mayor; J. A. Irwin, Reeve; Graham, Redden, Abernethy, Dunk, Tait, Councillors

1909 – William J. Doxsee, Mayor; A. H. McKeel, Reeve; Horkins, Smith, Carnahan, Fowlds, Abernethy, Councillors

1911 – C. L. Owen, Mayor

1912 – J. A. Irwin, Mayor

1914 – Armstrong, Mayor

1916 – Cairns, Mayor

1917 – William S. Russell, Mayor; Fowlds, Reeve; Smith, Palliser, Dolman, Mulhearn, Irwin, Councillors

1919 – Hay, Mayor

1921 – A. J. Meyers, Mayo.

1925 – A. J. Meyers, Mayor; Charles Davidson, Reeve; Charles W. Palliser, Deputy Reeve; W. J. Abernethy, R. H. Cole, G. A. Kingston, S. J. Moore, R. S. Southworth, W. S. Wiggins, Councillors

1927 – G. A. Kingston, Mayor; Charles H. Davidson, Reeve; Charles W. Palliser, Deputy Reeve; W. J. Abernethy, R. H. Cole, Alex MacDonald, Walter S. Wiggins, J. Nelson Stone, John O'Sullivan, Councillors

1929 – Charles H. Davidson, Mayor; J. M. Bygott, Reeve; J. N. Stone, Deputy Reeve; W. J. Abernethy, R. H. Cole, Alex MacDonald, John O'Sullivan, Walter S. Wiggins, J. R. Wilkinson, Councillors

1930 – Major J. M. Bygott, Mayor

1932 – Major J. M. Bygott, Mayor; J. N. Stone, Reeve (died and was replaced by Charles H. Davidson); N. Alex MacColl, Deputy Reeve; Harold N. Carr, J. K. Battisby, N. Thompson, E. C. McKeel, A. D. Bennett, F. F. Long, Councillors

1934 – Frank F. Long, Mayor

1943 – Frank F. Long, Mayor; Harvey M. Donald, William Brady, H. J. Taylor, Councillors

1945 – J. Ernest Ayrhart, Mayor

1947 – Harvey M. Donald, Mayor

1949 – J. Ernest Ayrhart, Mayor; Ralph J. Locke, Reeve; Oscar Mason, Deputy Reeve; Wilbert Kingston, Douglas Maybee, George Free, Fred Rutherford, William Nicholas, C. J. Maier, Councillors

1951 – W. A. Kingston, Mayor

1952 – Ralph J. Locke, Mayor

1956 – Ralph J. Locke, Mayor; Douglas Maybee, Reeve; F. M. Rutherford, Deputy Reeve; Peter H. Macmillan, Paul G. O'Sullivan, William R. Nicholas, Franklin S. Linton, George Nicholls, Isobel Tatham, Councillors

1956 – Douglas R. Maybee, Mayor

1958 – Fred M. Rutherford, Mayor; George Free, Reeve; Forrest R. Dennis, Morley Tanner, Morley Petherick, P. H. Macmillan, Jack Torrance, Sid Hopping, Councillors

1962 – Morley Tanner, Mayor

1974 – Harold Dunk, Mayor

1976 – A.C. (Cress) Newman, Mayor; Douglas Sharp, Reeve; Pearl Rutherford, Deputy-Reeve; Douglas Burgis, Eric Holmden; Helen Vice, Ian Beattie, Matthew Austin, John Wilson, Councillors

1978 – William Baker, Mayor

1980 – Bob Harvey, Mayor

1982 – Hector Macmillan, Mayor

1990 – Frank Linton, Mayor; Charles Ibey, Reeve; Eric Holmden, Deputy-Reeve; Catherine Redden, Ruth Brockman, Councillors

1991 – Catherine Redden, Mayor

1994 – Catherine Redden, Mayor; Everette Steele, Reeve; Lillian Turner, Deputy Reeve; Ron Cleverdon, Councillor

Campbellford Town Council, 1950.

Rear: Mayor – Harry Fowlds; clockwise around the table, Wes Sweet – Councillor, Ralph Locke – Councillor, Alex MacColl – Solicitor, P.H. Macmillan – Reeve, John F. McGregor – Clerk, Harvey Donald – Deputy Reeve, Walter Burgess – Councillor, Fred Macoun – Councillor, and Clarence Massie – Councillor.

Photo donated by Wes Sweet to Campbellford/Seymour Heritage Society Archives.

In 1998, the action of 1876 was reversed and Campbellford/Seymour once more became a municipality under one council. Mayor Cathy Redden, Reeve William H. Petherick, Deputy-Reeve William Thompson and Councillors Trish Baird, Harold Williams, Joe Watson and Betty Ellis currently provide leadership for the new municiplaity.

COUNTY WARDENS FROM CAMPBELLFORD/SEYMOUR

1872 – J. M. Ferris
1876 – John S. Clarke
1882 – Gilbert Bedford
1908 – Fred Peake
1914 – Alex Hume
1956 – Douglas Maybee
1977 – Kenneth E. Parr
1988 – William H. Petherick
1993 – Donald W. Clarke

LOCAL ARCHITECTURAL CONSERVATION ADVISORY COMMITTEE

On Thursday, January 20, 1983, a group of interested citizens met in St. John's United Church Auditorium to attempt to organize a heritage conservation group from which a Local Architectural Conservation Advisory Committee or LACAC could be selected. The meeting took place as a result of the active promotion of Margaret Macmillan. Mayor Hector Macmillan chaired the proceedings which resulted in the formation of the Campbellford/Seymour Heritage Society. In April 1983, a delegation of four people from the newly formed society appeared before Campbellford Council to request that a LACAC Committee be appointed by Council as required under provincial legislation. The same presentation was given to Seymour Council at a later date. The purpose of the local committee was to recommend to Council those area properties which should be preserved for historical or architectural value. The spokesperson for the group, Jack Connor, explained that the function of the committee was to make an inventory of buildings of local historic and architectural importance and to recommend to council which buildings or parts thereof should be preserved by means of designation. Such designation of a property under the Ontario Heritage Act of 1974 did not prohibit the development or change of that property, but provided council with a mechanism for controlling allowable alterations. Council was advised that provincial grants were available for preservation and maintenance of designated properties. Under the Heritage Act, a council could stop the demolition of a designated property but only for a maximum period of two hundred and seventy days after application has been made.

The initial committee of LACAC consisted of Jack Connor, Wallace Brown, Janet Derumaux, Susan Gibb, David Donald and Francis DeCarrol. Campbellford Council agreed to prepare a by-law to set up the LACAC Committee and contributed two hundred and fifty dollars to its budget. Councillor Gary Beamish agreed to sit on the Committee as council's representative and Clerk-Treasurer Mitch Stillman, was an ex-officio member.

The first designation made under the local LACAC on August 12, 1983, was the fire hall on Saskatoon Avenue, Part of Lot 7, East Factory Block, registered Plan 112. At the time of designation, the building was ninety-four years old and considered to be of architectural and historical significance. Council is now committed to protecting the hose drying tower, the standing seam roof, and the brickwork outlining the arches of the main door and windows. The fire hall was originally the water works and electric light station when built in 1889.

In 1984, with the help of summer students, an album was prepared by LACAC containing photographs of eighty-three Campbellford houses and businesses and seventy-nine properties in Seymour built in 1906 and earlier. These volumes were placed in the local library. Continual editing, correction, and updating of these volumes is of prime importance in recording and preserving local historic sites and buildings.

In 1987, twenty local citizens were presented by LACAC with a scroll recognizing their significant contribution to heritage conservation in preserving the historic features of their properties.

Designated properties include the following:

Campbellford

12–14 Front Street South	c. 1895
Baird/Davis Residence, 131 Queen Street	c. 1885
Baker Residence, 87 Booth Street North	c. 1882
Neil Burgess Law Office, 64 Front Street North	c. 1880
Fire Hall, 58 Saskatoon Street	1889
Heritage Centre, 113 Front Street North	1857
Kelly Residence, 113 Centre Street	c. 1885
Linton Residence, 308 Grand Road	c. 1870
Macmillan Residence, 26 Queen Street	c. 1857
Mill House/Chameleon, 37 Saskatoon Avenue	c. 1875
O'Rourke Residence, 126 Doxsee Avenue North	c. 1879

Seymour

Cenotaph, Trent River Village	c. 1923
Beesley/Miller, Concession 5, Pt. Lot 11	c. 1855
(Formerly De Haan Residence)	
Masson School, Concession 3, Pt. Lot 20	c. 1857
Oliver Residence, Concession 6, Pt. Lot 21	c. 1854
Strong Residence, Concession 5, Pt. Lot 23	c. 1867
(Formerly Potts Residence)	
Stonehaven, Buchanan Residence, Concession 6, Pt. Lot 21	c. 1853
Trent River United Church, Trent River	1878

THE TOWN CRIER

It takes an outgoing person to don 18th century breeches, clang a bell and deliver a proclamation to an assembly in a voice as loud as a booming stereo. Yet it is second nature to a small group of men and women who spend their off-hours as town criers. They are part of a tradition linked to ancient Greek runners and heralds. In European towns during the Middle Ages, and later in North America, a crier's bellowing call, "Oyez! Oyez! Oyez!," caused citizens to stop in their tracks to hear the news of the day. Whether proclaiming an impending war, a missing horse or goods for sale, town criers were revered for their ability to read when most people could not. Toward the end of the 1700s, the craft lost ground, a victim of printing presses, newspapers, and literacy. Toronto, however, retained a town crier until 1826, and Charlottetown employed one as recently as 1880. Currently, a renaissance is under way. About three hundred official town criers ply their trade worldwide, and in Canada approximately sixty have formal appointments. Half of those belong to the Ontario Guild of Town Criers. New Brunswick, Nova Scotia and Quebec have guilds, and there are criers in PEI and Newfoundland as well. Town criers take their profession seriously. As duly appointed officials, they are ambassadors of their towns.

Early in 1984, Mayor Hector MacMillan invited Jack Parsons, owner of the Motel Riviera, to assume the position of Town Crier for Campbellford, in conjunction with the Ontario Bicentennial Celebration. Jack Parsons was an imposing figure in his beautiful scarlet jacket, white breeches, black tricorn hat, black shoes with gold buckles and large gold belt. His white beard and long white hair gave him a most authentic appearance. Each town with a Crier sent that person to a regional Cryoff competition, the local one being at Peterborough. The top three from each Cryoff were sent to Ottawa, sponsored by Nordair, for the Provincial Championship. Parsons made it to the finals but was edged out by a Crier from Kingston. Jack made numerous appearances across Ontario that year and was officially appointed Town Crier of Campbellford by an act of Council on November 19, 1984.

Jack Parsons, first Town Crier of Campbellford from 1984–1994.
Photo courtesy of Jack Parsons.

In January 1985, six other Criers met here under the guidance of Bob Smith, Crier of Niagara-on-the-Lake, who was also chairman and planner of the 1984 Bicentennial Town Crier challenge. The purpose of the meeting was to plan the formation of The Ontario Guild of Town Criers which received its Charter in July of the same year. Between 1985 and 1989, Jack represented Campbellford numerous times in cities across Ontario, and as far away as St. John, New Brunswick. He also attended the Provincial Competitions in Collingwood/Stayner and Amherstburg. In 1988, Jack finished in fourteenth place at the World Championship in Halifax, in fifth place at the Provincial Championship in Toronto, and in first place at the Festival of the Forty in Grimsby. In 1989, Jack and his wife, Nancy, went to the World Championship in Ghent, Belgium, stopping at Blandford Forum, London and Rochester, in England.

In 1990, Jack won the award for the Loudest Cry at the Thirteenth Annual Halifax International Championship and also attended the third World's Championship in Fredericton. In 1991, he won the Best Uniform award at the North American Town Crier Championship in Decatur. He also continued to represent Campbellford in meets across Ontario between 1992 and 1994, as well as representing Campbellford at the North American Town Crier Championship at Nemacolin Resort, Pittsburgh. Jack retired as Town Crier in February 1995, after participating in a total of at least 332 events during his career.

In 1994, Jack Parsons officially handed over his prestigious role as Campbellford Town Crier to Tom Kerr, who farms land in Seymour Township formerly owned by Captain Tice, one of Seymour's early settlers. Tom donned a magnificent blue velvet coat and white breeches fashioned by his wife Rose-Marie.

⁓ Campbellford/Seymour Public Library ⁓

As early as 1858, the Township Council of Seymour sponsored library collections at locations such as Burnbrae and English Line. When the village of Campbellford was incorporated in 1876, the distribution of these collections was problematic. Finally the township established a Township Library in Campbellford in the Trent Block. A library board was set up and John A. Rutherford was appointed librarian and caretaker. On November 10, 1884, a meeting was held in the Town Hall to establish a Mechanics' Institute Library. It was moved by Rev. Arthur Browning and seconded by Mr. Cock, that subscribers of five dollars and up become trustees for the proposed Campbellford Mechanics' Institute, which in 1912 became Campbellford Public Library. A room was secured on Front Street from Mr. Cockburn at sixty dollars per year and Henry Rowed became the librarian and caretaker of the Institute. For a salary of eighty dollars a year, he was also to provide heat and light for the reading room and library. The Seymour Township Library was moved from the Trent Block to the new facility on condition that the residents of Seymour enjoy the same rights and privileges as village residents. Each council contributed fifty dollars to the support of the Institute. In 1885, Thomas Oliver became the new librarian and members of the board were A.B. Colville, Daniel Kennedy, A.G. Knight, D.J. Lynch, Charles Gillespie, R. Manning, Rev. Father Casey, Rev. Mr. Hinds, and John Tice.

Early in 1885, the Campbellford Mechanics Institute was opened to the public and the Campbellford Herald and many other newspapers and magazines were placed on its shelves. Lectures and entertainment were held to raise money and a place was provided for playing checkers. In 1886, John Clarke succeeded Thomas Oliver as librarian. In 1887, A.H. Rendle was appointed librarian and the provincial government grant was two hundred and fifty dollars. In 1888, the library moved to a room in the Ferris Block. Lydia Rendle became librarian in 1890, followed in 1900 by Miss Cooke.

In 1906, Andrew Carnegie was approached for a grant or donation to erect a new free public library. That same year, the Carnegie Foundation offered a grant of five thousand dollars. By 1911, the grant was increased to eight thousand dollars on condition that ten per cent of that amount be expended each year on maintenance.

In June 1911, the Mechanics' Institute gave its assets to the town under the terms of the Library Act. Rev. A.F. Reid was president of the board and W.A. Carnahan was secretary. The lot at the corner of Ranney and Bridge Streets was purchased for five hundred dollars. On May 30, 1911, a by-law was enacted to accept Carnegie's offer and on May 23, 1912, the cornerstone was laid by Rev. A.J. Reid. A portrait of Andrew Carnegie was donated to the new library by the Carnegie Foundation.

In November 1912, the formal opening took place and Hilda Bonnycastle was appointed librarian. Ora Haig served from January 1913 to May 1918, when Helen Campbell accepted the position. She retained it until 1934 when Lillian Benor was appointed. Lillian served until 1959. Other librarians over the years have been Jean Bodeau, Grace Rutledge, Rose Peacock, Mrs. Perry, Ann Caldwell, Pera Pritchard and Mae Bailey. The current librarian is Donna Wilson.

Campbellford/Seymour Library became a branch of the Northumberland County Library system in 1984. The other branches were Brighton Township (Codrington), Hastings, Percy Township (Warkworth), Grafton, Centreton, Alnwick Township (Roseneath) and Hope Township (Garden Hill).

In 1991, a large bequest made to the library by Mary Margaret West in the name of her grandfather, Samuel J. West, became the impetus for the expansion of the library. The town of Campbellford and the Township of Seymour hired Beckman Associates to conduct a study of library services and facilities. The survey indicated that the community wished to retain the original Carnegie building and to add an addition to it. Provincial government funding was secured for the project and a group of interested citizens formed Friends of the Library to raise funds from the community. Phillip H. Carter of Port Hope and Toronto was selected as the architect. The Bennett property behind the library was purchased and the building, formerly the Bata Shoe Company, was demolished. The library collection was moved in 1994 to the old Campbellford Chrysler building at the corner of Doxsee and Market Streets while the original building was renovated and the new addition was built.

The new library was opened on Sunday, September 14, 1995. In the original building, the old pressed tin ceilings and beautiful original hardwood floors were uncovered. This section contains the children's library on the first floor and meeting rooms on the second floor. The adult collection was housed on the main floor of the new building. An elevator was also installed. The new addition contains the adult circulating and reference collections and new computers. The new carpet is in the Campbell tartan in honour of the Campbell brothers who founded the community. The Rotary Club of Campbellford donated the funds for the restoration of the front entrance to expose the original pillars. The children of Campbellford/Seymour raised the money for the clock in the outside clock tower.

Northumberland Arts and Crafts purchased the children's furniture. Teachers from the High School bought the study carrels. The renovated and expanded facility demonstrates the community's commitment to the provision of library services.

— Campbellford/Seymour Fire Department —

In the early days, fire was the deadliest enemy of the pioneers. Remote settlements with long distances between neighbours and the lack of communication made it virtually impossible to contain any fire which erupted. The main source of heat in most homes was an open fireplace and light was provided by crude oil lamps which were always a danger. The use of combustible materials such as paper, shavings, hay, and feathers for insulation and mattress stuffing was a further hazard. When the land was being cleared, huge stumps were burned and might smoulder for days before rekindling. The only way to fight fire was a bucket brigade, often using a limited supply of water, supplemented by hoes, trenches and even wet straw. From the very beginning, fire plagued the town and township.

Because most of the buildings were of frame construction, almost every structure in the downtown section was incinerated at one time or another. As the frame structures were replaced, more substantial stone and brick buildings took their place. By 1874, the people were becoming more organized and the Campbellford Herald began to carry such comments as, "We take this opportunity to call attention to our city fathers and villagers generally to the need for fire fighting equipment." Another read, "Remember the old proverb: an ounce of prevention is worth a pound of cure." A third stated, "A small hand engine would not cost a great deal and might be the means of saving a vast lot of property. With the river flowing through the midst of the place, it would not be difficult to obtain plenty of water. There are, we doubt not, a number of individuals who would readily form an efficient fire company."

As a result of this pressure, a fire company called the Britannia was formed. Villagers purchased a carriage, pulled by man or horse and equipped with reel and hose, from Peterborough at a cost of six hundred dollars. This first piece of equipment still survives in storage.

After examining the effects of a disastrous fire in 1875, council in the following year voted to spend one thousand dollars to purchase a new fire engine that weighed five hundred pounds, carried about five hundred feet of hose and was capable of throwing two lines of water from one and a half inch hoses to the top of any four storey building. Despite this purchase, the very next year, the woollen mill burned. As a consequence, council made a grant of ten thousand dollars, payable in installments of one thousand dollars for ten years, supplemented by a bonus of five thousand dollars from the citizens, to have the mill rebuilt, thus ensuring employment for the seventy labourers who had lost their source of income.

The Fire Hall, built in 1878, is a designated heritage site. This building is constructed of brick with a unique onion dome tower, a prominent local landmark which had a practical use. Following a fire, the cotton covered hoses were carried to the top of the tower by the firemen who climbed ladders built into the wall. It was essential to dry the hoses thoroughly in order to prevent the growth of mold and preserve them for as long as possible. This tower is still used, but has been improved by the addition of a safety cage over the ladder and the installation of a heater to facilitate drying of both hoses and clothing. The large door to the Fire Hall has hinges formed of heavy metal in a colonial style; above is a rounded window and decorative brick. The second storey apartment, with its balcony and fancy railing, was originally occupied by the Fire Chief. This apartment is now a comfortable lounge with pictures of former fire department personnel and historic fires adorning the walls. No pole has ever existed in the building. The bell is inscribed, "Britannia Fire Co., Campbellford, 1877. McNeely Bell Foundry, West Troy, N.Y." The cost was seventy-five dollars for the bell and mountings plus freight costs of $3.18 and duty of $13.50. Originally, the bell was rung to alert everyone within range that a fire had been reported. Firemen and many local citizens rushed to report for duty. In later years a siren sounded, and today a pager system has been put in place. The new system assists the firemen by eliminating distractions and concerns for the safety of spectators. All of the firemen have always been volunteers, who hold regular jobs as well. Their commitment to the safety of local citizens is deeply appreciated.

On July 2, 1887, the following were the members of the Britannia Fire Company: James W. Dinwoodie, Thomas Blute, George Riddell, William Moyse, G. Locklin, H. Huycke, John Mott, H. Marsh, E. Nancarrow, G. Morrison, John Badgley, John Shannon, H. Williams, William Johnston, A. McDonald, J. Boland, S. Montgomery, G. Mitchell, E. Rellis, W. Morton, W. Keir, D. McLaughlin and Robert Patrick.

In January 1926, the Fire Department was reorganized by Town Council, reducing the number of firemen from seventeen to twelve: R.J. Bibby, R.A. Dunk, H. Davidson, J.M. Ferris, Joel McArthur, Harold Petherick, Joseph Poulton, C.B. Williams, and Clifford Weston. The Fire Chief was Charles Davidson, Assistant Fire Chief Vincent Farrell and Secretary Roy Bell. The salary for the Chief was seventy-five dollars per year while the men received fifty dollars per year for their services.

On May 1, 1985, firemen expressed their concerns about the state of the Fire Hall in its present location through a proposal to Town Council. It was suggested

Campbellford Volunteer Fire Department, 1917. Left to right: Vince Farrell, Mr. Bibby, Joel McArthur, Harold Petherick, R. Dunk – Deputy Chief, C. H. Davidson – Chief, Roy Bell. The fire truck is a 1917 Chevrolet Baby Grand, body by J. P. Bickel of Woodstock. Rene and Nel Davidson are in the background.

Donated by Mrs. Rutherford to the Campbellford/Seymour Heritage Society Archives.

that the section of the hall located between the water filtration plant and the oldest section of the Fire Hall be enlarged to accommodate four bays with large doors. Those making the request were the following members of the Campbellford Fire Department: Chief, Laurie Nesbitt, Deputy Chief, Tom Fox, Doug Stickwood, Arden Stephens, Gerry Radford, Paul Imperial, Mike Milne, Lionel Williams, Joe Kelly, Bill Bertrand, Don Petherick, Ed Stapley, Bob Wickens, Randy Dunkley, Bill Deschamps and Ken Robertson. Some renovations were subsequently completed.

Currently, the Fire Hall houses many types of vehicles and equipment which had formerly been the property of either the town or township. There had always been some shared expenses, but in 1988 the Fire Department decided to amalgamate Campbellford and Seymour Departments and share all costs. A 1946 Ford is used only for parades. There is a 1966 Fargo pumper as well as a 1991 model. A 1980 tanker makes more water available for rural fires. In 1996, Seymour made its final contribution in catch up costs by purchasing a 1995 pumper tanker. In addition, there is also a 1965 model one hundred foot ladder truck 665 which is hydraulically operated and was purchased from Cobourg when they upgraded in about 1989. The firemen make use of eighteen self-contained breathing apparatus, SCBAs, which provide fresh air through a face mask from tanks which are strapped on their backs. These tanks, which weigh about twenty pounds, are invaluable inside burning buildings. In addition to the trucks, two vans provide rescue and supplies. This responsibility was previously held by Northumberland County which recently opted out of this service. The Rescue Van is a 1979 Ford Van equipped with Jaws of Life and an aluminum boat and dry suits for water rescue. The Equipment Van is funded by Campbellford/Seymour.

A rural fire calls for the dispatch of a 691 Pumper, an 88 Equipment Van and a 695 Tanker Pumper. If the call is in town, a 691 Pumper and a 688 Equipment Van respond. Additional equipment is sent as needed. If the Department finds that additional manpower and equipment are needed, a call is sent to Northumberland Mutual Aid System for help.

The Fire Chief and Deputy Chief are elected by the members of the Department. The following have served in these roles over the years:

Year	Chief	Deputy Chief
1907–26	Charlie Davidson Sr.	Captain Irwin
1926–30	Charlie Davidson Sr.	Vincent Farrell
1930–47	C. B. Williams	Vincent Farrell
1947–50	Roy Bell	Vincent Farrell
1950–57	Alex MacDonald	Vincent Farrell
1957–78	Charlie Cork	Charlie Shaw
1978–92	Laurie Nesbitt	Tom Fox, Bob Wickens
1992–present	Bob Wickens	Doug Stickwood

~ Police ~

HISTORICAL BACKGROUND

The groundwork for the future development of organized policing was begun on September 17, 1792, by the first Parliament of Upper Canada, now Ontario. During the years following 1792, judicial districts, such as the Newcastle District, were established throughout the Province. Each was provided with a gaol and a court house. A high county constable was appointed to serve the needs of law enforcement in each judicial district. A constable assisted him in every parish, township and place. These constables were untrained and were paid through the judicial fee system. Their authority was confined to the municipality in which they served and their responsibilities were limited. Police in organized communities were paid a salary.

VILLAGE AND TOWN POLICE

One of the earliest village constables was Peter Shapter who investigated an incident at Meyersburg in 1878, involving a local teacher who was enamoured of one of his young female students. In 1882, the Campbellford Herald reported that, at a special meeting, Campbellford Council appointed A. Saylor of Madoc, "a man of splendid physique suitable for the job," a regular constable for the village at an annual salary of $300 plus expenses. On September 10, 1883, Thomas Bell was appointed Chief Constable for the village of Campbellford. In the later 1880s, Chief Constable Stillman was in charge.

In 1913, Constable Dickson was in charge of town policing, and the Herald related a story of him arresting a tramp who was a Scotsman over six feet tall. The tramp had frightened several local families as he begged for food and he had also assaulted the constable. When he appeared in court in front of Magistrate Squires, he was sent to Peterborough for trial because of the seriousness of his offenses.

By 1918, Charles Duncalfe was appointed Town Constable at a salary of twelve dollars per month. By 1932, the town employed both a Chief of Police, G. C. Bromley, and Night Constable, George Hardy.

It appears that the Depression forced the Town Council to reduce the police wages in 1933, Bromley's from $100 to $90, and Hardy's from $90 to $81. Hardy later became Chief and was assisted by W. E. Cargin and, in 1938, by W. Normington. In February 1944, Constable David Bowen succeeded in preventing break-ins at Davidson's Garage and Mason's Service Station. In 1952, Darrell Duncalfe, son of Charles Duncalfe, was chosen from a total of five applicants to serve on the Campbellford Police Force. W. E. Cargin became Chief in 1953, after being selected from among forty-six applicants. George Rose was Chief in the later 1950s. Sam Baird was the last Chief of Police with Lorne Thompson, Clarence Duncalfe and Jason Field serving as Constables. When the Ontario Provincial Police took over town policing in 1975, both Sam Baird and Jason Field became OPP officers.

CAMPBELLFORD OPP

The Ontario Provincial Police Detachment at Campbellford was formed in 1934 with responsibility for rural policing only. It consisted of one officer who worked out of his home. Until 1950, Campbellford Detachment was with the Belleville District and it then became a part of the Peterborough District. In 1952, the OPP set up an office at 238 Grand Road and the chief officer of the detachment resided on the premises. On March 31, 1975, the OPP took over responsibility for policing the town as well as the rural area. The office remained at the Grand Road location until 1994 when a new OPP building was constructed at 20 Industrial Drive, incorporating every modern facility. In 1998, an office was established in the Community Resource Centre at 36 Front Street South to promote community policing.

⁓ Campbellford Post Office ⁓

As early as 1828, the people of the district were served by a post office called Seymour Office, located at The 'Patch'. The mail was brought by stage from Colborne by way of Warkworth and from Brighton and Havelock. Stage routes were the only established means of transportation until 1879, when the railroad was built through the town.

For many years, the Campbellford Post Office, so designated in 1854, was located in rented property. The Ferris Block at the southeast corner of Front and Bridge Streets and later the Corkery Block further south on Front Street were two early locations. Rural post offices also were established in the hamlets of Seymour Township. Seymour East, changed in 1857 to Menie, operated from 1836 to 1914, Seymour West from 1836 to 1854, Burnbrae from 1855 to 1913, Polmont from 1886 to 1913, Hoard's Station from 1883 to 1946, Rylstone from 1865 to 1913, Stanwood from 1884 to 1914, Meyersburg from 1856 to 1971, Trent Bridge/River from 1874 and Crow Bay for only two years from 1885 to 1887. In 1875, pre-paid postage was introduced; formerly the recipient had paid the charges.

Many efforts were made to have a government building erected in the town of Campbellford, and finally, in July 1936, a new post office was opened. The Honourable J.C. Elliott, Postmaster General of Canada, turned the key in the new government building and reviewed the history of the Campbellford office in a very appropriate address, which he concluded with the remark, "This is your office, its success depends on you, and is your success." Mayor Long then presented him with a key which Mr. Elliott used to publicly admit the citizens of Campbellford to the office. Other speakers were W.A. Fraser, M.P. and H.W. Mix of Ottawa. The building was a spacious, well-proportioned building of which the citizens of Campbellford were proud. In 1971, it became the Town hall and today this building houses the Community Resource Centre.

In 1971, the Post Office was relocated to a modern facility at the southeast corner of Doxsee and Bridge Streets complete with air conditioning. Because there is no house delivery of mail within the town of Campbellford, the townspeople pick up their mail daily. Funeral notices are also posted at the Post Office so it becomes a focal point in the community where news and views are exchanged. Rural mail is delivered by vehicles operated by private paid carriers on a five day schedule. In 1998, the Post Office was computerized to expedite mail service, but private courier service is greatly expanding and poses a significant threat to postal service. In 1999, the perforated stamp will become obsolete as the new stamp books are self sticking. The cost of mailing a regular letter is forty-six cents plus goods and services tax.

POSTMASTERS

1837–1942 – St. John C. Keyes	1910–1912 – J. B. Ferris
1843–1846 – H. Rowed	1912–1915 – J. A. Loucks
1846–1852 – R. Rowed	1915–1927 – C. L. Owen
1852–1857 – James Boland	1927–1960 – J. M. Ferris
1857–1961 – James Archer	1960–1978 – Thomas Smith
1861–1863 – Mr. Platt	1978–1991 – David Wheeler
1863–1875 – J. M. Ferris	
1875–1909 – W. B. Archer	

LEAD HANDS
1991–present –   Nancy Snarr
Fred Garvey

Water and Light/
∼ Public Utilities Commission ∼

In the early years, the homes of the people, as well as stores and factories, were lighted by coal-oil lamps. In 1886, the Northumberland and Electric Company installed the first lighting system at their site at Ranney Falls. The nine lights used simple, direct current arc lamps. The Trent Valley Woollen Mill was lighted by gasoline vapour.

The merchants in the village of Campbellford had discussed the possibility of converting water power into electric power. The council was progressive enough to see the advantage of electricity for lighting and was one of the first municipal organizations to grasp the vision of public ownership. They formed a citizen's committee to aid them, and in 1889 an electric plant was started on a site donated by the late Robert Cockburn, located where the present water treatment building now stands. The contract for building the plant, supplying pipe and digging and laying drains, blasting the tail race and raceway was let to Niles, Hunting and Company of Hamilton for the sum of $19,500. The plan included the installation of twenty-two street lights, two miles of water lines and twenty-five fire hydrants. Pipes installed on the bridge were placed in wooden boxes filled with sawdust to prevent freezing. County Council ordered that these pipes be removed and buried in the river bed. J. W. Dinwoodie was paid $1,000 to relocate the pipes. The first plant went into operation as a public utility under the management of the Water Works and Electric Light Commission which held its first meeting on January 21, 1891. The Commission was composed of Reeve W. W. Armstrong, W.B. Archer, Dr. John Macoun, James Benor, and W. H. Ashton, with G.G. Eakins as Secretary and, the next year, Alex Donald, the Treasurer for the municipality in the Secretary's role. In 1891, a room was rented on the third floor of the Ferris Block for meetings of the Board of Education, the Water Works Commission and Council. By 1892, the Commission was considering the raising of the level of the water wheel to generate more power.

The use of electricity increased until there was insufficient power available to supply the demand. Charles Gillespie was successful in securing for the corporation the power site at Crowe Bay, where the Gilmour Lumber Company had formerly operated a saw mill. Here they installed a 2000 lamp machine, and in 1899 the second electric light plant came into being. Charles Dunk built the flume and Thomas Ford became the first operator. The Commission at this time was composed of C.S. Gillespie, Charles Dunk, James Dickson, Charles Brennan and Charles Benor. This plant, however, provided for lighting only, and it was not long before the increasing expansion in the use of electrical energy made necessary a further extension of the system. The poor service provided had impelled one citizen to parody "The Charge of the Light Brigade" and referring to the incandescent lamps, used the expression, "the thin red line."

By 1901, the Water Works and Electric Light Commission had the following members: Dr. Macoun, James Dickson, Reeve Charles Smith, P.J. Wims, William Morton and James Dickson, Chairman. Poor service resulted in general dissatisfaction. The Commission Board wanted to enlarge the plant at Crowe Bay but there was so much conflicting opinion that the Council submitted to the ratepayers a by-law whereby the Commission Board was abolished and management was taken over directly by the Municipal Council from January 5, 1906 until January 12, 1911. During this interval, the third and present electric light and power plant, which went into operation in September 1909, was constructed. The commission was re-established in an election of December 28, 1909 and took office as the Water and Light Commission. The first rural line was constructed to John Parks' Grist Mill at Hoard's Station. The Water and Light Commission also had charge of the water supply of the town, which was pumped from the Trent. In 1907, the Water Works got a water tank of sufficient size to hold three water carts full of water. Raw water was drawn from the river by suction pipes to the pumps whose fast-revolving impellers mixed chlorine gas thoroughly with the water. The chlorine was to kill bacteria, rendering the water fit for human consumption.

In 1920, the Commission asked the Westinghouse Company to furnish in writing a layout of a new street lighting system and an estimate of its cost. The old arc lamps would be replaced with one hundred incandescent lamps. Cost was approximately three thousand dollars. In 1947, the drilling and laying of underground cable was completed to facilitate the installation of traffic lights at the intersections on either side of the bridge. In 1948, street lighting was installed on Grand Road from Bridge Street to Victoria Street.

During this early period, the Commission always generated a profit. In 1950, the Town received a $12,000 grant from the Commission and, in addition, was given free water and light service to the community centre arena which the Town had taken over. Members of the Commission that year were: James Benor, Chairperson, Walter Wiggins, H.E. Hogle and A.J. Meyers. Percy Denyes was the Manager and James McMullen the Assistant Manager. Hylton Coxwell was the meter reader for many years, followed by Frank Osborne and William Glenn. In 1951, street names were installed on metal poles at intersections. In 1952, new metal light standards were installed at Front Street and the old wooden poles removed. In that same year, spearheaded by manager Percy C. Denyes, the PUC installed floodlights at the local tennis court. Robert J.A. McGregor was Chairman for several years, followed in 1956 by A. C. Newman. In 1957, traffic lights were installed at the intersection of Bridge Street and Doxsee Avenue. In 1959 Jack Storie, left after being employed in the Waterworks Department for fourteen years. Hector McArthur became chairman 1960, with Glynn Vandewater as Vice-Chairman. On December 21, 1960, it was decided to have a delegation interview Dr. A.E. Berry of the Ontario Water Resources Commission in Toronto early in 1961 to discuss the proposed new water works system for the Town. Arthur Evans, Manager, Hector McArthur, Chairman and Mayor F.M. Rutherford were named to the delegation. At a joint meeting of Campbellford Town Council and the PUC in late 1962, the building of a new filtration plant for the Town's water supply was authorized.

By 1971, the new sewage treatment plant was also in operation. Commissioners were: George Free, Glynn Vandewater, Hector McArthur and Ralph Locke. Upon Locke's death in 1973, Robert Clarke became a Commissioner. In 1974, a water line was extended to serve the new industrial park.

In 1984, George Free was Chairman with Commissioners Bill Murray and Brian Wilson. In 1985, a refurbishing of the water tower was undertaken. Improvements were needed at the sewage treatment plant to meet new standards.

These concerns were addressed through a sewer rehabilitation program, until finally, in 1992, the sewage treatment plant was approved to handle more housing units. These improvements have been continued in order to achieve separation of the storm sewers which often overflowed into the system.

In 1990, Cy Johnson became Chairman and the Commission adopted a policy that all commercial establishments in town install water meters by year end. In November of that year, the position of Line Foreman, which had been cut in the annual budget, was re-instated. By 1994, the Commission needed to undertake an updating of the town's water distribution system, replacing some piping which was seventy-five years old. In 1995, a major overhaul of the water filtration plant was begun and a new water storage tank was built.

Managers since the 1940s have included: Percy C. Denyes, Arthur Evans, George Van Bridger, William R. Graham, Bruce Craig and Mark Campbell.

Campbellford still owns its own power house, which is not connected with the Hydro-Electric Power Commission of Ontario. Campbellford has always been and still is rightly proud of its municipally-owned water and light system. The governing body is elected by the people of the town, each commissioner serving a term of two years. The Mayor also holds a position on the Commission. Current commissioners are Rosemary MacLennan, Ron Peters, Cy Johnson, and Bill Murray.

～ Waste Management ～

In the early days, there was very little garbage. Clothing was handed down and eventually made into quilts and cleaning rags. Old woolen material was recycled to woolen mills to be turned into blankets. Food packaging was minimal, food was preserved in reusable glass sealers, and food scraps were fed to animals. Bones were used for soup and then fed to the dogs. Each home or farm had a place where broken dishes and other discarded items were buried. Larger towns often had an abandoned place where dumping was allowed. No one cared about oil spills, gasoline leaks, leachate from landfill sites or any other form of pollution.

Documented information about early waste management sites in the Campbellford/Seymour is somewhat scarce and much of the following is based on the recollections of local citizens who remember the locations of various dump sites. One of the earliest was located at the end of Alma Street in Concession 6, Lot 8, somewhere beyond the present Campbellford/Seymour Works Department site. Donald Frederick recalls that in the 1930s local car dealers buried used Model T Fords in that dump because they were unable to sell them during the hard times of the Depression. Subsequently, a dump site was opened in the area between the Trent River and the Canal where the CNR spur line connected to the Gair Pulp Mill. In 1953, a new site was opened at Concession 5, Lot 8, where the Industrial Park is now located. This site was officially closed on October 1, 1974, but for some time before that dumping had been banned by the provincial government. The town's garbage was dumped into large containers which were trucked to a disposal site near Trenton. Seymour township agreed to allow the town the use of its waste disposal area which had opened in 1962 at Concession 7, Lot 13, just off County Road 50, provided the town agreed to pay half its operating and maintenance costs. By 1979, the wells of several nearby houses were contaminated and these were condemned by the Ministry of Natural Resources. The Town of Campbellford then extended the town water line to service these houses. The dump closed on October 1, 1986. A new site was opened on Concession 5, Part Lot 3, in May of 1984. This is now part of the Northumberland County waste management system. Garbage is presently picked up at the curb of each home for a fee of $1.50 for wet waste, while dry, recyclable waste is collected at no charge. Illegal dumping by those unwilling to pay the fee has become a problem in the area and requires extra pick-up by the Public Works Department along roadways and in ditches. Once a year, the Ministry of Natural Resources picks up hazardous wastes at the fair grounds; the Rotary Club provides personnel for this collection.

ENDNOTES

1 The exact location of Crosby's Hall could not be verified at the time of publication but the 1871 Census records that Samuel Crosby was a miller.

2 All general reference texts listed at the back of the book were consulted. Current or former members of Seymour Council were consulted and the photographs of previous councils on display at the current municipal office were also checked.

$\mathcal{S}$chools

A Brief History of
～ Campbellford Schools ～

The earliest school in the district appears to have been erected at "The Patch" near Ranney Falls some time prior to 1850. The teacher, James Boland, had approximately twenty pupils. Education in the town proper had its modest beginnings in about 1852, with the erection of a one-room log public school, known as S. S. #8, probably located in the parking lot of the present library on the northwest corner of Ranney and Bridge Streets. During this time period, a Miss Ogilvie, one of the three daughters of William Ogilvie, also operated a private school at her home, now the Canadian Legion Hall. At various times, over-crowding caused classes to be held elsewhere, such as in the basement of the Baptist Church, and the Town Hall of the day. In addition to Miss Ogilvie, some of the early teachers were Lydia Archer Rendle, Mabel Funnell Thomas, and Mrs. Kingston. The log school was destroyed by fire, and a stone building was erected in 1872 across Ranney Street in present-day Hillside Gardens Park at a cost of $5,500. The school trustees had acquired Lot 3 and Lot 2 in Block L between Ranney and Booth Streets in 1865 and 1872 respectively. As well as serving as a primary school, the first high school course was taught in this stone building.[1] In 1875, twelve out of fifteen pupils passed the high school entrance, and their teacher, head master Mr. Brisbin, was congratulated on his ability "to impart his knowledge so well."[2] Mr. Brisbin was succeeded in 1876 by Mr. Bristow and in 1877 by A. G. Knight, who is revered as one of Campbellford's most outstanding teachers.[3] In 1877, a four-roomed brick structure was erected in front of the stone building and became the high school. The first graduating class of Campbellford High School included Robert Levesconte, Will Hawley, William Horkins, Edward Cornelius Huycke, Marshall West, and Emma Connor.

In 1886, plans were made to separate the primary and secondary schools, and tenders were called for the erection of a new high school on Lot 1, Block L, adjacent to the existing school grounds, which had been acquired by the trustees in

1885. William Dunk was contracted to erect the structure at a cost of $6,300 plus $970 for the heating system. The trustees also acquired Lot 4, Block L in 1886, and added it to the school grounds. In 1890, there were three teachers on the staff of the high school, with an enrolment of 110 pupils. On February 14, 1889, the brick and stone primary school burned and a fine new brick building was erected to replace it. Opening on March 11, 1890, it was a three-storey building with three large classrooms on each floor. The stone for the basement was quarried from Mr. Locke's farm, two miles to the north of the village. The cost was $13,065, made up as follows: contractor's price – $9,775, desks – $792, steel girders – $385, furnaces – $1,625, architects' fees – $488. Mr. Bartlett and Mr. Benor were the contractors.

Room 1, Entrance Class, Campbellford Public School, October 21, 1924.
Teacher-Principal, Charles S. Haig.
Back row standing from the left: Bill Peake, Eldon Leonard, Leonard Smith, Stewart Anderson, James Heptonstall, George Sloggett, Rossmore Dunk, Arlington Phillips, Wesley Cochrane, Robert Poulton, Jack Boyd.
Next row seated from left: Alice McKelvie, Dorothy Reynolds, Margaret Cock, Morley Baker, Dorothy Henson, Fred Ingram. Next row seated from left: Hyacinthe Collinson, Goldie Nicholson, Edna Marks, Flossie Henson, Beatrice Baker, Walter Bibby.
Next row seated from left: Marguerite Reid, Dulce Carter, Nellie Haig, Grace Irwin, Jean McArthur.

Photo donated by Mrs. W. G. Campbell of Toronto to the Campbellford/Seymour Heritage Society Archives.

The high school continued in the Bridge-Ranney-Booth Street grounds until the construction of a new building at the north-west corner of Ranney and Market Street in 1923. At that time, the old high school building became part of the elementary school and accommodated primary classes. The other elementary school building erected in 1890 suffered the same fate as its predecessor, burning down on March 5, 1966. The students were accommodated at Kent School, Campbellford High School, and St. Mary's Catholic School and plans for Hillcrest, a new east side elementary school, were hastened. By 1968, all the students had been re-located to Kent School and the newly completed Hillcrest School. The remaining elementary school building became the Adult Retraining Centre, and was demolished in 1977.

— Town Schools —

The present high school was built in 1923 on the northwest corner of Ranney and Market Street at an estimated cost of over $80,000, and it was occupied in 1924. The staff consisted of E. H. Greig, Principal, and teachers Essa C. Dafoe, Kathleen B. Ferris, Kathleen B. O'Shaughnessy, Marion E. Smith, and Earl Stephens. The building was one of the best equipped schools in the entire district. On the ground floor, there were three classrooms, the principal's office, and an assembly hall. The second floor had three more classrooms, a science room, a

Campbellford High School, constructed in 1923.

From the postcard collection of the Campbellford/Seymour Heritage Society archives.

chemistry laboratory, an art room, and the teachers' room, also used as a library. The gymnasium was the envy of all visiting schools. In 1937, the basement lunch rooms were made into home economics and manual training rooms.

E. E. Darling, who became principal of the school from 1951 to 1961, recalls his days as a student in 1926. The young, capable, and dedicated staff at that time included Principal E. H. Greig, Earl Stephens (Mathematics), Kathleen Ferris (English), Kathleen O'Shaughnessy (French), Massie Wheaton (Commercial), Laura Stafford (Latin), and Mona Hammond (History). Two members of this staff, Kathleen Ferris and Kathleen O'Shaughnessy, popularly known as Big Kate and Little Kate, continued to teach at the school until retirement – a truly remarkable record! In a letter written for the fifty-year reunion booklet, Mr. Darling highlighted two outstanding achievements of the 1926–27 school year: first the successful showing of the graduating class in the Upper School examinations, which resulted in the majority of the class continuing on to university; and second, the production of the delightful musical operetta, "Tulip Time." He also remembers that students were responsible for their own transportation. There were no snow ploughs and no buses, so students, depending on the season or their location, relied on the family car or horse and cutter, "shank's mare," [4] and the train from Peterborough to Belleville. He remarked that the train made regular stops at Hastings and Campbellford and could be flagged down at Westwood and Godolphin. About forty students arrived at the Campbellford station at 9:40 AM, walked to school and were ready to start classes at 10 AM They were picked up for the return home at 7 PM.

Mr. Darling added the following anecdote:

> "Inconceivable as it may seem, three members of the Upper School class of '27 were – Percy Honey, Ronald Love and Ellis Darling. Surnames only were the acceptable staff approach to the students. This led to much embarrassment during the year." [5]

The depression years were lean ones for education. An advertisement for a teaching position frequently brought seventy-five to one hundred applications. In 1932, the year that E.E. Darling joined the staff at an annual salary of $1,700, teachers had their salaries reduced by $200. At the request of the Town Council, on February 5, 1932, the various boards and committees of Town Council, the School Boards, the Public Library, and Water and Light Commission met for the purpose of reducing expenditures. The following is the report of the High School Board:

> "Mr. Thomas E. Hall, Chairman of the Finance Committee, spoke first and went over the situation and showed that he could not promise any reduction of expenditure. George O'Sullivan, Chairman of the Board,

spoke and showed nearly all teachers were under contract on a fixed salary and that the Teachers' Federation controlled teachers' salaries, thus the Board's expenses were to a large extent fixed. However, it would be possible to reduce sundry expenditures." [6]

In the 1930s , the commuter train was withdrawn and school buses began to transport students to school. In the prospectus to elementary students for the year 1933, the high school bus routes were announced for the following year:

"The school will run two buses this next year; one from Roseneath to Hastings, and the other from Orland and Codrington, to Campbellford. These buses will be under the supervision of a careful driver. They will stop at all railway crossings. They will be heated. The welfare and safety of the students will be looked after as far as possible. These buses will arrive in Campbellford every morning before nine o'clock, and will leave shortly after four o'clock on their return trip." [7]

The most difficult bus route, and no doubt the longest, was the A. J. Meyers route to Alderville, Roseneath, Alnwick Township, and Hastings to Campbellford.

In 1939–41, the grade eleven and twelve students compiled a history of Campbellford – fifty-five pages of data, pictures, and poetry.[8] This publication has been an invaluable resource in researching and writing this new history of the town and surrounding area.

An interesting feature of the school in these years was the Adult Education Night Classes. Under the joint sponsorship of the Department of Education and the Department of Agriculture, these courses reached a peak of 22 classes with over 500 students, the largest held anywhere in Ontario! Classes were held in various locations in town such as the library, Davidson's Garage, and Jones' Welding Shop, as well as the high school. However, the sponsorship was withdrawn and the night school attendance waned.

The wartime baby boom and the thrust of technological change had its inevitable impact on the school. The Northeast Northumberland District High School Board was created on January 1, 1954.

The first major addition to the building was completed in 1960, consisting of a gymnatorium, new offices, and two additional classrooms. This addition was needed to accommodate the students from Warkworth High School which had been closed. The second major addition to the school was completed for the fall term of 1963, and was formally opened on December 8, 1963. It included a modern cafeteria, new staff room, music room, woodworking and metal shops, two new science labs, and one additional classroom. In 1970, the library, technical shops, and large family studies room were added. The building was not changed

Grade 12, Campbellford District High School, Feb. 17, 1959.

Front row: J. Johnston, R. Gibson, L. Little, A. Boyd, C. Horsman, C. Clark, C. Rannie, G. Parker, J. Hopping, C. Newman. Second row: M. Wilson, E. Stephens, B. Holmes, T. Holmes, T. Donald, D. Godden, P. O'Connor, D. Wood, M. Runions, J. Jacobs, S. Jewell, S. Post, A. Bell. Third row: B. Seymour, D. Miller, G. Ellis, L. Tatham, D. Dooher, W. Chapman, D. Haig, D. Peeling, L. Bright. Fourth row: G. Brunton, M. Jones, D. Kerr, R. Wright, D. Hopping.

Photo from high school yearbook, Trent 1959.

172

again until 1988, when the original 1923 building, by then known as the old wing, was torn down and a new structure put in place to link the 1960, 1963, and 1970 additions and renovate the existing structures. There was considerable discussion in the community about the possibility of including a theatre auditorium in the 1988 renovation, but this project proved too costly and was not approved by the Northumberland and Newcastle Board of Education.

The principals of the high school from 1922 to the present are listed below:

1922–1944	E. H. Greig, BA
1944	A. E. Robinson, BA
1945–1950	H. R. Hendershot, BA
1950	W. T. Armstrong, BA
1951	G. A. Keith, BA
1951–1961	E. E. Darling, BA
1961–1963	R. M. Hall, BPhE, MEd
1963–1967	L. S. Caughill, BA
1967–1969	T. J. Brennan, BSc
1969–1979	J. A. Jackson, BSA, MEd
1979–1981	Terry Hawkins, BA, MEd, EdD
1981–1986	Chas. Kennedy, BA, MEd
1986–1996	Chas. Clarke, DPRI, BA,MSc
1996–present	Diane Fair, BA, MEd

Sports and extracurricular activities for all students include the following: basketball, volleyball, curling, wrestling, hockey, chess, yearbook production, camera club, student council, music, and theatre arts. Another unique program at the school is Co-operative Education which allows students to earn credit courses by spending a specific time in work place settings in businesses and organizations in Campbellford, the town of Hastings, and Warkworth. Enrolment in the high school as of April 1999 is 672, and there are 68 teachers on staff.

CENTRE FOR INDIVIDUAL STUDIES

The Centre for Individual Studies began in Cobourg in 1986. At that time, there was a need for an alternative school for adults who wished to complete the credits they required for their Ontario Secondary School Graduation Diploma. The program, under the jurisdiction of the local school board, started with seven students in the basement of an elementary school. Since then, there have been five additional CIS campuses created at Campbellford, Port Hope, Brighton, Bowmanville and Peterborough. The success of the program is evident with a total student enrolment of approximately two thousand.

Campbellford CIS opened its doors in September 1987 at 37 Margaret Street and has been flourishing ever since. From this small campus, up to 1997, there have been ninety-seven graduates who have improved their literacy and computer skills, heightened their self-esteem and experienced job training through Co-operative Education.

In 1997–98, the enrolment in Campbellford was one hundred and twenty-four. The main building and a portable classroom are staffed by three full-time teachers, one half-time teacher, a part-time secretary, and a custodian. The students are adults, and also young people, who for a variety of reasons, cannot attend the traditional high school setting.

Campbellford CIS is a program which benefits the whole community. The cost of registration, books, and materials is minimal. There are many courses offered and students may work in a self-directed mode and/or in a traditional classroom setting. The operational hours from 8 AM to 5 PM allow students to create a flexible timetable to suit their needs. The Campbellford CIS offers Internet access to the entire community and welcomes inquiries and visitors.

KENT PUBLIC SCHOOL

The parcel of land that became the site for Kent School was purchased from the Lions Club of Campbellford. The club had obtained it from Ted Atkinson for the purpose of establishing a town park. The property consisted of five acres of the southwesterly section of the English Church "Glebe," Concession 7, Lot 10, Township of Seymour, Town of Campbellford. The purchase price was $5,000; landscaping was an additional $427.70.

Construction by a local contractor, Lorne Watson, began in the spring of 1958. The original building consisted of five classrooms, a kindergarten room, boiler room, teachers' room, supply room, and offices. The cost of construction was $130,000. Cox and Moffatt were the architects. The official opening for Kent School was held in January 1959. The Hon. William Goodfellow, MPP, was the guest speaker. Chairman of the Campbellford School Board was Hector Macmillan, Secretary-Treasurer was Chrissie Roberts, and board members were Helen Cowell, Ted Cryderman, Forrest Dennis, Dr. David Burgess, and Everette Steele. The teaching staff were: Flossie Bennett, Carole Benor, Carrolle Clements, Evelyn Connor, Joy Linton, Gladys Nicholson, and Principal Bert Whitfield. The secretary was Hazel Storey and Don Hoare was the custodian.

In January 1961, the land separating the school site from the Anglican rectory was obtained from Ted Atkinson for $2,000. In Seymour Township, changes were occurring that would ultimately impact on the school. In January 1965, the eleven rural school systems joined to form the Seymour School Area Board. Members of this board were Clem Milne, Chairman, Margaret Dart, Carl Free, Robert Lisle, Ray Pollock, and Ethel Clark, Secretary-Treasurer. The following year, in January 1966, the Campbellford School Board was amalgamated with the Seymour School Area Board to form the Seymour-Campbellford Area Board. The schools under their jurisdiction were Kent, the Bridge Street Junior and Senior Schools and the eleven rural schools in Seymour Township. Chairman of the newly amalgamated Board was Cy Johnson. Members were Clayton Duff, Carl Free, Robert Lisle, Bill Machesney, Bill Murray, Ray Pollock, and Ethel Clark, Secretary-Treasurer.

A crisis was created for the new Board when, on Saturday, March 5, 1966, a noon-day fire destroyed the nine room Bridge Street Senior School. Through wonderful co-operation from parents, teachers, and the community, students were accommodated in the following ways. There were six classes on shift at the Campbellford District High School, one class at St. Mary's School, one class at Bridge Street Junior School, and one class at the Parish Hall on Doxsee Avenue. These arrangements, organized by Bill Rothwell, Principal of the Bridge Street Schools, were in place until the end of the school year in June.

The Seymour-Campbellford Public School Area Board, faced with this circumstance, prepared and executed a number of initiatives. The decision was made to accommodate all the town and township students in two central schools, one on each side of the river. Students on the west side would go to Kent, which would receive an addition. It would be established as a junior school to Grade 6 with accommodation for special needs programs. A senior school to Grade 8, named Hillcrest, would be built on the east side of the river on property purchased from the Grant Anderson farm. Hillcrest would accommodate students from the east side and include all the Grade 7 and 8 students from Kent. The Grades 7 and 8 program would have the flexibility to offer courses such as wood working and home economics on a partial rotation schedule to prepare the students for high school experiences. Libraries would be established in both central schools, and become an integral part of teaching methods.

The addition to Kent School was started immediately. Preparations for the building of Hillcrest began. The Seymour-Campbellford School Area Board rented an office on Front Street North to be used as their central office, and as a supply room for all the schools. In this way, all aspects of administration necessary to consolidation could be co-ordinated in preparation for entry into the two central schools. Bert Whitfield was appointed Supervising Principal to assist the School Board with their initiatives. The two central schools, Kent and Hillcrest, were ready for occupancy by the time school opened in the fall of 1966. During the month of September, students and teachers moved into the buildings and a new partnership began. The eleven rural schools and Bridge Street Junior School were closed. The official opening for the Kent addition was held on Sunday, January 8, 1967 with Russell Rowe, MPP, as guest speaker.

Members of Kent School staff were: Bert Whitfield, Principal, Jerry Boise, Vice-Principal, Cozette Barnum, Carole Benor, Freda Donald, Eva Fraser, Joy Linton, Dorothy McCulloch, Eleanor Nelson, Carolyn Roberts, June Seaborn, Joan Sharp, Gearold Young, Gladys Nicholson who was the music supervisor, Christine Whitfield, the school librarian, Sherron Rutherford, the secretary, and Maurice Dunn and Don Hoare, custodians.

In January 1969, the provincial government brought the Northumberland-Durham County School board into existence. Cy Johnson and Howard Sheppard represented the area on the County School Board.

Kent Public School offered physical education programs, including intra-mural sports, with an on-site skating rink in winter for school and community use, library-supported curriculum studies, operation of morning and afternoon kinder-gartens, a music program and special education programs to fit individual needs. Consultants from the Ministry of Education Office in Kingston, as well as teachers and parents, became closely associated with school curriculum policies under the Hall-Dennis Report. Students had opportunities to see many distinguished visitors. Among these were John Robarts, Premier of Ontario, Earl Rowe, Lieutenant-Governor of Ontario, and Lester B. Pearson, Prime Minister of Canada.

In the 1980s, five portables were added to accommodate the addition of Grade 7 and 8 students. During this time, the school mascot, the Kent Kodiak Bear, was designed by parent, Kathy Stickwood. The motto, "Kent – Where Kids Count," was also adopted. In commemoration of the Ontario Bicentennial in 1984, a time cap-sule containing 1983–84 school year documents and a copy of the School Chronicle was constructed. This time capsule is to be opened in the year 2034.

In the 1990s, the landscaping in front of the school was changed and cement steps leading to the upper hill area increased the use of outdoor space for school and community. Declining enrolment reduced the portable classrooms to four. New primary playground equipment and basketball standards were added in memory of Brian Pugh, a popular, dedicated teacher at Kent School who passed away suddenly in September 1994. The Kodiak Bear lived on with the phrase, "Once a Kodiak, always a Kodiak," being inscribed on a plaque with a Kodiak Bear. Teddy bears were given to students and staff in times of illness or bereavement.

A big change in technology took place with the addition of a computer lab. The library was also computerized and all Grade 1 to 3 classrooms were equipped with four or five computers in conjunction with the Math and More Program. In the late 1990s, Grade 3 and 6 Provincial Tests began and a new Ontario Curriculum is presently being introduced.

The school has grown and now accommodates students in seventeen class-rooms. There are sixteen teachers, a principal, three educational assistants, one librarian, two supply staff, two secretaries, and two custodians.

Principals who have served at Kent School include:

Bert Whitfield, BA, MEd	1958–1983
Russ Kinch, BA, MEd	1983–1990
Mac Dallman, BA, MEd	1990–1993
Elvin Petherick, BSc, MEd	1993–1998
Debbie Clachers, BA, MEd	1998–present

HILLCREST PUBLIC SCHOOL

Hillcrest Public School was built at 55 Elmore Street in 1967. It offers junior kindergarten to grade eight programs and French Immersion for grades five through eight. Instrumental music is available, under the direction of Nancy Courtney, in grades five through eight, and the school band has won many awards for musical excellence. Students at Hillcrest are encouraged to participate in drama and environmental programs such as recycling and composting. Peer assistants function within the school to plan special activities for the students. A computer resource lab is available for student and parent usage. Beside the school is a ten acre playing field and students have the opportunity to participate in a variety of house league and extra-curricular sports activities. A range of counselling services is available to all members of the school community. Fund raising initiatives by students and parents provide computer upgrades and support local charities and school-related trips. Volunteers have contributed more than 2500 hours of involvement in many areas of school life. As of 1998, the school has a newly established school council comprised of parents, school staff and community representatives which serves as an advisory group to the school. The school is used by many local groups; the recreation department offers several evening activities in the school. In 1999, the school had an enrolment of 400 students in fifteen homerooms and was staffed by nineteen teach-ers, two educational assistants, two office staff, and two custodians.

Principals at the school included:

George McCleary, BA, MEd	1967–1983
William Pettingill, BA, MEd	1983–1986
Sherry Summersides, BSc, MEd	1987
James Harrison, BSc, MEd	1987–1990
Russ Kinch, BA, MEd	1990–1994
Richard Cameron, BA, BEd, MEd	1994–1998
Elvin Petherick, BSc, MEd	1998–present

HOME AND SCHOOL ASSOCIATION

During the late 1940s, parents, teachers, and school boards were encouraged to form Home and School Associations to address issues concerning the education of children. They were designed as study/discussion groups, with the teachers, as professional educators, providing leadership and guidance. Parents were asked to give their time and energy to organize such associations to support school activities. This was a revolutionary concept for the times, and parents of students in Campbellford public schools embraced the idea enthusiastically.

～ Separate Schools ～

The first Separate School in the Parish of Campbellford was established in 1903. This was a frame building on the Percy-Seymour boundary on Concession 7 of Seymour, and was known as Sacred Heart School or S.S. #12, Seymour. In 1913, it was replaced by a brick building which was blessed by Bishop M. J. O'Brien on October 28 of that year. In 1909, a second Separate School was built on Concession 10, Lot 5, of Seymour, on land deeded to the Diocese by Jeremiah O'Connor. This was known as St. Joseph's School or S.S. #3, Seymour, and was a brick building built at a cost of $3,000. It was blessed by Bishop R. A. O'Connor on June 18 of that year. During the 1920s, the enrolment at Sacred Heart School decreased and pupils were transferred to St. Joseph's. St. Joseph's and Sacred Heart Schools were used alternately, depending on enrolment, until 1935, when Sacred Heart was closed. When it was demolished, Father McCarney used the materials in the construction of the rectory of Assumption Parish in Otonabee.

Prior to 1920, there was no Separate School within the Town of Campbellford. In 1920, Father Whibbs purchased land at the corner of Bridge and Booth Streets as a site for a school. It was decided not to use this land for a school site, and the building situated here was moved to a new location on another parcel of church-owned land at 37 Margaret Street. The former residence was then converted into a two-room school known as St. Mary's. In 1921, Father Whibbs acquired the Callaghan home beside the rectory and converted it into a convent for the sisters of St. Joseph. Mother St. Peter was the first head of the convent and Sister St. Louis was the first principal of the school. Her assistants were Sister Amelda and Sister St. Marie. Sister St. Agnes Marie was the first music teacher at the convent.

In 1950, the two-room St. Mary's School was extensively renovated by removing the second storey, creating a flat roof, and applying stucco to the exterior. Installation of oil heating and improved washroom facilities were completed. Despite these improvements, the building was soon too small for the increased enrolment. By 1953, the room at the back of the rectory was being used as an additional classroom.

The four-room St. Mary's Separate School was built in 1956 at 35 Centre Street. On its completion in 1957, the old Margaret Street building was rented to the High School, St. Joseph's School was closed and the pupils transferred to St. Mary's. In 1958, Queen of the Most Holy Rosary Separate School at Codrington also closed and the remaining students were transferred to St. Mary's.

By 1965, increasing attendance resulted in the addition of two classrooms and a general purpose room for use of both the school and the congregation. Until this construction was completed, space in the rectory again became a classroom. In May 1968, school accommodation was again found to be inadequate and a second addition was planned. This new section was ready for occupancy in time for opening of school in September 1969. By 1998, St. Mary's had expanded to house ten classrooms and thirteen staff members.

By 1960, the old Margaret Street school building was no longer needed by the High School. It was then sold to the Rotary Club for use as a youth centre and a school for the mentally challenged. Eventually, the building was sold to the Association for the Mentally Retarded (ARC) and operated under the Northumberland-Durham Board of Education as Merryvale School. This facility closed in 1986 when the policy of the Ministry of Education was to integrate all students into the regular school system. Since 1987, the building has been used as the Centre for Individual Studies.

～ Rural Schools ～

The hopes and dreams of the early settlers in the area included schools for their children. A defined geographic area was called a school section and the children within the boundaries could attend the school. Trustees, usually three, were elected by the landowners to form a school board. A secretary-treasurer would be hired and an auditor appointed. Board meetings were held during the year as necessary, and an annual meeting for all of the taxpayers was always held at the end of the calendar year. The Board was responsible for the hiring of teachers, maintenance and repair of the school, provision of supplies, setting the mill rate for the school section, and hiring a caretaker for annual cleaning, daily sweeping, and lighting fires.

Each rural school had its unique history and development. In the Campbellford/ Seymour area, the amount of primary source material that has survived varies from school to school. Some of this material is privately held by former teachers and students, some of it is recorded in the Tweedmuir Histories maintained by the

Women's Institutes, and some of it survives only in the memories of the teachers and students who attended these schools. The following accounts include the events unique to the development of each school, based on the available material. In addition, descriptions of events and activities have been included with each school that, taken in their totality, recreates the unique experience and flavor of life in all rural schools.

OLD BURNBRAE SCHOOL, S.S. #1 AND SHEA'S SCHOOL

A tavern and the first old Burnbrae School were situated on the northeast corner, north half of Concession 6, Lot 20, known as Burnbrae Corner. Approximately seventy-five pupils attended in summer and close to one hundred in the winter. On June 2, 1885, the trustees decided to divide the section. A new school was built on 3/4 acre, on the northeast corner, Concession 7, south half of Lot 20. It was called Shea's School after Francis Shea who had lived there. The land which belonged to James Donald and his wife was deeded over to the trustees on February 11, 1886. The cost to build the school was $780.

Teachers included J.L. Service, John Graham, Janet Crosby, J.C. Mills, Mr. McFarlane, Ella Barnett, William Atkinson, L.M. Howson, H.M.C Mallory, L. Oulton, Leafa Totton, Elsie Ashton, Clara West, R.J. Miller, M.E. Johnston, B. McConnell, M. Hewitt, G. Meiklejohn, H. Haig, M. Upton, Earl Fairman, E.R. Cruikshank, William Atkinson, Clara Perry, Luella Matthews, Clarice Curtis, Miss O'Neill, Dorothy Curle, Rosena Grills, Mildred Dunk, Jean Wallace, Betty Thompson, Shirley Dunham, and Gearold Young.

When the schools were amalgamated in 1967, the building was sold to Watson Murray. The building is still standing and is used for storage by its current owners.

S. S. #1, Shea's School, on Concession 7, south half of Lot 20.

Photo donated by Hank Willis to Campbellford/Seymour Heritage Society Archives.

S . S . # 2 — PETHERICK'S CORNERS

The first school in the Petherick's Corners school section was a log building on Concession 8, Lot 23, built sometime after the earliest settlement of the area in 1832. Prior to 1854, school was taught by Mrs. Johnston in a log building on Will Wright's farm and also at her home at Concession 9, Lot 22, as well as by a Mr. Clark, a Bible Christian preacher. In 1854, a school was built somewhere on Concession 9 by Joe Garry, but it burned down about ten years later. School was then held in the home of William Petherick, Concession 9, Lot 20, until a building was erected on the southwest corner of Concession 10, Lot 21, in 1865. The first trustees were Daniel Petherick, William Arnold and George Finkle.

The new school had long benches on which the children sat, and a wood stove provided heat. Each year the trustees arranged for the delivery of wood for the winter. In 1899, the minute book read:

"........agrees under contrack to furnish seven cords of sound body wood, birch or maple, 2 ft. long, and three of pine or seder 2 ft. long sound and all the above to be split for the stove at one Dollar and nineteen cents per cord and to be delivered by the first of febury." "Received payment in full twelve dollars & fifty cents." [9]

Money to operate the school and especially to improve the building was borrowed from the residents of the community and repaid with interest.

The school was also used for elections and political meetings. The minute book records that, in December 1893, the trustees were paid eight dollars for two provincial elections and six dollars for two municipal elections.

The minute book of the secretary-treasurer suggests that discussions were held and motions were recorded in a business-like manner. The following summarizes some of the significant events and activities in the history of the school:

1885	—	Municipal Grant – $54.74
	—	Government Grant – $45.24
	—	Assessment on S. Section – $353.25
1900	—	The teacher's salary was $250.
1900–1950s	—	Caretakers during this period were members of the John Simpson family.
Dec. 1903	—	"A discussion then arose relative to certain parties living at too great a distance from the school and it was moved and sec'd that lot 24 in the 11th Con. And all that part of the Section lying north and east to the boundary also the north halves of lots 24 & 25 and all of lot 26 in the 10th Con. and all of lot 26 in the 9th Con. be detached from S. S. No. 2 for

the purpose of forming a new Section or union of Sections with a part of the Twp. of Rawdon adjoining." "Carried almost unanimously 21 votes." The above became part of "Rylstone School." [10]

Aug. 13, 1905 — First entry to mention telephone message relayed to teacher.

Dec. 1906 — Letter from inspector re "improving the school." "$600 was borrowed and by April screens were installed, windows repaired and hooks for coats & hats installed, maps purchased."

1910 — Legislative Grant – $85
— County Grant – $19.40
— Township Grant – $445

1912 — A new drilled well was installed.

1915 — A lobby was added and cement walks were installed around the school.

1938 — Sanitary toilets were installed.

1939 — Manual training equipment was purchased.

1945 — New slate blackboards and cupboards were added.

1950 — A telephone was installed.

1967 — S.S. #2 was closed.

A former pupil of S. S. # 2 once told his co-workers in Toronto that he had gone to a 'private' school. This certainly reflected the close-knit atmosphere among pupils and teachers at Petherick's Corners. William Petherick[11] remembers being related to all but two of about thirty students when he attended the school. His wife, Gladys (nee Clarke), was a teacher there in the 1950s and she was surprised to hear children referring to adults by their first names rather than the customary and more polite salutations. She soon learned the practice was not bad manners, but simply for identification purposes. "There were so many Pethericks and Barnums here they had to use first names so people would know about whom they were talking," she said.

Teachers at the school, and dates where known, are:

1884	Mr. Morris	1903	Mary Nichol
1885	A. M. Stanbury	1904	V. Crossley
1886	Samuel Brown	1905	J. H. Bissonnette
1890	Lottie Brooks	1905–1906	Ada Arnold
1891	Forbes Stillman	1907	Eva L. Fusee
1899	Miss Bell	1909	Miss Petrie
1900	Miss Doxsee	1912	Miss Love
1901	E. F. Skitch	1915	W. J. Doxsee

1916–1917	Hattie Redden	1934–1940	Harry Ewing
1917–1920	W. R. Atkinson	1940–1942	Norma Arkles
1921	Miss Armstrong	1942–1943	Vera Brisbane
1924	T. J. Barrie	1943–1952	Doris Reid (Stapley)
1924–1926	Everett Fairman	1952–1953	Roma Braithwaite
1926–1929	Nellie Bennett	1953–1956	Gladys Clarke (Petherick)
	(Petherick)	1956	Bessie Bland
1929–1931	Mary Peake	1857–1958	Doris Stapley
	(Rannie)	1959–1960	Norman Stewart
1932–1933	Dorothy Barnum	1960–1964	Joan Sharp
	(McCulloch)	1964–1967	Doris Brown

The building is now a private residence.

S.S. # 3 — CONNELLY'S SCHOOL

The boundaries of S.S. # 3 were south to Concession 9, east to the Trent River, west to Highway 30, including two farms to the west of the highway, and north to Concession 12. This made Connelly's one of the larger school sections in Seymour Township.

Many of the early settlers were of English, Irish, and Scottish background with the majority of Scottish descent. Settlement began in the 1830s with the Clark, Connelly, McArthur, Dunham, Macoun, Govan, Cochrane, Waddell, Mahoney, McCulloch, McCormack and McColl families.

Before 1850, the first school building in the section, constructed of logs, was located several lots east of the later site. About 1850, a second building was erected on Concession 10, Lot 9, on land purchased from P. Connelly. On this site, a log school was built which remained in use until 1868. This structure was heated by a fireplace. When the new building was erected in 1868, the old school was purchased by William Ivey and used as a stable. Later, when the property was owned by Charles Macoun, the building was sold to Frank Dobscha and the logs were used to erect a cottage at Puff Ball Inn.

In 1868, the brick structure was built, one of the builders being William Rooksby of Stanwood. A porch was added in the late 1890s, and became a part of the classroom when the attendance overflowed from the schoolroom. Steps across the north side were removed in 1926, and a cement walk and stoop were erected. In 1928, new slate blackboards were put along the south wall at a cost of $300. In 1928, additional land was purchased from the Dunhams to enlarge the play area. A new roof was installed in 1934 and the school was wired for electricity in 1937. In the summer of 1938, the door was changed from the east side to the north side to allow room for indoor toilets and cloakrooms on either side of the porch. Trees

S. S. #3, Connelly's School, Class of 1940, *taken September 13, 1940.*

Front row: Jack McCulloch, Don Campbell, ? Merrill, Goldy Lightle, Gerald Lightle, Elmer Kelly, Neil McCulloch, Fred Baker, Morris Kelly, Gerald Morrow, Fred Nicholas.

Second row: ? Merrill, ? Merrill, Isabel McCulloch, Joyce Bright, Iona Bright, Betty Clark, Barbara Long, Dorothy Long, Gwen McCulloch, Lois McCulloch, Freda McCulloch.

Third row: Everett Laundry, Keith Longmuir, Earl Merrill, Eugene Bright, Cecil Lightle, Ron Stanbury, Jack Long, Andrew McCulloch, Bert Kelly, Alec Rutherford, Ken Laundry.

Back row: Teacher – A.E.Maycock, Jean Macoun, Leta Kelly, Arlie Bright, Viola Merrill, Jean Laundry, Jean Wood, Betty McCulloch, Aletha Nicholas, Music Teacher – Albert Hazell.

Photo donated by Carolyn Free Donald to Campbellford/Seymour Heritage Society; identification by Alec Rutherford.

were planted on the land east of the creek. In 1935, John Kelly ploughed an area in the northeast corner for use as a school garden.

Music was first taught in 1930 by Albert Hazell. Many pupils went on to compete at the Music Festival.

Oratorical contests were also a popular event with students from Connelly's School capturing first prize on several occasions. Notable graduates include George Macoun, DDS, John Macoun, MD, and Father Frank O'Sullivan.

Trustees at Connelly's School included: George Anderson, Thomas Rutherford, Archie Clark, Martin MacArthur, George Longmuir, William Hooper, Duncan Clark, George Dunham, Archie McCulloch, Charles Macoun, William West, Thomas Dunham, Robert Waddell, Raymond Free, Howard Clark, Robert McCulloch, Reg. C. McCulloch, John Kelly and Douglas Rutherford. In December 1964, the three man board was terminated in favour of a Township School Area Board.

Teachers in the school, and dates where known, included:

	John Macoun
	John McGrath Sr.,
	Mr. Sykes,
	M. Service (Mrs. Albert Cassan)
	Maggie Brooks
	Miss Young (Mrs. Sparling)
1890	Emma Stanbury
1891	Maggie Donald
1893–1994	John McGrath Jr.
1895–1998	Matty Doxsee (Mrs. Charles Macoun)
1899–1901	Lizzie McGregor (Mrs. Walter Rutherford)
1902–1904	F. Barron
1905–1907	A. Van Volkenberg
1909–1910	Fred Wood
1911–1912	Maude Tufts (Mrs. H. Clark)
1913	L. McGregor
1914	A.G. Stevenson
1915–1918	Beatrice Borland
1919–1921	Nellie Jeffs (Mrs. Murray Meiklejohn)
	Annie Stevenson
1922	Jennie Ballantyne
1923	Vera Squires
1924–1926	Dorothy Huycke (Mrs. Ralph Locke)
1927	Alexis Allison (Mrs. Reg Craighead)
1928–1931	Earl A. Fairman
1932–1940	A. Everett Maycock
	Catherine MacDonald
	Alexis Allison
1955	Gwen McCulloch Coombs
1956	Shirley Osborne
1956–1961	Eva Fraser
1962	Gladys Petherick
1867	Dorothy McCulloch

Connelly's School closed in 1967 and the students were transferred to Campbellford. The building is now a private residence.

S. S. # 4 — W E S T ' S   S C H O O L

The first school building on Concession 7, Lot 3, was a log structure with a cottage roof. It was approximately fifty feet square with a big desk occupying most of one wall. The pupils sat on wooden benches around the desk which had sloping sides to hold their books and slates, while a stove near the entrance provided heat. This log school was used until the 1880s when it was dismantled and moved to the Abraham Free farm on Lot 4 where it was used as a pig barn until it disintegrated.

After initial bickering over location between the 'uprollers' and the 'downrollers', i.e. those who lived on the upper portion of the school section and those who lived on the lower portion, a new school was built halfway between them on the West property, in the centre of Concession 3 on the east side of Highway 30. The original indenture, dated July 2, 1867, made between William Melville, John McKelvie, and Abraham Free, states that these trustees of the Concession School Section #4 agreed to purchase the school property from William Clarke for a cost of ten dollars "to have and to hold in trust for a common school in and for School Section #4 according to the provisions of the school act of Upper Canada and for the education of the resident youth of the said school section." [12] The deed was dated January 2, 1874.

Early trustees were William Stillman, James Free, John McKelvie, John and George Rutherford. The first recorded annual meeting of S.S. #4 was held on December 26, 1883. At a special meeting on October 22, 1887, a motion was moved by James Free and seconded by William Stillman that the Free Methodists have the use of the schoolhouse for six dollars, provided that they take proper care of same. The minutes recorded the teacher's salary in 1887 as $400, while the following year, it had decreased to $325.

The new frame school burned to the ground. Local lore tells that on an extremely cold morning, the brothers who acted as caretakers put on a roaring fire which not only warmed the inside of the building, but the outside as well! According to the January 12, 1889 trustee meeting, a motion was moved by William Stillman and Thomas Free that the old West's Methodist Church be used as a temporary schoolhouse. On March 1, the decision was made to build a new schoolhouse on the old site, provided that the Board of Health approve the school grounds. The brick structure and basement were erected in 1890 by Charles Dunk and Louis Breault at a cost of $855. In 1896, a wood furnace was installed by Morton and Owen of Campbellford for $85. In 1899, hardwood was purchased at $4.50 a cord and softwood at $2.50 a cord. The furnace was replaced in 1947 by James Jacobs for $250. The cost of wood had risen to $16.50 a cord, so, in 1953, the wood furnace was replaced by an oil furnace.

Originally, ceilings and walls were whitewashed and later painted. In 1906, metal sheeting was applied to the ceiling and side walls. The blackboards were originally a painted surface. These were replaced in 1906 with slate blackboards. In 1910, a new floor was laid at a cost of $15.75. In 1951, a new floor was installed at the front of the school and a new front door hung. In 1906, a new stoop was constructed of cement and stone. Originally, windows existed only on the south and west sides of the building. These had wooden shutters in 1899, which were later removed. In 1948, a gift of windows on the north side of the schoolhouse was accepted from Angus Todd who was the teacher. Screens were added in 1958. In 1949, electricity was installed and a new lighting system added by Garneau and Dunsmuir for $550. New fluorescent lamps were installed by Garneau in 1956.

A well was dug at the time of construction of the building, and, in 1910, it was cased at $1 per foot. A pump was installed for $10. A new well was drilled in 1952 at the north of the walkway but the water has since become unpotable. A cistern was built into the southeast corner of the basement in 1944. A motion was made in 1901 to have two brick closets (outside toilets) built but this was rescinded and wooden closets were built instead. At some later date, two brick closets were built onto the east side of the building. These were still there until after the new 1950 addition was placed on the south side of the school. This contained two toilet rooms, as well as a storage room, often referred to as the teacher's room. Wash basins were installed in 1953.

In 1937, land lying to the south of the school yard was purchased from George Elmhirst for $15. Improvements to the grounds north of the school were made in 1942. At this time, some tombstones from the old cemetery on the property were moved to West's Cemetery across the road but some were missed and remain on the school site to this day. Many fences have surrounded the property. The first, mentioned in 1897, was a board fence four and a half feet high. This was replaced in 1909 by a Maple Leaf fence across the front at $1.30 per rod. Two gates were purchased at the time costing $6.30 and $3.50. The fence was later replaced by a galvanized wire fence. The back and northern portions of the fence have been removed in recent years and the grounds cleared of brush and debris. Trees and hedges were planted over the years but only a few originals survive.

The last trustee meeting of S.S. # 4 was held on December 30, 1964. When the rural schools closed in 1967, students were bused into the amalgamated town schools. Pupils from the former West's School attended Grades 1 to 6 at Kent School and Grades 7 and 8 at Hillcrest.

The Seymour West Women's Institute bought the school property in 1967 for $200. The indenture was dated December 13, 1968, between the Public School Board of the Township School Area of Seymour and Campbellford and WI trustees Faye McKelvie, Ruby McCulloch, and Eileen Rutherford. The deed was registered on February 7, 1968.

Teachers were required to light the fire daily in the early years and were compensated for same. According to the trustee records, a dispute over the sum paid for lighting fires caused teacher, George Sanborne, to resign. He wanted $15 and the trustees would only pay $7, but ended with a motion to pay five cents a day. The first paid caretaker was Stuart Nelson in 1913 for $25 annually. In 1961, Howard MacDonald, a student, was paid $175 as caretaker, which included cutting the grass during the summer. The WI revived the tradition of Christmas Concerts in 1975, and has continued to include one as part of their family night each December.

The following is a list of teachers from 1882 to 1929 as taken from the original trustee treasury book, and from 1951 to 1967 as taken from the Tweedsmuir History:

1880	R. J. Sykes	1902	J.D. (Douglas) Carlaw
1882	Edward J. Free	1904	Fred O'Connor
1882	John Graham	1905–1906	Claude Winters
1884	Miss Stephens	1907	Gertie Buchanan
1886	William Scarlett	1907–1908	Archie Peebles
1887	William G. Armour	1908–1909	Eva Fusee
1889	H. Anderson	1909	Stirling Waterman
1889	M. Scarlett	1909–1915	Amy Salisbury
1890	Charles Dunk	1916	Hazel Atkinson
1891–1893	John Graham	1916–1917	M. Jordan
1894–1895	George C. Sanborne	1919–1922	Beatrice Borland
1895–1896	Effy Stewart	1922	O. Doxsee
1896	Della Sanderson	1923–1926	Freda Nelson
1897	R.J. Sykes	1926–1929	Harold Dunk
1898	E. C. Hanna	1929–1951	Angus Todd
1899	R. McLean	1951–1955	Robert Moorcroft
1899	R.H. (Dick) Bonnycastle	1955	Mrs. Davis
1901	Mabel McBride	1958–1967	Cozette Barnum

S.S. # 5 — ENGLISH LINE

This school building is located at Concession 2 , north part of Lots 13–14, and the school boundaries were south to the Trent River, east to Robert Diamond's farm at Concession 2, Lot 16, north to Concession 5, west to the Trent River, an area approximately nine square miles. The first settlers in this area were retired British army officers who had previously settled along the Atlantic seaboard. The English from north Devonshire formed the majority, along with a few settlers from Scotland and Ireland.

The first school was built of logs across the road from the later location. In 1861, a frame building took its place, built by Robert White for $395. In 1884, it was sold to James Benor for $45 and removed from the site and used as a shed. In 1884, the present brick school was erected by James Benor for $1324. William Dunk received $10 for drawing up the plans. In 1907, the ceiling was repaired by Preston Metallic Co. for $96. Two wood stoves provided the heat. In 1930, the building was wired for electricity by Mr. Denyes from Campbellford. Orville Grills excavated the basement in 1937 and Lindsay Fry completed the work. At first, the grounds contained 1 1/4 acres. An additional acre was later added. A well was sunk by Benjamin Moir in 1871, and a woodshed and ash-house was completed by M. S. Cassan for $95 in 1904. In 1926, a stable to accommodate six horses was built at the foot of the school hill. The school is now a private residence.

Teachers from 1861 until its closing in 1966 were Mr. Mallory, Mr. Pollock, Mr. Rutherford, Mr. O'Sullivan, Mr. McLeod, Mr. Service, Mr. Walker, Mr. Graham, Wiggie Holmes, Tom Johnston, Walter Smith, Mr. Henderson, Miss Service, H. L. Dougan, Mr. Scarlett, C. J. Boyce, L. M. Sharpe, Claude Winters, Mr. Shapley, Charlie Haig, Nellie Turner, Grace Payne, Della Lisle, Ida Thompson, Gertie Costley, Mae Hubble, Lillian Locke, Miss Davidson, Clara Pettey, Flossie Rutherford Scott, Violet Patrick, Mildred Curtis, Verna O'Neill, Mr. Bick, Mr. Finlay, Helen McMullen, Florence Rannie, Esther Meiklejohn, Doris Potts, and Eva Fraser.

Three famous graduates were S. A. Peake, Surgeon, A. E. Forrest, President of Great North Western Life Assurance Co. and Frank Forrest, Vice-President of the same company.

Doris Potts remembers:
— music was introduced in 1930 by Albert Hazell
— entering exhibits in the Campbellford-Seymour Agricultural Fair
— ball games with neighbouring schools
— belonging to the Red Cross Society and following parliamentary procedures at the meetings
— entertaining parents and neighbours at Hallowe'en and Valentine parties
— enjoying an ecumenical religious education course
— skating on the neighbour's pond at noon hour
— finding a skunk in the basement after a weekend. It had eaten the seed collections.
— Christmas concerts presented at the local church with a twenty member, fully uniformed, rhythm band
— burning maple blocks of wood in the basement furnace
— cleaning the school yard on Arbour Day, the first Friday in May, then hiking to the neighbouring woodlot for a treasure hunt in the afternoon
— singing at the Music Festival
— having a picnic at Bradley Bay on the last day of school

S.S. # 6 — MEYERSBURG

The first Meyersburg school was built on Concession 2, Lot 13, and was a wooden structure about twenty by fifteen feet. It contained long wooden benches and desks in two rows with one centre aisle. There were three windows on the east and three on the west side of the room. It was used for church services by the Wesleyans and other community gatherings. In early days, Timothy Finlay from Ireland came and taught in the Meyersburg School. John Rutherford and Eliza Stone also taught in the early years of the school. A burying ground, which eventually contained seven graves, was started at the back of the school. That first school house was bought by John Jones for $12 and moved to his property beside Highway #30 to be used as a drive shed.

A second building was built in 1873 on the same site. It was of brick construction and considerably larger and more up to date. The room was lighted by six large windows, three in each side as before. The same long benches were used and it had a long painted blackboard across the west end. The classroom was heated by a box stove. Unfortunately the building was poorly constructed. After only twenty-five years, the walls and ceiling began to show signs of weakness in the masonry. The outside walls on two sides had to be propped up with poles. The school was torn down in 1900. More bricks were added to the old ones and constructed into a new school with strong three-brick walls. George Skinkle was the contractor and the cost of building the third school was $1,193.

In the 1920s and 1930s, desks were screwed to the floor in rows with the front of one attached to the back of another. They were large enough for smaller children to sit two in a seat. Extra lighting was provided by gas lanterns when needed, although Meyersburg School had good light on most days from its modern windows. The heat source was a furnace with a large register in the classroom floor. There were good quality slate blackboards at the front of the classroom and ones of lesser quality on the sides. There were benches at the back of the school room and hooks for coats and hats. Water was pumped from the well when it was potable, or carried from Garnet Hay's place when the school's well was not of good quality. A large crock-type container with wide dark blue stripes, sort of a barrel shape, had a spout at the bottom so the pupils could pour out a fresh drink. A bird feeder was attached to the front west window where chickadees and nuthatches would come any time, but the blue jays only appeared early in the morning.

In those days, there were no grades – children started in Primer Class and then went on to First Class, Second Class, Junior Third, Senior Third, Junior Fourth and Senior Fourth for a total of seven years. At the end of Senior Fourth, students tried Entrance Examinations set by the Ontario Department of Education to go on to high school. Penmanship was an important skill the pupils were expected to develop. Printing was not always widely taught. Unfortunately in the 1920s and 1930s children who were left handed were generally forced to write with the right hand. In some cases, the teacher would crack the knuckles of the left hand with a pointer. In art classes, pupils were expected to copy exactly what the teacher drew on the blackboard – creativity was not encouraged. Maps also had to be copied by the older students. They studied history, geography, geometry, literature and composition and spelling. Spelling bees were a regular occurrence. Grammar, memory work, and book reports were part of the curriculum. Younger children were expected to learn reading, writing and arithmetic. They were drilled in addition, subtraction, multiplication and division. Christian religious education was being taught still in the 1960s. Vocal music was conducted by the teacher who might use a pitch pipe or could accompany the students on the piano. Children learned to work on their own while the teacher worked with other grades.

The children brought lunches to school, usually eating at morning recess so they would have a longer time to play over the noon hour. In good weather, at lunch time, they went out to play 'scrub' on the ball diamond. In winter, they played snow tag. On rainy or stormy days, the pupils stayed inside and played games – sometimes 'Hangman' on the blackboard or 'I Spy' or 'Pass the Secret On'. Everyone had to learn to get along with a variety of age groups.

Special celebrations were held throughout the year. On the first Friday in May, the school celebrated Arbour Day by cleaning up the school yard – it was always a day of fun after the work was done. In December, Bob and Bill Scott put up the stage, and practice for the Christmas concert began. It was hard work for the students to memorize parts for plays and skits, songs and dances. Santa Claus would arrive at the end of the program with candy for all the children. Garnet Hay and Reg Hay were great Santas.

In the spring, textbooks and supplies for the upcoming year were ordered and were stored in a large cupboard. Copies were made on a jelly-like hectograph pad. Material was written or printed on special carbon, laid on the jelly and then copies were taken until they became too faded. These pads could be used a number of times before they had to be discarded.

Teachers in Meyersburg School from 1878 to 1967 were John Shannon, George Simmons, William Armour, William Beattie, Edward McGrath, Martin Sutherland, Mat Doxsee, Miss Peters, J.R. English, Miss Reilley, Verna Free, Nellie Turner, Jennie Partridge, Grace Payne, Zella May Hanna, Ada Arnold, Ada Locke, Laura Patterson, Edna Connor, Jen E. Dillworth, Constance McKelvie, Delma Kimmerly, Helen Peake, Rosena M. Grills, G.E. Sloggett, Shirley Wright, Lillian E. Burgis, Helen Glover, Gwendolyn A. Coombs, Bernadene Logan and Marion A. Smith.

When the last teacher, Marion Smith, was hired, Ed Rutherford, the secretary, and two other board members, Bill Bateson and Carl Stoddart, went to her parent's home in Belleville one evening in May 1963, to conduct the interview. When she was hired, June Goacher took her in as a boarder. She walked to school every day, except when, in bad weather, Laurie Nesbitt gave her a ride on the high school bus.

Teachers in the Seymour Township schools had an association which would meet once a month at one of the schools. At these meetings, problems and ideas were shared.

The rural schools closed in September 1967 and all students moved into town schools. The Meyersburg School and property was purchased and converted into a home.

S.S. # 7 — MASSON'S SCHOOL

The first school was a log building on David Allan's property on Concession 2, Lot 21. James Nealon lived in the lower part, and school was taught overhead. Miss Main was the first teacher. There were benches to sit on but no desks or blackboards. Property for a new school was bought from Thomas W.S. Masson in 1855. The building, thirty-six by twenty-four feet, was erected in 1856 by Elijah Chard and was made with stones from the surrounding neighbourhood. A brick porch, built by Robert Sharpe and Hiram Doxsee, was added in 1893. Half an acre of land across the road was purchased in 1873 from the David Allan Estate for $47.50 for use as a playground.

The large desks faced east and there were two windows on the west side. Painted boards were the first blackboards and pupils wrote on slates. A slate blackboard was purchased in 1902 for $24. In 1909, Robert Sharpe erected a picket fence around the property. A cement platform outside was added in 1915, and a horse stable was built in 1926. Music lessons taught by Mr. Albert Hazell began in 1931. In 1937, two of the windows on the north were closed and five large ones were put in the south side by Lindsay Fry. Foolscap paper for examinations was bought for 12 cents a half quire. The health unit began work in 1945. In 1947, two swings were donated by Campbellford Kinsmen Club. Electricity was installed in 1951.

First ratepayers included Thomas Keith, John Massie, William Massie, William Robertson, George Johns, Andrew Milne, James Haig, John Doxsee, Alec Ingram, Peter Donald, William McKenzie, Thomas McAvilla, Thomas Fry, T.W.S. Masson, George Milne, George Innis, Stephen Scott, Gilbert Sharp, George Stollery, William French, Thomas Haig, David Peterson, Asa Williams, David Allan, and Henry Locke.

Teachers from 1880–1885 were H. Pollock, V.A. Coleman, Henry McCullough, John Bell, Duncan McColl, L.G. Young, and John Brown.

Teachers from 1880–1900 were Archie Graham, John Graham, Miss Ealey, Emma Stanbury, Miss McGregor, and Bella Crosby.

S. S. #7, Masson's School, located at Concession 2, Lot 21.
Photo donated by Hank Willis to Campbellford/Seymour Heritage Society.

Teachers from 1900–1997 were Miss Davidson, Lottie Grass, L. Nicol, Carrie Wheaton, Olive Frederick, George Short, K. Green, J.M. Warwick, E. Anderson, Emily Masson, Jennie Masson, Pearl McAdam, Ida Thompson, Mary Masson, W.K. Bunner, Elizabeth Weir, Victor Masson, M.J. Smith, Anna Creighton, Emily Masson, Bertha Clark, Thomas Chaplin, Lenora Williams, Agnes Thomson, Lillian Locke, Clair Curtis, Ella Cock, Doris Rannie Potts, Gwendolyn Beckell, Frances Mahoney, Milton Blakely, H.E. McDonald, Joyce Grills, Mary Rannie, Eva Fraser, Madeline Simpson, Lois Hicks, Betty Miluck, and Catherine MacDonald.

The inspectors were Mr. Scarlett, Mr. O'Dell, Mr. Boyes, A.A. Martin, Sam Sutherland, C.W. Young and D. Rikley. Clayton Thompson was secretary-treasurer when the rural schools closed in 1967 and became part of the Seymour Campbellford School Board. Pupils were taken by bus to attend Hillcrest Public School in Campbellford. The building is now a private residence.

Doris Potts remembers:
— watching a trustee pull out and dispose of snakes from the school well
— going to Fred Stollery's for the day's supply of water
— following the "common cup" with chlorine for purification issued by the Department of Health
— finally getting earthenware water tanks
— hot lunches for which the teacher supplied the meat and each pupil brought a vegetable for the pot
— going to school in bare feet

— Oscar Rannie finding a band of gypsies in the schoolyard when he arrived to light the fire

— dealing with a boy who met and challenged a skunk on the way to school

— taking part in school fairs when classes were judged for marching and exercises besides exhibits of baking, flowers and vegetables

— riding to school over snow-blocked roads with the farmers driving teams of horses with long sleighs

— bobsled rides down the school hill

— gathering wild strawberries along the railroad track on the way to school

— maple trees being planted by Edward Rannie in 1890

— the tapping of these same trees in 1940 by the teacher and students, the production of syrup on the box stove in the school, and finally a meal of pancakes and syrup

— Tom Chaplin teaching cricket

S . S . # 9 — S T A N W O O D

The school was erected on Concession 13, Lot 19, Seymour Township in 1882. Daniel Rowe was the contractor and the cost of the brick structure, wooden seats, and blackboards was $500. New seats were installed in 1912 along with slate blackboards. In 1915, a lot was purchased from D. Akins to enlarge the playground. First Chairman of the School Board was R.D. Rutherford, who also acted as Secretary. Among the early settlers were Peter Loucks, J.H. Lisle, James McAlpine, Henry Redden, J. Dewey, L. Breau, J. Jacobs, H. Deacon, C. Keller, T. Levecque, W. King and Daniel Rowe. Some of the Secretaries down through the years were John MacKenzie, C.D. Lawrence, Harold T. Rutherford, Thomas McKeown, Robert Lisle, C. Stephens, H. Dickinson, C. Rowe, and Warrington Hay.

Teachers from 1882 were Annie Stanbury, Alex Todd, J. Little, Isaac Brooks, L. Little, Della Sanderson, Mrs. C. Lawrence, William Skitch, Frank Sanderson, Thomas Murphy, Miss Hudgins, A. Van Volkenburgh, Miss Jordan, Annie Stephens, Arthur Armour, Miss Currie, Miss Weatherill, M. Anderson, W.R. Atkinson, Mr. Reynolds, A. Arnold, Miss Duff, Mrs. W. Rutherford, Daisy Sparkes, L. Milne, Mr. MacCrimmon, G.A. Philp, Eleanor Johnson, Madeline Lisle Simpson, Mac Hay, Gwen Rutherford, D. Amblin, Cora Reid, Rosena Grills, C.M. Bongard, H. Baker, Eva Fraser, F. Althouse, R.G. Wilson, G. Clancy, Vivian Graham, and Doris Stapley.

Thomas Murphy, who taught in 1902–1903, went on to become an M.P.P. and Minister of the Interior in 1937. Graduating students who entered the teaching profession include Annie Stephens, Arthur Rowe, Dorothy Redden, Madeline Lisle Simpson, Jerry Boise and Mac Hay. Russell Rowe, a pupil of S.S.#9, became a teacher before moving into provincial politics as representative from Northumberland and Speaker of the Legislature.

Average enrollment was thirty to thirty-five pupils for the eight elementary grades. For a while, during the 1930s, the first two grades of high school were also taught, increasing the already hectic schedule of the country school teacher. Pupils faced long walks to and from school — over two miles in many cases. Winter time could be difficult as only the main roads were ploughed. When snow drifts clogged sideroads many pupils would resort to travelling the fields. One teacher, Miss Sparkes, often snowshoed from her home to the school — a two-mile trek.

A big box stove squatted near the back of the room. It was surrounded on three sides by a solid wooden screen, the inside surface of which was lined with tin. The older boys were detailed, a week at a time, to keep the stove fueled. There was an unspoken competition among the "firemen" as to who could stoke the hottest fire. The pinnacle of success was reached when the super-heated tin liner caused the wood screen to start smouldering. This created a break in the tedium of study. Pupils would dash outside and fetch in buckets of snow to cool down the screen. These diversions could be staged one or two times per winter without the teacher becoming suspicious.

During the winter months, the children were allowed to bring a dish to the school to heat for lunch. The stove top would be covered with a variety of cookware before the noon break. Savory smells filled the air as baked beans, creamed corn, scalloped potatoes, hamburger, macaroni, and sausages bubbled, burped, and sizzled.

Two large blackboards covered the wall on each side of the platform which held the teacher's desk. Above the blackboards were two pull-down maps, one of Canada and one of the world. Additional blackboards lined each of the side walls. Shelves on the back wall provided space for the small library, and storage for the brown bags, lard tins, and honey pails that carried the lunches. There were a few coat hooks, with the overflow often spilling onto the floor. The addition of an entry porch provided the extra storage space.

In the mid-1930s, the local school board paid for some of the school supplies. This practice was discontinued after a few years, but while it lasted, was a bonanza for pupils. Scribblers, pencils, erasers and rulers, bought in volume, were secured in a cupboard. The free supplies were doled out carefully and extravagant use was discouraged. One lad, who had a habit of chewing pencil ends as he agonized over his school work, could be seen occasionally writing with a very short pencil stub. He had used the pencil at both ends and was not yet eligible for the next issue.

Junior graders looked forward to the time when they would be allowed to use pen and ink. Initial enthusiasm was somewhat dashed when they finally got to write with the scratchy straight pens. Sharp nibs punched holes in the paper and released blobs of ink unexpectedly, while ink-stained fingers struggled to master the cranky instrument. Fountain pens were starting to appear — the "Cadillac" of pens. With considerable relief, the straight pens were retired and new Sheaffers and Parkers were used.

Recreation at school followed seasonal patterns. 'Shinny' and sleigh riding were predominant winter activities. Icy road conditions brought out sleds and sleighs. Lunch hours would be spent racing down the hill just west of the school. Ending the run at the base of the opposing hill, the children would climb to the top and swoop back again toward the school. Boys with home-made bobsleds became instantly popular, as requests for rides were numerous. When warmer weather prevailed, there was a trek to a nearby bluff. The steep slope was ideal for 'bottom sliding'. Once the snow was 'butt' packed into deep smooth ruts, the students were ready for action. Overnight freezing would provide a fast icy slide. The bluish tint to the slides was easily explained, as most of the boys wore denim overalls, which now had bleached-out seats.

The 'shinny' brand of hockey was played on many surfaces – on frozen ponds, on crusted fields or on the packed snow of the school yard. The shinny battles continued until bare ground and mud replaced winter's snow and ice. By that time the National Hockey League playoffs were winding down and it was time to toss away the home-made hockey sticks. The hockey heroes imitated by the teams were retired for another season. The list of favourites were mostly Maple Leaf stars such as Syl Apps, Gordie Drillon, Turk Broda, and Red Horner.

With the coming of spring and the rising of the sap, a yearly ritual took place. Out came the jack knives to hack off small limbs from a nearby basswood tree. For a few days, whistle-making was of prime interest. The whole musical scale was represented by honkers as large as a lad's wrist and tweeters the size of a baby finger. Softball then took over the remainder of the term and resumed when school returned in the fall. Occasionally a game was arranged with another school. A friendly rivalry existed between S. S. #9 and S.S. # 3 – Connelly's in particular. Games were keenly contested by mixed gender teams.

Stanwood was probably one of the few rural schools to have students playing cricket. The inspiration came from Jerry Boise and English boys' magazines which featured cricket items. From illustrations, the players were soon carving out their own cricket bats. Broom handles disappeared from home to reappear as wicket stumps. Thread spools, filched from sewing baskets, were turned into the "bails" that topped the wickets. The British would say "it's not cricket," but certainly it was the Canadian version.

A much anticipated indoor school event was Valentine's Day. Students applied their artistic skills and imagination in drawing up cards. School work was suspended in the afternoon for games and the Valentine exchange. "Store-bought" cards were a luxury during the Depression. The card exchange served to express affection that children were often too shy to display in another fashion. It was also a popularity poll and pupils receiving the most cards basked in their elevated status. For those receiving few cards, the message was not so kind.

An occasional visit by the school inspector was cause for students to be on their best behaviour. Although Mr. Martin was a quiet, unassuming man, the teacher was usually a little tense until he made his report and left. Sometimes the teacher would organize a spelling bee or a geography match. A spirited contest would result as pupils strove to impress inspector and teacher alike.

Arbour Day was regarded as a harbinger of spring. Though not an official school holiday, it was a departure from the regular routine. On the first Friday in May, school books were set aside and a general clean-up took place. While the senior girls dusted the classroom and cleaned windows, the older boys were sorting out the woodshed, stowing away the remaining wood as fuel for another season. Junior pupils busied themselves raking up the schoolyard and collecting the debris left in the wake of the departed snow. With the clean-up complete, it was a free day to use as the children pleased – a chance to explore spring freshets and newly-formed ponds, to look for signs of new life stirring on sunny woodland slopes. Lunch was a picnic. Some teachers liked the idea of planting a tree or shrub to mark Arbour Day. Somehow the plants never seemed to thrive long enough to reach maturity.

One of the highlights of the school year was the Christmas Concert. For several weeks before the event, time would be set aside for practice. There would be plays or skits, recitations and readings, a chorus, and maybe a pantomime. All pupils were included in the activities. As the time drew closer, some of the local farmers would meet at Stanwood United Church and assemble a rough planked stage across the front of the church. Final rehearsals were held in the unheated building. On the night of the concert, the Church would be filled to capacity. A towering Christmas tree decorated with garlands, streamers, and ornaments glittered and sparkled in the light of the hissing gas lamps. The children waited behind the curtained dressing rooms on either side. Some small tyke would move nervously to centre stage and whisper the introduction, while the audience strained to hear, and then the show was on. The children struggled through their lines, helped considerably by the prompters. The audience applauded everything, both good and bad. The finale was usually performed by a number of youngest students dressed as alphabet blocks. Trooping on stage, they would attempt to spell Merry Christmas or some such Yuletide greeting. Often it was misspelled as they lined up in the wrong sequence, which added to the festivity. Everyone waited in growing excitement for Santa Claus to make his entrance. Suddenly he was there, bounding down the aisle and making his way to the great tree. Within short minutes the pile of gifts there had disappeared, bags of candy had been distributed, and Santa was on his way. It was a role that Robert Lisle often performed and enjoyed equally with the children.

S . S . # 1 0 — T R E N T R I V E R

Some of the early settlers in the Trent River area were Nelson Wood, Michael Van Volkenburg, Lawsons, Gibsons, Thompsons, Killbanks, R. Nixon, Launts, Staceys and Carnrites. The need for a school was soon evident and a log building thirty feet by forty feet was erected in 1869 and used both as a school and a church. Trustees were M. Van Volkenburg, James Thompson, and Frank Leigh. The building was located on Concession 13, Lot 5, on the southeast corner of Nelson Wood's farm. The grantor of the deed was Thomas Wood. A box stove was situated in the centre of the room. Blackboards were simply pine boards painted black. Slates and slate pencils were used by the pupils. There were few text books and no library books. The teacher was well supplied with ironwood and beech gads[13] which were needed for discipline purposes.

The earliest teachers were Jennie Patterson, Margaret Elliott, Miss Armour, H. Pollock and George Spencer. After ten years, this old school was abandoned and a new site was selected for a brick building on Highway 30. An addition was later made to the west side of the new structure. The half acre of land included a side hill and very stony soil.

Throughout the years, the course of study included Arithmetic, Reading, Geography, History, Writing, Physiology, Spelling and Drawing. Text books were improved to the benefit of both teacher and pupils. School fairs and the study of agriculture were popular. Music was introduced in 1930 under Albert Hazell. Public speaking at oratorical contests was sponsored by the Trustees and Ratepayer's Association.

In 1932, an additional half acre was added to the school grounds. The old wood shed was moved to the rear of the building in 1933. In March 1937, the school was wired for electricity. A school garden was begun in 1936. Trees were planted and the lawn improved. In August 1944, a basement was excavated and a new furnace installed. The west end was divided into two cloakrooms and a porch. Few, if any, changes were made to the original accommodation with regard to heating and seating. The old box stove was used until 1944 and the double seats were still in use until 1959. The classroom was thirty-four by twenty-six feet with seats fastened to wooden skids so they were movable.

In 1945, a bulldozer was able to level and grade the grounds which for years had defeated the equipment available to the early settlers. In 1946, a small additional piece of land was purchased from T. J. Brown, and a new fence installed along the east side. On Arbour Day, May 3, 1946, a tree planting ceremony honoured those who served in World War II.

The building was used until 1959 when a new structure was built in Trent River Park. The old building was sold and is currently a residence. The new building was only used for a short time until all pupils were transported to Campbellford in 1968. It too was sold and became a residence.

S.S. # 11 — BURNBRAE

This school section was very large with up to seventy-five pupils in attendance. In June 1885, a meeting was held to divide the section into two. A contract was given to William Stewart Sr. to build a brick school on the southwest corner of Concession 6, Lot 22, on land purchased from the Craighead farm opposite the Burnbrae Church. Austin Huycke was the teacher in 1889 at a yearly salary of $250. Between 1900 and 1940, salaries rose from $275 to $1,100. The yard was fenced in 1906. Slate blackboards were installed in 1910. Agriculture was on the curriculum from 1917 to 1920. George Craighead was the caretaker for many years.

The school was burned in 1958 by two Toronto teenagers. Classes were held at Menie in the Women's Institute Hall. The contract for a new school, which opened in 1960, was given to Fred Fry. At that time, the inspector was C.W. Young and Frank Potts was the secretary-treasurer. The new building became a private home in 1966 when the rural schools were closed.

Teachers included A. Graham, O. Sharpe, Miss Crosby, Miss Coleman, Miss Hubbell, A.H.S. Huycke, Miss Huycke, J. Boyd, J. Bell, J. Masson, Thomas Third, G. Laidly, M. McMullen, E. Masson, P. Thompson, G. Thompson, V. Pearson, G. Stinson, N. Jeffs, G. Hamblin, A. MacAlpine, Beatrice Borland, H. Thomas, Jean Craighead, Malcolm Hutcheon, and Fern Weatherill.

Shirley Twigg remembers:
— starting school at age 5 so that she would not be the only first grader, and walking four miles every morning and afternoon to get there
— the pot-bellied stove being held together by a wire because it was cracked
— indoor chemical plumbing being installed along with a wash basin for hand washing
— desks with ink wells
— playing 'Nickety Hen Over the Pig Pen' and 'Fox and Goose' in the snow
— taffy pulls at Gilbert Ketcheson's woods
— cooking potato soup, which included a pound of butter, and also hot chocolate on a two burner hot plate
— daily repeating of the Lord's Prayer and the singing of God Save the King
— girls wore dresses in both summer and winter when heavy stockings and picky underwear were added

– making maps from flour, salt and water, colouring the rivers blue

– pupils were unsupervised during lunch hour as the teacher went home for lunch

UNION SCHOOL #7 — SEYMOUR/RAWDON

This school was located on Concession 3, Lot 26, Seymour Township on land initially owned by William Doxsee and currently owned by the Parr family. No documentation is currently available about this school. The stones from the foundation and well have been incorporated into the stone fence on the property.

UNION SCHOOL #12 — PERCY/SEYMOUR/FLEMING'S

This school was located on Concession 13, Lot 21, of Percy Township. It was first built in 1853 on land belonging to the Fleming family. The original school burned and was replaced with a new structure in 1869. Seymour ratepayers who sent their children to this school included William Brown, John Rutherford, Robert Fisher, James Longmuir, and the Waters family.

UNION SCHOOL #18 — RYLSTONE

Between 1865 and 1870, a log school was erected on Concession 11, Lot 22, Rawdon Township. In 1903, pupils from the northeastern portion of Seymour Township who had previously attended the schools at Petherick's and Stanwood became part of a joint school section with their neighbours in Rawdon Township. Attempts to erect a new building were not successful until 1919–1920.

In September 1921, the Union School was opened to students of Seymour and Rawdon Townships, with Anna Gow as the first teacher. The site chosen was Concession 11, Lot 26, Seymour, on the west side of the road dividing the townships. The first trustees were Andrew Thomson, Harold Barnum, George Gibson, and secretary-treasurer, F.M. Rutherford.

Indoor toilets were installed in the basement in 1938 as well as four rows of fluorescent lights plus four floodlights to improve the poor lighting system. In 1940, the building was given a covering of stucco.

School fair work was begun in 1925 and continued until 1967, except for the war years. Grade 9 lessons were introduced in 1930. In 1937, Albert Hazell was hired for one half hour a week as the first music teacher. Don Pollock also taught music in this school for several years until its closing in 1967.

The teachers who taught at the school and their annual salaries are as follows:

1922–1923	Augusta Morton	$1,000
Sept.–Dec., 1923	Mrs. Thomas Reid	1,000
Jan.–June, 1924	Flossie Scott	900

1926–1928	Evelyn Bonnycastle	900
1928–1932	Helen Bateman	900
1932–1934	Margaret Cock	900–1,000
1934–1939	Russell Rowe	750
1939–1940	Helen Hendy	660–740
1940–1943	Ruth Murray	725
1943–1944	Gladys Elmhirst	750
1944–1945	Jean Barlow	1,000
1945–1947	Mrs. Doug Clancy	1,100–1,150
1947–1948	Evelyn Mellville	1,500
1948–1949	Joyce Grills	1,500
1949–1950	Mrs. Hopkins	1,500
1950–1951	Miss Atkinson	1,800
1951–1968	Cora Reid	4,000

In 1967, the school was closed and the Seymour children were bused to Hillcrest in Campbellford. The school building was sold to the Rylstone Women's Institute in 1968 for use as a hall. Rawdon residents were initially sent to the Twelfth Line School and the Ninth Line School in Rawdon. When the Rawdon schools closed in 1969, the students were all bused to Marmora schools.

ENDNOTES

1 *Abstract Index to Deed, Village of Campbellford, Lot #1-4, Part of Township Lot No. 10 and 11 in the 6th Concession of Seymour in Block L. Booth St. according to Plan made by C. F. Caddy*, registered 10 April 1885 as #771/2 , amended 1890.

2 F. G. DeCarrol, *Reflections: Campbellford Centennial Year – 1976* (Campbellford: np, [1976]), p. 139

3 *Peterborough Examiner*, Monday, October 15, 1923.

4 On foot.

5 *Campbellford High School 1923–1973* (Campbellford: Campbellford Herald, 1973), pg. 8.

6 *Campbellford High School 1923–1973* (Campbellford: Campbellford Herald, 1973), pg.1.

7 *Campbellford High School 1923–1973* (Campbellford: Campbellford Herald, 1973), pg.1.

8 *History of Campbellford* (Campbellford.: Classes of 1939–1940, Campbellford District High School, 1940), p.1-8.

9 Excerpts are from the minute book of S. S. #2, Petherick's Corners, now in the possession of William and Gladys Petherick, R. R. # 2, Campbellford, Ontario K0L 1L0.

10 Ibid.

11 William Petherick was Reeve of Seymour Township from 1980-1997 and became Deputy Mayor and Reeve of Campbellford/Seymour in 1998.

12 *Deed of Indenture between Trustees of S. S. #4 and William Clarke, dated July 2, 1867, dated January 2, 1874.* This original document is preserved in the Tweedmuir History of the Seymour West Women's Institute.

13 Gad is an old word for a cattle prod.

Chapter Seven

Churches and Cemeteries

— Anglican —

CHRIST CHURCH (ANGLICAN) PARISH

Early settlers of the Anglican faith had no church building, and only occasional visits from travelling missionaries. They travelled on foot and by horse to meet in farm homes, mills and barns, wherever church services could be held. The earliest known account of Anglican services held in Seymour Township is dated June 7, 1835. From 1835 to 1850, services were held in various locations, such as at "The Patch" near Ranney Falls, over John Gibb's store, in a sitting room of Wellman's Hotel and in Captain Levesconte's home on the English Line. Sunday School was often held in the early schoolhouses. Rev. Bowers was the first resident clergyman for the area and lived in a log house on Concession 4, Lot 5, opposite the Henry Bonnycastle farm. There was considerable discussion about the possible location of a permanent church, but this was resolved when the Rowed family donated the area known as the 'Glebe',[1] located on Concession 7, Part of Lot 10. The donation consisted of a house to be used as a rectory and twelve acres of land. Rev. John Samuel Clarke, who served as minister of Seymour and Percy from 1853 to 1856, was the first clergyman to reside in the rectory. The early settlers supplied the labour to build the stone and timber church, assisted by a gift of money from the Church of Ireland. George Ranney, a local mill owner, donated the lumber and Elizabeth Rowed Carlow gave the timber. The church was opened in 1854, without pews or a pulpit, and the congregation was seated on pine boards placed on blocks of wood. The minister stood on a raised board, and used a rough wooden desk for a lectern. When pews were added, the desk was replaced by a butternut pulpit.

In 1861, the church was consecrated by Bishop Strachan, freed from debt, and a gallery was added. The first rectory burned in 1871 and a new one was built on the hill behind the church. Between 1875 and 1883, the chancel and bell tower were constructed.

An early photograph of Christ Church, before the addition of the Parish Hall.
Photo courtesy of Ann Rowe.

In 1886, the former Bible Christian Church on Doxsee Avenue North, owned by the Methodist congregation, was acquired as a parish hall. It was a busy place, used by the whole community for social occasions, until it was sold in 1970. In 1954, to provide the minister with more comfortable accommodations, a new rectory was built adjacent to the church. A new parish hall, attached to the church, and named for Arthur Jenkins, a former warden, was consecrated in 1972 by Bishop Snell. In 1983, a new organ was purchased and in 1991, through the efforts of the organist, Ken Laird, a keyboard was added. Two parishioners were honoured – Bruce Elmhirst for serving fifty years in the choir and Ethel Higginson, on her retirement, after thirty-five years as church secretary.

Since 1991, there has been growth in the Sunday School and Youth Group. In 1994, the 140th anniversary year, a program was started to restore and enlarge the Parish Hall. The roof of the church was re-shingled, the church office moved from the Rectory into the church hall and the bell tower repaired. The Arthur Jenkins Hall was expanded to accommodate a new kitchen and washrooms for the handicapped. A parking lot at the rear of the hall and ramps have made the facility more accessible. Bishop Douglas Blackwell dedicated the extension on March 17, 1996. In November 1996, the church started the final phase of hall expansion. The building provides three Sunday School rooms, a Nursery, an Adult Fellowship room, and offices for the Rector and Secretary. In 1996, new pews were installed in the nave and the best of the old ones were put in the balcony. New lighting, and a stair rail were added to the balcony and the wainscotting and floor of the nave were painted.

The Victory Bells at Christ Church have been sounded by Harry Bennett to recognize important occasions over the past seventy-seven years. Harry helped his father, Charlie, ring the bells to celebrate the end of World War I in 1918. In 1945, Harry and his father rang the Victory Bells again for World War II. On the 50th anniversary of VE Day, May 8, 1995, Harry and his son Rich, rang the bells in remembrance.

The church property was originally the site of the earliest Anglican cemetery, including a burial vault. The cemetery was closed in the 1870s and a new one opened on the hill further up Church Street. Land was added to the new cemetery site in the late 1880s. In 1984, the Anglican Church Women underwrote the expense of the restoration of the burial vault. In 1994, the old gravestones were removed to the new cemetery on Church Street.

CHRIST CHURCH ANGLICAN CHURCH WOMEN

In 1967, the Diocese amalgamated all women's groups under the umbrella of the Anglican Church Women. Prior to this, there had been an active Women's Auxiliary, a Parish Guild, and a Chancel Guild.

This new group meets monthly providing fellowship, support for the Church, assistance with missionary projects, and services to the local community, including the food bank. Twice a year the group sends layettes and supplies to the Downtown Church Workers in Toronto. Financial support is also provided to church related houses in Toronto. A foster child in Africa has been supported for many years. Rummage sales, bazaars, and catering as well as a monthly dinner for seniors, are the organization's main sources of income. An annual fellowship gathering of women from other local churches is sponsored by the Anglican Church Women.

～ Presbyterian ～

PRESBYTERIAN CHURCH

Pioneer families gathered for worship in their homes or those of their neighbours. Because of the scarcity of ordained clergymen, travelling missionaries covered vast territories. Prior to 1791, the Church of England occupied a privileged position in Upper Canada. However, in 1798, Presbyterian and Lutheran ministers were extended the right to perform marriages.

Presbyterianism in Campbellford/Seymour dates back to September 17, 1836, when a meeting of the inhabitants of Seymour was held at the Ferry House Tavern in Seymour for the purpose of establishing a church according to the National Establishment in Scotland. Fifteen gentlemen were chosen to form a committee for

General and Particular Management. Initial plans called for three churches, one on the west side of the river at Walter Govan's lot on Concession 9, and two in Seymour East, one at Gilbert Ketcheson's lot on Concession 5 and one at Couch's place near the river. Walter Govan communicated with the Church of Scotland.

A missionary tour of Seymour was conducted in 1836-37 by the Reverend Dr. Robert McDowall, a United Empire Loyalist from Fredericksburg on the north shore of the Bay of Quinte who was associated with the Dutch Reformed Synod of the United States. At that time, he was the only Presbyterian minister in Upper Canada. A resident minister was not available for Seymour for some time. From 1838 to 1844, Rev. James Ketchan of Belleville was appointed a missionary to the Townships of Seymour and Huntingdon. Rev. Robert Neill had arrived in Canada in 1837, sponsored by the Glasgow Colonial Society. His father-in-law, Rev. Urquhart was the minister at Cornwall. Neill spent some time in Lower Canada (Quebec) and also served as an assistant to Dr. Machar in Kingston. During this time, he ministered to several prisoners awaiting trial for treason following the Battle of Windmill Point near Morrisburg in 1838. On January 29, 1840, the Reverend Robert Neill – better known as Dr. Neill – was ordained in Seymour at the Allan property, just west of Hoard's Station, by the Auld Kirk Presbytery of Kingston. He preached his first sermon with a packing box for his pulpit. In addition to his work in Seymour East, he conducted services in the home of Walter Govan, Seymour West, and in the school house at Campbellford. He ministered to these congregations until 1858 when the Campbellford group formed its own church. For nearly forty-six years, this devoted man laboured faithfully and left a deep impression on the entire community. In November of 1885, he retired from active service and five years later died in Campbellford. At his request, Dr. Neill was buried in the very place where the pulpit of the old church at Burnbrae stood.

ST. ANDREW'S PRESBYTERIAN CHURCH, BURNBRAE

The first church in Seymour Township was a frame building constructed in 1840 on five acres of land at Burnbrae donated by Gilbert Ketcheson. This was a Church of Scotland or Auld Kirk congregation. The little frame church served the congregation until 1866 when it was replaced by a stone building which could seat four hundred people. On Friday, April 17, 1896, this structure burned during an electrical storm. Lightning struck the spire which was beyond the reach of the fire fighting equipment. An attempt was made to chop off the spire without success. The church had a new organ and had been recently redecorated. Everything was removed from the basement. Neighbouring farmers summoned by the ringing of the bell removed the pews, choir chairs, pulpit and chandelier. The present brick structure was erected at that time with bricks being drawn from Tweed by volunteers.

A Sunday School was established in 1838 in Seymour East at Robert Boucher's home on Concession 4 with Alex Menzies as Superintendent and an attendance of thirty to forty children and adults. A second Sunday School opened in Seymour West with J. Tice as Superintendent and an attendance of fifteen to twenty in attendance.

From approximately 1885, the Burnbrae congregation was affiliated with the Presbyterian Church at Rylstone as one pastoral charge. At church union in 1925, Rylstone congregation chose to join the United Church, ending this relationship.

The first manse was a stone house located at the rear of the cemetery. The large brick house beside the church was built in 1920. The old stone house was rented for many years until it was dismantled in the early 1980s and moved to Warkworth area. Each stone was numbered for re-installation. The adjacent cemetery opened in the early 1840s and is still in use today. Records date from 1852. The burial ground, marking the final resting place of many of the early pioneers of Seymour Township, is a peaceful rural setting maintained with loving care over the years.

ST. ANDREW'S PRESBYTERIAN CHURCH, CAMPBELLFORD

On March 10, 1857, in a meeting at the William Ogilvie house, now the Legion Hall, the congregation in the Seymour Bridge area withdrew from the Seymour East Charge. The first Presbyterian Church in town was a frame structure on a stone foundation, forty by twenty-six feet, erected on the site of the present church. This was a Canada Presbyterian or Free Church known as Seymour Congregation until the Village was incorporated in 1876 and was served by the minister of the Warkworth Charge. Thomas Rutherford drew the logs, timber and lumber with a yoke of oxen named Buck and Bright. He drove in from Seymour West, worked a twelve hour day, and then headed for home. The cornerstone was laid on July 4, 1859, and the building was dedicated in May 1861. On June 21, 1858, Rev. Thomas Alexander was ordained as minister of Percy-Seymour with his residence in Percy. He remained on the joint charge until 1865 and retained Warkworth until 1872. For a few years, Seymour Charge was covered by supply ministers including Rev. David Beattie. In 1872, for economic reasons, the charges were once again twinned and Rev. Beattie declined the dual responsibility due to his advancing age. He moved on to Rylstone and later to the Madoc area before his death in 1892. In 1875, the two distinct branches of Presbyterianism in Canada united to form the Presbyterian Church in Canada. Seymour Congregation and Warkworth remained twinned.

St. Andrew's Presbyterian Church, ca 1900.
Photo donated by Bernice Hardy to the Campbellford/Seymour Heritage Society Archives.

When the second building was erected, the old frame church was sold and moved in 1883 to the A.J. Meyers property on south Front Street where it was used as a warehouse for carriages and farm implements. The cornerstone for the new structure was laid on June 14, 1882, on the lot north of the old church. William Dunk was hired as the contractor. This was a brick building with a stone basement, seventy by forty-two feet, capable of seating six hundred and fifty persons. The new structure opened on January 28, 1883.

In 1885, Campbellford became a separate charge and entered upon a new era. There was a considerable increase in the population of the village, and the congregation was fortunate in securing Rev. John Hay. The first organ was added in 1884, with James Dickson as choir leader and Miss Dinwoodie as organist. In 1890, it was necessary to enlarge the building by the addition of fifteen foot wide wings on the entire length of the north and south sides. The pews were re-arranged in a semicircular form. During these renovations, services were held in the Music Hall. In the same year, the Sunday School purchased a new library. In 1892, a generous bequest from Marion Gibb erased fully the church debt. It also funded the building of a manse in 1895 on a lot purchased from Father Quirk of St. Mary's Roman Catholic Church. The contractor was James Benor of Campbellford.

An alcove for the organ and choir were added in 1902. A new Casavant pipe organ was added in 1909. This instrument has provided accompaniment for cantatas and recitals with ecumenical participation throughout the years. On June 14,

1908, the golden jubilee of the formation of the congregation was held with special services. The event was celebrated by a printed historical booklet. In 1912, renovations were made to the auditorium, Sunday School rooms, and sheds.

During the Great War, the use of the church was given to various organizations. On September 19, 1920, a bronze war memorial tablet with the names of twenty young men from the congregation was unveiled. At the back of the church is a Roll of Honour, listing the names of one hundred and six men of the congregation who were in active service in the Great War.

In June 1925, the congregation rejected union with the Methodist church and many members left St. Andrew's to join the new United Church, including the minister, Rev. C. F. McIntosh. For many years, Burns Night events and suppers have been popular events. St. Andrew's continues in the Presbyterian tradition.

WOMEN'S ORGANIZATIONS OF ST. ANDREW'S PRESBYTERIAN CHURCH

Ladies Aid Society

In 1876, during the ministry of the Rev. John Hay, the first Ladies Aid Society was organized. Projects were many and varied, and under excellent leadership were most successful. The Society and its successors have always taken an active part in the activities of the church, helping financially with the upkeep of the church, assisting families, celebrating anniversaries, and providing help and comfort to the bereaved.

In 1940 the Seymour West Ladies Aid Society was formed at the home of Mrs. Ray McCulloch. Projects were quilting and catering for banquets and weddings, with the proceeds going to the Board of Managers of the Church for renovations and upkeep. In 1975, this group amalgamated with the Campbellford St. Andrew's Ladies Aid.

Women's Missionary Society

In 1886, during the ministry of Rev. John Hay, the Women's Foreign Missionary Society was organized with a membership of twenty-six. In 1889, the "Happy Workers" Mission Band was organized with Mrs. (Rev.) Robert Laird as leader and a membership of thirty-seven children. In 1901, a Young Women's Mission Band was organized, but was disbanded in 1908. In 1910, a Young Ladies Home Mission Circle was organized with Mrs. (Rev.) G. A. Brown as president. In May 1914, at the General Assembly in Toronto, the formation of the Women's Missionary Society took place, amalgamating the Women's Foreign Missionary Society, the Women's Home Missionary Society, and the Women's Missionary Society of Montreal. The St. Andrew's group was organized on June 9, 1914. As part of the amalgamation, the Young Ladies Home Mission Circle that was formed in 1910 became known as the Young Ladies Mission Circle. During the Great War (1914–1918), Red Cross work and the packing of bales of clothing, hospital supplies, and Christmas boxes was the chief work of the "Young Ladies. In 1951, the Young Ladies Mission Circle became the Evening Auxiliary. Many missionaries have spoken to the Women's Missionary Society over the years: Mrs. Johnston Goforth, Rachel McLean, Freda Matthews, Bessie MacMurchy, Beatrice Scott and others.

In December 1949, Rev. A. E. Toombs was inducted as minister of St. Andrew's Campbellford and Burnbrae. Rev. Toombs and his wife Selena were retired missionaries with 22 years service in the Bhiel Field of India. Through their 16 years in Campbellford, Mrs. Toombs, an active Society member, shared many of their experiences as missionaries to the Bhiels. In 1957, the Society sponsored the first Robbie Burns dinner. This event continued until 1975, featuring many memorable guest speakers and entertainers; one of whom was Keiller MacKay, Lieutenant Governor of Ontario. In 1970, Mrs. Rev. W. McBride organized the first Ecumenical Christmas Program which continues each year hosted by different congregations.

In 1973, the Women's Missionary Society and Evening Auxiliary amalgamated as the Women's Missionary Society of St. Andrew's. This organization raises money toward an allocation set by headquarters in Toronto in support of missionaries and missions throughout the world. Subsequently, the Women's Missionary Society and Ladies Aid amalgamated to form the Presbyterian Ladies Association.

RYLSTONE PRESBYTERIAN / UNITED CHURCH

The Rylstone community occupies a unique position on the boundary of Seymour and Rawdon Townships as well as the county boundary for Northumberland and Hastings Counties. The first services in the community were conducted twice a month by an Anglican minister, Rev. Gandier, in an upper room of David Allan's house. Later, the log school on Concession 11 of Rawdon was used.

The first Presbyterian church building at Rylstone was a frame structure erected on a half-acre of land donated by Robert C. Rutherford on December 1, 1869 and located on Concession 11, Lot 24. Trustees were Alexander Dunn, William Meiklejohn, and James Donald. This was a plain, unpretentious building which served the needs of the community for many years. There was no organ in this church. Singing was led by a precentor who sounded the correct pitch on a tuning fork. The offering was received in a pouch suspended from a long pole rather than on collection plates. The old building was still in use as a church hall on August 5, 1937, at the 50th Anniversary celebrations of the Women's Missionary Society.

Land for the new church building, located at Concession 10, Lot 24, was donated in 1893 by William and Ann Thomson, who also provided land for the adjacent cemetery. The new Rylstone Presbyterian Church was dedicated on

October 8, 1893. In 1925, the congregation decided to become part of the United Church of Canada and the former relationship with the Burnbrae congregation was severed. Rylstone became part of a circuit which included Springbrook and Stanwood. Two ministerial candidates have come from the Rylstone area – Grant Meiklejohn in 1940, and Ronald D. Barnum in 1962.

In 1968, the church at Rylstone was closed and the congregation joined with Stanwood and Springbrook to form the Springbrook Charge. The building was demolished in 1976. A memorial plaque now marks the site of this very active congregation. The cemetery is well maintained and continues to be in use.

～ Methodist/United ～

EARLY METHODIST CONGREGATIONS

Early Methodist activity in Seymour came from the circuit riders who travelled the area on horseback. Methodist worship in those days was fervent and evangelical. It was the custom of the people to voice their assent to the words of the preacher by such interjections as "Amen" or "Hallelujah." The old fashioned class meeting was conducted by lay leaders for the two-fold purpose of discipline and fellowship. Such things as card playing and dancing were forbidden to the Methodist people. If a church member did not conduct himself according to the Methodist conception of Christian standards, his name would be removed from the membership roll. If a church member became negligent in regard to attendance at worship or participation at the Lord's table, his name would be dropped from the roll. Prayer meetings were a regular feature of church life, and the layman who could not pray in public was the exception rather than the rule. Although Methodists were strict in their standards of conduct, they were not gloomy but cheerful and sociable, and thoroughly enjoyed their tea meetings and gatherings.

Meetings were often held at "The Patch," near Ranney Falls. The Seymour circuit was supervised from Asphodel (Norwood) and later from Percy before it became a separate circuit. Homes, barns, schools and lodges provided places of worship until a church building was erected. The first recorded structure was a Wesleyan Methodist church built in 1847 on the site of West's Cemetery, Concession 7, Lot 5. The 1851 census describes this as a frame building owned by the Wesleyan Methodists, capable of seating two hundred persons. In the late 1860s, a split in this congregation led to the creation of a separate Methodist Episcopal group which met across the road in the school. There is some indication that they may have erected a building but no proof. In any case, this was the first Methodist Episcopal congregation in Seymour Township. It seems likely that this group formed the nucleus of the Campbellford congregation which erected the brick building on Queen Street beside the river in 1874. The Wesleyan Methodists continued to meet at West's Corners until the 1884 amalgamation when they rejoined with the Methodist Episcopal congregation and St. John's Wesleyan Methodist congregation in Campbellford to form the Methodist Church.

West's Cemetery was established by trust deed on March 15, 1849. Samuel and Margaret Gilpin who owned the property, conveyed the land to five trustees of the Wesleyan Methodist Church, namely Edward Stanbury, Charles Jones, William West, James Upton and Matthew Hawkin. The cemetery continues to be used occasionally and has been maintained through the estate of the late Mary Margaret West, a descendant of the Gilpin and West families.

Meyersburg was also the site of a Methodist congregation. The Wesleyans had worshipped in the old schoolhouse for many years. Behind the building, which is now a residence, are seven unidentified graves. On September 7, 1891, land was donated by John Ham Sills, Ephraim George Sills and his wife, Sarah on the westerly side of Main Street. The Trustees were Robert Jones, Josiah F. Fraser, George Potts, Nelson Simmons, Thompson Armstrong, George M. Clark and William M. Bateson. The Trustees were required to build a fence around the property at their own cost and no barbed wire was to be used. The minister at the opening was Rev. Mathew Elijah Wilson, who was the minister of the Norham Circuit where he resided. Meyersburg Church operated from 1891 to 1941. In 1950, the church building was moved to Batawa to serve as its municipal library.

HOARD'S UNITED CHURCH

The first church at Hoard's Station was a Methodist Episcopal building erected in 1871 on the present site at Concession 3, Lot 24, donated by Stephen Scott, in whose honour the church was named Stephen's Methodist Episcopal Church. This congregation was one of twenty-six appointments on the Stirling Circuit, served by two ministers and numerous lay preachers. Stephen Scott was a gifted musician and led the singing, assisted by James Barnett and James Landon. After the amalgamation of the Bible Christian, Wesleyan Methodist and Episcopal Methodist faiths in 1884, Stephen's Methodist Church was moved to the Seymour Circuit in 1890. In 1894, an organ was purchased with money raised from a Harvest Supper held in Jeffs' woods. Throughout the years, improvements were made to the building. At the creation of the United Church in 1925, the congregation was increased with the addition of ten families from Burnbrae Presbyterian Church who were in favour of church union.

At the annual meeting in January 1955, discussion began about the inadequacy of the existing building. By June 1955, a decision was made to build a new church. During June 1956, Stephen's Church was demolished and the salvaged

Hoard's United Church, Concession 3, Lot 24, celebrated its 100th Anniversary as a congregation in 1971.

Photo from Campbellford/Seymour Heritage Society Archives, originally from the files of the Campbellford Herald.

material sold. Wilfred Spencer and Co. were given the contact to erect a new brick church. The cornerstone for the new structure was laid in the fall of 1956. During construction, the congregation worshipped with Tabernacle United Church on English Line. The basement was completed by volunteer labour under the supervision of James Grills. By December 1956, the lower level was used for worship while work proceeded on the upper sanctuary. Dedication of the new Hoard's United Church was held on May 5, 1957 with an overflow congregation. Many memorials and gifts were presented during the service. In 1969-70, a new kitchen area was constructed to improve the ability to prepare and serve meals. In 1971, Hoard's celebrated the 100th Anniversary of organized church life. Rev. Percy Lambert, the only surviving former minister, came from New Bedford, Massachusetts to preach the sermon. In 1974, the Seymour Pastoral Charge celebrated the 25th Anniversary of Rev. Gordon J.A. Whitehorne's pastorate.

Active groups at Hoard's United Church over the years included the women's organizations, Sunday School, Baby Band, Mission Band, Messengers, Young People's Union and AOTS Men's Club. The choir has provided inspiration throughout the years under the recent leadership of Doris Potts, Norma Thompson and Lois Heagle. For many years, Frank Heagle and later his son, Gerald, have kept the grounds and building in attractive condition. The cemetery was established in 1959 on adjacent land donated by Harry Parr. The first burial on July 15, 1959, was Mary Eleanor Whitton, born in Enniskillen, Ireland and a resident of Snarr's Nursing Home. Grace Gunning funded the building of the stone gates in 1971. Since no cemetery had existed for the previous church, most burials prior to 1959 were at English Line Cemetery.

WOMEN'S ORGANIZATIONS OF HOARD'S UNITED CHURCH

Throughout the years, various women's organizations were active including the Ladies' Aid, founded in 1913 by Mrs. Bunner with Mrs. A. H. Parr as the first President. The Ladies' Aid became the Women's Association in 1925, following church union. The Women's Missionary Society was organized at the same time by the woman who had come over from Burnbrae Presbyterian, with Mrs. William Rannie serving as the first President. The two groups met jointly after 1934, and in 1962 amalgamated to form the United Church Women. Several members have served on the Presbyterial and Conference Executive: Betty Thompson, Presbyterial President – 1964-65, and Conference President – 1972–73; and Norma Thompson, Presbyterial President – 1990–91. The 1998–99 executive is Joanne Brown, President, Marie Forgrave, 1st Vice-President, and Nancy Ballard, 2nd Vice-President. The contribution of these women to the life of the congregation has been significant.

ST. JOHN'S UNITED CHURCH

In 1865, under the leadership of Rev. Isaac Weldon of the Wesleyan Methodist Conference, the first church and sheds were built on Bridge Street at the present site of St. John's United Church. By 1880, money was being raised for a new building which was completed and dedicated in 1883. The minister's salary was raised by annual pew rents. With the union of the Bible Christian, Wesleyan Methodist and Episcopal Methodist Churches in 1884, the buildings used by the Bible Christian congregation and the Methodist Episcopal congregation were closed and eventually sold. The new building became the Methodist Church of Canada. The contractor for the building was William Dunk. The structure measures sixty-six by forty-two feet with two towers eight feet square with a gallery and a semi-circular choir loft. The pews have iron ends and are ash panelled trimmed with butternut and upholstered cushions. In late 1886, a new parsonage was built and the trustees decided to fill and level the ground at the front of it and

St. John's United Church on Bridge Street West, taken sometime before 1955.

Photo from postcard collection of Campbellford/Seymour Heritage Society Archives.

add drivesheds for horses. In May 1889, the grounds were spruced up for Arbour Day by removal of stones, planting of maple trees and repairing the fence. A Mission Band was organized in 1889 as well as the Afternoon and Evening Auxiliary of the Women's Missionary Society. New steps were installed at the front of the building in 1890 and the lighting was converted to electricity. In 1905, there were twenty Sunday School classes. Sunday School concerts, garden parties, bazaars and fowl suppers formed an important part of congregational life. In 1908, the first pipe organ, installed in 1900, was replaced, thanks to a generous donation from the Ladies Aid.

In 1925, the union of the Presbyterian, Congregational, and Methodist churches was completed. Although St. Andrew's chose to remain an active Presbyterian Church, many members who had favoured the union moved to St. John's. Albert Hazell became the organist and choir leader. A new addition was built in 1928 at the rear of the main building containing the present Choir and Malcolm Lounges and the small kitchen area. In the 1940s, hymn boards and new seat cushion covers were added and the pipe organ was replaced by an electric model.

During 1955, a major expansion program added an auditorium, boardroom and washrooms. This was needed to house the huge Sunday School which filled the auditorium – nine year old and older children at ten o'clock, followed by the younger children at eleven o'clock during the church service. Midweek activities were held for Young People's Union, Young Adults, Mission Band, Epworth League, Women's Missionary Society, Women's Association and other groups. In 1960, a new kitchen was added to the north end of the auditorium as well as a new stone-faced entrance to the sanctuary.

In 1991, the Mary Johnston Trust Fund for Christian Outreach enabled the congregation to assist a member to study for the ministry. A new parsonage was purchased and the former building to the west of the church was demolished to provide parking. The new parsonage, located in Parkview Estates, has since been sold and the minister now is provided with a living allowance. In 1993, a generous bequest from Mary Margaret West in memory of her grandmother, Martha Emily Gothard West, led to the installation of an elevator to the sanctuary, a canopied entrance to the elevator from outdoors, and other renovations throughout the building. Stained glass windows have been dedicated in loving memory of former church members.

Through the years, eight young men from the congregation have been ordained for the Christian ministry – Aylmer Frederick, Percy Shafter, Alfred Trueblood, Harry Turner, Robert Nicholls, Earl Taft, Ronald Barnum and Ronald Pierce. A ninth candidate, Jamie York, is presently completing his qualifications for ordination.

As the new millennium approaches, a program rich in ministry and music dominates. Under the capable leadership of a new minister, Rev. James Cullen, and organist and choir leaders Brian Finley and Donna Bennett, the future looks bright for the congregation of St. John's.

STANWOOD UNITED CHURCH

Previous to the Methodist union in 1884, there were three Methodist classes meeting in the Stanwood area. The Bible Christians worshipped in a small frame church, sometimes called the White Church, located near the cemetery on land donated by James Jacobs at Concession 13, Lot 20, west half, about a half-mile north of the present building. The Episcopal Methodists were situated near the old blacksmith shop, just east of the store on Concession 13, Lot 20, east half, later the home of Mr. and Mrs. Albert Hay. The Wesleyan Methodists did not have a building. Their services were held in the homes of their members and in the school house. Until Zion Church was built at Petherick's Corners in 1878, many people from the Petherick's area walked to the White Church. When a minister was not available, Amos Barnum and other laymen led the service. In 1884, after a prolonged debate, these three communions united and, henceforth, were known simply as the Methodist Church. This union occurred during the pastorate of Rev. Dingman. Prior to that time, the following ministers had travelled the circuit : Rev. J.C. Ash, Rev. David Potter, and Rev. T.J. Edmison. It seems likely that the Bible Christian (White) Church closed at this time, and that the congregation of the three former denominations met in the former Methodist Episcopal building until the present church was erected.

The current building at Stanwood, also known as Bethel East, was built in 1903 on land purchased from John S. McKeown and his wife on November 18, 1902. The trustees were James McAlpine, Joseph McKeown, Billa Loucks, Hamilton Johnston, Charles D. Lawrence, Thomas H. Rowe, Daniel Loucks,

James Aikens, and James E. Johnston. The erection of the church was made possible through the generous support of the community. Not only did the members provide financial support but they also assisted in hauling stone from the Crowe River for the foundation, brick from West's Corners and lumber from Marmora. The masons were George Alfick and C. Hoskins and the carpenter was Alfred Dunk. The church was completed during the pastorate of Rev. Charles Fusee, who passed away while serving on the charge. Following the dedication service, a fowl supper was sponsored by the ladies to assist with the cost. Tables were set up in the basement and also in the new buggy shed, which had been built at the same time. Over five hundred people attended the event. Each lady of the congregation was asked to cook between ten and thirteen fowl and to bake the same number of pies. The new Stanwood Church was part of the Seymour Circuit from 1903 until 1925.

At this time, during the pastorate of Rev. C.D. Daniels, another union took place between the Methodists, the Congregationalists, and most Presbyterians, which formed the new United Church of Canada. Stanwood became part of the Springbrook Pastoral Charge along with the former Presbyterian Church at Rylstone. This placed Stanwood in the Belleville Presbytery. This affiliation continued until 1968 when Stanwood was reunited with the Seymour Pastoral Charge in the Cobourg Presbytery.

Sunday School was active throughout all these years. In 1934, Charles Lawrence was Superintendent, Allan Rutherford was Secretary and Verna Rowe was Treasurer. The teachers were: Bible Class – Daisy Sparkes, Assistant – Mr. Foley, Intermediate Class – Mrs. John Rowe and Mrs. John Lain, Junior – Mrs. Garnet Redden, and Primary – Mrs. Murray Petherick.

The first meeting of the Young People's Union, organized in 1944, was held at the home of Mr. and Mrs. Harold Simpson. Meetings were held monthly in the homes of the members as well as in the school house. In 1945, the membership was forty-six. The group was actively involved in the community until 1954.

The small cemetery on the site of the old White Church was, for many years, a free burying ground. Many of the early monuments are now gone. In more recent years, the cemetery has been improved and it is still used occasionally.

WOMEN'S ORGANIZATIONS OF STANWOOD UNITED CHURCH

There was a Ladies Aid until the 1920s when it disbanded due to lack of support. In June 1929, Daisy Sparkes, a teacher at Stanwood School, organized the Stanwood Sewing Circle. Six meetings were held that year with a membership of thirteen. The officers were: President – Daisy Sparkes; Vice-President – Mrs. Dan Brown; Secretary – Mrs. Carman Redden; Treasurer – Etta Petherick; and Organist –

Mrs. Stanley Keller. These women completed nearly 250 quilts. They were given to the Salvation Army, used in the war effort, and packed in bales to be sent to refugee areas and to the far west. The Sewing Circle continued until 1962 when the United Church Women was formed.

TABERNACLE UNITED CHURCH

The first congregation in the English Line area was a Bible Christian group, who purchased land located on Concession 3, Lot 15, on August 2, 1855 from Thomas and Grace Grills. The frame building was located just east of the present structure within the bounds of the cemetery. The 1861 federal census describes the church as "a frame chapel belonging to the Bible Christians with seating for one hundred and fifty, with a worth of $600." Trustees for this transaction were William Heard, George Stollery, James Finch, John Martin, Richard Sloggett, Joseph Grills, Nathan Grills, George Potts and Robert Davidson, all of Seymour Township.

The Bible Christians were a small Methodist sect mainly from the parishes of Devon and Cornwall, England, homeland of many settlers on Concessions 1, 2 and 3. Many probably were following the faith of their fathers. In 1833, John Hicks Eynon and his wife, Elizabeth Dart, had established five missions in the Cobourg area. By 1847, this had grown to twenty-four church buildings and numerous additional preaching places. This group was extremely evangelical with Ministry and lay personnel holding common powers and privileges. They resisted all connections between church and state and showed a preference for free prayer and gospel hymns. Even in these early times, this faction encouraged the ministry of women. The Seymour Bible Christian Circuit included these churches – Tabernacle, Campbellford, the White Church at Stanwood, Salem in Rawdon Township, one located on the Dunham property at Concession 11, Lot 8, Seymour and another on the Turner property on Concession 5, Lot 3, Seymour. Quarterly meetings were held with representation from each congregation. In 1875, the circuit, represented by trustees Joseph Temple, John Clark, and Edward Stephens, authorized Pastor Joseph Archer to purchase Lot 13, Block 11, Rear Street and a brick parsonage was constructed for the use of the circuit ministers. In 1881, it was decided to close and sell Salem Church on Concession 4, Lot 24, Rawdon Township. The Campbellford Bible Christian congregation joined St. John's Methodist Church as part of the union of 1884 and the church building was closed. The remaining congregations entered the union as well and became the Seymour Methodist Circuit.

By 1893, the Tabernacle congregation saw the need for a new building and Thomas and Grace Grills once again deeded property west of the old church for one dollar. The Tabernacle Church continued to thrive and, in 1925, joined its fellow congregations in the new United Church. Sunday School, Women's Association, Young People's Union, and the choir were active groups in the congregation. In 1956, Mrs. Harry Grills resigned as choir leader and organist, a position she had held for twenty-five years. The church shed which was no longer in use was sold in 1970 to Bill Johnston. The former Bible Christian parsonage on Doxsee Avenue, formerly Rear Street, was sold in 1988 and a new home purchased at 233 Ireton Street.

In 1968, the Seymour Charge entered into an amalgamation with St. John's in Campbellford to form the Campbellford-Seymour Charge under a team ministry. This organization ended on June 30, 1975, when Seymour once again became a separate pastoral charge from St. John's Campbellford.

The cemetery adjoining Tabernacle United Church, known as English Line Cemetery, was on land donated by Thomas and Grace Grills in 1859. It has been in continuous use since that time, with additional property acquired in 1951 and in 1965.

WOMEN'S ORGANIZATIONS AT TABERNACLE UNITED CHURCH

The Ladies Aid was organized on February 3, 1913. It provided active support for the war effort in the form of bandages, hand-knitted items, sheets, and quilts. The Ladies Aid became the Women's Association which took on additional fund raising activities by providing meals at the livestock sale barn in Hoard's Station, and bake sales at Hendrick's Resort. In 1962, the Women's Association became the United Church Women, which continues to provide service to the community.

TRENT RIVER UNITED CHURCH

The Trent River United Church was built in 1878 by the Methodist Episcopalian congregation of the area and is now the only church in the village of Trent River. At the time of construction, the Methodists were divided into three groups: the Methodist Episcopalians, the Wesleyan Methodists, and the Bible Christians. Each group had its own church building in Seymour West. In 1884, these groups amalgamated to become the Methodist Church.

The Methodist Episcopalians were initially located at the corner of Concession 14, Lot 5, on present-day Highway 30. When they moved to the new church in Trent River in 1878, the old building was no longer used. On January 5, 1903, the current owners, John Dunning and his wife, sold five and one-half acres to John A. Ferris, Matthew W. March, and Richard Bartlett, the trustees of I.O.O.F. #248.

On August 1, 1874, George Gibson and his wife, Agnes sold land on Concession 13, Lot 6, to the Trustees of the Tilton Seymour Congregation of the Wesleyan Methodist Church. The Trustee Board consisted of Adam Davidson, Peter Killbanks,

Oliver Tyler, Thomas Henry Scriver, Nelson Wood, Duncan Thompson, James Thompson, William Wood, Thomas Wood, and William Henry Davidson. This church was on the same site as Centre Cemetery and was locally referred to as Wesley or Centre Church. In 1925, all the Methodist congregations became part of the United Church and Centre Church was closed. The cemetery continues to operate.

The Bible Christians initially worshipped in a building on the Henry Dunham farm opposite Clark's Cemetery on Concession 11, Lot 9. This land was a Crown Patent, dated July 8, 1869, for half an acre to Archibald Thompson, Neil McCulloch, John Clark, Archibald Clark, and Neil McNaughton, Trustees of Clark's Bible Christian Church. However, the structure was obviously there earlier, as the 1861 census describes "a Bible Christian Church, built of wood, capable of holding 100 persons." The adjacent cemetery, known as Clark's, was opened prior to 1863 but has seldom been used in recent years.

Other Methodist congregations operated in the area and some of their members became part of the Trent River Methodist Church after 1884. Bethel Methodist Church was built in 1887 on the Longmuir farm on Concession 11, Lot 7, during the pastorate of Rev. Hie. It was part of the Hastings Circuit. In 1891, William and James West, the current owners of the land, sold the south half to trustees Edward Stanbury, John McCulloch, Jessie Campney, John Phillips, and William McConnell for $460. This church operated until 1928, shortly after the formation of the United Church. The brick building was later demolished by John Brown.

A Free Methodist Church also operated in Trent River. On October 24, 1896, Eliza Ann Stacey Free, gave land on Concession 14, Lot 6, for its construction to Clark Johnson, Bruce E. Heard, and Ira Loucks, Trustees of the Trent Bridge Congregation of the Free Methodist Church of Ontario. Further information is unavailable at this time about the fate of this congregation.

The exterior walls of the present Trent River United Church are bricked in a very attractive relief pattern, outlining simple Gothic windows. Buttresses, inset with limestone dripcaps, reinforce the side walls. The base of the bell tower forms the entrance vestibule. Angled brick columns flank the door. The steeple no longer exists. The interior of the church is plastered, and the ceiling decorated with a plaster molding, which encloses an elaborate medallion. In 1878, the church had a great steel stove which accommodated cord wood lengths, and two long strings of stove pipes heated the church. John Ruttan, the leader of the young men's classes, organized a wood bee every winter with all of his boys, to cut and haul to the church enough wood for the following winter. John Ruttan was caretaker, and fired up this big stove. Over the years, additional renovations were made to the chimney, the front door, the eavestroughing, the windows, the vestibule, the dining hall, and the heating system.

In 1978, the Trent River United Church celebrated its hundredth birthday with Rev. Asbell as the guest speaker. The centennial committee was very active, organizing a variety show and a float for Norwood Fair Parade. All former choir members were invited to join the centennial choir, accompanied by Wallace J. Brown. After the church service, everyone was invited to Knapp's Museum, now The Pine Cone, for a lunch and social time. Roy and Doris Glenn provided the music on the grounds. Frances Brown and Thomas Wight, the seniors, were invited to cut and serve the centennial cake.

In 1984, the little church became a designated site under the Ontario Heritage Act as a building of both architectural and historical importance. This made the church eligible for restoration funds from the Province of Ontario and its important architectural features are protected. Funds were received to repair the ceiling of the church which was restored to its original style by the Dudleys of Warkworth.

The United Church Women have always provided strong financial support for the church, holding pot luck dinners, strawberry socials and fall suppers. Some of the ministers who served on the Havelock-Trent River Charge were R. B. Denike, William H. Learoyd, William Tucker, Joseph Rae, George McColl, Charles H. Coon, Thomas W. Joliffe, Isaac Puffer, Henry McQuade, Joseph C. Bell, William Johnston, Joseph Real, Charles DeMill, C. Adams, E. Seymour, W. Archer, S. Kemp, A. McLaughlin, J. Wilkinson, F. Vanderburg, A. Newman, H. Allen, R. Beech, J. King, J. Hicks, P. P. Miedema, William Fletcher, T. Asbell, G. Phillips, J. Hopkins, A. Doerksen. In June of 1997, Rev. Barbara McMath became the minister and continues in that role.

ZION UNITED CHURCH, PETHERICK'S CORNERS

Zion Episcopal Methodist Church was built in 1878 on Concession 9, Lot 20, on land donated by William Petherick. The building of the church was made possible through generous donations from members of the community. Many local men hauled brick and stone as well as giving financial assistance. James Benor was the carpenter. William Reynolds constructed the foundation of stone with the upper structure of brick from West's Brickyard. The first Trustees were Gilbert Wright, Daniel Petherick, William Cleugh, John Arnold, William Petherick Jr., James Watson, and Edward Hall. After the dedication of the structure, a meeting was called and a subscription was taken up to cover the entire debt of the church. A lunch was served to each one in a paper bag consisting of an apple, bun and cake. Because the church was located on a hill, the construction committee did not realize that the ground was actually quite wet. As a result, the walls settled and cracked. John Bailey, who had a shop on the corner, offered to make and install support rods. The spire which was originally on the building was also removed to relieve stress on the walls. John Simpson and Dan Petherick performed this task for five dollars. Because the church is located on a windy site, there is a story that the steeple took off and landed upside down in the old cemetery.

In 1884, the three Methodist sects united to form the Methodist Church, and Zion was one of four churches on the Seymour Circuit. The minister was responsible for three services each Sunday and one congregation would have a local preacher, such as Mr. Winters or Amos Barnum. Mr. Winters had an evangelistic club of young men who sometimes came to Zion to conduct the service on an unstaffed Sunday. Prayer meetings were held every Wednesday night. Amos Barnum usually led the prayer meeting as well as requesting testimonies before the Sunday service. Ministers on the Seymour Methodist Circuit were Rev. Garett J. Dingman, J. Anderson Chapman, George Dunkley, William B. Tucker, Robert L. Edwards, Dan Williams, Richard Courtice, Moses Metherell, William J. Sanders, Charles Fusee, Harry Frost, Francis W. White, William J. Wetherall, John Bunner, Milton L. Hinton and John Glover. During the pastorate of George Dunkley, a revival service was conducted by the pastor which lasted for twelve weeks, with crowds present every night.

The church was first lit with about sixteen coal oil lamps with one being a chandelier in the centre holding four lamps. Heat was provided by two wood burning box stoves. The lamps were later replaced with electricity and the wood stoves with oil stoves. The ceiling of the sanctuary was lowered. A shed was built with a private stall for the minister's horse. Before the advent of the automobile, entire families would ride to church in democrats or buggies. The democrats were high, so two stands were built with steps to enable the women to get in and out. Many people walked several miles to attend services. There was also a small kitchen, built at the back of the building, where tea meetings were held.

Sunday School was very active for many years with a record attendance of ninety. Superintendents included Amos Barnum, Thomas Fry, John Arnold, William Petherick Jr., Will Forde, Aylmer Petherick, and Karen Ingram. In 1952, the church was filled to capacity for the dedication service and opening of the new Sunday School Hall. Mrs. Bick, the minister's wife, started the Women's Association or Ladies Aid. Mrs. John Simpson was President for twenty-five years and missed only one meeting because of a death in the family. Young People's Union was also active throughout the years.

In 1925, the congregation entered the new United Church. Ministers since that time have been Charles D. Daniels, Fred G. MacTavish, Dr. Reddick, J.R. Bick, P.J. Lambert, Gordon Whitehorne, Lance Woods, Gordon Ballantyne, Wendell Sedgwick, Margaret Pogue, Donald Jones, Clive Wilson, Winnifred Bridges, David Spivey, Ross Bruleigh, Earl Taft, and David Shepherd.

In 1996, a decision was made to close Zion Church because of declining attendance and the need for renovations. At the last service on April 14, 1996, Rev. Gordon Whitehorne described the closing as a "casualty of the times."

No dates are available for the old cemetery beside the church but it seems likely that it was used from the 1860s or earlier until 1886, when the wet ground proved unsatisfactory and the new Zion Cemetery opened on the opposite side of the road. Until 1910, there were two separate sets of trustees for the church and the cemetery. In 1910, the graveyard trustees resigned and their responsibilities were assumed by the trustees of the church, who continue to look after the cemetery now that the church is closed. The cemetery continues in use to the present time.

⌐ Roman Catholic ⌐

ST. MARY'S ROMAN CATHOLIC CHURCH

The third oldest Roman Catholic parish in Northumberland County is St. Mary's of Campbellford. The parish presently includes the Township of Seymour with the exception of the northern area in Concessions 13 and 14, and the area south of Concession 3 and west of the Trent River.

The first Masses were celebrated by an itinerant priest, Father Vaughan, in 1846 in a school house and later in the farm house of Michael O'Sullivan. In addition to the visitations of Father Vaughan, curates of St. Michael's Parish of Belleville served the area. In 1847, Father Bernard Higgins was given charge of the areas known today as Campbellford, Hastings, Warkworth, and Norwood, his place of residence being Hastings. He celebrated Mass every second Sunday in Campbellford and Warkworth. Father John Quirk, pastor from 1862 to 1879, built the first church in Campbellford. In 1879, the Missions of Campbellford and Warkworth were detached from Hastings, and Campbellford was raised to the status of parish with Warkworth as a mission. The first pastor of the new entity was Father D. J. Casey who built the present rectory. In 1894, Warkworth was detached from Campbellford and affiliated with the Parish of Burnley. In 1895, Father W. J. McCloskey became the third Pastor of Campbellford. During his pastorate, two native sons of the parish were ordained to the priesthood in St. Mary's Church by Bishop R. A. O'Connor – Rev. Joseph O'Sullivan on December 19, 1896, and Rev. Francis J. O'Sullivan on November 4, 1897. Father McCloskey helped to acquire a bell which was blessed by Bishop O'Connor on October 20, 1898.

During the early hours of Christmas morning, 1899, fire destroyed St. Mary's Church. An altar stone, a chalice, and vestments were sent by train from Peterborough to Campbellford in time for the celebration of Mass in a hall at eleven o'clock on Christmas Day. On the day following Christmas, Bishop

O'Connor came to Campbellford to attend a meeting of the parishioners and preliminary plans were made for the rebuilding of St. Mary's. At this meeting, fourteen hundred dollars was pledged for restoration and in two weeks the fund had reached a total of six thousand dollars. Thomas Hanley of Belleville was engaged to prepare plans for a church of brick construction, and later the contract for building was awarded to Richard Sheehy of Peterborough who recommended the use of stone instead of brick.

The contract price was approximately $14,000, which covered sub-contracts for carpentry, plastering and painting to James Benor of Campbellford. By May 20, 1900, construction was sufficiently advanced for the laying of the cornerstone by Bishop O'Connor. The ceremony was attended by three thousand people and the sermon for the occasion was preached by Father R. J. Teefy, Superior of St. Michael's College. On November 4, 1900, the completed church, built and equipped at a final cost of $21,000, was dedicated by Bishop O'Connor. Built on a site commanding a view of the town, the church is one hundred and twenty feet in length, and fifty feet in width. It has two towers, one capped with a spire which rises one hundred and thirty feet from the ground. On the occasion of the dedication ceremony, the sermon was preached by Bishop McEvay of London, a for-

St. Mary's Roman Catholic Church, dedicated November 4, 1900 by Bishop O'Connor of Peterborough.

Photo courtesy of Ann Rowe.

mer priest of the Diocese of Peterborough. Fourteen hundred persons crowded the church, its gallery and vestry on that memorable day.

In August 1903, Father McCloskey died in Campbellford and was buried beside the church which he had built. In 1911, Father Whibbs built a frame chapel at Healey Falls to serve the spiritual needs of the labourers who were working on the Trent Canal. On June 18, the chapel was blessed by Bishop R. A. O'Connor. At a social on July 27, 1911, the mortgage on the church was burned in the presence of Bishop O'Connor, the original debt having been liquidated in eleven years. In 1912, the Mission of Keene was attached to Campbellford for a period of two years. In 1921, Father Whibbs purchased the property for the convent and school.

The Rector of St. Peter's Cathedral, Father C. J. Phelan, became the fifth Pastor of Campbellford. During his term a new lighting system was installed in the church, the interior was completely redecorated, and debt incurred since the retirement of the original debt was wiped out. Father Phelan died suddenly on December 13, 1934, and on May 17, 1935, Father V. J. McAuley, Pastor of Ennismore, was named to succeed him. A few months later, Father McAuley observed the Silver Jubilee of his ordination to the priesthood. During his seven year tenure, the landscaping of church property was completed. In 1937, the parish was host to the Diocesan Eucharistic Congress and, in the following year, to the Holy Name Rally for the Southern Deanery of the Diocese.

In 1942, Father Joseph Collins, formerly Pastor in the northern Parishes of Parry Sound and Trout Creek, was appointed to Campbellford. During his pastorate, the church heating system was improved and numerous improvements were made to the parish house. On October 17, 1945, Father Collins observed the Silver Jubilee of his ordination to the priesthood. The observance was deferred from June until October because of the consecration and installation of Peterborough's seventh Bishop, Gerald Berry, in June 1945. On May 31, 1947, a native son of the parish, Rev. Joseph O'Sullivan, was ordained to the priesthood by Bishop Berry in Peterborough and celebrated his First Mass in St. Mary's Church. In April 1948, Father Collins was transferred to St. Michael's Parish of Cobourg.

Father J. C. Moloney, former Pastor of Huntsville, succeeded Father Collins. During his pastorate, the parish cemetery received considerable attention: a new fence was erected, a mortuary chapel built, and the grounds landscaped. The former rectory kitchen was abandoned in order to conserve heat, but later converted into an assembly room which eventually became an emergency classroom. A program of church repair and improvement was begun and continued over a period of years. After the construction and opening of the new St. Mary's School in 1956, the convent of the Sisters of St. Joseph was renovated and enlarged at a cost of $13,000. On June 21, 1953, a native son of the parish, Rev. Thomas Hoey, of the

Society of Jesus, was ordained to the priesthood in Toronto. During the latter part of his pastorate of fourteen years, Father Moloney was absent from the parish for two months during which time he visited the Holy Land. The parish was placed in charge of the Redemptorist Fathers during his absence. In September 1962, Father Moloney requested a smaller parish and was transferred to Norwood.

Father Joseph Walsh, former Pastor of the Parishes of Kinmount and Wooler, became Campbellford's ninth pastor. He placed the assembly room at the rectory at the disposal of the School Board. In 1965, in keeping with the directives of the Second Vatican Council, a new altar facing the congregation was erected and a public address system was installed. At the close of the year 1969, the parish statistics recorded one hundred and seventy families and six hundred and eighty persons in the parish. In June 1971, in a diocesan reorganization of clergy, Father Walsh was transferred to the Parish of Downeyville, and Father James Houlihan, former Pastor of Lakefield and St. Anne's of Peterborough, was appointed to Campbellford.

In the autumn of 1971, Father Houlihan initiated a renovation of the sanctuary of St. Mary's Church according to the requirements of the new liturgy. The main altar, the side altars, and Communion railing, were removed. A platform was constructed to accommodate seats for the presiding priest and the servers. In the foreground of the sanctuary, a new altar was installed with lecterns on either side and the side altars were replaced by a Repository for the Blessed Sacrament and a new Baptismal Font. Panelling of red oak was installed. The altars, Baptismal Font, seating accommodation, and lecterns are made from red oak, the design and execution being the work of Gordon Burns. The entire sanctuary floor was carpeted and a few pews were removed to provide greater accessibility to the centre and side aisles of the church. The Stations of the Cross were reduced in size and painted in one colour to blend with the church walls.

Father Houlihan left St. Mary's in October 1976, and the pastors who succeeded him over the following years were: Father Vernon Perdue – October 1976 to January, 1981; Father John J. Hickey – January 1981 to 1988; Father Clarke J. Hudson, 1988 to June 1990; and Father Clair L. Hickson, June 1990 to the present.

The burial ground for this church is located between First Street and Burnbrae Road on the eastern edge of Campbellford.

ST. MARY'S CATHOLIC WOMEN'S LEAGUE

The Catholic Women's League was organized nationally in June 1920 under the patronage of the Canadian Conference of Catholic bishops. The Catholic Women's League at St. Mary's Church was chartered in 1927. The branch was organized on October 30, 1927 and the first president was Mary O'Sullivan, the mother of local resident, Paul O'Sullivan and Father Joe O'Sullivan, the former rector of St.

Jerome's Church in Warkworth. The rest of the executive consisted of: Chaplain, Rev. C. J. Phelan; First Vice-President, Mrs. James Kerr; Second Vice-President, Marguerite Anderson; Third Vice-President, Mrs. Peter Corkery; Recording Secretary, Kathleen O'Shaughnessy; Corresponding Secretary, Mrs. Matt Mulhearn; Treasurer, Mrs. P. J. O'Connor. In 1931, the Diocesan Convention of the Catholic Women's League was held at St. Mary's. Marguerite Anderson, President of St. Mary's branch, occupied the chair and welcomed the delegates. In 1937, a newspaper article noted that a euchre party was held in the Catholic Women's League rooms in the Irwin Block. The gentlemen's prize was won by Owen Brahaney and the Ladies' award by Mrs. Robert Lee. That year the organization also held a tea at the home of Mrs. James Heffernan on Grand Road. The hostess was assisted by Mrs. T. Forestell, Mrs. D. N. O'Keefe, Mrs. Edward O'Connor, and Celestine Forestell, and Kay Hoey. Mrs. P. J. O'Connor and Mrs. Edward Forestell poured tea.

In 1940, the Catholic Women's League elected the following officers: Honorary Chaplain, Reverend J. C. Moloney; President, Helena Smith; First Vice-President, Mrs. F. G. Macoun; Second Vice-President, Mrs. Howard Wilson; Third Vice-President, Mrs. S. J. Bibby; Recording Secretary, Mrs. Russell Long; Corresponding Secretary, Mrs. Emmett Kelleher; Treasurer, Kathleen Doherty; Councillors, Mrs. Andrew Clarke, Gladys Monaghan, Mrs. Ed. Collins, Mrs. Charles Forestell, Mrs. Allan Coveney, and Mrs. Joe Kelleher. By the 1950s, the League's meeting rooms were in the Turner Block where they sponsored regular bingo games as fund raisers. In 1951, Kathleen Doherty became President, succeeding Helen Smith. In 1962, it was noted in a newspaper article that the Catholic Women's League held a Citizenship Tea in St. Mary's Parish Council rooms. The President, Mrs. E. Kelleher, welcomed the many guests.

In 1977, St. Mary's Catholic Women's League marked the fiftieth anniversary of its charter. The anniversary Mass was celebrated by Bishop James Doyle, assisted by Revs. V. Perdue, J. Houlihan, J. Walsh, J. O'Sullivan, C. Kay, and J. Scott. The lay reader was Maureen Dikun, and those participating in the Offertory procession were Marie Dunkley, Vivian Pirri, and Mrs. John Clancy.

Presently St. Mary's Catholic Women's League has 104 members who work together to foster the ideals of their organization – "For God and Canada."

The group raises fund through an annual Christmas bazaar, luncheons, rummage sales, and the provision of lunches at Hoard's Station Sale Barn. Donations are made to community organizations, St. Mary's Church, needy families, and fire victims. Children at St. Mary's School are also assisted in their preparation for receiving the Sacraments.

The 1999–2000 Honorary members are: Helen Calnan, Irene Hawley, Ann McKinnon, Jean Mahoney, and Kaye Kelleher.

The executive for 1999–2000 are:

President	Pamela Goudreault
Past President	Dianne Craig
First Vice-President	Rosemarie Boxell
Second Vice-President	Christine O'Brien
Secretary	Peggy Duck
Treasurer	Monica McKelvie

~ Baptist ~

CAMPBELLFORD BAPTIST CHURCH

In 1873, only a small number of the inhabitants in the area declared their religion to be Baptist. For a few years, they met informally in an office on the second storey of the "Fletcher Block." The location of this block is somewhat unclear, but it is thought to be the building known later as the Irwin Block, in which the Fishing Hole Drop-in Centre is currently located. In 1884, the *Canadian Baptist* magazine carried an article written by William Peer, who shortly thereafter became the first pastor of the Campbellford Baptist Church. In the article, he wrote:

> "The few Baptists that live in and around Campbellford...[a] thriving town of over two thousand inhabitants, have banded themselves together and purchased a magnificent brick house in which to worship. The house was built at a cost of over four thousand dollars, and has a splendid basement for Sunday School purposes."

W. A. Kingston, in *The Light of Other Days*, notes:

> "In 1884 when the Methodist Churches united, the Methodist Episcopal building was sold to the Baptist congregation for $2,000. The church was prosperous and the building was shortly paid for."

In an early church minute book, on October 9, 1884, the following appeared:

> "The opening services of the church in Campbellford took place on Sunday, September 28th. The day was very unpropitious, but the attendance was excellent in all the services. The Rev. E. W. Dadson preached with freshness and vigor morning and evening, and the Rev. Geo. Richardson talked about 'The Believers Riches,' in the afternoon, in such a way as to delight and profit all who heard him. It is quite a neat building, and not badly situated. This is a very excellent move, and we trust that our Brother Peer will realize all his hopes."

From 1884 until September 1995, the congregation of the Campbellford Baptist Church met in the building at 67 Queen Street, formerly known as George Street. In the early 1900s, it was necessary to remove the steeple.

In 1986, at the spring business meeting of the congregation a Long Range Planning Committee was formed "to look into possibilities regarding the acquiring of larger facilities." Due to the limited size of the Queen Street property, and no possibility of purchasing land adjacent to the church, searching for larger facilities was a priority. The Committee was formally appointed at the Annual Meeting in January 1987, and over the next four to five years searched for a suitable property. On October 1st, 1993, the Co-op building became available. The main building was the right size, and the land was adequate for parking. Additional buildings could be constructed at a later time.

The 1993 Congregational Meeting approved a motion stating: "That the congregation of the Campbellford Baptist Church approves the purchase of the Co-op property from United Co-Operatives of Ontario on the west side of Grand Road, known as 166 Grand Road, Campbellford...and for use as a church property, ..., dated November 26, 1993. Carried." On March 25, 1994, the transfer of the deed took place, and the Trustees, on behalf of the congregation of the Campbellford Baptist Church, assumed ownership.

On Sunday, March 27, 1994, a "Brief Service of Thanksgiving, Prayer and Dedication," was held at the newly acquired property on the occasion of the "possession of land and buildings..., the future new home of the Campbellford Baptist Church." Throughout 1994 and 1995, renovations proceeded with over 13,000 volunteer hours donated by members of the congregation, community, and friends. On Saturday, June 4, 1994 over thirty people were on hand to rebuild the "Western Wall" of the building. Work began before 8 AM, and the last piece of scaffolding was taken down at 8 PM. The last worship service in the former building was held on Sunday, September 10, 1995. The building was full, with the congregation sitting on borrowed chairs, the pews having been removed for installation in the new building.

The first worship service at the new location was held on September 17, 1995, with a large attendance. The Grand Opening was held on October 22, 1995 on the occasion of the celebration of the 111th Anniversary, including people from the community, other churches, and sister Baptist churches in the Trent Valley Association and Convention. The over six hundred fifty people in attendance provided an offering in excess of $12,000 to be used for payment on the mortgage.

On May 10, 1996, the Queen Street building, home of the congregation for 111 years was sold to "Cathy's Floral Design," a flower shop owned by Cathy Hare.

⌒ Other Denominations ⌒

GLAD TIDINGS PENTECOSTAL CHURCH

The Pentecostal Church in Campbellford began in 1935 in the form of home prayer meetings. In addition, members of the Pentecostal church in Peterborough held tent meetings which were met with a favourable response from the community. In the fall of 1939, the District Officials of the Pentecostal Assemblies of Canada organized the Campbellford congregation. In 1940, property was purchased on Bridge Street West and a basement church was built. Many tons of stone were hauled in from the country to build the foundation of the existing church building, and exposed portions of those first walls reveal how well they were built. In 1951, the church launched a building program to enlarge the existing basement church and build an upstairs auditorium. Over the years, the property has been expanded for parking, with a total renovation and expansion of the church facility in 1974. In 1988, a new rear entrance was added as well as modernization of the complete facility. In 1997–98, the church property received further improvements, and a donation of land to the west for future growth and development.

This is a family church with ministry available to all age groups, including such programs as King's Kids, Youth Group, and Adult Bible Study. There are also Women's Ministries and Men's Fellowships.

PLYMOUTH BRETHREN (GOSPEL HALL)

The movement known most often as The Brethren had its roots in Dublin, Ireland, about 1830. The local work of this group commenced in 1891 with the pitching of a tent in the area of an old tannery beside the river. For three successive summers, the gospel was preached under canvas by leaders W.H. McClure, W.H. Hunter, and Mr. Moneypenny. The resulting converts formed the nucleus of the present assembly. The small congregation secured rented space in the J.A. Irwin Block where they continued to meet until 1920.

Land on Rear Street was purchased by John Diamond from Robert Linton and the present frame building was erected. John Diamond, a retired farmer from the Norham area, was an elder for many years in the Gospel Hall assembly. Other surnames associated with this denomination were: Diamond, Clark, Thain, McDonald, Kennedy, Miller, Bayes, Gibson, Scarlett, Patton, Irwin, McNaughton, Owens, Hall, and Sinclair.

On Sunday, Sunday School was held first, followed by the Breaking of the Bread and an evening service. There was also a midweek service.

FREE METHODIST CHURCH

The Campbellford Free Methodist congregation appears in 1906 as part of the Warkworth Circuit under the leadership of Amanda Hughes and Gertrude Pratt. Initial gatherings were probably prayer meetings in the home of Ira and Emma Loucks, staunch supporters. About 1907, the congregation was organized with seven members under the district chairman, A.H. Norrington, who had married Amanda Hughes. With the decline of the lumber industry, the Loucks family moved from Healey Falls to Campbellford and services were held in a hall over the Smith and Russell Feed Store at the corner of Bridge Street and Doxsee Avenue. In 1908, Gertrude Pratt and Aggie Kearns served the congregation under the official Warkworth–Campbellford pastor, Charles Cunningham. By 1909, Campbellford was a separate circuit assigned to Ethel Davey.

The congregation continued to grow under Kate Clark from 1915 to 1917. In 1917, the congregation erected their first building, a cement block structure on Queen Street, south of the cenotaph. Kate Clark went on to Galt where she died suddenly in November 1917. It was felt that the burden of the new church construction and her untiring work in the Sunday School had been responsible for her early demise. The building was destroyed in a disastrous fire in January 1953. A decision was made not to rebuild on the existing site but to construct a new building on 67 Ranney Street North which officially opened on October 17, 1954.

The Free Methodist Church, located on Ranney Street North.

Photo from Campbellford/Seymour Heritage Society archives, originally from the files of the Campbellford Herald.

JEHOVAH'S WITNESSES

Early meetings of the Jehovah's Witnesses were held in a store on Bridge Street West. In 1970, a hall was built on Victoria Street to house the congregation. The donation of four acres of land was the first step in assisting the group to build a new hall in Percy Township on County Road 25. On an August weekend in 1993, hundreds of Jehovah's Witnesses from across eastern Ontario helped their brothers and sisters from Campbellford area construct the new building. Many of the seven hundred volunteers who turned out were skilled tradespeople. The new hall was sufficiently enclosed that an abbreviated worship service was conducted on Sunday afternoon. The new hall is home to about eighty members. It has a seating capacity of two hundred and includes a library and training centre.

SAVED ARMY

In 1884, the Saved Army announced its intention to come to the village of Campbellford. It arrived in the summer of that year and held meetings in the Music Hall. The Saved Army was a revival group of Methodists who worked in co-operation with the local Methodist clergy. Lieutenant Pengelly was in charge of the Campbellford events along with two young women. The services drew large attendance or 'audiences'. Services included 'knee drill' and parades were held to local churches. The Saved Army left the area after one year due to lack of financial support.

SALVATION ARMY

The Salvation Army was founded in England in 1865 by William Booth, a former Methodist minister. In 1882, he sent an American officer to London, Ontario, to launch the Canadian campaign. The Salvation Army arrived in Campbellford in the spring of 1885 and rented as their barracks the former Bible Christian Church on Rear Street. Huge crowds of up to 800 were lined up to attend the meeting in April 1885. Captain Wright and "Faithful Nellie" were the leaders. In November 1885, the old building was sold to the English Church to be used as a Parish Hall. In the summer of 1886, the Salvation Army used the old roller skating rink and also rooms over Irwin's Store as a base. In 1888, a former livery stable at 92 Bridge Street East was purchased. The first officers to be stationed in the new barracks were Captain Lottie Ogilvie and Lt. Edith Hartley. This location is still in use. A rented house was at first used for the officers but, in 1902, the roof of the hall was raised to provide living quarters on the second level. Unfortunately, the newly created area was cold and damp and was vacated soon afterward.

Open air meetings were common and the Salvation Army Band was often seen in parades and on the local street corners. In July 1891, a special camp meeting was held in Beattie's Grove on Highway 30 with two daily meetings and four on Sunday. It was usual to hold daily meetings every evening, and Thursday and Saturday were the nights for parading the streets. A regular meeting was also held on the English Line. Both instrumental and vocal music were an important part of worship. Singing was often accompanied by brass instruments, bass drum, and the timbrel or tambourine. Many converts joined the ranks. An important vow of temperance was part of the commitment. In 1884, the War Cry became the official publication for the Salvation Army in Canada and Bermuda.

Officers were constantly on the move to new assignments. Some of the names from early years were Captain and Mrs. Houselander, Captain and Mrs. Sharpe, Captain Charlong, Captain Matthews, and Lieutenant Morgan. In 1934, the Army celebrated its 50th anniversary of work in the town.

In the 1950s, after the barracks was raised, a new basement created, and renovations completed throughout, it became the location for Vacation Bible School for the community. With the support of the larger community, the Salvation Army is particularly active in disaster relief. In addition, Christmas hampers have been distributed in the community with the support of many organizations and individuals. They operate a used clothing store on 53 Bridge Street East. The annual Red Shield Appeal and, more recently, Coats For Kids, also receive wide support. In 1994, the local corps celebrated its 110th year of continuous service to the community.

THE CHURCH OF JESUS CHRIST
OF LATTER DAY SAINTS

In the year 1832, the Church of Jesus Christ of Latter Day Saints was organized. That same year there were several missionaries of the church in Canada. Approximately one hundred years later, there were congregations large enough to form branches of The Church of Jesus Christ of Latter Day Saints in the Southern Ontario area. Over the years, these congregations have grown and cities such as Belleville, Trenton, and Peterborough have had to expand their buildings to hold the numbers of members attending.

On January 26, 1992, the number of people travelling from the Campbellford area, to attend services in one of these other areas, was such that it was deemed appropriate to commence holding services in Campbellford. The first meetings were held in the Hillcrest Public School until the former Allen Insurance office space on Doxsee Avenue South was made available. In the near future, a building is to be erected on land purchased on part of Concession 6, Lot 12, Township of Seymour, and part of block 106, Town of Campbellford.

The branch was organized with Gary Rowan serving as its first Branch President, Osborne Turnbull as first councillor and Douglas Shepherd as second councillor. The first official meetings were held February 2, 1992, with thirty-eight people in attendance. Since then, the church has experienced growth and a semi-permanent location for meetings was established in a business plaza on Doxsee Avenue South.. Since the church has no paid ministry, the Branch President, Tim Holt, represents the head of the local branch, with Andrew Turnbull as first councillor, Osborne Turnbull as Sunday School President, and Ronald Solmes as first councillor. Margaret Ann Rowan is President of the Relief Society and Wendy Solmes is first councillor. Christine McLaughlin is Young Women's President, with Jennie Peters as first councillor and Christine McCartney as second councillor. Carl Stoltz is Young Men's President, Rachel Shepherd is Primary President, and Deborah Holt is the Seminary Teacher, conducting scripture study for high school youth. Programs during the week as well as on Sunday ensure that all members of the branch are supported and encouraged to grow and fulfill their individual potential.

An important part of the Church mission is genealogical research. On January 7, 2000, a Family History Centre opened in Campbellford. Researchers can now access the FamilySearch data bases and order microfilmed materials from the main library of the Church in Salt Lake City.

~ Cemeteries ~

MOUNT PLEASANT CEMETERY

This is the largest cemetery in the area, with burials from most Protestant denominations. When the cemetery originally opened in 1878, it was a private company owned by McCombs. In 1948, it became a registered burial site operated by an elected board.

ADDITIONAL BURIAL SITES

Several other small cemeteries are located in Seymour Township. The Keller Cemetery, on Concession 12, Lot 15, overlooking Healey Falls is the burial site for five generations of descendants of Christopher Keller, one of the original settlers in this area. The property was given to the Kellers by Thomas Rowe who owned the adjoining farm. The cemetery is still owned and maintained by the Keller family.

The Atkinson Cemetery, a private burial ground overlooking Crowe Bay, is located on land that was a Crown Grant to Thomas Atkinson in 1832 on Concession 8, Lot 15.

Polmont Cemetery on Concession 13, Lot 5, Govan Cemetery on Concession 9, Lot 9, Ivey Cemetery on Concession 7, Lot 5, Bell Cemetery on Concession 8, Lot 6, as well as many other unmarked pioneer burial sites dot the

Township of Seymour. Three known locations are the Macoun burial site on Concession 10, Lot 7, the Hoard family site on Concession 2, Lot 26, and the Dunk burial lot on Concession 7, Lot 18. Grave markers from these known locations have been removed to nearby cemeteries. Transcripts of most of these burial sites and the other cemeteries mentioned above are available in written and computerized format at the Campbellford / Seymour Heritage Centre.

ENDNOTES

1 Land owned by a parish church was referred to as Glebe.

Chapter Eight

$\mathcal{O}$rganizations

~ Service Clubs ~

CAMPBELLFORD KINSMEN CLUB

The Kinsmen Club of Campbellford was formed in August 1944, at Villa Trent. Twenty-five members signed the charter, with Forrest Dennis as President, Jack Fink as Vice-President, Ken Kingston as Secretary, W. J. Callaghan as Treasurer, and Roy Barnum, Roy Smith, and Harold Dooher as Directors. Other presidents in the 1940s included Joe Smith, W. J. Callaghan, Gord Walroth and Paul O'Sullivan. The first major project was a street dance held on July 20, 1944. Since its beginning, the club has been active in Blood Donor Clinics, Salvation Army activities, and Hallowe'en parties for children. Milk for Britain was a big project in 1944. The first Kinsmen hockey team was coached by Owen Hendy and played its first game in the old Davidson Arena on December 5, 1944.

In the early 1950s, the club began the Turkey Bingo which is still held annually. School bus trips for grades 7 and 8 to Toronto and Ottawa in the spring were also started. Presidents in the 1950s included John Hill, Ray Hall, Cyril Johnson, Jack Tinney, Dante Pace, Bev Collins, Bert Greenhalgh, Francis Barton, and Graydon Bell. During this time, the Club also supplied playground equipment to schools in the area. They initiated the Century Club, a fund raising project. The Kinsmen purchased their first hospital bed and wheelchair for their loan cupboard in 1957.

Presidents during the 1960s included Edgar Brown, Garry Holmes, Dante Pace, Gord Gilders, Tom Holmes, Gerald Locke, Keith Stephens, Keith Algar, and Doug Stickwood. The early 1960s saw the club membership drop to five, but hard work corrected this deficiency. During 1963–64 it was decided to build the new Kinsmen Ball Park on the fair grounds. The annual Kinsmen Stag was first held in October of 1964. The club officially adopted red jackets as their club costume. New bleachers were installed at the ball park in 1967. The Kinsmen weekly bingo was started on Wednesday, October 12, 1967. That year, $1,405.68 was spent on playground equipment and $900 on bus trips.

During the 1970s, the following were presidents: Brian Runions, Glen Splaine, Bill Mallory, Don Pearson, and Bob Reid. The Kinsmen took part in two industrial home shows, during which Roxanne Rothwell and Eunice Chrysler, both Miss Kinsmen, were crowned Miss Home Show. In 1971–72, new air conditioners were installed in the Senior Citizens' rooms. The Club also held its first Annual Winter Carnival which has since become an annual event. The Kinsmen started a T.V. Bingo with the co-operation of Redden's Radio and T.V. Plans were made to construct a building at the ball park to house change rooms, washrooms and a canteen. This was completed in 1973–74 at a cost of over $14,000. In addition, the Club donated $5,000 towards the new Community Swimming Pool. In 1974–75, the lights at the Ball Park were rewired. Additions were purchased for the Kinsmen loan cupboard which now consisted of over fifteen wheelchairs, hospital beds, commode chairs, and other equipment.

In 1985, the Kinsmen decided to rename the ballpark in memory of Brian Runions. The following article appeared in the Campbellford Herald:

"The Campbellford Kinsmen Club plans to rededicate and rename its ballpark "The Brian Runions Park" in honor of its longtime member who died last June.

Gene Brahaney, who is organizing the ceremony to rename the park, says he hopes the event will serve as a "lasting tribute to one of our community who so tirelessly worked for the community's betterment through his work in Kinsmen activities, minor hockey and softball, the Salvation Army, Campbellford Figure Skating Club and Campbellford District High School.

Those of us who have been blessed to know 'Shack' as a friend since high school days don't need to be reminded what Brian stood for," Brahaney says.

Initial plans are for the ceremony to be held next year during the Victoria Day weekend in conjunction with the Kinsmen Spring Dance and mixed slo-pitch tournament. Brahaney said his committee welcomes any suggestions.

It is the Kinsmen Club's desire that the people of Campbellford/ Seymour will support this idea and be present next May to show the Runions family and their relatives and friends how much his efforts to make our community a better place are appreciated." [1]

The present club membership is 41 and is supported by a strong and helpful auxiliary, the Campbellford Kinette Club.

CAMPBELLFORD KINETTE CLUB

The Campbellford Kinette Club was chartered in January 22, 1971 under the sponsorship of the Campbellford Kinsmen Club. Charter President was Diane

Splaine, and charter members included Barbara Linn, Linda Robertson, Peggy
Pace, Sharon Smith, Ruth Exton, Megan Collins, Judy Mallory, Helen Stephens,
Sharon Peeling, Donalda Runions, Anne Locke, Ruth Grills, Theresa Craig, Pat
Cutts, Gerry Hooper, Paula Meier, Diane Ritchie, Helen Brahaney, and Gloria
Reid. The motto of the organization is "Serving the Community's Greatest Need."

At Christmas of 1971–72, the club began its annual fund raising project called
"Eat, Drink and Be Merry," which was a draw for a picnic hamper filled with wine
and cheese. In 1973, the Kinettes took over the Woodgreen Project, which
involved bringing underprivileged children from Toronto to the Campbellford
area for a week's vacation in August. This has also continued on an annual basis.
Other fund raising events include bake sales, raffles, ball park concession sales,
and co-operating with the Kinsmen in fund raising events, such as the winter carnival, bingo at the Campbellford/Seymour Arena, the TV Auction, and Kingo. The
club supports most local charities, sports programs, and provides school graduation prizes. Donations are made to the hospital, the Cancer Society, CNIB, the
Red Shield Appeal, the Heart and Stoke Foundation, the Kidney Foundation, and
major district and national programs such as Cystic Fibrosis.

In June 1976, the Kinsmen and Kinettes hosted the District Spring
Convention as a camp-out at the fair grounds in Campbellford. Approximately
500 Kinsmen and Kinettes from Campbellford and Quebec City attended.

The Kinette Club is no longer responsible to the Kinsmen Club but is independent and pays district and national dues. There are still four charter members
in the club – Donalda Runions, Sharon Peeling, Helen Stephens, and Anne Locke.
Presidents since the charter include:

Diane Splaine	1971
Anne Locke	1971–1972, 1979–1980, 1991–1992, 1997–98
Helen Stephens	1972–1973
Carol Pearson	1973–1974
Donalda Runions	1974–1975, 1981–1982, 1995–1996, 1997–1998
Gloria Reid	1975–1976
Judy Mallory	1976–1977
Helen Brahaney	1977–1978
Sharon Grills	1978–1979
Karen Phillips	1980–1981
Sharon Peeling	1982–1983
Penny Paul	1983–1985, 1987–1988, 1990–1991, 1996–1997, 1998–1999
Sandie Puddephatt	1985–1987
Ann Fone	1988–1990, 1992–1995

CAMPBELLFORD LIONS CLUB

On November 23, 1953, the Lions Club of Campbellford under the sponsorship of the Norwood Lions Club, was chartered with 31 members, and Vern Rose as Charter President. Over the years the Club has had as few as 20 members and as many as 55 members. Membership is by invitation only and must be reviewed by the Club's Board of Directors as well as the full membership. The Lions motto is: "We Serve."

The Campbellford Lions took on many fund raising activities, with one of the first being a Summer Carnival in 1954. The Carnival was an annual event until it became evident that the liability was more than the Club wanted to face. It was also becoming more and more difficult to find a suitable location. Another of the early fund raising projects was to canvas door to door selling peanuts, enabling the club to raise money for charity. Other innovative fund raisers included circus sponsorship, and draws for money, golf clubs, a replica car, and TVs. For twenty-four years Community Birthday Calendars have been sold, enabling the community to join in celebrating special events such as birthdays and anniversaries. In 1924, at the Lions Club International Convention, Helen Keller challenged the International Association to be "Knights of the Blind." The Lions Club of Campbellford also embraced this cause, and over the years has supported the blind by supplying glasses for needy people in the local communities. As well, used eye glasses are calibrated and sent to third world countries. Monies are sent to the Lions International programs to support Eye Clinics around the world, so that blind children could have operations to give them sight. Money is also sent to Leader Dog School so that the blind can have the use of guide dogs. In recent years the Lions Canadian Foundation fostered a breeding and training program to supply Guide Dogs for the Blind, and Hearing Ear and Special Skill Dogs for the handicapped. In the mid 80s the Club supported a local resident in attending a Guide Dog School to learn how to use and care for a Guide Dog. This dog enabled the recipient to function independently for many years.

In 1956, the Club purchased property on Kent Street with the intention of developing a community park. However, this property was sold to the school board for the construction of Kent Public School. The Lions then purchased the property on west River Road (Queen Street) which became "Lions Park." During the 1970s property to the north was also purchased for facility expansion. This is a community park for all, and before the town swimming pool was built, the beach was used for swimming classes. Each summer there are 30 to 50 family picnics held on week-ends and donations are received from appreciative families. The Club invests between $6,000 and $7,000 annually to maintain the park.

Over the years, the Club has supported many worthwhile charities, other than the CNIB. Boy Scouts, the Salvation Army, the Venture Van as well as minor

Cooling off on a hot summer day at Lions Club Beach on Queen Street.

Photo from Campbellford/Seymour Heritage Society Archives, originally from the files of the Campbellford Herald.

hockey, figure skating, the hospital, schools, the town pool, and many individuals in need have also benefitted from Lions Club support.

Bill Oliver and Leith Crue have served as Zone Chairmen, Eric Holmden as Deputy District Governor, and James T. Clarke as Governor. Several Campbellford Lions have acted as Chair on many district committees. In 1958, the Club sponsored the forming of the Havelock Lions Club.

Past Presidents

Vern Rose	1953–54	Ray Sharpe	1968–69
Bill Peake	1954–55	Bruce Sharpe	1969–70
James T. Clark	1955–56	Don Hughes	1970–71
Bruce Connor	1956–57	Don Pollock	1971–72
Harold Peters	1957–58	Clarence Irwin	1972–73
Les Baker	1958–59	Jack Perry	1973–74
Preston Hall	1959–60	Mel McKeown	1974–75
Robert Bennett	1960–61	Paul Jolliffe	1975–76
Bruce Wallace	1961–62	Jim Kerr	1976–77
Bill Oliver	1962–63	Frank Keeler	1977–78
Ray McKinnon	1963–64	Eric Holmden	1978–79
Leith Crue	1964–65	Paul Simpson	1979–80
Bill Machesney	1965–66	Bill Oliver	1980–81
Al Amsbury	1966–67	Orion Clarke	1981–82
Jim Dikun	1967–68	Al Creasy	1982–83

Past Presidents (continued)

John Petherick	1983–84	Steve Wilson	1991–92
Bill Elliott	1984–85	Bill Elliott	1992–93
Lloyd Gaskin	1985–86	Bill Elliott	1993–94
Eric Holmden	1986–87	Les Burtt	1994–95
Gary Rowe	1987–88	Bob McGregor	1995–96
Gary Rowe	1988–89	George Scott	1996–97
Bob McGregor	1989–90	George Scott	1997–98
John Stocker	1990–91		

CAMPBELLFORD LIONESS CLUB

The Campbellford Lioness Club was formed in 1967 at a meeting at the home of Ede Amsbury, with 23 women in attendance. The charter executive was: President, Helen Anderson; Vice-President, Joan Donnelly; Secretary, June Bovay; Treasurer, Pat Irwin; two-year Directors, Ede Amsbury and Mildred Baker; and one-year Directors, Mary Hughes and Dorothy Machesney. The motto of the club is: "Serve Others." Members work closely with their sponsoring Lions Club and Lions Clubs International to serve the community. In 1998, the membership was made up of 40 women of all ages, representing various careers and life styles. The local club supports charities such as the CNIB Leader Dog Program, the Heart and Stroke Foundation, Meals on Wheels, Community Care, the Lions Club 'Sight First' program, and the local food bank. One of the club's outstanding activities is the creation of a 'silent' helping fund in all local schools to assist needy children.

ROTARY CLUB OF CAMPBELLFORD

The Rotary Club of Campbellford was formed on November 16, 1928, and was admitted to membership by Rotary International on December 26, 1928. The local Club was organized largely through the efforts of Belleville and Trenton Rotarians under the leadership of Mackenzie Robertson. The first informal luncheon took place at the St. Lawrence Hotel on Front Street. Harold N. Carr, who at that time operated the Trent Valley Creamery, and was a close friend of "Mac" Robertson, was a key figure in the early efforts to form this club. "Charter Night" was January 14th, 1929. At first, the meetings were held on Friday at noon, but this was later changed to Monday and the original meeting place was the St. Lawrence Hotel. The first president of the Club was Dr. H. Bruce Longmore.

Rotary's motto "Service Above Self" held great appeal for the business and professional men of that era, who felt that by joining together in a common cause much could be done to alleviate the distress of many of the crippling diseases and congenital deformities of children. In fact, until the government made its comprehensive medical plan available on a province-wide basis, Rotary's main thrust was to raise funds for the help of disabled children.

The Club also earned considerable distinction for the tonsil clinics that were held in the town's first hospital on Front Street North. This hospital was established largely through the efforts of Rotarian Dr. Elmer A. (Stu) Stuart, president in 1943–1944, and Dr. Bruce Longmore. At least one of the present Rotarians was born in that hospital.

The opening of the present Campbellford Memorial Hospital in September 1953 was facilitated by the efforts of club members Archie Meyers, Bud Davidson, Russell Bale, Ralph Locke, who became a District Governor of Rotary, Harvey Donald and Ernie Ayrhart, and the financial contributions of the Club as a whole. The Club also supported the Hospital with the contribution of $15,000 toward the building of the new emergency wing.

Other projects in the health field included the Five Counties Children's Centre in Peterborough, which received a large portion of the Club's finances from 1974 to 1978. Following completion of the Centre, the Campbellford Rotary Club has provided both financial assistance and directors for its board of management. Later, the Northumberland Children's Centre was assigned the responsibility for most of these children's services within Northumberland County, and the Club has provided representation on this board as well as financial assistance. The Rotary Club of Campbellford is also active in the annual Easter Seals Campaign, and administers the distribution of the funds raised in this area to assist eligible children.

Another youth related project has been the complete renovation and enlargement of the "Scout Hall" in Kennedy Park. The building is now known as the "Rotary Youth Centre" and is being used by the Scouts, Cubs, and Beavers, and as a Day Nursery and summer Day Camp.

One of the most popular projects of the Rotary Club of Campbellford has been the "Rotary Trail." This three-kilometre walking trail around the Trent Canal, which was the idea of Rotarian Charlie Thompson, is used by a large number of people on a daily basis, both summer and winter. The construction was under the supervision of Kal Ojamae. Both Kal Ojamae and Charlie Thompson later became Presidents of the Rotary Club of Campbellford.

Many Campbellford/Seymour institutions and groups have received financial assistance from the Rotary Club of Campbellford, among them the Campbellford/ Seymour Fire Department (Rescue Van), Ferris Provincial Park (Picnic Shelter), Campbellford District High School (Many student projects), the Campbellford/ Seymour Library (Restoration of the original entrance), the Venture Van, and the Heart Catheter project. Major fund raising projects over the years have ranged

Prime Minister Lester B. Pearson and his wife, Marion, attend an assembly of the school children of Campbellford in 1965, organized by the Rotary Club. Foreground, left to right: Pauline Jewett,,M.P. for Northumberland; Morley Tanner, Mayor; Lester B. Pearson; Marion Pearson; Cy Johnson, Rotary Club President. Background, left to right: Pat Quinn, Chairman of the Catholic School Board; Clem Milne, Chairman of the Seymour Township Public School Board;Wayne Gunter, Chairman of the Campbellford Public School Board.
Photo courtesy of Cy Johnson.

from street carnivals and The Trip of the Month draw as well as participation in the famous Boston Marathon.

The Rotary Club of Campbellford's involvement in the Boston Marathon, which is twenty-six and a quarter miles long, was a fund raiser suggested in 1976 by Neil Burgess in honour of the late Rotarian Bob Pope. Neil and Bob McKrow canvassed individuals and businesses to sponsor a runner for the 1977 race. Many supportive members assisted with this successful project, raising over $100,000.The other runners over the twenty years of Rotary's involvement were:

1977	Neil Burgess	1982	John Austring
1978	Pat Kelly	1983	Mary Dunford
1979	John Bateman	1984	Tena Michel
1980	Vic Conte	1985	Joe Fuger
1981	Kimberly Hulsman	1986	Dr. Mike Morris

1987	Kristina Hook	1992	Pat Watters
	(a Swedish exchange student)	1993	Steve Sharpe
1988	Dr. Bob Henderson	1994	Dr. Richard Pallen
1989	Paul Irwin	1995	Rob Pope
1990	Gary Stewart	1996	John Sharpe
1991	Bob Crate		

Since Rotary is an international organization, the Campbellford Club has been an active contributor to many of the Rotary world wide projects. Contributions totaling more than $8,000 have been made to the Polio Plus campaign, which is working to eradicate polio. Other projects include the Hospital of Hope in the Dominican Republic, housing projects in India and a hospital in Ethiopia. An exchange student program is also in place through which a Campbellford student is sent overseas to spend a year, and an incoming student from another country spends a year in Campbellford.

Past Presidents and Paul Harris Fellows of the Rotary Club of Campbellford

1928–1929	Bruce Longmore	1952–1953	Frank DeCarrol
1929–1930	Alex MacColl	1953–1954	Bud Davidson+
1930–1931	Harold Carr	1954–1955	Bill McComb++
1931–1932	Stanley Neal	1955–1956	Arn Bright
1932–1933	Clarence Williams	1956–1957	Leo Doherty
1933–1934	Rev. Rob Tait	1957–1958	Cliff Gibson+
1934–1935	Elie Brunelle	1958–1959	Grant Anderson
1935–1936	Dwight Bennett	1959–1960	Paul O'Sullivan
1936–1937	Tom Hall	1960–1961	H.L. Macmillan+
1937–1938	Charlie Davidson	1961–1962	W.R. Dawson+
1938–1939	Harold Neale	1962–1963	Roy MacLaren+
1939–1940	Arthur Armour	1963–1964	Don Meyers+
1940–1941	Steve Maguire	1964–1965	G.W. Rutherford
1941–1943	Percy Denyes	1965–1966	Cy Johnson+
1943–1944	Dr. Stu Stuart	1966–1967	Tom Smith+
1944–1945	Bert Taylor	1967–1968	Chuck Davidson+
1945–1946	Ralph Locke	1968–1969	C. Stephens
1946–1947	Jimmy Benor	1969–1970	Gordon Whitehorne
1947–1948	Owen Watson	1970–1971	Don Bennett+
1949–1950	Charles Calver	1971–1972	John Coxwell
1950–1951	Art Loucks	1972–1973	Al Weaver+
1951–1952	Frank Linton+	1973–1974	Bill Mulholland

<u>Past Presidents and Paul Harris Fellows of the Rotary Club of Campbellford (continued)</u>

1974–1975	Carl Sherk	1988–1989	Cy Johnson+
1975–1976	Ken Hulsman	1989–1990	Chuck Davidson+
1976–1977	Elton Hutchinson+	1990–1991	Charles Clarke
1977–1978	Denton MacArthur	1991–1992	Lynn Forgrave+
1978–1979	Jack Connor+	1992–1993	Steve Sharpe+
1979–1980	Gerry Ireland	1993–1994	Tom Holmes
1980–1981	Thornton Waters+	1994–1995	Kal Ojamae+
1981–1982	George McCleary	1995–1996	Dan Derumaux
1982–1983	Wayne Gunter+	1996–1997	Joe Fuger+
1983–1984	Bruce Sharpe+	1997–1998	Dave Carlaw
1984–1985	John Austring+	1998–1999	Charlie Thompson
1985–1987	Bob Connor+	1999–2000	John Gabriel
1987–1988	John Parsons	2000–2001	Wallace Brown

+ **Named Paul Harris Fellows in honour of the founder of Rotary for worthy efforts in the community.**

In September 1992, Florence Headrick was the first non-Rotarian to receive the Paul Harris Award for her medical missionary work in Haiti, Ecuador, and Albania.

ROYAL CANADIAN LEGION, BRANCH 103 — CAMPBELLFORD

In 1926, the former Ogilvie property which became the Armouries, was assigned by the Town of Campbellford to the British Empire Service League for the sum of one dollar and granted a charter as the Canadian Legion of the British Empire Service League. It was signed by the charter members as noted, on the 25 day of July 1927. Charter Members are as follows:

A. Linton	Raymond Connor
Thomas Hyland	Harry Free
G. A. Thompson	J. E. McEachern
J. M. Bygott	Earle J. Johnstone
R. C. McCulloch	J. T. Dutton
Charles Holmes	Earnest Tom Cleverley
A. T. F. Thomas	George H. Free
Arthur Messenger	

During World War II, the Legion was less active because many members were posted to war service. Meetings were sparse and were held mainly on Friday nights. In 1945, when some of the World War II veterans started to return, they joined the Legion and regular monthly meetings were instituted. In the mid 1960s, the property became licensed and operates, to this day, seven days a week.

The main purpose of the Legion originally was to care for veterans and their families. The organization became very knowledgeable about pensions and benefits owed to service personnel, and often interceded on their behalf. Locally they raised funds for their own needy members. A club atmosphere in the Legion hall and an active sports programme gave the men and women a place and a reason to gather in comradeship. The Canadian Legion was a powerful lobby group to parliament to ensure veterans and others serving in the wars would be, in a small way, repaid for their duties in serving Canada. As the older members died and no longer needed care, the Legion turned its attention to fund raising for community programs.

Currently the Legion sponsors a Seniors' program, the Poppy-Remembrance Campaign, and a Youth Program which includes a public-speaking contest for the area. The organization, along with the Ladies Auxiliary, is involved in fund raising for local charities. One of the more popular fund raisers is provision of inexpensive meals, which are prepared in the modern kitchen upstairs in the hall. An example is the Fish Fry – all you can eat for $6.00! The Legion also sponsors a chilifest where the best cooks in the area compete to win an award for the best recipe.

On November 11 of each year at 11 AM, the Legion holds its annual Remembrance Day observance at the Cenotaph on Queen Street. In 1998, Rev. Douglas Hall, padre of the Legion, said:

> "There are few proud men and women left to pass on countless personal tales they wrote of deeds conducted in the name of freedom and to relate the horrors of war. Were it not for the sacrifices made by so many Canadians and their allies, too often at the cost of their lives, we would not enjoy the freedom which we readily accept today as our social right. Even today, after two world wars more than one-third of the world is still engaged in open warfare. Obviously people have not remembered the lessons written in blood."

Executive members of the 1998–99 term are:

President	Joy Herrington	Secretary-Manager	Gail Cleary
Past President	Gary Wilson	Treasurer	Charles Ibey
First Vice-President	Elwood Irwin	Executive	Nancy Wilson
Second Vice-President	Dave Herrington		Eileen Bell
Third Vice-President	Lynn Woodcock		Mark Mechetuk
Padre	Douglas Hall		Mike Marshall
Secretary	J. E. Dewey		Douglas Hall

ROYAL CANADIAN LEGION, BRANCH 103 — CAMPBELLFORD — LADIES AUXILIARY

The inaugural meeting of the Ladies Auxiliary to Branch 103, Canadian Legion, was held in the Legion Hall May 15, 1951, as a result of the diligent efforts of Ruth Atkinson, a Silver Cross mother. Assisted by the Ontario Provincial Command Ladies Auxiliary of Toronto, the local Auxiliary was created with the following executive: President – Helen Hazell, First Vice-President, Ruth Atkinson, Second Vice-President, Nell Atkinson, Secretary – Beatrice Horsman, Treasurer – Lillian Shaw, Standard Bearer – Mae Phillips, Executive – Dorothy Mills, Katie Massie, Lottie Shaw, and Margaret Field Ingram. Other charter members included Agnes Blake, Jennie Rowe, Irene Torrance, Lily Baker, Ellen Donald, Jane Sutton, Euphemia Hollings, Leticia Sanders, and Jennie Seabrooke. The first general meeting was held May 30, with 23 members being initiated.

The first fund raising projects of the Auxiliary included selling draw tickets, holding a tea and bake sale, and staffing a refreshment booth at the Branch Carnival, where ice cream cones were sold for 5 cents, pop for 10 cents, and hot dogs for 15 cents. Members did sewing and knitting for the hospital, located then at 123 Front Street North, and card parties were held to raise money to purchase blankets for the hospital. In March 1957, the Auxiliary prepared the first Cancer Campaign in partnership with the local firemen and the following year, took over canvassing Ward 4, which continues today. They also established a Disaster Fund. In 1959, the Auxiliary started making sandwiches and hot chocolate for the Santa Claus parade. They gave a gift to the first baby of the New Year and made baby layettes for needy mothers. On-going fund raisers include teas, bake sales, cooking schools, rummage sales, card parties, and an Annual Penny Sale, as well as catering dinners at the Legion.

Funds raised were used initially to improve Legion kitchen facilities. Bursaries were also donated to the local schools to assist students in their educational ventures. The Auxiliary has always worked co-operatively with Legion Branch 103 to assist local veterans and their families through the Poppy Fund, the Children's Picnic, Christmas parties, and lunches for bereaved families. The Auxiliary has also supported Meals on Wheels since its formation. The Auxiliary has always had an active sports program and has twice hosted a Provincial Bowling Tournament. They have supported a girls' hockey team and other youth groups.

Members have also enjoyed bus trips for shopping, dinner theatre, the Ice Capades, the Royal Winter Fair, the CNE, and the Blue Mountain pottery factory.

Executive members of the 1998–99 term are:

President	Helen Stephens	Sports Officer	Ruth Stevens
Past President	Lillian Adams	Executive	Nancy Brunton
First Vice-President	Jessie Parcels		Evelyn Hagerman
Second Vice-President	Eileen Carlaw		June Hagerman
Secretary	Dolly Mills		Isobel Glover
Sergeant-at-Arms	Helen Glenn		Carol Rowe
Treasurer	Jean Powney		

IODE – Imperial Order Daughters of the Empire

The mission of IODE, a Canadian women's charitable organization, is to improve the quality of life for children, youth, and those in need through educational, social service, and citizenship programs. The vision of IODE is to improve the physical and emotional health and expand the educational opportunities of all Canadians within a unified country. The Campbellford/Seymour area has been fortunate to have two chapters of such dedicated women.

IODE — CAMPBELLFORD CHAPTER

On September 4, 1914, the Campbellford Chapter of the IODE was formed. Charter members included Olivia Free, Jessie Jenkins, Mary Kerr, Gertrude Haig, Josie Turner, Sadie Archer, Margaret Stewart, Annie Armstrong, Nellie E. Ashton, and Elizabeth Robertson.

Early activities of the Campbellford Chapter focused primarily on the war effort. The Chapter sent knitted goods to the Red Cross and Christmas boxes to servicemen from the local area. Hospital supplies such as quilts, towels, pyjamas, face cloths were sent to the IODE Hospital, and donations were made to the Prisoner of War Fund.

Locally, donations were made to the public library, and prizes were awarded to students graduating from the high school. Two adopted schools were also furnished with books for libraries, and contributions were sent to the Children's Aid Society at Port Hope.

In February 1922, the Campbellford Chapter of IODE, along with the Bemersyde Chapter, as well as representatives from both the Campbellford and Seymour Councils, formed a Memorial Committee to establish a monument to those who served their country in World War I. A Memorial Fund was set up and after four years, the Committee was able to organize the erection of the Cenotaph on present-day Queen Street. It was designed by Alfred McKeel of Campbellford and built by the McCallum Co. of Kingston. On it were inscribed the names of those who fell in World War I. The monument was unveiled on June 20, 1926 at a special service.

In March 1928, after fourteen years of service, the members decided to discontinue the Chapter.

IODE — BEMERSYDE CHAPTER

Bemersyde Chapter, Imperial Order Daughters of the Empire, was formed in Campbellford in March 1918. The application for the charter was received at head Office on March 12th, 1918, and Charter 771 was granted by the National Chapter on April 6, 1918. The charter members were Florence Benor, Ruth Diamond, Lulu Gay, Georgia Hay, Kathleen Locke, Beatrice Mitchell, Grace Moore, Zita Rallis, Dorothy West, and Rita Wood. The motto chosen was "Excelsior" and Rita Wood was elected as the first Regent.

The name of the Chapter – "Bemersyde" – was chosen to honour Sir Douglas Haig, Commander-in-Chief of the British Forces in France from 1915–1918. Bemersyde was the ancestral home of the Haig family for seven centuries in Scotland, and the Haigs were one of the pioneer families of Campbellford/Seymour. Gertrude Haig and Sadie Archer, members of the existing Campbellford Chapter IODE (1914–1928), were instrumental in forming Bemersyde. Both women were made Honorary Regents in later years.

Early projects to raise Chapter funds included raffles, plays, and dances held in the Music Hall, now the Masonic Temple. The IODE Ball was instituted and became an annual event. During the 1920s, money was donated to the Navy League, the Salvation Army, and $10 was given as a prize to "Miss Campbellford." Children's books were purchased for the Library, and this marked the beginning of support for education by Bemersyde Chapter. Support to the Memorial Fund resulted in the erection of the present Cenotaph, which was unveiled and dedicated on June 26, 1926.

Just as Citizenship, Education, and Services are the three main areas of concentrated activity nationally and provincially, it is easy to trace these patterns in the Bemersyde Chapter in the 1920s and 1930s. Membership increased to forty-five in 1937. Four awards of three dollars each were given to "top" boy and girl in the public and separate schools and $300 was provided for bursaries in the high school.

Bemersyde's fifty members commenced the busiest and most dedicated period in their history in 1939 when the war began. Bales of clothing were donated and collected for shipping to Britain; members formed sewing circles; ditty bags (small cloth bags containing toilet articles), and bandages were sent to the Navy League.

Tag days and countless parties, socials, and dances were held to raise money for the war effort. War brought drastic changes into the lives of all members and their families, as husbands, sweethearts, brothers, and fathers went into the services. By 1942, Bemersyde Chapter members were engrossed in knitting socks, sweaters, helmets and gloves. They collected woollen articles for blankets for men in minesweeper crews, gathered salvage, packed hundreds of parcels, filled countless ditty bags, and sent cartons of knitted good to Provincial headquarters in Hamilton. Cigarettes, magazines, and food parcels were sent to local servicemen, and over three hundred airmen were entertained for weekends from nearby Trenton Air Station. It is rumoured that many romances in the area started with these visits. After the war ended, Bemersyde members generously sent boxes of food and clothing to refugees in England, Holland, and other war-devastated nations.

The war over, members once again concentrated on community projects. A table and couch were purchased for the local Public Health Unit. The newly-built Campbellford Memorial Hospital received $1,000 to furnish a semi-private room. Fifty white blankets were purchased and countless knitted baby sets and diapers were donated to the nursery, as well as a much needed incubator. A suction-pump and instruments were purchased for the operating room.

Bemersyde members donated money to buy uniforms for the Campbellford Citizen's Band. During Campbellford's Centennial Year in 1956, the Chapter hosted a garden party for all the "old boys and old girls" at the home of Mayor Ralph Locke and his wife, Dorothy, and served a luncheon there to the Lieutenant-Governor and his wife, the Honourable Louis and Mrs. Breithaupt. Centennial costumes were the vogue for the week, and chapter members gathered at the newly constructed Community Centre to serve lunch and to pose for a Chapter portrait.

During the 1950s, parcels for overseas continued and knitting was sent to headquarters. Members Marion DeCarrol and Florence Benor were elected provincial Councillors. The 1960s saw flags presented to schools and the Boy Scout troop. Clothing and "sunshine" parcels were distributed locally, Christmas trees and parcels were given to the hospital and nursing home, and books were collected for the forces still stationed in Germany. Toys and musical instruments for a rhythm band were donated to Merryvale School, and the Chapter adopted their first classroom in a native school in northern Ontario.

In 1968, Bemersyde Chapter celebrated 50 years of service to IODE. By the mid 1970s, $4,000 had been raised for interest-free loans to students continuing post-secondary education, another classroom was adopted at Massey, Ontario, and knitted articles and books were sent to the Friendship Centre for Native Canadians.

To commemorate the 75th anniversary of the National Chapter of Canada IODE, Provincial Chapters across Canada were asked to sell the IODE rose, a red floribunda rose originated and grown only for IODE, and use the monies raised in each province for a program of their choosing. Thus the "Concern for Children" fund began to provide research into genetic medicine, and the first "Tour of Homes" was held. A radiant-heated bassinet was purchased in 1979 for Campbellford Memorial Hospital to celebrate the "Year of the Child." Earlier a centrifuge machine had been donated to the laboratory. The title of the organization was officially changed to IODE.

In the 1980s, Labrador became the main focus of the National Chapter and a classroom in the Wm. Gillett Pentecostal School, Charlottetown, Labrador, was adopted and support is still on-going. Over the years, clothing, treats, books, toys, tapes, art supplies, and rhythm band equipment have been generously donated.

Awards to students at the elementary and high school level continue to be given annually for scholastic achievement. Interest-free loans are still available for post-secondary study, and framed portraits of the reigning monarch are provided for schools. Oral communication awards are donated to all local schools. Financial support is given to the Northumberland Music Festival. A wreath is still placed at the Cenotaph each Remembrance Day.

A newly purchased oak book cart, suitably inscribed, was donated to the new addition of the Campbellford/Seymour Library, and the "Born to Read" program, bags of books for new-borns and moms, are provided by Chapter members and distributed by the Library.

Bemersyde Chapter undertook to furnish the waiting room at the recently expanded Campbellford Memorial Hospital at a cost of $5,000, and purchased a $3,000 infusion pump. Visits and treats are provided monthly at the nursing homes, and cash donations are given to Meals-On-Wheels, the Food Bank, and the Salvation Army Christmas hampers, as well as for the purchase of candy for the Santa Claus Parade, and the purchase of bedding for fire-victim families. Nutritional snacks, called "Food for Thought Baskets," are also provided to elementary schools.

Along with other local service organizations, Bemersyde IODE helped to erect two signs at the entrances to town, and also purchased and maintained a lighted candle for the "Festival of Lights Showcase" at Old Mill Park. Chapter funds are distributed annually to help fund the many varied projects undertaken by the Provincial and National Chapters of IODE.

At present, Bemersyde Chapter has two members who are councillors of the Provincial Chapter of Ontario IODE and the National Chapter of Canada IODE. Marie Locke was elected President, Provincial Chapter of Ontario, in 1993, and at present is the Membership Officer for the National Chapter of Canada IODE. Marilyn Murray was elected Vice-President, Eastern-Area, Provincial Chapter of Ontario IODE, in 1993, a position she still held in 1998.

Regents 1918–1998

Rita Wood	Ruth Vandewater
Hazel Atkinson	Pearl Rutherford
Hattie Hawthorne	June Bennett
Bird Ironside	Evelyn Connor
Eleanor Ferris (Douglas)	Marilyn Murray
Helen Cowell	Maythel Peeling
Flossie Scott	Marie Locke
Enid Loucks	Rita Lines
Marion DeCarrol	Ruth Hamilton
Florence Benor	Cozette Barnum
Helen Anderson	Eva Fraser
Georgia Maybee	Betsy Thompson
Helen Vice	Annabelle McCormack
Thelma Kingston	Shirley Simpson

~ Women's Institutes ~

The Federated Women's Institute of Ontario, more commonly known as the Women's Institute, has a fascinating history. From a cold night in February 1897 in Stoney Creek, Ontario, when the WI held its first meeting, until 100 years later in 1997, the organization has pioneered in the field of women's issues. Traditionally, it has always had a strong connection to the Provincial Department/Ministry of Agriculture. With nearly thirteen thousand members province-wide, this is a grassroots organization which focused mainly on education, communication, finance and lobbying efforts. Three hundred and ninety-nine new members joined in 1997 alone. The organization has enriched the lives of women in rural communities and gathered together a history of their areas, with minute books, scrapbooks, and history books containing research and current events. The W. I. motto is "For home and Country."

During World War I, WI branches were mobilized to undertake war work because of experience in working together on practical projects. During the depression years, 1930–39, many branches turned their attention to the viability of their community social life. Social gatherings provided an outlet for the stress of economic hard times, and local relief played an important role in many branch activities.

In 1925, a special committee of the WIO was formed to be known as the Committee for Historical Research and Current Events. Every branch was encouraged to keep a history, which included individual farms, industries and public buildings, first settlers, schools, and churches. In 1947, every WI branch in Ontario was asked to prepare a volume of history about the community before the celebrations for the 50th anniversary of WI took place. Lady Tweedsmuir, recently widowed, was delighted to approve the idea that the books should be named for her late husband the former Governor General of Canada, thus the Tweedsmuir Histories were born. The Tweedsmuir History books are invaluable because of the important role these books play as chronicles of local history. These books, which are collections made by each WI branch, contain a history of local communities found no where else.

At the annual Trent Valley Area convention, held on October 15, 1998, in Belleville, one hundred and seventy-three members participated. Trent Valley encompasses the districts of Hastings, Prince Edward, Northumberland and Peterborough Counties. Plans were announced for members to take part in the Associated Country Women of the World Conference to be held in 2001 in Hamilton. The Federated Women's Institutes of Ontario now have their own provincial office in Guelph, independent of the Ministry of Agriculture and Food. A revised vision statement "Working together shaping tomorrow's world" and strategic goals set clear direction for policy changes, while taking advantage of technological advances. The structure of the provincial board has been significantly reduced in size and a Provincial Advisory Council will liaise between members, committees, and the Board. The Institute is ready for the millennium.

RYLSTONE WOMEN'S INSTITUTE

The Rylstone Women's Institute began on February 24, 1924, at the home of Matilda Spencer. Afternoon meetings were held the first Thursday of the month in the homes of members. The following is the first executive for 1924–25: President – Margaret Meilklejohn, Vice President – Cora Barnum, and Secretary – Pearl Rutherford. Membership was thirty-four and average attendance was seventeen.

Projects completed over the years included the compilation and sale of cookbooks, the distribution of first aid kits to community schools, the packing of bales for the needy in the north, and the furnishing of a room in the first Campbellford Hospital. Boxes were packed and sent to soldiers overseas during World War II, quilts were given to local brides and the Red Cross, boxes were packed for British Flood Relief and fire victims, and $1,000 was donated to Campbellford Memorial Hospital. Donations were sent to many charitable organizations such as the Heart and Stroke Foundation, the Salvation Army, the Agricultural Society, the Northumberland Music Festival, the Stirling Festival of Sacred Praise, the Hospital Auxiliary, Women Feed the World, Pennies for Friendship, 4H Clubs, the Erland

Lee and Adelaide Hoodless Museums in Guelph, the Hastings County Museum, now Glanmore National Historic Site in Belleville, and others.

Guest speakers came from all walks of life and many craft experts shared their skills and techniques. Short courses were presented on bread making, braiding, needlepoint, candle wicking, indoor gardening, and cooking.

Unfortunately, membership has declined in recent years. Meetings are held on the first Wednesday of the month. The former schoolhouse of Union School #18, Concession 11, Lot 26, acquired in 1968, is presently the meeting place of the Rylstone Women's Institute. It is owned and carefully maintained by the Institute and used for community events. Executive officers in 1999 were: Dorothy Thomson, President; Donna Phair; Secretary; Marie Findlay, Treasurer.

SEYMOUR EAST WOMEN'S INSTITUTE

The first institute, known as Menie Institute, was organized in 1907 by Martha Macoun of Seymour West. Eliza Meiklejohn was the first President. Succeeding her were Mary Rannie, Ellenore Clancy, and Minnie Oddie. This first group met and hosted many entertainments in Lamb's Hall at Menie on Concession 4, Lot 22.

During World War I, the Institute was responsible for a hospital ship, and boxes of food were sent to soldiers at the front. In 1913, the Institute undertook to beautify Burnbrae Cemetery by planting shrubs and flowers. At the end of World War I, the Institute became interested in establishing a public rest room in Campbellford, as well as a hospital. The hospital was opposed by Dr. Thomas W. Carlaw and plans for both were abandoned. This first institute was disbanded in 1918.

A new group was formed on November 1, 1933, when forty-five ladies met at the home of Lena Thompson who became the President. The organizers were interested in fostering community friendship and goodwill, and in developing a broader view of life and a wider knowledge of child welfare. In co-operation with Rylstone and Seymour West branches, a room was furnished in the former Campbellford Hospital on Front Street North. School fairs were encouraged as well as a special prize list for the local fair. Quilting was a favourite pastime. From the beginning, young women were encouraged to participate in the 4H activities and to take part in local Achievement Days.

The Seymour East Institute met for many years in the homes of the members. In 1949, the former T.S. Little property at Concession 5, Lot 23, was purchased and converted into the Institute hall. Monthly meetings and many community events took place here. Eventually, It was decided that this hall was too expensive to maintain and, in 1998, the property was sold. Executive officers in 1999 were: Jessie Poulton, President; Gladys Valleau, Secretary; Joan Riseborough, Treasurer.

SEYMOUR WEST WOMEN'S INSTITUTE

In July 1912, a group of Seymour West women met at the home of Jennie Longmuir to form the Seymour West WI Branch. Eight members elected Martha Jane Macoun as President and Jennie Longmuir as Corresponding Secretary. By the first anniversary in 1913, over ninety members gathered at the Macoun home. Jennie Macoun would lead the Branch through nine of the formative years and would go on to the provincial level as a board member and, in 1919, as the first Corresponding Secretary of the Federated Women's Institutes of Ontario.

Over the years, the members have been active in catering, holding garden parties, and assisting in canvasses for cancer, tuberculosis, and the blind. They have promoted school oratoricals and music, 4H activities, war relief efforts and hospital support. There was serious competition between branches on occasion, as the following tale illustrates. At a school fair competition, a woman setting up a display of woodchuck tails feared that another woman would win the prize over her school. Prior to the judging, the door had been locked. She nimbly climbed out the window, went home for some forgotten tails, climbed back in, added the smelly tails to her exhibit, and won the prize for her school!

In 1968, as a result of negotiations between the School Board, the Township Council, and the Ministry of Education, the former West's School, S.S, #4, on Concession 7, Lot 6, became the Seymour West Institute Branch hall. Over the years, the hall has been renovated and furnished through voluntary effort.

The Institute continues to support many community projects, such as the local hospital, library, and music festival. One thousand dollars was donated to the Campbellford Memorial Hospital for the equipment for a hospital room. The Branch has sponsored a homemaking club, and has undertaken the cleanup and care of two cemeteries in the community. In addition, there have been numerous day trips, picnics and other pleasurable activities. In 1975–76, an ambitious endeavour involving an old fashioned Christmas Concert was presented to the community. This has continued in the form of a W. I. family night dinner and concert. As the Branch and the community grows, so does the Tweedsmuir History. From the first volume, which was begun in 1963, the number has grown to nine volumes.

Executive officers in 1999 are: Shirley Little, President; Marion Hay, Vice-President; Pat Lloyd, Secretary.

TRENT RIVER WOMEN'S INSTITUTE

The Institute was formed November 21, 1929, by District President Mrs. John A. Sexsmith, accompanied by Mrs. Arthur Russell and Mrs. William Anderson of Belmont Institute, at the home of Annie Wight. Ten members were present at the initial meeting and the officers elected were: President – Mrs.

George Brooks, Vice President – Mrs. Thomas Tyler, Secretary/Treasurer – Mrs. Harry Mann, District Director – Mrs. Frederick Scott. Since 1929, meetings have been held every 2nd Thursday of each month. Two life members are still living – Annie Greenly and Doris Little.

Many projects have been completed during the past 69 years. Institute members were a very active group during World War II. They took care of twenty-five area servicemen with parcels, gifts, needed articles of clothing, and food packages. Those returning from overseas were honoured with gifts of rings, watches, pens, and pencils from money raised by quilting, card parties, entertainment, and donations. Approach signs to the village were erected in 1930. School zone signs, first aid kits, and flags were donated to two schools. The Institute was instrumental in the installation of seven street lights in the village, and in the purchase of a community hall in 1950. A Baptismal font was donated to Trent River United Church in 1947. Each November 11, Trent River Women's Institute donates a wreath and participates in the memorial service held at the Cenotaph.

Recently donations have been made to the following: the Manitoba Flood Relief Fund, Peterborough Heart Catheter Fund, the Campbellford Memorial Hospital, the new library in Campbellford, the Havelock and Norwood Fire departments, the Havelock Food Bank, the School Ecology garden, and Pathfinders. Members have volunteered for the Cancer society, and knitted hats, gloves, and baby clothes to raise funds for Community Care, Havelock.

February 19th, 1997, was the centennial of the Women's Institute which started in Stoney Creek in 1897. Women's Institutes throughout Ontario celebrated at their own branches. On June 7 and 8, Peterborough District met at Lang Village for two days during which visitors could enjoy entertainment, view the Tweedsmuir Books, and watch quilting. On Sunday, a service was held in the church at Lang Village.

On June 21, 1997, Trent River members attended a convention held in Hamilton. The convention was attended by nearly two hundred members from seventy countries. Many dignitaries spoke and good wishes were sent to the convention by Queen Elizabeth II. Trent River's Centennial project was a quilt made by President Edna Lee who embroidered, by hand, seven hundred and four names. The names were collected by the Trent River WI members, charging one dollar per name and the money was donated to the District. The motif was "School House and Maple Leaf." The quilt was finished with the help of Belmont and Havelock WI members. To conclude the Trent River WI celebration of the centennial of the WI, a flower show and afternoon tea was held in Trent River Church Hall on July 19th, 1997. Three senior residents of Trent River were judges of the flower show. Certificates for fifty years of membership were presented to Annie Greenly and Doris Little. A thirty-year pin was presented to G. Graham.

Trent River Women's Institute members attending celebrations of the Centennial of the Women's Institute organized by the Peterborough District at Lang Pioneer Village in June 1997. Left to right: I. Tyler, Margaret Pollock, G. Graham, Joan West, Edna Lee.

Trent River continues to participate in many community projects although the following members are all that remain: Past President – M. Jeffry, President – Edna Lee, Secretary/Treasurer – Joan West, Public Relations – G. Graham, District Directors – I. Tyler and G. Graham, Life Members – Annie Greenly and Doris Little. Unfortunately Margaret (Dutch) Pollock, who fulfilled the role of Auditor and Curator of the Tweedsmuir History, passed away in November 1997.

⁓ Masonic Lodges ⁓

FREEMASONS — GOLDEN RULE LODGE #126

In late 1859, several local men, including some from Masonic Lodges in nearby towns, took the initial steps to form a Lodge in Campbellford. The first meeting was held on Tuesday, February 7, 1860, at which time Brother J. M. Lindsley was installed as Worshipful Master, under the direction of the past masters from Stirling and Trenton. The Lodge was named Golden Rule Lodge and numbered 126 on the register of the Grand Lodge. At that time, the Lodge rooms were located in what was then known as the Corkery block, later known as the

Doherty block. This property was situated on the west side of Front Street South next to what was then known as the Armstrong Block and is now the Cottage Country Store. The Doherty Block was demolished in 1996.

Masonry flourished in Campbellford and, Golden Rule Lodge was to become one of the strongest lodges in District 10, which was comprised of four lodges in Peterborough, and one each in Lakefield, Keene, Millbrook, Norwood, Havelock, Campbellford, Hastings and Warkworth. In 1923, the Lodge rooms were moved from the Corkery block to rooms over the former Anderson's Hardware on the west side of Queen Street. This location now houses Redden's Cable TV.

In 1936, the Masonic Order purchased the former Music Hall on the northwest corner of Front and River Streets and it remains the location of the Masonic Temple to this day. Many alterations and renovations had to be made in order to prepare a new upper floor as a meeting place. A committee was formed under the capable leadership of Brother Archie Meyers, who was a qualified engineer, and steel work was installed to support the new top floor. The new temple was dedicated in 1938 by the Grand Master, Most Worshipful W. J. Dunlop. The Worshipful

Officers of the Golden Rule Lodge, No. 126, 1926. Back row, left to right: Treasurer, J. Maynard; Immediate Past Master, P.C. Denyes; Senior Steward, H. McDonald; Secretary, Frank C. Bonnycastle; Inner Guard, T. E. Hall; Organist, E. C. Dolman; Chaplain, R. Lowery. Middle row, seated, left to right: Junior Deacon, S.H. Neale; Junior Warden, J.A. Murray; Worshipful Master, George H. Free; Senior Warden, R. H. Harry (Hardy); Senior Deacon, W.S. Wiggins. Front row, left to right, on floor: Tyler, S. Clegg; Junior Steward, J.O. Benor.

Photo by Frank Bonnycastle, from Campbellford/Seymour Heritage Society Archives.

Master that year was Frank Menzies and the District Deputy Grand Master was F. F. Long. The Lodge continued to flourish, particularly after World War II, when young men were returning from overseas.

In 1960, the Lodge's centennial year, the Lodge room was completely redecorated. A low platform with red cedar floor was built around the perimeter of the room and theatre-type seats acquired from the demolished Shea's Theatre in Toronto were installed. Each member was asked to buy a square yard of new carpet and the room was given a new floor cover. Over the last few years, several other improvements have been put in to accommodate the provincial court, i.e. judge's chambers, air conditioning and more washrooms. This hall has always been a favourite place to hold dances and celebrations and continues to be used in that capacity. The building is truly a landmark of the town.

FREEMASONS — IONIC CHAPTER #168
ROYAL ARCH MASONS

In 1909, a Masonic Chapter of Royal Arch Masons was formed after a petition by Masons William Smith, Dr. E. J. Free, T. A. Brown, and W. E. Carnahan was forwarded to Grand Chapter. Excellent Companion W. Smith was the charter First Principal.

The following Excellent Companions have served as Grand Superintendents of the District:

1919 – D. F. Robertson	1959 – T. H. Burgis
1922 – I. A. Humphries	1972 – J. Meier
1932 – L. B. Glover	1983 – A. Lauesen
1943 – J. O. Benor	1994 – Roy Ballard
1951 – W. H. Brady	

The Officers in 1998–99 were :

First Principal	– Very Excellent Companion William Hay
Second Principal	– Very Excellent Companion John Haig
Third Principal	– Excellent Companion John Van Allen
Scribes	– Excellent Companion Jack Parsons and Very Excellent Companion Pieter Wilmink
Treasurer	– Right Excellent Companion Alf Lauesen

ORDER OF THE EASTERN STAR — CAMPBELLFORD CHAPTER NO. 278

This Chapter was instituted on April 27, 1953, and a meeting for constituting the Chapter and for the installation of officers was held on October 14, 1953. The following officers were installed:

Worthy Matron	Marguerite Burgis	Worthy Patron	Harry Burgis
Associate Matron	Irene Brady	Associate Patron	William Brady
Secretary	Pearl McComb	Treasurer	Ann Haskin
Conductress	Alma Wallace	Assoc. Conductress	Nellie King
Chaplain	Marjory Pierce	Marshal	Barbara Steele
Organist	Frances Nicholls	Adah	Florence Hopping
Ruth	Gertrude Cochrane	Esther	Betty Connor
Martha	Eileen Hazell	Electa	Martha Nicholas
Warder	Bernice Adams	Sentinel	Claude Fairman

The Chapter was active in fund raising for the local community as well as the Grand Chapter of Ontario, donating funds to associations for kidney, heart, cancer, multiple sclerosis, the mentally challenged, rheumatism, and arthritis. They also make donations to the Hospital for Sick Children, the Burns' Institute, the Grand Benevolent Fund, the Florence Nightingale Home, and the Estarl Fund which is an award for a Theology student.

The Campbellford Chapter was honoured with the following appointments:

Grand Representatives – Irene Brady, to the State of Wisconsin
    Helen Meyers, to the State of Arkansas
    Marguerite Burgis, to the State of Vermont

Pages for Grand Chapter – Alma Wallace, Gloria Fox, Carolyn Sheridan
Grand Page for General Grand Chapter – Marguerite Burgis, in Milwaukee,
    Wisconsin
Grand Organist – Bruce Barnum, 1967–68
Grand Chaplain – Marguerite Burgis, 1974–75
District Deputy Grand Matron – Marguerite Burgis, 1968–69

In 1987, the Campbellford Chapter was disbanded and interested members moved to Warkworth, Havelock, and Tweed.

~ Loyal Orange Lodge ~

The Orange Lodge has a long and colourful history in the Campbellford/ Seymour area. The precursor of the Orange Lodge in Seymour was an organization known as the Sons of Temperance, #298, Seymour Division. This organization came to Upper Canada in 1848, and was incorporated by Parliament in 1851 and 1856. The aims of the Sons of Temperance were to campaign against the use of alcoholic beverages, to elevate morality, and to provide mutual assistance. The

Seymour Division was instituted July 9, 1851, at the Chapel at Gilpin's Settlement or West's Corners. The organization appears to have become inactive by 1857 when #298 was granted to a new division in York.

Seymour West Orange Lodge, #523, was founded July 14, 1853. Internal conflicts within the Provincial Lodge resulted in the issuing of a new warrant in 1856 and, thereafter, the Seymour West Lodge is referred to as #526. On December 6, 1859, discussion began with regard to the construction of a Lodge room which was eventually erected, probably in 1864, on the John Free farm on Concession 8, Lot 3. When John Free died in 1888, a decision was required with regard to the building since neither the Lodge nor John Free actually had title to the property. For several years, the members planned to move the structure into the village Campbellford. This proved to be too expensive and, by 1897, the Lodge had moved to rented quarters in the basement of the Baptist Church in Campbellford. Orange Lodge #36 already existed in Campbellford at that time, having been chartered in 1847 under James Maxwell Levesconte. Lodge #36 met in rented quarters in the Trent Block. The two separate Lodges co-existed until December 1930, when the two amalgamated under #526. In 1931, meetings were held in the Turner Block and, in 1933, the Lodge rented the Ladies Orange Benevolent Lodge hall.

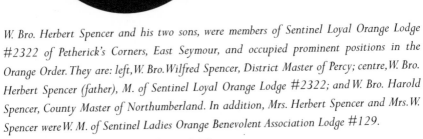

W. Bro. Herbert Spencer and his two sons, were members of Sentinel Loyal Orange Lodge #2322 of Petherick's Corners, East Seymour, and occupied prominent positions in the Orange Order. They are: left, W. Bro. Wilfred Spencer, District Master of Percy; centre, W. Bro. Herbert Spencer (father), M. of Sentinel Loyal Orange Lodge #2322; and W. Bro. Harold Spencer, County Master of Northumberland. In addition, Mrs. Herbert Spencer and Mrs. W. Spencer were W. M. of Sentinel Ladies Orange Benevolent Association Lodge #129.
Photo courtesy of Jack Spencer and Dorothy Thomson

There were several other Orange lodges operating before the turn of the century: #1369 (Polmont) at Concession 12, Lot 5; #1338 Victoria (Stanwood) at Concession 13, Lot 20; #1114 (Burnbrae) at Concession 6, Lot 20; and one other which operated briefly in the Healey Falls area. In 1912, #2322 Sentinel Lodge was built at Petherick's Corners at Concession 9, Lot 21. All Lodges today attend Campbellford #526.

Each Lodge possessed a branding iron and, many years ago, an Orangeman was branded on the skin over his heart to prove his faith. Each Lodge also possessed a box containing black and white balls and when a new member sought admission to the group, each member chose a black or white ball in a secret vote and thus the newcomer was either chosen or rejected. One black ball in the ballot box meant the prospective member was 'blackballed' – hence the term which is still used today.

Each Lodge kept careful records and, in 1987, the Campbellford Lodge sent to the Archives of Ontario 23 volumes listing members names and minutes of meetings from #36 (Campbellford), #1114 (Burnbrae), and #526 (Seymour West) covering 1850–1948.[2]

The Lodge in Campbellford, #526, exists today and meets the last Wednesday of every month at 120 Grand Road at 8 PM In 1998, there are fifteen members as contrasted with forty-three in 1929. Over the years, the religious purpose of the Lodge has declined in importance and it has expanded its mission of charitable works. The Lodge supports a research centre at Richmond Hill and a day care centre at Sick Children's Hospital in Toronto. They care locally for elderly, needy members and those who are disabled.

In July 1994, Campbellford hosted seventy lodges of the Loyal Orange Association of Canada in a district walk, an annual event that commemorates the victory of William of Orange at the Battle of the Boyne in 1790.

～ Oddfellows and Rebekahs ～

I O O F

Campbellford Lodge No. 248 of the Independent Order of Oddfellows was instituted on October 8, 1885, and met on the top floor of the Ferris Block, which is located at the southeast corner of Front and Bridge Streets below the bridge on the riverside. The Lodge met weekly on Friday nights until 1954 when a decision was made to purchase the building at 22 Doxsee Avenue South. The top floor was renovated for a modern Lodge Hall and the lower floor was leased by a series of tenants, Brewers' Warehouse, a butcher shop, Canadian Tire, and the local Health

Unit. In 1988, the Health Unit took over the top floor and the Lodge met for the next eight years in the basement of the Masonic Lodge on Front Street South. In 1997, the former Jehovah Witness building at 240 Victoria Street was purchased and modified to include a basement at the back and a kitchen. The grand opening was held on April 12, 1997, with the Grand Master of Ontario, Brother Ron Wannamaker, and Campbellford Mayor, Cathy Redden, officiating. Meetings are held the first and third Thursday of every month.

Campbellford Lodge No. 248 belongs to Madoc District No.45 and includes Lodges in Stirling, Tweed and Madoc. The emblem of the Lodge consists of three intertwined links representing friendship, love, and truth. Membership is conferred on an initiatory and first, second, and third degree basis. There is a Lodge memorial just inside the gate of Mount Pleasant Cemetery. Campbellford Lodge also sends two delegates each year to the Grand Lodge Sessions.

The major part of Lodge activity in the community is the provision of medical aids and devices for the sick. The Lodge also does fund raising for awards such as the Harold Smith Bursary of $250 given to two graduating students each year and two additional bursaries of $200. The Lodge supports the Salvation Army at Christmas. A recent donation of $5,000 was made to the fund for the Heart Catheter for this area which will be located in Peterborough. Along with the Rebekahs, the Oddfellows also support a seniors home in Barrie which is a modern facility of 157 beds and 20 individual apartments.

Charter members were Joseph Townsend, George Boyce, James Carr, Charles Gillespie, Harper Shaw, and George Eakins. The first Noble Grand was Joseph Townsend in 1885. Other members who have gone on to their last degree are the following Brothers:

Ducky Shaw	Joe Poulton, Sr.	Joe Poulton, Sr.	Earl Craighead
John McGregor	Perce Sherwin	J. B. Ferris	Earnie Haig
Sam Flint	Wally Rutherford	Roy Loucks	Cress Newman
Oscar Campbell	F. Rutherford	Ralph Stephens	Ralph Atkinson
Ray Archer	Harold Smith	Bill Nicholas	J. R. Irwin
Ernie Archer	Alf Burgis	Harold Petherick	Grant Anderson

The Ancient Mystic Order of Samaritans (AMOS) is also affiliated with the Oddfellows Lodge and to become a member requires membership in the IOOF. The motto of AMOS is "We Never Sleep" and the emblem is the Owl which features prominently on the float used in many local parades. Members wear a fez with different coloured tassels designating different offices. AMOS supports the Campbellford and District Association for Community Living.

IOOF — LOCH LOMOND
REBEKAH LODGE #248

The Rebekah Lodge, the women's branch of the Independent Order of Oddfellows, is a worldwide organization promoting Friendship, Love and Truth. The Loch Lomond Rebekah Lodge #248 was instituted on May 23, 1923. The first Noble Grand was Sister Lillian Moore. Dues were two dollars at the start, raised to five dollars in 1926, and now stand at fifteen dollars. Meetings were initially held in the Ferris Block Lodge rooms. In 1953 the Lodge rooms were moved to the I.O.O.F. Hall on Doxsee Street South and the Rebekahs assisted in furnishing this new facility. Fund raising projects included catering for the Lions' Club dinners for over 30 years, and holding euchre parties, bridge tournaments, quilting bees, dances, and bingo games.

The current fund raisers are bazaars and luncheons and, in co-operation with the Oddfellows, lunches at Hoard's Station Sale Barn three days a year. Money raised at the Sale Barn is for the Humanitarian Committee, which supplies wheelchairs, crutches, walkers, and other aids to anyone in the community who had a need. Other projects include the support of a child through WorldVision, two $200 bursaries to graduates of Campbellford District High School, and donations to Meals on Wheels, Venture Van, the Legion Poppy Fund, the Northumberland Music Festival, Community Care, the Heart Catheter Fund, the Salvation Army, the Five Counties Children's Centre, the Fare Share Food Bank, and the Festival of Lights. Thousands of dollars have been raised over recent years for Camp Trillium, a summer camp for children with cancer, as well as for a new camp at Rainbow Lake. Every Christmas, fruit baskets are distributed to sick and shut-in members.

Loch Lomond Lodge is a member of District #4 which includes Belleville, Havelock, Stirling, and Madoc. District Deputy Presidents from Campbellford include Irene Torrance (1967–68), Evelyn Hopkins (1970–71), Carlyn Sheridan (1972–73), Ruby Gill (1979–80), Susan Gordon (1984–85), Veleta Ibey (1992–93), and Mildred Campbell (1996–97). On April 12, 1997, the grand opening of the new Oddfellow/Rebekah Hall at 240 Victoria Street was held. The Lodge celebrated its seventy-fifth birthday on May 30, 1998. There are seventy-one active members, including some fifty-year members – Madge Tanner, Ruby Gill, Helen Abernethy, Helen Pickering, and Phyllis Reid. Meetings are held the second and fourth Thursday of each month.

～ Youth Organizations ～

SCOUTING AND GUIDING ORGANIZATIONS

Scouting in Campbellford was first established in 1922, and is completely run by volunteers who serve as uniformed troop leaders as well as providing behind-the-scenes support. The Campbellford organization is part of the Scouting District of Trent Valley, which encompasses Havelock, Norwood, Warsaw, Campbellford, Warkworth, and Hastings. The Campbellford movement is fortunate to be sponsored by the Campbellford Rotary Club which provides financial assistance as well as a location for meetings at the Rotary Youth Centre in Kennedy Park.

Scouting is for youth members between the ages of 5 and 26, and is divided into Beavers, aged 5–7, Cubs, aged 8–11, Scouts, aged 12–14, Venturers, aged 15–17, and Rovers, aged 18–26. Each section uses the programs designed for them by the national association, which are organized in increasing challenge and learning levels by age and ability. In 1992, Scouting in Canada became co-educational. The young people who join Scouting are assured of a full program of crafts, games, challenges, camping, canoeing, community service, and more.

Guiding is for girls and young women only, and is still going strong after an eighty year history in the Campbellford area. It was started locally in 1919 by Grace Payne and stressed allegiance to country, quasi-military drills, uniforms, and formal educational and achievement programs that were designed and tested by outside experts. The program is less formal now, and stresses self-respect and respect for others. Guiding offers programs for Sparks, aged 5–7, Brownies, aged 7–9, Guides, aged 9–12, Pathfinders, aged 12–15, Senior Branches, aged 15–18, and Guide Leaders, over 18.

The Campbellford and Warkworth branches are now combined and are called Sugarbush. The young people enjoy meetings, hikes, and exchanges in Canada and abroad.

CAMPBELLFORD DISTRICT HIGH SCHOOL ENVIRONMENTAL CLUB

Environmental awareness and action have existed at Campbellford District High School for many years, with courses in Environmental Science and Outdoor Education available to students in senior grades. The Trent Valley region provides a natural setting for field studies and recreational pursuits such as camping, hiking and canoeing.

As society has become more concerned about issues such as air and water pollution, waste disposal, and forest destruction, the Northumberland/Newcastle Board of Education mandated all schools to practice environmentally-friendly habits, with a staff member from each school appointed as an environmental representative. The extra-curricular CDHS Environmental Club which has operated since 1995 is a natural vehicle to advance environment education. The mission statement for the club includes "environmental education, awareness and action for club members, the school population and the community." The enthusiasm among the students was tremendous and resulted in several worthwhile projects.

Each school year begins with the club reviewing needs within the school grounds. Recycling, gardening, and cleaning are the focus before cold weather arrives. Club members oversee the recycling within the school throughout the year, and studies have shown that over fifty per cent of waste materials are being diverted away from landfills and into the "wet-dry" facility at Grafton. In return for financial assistance from the Campbellford Rotary Club, the students have laboured in the community, particularly in cleaning the riverbanks near the Rotary Trail on Grand Road.

Club members keep information on file about environmental concerns. In 1997, a Federal government program called Action 21, "Rescue Mission: Planet Earth" caught club members' attention. This was a detailed study of sixteen indicators that students applied to the locality. Once finished, the project was submitted to the United Nations where it was added to many other projects from around the world. The students were amazed to realize that human conditions in other areas of the world are much worse than those in Canada. Fresh water, forests and plentiful food supply are enjoyed at present, but careful management of the environment is needed to maintain this quality of life for future generations.

On April 15, 1998, as an exciting conclusion to the Action 21 project, environmental education students at CDHS were treated to an afternoon with Environment Minister Christine Stewart, MP for Northumberland. Ms. Stewart was presented with the Club's completed project, and in return, she donated the CD-ROM "State of the Environment" and the book "Get a Life."

With such a rich tradition of environmental education at CDHS, it is hoped that such programs will continue in the future.

⁓ Other Organizations ⁓

FRIENDS OF FERRIS

On May 3, 1994, the Province of Ontario made the decision not to open Ferris Park for the 1994 season due to lack of funds. The park had an operating deficit the previous year of more than $30,000. On May 12, 1994, Steve Sharpe, and a group of other concerned citizens, including some from Town Council, formed an ad hoc committee to approach the Ministry of Natural Resources to see how the park could be kept open. On June 21, 1994, the Province agreed to allow the Town of Campbellford and the Township of Seymour to manage Ferris Park and a one year agreement was signed. During this period of time, other concerned members of the community volunteered to assist the ad hoc committee in helping to run the park and referred to themselves as the Friends of Ferris.

The Town and Township formed a management committee to oversee the operation of Ferris Park with Lillian Turner as chairman. Other council members from both Campbellford and Seymour were David Linton, William Thompson and Harold Williams. The committee also included Steve Sharpe, representing the BIA, and Bob Scott, representing the Friends of Ferris. The Province was satisfied with the ability of Campbellford/Seymour to operate Ferris Park and a five year agreement was signed in April 1996.

The Friends mandate reads as follows:

This Charitable Organization is established to raise funds to assist with the promotion of Ferris Provincial Park and the capital expenditure projects for the park. This Organization will also supply volunteer labour for events and/or acceptable support activities. This Organization will produce a newsletter to inform members about what is going on within the park and to suggest ways local residents can contribute to the health and beauty of the park. This Organization will also promote and protect the resources of the park.

The first elected Friends Chairman was Richard Pearson, followed by Bob Scott. The Friends have worked at several fund raising activities such as the Duckie Races on Canada Day and the Giant Yard Sale in September. The Yard Sale has attracted a few thousand visitors to this area over the past four years.

At the January 1999 Annual Meeting, chairman Betty Taylor read the Friends impressive accomplishments. Various events, media coverage, and the interaction of volunteers with the public at events have all contributed to the realization of their mandate. The August 1999 Teddy Bear Picnic under the Rotary shelter, attracted people from Toronto to Kingston. The Public Utilities Commission assisted the Friends in the set up of osprey nest platforms, with more planned for the future. Many trails have been developed with proper signage to direct visitors. Benches have been bought and installed so that visitors can reflect on the surrounding beauty. A large expenditure was the purchase and installation of playground equipment. A picnic shelter was also built.

The 1999 executive is: President, Beverley Vye; Vice-President, Jean Tilney; Secretary, Marilyn Scott; and Treasurer, Barbara Geen.

CAMPBELLFORD SENIOR CITIZENS CLUB

In 1960, a group of senior citizens opened a drop-in centre at the corner of Bridge and Queen Streets. The room was available for seniors to play cards in the afternoon, bingo in the evenings, and pot-luck suppers and dances were held occasionally. In 1964, the group decided to form an official Seniors' Club, and elected executive members as follows: President – Harry Cassidy, First Vice-President – Flossie Scott, Second Vice-President – Lottie Shaw, Treasurer – Forrest Dennis, Secretary – Jo Skinner, Correspondence – Kaye Forestell, and Past President – F. M. Rutherford, who had been involved in the start of the informal drop-in centre.

The purpose of the Seniors' Club is to improve the quality of life for older citizens. Initially the eligibility age was 60 and over; the annual fee was a dollar and, by 1972, there were 244 members. Bill Moon donated the Club's first TV set in 1967. Money was raised from the proceeds of bingo, bus trips, Christmas dinners, and card games. The Treasurer's books were audited annually by Rev. D. Mansell Smith and Joe Smith.

In 1976 the seniors needed a new meeting place for their growing membership. A building fund was established, and the members met with the Town of Campbellford Council to request an accessible area on which to erect a building. The Town agreed to build the Seniors' Club on the east side of Grand Road adjacent to Old Mill Park, opposite the Chamber of Commerce building. Until 1980, planning continued for the new building which was named "The Forrest Dennis Senior Citizens Centre." In April 1981, $10,000 from the building fund was given to the Town of Campbellford towards the cost of construction.

The formal opening of the new Centre was July 2, 1981. A new television set was donated by A. D. Bennett's furniture store and a piano was purchased for $2,800. It was agreed by the Seniors' Club and the town that Campbellford would pay the taxes, heat, insurance, and utility costs for the building, and the Seniors Club would be responsible for the general upkeep and cleaning. The executive for the club was given full authority to determine the use of the building, and other groups may obtain permission to use the club rooms.

In 1986 the age of membership was dropped to 55 years and older, and annual dues were raised to ten dollars. Anyone aged 90 could have annual dues waived after faithful membership for a number of years. At present, the Centre is a very active place, with the following activities being scheduled throughout the week: bridge games, Campbellford Little Theatre rehearsals, line dancing, Euchre Clubs, Harmonica Club rehearsals, Seniors' Glee Club. Seniors' exercise classes, shuffleboard, cribbage games.

In 1960 the United Senior Citizens of Ontario formed a club, with their head office in Toronto. The various local Seniors' Clubs pay two dollars annually per member and in return their interests are represented by the USCO at the provincial level at Queen's Park. The USCO produces a monthly magazine called "The Voice" at a cost of fifteen dollars annually to keep the various clubs up to date on current issues.

The executive for 1999–2000 is:

President	Joyce Stephens	Sunshine	Helen Haig
Vice President	Shirlee Pidgeon	Kitchen	Marie Mackey
Secretary	Verna Petherick	Rentals	Audrey Howell
Treasurer	Pam Dunn	Entertainment	Helen Haig
Past President	Steve O'Henly	Membership	Jean Pettifer
Travel	Joyce Stephens		

ENDNOTES

1 Campbellford Herald, December 4, 1985.
2 Archives of Ontario. F878, *Inventory of the Papers of the Loyal Orange Association of British America. Loyal Orange Lodge No. 526, Seymour Township, Ontario*, July 1993.

Chapter Nine

Communications and Transportation

— Communications —

NEWSPAPERS

The Campbellford Herald

The Kingston family owned the Campbellford Herald for seventy-three years. It was pur-chased by George A. Kingston, left, in 1904, and after his death in 1936, his son Wilbert Kingston, centre, took over its operation.When Wilbert died suddenly in 1968, his younger brother, Kenneth, right, took over and operated the newspaper until it was sold in 1977 to Northumberland Publishers.

Photos from Campbellford/Seymour Heritage Society Archives, originally from the files of the Campbellford Herald.

Herald, Campbellford – Expired Dec. 24, 1996, in its 124th year, following a lengthy illness due to poor circulation. In attendance were staff members John Campbell, Nancy Allanson, Jean Convey and Mark Hoult. Retiree Jim Bell, a Herald employee for 45 years, sent his regrets.

So might have begun an abbreviated obituary of the Herald in its final edition. That a small business survived for 123 years is indeed impressive but many Canadian weekly newspapers born in the 1800s achieved a remarkable record for longevity. It wasn't until the latter part of the 20th century that these venerable institutions fell victim to younger rivals for advertising dollars.

The Campbellford Herald was launched as a broadsheet on Dec. 9, 1873 by the Vosper brothers, J. T. and T. J., who declared: "A feeling has for some time existed in the minds of the people of this village that a local organ was required in this place, to advance the interests and promote the well-being, morally and intellectually, of the people." The founders further noted that "the rapid growth of Campbellford, the improvements and progress of the surrounding country, bid fair to ensure the safety and success of the undertaking."

Their venture was a bedrock of stability through its first century of existence, with ownership being a family affair, first with the Vospers and then the Kingston brothers, Wilbert and Ken.

When Northumberland Publishers, based in Cobourg, purchased the Herald in 1977, the weekly's evolution as a chronicler of community life quickened. Regular reports from local organizations, such as women's institutes, and various communities – Stanwood, Springbrook and Wellman's Corners, for example – still made their way into print but there was a marked shift in emphasis toward more 'hard' news and features. The editorial mix included columns by Marjory Scriver (health issues), Betty Thain (cooking), Neville Edwards (humour) and Margaret Santon (gardening). Especially popular with readers were the children's Christmas writings and, later, the graduation supplements.

In 1983, the Herald got its third owner in six years when the St. Catharines Standard purchased Northumberland Publishers. Changes in ownership brought with them greater capital and editorial resources, making it possible for the Herald to remain contemporary despite its advanced age. The newspaper made itself over many times, and there was always an infusion of young writing talent to invigorate the business.

But as much as the Herald changed in look and content support for the community organ withered. The two free distribution weeklies that arrived on the scene in 1985 siphoned off its readers, and declining readership in turn drove away advertisers. Paid circulation, which had hovered around 3,650 in 1985, had shrunk to little more than 1,600 by 1995.

In February 1996, the Herald revamped itself for the last time, becoming a tabloid. It wasn't enough for the weekly's new owner, Southam Inc., Canada's largest newspaper publisher, which bought the St. Catharines Standard a few months later. Notice of the Herald's imminent demise was made public in the newspaper's Nov. 27, 1996 edition when Earl Bateman, president and chief operating officer of Southam's Ontario Community Network, announced it was selling the weekly and its sister newspaper, the Warkworth Journal (acquired by the Standard in 1989). The pair had "performed poorly for several years and efforts to make them profitable (had) failed," he said. "Sinking revenue and subscriptions, combined with the distribution of several free total market publications, makes it difficult for them to compete."

Two inquiries were made regarding their purchase but no buyer stepped forward. The two newspapers made a quiet exit on Christmas Eve.

– by John Campbell, last editor of the Campbellford Herald

The Campbellford News

On Thursday, April 8, 1886, the Campbellford Herald acknowledged the inaugural issue of The Campbellford News, an eight-page journal, edited by A. Neal Clarke, former proprietor of the late Hastings Observer. At the time of publication, no additional information was available about the fate of this newspaper.

The Campbellford Gazette

By 1896, Robert A. Latimer, a former member of the editorial staff of the Perth Courier, was the editor of The Campbellford Gazette. At the time of publication, no additional information was available about this paper.[1]

Campbellford Despatch

This weekly newspaper was likely produced between 1898 and 1912, and came out each Thursday at a subscription cost of 50 cents per year in advance. H.B.R. Dryden was the editor, and there is mention of an office on Front Street. The newspaper's name, 'Despatch,' is not an incorrect spelling but a variation of the word 'dispatch', commonly used at the time. Over the course of its publication the newspaper was variously known as 'The Campbellford Despatch, 'Campbellford Despatch,' and 'The Despatch.' The paper contained local advertisements, but reporting was heavily national and international, with major local events appearing from time to time on the front page.

The Campbellford/Seymour Heritage Society has been the recipient of five issues of this newspaper dating from 1899 to 1912. The February 23, 1899 edition is named 'Campbellford Despatch' and is Volume 1, Number 33, which seems to indicate that the first paper was published in July of 1898. The September 12, 1901, Volume 4, Number 8 publication states that the subscription had risen to one dollar per year, in advance, with H.B.R. Dryden still editor. This paper was now called 'The

Campbellford Despatch'. Unfortunately, the 1904 issue in the possession of the Heritage Society is only the top half of the publication. This paper is dated November 3 and is Volume 7, Number 16. This publication is named 'The Despatch' and is still one dollar per year. There is no mention of the editor or address.

The Thursday, July 5, 1906, Volume 8, Number 52 publication of 'The Campbellford Despatch' was still one dollar per year with H.B.R. Dryden now referred to as editor and proprietor. The headlines read, "Campbellford Now a Town" and the sentence below reads "Glorious Inauguration and Old Boys Reunion." This statement follows the headlines:

> "Monday July 2nd, 1906, will long be Remembered – Greatest Event in the History of Campbellford – 10,000 People Participate in the Inauguration of the Town."

The November 14, 1912, publication, listed as Volume XIII, Number 37 and entitled 'The Despatch', named A. F. Sheppard the publisher. The lead story was the drowning at Ranney Falls of Maxwell and Donald Doxsee, sons of Mr. and Mrs. Ernest Doxsee. A picture of Ranney Falls accompanied the article.

The editors worked diligently to obtain subscriptions. When the paper was just fifty cents per year, and payable in advance, there was an interesting offer made to new subscribers. They would receive a one hundred page book full of 'Stories, Humour and Statistics,' retail value fifty cents. The paper boasted about having the very latest type faces and improved machinery for turning out a fine newspaper.

Information as to how long this paper stayed in operation is unavailable. This paper probably operated in direct competition with the Campbellford Herald, which emphasized local news as opposed to the national and international news that predominated in the 'Despatch.'

The Community Press

The Community Press had its first run from 40 Mill Street, Stirling, on April 16, 1985. Four thousand copies were distributed within a ten mile radius of the village of Stirling. Alan Coxwell was instrumental in the establishment of the newspaper. His grandfather, Hylton Coxwell, was a stringer in the 1930s for both the Toronto Telegram and the Toronto Star. Alan and his business partner, John Seckar, were focused on reporting events and issues of interest to their local readers. The staff, which included Heather McGee, Terry Bush and John Bennett, lived in the area and kept themselves attuned to the concerns of the local population. The first proof reader for the Community Press was Shirley Crane, who had retired from teaching. Her complaints about the spelling and grammar errors in the Press resulted in her being offered the job. The late Al Clunie also came on board as part of the Press team.

By 1992, the print run had grown to twenty thousand, and now included a Western edition serving the area from the edge of Peterborough to Campbellford, and an Eastern edition serving Tweed and south to Highway 401. In late 1992, the Quinte edition was born and the paper now covers Belleville, Trenton, Brighton and the southern rural areas. The Community Press is still growing and now is being read in fifty-seven thousand homes each week. Included in the paper's distribution are weekly special flyers from local businesses.

The mandate of the Community Press is to deliver readable local news to the communities it serves. The weekly Community Press remains wholly independent and now produces three editions.

The Campbellford Courier

– as it appeared in the Campbellford Courier

First issue of Courier published Sept. 25, 1985

Wednesday, Sept. 25th, 1985, was a special date in the history of Campbellford. It marked the creation of the Campbellford Courier, giving the community an alternative voice in the publishing field. Prior to the Courier's entry the Campbellford Herald had been the area's only weekly community newspaper.

The introduction of the Courier marked the eighth weekly newspaper launched by owner and publisher Joe Cembal in the area. The company's head office is located in Marmora.

Cembal, who formerly worked for MacLean-Hunter Publications in Toronto, said his decision to move into the Campbellford market would fill a void not already covered by his other seven weeklies.

The other area newspapers in the Cembal Publication family included the Stirling News-Argus, which at that point in time had been published for over 105 years; the Marmora Herald, continuously published for over 108 years the Norwood Register, 111 years, the Havelock Citizen, 15 years; the Hastings Star, 13 years; and the Kingston Heritage, which had been published for over 10 years.

All of the newspapers are produced out of head office in Marmora.

Cembal said it was his intention of producing a newspaper in Campbellford which placed emphasis on editorial and news coverage as well as 100 per cent coverage of every household in the area.

POST CARDS

An interesting method of communication used between 1900 and 1912 was the post card. Most cards were 3.5 by 5.5 inches but a few were larger or smaller. They were printed on heavy, good quality paper, with one side featuring a picture and the reverse side a blank space for the sender to write a short message and the address of the receiver. At first, the post offices did not like these one cent messagesage bearers and written messages were forbidden. However, as the post card craze caught on, the post offices relented and messages were permitted. These cards are prized items for collectors today. Some post cards are prized for their historic pictures of early towns, villages, and buildings. Others are collected for their valuable stamps or post-marks as well as their interesting messages. The many pictures, which were produced in colour as well as black and white, provide a valuable source of history. There were also humorous, sympathy, birthday, and other special occasion cards for St. Patrick's Day, Valentine's Day, or Christmas. In addition, it was common to have a photograph of a person or group printed on a post card. The cards were printed in many European countries as well as in the United States and Canada. Some of the humorous cards were considered to be quite risqué for the time, especially those from overseas. Today these cards sell for several dollars or more. Dealers in every country exchange post cards so that those sent from a particular location are often returned to a dealer in that area. Albums, containing black or grey pages with slots, were also produced in the early 1900s for collectors to store their treasured items. Some could hold up to one hundred cards.

Carolyn Donald has a wonderful collection of post cards from A. E. Stephens of Campbellford to her great aunt, Mary Free of Polmont. These post cards document the story of a courtship which extended from 1911 to 1918. This couple was eventually married in 1922. The messages included requests for meetings at church and picnics. Toward the end of the courtship, a lovely card, beautifully embossed with flowers, includes a printed message, "To My Dearest." This sample of a prepared title reflects a trend which continues today as people are often reluctant to express their personal feelings in writing.

TELEPHONE

In 1886, the North American Telegraph Company, headquartered in Kingston, Ontario, was given the power to establish, construct, purchase, lease or work any lines of telegraph or telephone from and to any place or places in Canada. In 1888 construction crews of the Bell Telephone Company of Canada extended the first long distance line from Belleville, through Stirling, Campbellford, and Hastings. This line was extended to Peterborough in 1889.

About 1889, the first telephone line became operative in Campbellford. This was a private line from Charles Smith's Flour Mill to the railway station. Then two additional services were run to the station, one from the Trent Valley Woollen Mill and the other from G.G. Eakins' Drug Store. Later, these were connected and Mr.

Eakins became the manager. The switch for the system was in his drug store. Then, by 1890, as the number of telephones slowly increased, J. Nicol, who ran a book store, had charge of the first real exchange.

Campbellford and Warkworth were connected by telephone and telegraph in 1890. By 1893, the town had long distance communication with Belleville through Stirling and Foxboro and with Peterborough through Hastings and Keene. Through these connections, the local telephone user could reach hundreds of other towns and cities.

By 1895, Campbellford's small telephone exchange, with fifteen customers, was located in F. W. Wood's Drug Store on Front Street South. Under F. W. Wood's supervision the customers mushroomed to fifty-two by 1900, and they were proudly listed in a pocket-sized directory for Eastern Ontario.

Reports of the Company gave the long distance charge for a call from Campbellford to Peterborough as thirty cents, while a call to Ottawa was eight-five cents, and one to Kingston fifty cents for a five-minute conversation.

Starting in 1910, telephone service was provided all night and for a two hour period on Sunday. This service existed with a patching system within "off" hours. Mulhearn's Livery was connected with the Windsor Hotel and F.J. Kent's Livery with the St. Lawrence Hotel.

Campbellford listings in the Bell Telephone Company of Canada Official Telephone Directory, District of Eastern Ontario, 1900, p. 44–5.

Directory courtesy of Helen Wood and Vera Newman.

CAMPBELLFORD. 44

†CAMPBELLFORD, F. W. WOOD, Local Manager.

29	Archer, W. B	Residence	Booth
30	Bailey, A. E	Residence	Rear
51	Burrows, G. E	Residence	George
24	Cairns, J. W	Druggist	Bridge
19	Callaghan, Thos	Residence	Booth
20	Carlaw, Dr. T. W	Physician	Bridge
17	Colville, A. L	Office	Bridge
9	Colville, A. L	Residence	Booth
6	Connelly, D	Store	Front
34	Cooper, W. E. (Rev.)	Rectory	Church
1	Coyne, I. & Co	Store	Front
39	Crowe, Edward	Store	Bridge
27	Cumming, W. W	Residence	George
3	Denike, R. B. (Rev.)	Residence	Church
2	"Despatch"	Office	Front
38	Elcombe, E. W	Store	George
21	Fire Hall		Mill
18	Ferris, J. B. & Co	Store	Front
37	Ferris, J. B	Residence	Saskatoon
28	Fowlds, H. M. & Son	Elevator	Bridge
22	Gibson House	Hotel	Bridge
35	Grand Trunk Ry	Station	
16	Hay, Geo. A., V.S	Residence	Booth
25	Haynes, W. H	Residence	Front
44	"Herald"	Office	Bridge
52	Higginson Bros	Store	Front
42	Johnston, J. W	Residence	Booth
50	Kent, J. N	Livery	Front
11	Macoun, Dr. J	Physician	Frank
47	McCloskey, (Rev. Father)	Residence	Booth
43	Morten & Owen	Hardware	Bridge
48	Mulholland, A. A	Residence	George
5	Mulhearn, B	Livery	Front
15	Nancarrow Bros	Store	Bridge
7	Naylor, T. J	Residence	Stirling rd
45	Northumberland Paper & Elec. Co		River Front
41	Owen, C. L	Residence	Frank
33	Queen's Hotel		Front
10	Rankin, W. E	Residence	Grand rd
14	Rathbun Co. (The)	Office	
8	St. Lawrence Hall	Hotel	Front
26	Scherk, Dr	Residence	Front
36	Shannon, R. S	Store	Front
12	Smith, Chas. & Sons	Flour Mill	Mill
46	Smith, Chas	Residence	Mill
31	Standard Bank	Office	Front
23	Stewart, Wm	Livery	George
49	Tait & Douglas	Hardware	Front
13	Thomas Bros	Store	Bridge
40	Trent Valley Woolen Mills, Office		Bridge
32	Windsor Hotel	Hotel	Front
4	Wood, F. W	Residence	Front

There were two hundred sixty-three customers in Campbellford with R.H. Simpson becoming the manager.

In 1910, the North American Telephone Company leased its telephone exchanges, lines, and other telephone property to the Bell Telephone Company of Canada. On February 14, 1911, this same property and business was sold to Bell. W.E. Brewster was the manager for the next eleven years, followed by L. Pierce.

In about 1912, "Mr. Telephone" started his long and popular career in Campbellford. Wilbert Daniel (Webb) Wood was born in Hastings County in 1887. As a young man, he worked with "gangs" installing hydro and telephone poles throughout the country. When he stepped off the train in Campbellford, he was hired immediately, and he spent the next forty years serving the needs of the residents of Campbellford/Seymour. Over the years, he worked as an installer, a telephone repairman, a switchboard repairman, a business office representative, and finally as the telephone manager in 1928. Webb retired in 1952 after forty years of service. Daughters Helen Wood and Vera Wood Newman recall stories of how the farmers manipulated Webb into breaking the trail on the snow covered roads by pretending telephone repairs were necessary. In winter Webb hired a horse, "Little Joe," and a cutter from Rutherford's Dairy, and with his spurs, test set, bag of tools, and bear-paw snowshoes set out to repair broken lines.

In Campbellford, the magneto system, which required customers to crank the generator on their phones to reach the operator, had always been used. By April 17, 1940, the phone system was converted to common battery operation and the 880 customers merely lifted the receiver for service.

On December 2, 1962, Campbellford/Seymour telephones were changed to the dial system. Telephone numbers became numerical only, and all local telephone numbers were now seven digits. Direct Distance Dialing was also introduced, enabling customers to dial their own long distance calls without operator assistance. On December 15, 1968, long distance charges ceased on calls to Warkworth, Hastings and Havelock. In June 1978, Bell announced the addition of one thousand more telephone directory numbers, adding this to two thousand, seven hundred directory numbers then in effect. The number of subscribers on a multi-party line was cut to a maximum of four. In 1988, Bell Canada modernized its facility on River Street. Improvements also included relocating cable to allow road construction between Campbellford and Petherick's Corners and placing additional cable and a new digital switch at Meyersburg. Local plans through the 1990s included modernizing facilities in the Centre Street and First Street area, installing a fiber optics link between Campbellford and the national fiber optics transmission system, reconstruction of a pole line to incorporate P.U.C./Hydro facilities, and replacement of Campbellford's analogue switching system with state-of-the-art digital technology by 1993.

The Bell Telephone Company of Canada was one of the few companies that employed and trained women before World War II, and as such played an important role in the empowerment of women. The company was known its for its progressive treatment of women in the form of promotions, provision of benefits, and payment of fair wages. Employees also had the benefit of being able to transfer to Bell positions in other localities, either as a promotion or for personal reasons.

Gert Heffernan, who was employed by Bell in Campbellford from 1920 until about 1952, was interviewed in July 1994 about her experiences with the company. Gert, then 90 years of age, recalled some of the highlights of her employment. When she began her job with Bell, Mr. Brewster was manager, Jennie Ranney was secretary, and Bob Whalen and Webb Wood were in charge of installation and repair. She recalled the first night operator being Bill Peeling, a high school student who worked for a few hours when needed. Over the years, chief operators were Mary Maguire, Miss Nelligan, Doris Dewey, Miss Curran, Jennie Ranney, Flossie McComb, Orpha Clegg, Josie Milner, Viola Noland and herself. Caretakers included Claude Duncalfe, Bob Bullen, Neddie Flint, Edna Waters, Gerald Sharp, and Johnny Runions. Gert, Goldie Loucks, and Lorna Dewey were also amazing in that they recalled the names of close to seventy operators, the last hired being Verda Thain. Some of the "local boys" who worked for the Bell Telephone Company of Canada were Joe Clark, Harry, Bud, and J.P. Wood, Maclean Shillinglaw, Ken Grills, and Alex, Jack, Eric and Evan McCulloch. "The Men" who worked with Webb Wood were Ross Kemp, Tom Hall, Stewart Hagerman, Mickey Kirkpatrick, Bill Merritt, Royden Henderson, Reg Seymour and Everette Steele.

Bell Telephone Operators in Campbellford

With the help of Gert Heffernan and Goldie Loucks, the following women were identified as operators in the Campbellford Office:

Pearl Maguire	Hazel LaBrash	Elsabeth Whitton
Carrie Barnum	Ina (Sales) Arnold	Betty (Jeffs) Fry
Betty (McCulloch) Ames	Stella Donald	Shirley (West) Scott
Mary Hughes	Winnie Fry	Ann Hoey
Laura O'Shea	Flossie (Henson) Hinton	Ruth Allanson
Mary Taylor	Lena Duncalfe	Dorothy Lloyd
Jessie Cassan	Lottie Bennett	Edith Pullan
Rose Hollenby	Alice (Tripp) Donald	Helen O'Shea
Nell Barrie	Gladys Hankenson	Ruby Ellis
Kate Barrie	Geraldine (McMullen)	Barbara (Mumby) Fry
Clara Rowe	Mackenzie	Verda Thain
Tress (Rowe) McArthur	Jean (Smith) Cotton	Cora Barnum

Bell Telephone Operators in Campbellford (continued)

Maude Maguire	Flora Graham	Marge (Fleming) Locke
Joan Joyce	Pat (Hogle) Curle	Audrey Blakely
Joan Haig	Joyce (Poole) Stephens	Shirley (Dunk) Sager
Bessie Bedford	Grace McNaughton	Olive Radley
Marion Haig	Mamie (Winstanley) Murray	Helen Haig
Alice McKelvie	Loretta (Sarginson) Collins	Joyce Clancy
Betty Fairman	Helen Hazell	Nancy (Peake) Ruttan
Nellie Stephens	Goldie (Glenn) Loucks	Shirley MacDonald
Ida (Wilson)	Teresa (Dunlay) Shaw	Yvonne (Petherick) Jackson
Darrington	Isobel (Stephens) French	Harriet Haig
Helen Long	Lorna (George) Dewey	Noreen (McCann) Coxwell
Ruby Simpson	Doreen (Smith) Lisle	Marilyn (Stephens) Pollock

RADIO AND TELEVISION

CKOL Radio

The driving force behind the establishment of CKOL Radio in Campbellford was Dave Lockwood. The station had its origin in a 1988 market study which showed that the community was not properly provided with local news and information on a regular and current basis by radio facilities outside of the area. Also, radio advertising rates were not geared to the small merchants of Campbellford/ Seymour whose true market area was within a twenty minute drive. Within that twenty minute drive the study showed there was an audience of approximately 24,000 people in the summer months and about 14,000 in the winter.

Part of the process to start a radio station involved licensing with Canadian Radio and Television Commission, the CRTC. An application was filed for approval of a Community radio station, and the music format which it would follow. The CRTC has a list of the different types of music that stations choose and one of the first problems encountered with CKOL was that it did not fit any of the categories, such as country, oldies, rock and roll, classical, or any one type of music. The aim was to provide listeners with a variety of music, and, with the exception of alternative, or hard, or acid rock, the station has met this objective. The CRTC was eventually convinced of the viability of this approach and the license was granted. CKOL 98.7FM officially went on air for the first time on July 1, 1992, broadcasting from Old Mill Park.

Community radio provides coverage for local events and air time for local artists. Many local musicians have been invited to the studio for interviews and an opportunity to play their music. Local politicians participate in open-line shows and community groups are interviewed about their up-coming events. Since the beginning, the station has relied on volunteer broadcasters. Financially, the station relies on advertising revenue, donations, and fund raising campaigns. Currently all are in short supply and the station relies on a few loyal, hard-working supporters. Supervisory staff control operations to assure that listeners will be properly served and the requirements of the CRTC are met.

Television and the Internet

Looking back over the last century, there has been a vast change in the way the citizens of Campbellford access the outside world. Even as little as fifty years ago, to see events in far off places as they were happening meant actually being there. There were movie newsreels at the theatre which showed "current" events. But to really see something "out there" meant physically traveling – usually by train or bus. Times have changed, and local citizens can now stay very much in touch with the rest of Ontario and the world, and see things as they happen without leaving their living rooms – thanks to two modern marvels: Television and the Internet.

In the more remote areas of Campbellford/Seymour, many television viewers are dependent on television antennas, rotary dials, and 'bunny ears' for their television reception. Some residents, especially those located closer to the town, have access to cable TV to provide them with a reliable and varied television service. This began in Campbellford in July 1966, when Redden's Cable TV opened at 16 Queen Street. Owner-manager, Brian Redden, is kept busy providing access to over thirty different channels, ranging from CNN, ABC, CBS, NBC, and PBS, through TNN, CBC, CTV, TVO, and TSN, and local Community News and Advertising.

An alternative to cable viewing, and a comparative newcomer to the television scene, is the Home Satellite Receiver. This is a small dish-shaped antenna, mounted usually on the roof of the house, which receives signals from satellites broadcasting a large number of TV channels, perhaps as many as 200. As with cable, customers can choose optional "packages" of stations, through such servers as StarChoice and Bell ExpressVu. Ken's Stereo and TV, in business at 29 Front Street South since 1983, has been providing and servicing Home Satellite systems since 1995. Recently, Redden's Radio Shack has also begun to provide this service as well.

Television is, of course, an essentially passive medium. Even with cable or satellite the choice of programs is limited. However, for those who like to take a more active role, the Internet gives the opportunity for interaction. Browsing the tens of thousands of Websites, as well as participating in discussions with other people via electronic mail or interactive 'chatrooms' requires two things: a personal computer with the appropriate software and hardware, and an account with a company called an Internet Service Provider, or ISP, such as *www.redden.on.ca*.

Cornerstone Computer Systems, at 13 Front Street North, is the oldest established computer store in town. Its owner, Denis Gale, was a Business Systems Engineer before opening the business here in 1995. Cornerstone sells and services computer hardware and software, does upgrades to customers' machines, offers a general consulting service, and is also an agent for the Kawartha ISP, *www.kawartha.com.*

DR Computers, run by Dave Lloyd, is at 30 Doxsee Avenue South. The "R" initially represented early partner Rod Williams, but now represents Dave's daughter Rhiannon, who helps out when she's at home. Familiarly known as Doctor Computer, Dave has been selling and servicing PCs since March 1996, and is also an agent for Accel Computers, an ISP in Peterborough, *www. accel.net.*

Ashford Computer Services has been owned and run by Brian Ashford since 1997. It offers computer sales and servicing, general consulting, and also rents video games. Brian can arrange an Internet account with the newest ISP available locally, a company called Nexicom from Millbrook, *www.nexicom.net.*

Campbellford has something to suit everyone's taste in modern "world watching": conventional television reception, reliable cable television service; more avant garde TV offerings via a satellite dish; places to shop for a new computer, or to upgrade or service an old one; and a wide choice of Internet Service Providers.

～ Transportation ～

ROADS

The first roads followed trails made by animals going from their feeding grounds to watering places. Later men walked these primitive routes, marking their progress through the forest by blazing trees. County Road 31 from Hoard's Station to the Hastings-Warkworth highway follows the route of an old Indian trail. As settlement progressed, a few families had access to an ox and two wheeled cart.

Following the surveys of the township, fourteen concession roads, running west to east, and located seven-eighths of a mile apart were laid out. These were joined by sideroads, running north and south, at various intervals. The first task was to clear the allotted width by cutting trees and filling the holes left after their removal. Brush and stone were used to reduce the size of the holes. The dirt surface was soon worn into ruts and bumps. As the settlers became more prosperous, travel was by horseback or by wagons, carts, and democrats.[2] Wet weather caused mud and made travel very difficult. Some surfaces were covered with gravel or broken stone. When roads passed through swampy areas, cedar logs were laid crosswise side by side as closely as possible and filled in with earth. These were known as "corduroy roads." As the logs settled into the boggy areas, a bumpy but adequate road emerged. Maintenance was assigned to a pathmaster for each beat or assigned territory. Gravel was hauled in horse-drawn wagons and spread by road workers using shovels and rakes. Grading and ditches were handled by two men using a two-handled metal scraper.

As automobiles became the preferred mode of travel, improvements in the road surfaces were critical. Highway 30 was completed from Meyersburg to Campbellford prior to 1934. In that year, contracts were let to two companies for the section from Campbellford to Trent River. The work commenced at either end and the two groups met. A gravel surface was completed by that fall and later the road was paved.

In 1936, the road on the east side of the river was paved to the Rawdon boundary. Later, Hastings County completed the stretch into Springbrook.

In 1961, the West River Road was designated as a Development Road by the Department of Highways. The surface was completed to Healey Falls and the next year the county extended the work to Highway 7.

In recent years, taxes cover the cost of road maintenance by the hiring of crews for road work and snow ploughing. Machinery such as bulldozers, graders, dump trucks, and ploughs now do the labour which, in early times, was all done by hand.

STAGE COACHES

Before automobiles became the common means of transportation, stage coaches connected Campbellford/Seymour to neighbouring communities, such as Colborne, Warkworth, Brighton, Hastings, and Havelock. They were used to carry both passengers and the mail. One of the earliest references to stage coaches comes from the Campbellford Herald in 1876. It notes that Mr. Wade, the long-time owner of the stage line between Brighton and Campbellford which carried the mail, was selling the line to Mr. I. C. Sanford of Brighton. In 1878, H. Huycke established a stage coach line between Campbellford and Hastings, and planned a tri-weekly service. At some point before 1894, Henry Clegg operated the Campbellford-Havelock stage. He found himself unable to stand the rigours of daily trips and sold the line to Thomas Rainie of Campbellford. The Herald noted that "Mr. Rainie has fallen into a good job." In 1904, the Campbellford-Havelock stage, operated by C. H. Coveney, left Campbellford daily at 8:00 AM and arrived in Havelock at 10:30 AM, in time to catch the CPR train. The stage returned daily at 3:30 PM, and a one-way fare was fifty cents.

In 1910, Leonard Carr, Jr. took over the Campbellford-Brighton stage from John Weese, who had operated it for many years. The stage left Campbellford at 5:30 AM, made stops to pick up and deliver mail at Meyersburg, Codrington, Orland, and Hilton, and arrived in Brighton at 9:20 AM. The return trip left at 1:00 PM and arrived in Campbellford at 5:30 PM. The fare was $1 one-way and $1.75 return. The coach was designed to carry six passengers, but often carried twelve, and on one occasion, seventeen. When King Edward died in 1910, the stage, like all other vehicles carrying the Royal Mail, was draped in black during the period of mourning. Carr left the stage coach business in 1914. Later operators were a Mr. Williams, and William Sloggett. In August 1915, George McComb purchased the Havelock stage from John Lawrence. It is unclear how long the stage lines continued to operate.

RAILWAYS

In the early 1870s, the Grand Junction Railway obtained a charter to build a rail link from Belleville to Peterborough where it was to join the Midland Railway, and form part of the grain route from western Canada. The section from Belleville to Campbellford was completed in 1878 and extended to Peterborough in 1880. The original line followed a long and circuitous route through the village of Campbellford, with level crossings at Booth Street, Rear Street, Front Street, Queen Street, Canrobert Street, and Sebastopol Street, and an overhead bridge at Ranney Street. A curved wooden-trestle bridge spanned the river from a point just to the north of Market Street (Lots 25 and 26 of the Kirchoffer and Cockburn Subdivision Plan, 1877) on the east bank to a site on the west bank just to the north of Napier Street (Lots 62 and 63 of the Rowed Subdivision Plan, 1867–68). On May 15, 1878, a tender was put out for the construction of three station houses – one at Hoard's Station, and one in each of the villages of Campbellford and Hastings. The latter two were built by J. W. Dinwoodie of Campbellford.

The first train arrived in Campbellford on Saturday, December 7, 1878 before the bridge was completed. It was not until June 10, 1879, that the first train crossed the Trent River at Campbellford and arrived in the nearly completed station house located on the north side of the Hastings Road (present-day Bridge Street or Hwy. 30) just to the west of Simpson Street, with Engineer Harry Kelly at the throttle of Engine No. 38. The first shipment of grain occurred on Thursday, October 23, 1879 and was a car load of barley sent from Hoard's Station by Thomas Walker of Rawdon Township. On July 8, 1879, nineteen tons of cheese were shipped from Campbellford. The first train from Belleville to Peterborough went through Campbellford on December 6, 1880.

The Grand Junction Railway experienced financial difficulties and was leased in 1881 by its rival, the Midland Railway, which was by then already in the control of the Grand Trunk Railway. This lease was converted into ownership in 1883, and eventually the combined assets of the two railways were integrated into the CNR system.

By 1889, it was evident that the line through the village was unsatisfactory; grades, curves, street level crossings, and in winter, snapping bridge bolts created too many problems. It was decided to reroute the rails to a more southerly location and to move the station. Property was purchased from Adam and J. W. Dinwoodie on the east side of the river and from the Cumming Estate and J. C. Gibson on the west side. The new line opened in 1899 and included a bridge over the Trent River between Picnic Island off the east shore and a site opposite the new Canadian Tire Store on Grand Road on the west shore. The section of the old line on the east side of the river was retained as a spur line to the Rathbun saw mill, located near the site of the present high school. The station, now owned by the Grand Trunk Railway, was relocated to the north-east corner of Alma and Simpson Streets.

Original route of the Grand Junction Railway through Campbellford, completed 1878.

Prepared from National Archives of Canada national Map Collection, #156716. Reproduced with permission.

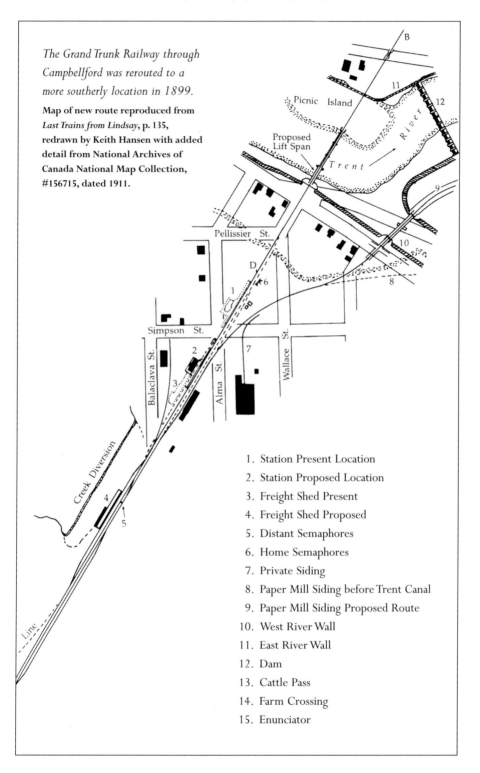

The Grand Trunk Railway through Campbellford was rerouted to a more southerly location in 1899.

Map of new route reproduced from *Last Trains from Lindsay*, **p. 135, redrawn by Keith Hansen with added detail from National Archives of Canada National Map Collection, #156715, dated 1911.**

Picnic Island

Proposed Lift Span

Trent *River*

Pellissier St.

D

Simpson St.

Balaclava St.

Alma St.

Wallace St.

Creek Diversion

Line

B

1. Station Present Location
2. Station Proposed Location
3. Freight Shed Present
4. Freight Shed Proposed
5. Distant Semaphores
6. Home Semaphores
7. Private Siding
8. Paper Mill Siding before Trent Canal
9. Paper Mill Siding Proposed Route
10. West River Wall
11. East River Wall
12. Dam
13. Cattle Pass
14. Farm Crossing
15. Enunciator

When the decision was made to complete the Trent Canal, it included a control dam south of the railway bridge. This dam would raise the water level, so that a moveable span was considered necessary to allow the passage of river traffic. The original intent of the railway was to replace the span on the west bank of the river with a bascule or lift bridge and to erect a second lift bridge across the canal to allow access to the industries on the island between the river and canal. Only the second lift bridge was actually built and it was known locally as the 'Low Black.' The Grand Trunk Railway decided not to build the other moveable span, but to completely replace the old bridge with a new, stronger structure to accommodate the grain traffic. The Dominion Bridge Company erected the new bridge in two phases. In 1917, the three spans over Saskatoon Avenue were completed and in 1918, the eight remaining spans over the river, canal, and the road on the west bank were completed. In 1914, a new station was also built about 100 yards south of the existing station on the south-east corner of Simpson and Alma Streets.

The presence of the railway helped to create an economic boom in Campbellford during the early years of the twentieth century. Lumber, grain, hogs, paper, apples, lamb, cheese, and eggs were all exported from the area, headed on their way to such places as Glasgow, Liverpool, Buffalo, Montreal, or just Belleville. From 1914–1918, four passenger trains stopped in Campbellford on a route that linked Belleville and Toronto. Twice daily the trains ran in both directions, a great benefit to the town at a time when cars and trucks were rare. The grain movement from the Lakehead sustained the rail line through Campbellford for many years. Wheat was taken from Fort William by boat to Midland where it was then shipped by rail through Lindsay and Campbellford and on to Belleville. This movement continued from about 1910 until the late 1950s. The carloads of wheat from Western Canada during the 1930s also brought with them the unemployed 'hobos' who were grim reminders of the hardships of the depression. During the 1930s, Major Bygott was the station agent in Campbellford. He was followed by Art McConnell and C. L. (Charlie) Redden who was there in 1969 when the station was closed. In Campbellford, there usually were seven or eight full-time employees, and in the summer, the section gang usually took on student help. In addition, there were track gangs who would come through on boarding cars to maintain the track and do maintenance on the bridge using heavy equipment.

The advent of air travel, increased automobile travel, and the development of roads and trucking decreased the viability of the railway system both for freight and passengers. Government subsidization, while used in the short-term to sustain local runs such as the Campbellford line, was not the long-term solution. When the route and station were closed in 1969, the effect on the local population was minimal. The black lift bridge on the spur line to the island was torn down in December 1972. There was some local effort to save the station as a museum, but

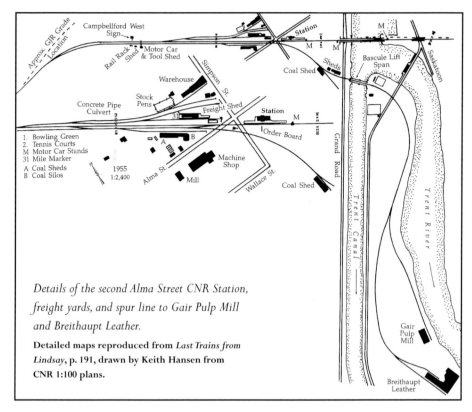

Details of the second Alma Street CNR Station, freight yards, and spur line to Gair Pulp Mill and Breithaupt Leather.

Detailed maps reproduced from *Last Trains from Lindsay*, p. 191, drawn by Keith Hansen from CNR 1:100 plans.

nothing came of it, and it was demolished by Ed Little in July 1982. The bridge on the main line was removed in April 1987, and all that remains today are the two piers that can be seen while driving along the canal on Grand Road.

Working on the Railroad – Recollections about Charlie Redden and his times

Based on an interview with Brian Redden by Marilyn Scott, Nov. 11, 1998.

Brian's father, C.L. Redden, known to the railroaders as Charlie, was employed for forty-five years on the railroad. He worked at almost every station on the main CNR line between Cornwall and Thunder Bay. At the beginning of his career, he and his wife lived in a trailer going from station to station to fill in for operators on vacation. Brian was born in Campbellford, but Brian's older brother, Bev, was born in Agincourt when Charlie was the operator there. As Charlie got more seniority, he became the full-time operator at a station.

In the 1930s and 1940s, Charlie was the night operator at the Campbellford Station. He was promoted to Agent-Operator, and worked at Marmora Station, Brennan, and Hastings before returning to Campbellford in 1960. To become a telegraph operator, Charlie trained at the Dominion Telegrapher's school in Toronto for approximately eighteen months. Periodically, he had to go some place on the main line for an upgrading test and the children would go with him. There were two telegraph systems, one for the public and one for railroad business, and there could be three or four wire messages a day. Once, during a murder trial, Charlie had to send all of the press releases to the station in Toronto. He also looked after the dispatch phone for train orders, which was used to relay orders to the track people from the chief dispatch in Belleville.

In a small town such as Campbellford, the position of station agent was combined with the telegraph operator's responsibilities. As station agent, Charlie had to know how to signal the trains to stop, as there were no two-way radios. Charlie's last duty before leaving the station at night was locking up and putting up the signal. Another of Charlie's responsibilities was to stand on the platform to look for hot boxes and problems on passing trains, such as a hose being loose. He would signal to the conductor in the caboose that there was a problem and he also would signal the engineer as the train approached to let them know that he was there. This meant that the engineer would know that the train was being inspected as it was going by.

There were daily passenger trains – morning, afternoon, and evening. The freight trains went straight through. The passenger trains had a baggage car and an express car. They let the passengers out and the baggage was loaded on the wagon. There was a seal on the baggage door and the operator took that off and then they could load the baggage on the wagon. The express car had parcels and a delivery truck pulled up beside the express car and unloaded the packages.

Charlie used to hoop the trains, so that the trains did not have to stop. A hoop was a pole-like device with a wire clip on it and there was one for the engineer and one for the caboose. Usually it was used to relay a telegram. Charlie would write out the message on a special form, fold it in a special way, and put it on the little clip. He would go out and hold the hoop up, and the engineer would put his arm out and grab the hoop, and at the same time pull the message out, and put his hand back and throw the hoop down. It was the same thing with the shorter one for the caboose. The train might go quite a distance before they threw the hoop down. Brian himself recalled having to go sometimes about five hundred feet to retrieve the hoop, because the train was moving along at a good speed and did not slow down much. It was often a scary operation because of the steam and noise generated by the 'double headers,' which were trains drawn by two steam engines.

Brian recalled several incidents and stories that occurred while Charlie was station agent. In the 1960s, there was a major train derailment at Trenton on the main line. There were box cars in the canal and the extensive damage shut down the line. The trains were rerouted through Campbellford, first one way and then the other.

Peter Monaghan, who worked as a section man for the CNR for fifty years in Campbellford, told him about the days when the carloads of wheat which were shipped from western Canada during the 1930s also brought with them the unemployed hobos. One day one of these men fell asleep in a railway car and was unwittingly locked in. It was very cold outside and the poor man was trapped inside, pounding on the door for help, until Peter heard him and released him.

Mike Walmsley, a driver with Express Car, averted a potentially disastrous derailment near Campbellford. Near the intersection of Highway 30, County Road 35, and the present Bannon Road, the railway tracks crossed over Trout Creek on a trestle. Mike was fishing nearby and heard the noise of a rail splitting, probably due to the heavy traffic. If another train had gone over the trestle, the train would have derailed and landed in the creek. He alerted Charlie who put the semaphore on to stop the train. After the problem was repaired, Mike was recognized for his quick action by the CNR.

In the 1960s, a robbery occurred at the station. The intruders took a steel bar with an edge on it and cut into the door like opening a can of beans. They were never caught. Fortunately, not much was taken, since Charlie made a bank deposit for the station every day.

The station was of wood construction, with a high basement under one third of it. At one time there was a fire. Roy Hoard and the section gang were burning grass around the station at the end of the day. They thought they had extinguished all the flames, but some had spread under the station and the express shed. About an hour after Charlie left, some one saw smoke coming out from under the station and telephoned him. Charlie could see the smoke from his house. He was running down the platform shouting "I've got the key!!! I've got the key!!" just as one of the firemen was about to put an axe through the door. Since there were still trains going through, he had to call the head office at Belleville to let them know what was happening. He went down to Ray Hoard's house to make the call. Mike Walmsley, who was also a fireman, believed that Charlie was still inside the station and, using an air pack, he crawled around the station on his hands and knees looking for Charlie. When Charlie came back from making the call, Mike was glad to see him. The CNR decided to repair the station even though its closing was imminent. The floor joists, walls, and windows were replaced immediately by a team of thirteen carpenters. While the work was being done, a desk was moved to the waiting room to serve as an office. It was quite smoky and the working conditions were very poor.

By 1968, the rail line was not economically feasible, and the company decided to close the station. Due to regulations, they still had to have an Agent Operator for one year. Charlie stayed in Campbellford until 1969 when the station closed, residing with his family at 246 Gravel Road, in a house he bought in the 1940s.

AMES COACH LINES

In 1934, Kenneth Ames came to Campbellford and started a bus line which provided service to Brighton and Havelock. In the early years, the departure times were set to allow passengers to connect with train times. Fred Ames, son of Kenneth, left school at age fifteen, and, because of a shortage of trained bus drivers during World War II, obtained a special licence to drive a bus. Ames Coach also operated school buses to the local elementary and secondary schools. After Kenneth Ames died in 1963, Fred took over the family business. In 1991, the charter rights were sold to Franklin Coach Lines of Belleville. Fred's son, David Ames, now operates the company which is presently involved only with school buses.

AIR CONNECTIONS

The new Trans-Canada Airlines was created in 1938 under control of the C. N. R. Eighteen months later the first regular cross-country services were launched and the passengers had to don oxygen masks when flying over the Rocky Mountains. In those days all stewardesses were required to be registered nurses, a rule which lasted until 1957. In this same year Trans-Canada Airlines became the first carrier to adopt the turbo-prop Vickers Viscounts. Subsequent aircraft included the Vanguard, the DC-8, and various Boeing aircraft up to the 747 and the 767 jumbo jet.

Elizabeth Free Loukes who was born in Campbellford in 1921, the only child of Dr. Fred and Mary Dickson Free, was one of the early employees of TCA. After her nurse's training at the University of Toronto Nursing School, Elizabeth joined TCA as a stewardess in August 1944. The following experiences about her time with TCA were recorded in her diary.

"My first posting after finishing my stewardess training in Winnipeg was to Winnipeg flying the Winnipeg to Toronto northwest route. At this time, this was the longest leg of TCA's flight across Canada, taking approximately five to eight hours depending on the wind direction! The aircraft was either the Lockheed Lodestar 10 series or Lockheed 14 series at this time. Each had a crew of three: the Captain who usually was a former bush pilot, the First Officer who was often repatriated from the RCAF, having finished his air force tours and the Stewardess whose qualifications required that she be an RN, be under five feet, five inches tall and one hundred and twenty-five pounds, single, and no eyeglasses. The height and weight requirements were due to the small cabins, especially the tail section where the meal preparation took place.

My first experience was a scary one – the only time I was frightened during my employment. It happened in mid-winter at Armstrong, Ontario on a flight from Toronto back to Winnipeg. Before take-off in Toronto, the flight was cleared to go by the weather forecasters, although the temperature was near freezing. Somewhere between Porquis Junction and Armstrong the temperature changed a few degrees and freezing rain built up on the plane causing problems landing in Armstrong, the icing having changed the contours of the plane. The Captain made two attempts, and just as the wheels were about to touch down, the aircraft shuddered and shook making it impossible to set down. I went to the cockpit to ask the Captain what to tell my passengers. I noted the front screen of the plane was completely iced over, the side window was open, and the crew was very busy. The Captain just told me bluntly to go back and sit down which I did. Fortunately there were only five or six men aboard, no women, and no one was asking any questions. I had lots of time to think, knowing that Armstrong air strip was very short. If altitude could not be attained before running out of runway, the plane would go into the bush. Also Armstrong had been the site of one of TCA's few accidents in 1941. On the third try, the plane landed safely. The men filed out of the plane, never speaking or asking anything. Inside the little airport building, the pilots were pale and shaken. It had been very difficult for them to hold the plane during the shaking – quite a feat of strength for both of them. The crew stayed in Armstrong until the weather cleared, the plane was de-iced and the flight proceeded to Winnipeg.

Another flight that remains in my memory occurred on the Intercity run – this time between Toronto and Windsor. Some Norwegian Air Force personnel on leave over here chartered a plane to fly them to Windsor where they would pick up an American plane to take them on holiday in the USA. They were in high festive spirits, focusing much of their attention and teasing on me. There was also a language barrier. They were entitled, of course, to the usual meal served, which I attempted to do. Remember this plane was very small, one narrow aisle with five or seven single seats on each side. My small serving space was in the tail section; therefore I had to go up and down the narrow aisle many times to carry each one a tray. Each trip I made several young men would try to grab me with lots of teasing – all good-natured, of course, on their part – but wearing a little thin on my part. I complained to the Captain, hoping he would intervene on my behalf. However, he just grinned and suggested I tell them "that sort of thing is not included in TCA's service!"

Elizabeth left TCA in June 1945 to marry Lloyd Richardson of Campbellford. Currently she is living in Roseneath with her second husband, John Loukes.

ENDNOTES

1 J. Castell Hopkins, *Encyclopedic Canada*, Vol. 5 (Brantford and Toronto: Bradley-Garretson Co. Ltd., 1896, p. 181.

2 A democrat is a two-person carriage drawn by one horse.

Chapter Ten

Health and Social Services

～ Hospitals ～

CAMPBELLFORD HOSPITAL

There appears to have been a hospital in Campbellford as early as 1918, as evidenced by a reference in the Campbellford Herald in the summer of that year. The hospital was apparently located in what was then the residence of a Mrs. O'Sullivan, later the home of the Malcolm family at 72 Bridge Street West.

In 1935, Dr. E. A. Stuart saw the need for a hospital in Campbellford. That summer he contacted the town council and inquired about renting the old Mulhearn property at 123 Front Street North. At a council meeting on August 24, 1935, it was decided to rent the property to Dr. E.A. Stuart to be used as a private hospital. The rent was to be $15 month. The town agreed to pay not more than $700 to convert the house to a hospital, and this amount was to include a new furnace. In this agreement, the town also reserved two beds for indigent patients and agreed to pay Dr. Stuart $25 per month for the maintenance of these two beds. The original doctors at the hospital, in addition to Dr. Stuart, were Fred Free, H. B. Longmore, F. B. Brintnell, C. A. Bright, and C. MacNeill.

Prior to this establishment of the hospital, if the confinement or illness required hospital care, patients were taken either to Belleville or Peterborough. Many readers will remember someone in their family being in the hospital for weeks while the scarcity of cars and poor condition of the roads kept visitors from home to a minimum. Local citizens and organizations provided immediate support for the hospital.

The following are reminiscences of some of the early staff of the hospital.

Rita Smith, 1947

Although I only worked at the old hospital for a short time, I remember fondly the mothers and babies upstairs. The babies were lying crossways in the cribs and the mothers stayed in bed at least eight days. There were ten beds in the hospital. The operating room and another where we kept surgery patients were downstairs.

They say climbing stairs is good for your heart and I think we who worked there should have good hearts as we climbed those stairs many times a day.

Dr. Longmore donated a great deal of the equipment to the hospital at the beginning. He would always have such a polite manner with nurse and patient. One time my sister became very ill suddenly and Dr. Longmore decided it was a ruptured appendix after we got her to the hospital. He said there was not time to take her to Belleville so with the family's permission he operated and saved her life. That was only one life saved among hundreds. One time he called me to go with a patient to Peterborough hospital. The roads were so bad we went via Port Hope, taking hours to get there. We made it and the patient lived.

In those days we boiled the kits in a copper boiler on the kitchen stove. It may have seemed primitive but the love and care we bestowed on the patients was sincere. We did our best under trying conditions. Often we had to launder the bedding as one patient left to put it back on the bed as another arrived.

The housekeeper, Flora Smith, cooked the meals, cleaned the house and did the laundry.

Kay Brahaney, 1939–1943

I hired a taxi to take me from Hwy. 30 to the hospital. I walked from the house to the highway many times during the winter. The roads were not snowploughed.

The charge nurse was responsible for the bills, and purchasing of food. She was requested each month to deal with a different merchant in the town. The coal for the furnace was purchased from different dealers as well. Milk was bought in the same way.

They were very short of linens, thus involving frequent laundering.

After the second world war the baby boom forced the need for three shifts at the hospital. On many evenings the nurses were busy painting empty rooms, free gratis, after they had worked their regular shifts.

We found Mr. Harvey Donald a wonderful man to work with. His greatest ambition was to have a larger hospital to serve the needs of the town.

One time when I was on duty Dr. Stuart brought in a patient who had driven into the Trent River. The doctor had jumped in and saved the man's life.

Nurses carried trays up the stairs to obstetrics patients, brought babies to their mothers and prepared all the formula.

According to the records the first baby born in the Front Street hospital was Junor Bennett, son of Mr. and Mrs. Alfred Bennett of Meyersburg.

When the hospital first opened Miss Marguerite Bibby, later Mrs. Jas. J. Calnan, now deceased, was the first nurse on duty. She slept in, and did twenty-four hour duty. The housekeeper lived out and came to work each morning. The hours were long, sometimes twelve to fourteen. The laundry was all done at the hospital and dried on the clothes lines in the backyard.

The food supplies were purchased locally, each merchant supplying the necessary groceries one month at a time. Mr. Clayton Rowe was the general handyman. He collected the mail, looked after the grounds and kept everything in working order in the hospital.

Etta Windover

I started working at the hospital on Front Street in 1943. I was a practical nurse and spent my life trying to help people. Living in Norham often presented a problem getting to work but I usually managed to get there somehow or other. Mrs. Jean Ireland was the RN at that time working from 8 AM to 4 PM. I was on duty from 4 PM to 8 PM. I recall Mrs. Lee coming on week-ends or helping to relieve a nurse or give a hand with the extra load. She was a wonderful lady. Mr. Harvey Donald was around there and often discussed how wonderful it would be to have a new hospital.

Some of the nurses in the forties were Eleanor Kay Brahaney, Ona Arnold and Helen Gorman. At one point when Helen Gorman was the nurse on duty we had two sets of twins and one set was premature. They put the crib under a large light bulb with a screen over the crib and lots of blankets to keep them warm. If my memory doesn't fail, they are still living. They were fed with an eyedropper and taken home in baskets. It was a great accomplishment for the staff to save those children. We often put four babies crossways in the cribs.

Clayton Rowe was the caretaker. He shovelled coal into the furnace basement, got the mail for the hospital and kept the outside presentable. In the early morning when the furnace got low it would be chilly.

Dr. H.B. Longmore was a wonderful doctor. He kept up with the latest methods and was always interested in new ideas.

When Margaret Milne came to the hospital from New York, she had a tremendous amount of experience and was a great asset to the hospital as well as being a lovely lady to work with. I remember Margaret Bateson and Grace Edgar being there for a while as well.

The nurses were always fair with me, never taking advantage. I enjoyed my association with them. It was hard work climbing those stairs with trays, etc. but I made many lasting friendships.[1]

CAMPBELLFORD   MEMORIAL   HOSPITAL

A concise early history of Campbellford Memorial Hospital was written by Frank Linton, a long-time member of the Board of Directors, and appeared as a supplement to the Campbellford Herald in 1978. The following is a transcript of that account:

It was some time after the maternity hospital was opened on Front Street that the idea for a general hospital was spawned in Campbellford.

At the end of the War, people began to talk of a hospital and what a fine memorial it would make for those who had paid the supreme sacrifice. Service Club members, wrapped in the tissue of community service, saw it not only as a memorial, but as a symbol of a better Campbellford.

It was not until July 1945 that the first formal meeting was held with some of the Town's leading businessmen on hand – Mayor F. Long, Harvey Donald, who was to become the first President; W. J. Callaghan; F. W. Burgess; Roy Bell; W. J. Duncan; Frank Lee; and H. M. Fowlds. Seven months later, a second meeting was held and three new faces appeared. One of these, A. J. Meyers, was destined to play the leading role as Chairman of the Building Committee. However, from the time of that first meeting in July of 1945, no one realized that it would be eight years, one month and nineteen days before the first patient walked through the doors of Campbellford Memorial Hospital.

Early in 1946, Chester C. Woods, architect, was engaged by the Board and with further meetings, it was decided that a 30 bed hospital should be built at a cost of $5,000 per bed. A campaign committee, with little idea of the frustrations they were to face in the next seven years, was formed and had as their objective, the sum of $150,000; approximately one-third of the final cost of the building, by April 1954.

By the date of the Annual Meeting in February '46, the Campaign Committee had raised a total of $6,000 with another $9,500 in promissory notes. This left the Building Committee a long way from from letting out any building contracts, so that by March of that year, plans were scaled down to a 20 bed hospital with five nursery beds. Mr. A. J. Meyers, who drafted these plans, had the concurrence of the committee which felt that this was a far more realistic approach in view of the difficulty of raising money.

However, by October 1947, cost estimates had again risen, this time to $240,000 and a plan was devised to canvass by mail some 113 different firms who did business in Campbellford. This met with very limited success so that by February 1948, it was decided to award the contract for the footings and foundation walls to W. Spencer & Sons in the amount of $9,680. Funds available had grown by this time to over $40,000 and the committee felt that if some actual progress was shown, people would be more inclined to make donations. At this time, comprehensive plans were made to canvass the Township of Seymour and send a delegation to the councils of Percy, Rawdon and Hastings Village with a request for financial assistance.

At the end of May, public subscriptions had grown nearly $25,000 and this was augmented by a $40,000 grant from the Town of Campbellford; $20,000.00 from the Township of Seymour; a Provincial grant of $33,000 and pledges amounting to another $15,600; now making the total funds more than $133,000. The actual building had progressed to the point where the walls had been constructed to the bottom of the sills, and the lower storey including windows and floor slab was complete. It was not until May 1949, that tenders for the second storey and roof were awarded.

By the Winter of 1949–50, the building had been closed in but since there was no provision for heating, a large box stove was placed in the centre of the structure to keep out the frost. This was done at the suggestion of the building chairman, A. J. Meyers who not only provided the stove, but also the necessary fuel as a further contribution to the hospital.

In November 1952, it was discovered that the ground floor wing had been designated partly as an apartment for the live-in director and storage facilities. This could be used instead for twenty-two chronic patient beds and for this a grant of $3,500 per bed was available through the Provincial Government. This temporarily solved the financial problems as tenders for the modifications to the ground floor were let, and a purchasing committee to obtain the necessary furnishings and equipment appointed.

With the financial concern apparently resolved, a joint meeting of the building committee and the old hospital board was held in November 1952 when on the advice of W. Spencer, an opening date of April 1953, was suggested. Much direction and guidance on the purchase of equipment and furnishings was provided by those who had for years struggled to help the maternity hospital meet the minimum requirements of the community. Now these same people, Mrs. Jesse Locke; Mrs. R. E. Fox; Mrs. W. F. Scott; were to play an active part in the finalizing of the plans to open the new hospital and they, together with Mayor George Free; Dr. C. A. Bright; and Dr. W. W. Baker sat on the many meetings that were still to be held before the actual opening.

In May, Mrs. Margaret Daniels became the first full time employee of the hospital. Weekly meetings kept the committee busy until early August and the hospital was still to open without a high speed sterilizer, an X-ray or an elevator.

Room rates established in August – $6.50 per day for ward; $8.50 for semi-private; and $10 for private. On opening day, the staff comprised of 10 RN's;

Campbellford
Memorial Hospital

OFFICIAL OPENING
— AND —
DEDICATION
SUNDAY, AUGUST 23 - 1953

After the Dedication the public is invited to inspect Hospital.

Brochure for the official opening and dedication of Campbellford Memorial Hospital, August 23, 1953.

From the Campbellford/Seymour Heritage Society Archives.

1 ward aide; 1 orderly (who doubled as janitor); 1 engineer; 2 part-time in the laundry; 1 bookkeeper, and 4, including the cook, in the kitchen.

From the time operations began, it became obvious that the income received from patients was not going to be sufficient to make the hospital self sustaining, so by April of 1954, the Town was following the pattern of other municipalities by giving a monthly maintenance grant of $450. This was followed with a grant from Seymour of $150 a month and Percy in January 1957, with $100.

At the Annual Meeting in 1954, tribute was paid to A. J. Meyers for his untiring efforts as Chairman of the Building Committee and his personal contributions towards the building of the hospital. Mr. Meyers was made an Honorary Chairman of the Board until the time of his death in 1973, when the Campbellford Herald, in a well deserved tribute, pointed out the devotion of his time to this project during the early building stages, "and even his personal substance when disaster threatened the enterprise."

Ms. E. Wood was appointed Nursing Superintendent following the resignation of Mrs. Daniels and later that same year, Mr. E. Bureau, who was later to be appointed Administrator, was engaged as office supervisor. It was during Mr. Bureau's term of office, the Provincial Government introduced its universal health care program which began in January 1959. By early 1961, the full effect of the OHSC was being felt in the hospitals across the Province and Campbellford was no exception. Over-crowding, beds in corridors, a shortage of nurses, was a common complaint of the hospital administrators, so it was not long before plans for expansion were under way. Early in 1963, the Board began planning for the expansion which began during S. N. Carr's term as Administrator. In fact, Mr. Carr's ten years as chief executive were probably the most difficult years in the hospital's history. Not only did he have to deal with the ordinary day-to-day problems of management, but he had to act as liaison with the architect and building committee, make sure that patient care was being maintained at a high level even while the kitchen was being disrupted, the laundry demolished, dust and dirt from construction making constant inroads to the corridors.

During this time, Dr. Ivison Taylor of the Hospital Accreditation Council accepted an invitation to visit the hospital which he found to be "well equipped and could easily become accredited." However, this elusive goal is still being pursued by the Board as of the time of this writing. Recognizing the need to provide better facilities for the long stay patient, pediatrics, obstetrics and the outpatients, the Board adopted this as a guideline for long range planning.

Upgrading of services continued and at this same time, Campbellford made history being the first hospital to send electrocardiogram tracings by long distance telephone to Belleville for interpretation. The first actual case was transmitted on December 16, 1965. In the meantime plans for a major expansion were being made and the firm of Craig, Zeidler and Strong had been retained with preliminary plans to increase the bed capacity from 65 to 79 and the out-patient area, laboratory and storage facilities, estimated to cost $820,000. It was three more years before the plans were finalized and the cost has grown to $1,682,510. With the memory of the problems of raising funds for the original construction in the '40 s and '50 s, this was a project beyond the wildest dreams of that dedicated group headed by A. J. Meyers, who made it all possible.

In conclusion, we should pay tribute to those who in many different ways, contributed to the building which stands as a memorial to their dedication – P. C. Denyes; R. J. Bale; Drs. O. C. Watson; W. W. Baker; H. B. Longmore; and Arnold Bright; Messers Frank Lee; H. M. Fowlds; Wm. J. Duncan; N. Alex MacColl; J. A. Murray; Melville Wight; J. E. Ayrhart; W. F. Scott; A. D. Bennett; R. J. Locke and C. H. Davidson.

Franklin S. Linton was Secretary of the building Committee from 1947. He became a member of the Board of Directors in February 1953 and served as Secretary until 1971. He was Chairman of the Board of Directors from 1972 until 1976; serving the hospital a total of 31 years.

Currently, the programs and services provided by the hospital include the following:

Medical Unit	Surgical Unit
Operating Suite	Emergency Department
Intensive Care Unit	Pediatrics
Physiotherapy	Laboratory
Radiology and Ultrasound	Nutritional Services
Pharmacy	Discharge Planning
Patient Education	Public Education Services
Smoking Cessation Program	Pet Therapy Program
Mental Health Services	Ambulance Services
Pastoral Care Services	Four Counties Addiction Services Team
Ambulatory Care Services	

The Obstetrics Department was closed in June 1988, and babies are now delivered in Peterborough or Belleville.

In June 2000, Campbellford Memorial Hospital will be taking part in the accreditation process offered by the Canadian Council on Health Services Accreditation. The process is designed to help health service organizations across Canada examine and improve the quality of care and services. The hospital does this by comparing itself against a set of national standards of excellence.

MY YEARS AT CAMPBELLFORD
MEMORIAL HOSPITAL

Excerpts from an article by Marlene Bailey, RN

The summer of 1959 I received a phone call from Miss Vera Eidt, Director of Nurses at Campbellford Memorial Hospital, inquiring as to whether I would be available for work at the hospital for the next few days. As a recent graduate nurse from Belleville General Hospital I was eager to pursue my nursing skills (career) and felt I could continue my present shifts in the Obstetrical Unit at Belleville Hospital along with a few shifts at Campbellford. I arrived for duty at 7 AM the next day and was greeted by Doreen Mahoney, the very kind and cheerful head nurse on the first floor. Following a brief introduction to the staff and hospital, I was given a patient assignment. How times have changed! No compulsory orientation programs such as Health and Safety, and Nursing In-service training. I was expected to be available and competent to work in all patient care areas but was rarely allowed to enter through the doors of the very sterile maternity unit.

The hospital in 1959 consisted of two floors. The ground floor included laundry, dietary, and pharmacy departments plus a patient care area for long term care. The main or first floor contained a medical/surgical unit which included pediatrics. The obstetrical department under the efficient supervision of Gertrude McCulloch was located at one end. Emergency and operating rooms were also on this floor under the capable management of Margaret Little. Stewart Carr was CEO and his friendly smile and pleasant nature earned the respect and admiration of the staff.

Within a short time it became apparent it would be impossible to be available for work in two hospitals as there was no shortage of shifts at Campbellford. I continued working part time for the next ten years and I found the work rewarding and challenging. I took time off for three pregnancies which did not include maternity leave. One day I was summoned to Miss Eidt's office to be informed that she really could not afford another pregnant nurse.

All types of illnesses were accepted and treated at the hospital with very occasional transfers to other facilities; these included complicated pregnancies and some very sick children. A severe burn case was admitted from a fire at the chocolate factory during its construction. This man remained in hospital for months but eventually was discharged home. A number of leg ulcers were treated successfully with white sugar and plastic wrap dressings. Rehabilitation and health teaching were every staff member's responsibility. It was not uncommon to arrive on the ward in the AM and discover the corridor lined with patients on stretchers as all of the beds were full. Many of these patients were cared for on stretchers until discharge.

The physicians were a very integral part of the health team and often responded to calls seven days a week any time of the day or night. Doctors on staff during the 1960s included Dr. T.K. Hackett, Dr. David Burgess, Dr. W. Baker, Dr. Jolliffe, Dr. A. Kaufmann, Dr. T. Cunningham, Dr. R. Pritchard and Dr. L. Patterson.

Following the birth of my fourth child I made a decision to become a full time mother and home maker. This decision was soon rescinded when I was encouraged to fill in for a time at a local nursing home. Working with the elderly helped me to realize a special interest in geriatrics. In 1975 I returned to Campbellford Hospital and resumed my nursing in medicine, surgery and long term care.

Richard Quesnel was CEO and Grace DeCarrol was the Director of Nurses. Many changes had taken place during my absence from the hospital, but the most significant was the new addition. In 1972 a second floor was added to the hospital which included an Obstetrical unit, Chronic Care floor, Pharmacy and Physiotherapy department plus a beautiful chapel and activity room for long term care patients. The first floor consisted of the medical/surgical and operating room units and the ground floor now contained the administration offices, emergency, ambulance, dietary, x-ray and laboratory departments. The laundry services were purchased from Peterborough.

In 1977, I accepted the position of Head Nurse on the chronic care unit and functioned in a number of capacities over the next ten years, some of these included Discharge planning, Head Nurse of Obstetrics and Nursing Supervisor.

I worked with many capable and caring nurses during these years. Some of these included Marg Gummer, Emma Gowley, Joyce Kahler, Bev Sharpe, Faye Vandervoort, Jeanne Bryett, Diana Ballard, Florence Headrick, and Maureen Dikun in supervisory capacities. Many other very skillful, compassionate health care workers became a very important and memorable part of my nursing career. Orderlies were also very involved in numerous aspects of patient care but were phased out in the late 1980s. Ken Sisley taught me many procedures I could not learn in nursing school. Elmer (Skip) Pugri was the last orderly to be at the hospital. Jean Stubbs was Director of Nursing from 1980 until 1993 when Ruth Dixon assumed these duties. The hospital completed another major addition in 1987. The ground floor contained a large modern emergency department, laboratory, radiology and expanded dietary services. Below these areas pharmacy, central supply, housekeeping, ambulance, maintenance and the morgue were relocated.

In 1986 I resigned from my full time position and accepted a part time Utilization Co-ordinator role. Until my retirement in March 1997, my role at Campbellford Hospital included a variety of tasks, most notably discharge planning and public relations. In these positions I communicated regularly with other community health agencies to facilitate appropriate outcomes for patients and families and to promote public awareness of the hospital.

From 1991 until 1996 the old Obstetrical Unit known as the Reynolds Wing became a Mental Health Clinic and in 1996 "The Wellness Centre" located across the street from the hospital opened as the new clinic. In the spring of 1996 the Reynolds Wing on the second floor became a Self Care Unit and in the fall of 1997 the Chronic Care Unit was closed. In 1999 a Long Term Care Unit will re-open on the 2nd floor. Restructuring has become a common word in health care these days and consequently many changes are taking place. Hospital beds have been decreased and jobs lost. Some of the changes occurring are pleasant and many are painful but the friends I have made and memories stored of my years at Campbellford Memorial Hospital will remain forever.

AMBULANCE AND EMERGENCY SERVICES

Don Bennett gave the following information about early ambulance service in Campbellford:

"My father started the ambulance service. He was A.D. Bennett and he started it when he came to Campbellford in 1926. The ambulance was a coach car, with two big doors. He cut the side and took the back seat out and put a bucket seat in front. The car had big doors, so you could put the stretcher in through the side door, with the patient on the stretcher. The patient's feet were beside the driver and his head where the back seat would have been. There was room for a doctor or nurse to sit and there was a folding seat in case both a doctor and nurse were needed. Over the years, he replaced the vehicle several times. He was in the ambulance business from 1926 to 1965. It was not a profitable business. The charge to Peterborough or Belleville was $10, $30 to Toronto, and $2 for a local call. Often we did not get paid. Sometimes the driver would be called out in the middle of the night to accidents, but the police would have already taken the patient for treatment. The regular drivers were A.D. Bennett himself and his assistant, Wilbert Dalgleish. Dalgleish and his patient were both killed in the ambulance on a trip to Toronto in 1945. The nurse who accompanied them, Theresa Lee, survived but she was seriously injured.

I drove the ambulance myself before I went into the army. I became the second driver, when I got out of the army. I recall one particular incident before the war. Dr. Stewart called and said that a man named Sampson had his foot run over by the train on Centre Street and needed to go to Belleville. Dr. Stewart said, "We must go fast, so I will drive ahead of you." He was going through intersections without stopping and it was very scary. We had to stop every fifteen minutes so Dr. Stewart could loosen the tourniquet, as it was important to maintain the circulation in the foot.

In 1965, when we sold the funeral business to Al Weaver, the ambulance was also for sale, but Weaver only wanted the funeral business. The firemen took over the ambulance service until 1979 when the government took it over. The government brought in more drivers, more vehicles and located the ambulances at the hospital. Unlike us, these drivers were given the training that we had to learn on the job."

After Bennett's gave up the ambulance service, another local provider of ambulance service was the Ranson family. The Hastings Volunteer Fire Department also provided ambulance service for the Campbellford area. In 1970, the Ministry of Health located an ambulance vehicle at Campbellford Memorial Hospital. This was a blue and white Ford Van, equipped to handle two patients on stretchers, a jump seat for the attendant, and an unusual sounding siren for emergency use. Paul Dorie joined the staff that year. For two years, the service operated with one vehicle, and Hastings continued with the volunteer service. Since 1972, the service has gradually expanded until, in 1999, there are three ambulance vehicles, eleven full-time and nine part-time qualified attendants. In 1995, Paul Dorie received the Emergency Medical Services Exemplary Service Medal from Governor-General Romeo LeBlanc at a ceremony in Rideau Hall in Ottawa.

In 1998, the 911 emergency system went into effect in this area. Each property in rural locations has been given a unique civic address which is posted on a blue and white sign on the roadways, and the town locations use their street address. This is used for emergency fire, police, or ambulance calls, which are received by a Central Emergency Reporting Bureau and then forwarded to the appropriate agency.

CAMPBELLFORD HOSPITAL AUXILIARY

The Campbellford Hospital in 1943 was a fledgling institution meeting a great need in the community. On June 11, a group of ten dedicated and caring women saw and met the need for volunteers in the Hospital. They banded together, under the leadership of Theresa Lee, who became the first Auxiliary President. Theresa was a registered nurse who served overseas in World War I. The Auxiliary assisted with many tasks such as making sheets, bandages, drapes, and linens which were in short supply. They sometimes helped with laundry, cleaning, and painting and held fund raising events. As the Hospital expanded and employed more staff, the main role of the Auxiliary changed to the provision of financial assistance.

In 1953, when the Memorial Hospital opened, the Auxiliary supplied all of the required linens. They also made feather pillows and all of the draperies for the windows. The Auxiliary, with community assistance, provided furnishings for many of the rooms, including the Solarium, the Quiet Room, and two Common Rooms. Six modern beds and a second operating table were also supplied.

In March 1957, the Auxiliary widened its horizon and joined the Ontario Hospital Auxiliary Association. Spring Conferences were held in each Region annually, with Campbellford hosting this event in 1971, 1975, 1982 and 1987.

The Gift Shop was opened in 1970 and has become an integral part of the Hospital. Quilting has been a major fund raiser since 1975. Dorothy Stanish, with the help of Laura Dunk and Irene Stephens, launched the sewing of baby quilts to be sold in the Gift Shop. Approximately $7,000 has been realized since 1992 through the quilters' efforts. A 50th anniversary commemorative quilt made by this group is displayed on a hallway at the hospital.

In 1986–7, a major reconstruction and extension of the Hospital took place. This included a modern Emergency Unit, X-Ray Department, Laboratory, Ambulance Department, and office space. Construction and decorating of the extension was completed in June 1987. Auxiliary volunteers happily assisted at the official opening.

The Auxiliary has demonstrated steady growth. Today, the membership is approximately 140, including several members with twenty-five years of service. Over the years the Auxiliary has contributed approximately $734,000 to the Campbellford Memorial Hospital.

Past Presidents List

1943–49	Theresa Lee		1984–86	Joan Eady
1949–59	Lillian Fox		1986–87	June Bennett
1959–72	Lillian Scott		1987–89	Daisy Moulton
1972–74	Eva Locke		1989–91	Audrey Jackson
1974–75	Mary Reynolds		1991–93	Joan Sampson
1975–77	Ruth Craighead		1993–95	Edith Helm
1977–79	Dorothy Stanish		1995–97	Marilyn Scott
1979–81	Marion Rushbrook		1997–99	Joan Risebrough
1981–83	June Bennett		1999–2001	Carol Wyndham
1983–84	Thelma Johnston			

CAMPBELLFORD MEMORIAL
HOSPITAL VOLUNTEERS

In 1991, a volunteer services programme was launched by Campbellford Memorial Hospital. Volunteers are recruited to welcome and assist relatives and others who are visiting patients, and to act as escorts for patients who must attend various departments, such as X-Ray and the laboratory. They also deliver reports and specimens between the floors and the laboratory. They provide assistance to patients in acute care by reading and writing letters, circulating the library cart, filling water jugs, distributing and collecting menus, and doing some friendly visiting. The yellow smocks worn by the volunteers which they wear while on duty distinguish them from the Hospital Auxiliary Volunteers. Volunteers provide coverage six days of the week. The present co-ordinator of the volunteer programme is Wendy Ellis.

CAMPBELLFORD MEMORIAL
HOSPITAL FOUNDATION

The Campbellford Memorial Hospital Foundation was established in 1985 to provide financial support to the work of the hospital, the affiliated multicare facilities, and related health service agencies in Campbellford/Seymour. All money donated to the Foundation is applied to areas of need such as renovations, equipment purchases, and health education. Foundation funds are not applied to operating expenses which qualify for government funding. In 1998-99, the Foundation accepted the challenge of providing the financing for the construction of the Campbellford Memorial Health Centre. Wendy Warner is the current Director of Development for the Foundation.

～ Doctors of Campbellford/Seymour ～

Over the years, many physicians and surgeons have served the Campbellford/ Seymour community. Those for whom documentation was available are described below.

Dr. Robert Denmark was born in Tichfield, England in 1809. He became a surgeon in the Royal Navy, arriving in Seymour in 1839. Although he did not deliberately set up a medical office, he did respond to calls for assistance. He subsequently married the daughter of Dr. Rowed, another surgeon of the Royal Navy. Mrs. Denmark died in 1847, followed soon after by her husband's death in 1852. At one time during his brief practice, he was assisted by Dr. Mungo Ponton, who had been a Scottish officer with the Cameron Highlanders and received 600 acres of land in Seymour Township as a military grant.

Dr. Demorest arrived in 1853 from Prince Edward County. He set up a practice in Warkworth which provided much of the early medical care to the Campbellford/

Seymour area until his death in 1860. Dr. Patrick Fergus, born in 1811 in Ireland, had arrived in Seymour by the 1851 census. He established his practice at The Patch. Dr. Fergus is mentioned as being paid by the Fowlds Store in Hastings for attending a worker from one of the Percy lumber camps.

About 1860, Dr. Lyons arrived on the scene. He built the stone house later owned by Dr. E. A. Stuart. Dr. Lyons passed away in 1882. For a short time in 1861–1862, Dr. Eid provided medical care but left for the lure of the Australian gold fields.

Dr. John Massie was born in Scotland in 1833 and emigrated with his parents to Canada West, first to Kingston and subsequently to Concession 14, Lot 19, Seymour Township. After a short teaching career in Castleton, he graduated in Medicine from Queen's in 1865. For eight years, he practised in Colborne, followed by eight years in Campbellford, from 1873 to 1881. He relocated to Norwood for two years, after which, due to failing health, he moved his practice to Keene. He was a recognized poet, mentioned in Ross' *Scottish Poets in America*. Despite this recognition, Dr. Massie is buried in an unmarked grave at Burnbrae Cemetery.

Dr. George A. Pettigrew, a native of Asphodel Township, graduated from the University of Toronto in 1875 and set up a practice in Campbellford. In 1881, he relocated to Norwood where he passed away in 1911.

In 1882, Dr. Irvine Dorland Bogart moved his practice from Hastings. He married a local girl, Rose Anne Rendle, and built a home at Bridge and Rear Streets opposite T. J. Horkins store, where he resided until his death on May 20, 1900 at age 65. At about the same time as Dr. Bogart, Dr. Samuel Wallace commenced his practice on the site of the Wallace Block where he continued until his death in 1888. The drug store portion was purchased by Dr. W. F. Loucks who relocated to Front Street in later years. In 1884, Dr. J. W. Byam also practiced at Bridge and Front Streets. Dr. P. D. Goldsmith had a medical practice and Dr. James N. McCrea (McCrae) from Warkworth also had an office in the St. Lawrence Hotel. During the typhoid outbreak in 1889, Dr. James Loucks and Dr. J. W. Knight are mentioned as treating patients. For one year, in 1889–1890, Dr. Fred Bradd who had just completed medical school at the University of Toronto worked in the area before relocating to Peterborough. In 1891, Dr. John Macoun, born in 1860, was a physician in Campbellford. By 1892, a Dr. M. Gallagher is also mentioned as being located in Dr. Perry G. Goldsmith's former offices.

Dr. Edward J. Free was born August 13, 1859, the son of Abraham and Elizabeth Free of Seymour Township. After teaching for a short time at West's School, he attended the University of Toronto Medical School from which he graduated in 1886. For a short time, he practised in Ameliasburgh Township, later moving to Warkworth where he married Olivia Jane Sanborn in 1888. He moved from there to Campbellford where he practised for forty years. He was a member of the

Board of Health, the Board of Education, Medical Officer of Health and doctor for the railway workers in the area. Two of his five children lived to maturity – Fred, who became a doctor and John. Dr. Edward Free passed away in 1930.

The Campbellford Herald of May 1899, mentions Dr. J. H. Knight on Tice Street and Dr. W. P. St. Charles in the Wallace Block.

Dr. Thomas W. Carlaw, son of T.B. Carlaw, graduated as a medical doctor from Trinity College, University of Toronto, in 1893. This knowledgeable and active practitioner operated his practice from a building on Bridge Street, subsequently used by Dr. Free. Following Carlaw's basic medical training , he continued to keep abreast of new developments, spending a year in Glasgow and Edinburgh, where he earned additional certification, and travelling for other courses of a shorter duration in New York and Chicago. Unfortunately, this young man passed away in 1909, probably from a contagious disease contracted while tending his patients.

In 1892, Dr. Andrew Haig opened a practice in a house built by A. T. Green on Front Street. He was a native of Seymour, born in 1865, who received his MA and MD degrees from Queen's University and subsequently studied in London, England. In 1900, Dr. Haig was appointed superintendent of Kingston General Hospital, being the second Seymour Township native to receive this honour, Dr. Third being the first. Dr. Haig was succeeded by Dr. F. Hershy Scherk, who then left Campbellford in 1906.

Dr. Richard Henry Bonnycastle was a native of Campbellford, born on February 10, 1881 in Seymour West, the son of Frank Edward Bonnycastle. He received his education locally and graduated from University of Toronto Medical School in 1905. He returned to his home town to set up a practice in the Sharp home on Front Street North where he earned a reputation as a skillful and clever doctor. Prior to World War I, he served as Medical Officer of Health. In November 1914, he joined the Canadian Army Medical Corps and transferred to the Royal Army Medical Corps in May 1915. He reached France in July 1915 and served with the 47th Field Ambulance, 15th Division and the King's Own Scottish Borderers. During his service, he attained the rank of Major. He returned to Canada in May 1916 and again transferred to the Canadian Army Medical Corps, serving for a time with the Discharge Depot in Quebec. While serving at Valcartier, he acted as Medical Officer for the Canadian Forces stationed there. After devoting a year to the duties of this position, he returned to his practice in Campbellford. Dr. Bonnycastle died quite unexpectedly on October 7, 1917, at the age of thirty-six after a short illness, leaving his widow, Winnifred Evelyn (Freda) Carlaw and two young sons, Desmond and Murray.

Dr. George Barnes Archer, born in the local area in 1880, chose to work in the mission field. After graduating from the University of Toronto, he specialized in eye surgery. He was given a gold watch from the community when he set out in 1914 as a medical missionary for the Anglican Church in Ranaghat, India. He married Ethel Edwina Dickson from the United States but both Ethel and their infant child died tragically in childbirth while they were in India. Dr. Archer then joined the armed forces and served in World War I. After the war, he returned to India where he served in leper colonies until his death. During his time in India, he sent watercolour cards of the country to his relatives in Seymour. Dr. Archer was murdered in India in 1944 while sleeping on his own verandah.

Dr. H. Bruce Longmore began his practice in the 1920s. He was a member of the staff of the original hospital in 1935, often being called into consultation on difficult medical problems. Dr. Longmore was a wonderful family physician, on call at any hour of the day or night. Gwen Dubay recalls Dr. Longmore singing "I Want a Girl" to her when he came to the Jacobs home to pay a call on her during an illness. Dr. Longmore was highly respected and many local mothers named their children in his honour. The community was saddened when he passed away in 1952.

Dr. Ernest Victor Frederick, born in Campbellford in 1880, graduated from the University of Toronto in 1906 and studied in London and Albany. He set up a practice in Peterborough which he maintained until serving overseas in World War I where he contacted malaria. In 1921, he attempted unsuccessfully to set up a group practice which included a doctor from Keene , Dr. Middleton, a dentist, and Dr. Edward Free from Campbellford. In 1923, he relocated his practice to Campbellford for a short time before moving on to Los Angeles, Toronto and finally back to Peterborough.

Dr. Fred deFurlong Free, son of Dr. Edward Free, was born in Warkworth in 1895. At age seven, he developed polio, requiring him to wear a leg brace. He attended University of Toronto from which he graduated in medicine in 1919. After interning at Toronto General Hospital, he began practising in Campbellford. Dr. Fred Free was on the staff of the original Campbellford Hospital in 1935, served as Medical Officer of Health and as doctor for the C.N.R. workers. He died in 1957 of Asian flu at age sixty-two and was survived by his wife, Mary Helen Dickson and one daughter, Elizabeth.

Dr. F. Bruce Brintnell practiced in Campbellford in the 1920s. He was on the staff of the original Campbellford Hospital in 1935, then moved to Warkworth where he resided until his death. Another physician of the 1920s period was Dr. Elmer Richardson who left to practice in Oshawa.

Dr. E. A. Stuart trained in New Brunswick and subsequently opened his medical practice in Campbellford in the early 1930s. He rented the Brian Mulhearn property at 123 Front Street North in 1935 and converted it into the first hospital in the area. Later, he relocated to Saint Andrew's by the Sea and following that, to Vancouver. Another staff member of the original hospital was Dr. C. MacNeill.

Dr. Ward Baker was born in Percy Township in 1907 and graduated from the University of Toronto in 1932. He interned at Syracuse Memorial Hospital and Montreal Children's Hospital. After working in Montreal and Timmins, he returned to the local area in 1941 and set up a medical practice in a portion of the Walter Wiggins house on the corner of Bridge and Canrobert Streets, where he also resided. In 1944, he was assisted for a short time by Dr. Kenneth Drummond who relocated to Havelock. At the old hospital, Dr. Baker delivered babies, performed minor surgery, and set simple fractures. He continued in this location until 1969, when he moved to Peterborough, continuing to practice as an operative surgical assistant until 1989. At this time, Dr. Baker and his wife, Dorothy, returned to Campbellford where he passed away in 1992.

Dr. Roy F. Jolliffe practiced in Campbellford from 1944 until his retirement in 1971. He continued to serve as surgeon for the Warkworth Penitentiary until his death in 1979.

Dr. Charles Arnott Bright graduated from the University of Western Ontario in 1936. He came to Campbellford and set up a practice in the Meyers Block on Front Street South. Dr. Bright was on the staff of the original Campbellford Hospital but later trained in Psychiatry and moved to Ossington, New York in the early 1950s. He retired to New Mexico.

Dr. Bertha G. (Betty) Bright, sister of Dr. James Loynes of Belleville, graduated from the University of Western Ontario in 1937. She practised in Campbellford with her husband, Dr. C. A. Bright, in the 1940s, raising two sons, Jim and Bob. She now lives in retirement in Belleville.

Dr. James Rae Anderson was born in Campbellford in 1920 and graduated from the University of Toronto in 1943. He interned at Toronto General Hospital, Christie Street, and Sunnybrook before returning to Campbellford where he set up a practice on Bridge Street East across from the library. In 1953, this practice was purchased by Dr. David Burgess. Dr. Anderson moved to Simcoe County as Assistant Medical Officer of Health. He was appointed Medical Officer of Health for Peterborough County in 1962 where he served until 1966 when he became an editor for the Canadian Medical Association Journal.

Dr. Charlotte M. Horner, born in 1913, graduated from the University of Toronto in 1939 and subsequently undertook post-graduate training in Public Health. After serving with the RCAF in Gander and Halifax, she attained the rank of Flight Lieutenant. In 1945 she was appointed Acting Medical Officer of Health for Northumberland Durham Health Unit situated in Campbellford. In 1952, on the retirement of Dr. MacCharles, she became Medical Officer of Health. At this time, the Health Unit was moved to Cobourg. When the Haliburton, Kawartha, Pine Ridge Health Unit was formed in 1969, Dr. Horner remained until her retirement in 1973. She lived on her farm Charbrook, north of Cobourg until 1989 when she moved to Cobourg where she passed away in 1993. Dr. Horner was very active in Campbellford and could often be seen riding her horse about the town. She was a frequent visitor to local schools and administered inoculations to the students.

Dr. David Burgess was born in Philadelphia in 1916 and received his medical degree from Guy's Hospital in London, England in 1941. He interned at the Royal Surrey Hospital in England and became a medical officer with the Royal Air Force during 1942 and 1943. Because he was American, he then served in the US Army Medical Corps from 1943 to 1947, rising to the rank of Lt.-Colonel. At that time, he left the military to serve a rural practice in Bromley, Kent. Britain was then at the beginning stage of the move to socialized medicine so Dr. Burgess decided to emigrate to Canada, along with his wife, Pat, and sons, Simon and Neil. His first Canadian experience was in the remote community of Treherne, Manitoba, where he was the only doctor for eighty miles. He was called upon to deal with all kinds of medical treatments including dental care. The area also included a large French speaking population. In his role as coroner, he had many interesting experiences including an inquest, held in a school, into the death of a native. The presiding RCMP officer called upon all to "Rise for the King." Everyone stood, including Dr. Burgess. The officer then requested that the doctor be seated as he explained, "Not you, sir, you are the King!" The family remained in this remote and primitive setting until 1951, when they moved to Didsbury, Alberta. After investigating the potential of Vancouver as a possible practice site, Dr. Burgess decided that the rainy climate was not suitable. He then read of the availability of Dr. Anderson's Campbellford location and he purchased the huge brick home and the medical practice for $12,000, a sum considered to be exorbitant for the time. Dr. Burgess devoted the years from 1953 to 1981 to his medical practice in Campbellford. At that time, he relocated to Toronto after suffering injuries in a serious car accident. He later retired to Campbellford and Warkworth.

After Dr. Longmore's death in 1952, Dr. Ritchie took over the practice for a short time. In 1957, Dr. A.F. Kaufmann set up a family practice in the former Longmore home on Queen Street. Dr. Kaufmann was a skillful and caring physician who served the local area until ill health forced his retirement. He passed away in 1991.

Dr. Thomas James Kirkwood-Hackett, born in Ireland, graduated from Dublin in 1953. He set up a practice on Front Street North in Campbellford. Later, Dr. Hackett relocated to Doxsee Avenue South. He has served the community for many years, as well as acting as Regional Coroner.

Dr. Thomas Alexander Irving Cunningham, born in England in 1914, graduated from medical school in Ireland. After serving his internship in England and Ireland, he set up his practice in 1965 in Campbellford where he continued to serve until his death in 1977.

Dr. Alice (Yakushavich) Scott was born and raised in La Pas, Manitoba and served in the Royal Canadian Air Force during World War II. She graduated from the University of Manitoba with a BA in 1945 and from McGill in 1950 with an MD. She resided in Campbellford from 1968 and retired from practice in 1988. She died on October 13, 1999, in her 78th year.

Dr. Anthony Leslie Shellam, born in India in 1944, grew up in Campbellford. He graduated from the University of Toronto in 1969 and interned at Wellesley Hospital and the Hospital for Sick Children. In 1971, he served on the courtesy staff in Peterborough and on the active staff of the Campbellford Memorial Hospital. Tony served as Assistant Professor of Family Practice at Toronto Western Hospital until his death in 1994.

Dr. Robert O'Dowda Stephens was born in Toronto, graduated from medical school in 1947, and interned at Toronto Western Hospital. He has a diploma in Tropical Medicine. In the summer of 1977, Dr. Stephens and his son-in-law, Dr. R. W. Henderson, set up a practice at 79 Bridge Street. Dr. Stephens retired from the practice in 1990, but has continued to work part-time as a locum and as a consultant for community and international medical issues. Dr. Stephens has served as the Executive Director of the Christian Medical and Dental Society and the Evangelical Medical Aid Society (EMAS), which co-ordinates contributions of needy medical equipment to Third World countries. In 1998, he was the winner of the prestigious Sir William Osler Award. He is also involved with the Medical Assistance Plan (MAP) under the auspices of the Canadian International Development Agency (CIDA).

Dr. Robert Wayne Henderson, a native of Kelowna, B.C. graduated from the University of Manitoba in 1973. He interned at McMaster and came to Campbellford to set up his practice with Dr. R. Stephens at 79 Bridge Street East in 1977. Dr. Marnie Haig also worked in this practice from 1979 to early 1981. In 1992, Dr. Henderson and his associates established Hillside Family Medicine in the lower floor of the Multicare Lodge at 174 Oliver Road. He has also served as an Associate Professor in the Department of Family Practice at the University of Toronto, which involves the supervision of resident doctors in family medicine. In that capacity, he has successfully attracted several new doctors to the Campbellford/Seymour community. After completing a residency in family practice in Campbellford, Dr. Brenda Smith graduated from the University of Toronto in 1992. She served at Hillside Family Practice from September 1992 until July 1999, when she moved to Courtice. Dr. Harvey R. Williams graduated from the University of Toronto in 1994 and joined Hillside in July 1995. He had also completed a residency in family medicine under the supervision of Dr. R. W. Henderson. Dr. Flora Ricuitti and Dr. William Shannon came to Campbellford in a similar fashion. Dr. Ricuitti graduated from the University of Toronto in 1995 and worked at Hillside from February 1996, until June 1997, when she moved to North York. Dr. Shannon graduated from the University of Toronto in 1996 and joined Hillside in August 1997. This medical clinic has moved into new quarters on Isabella Street across from Campbellford Memorial Hospital.

Dr. David Clyde Rosen, a native of Montreal who graduated from Toronto in 1972, practised in Campbellford from 1978 until 1980 when he relocated to Credit Valley Hospital in Mississauga.

Dr. Isadore Michael Kaufmann graduated from Toronto in 1979. He came to Campbellford in June 1981 and subsequently set up his office on Doxsee Avenue South. He practiced there until 1995 when he left the local area.

Dr. Hein DeHaan, born in the Netherlands, graduated from the University of Capetown, South Africa in 1958 and served his internship there. After practising in South Porcupine, he located in Campbellford in 1980 in the former veterinarian's office at 84 Bridge Street East. He continues to practice family medicine in this location.

Dr. Michael J. Morris of Warkworth served as the Chief of Staff of Campbellford Memorial Hospital during part of the 1990s. He graduated from the University of London, England, in 1973.

Dr. Scott MacLeod, a native of Winnipeg but raised in Peterborough, graduated from the University of Toronto in 1977. After interning at Toronto Western Hospital, he arrived in Campbellford in 1981 to set up office on 23 Front Street South. He served as Chief of Staff of the hospital during part of the 1990s. He also served as coroner and maintained his interest in aviation despite his busy schedule. In 1996, he moved to practice in Virginia.

Dr. Paul Humphrey Minc graduated from the University of London, England in 1956. His office is currently at the Campbellford Clinic on Doxsee Avenue South.

Dr. Graham Morris graduated from the Royal Infirmary Medical School in Aberdeen, Scotland in 1966, received his Fellowship from the Royal College of Surgeons in England in 1970, and from the Canadian College in 1971. He practised as a general surgeon at the Arnprior and District Memorial Hospital and at Campbellton Regional Hospital in New Brunswick until 1991 when he relocated to Campbellford. His surgical skills were much appreciated at Campbellford Memorial Hospital and he also introduced laparoscopy to the local area. He retired from the hospital in 1999.

Dr. Norm Bartlett, a native of Huntsville, recently joined the Emergency Department of Campbellford Memorial Hospital. He did his pre-med studies at the University of Western Ontario where he earned a Master's degree in

Biochemistry. He attended the University of Toronto for his medical training. He served as a Resident at Kingston General Hospital and received special certification in Emergency Medicine.

～ Dentists ～

1875	J. F. Taylor
1891	Dr. Mallory
1901	J. McBride, Owen Watson, W.R. Glover, R. A. Sykes, H. O. Richardson
1925	C. V. Bussey
1950s	Lloyd Richardson, Ross Richardson
1965	Ralph W. Vandervoort
1966	D. J. Hughes
1976	Dan Derumaux
1976	Robert Rawluk
1995	Cheryl Byrne

View of Campbellford Memorial Hospital and the Multicare Lodge from Candy Mountain, 1999.

Photo courtesy of Michel Proulx

⁓ Assisted Living Facilities ⁓

CAMPBELLFORD MEMORIAL
MULTICARE LODGE

In 1980 the hospital board saw the need for a housing project which would enable seniors to live independently with support services. The result was the construction of the 49-unit Campbellford Memorial Multicare Lodge. In March 1992, the first tenant moved in and there has never been an empty apartment since. In 1998 there were sixty-one residents residing at the Lodge. Thirty apartments have the rent geared to income, and nineteen charge market-value rent. Support services are available to all tenants within the building. The first-floor office area provides accommodation to Hillside Family Medicine, a hairdressing salon, Campbellford and District Community Care, the Red Cross, Therapacc Inc. Rehabilitation, Five Counties Children's Centre, Northumberland County Community Care, and Campbellford and District Palliative Care.

Multicare is funded by the Ministry of Health and the Ministry of Housing. The Multicare Lodge has a Board of Directors which consists of Campbellford Memorial Hospital board members and members from the community. Mary Johnston is recognized for her generous bequest in 1991 which provided for the connecting bridge from the hospital to the Multicare Lodge. This bridge provides access for residents to purchase meals, housekeeping, and maintenance service from the hospital. Twenty-four hour emergency response has helped to provide a safe and secure living environment. Each living unit has two emergency buttons which ring directly into the Hospital switchboard.

SELF CARE LIVING ACCOMMODATIONS

In May 1996, the Campbellford Memorial Hospital Auxiliary donated $35,000 to assist in the establishment and renovation of nine self care rooms located in a separate wing on the second floor of the hospital. Individual rooms are equipped with private baths, tub and handrails, bed, dresser, chair, lamps and ceiling fans. Residents are encouraged to furnish their own rooms, or add to the furnishings with plants, pictures and other decor. All meals are prepared and served in the common dining room, with afternoon and evening nourishment also being provided. Some other amenities included in the monthly rate are weekly housekeeping, emergency call system, with professional nurses being available 24 hours per day, parking at no additional cost, medication pick-up from pharmacies, transportation for appointments, mail service and 24 hour security. This creates a unique seniors' living accommodation, providing independence, with the assurance of personal support.

RETIREMENT AND NURSING HOMES

In the 1960s, Morley Tanner bought Hillside Terrace Apartments and converted it into a nursing home. It initially had twenty-eight beds, but this was increased to forty-five. Tom and Ethel Ranson were licensed to run the nursing home. Ethel Ranson was the nurse in charge and there were forty staff. Later, after the opening of Carewell Nursing Home, this facility became a retirement residence only. It closed in 1999.

Carewell Nursing Home was built in 1979 at 320 Burnbrae Road East. It was recently purchased by Omni Health Care Limited of Peterborough, which operates fourteen facilities in the area, and the name was changed to Burnbrae Gardens. It has room for forty-three residents.

～ Community Health Services ～

HALIBURTON, KAWARTHA, PINE RIDGE DISTRICT HEALTH UNIT:

Excerpt from an article by Dr. Donald Mikel, former MOH

Before public health units existed, municipal councils hired physicians, and inspectors to protect health in an era of early industrialization and urbanization. These health professionals focused their attention on controlling epidemics, ensuring the safe supply of drinking water, and the safe removal of garbage and sewage. The Victorian Order of Nurses (VON) did not have a branch in the area, nor were there any other community nursing services. An appointed municipal doctor was responsible for the immunization of children in the schools, and placarding the homes of those with a communicable disease. Many risks to public health existed during this time. Huge epidemics of measles, scarlet fever, and polio were unfortunate annual events that touched many families. Although there was a law requiring that all milk be pasteurized before it could be sold, all too often raw milk was still being consumed.

As World War II began to wind down, the Ontario Department of Health began to make plans to improve this situation. The vision of establishing and administering health units on a county level, staffed by public health professionals, was adopted. In June of 1945, at its regular meeting, the Council of the United Counties of Northumberland and Durham decided to approach the province for the establishment of a health unit. The province agreed to the idea, and in 1945, this health unit became one of the first health units established in the province. In August, the United Counties of Durham and Northumberland Board of Health was appointed to begin organizing the Health Unit which would assume responsibility throughout the United Counties starting September 1, 1945. At that time, there was a population of about 50,000 people living in an area of 1,353 square miles for the United Counties of Durham and Northumberland.

The first Board of Health consisted of the Warden, C.R. Carveth, three county councillors and one Provincial Appointee. The Ontario Department of Health estimated it would take $60,000 to operate the Health Unit yearly. The required number of nurses was based on one for every three to four thousand people with the expectation that they would provide some in-home nursing care. On the recommendation of the Provincial Department of Health, Dr. Clarence W. MacCharles was hired to be the first Medical Officer of Health (MOH) along with two assistant MOHs. Louise Steele was appointed Nursing Supervisor and was joined by three public health nurses.

When the war ended, cars, refrigerators for vaccine, and office furniture were in very short supply. Nurses had to catch rides with teachers, neighbours, parents, or their supervisor to get to their destinations. In the early days, public health nurses travelled under adverse conditions to remote areas to visit homes and schools, sometimes having to quarantine homes of families with scarlet fever or whooping cough. From Bowmanville in the west, to Campbellford in the northeast, and north to Lake Scugog, the nurses were scattered in little offices in small places like Orono and Millbrook. There were only seven nurses at the time, and they put in many overtime hours from 1945 to 1946.

Three sanitary inspectors were also hired. They soon found a great many of the schools had unsafe water supplies, unsatisfactory sewage disposal, deficient lighting, and other poor conditions. Some buildings needed major repairs or complete replacement. Inspectors began meeting with the numerous school boards at once to recommend improvements.

Early in 1946, a vigorous immunization program was launched. The MOH immunized 5,000 elementary school children against diphtheria, and 4,300 against smallpox. Over 1,000 infants and preschoolers were immunized against diphtheria and whooping cough, and 786 against small pox.

Meanwhile, the health inspectors wrote by-laws to regulate municipal water supplies, slaughterhouses, dairies, municipal garbage disposal, hotels, tourist camps, and eating establishments. The bylaws were enacted by the various municipal councils and served a very useful purpose, until they were replaced by provincial legislation.

In 1946, the head office of the Health Unit moved from the County Building in Cobourg (then Victoria Hall) to a small house on the west side of George Street in Cobourg. Also in 1946, an agreement was made with the provincial Chest

Clinic in Belleville to provide X-ray service for tuberculosis diagnosis and control in several centres in the county. In addition, portable x-ray units travelled throughout the county to assist in the control of tuberculosis. As well, prenatal classes were started and "well baby" clinics were offered. After the war, there was a big increase in the incidence of venereal disease, so there were many cases and contacts to be followed up.

By 1949, the staff was gradually built up to an appropriate level, and a few of the tiny offices such as Warkworth and Blackstock were discontinued. Dr. Charlotte Horner was appointed Medical Officer of Health in 1952. Without assistant MOHs, she relied on community physicians to help with immunization. In addition, there were many changes in the leadership of the Sanitation Department in those early years. In 1947, Hugh McIntyre, the Chief Inspector, retired, and R. Groot replaced him. Jack Finlayson was appointed Chief Inspector in 1949. Dr. R. Damude, a public health veterinarian, was on staff from 1949 to 1952. He was responsible for animal diseases as they relate to humans. He tested milk, both raw from the producers and pasteurized from the dairies. He was concerned about mastitis, brucellosis (undulant fever), and tuberculosis in the herds. He was also responsible for inspecting slaughterhouses and all meat that was sold to the public.

The Health Unit dealt with epidemics both large and small. The last severe poliomyelitis outbreak occurred in 1951, just before the Salk and Sabin vaccines were discovered. There were usually a few cases each year. For instance, in 1947, there were eight cases resulting in one death in the United Counties. But in 1951, there were 51 cases, half of them resulting in paralysis and one death. The smaller hospitals refused to admit these patients, and the Toronto hospitals were flooded with patients from this province-wide outbreak. As a result, most infected patients were treated in their homes. All of these homes were placarded and quarantined. The public health nurses courageously gave considerable assistance in the bedside care of these patients in quarantined homes.

In the late 1950s, rabies spread from the Northwest Territories to Southern Ontario, infecting skunks, and foxes which, in turn, infected cattle, dogs, and cats, thus endangering the human population. The health inspectors had a busy year in 1958, diligently tracing all contacts, and ensuring that they received the proper treatment to prevent a certain and extremely unpleasant death. It is in no small measure owing to public health units that there have been very few deaths from rabies in Canada.

By 1955, Dr. Horner was pioneering nursing care in the home. This was done by the public health nurses long before the province introduced a home care program that currently exists.

In 1956, the Health Unit left its offices at 175 George Street and moved into the then new United Counties' Building on William Street in Cobourg. The space and physical conditions there were a great improvement over the previous offices. The Health Unit remained there until 1992, when it moved to its present location at 200 Rose Glen Road, Port Hope.

In 1962, provincial regulation allowed nurses to give immunization and tuberculin tests. This was of great benefit to Dr. Horner, who was finding it increasingly difficult to recruit community physicians to do the immunizations necessary in both the schools and the clinics. Nurses also took over the screening for tuberculosis.

In 1966, Louise Steele retired after nineteen years of service and was replaced by Betty Flaxman. The public health nursing department had a staff of twenty, including nursing supervisors and a senior nurse. They were deployed from six offices – Bowmanville, Brighton, Campbellford, Cobourg, Millbrook, and Port Hope. They carried out thirteen programs including dental health and nutrition, which later became separate departments. Miss Flaxman remained as Director of Nursing until 1980, at which time Betty Collins was appointed and held this position until 1987. Sharon Thompson was hired shortly afterwards and remains the current director.

In 1966, inspection services included the Chief Public Health Inspector, a senior inspector and four public health inspectors. There was also a hearing technician, and ten clerical staff persons. Thus, including the Medical Officer of Health, staff totaled 38. The annual expenditure for that year was $236,755.73.

In 1967, health districts were introduced by the Provincial Government, and County Boards of Health were encouraged to consolidate with each other. For inducement, the province's share of the funding for public health increased from 50 to 75 percent of the budget. There were other advantages. For example, these districts could save considerable money by not requiring duplication of senior jobs, and by sharing specialized positions. During a period of one year, in 1968, the public health unit of Victoria – Haliburton was organized and operated. Dr. A.G. Bailey was hired as the Medical Officer of Health along with E. Tindale, Nursing Supervisor, and William Hogle, Chief Inspector of Public Health. This health unit operated only briefly for 12 to 14 months until 1969, when the United Counties' Council began to explore the feasibility of amalgamating with Victoria-Haliburton and with the Peterborough County-City Health Units. Peterborough City and all the counties, except Peterborough, were unanimously in favour of this move. Northumberland-Durham and Haliburton-Victoria went ahead, and in 1969, the Haliburton, Kawartha, Pine Ridge District Health Unit was formed. The boundary now is a bit smaller, as the Bowmanville and Millbrook areas were later transferred to other jurisdictions – the former to Durham Region, the latter to Peterborough County.

Over the years, it became necessary to have a full-time Business Administrator to manage accounting, personnel, plant and equipment. Hugh Good filled that position until his retirement in 1982. Susan Bickle currently assumes the responsibility.

In 1970, Dr. Dennis Warrick was hired as the Director of Public Health Dentistry, along with a hygienist. This department made a dramatic impact on the dental health of the three counties. He began a vigorous program of dental education and fluoride rinsing in the schools, testing of well water for fluoride, and the recommendation of fluoride supplements to the children who required it. Later, clinics were established where certified dental assistants treated children's teeth with fluoride applications. These programs have been responsible for a significant reduction in dental caries.

Dr. Warrick also began a program of custom-made mouth guards to protect the teeth of young athletes from sports injuries. They were made at a minimal cost to the student. With this money, and the money raised through service clubs, a fund was established to defray the dental costs for the treatment children whose parents were not eligible for welfare. Dr. Warrick and some of his colleagues successfully lobbied the Ministry of Health, to provide government funding for treatment programs for these children. Dr. Warrick retired in 1994 and was replaced by Dr. Bill Ryding as Director of Dental Programs.

Other senior staff changes occurred from time to time. Jack Finlayson, Chief Inspector, retired in 1974 and was replaced by Ron Chartrand as the Director of Health Inspection Programs. The Home Care Program for acutely ill persons was formally established in 1970. In June of 1972, the Home Care Department was established, separate from the Public Health Nursing department. Marlene Edwards was appointed as the Director of Home Care Programs and held this position until she retired in 1995.

In 1974, a public health nutritionist from the Durham Health Unit came for one day a week to consult with nurses and others on nutritional matters. By 1977, the demand for these services indicated that this Health Unit required a department of nutrition. A full-time nutritionist has been on staff since 1977 and in 1989, the responsibility for health promotion was added to the nutrition department. Leslie Orpana has been the Director of this department since 1980.

Dr. Horner retired as Medical Officer of Health in 1974. A permanent replacement was not hired, as it was thought that amalgamation with Peterborough County-City Health Unit would still take place, and that the appointment of a new MOH would not be required. However, in 1977, the Director of the Public Health Branch of the Ministry advised the Board of Health that further negotiations with Peterborough would be pointless and recommended finding a permanent MOH. Dr. Donald Mikel was then hired, and he served as MOH until his retirement in 1992. The current MOH, Dr. Alex Hukowich, was hired in January of 1993.

To provide epidemiological support to the Health Unit's programs and services, the Department of Epidemiology and Statistics was established in 1989, and John McGurran was hired as director. This department also provided technical computer support.

Throughout the years, the highest quality of public health services has been and will continue to be, delivered to the population of the community. This is attested to by the fact that in 1982, the Haliburton, Kawartha, Pine Ridge District Health Unit was the first health unit to be accredited in Ontario and has retained the highest level of accreditation since 1984.

CAMPBELLFORD & DISTRICT COMMUNITY MENTAL HEALTH CENTRE / COMMUNITY WELLNESS CENTRE

The Campbellford & District Community Mental Health Centre is an adult outpatient mental health program which operates out of the Community Wellness Centre on Oliver Road across from Campbellford Memorial Hospital. The Centre opened in January of 1991, with a broad mandate to enhance the quality of life for people struggling with mental illness. While the program is administered through Campbellford Memorial Hospital, the Centre operates semi-autonomously and has a separate community advisory committee. The Centre currently has a staff of five:

Dr. Gene Duplessis, PhD, Director
Ray Scott, MA, Case Manager / Crisis Worker
Sandra Leggat, MA, Case Manager / Crisis Worker
Kathryn McLay, RN, BA, Case Manager / Crisis Worker
Robin English, Secretary-Receptionist / Psychosocial Rehabilitation Resource

Dr. Michael Kaufmann was the original chair of the Centre's community advisory committee and worked intensively with the program for the first five years of its operation. When Dr. Kaufmann's work took him to Toronto, another founding member of the community advisory committee, Maureen Dikun, assumed the role of chair.

The Centre has been busy from day one. The staff use a holistic approach to treating mental illness and offer a wide range of interventions. These interventions include counseling, crisis intervention, case management, skills training, group therapy, crafts, exercise, art therapy, women's programs, yoga, meditation, horticultural therapy, and support for family members. To date, over one thousand area residents have been served by the Centre!

Community Wellness Centre on Oliver Road, 1999.

Photo courtesy of Margaret Crothers.

Numerous professional articles have been published on work conducted at the Centre. In 1993, Dr. Duplessis co-ordinated the development of a book on excellence and innovation in the field of community mental health. The book, *What Works! Innovation in Community Mental Health and Addiction Programs*, was published by the Ministry of Health for all community mental health programs in Ontario.

Campbellford went through a long period where there were no local psychiatric services, and residents had difficulty accessing psychiatrists elsewhere. In response to this problem, the Centre pioneered telepsychiatry in Ontario. Telepsychiatry involved the use of teleconferencing technology to link psychiatrists at the Clarke Institute of Psychiatry with patients in Campbellford. This work was featured on the CBC's Undercurrents program and has been the subject of numerous media reports.

HALIBURTON, NORTHUMBERLAND, AND VICTORIA ACCESS CENTRE

The Access Centre was formed in 1997 as part of a decision by the Ontario Ministry of Health to make health care services more easily accessible to the community. It combines home-care services and long-term care facility placements. It also provides information on visiting nursing, occupational therapy, physiotherapy, speech therapy, homemaking services, and school health support services. The Centre is located at 22 Doxsee Avenue South, but will move to the new health centre in April 2000. Diana Rutherford is the Board Member from Campbellford, the Team Secretary is Jackie Oliver, the Case Manager is Carolyn Lee, and the Manager of Client Services is Judith Layzell.

VICTORIAN ORDER OF NURSES

In 1973, the VON opened an office in Cobourg at the request of the Medical Office of Health. The Quinte Branch of the VON was asked to expand into Northumberland County. For many years, the VON was the sole provider of visiting nursing care in the County, and each municipality had its own local office. In 1996, the Ministry of Health created the Access Centres across Ontario and the VON offered its services through this new facility. In 1999, the VON closed its Campbellford office and centralized its operation in the Trenton office. It continues to offer home nursing care and foot care clinics to the local area.

CAMPBELLFORD AND DISTRICT PALLIATIVE CARE

Palliative Care is active, compassionate care given to people experiencing life threatening illness that no longer responds to traditional curative treatment. The programme provides physical, emotional and spiritual support to clients and their families. The late Marie Reid is credited with writing the original plan for a Palliative Care Program in Campbellford and without her vision, this program may have never started.

Campbellford and District Palliative Care is a community based hospice that services the northwestern part of Northumberland County and the Townships of Asphodel and Belmont. The program started in 1991 and was originally located in Campbellford Memorial Hospital and sponsored by the Campbellford Memorial Hospital Foundation. Since that time, Campbellford and District Palliative Care has relocated to 174 Oliver Road in the Multi-Care Lodge. The present funding sources include the Campbellford Memorial Hospital Foundation, Ministry of Health Long Term Care, donations and fund raising.

The program is managed by two paid staff and a Board of Directors made up of representatives from various health and community organizations. At present, the group is fortunate to have the help of thirty volunteers who form the backbone of the organization. The specially trained volunteers assist both the client and family from the time of diagnosis through to the bereavement period. Since the program started, more than two hundred and sixty-one clients and their families have been helped by the dedicated volunteers. Each year one or two training programs are offered. Currently, the program is expanding to provide a Caregiver's Support Group and a Bereavement Support Group. Campbellford and District Palliative Care has been extremely fortunate to have dedicated people from the community who give so willingly of their time to be members of the Board of Directors and Palliative Care volunteers.

From 1991 to 1993, the Chairperson was Diana Rutherford and the Co-ordinator was Judith Mueller; from 1993 to 1994, the Chairperson was Linda Moroz and the Co-ordinator was Judith Mueller; from 1994 to 1997, the Chairperson was Trish Baird. In 1996, Judith Mueller resigned and Tracy Graham became Co-ordinator until March 1998 when Karen Marten took over the Co-ordinator's role. Maureen Dikun became Chairperson in 1997. Leone White has been secretary since 1995.

CAMPBELLFORD AND DISTRICT COMMUNITY CARE

Community Care is a non-profit organization designed to provide supportive help and outreach programmes in Campbellford/Seymour, Hastings, Warkworth and the township of Percy. The services provided include transportation, home help, friendly visiting, Diners' Club, information and referral assistance, fun and fitness, respite care, Meals on Wheels, telephone visitation, education seminars, a wandering persons registry, and a visiting library.

Community Care opened in 1984 at 44 Front Street North. Steering committee members were Richard Quesnel, Lorraine Capstick, Daisy Moulton, George Free, John Crawford, Norma Stewart, Judith Layzell, Maureen Dikun, and B. Bennett. After the Multicare Lodge was completed at 174 Oliver Road, the office moved to Unit 15 in the lower floor. There are satellite offices in Hastings and Warkworth.

～ Social Service Organizations ～

BLOCK PARENTS

In 1984, a group of concerned parents decided that it would be advantageous to the town and to its children that a Block Parent Association be formed. The group was assisted by Constable Glen Yewer of the Ontario Provincial Police. The schools were very co-operative and the teachers used the information provided by the group to educate the children about the program. The OPP Community Officer also spoke with children in classrooms about personal safety issues and showed demonstration videos. Community outreach was very successful and by 1986 there were 150 Block Parent homes which provided a good safety net covering the town. Block Parents are responsible adults who are willing to volunteer their homes as a refuge in an emergency. They place the distinctive Block Parent sign in the window when they are home and provide a safe haven for children at risk. There have not been any major incidents, except the occasional aggressive dog chasing a child, a bully throwing stones, or children falling and hurting themselves.

CAMPBELLFORD AND DISTRICT
ASSOCIATION FOR COMMUNITY LIVING

The Campbellford and District Association for Community Living began in 1960 as a result of the organizing efforts of Mary Cook of Campbellford. The mission of the Campbellford and District Association For Community Living is to advocate for local individuals with challenging needs and to assist them to be full participants in the community. Also, many children with challenging needs had the ability to learn but no provincial funding was available for their education. Parents of these children faced the decision of placing their children in institutions or paying the fees to educate them to schools operated by the Ontario Association for the Mentally Retarded. Mary contacted William Kirk, the president of OAMR, who agreed to attend a public meeting in Campbellford in January 1960. The Campbellford and District Association for Retarded Children was established in April 1960. The first executive consisted of: Reverend Owen Barrow – President, Eva Weir – Secretary, Rev. Gordon Whitehorne, Dr. Baker, Marguerite Beattie, and Alma Older. Other supporters were Catherine MacDonald, Mary Rannie, Bill Pettey, and Bill Rothwell. Hector Macmillan of the Campbellford Rotary Club proposed to raise funds throughout the district, taking in the communities of Hastings, Warkworth, Havelock, Norwood, Castleton, Codrington, Stirling and Campbellford.

In September of 1960, the Association opened the Merryvale School, the first school for developmentally handicapped children in Northumberland County. The first teacher was Gwen Laurason. In April 1968, the Ministry of Education assumed responsibility for the school's operation. In 1972, Betty Langford was appointed principal of Merryvale School and she remained in that position until the school was closed in 1985. She and her students were transferred to a self-contained classroom at CDHS, and Betty remained there until her retirement from teaching in 1996.

In the early 1960s, the Campbellford and District Association also began a sheltered workshop for developmentally handicapped adults at the former high school on Bridge Street East. When this building was torn down in 1977, the workshop re-located to 36 Front Street North prior to the move in 1979 to the present location at 27 Doxsee Avenue North. A prominent feature of the Doxsee Avenue workshop was the furniture repair and stripping program.

The Association was incorporated by Letters Patent from the Province of Ontario as the Campbellford and District Association for the Mentally Retarded in June 30. 1970. In March 1988, the members again voted to change the name to the Campbellford and District Association for Community Living. The CDACL has progressed with many changes being incorporated into its mandate. With the provincial direction of closing institutions, the Association opened a group home in Hastings and built a new home in Warkworth. This enabled residents to experience living as members of a community. During the summer of 1997, the Hastings residents purchased an apartment complex in Campbellford and added a Transitional Youth Program in this building.

In 1987, a Life Skills program was initiated in Havelock. A similar program was implemented in Campbellford after the furniture repair and stripping workshop was closed in 1989. A new business venture, an office supply store, was also started at this location with some of the members staffing the store. This business is currently in the process of becoming a co-op venture with all members sharing in the ownership. The Life Skills program has changed to the Alternative Project focusing on community involvement. This includes community-based recreational activities, volunteering in the community and hosting dinners at the Diner's Club. Part-time employment has been obtained by some of the participants through the Supportive Employment Programme and several people have worked on summer projects through the Environmental Youth Corps.

The Association, whose head office is located at 99 Centre Street in Campbellford, has recently extended its boundaries to the Brighton area, initiating the Brighton Summer Project and continuing this program on a part-time basis during the fall of 1997. The Association continues to grow and face the challenges of the future. In 1998, the Supportive Employment Programme of CDACL relocated to the newly established Resource Centre in the former Town Hall. The Campbellford and District Association For Community Living continues to ensure that each individual has the opportunity for growth and self development, personal and individual choice, and the availability of supports to develop personal skills to live, work and participate successfully in the community.

Mary Cook has received several awards and plaques to honour her contribution to assisting the mentally challenged in the community.

CANADIAN CANCER SOCIETY, CAMPBELLFORD BRANCH

The initial proposal for a cancer society in Campbellford was made by Rev. A. E. Toombs and Muriel Ellis in 1957 at a Home and School meeting. Representatives from the Peterborough Unit of the Canadian Cancer Society were subsequently invited to a meeting at the Legion Hall to discuss formation of a local branch. At a later meeting in 1958, the following executive officers were chosen: President – Ron Hazell, Vice-President – Rev. A. E. Toombs, Secretary – Murray Locke, Treasurer – June Bennett. In 1961, Kathleen Doherty was appointed Chair of Patient Services. The Legion Hall was used to make and store bandages and dressings, which, at that time and for many years, were made from sterilized old bed sheets lined with newspapers.

In 1959, the local branch held its first door-to-door canvas, collecting a total of $1,047.90. These proceeds went toward transportation costs of patients going to Toronto and Peterborough. Later, proceeds from canvassing and 'In Memoriam' donations were used to pay for wigs, colostomy supplies, dressings, and some drugs. Now, with government involvement, these needs are met through the Assistive Devices Programme and the Trillium Drug Plan. Transportation is still provided free by the Society for cancer patients. Trained volunteers also provide peer support, enabling patients to talk with others who have dealt successfully with cancer. A breast cancer support group was formed in 1995 for newly diagnosed patients. Current fund raising consists of the annual door-to-door canvassing, the sale of daffodils, a curling bonspiel, a golf tournament and 'In Memoriam" donations. The total receipts for 1997 were $30,655.57

In 1998, the officers of the Campbellford branch were: President – Paul Philp, Secretary – Nancy Sparling, Treasurer – Ellenor Allan, Patient Services – Fran Douglas, Campaign – Betty and Bob Pearce, Transportation – Joan Ibey.

CHILDREN'S AID SOCIETY

There is evidence to suggest that there was a local Children's Aid Society in the Campbellford/Seymour area in 1915. The Herald reported that a local branch was organized with the following officers: President, C. L. Owen; Secretary, A. J. Jenkins; Treasurer, R. C. Weston; Committee, the doctors of the town. No further information about this group was located and it is uncertain at what point the Children's Aid Society of Northumberland in Cobourg took over responsibility for child welfare issues. There is, no doubt, a long history of developments in this area which could be written.

COMMUNITY RESOURCE CENTRE

In 1998, the Resource Centre was established at the old Town Hall at 36 Front Street South through the combined efforts of several levels of government and local organizations. Human Resources Development Canada has been an integral supporter of this initiative, along with the Municipality of Campbellford/ Seymour. The Campbellford and District Association for Community Living moved its Supportive Employment Programme to the new location. Industry Canada approved a $30,000 grant to provide four Internet sites in the area, two of which are at the Resource Centre, to assist the community to get "online." The Trillium Foundation Access Fund has provided $47,000 to enable the Resource Centre to become physically accessible.

The services available at the Community Resource Centre include the following:

— Human Resources Development Canada Services (Job Kiosk)
— Campbellford and District Association for Community Living
— Supportive Employment Program of CDACL
— Career Edge/Employment for Youth
— Community Access Program – Internet Access and Training
— Computer Training
— Ontario Provincial Police – Community Policing Office
— Northumberland Services for Women
— Northumberland County/Ontario Works
— Community Advocacy Services
— Loyalist College Continuing Education
— Adult Basic Literacy Programme
— Northumberland Child Development Services

FARE SHARE FOOD BANK

On March 6, 1990, Jean Loucks, Donalda Graham, and Hilda MacPherson from the Mission and Outreach Programme of St. John's United Church met to discuss the possibility of creating a food bank for Campbellford/Seymour and the surrounding district. A committee of women visited the Cobourg Fare Share Food Bank to study how the issues related to a food bank were handled in that area. On October 2, 1990, an open meeting was held at St. John's United Church in Campbellford where two volunteers from the Cobourg Food Bank were guest speakers. On November 2, 1990, a Board of Directors and Committee members were named to operate a food bank for the area. It was decided to rent the former Dairy Corral building at the corner of Centre Street and Cockburn Street for the headquarters of the operation. Subsequently, the Food Bank's headquarters moved to a location at 28A Doxsee Avenue South off the public parking lot behind Haircrafters beauty salon.

The Fare Share Food Bank was first opened on January 9, 1991 for the communities of Campbellford, Hastings, Warkworth, Seymour and district. Its mission is to provide frozen and non-perishable food for people temporarily in need. To facilitate the collection of the food, barrels are located at various permanent and temporary locations throughout the area.

The first executive and directors were as follows:

President	Doris Thompson
Secretary	Jean Loucks
Treasurer	Don Bennett
Press/Publicity	Doris Thompson, June Bennett

Directors	Trish Baird	Jean Loucks
	George Bibby	Donalda Graham
	Bert Purvis	Cathy Henderson
	Al Weaver	Meg Pammenter
	Don Bennett	Doris Thompson
	Madeline Simpson	

In 1998, during the month of October, the food bank supplied 109 clients, of whom 28 were new to the area. At the annual meeting on October 27, 1998 at St. John's United Church, the following executive was elected:

President	Reg Murdoch
1st Vice-Pres.	Lillian Adams
2nd Vice-Pres.	Clifford Richardson
Secretary	Bonnie Wilson
Treasurer	Joyce Blackbourn
Directors	Vic Dawson
	Thornton Waters
	Nancy Nicholson
	Don Bennett
	Rev. Jim Cullen

THE FISHING HOLE

A group of local residents, who saw the need for a safe and supervised centre for young people, organized the Fishing Hole as a satellite chapter of the Northumberland Youth for Christ. The Youth for Christ mission statement is as follows: "As members of the Christian community, we will communicate to youth the life changing message of Jesus Christ, showing concern for their whole person and challenging them to become his disciples." The Fishing Hole opened its doors on September 15th, 1998 at 45 Front Street North through the generosity of the owner, Phil Monner. Day one saw fifteen people come through, and day two saw thirty-one. By the end of the first week two hundred and sixteen visits were recorded.

In early 1999, an average of 350 to 450 people visit weekly, with the centre being open just sixteen hours per week. Limited night time use is being planned, contingent upon volunteer help becoming available. The teens have become involved in renovations within the building and the plan is to set up an area where school work and research can be completed using donated computers. Ping pong tables are in place, and there is space for a pool table if one can be found. There are simple rules at The Fishing Hole; respect yourself, respect others, and respect the property. Few problems have occurred and peer pressure initiatives often solve problems.

Peter Panabaker is the only paid staff member at The Fishing Hole, supported by approximately fourteen volunteers. His wife, Mary, interviews and trains all volunteer staff. Staff is selected to represent various religious denominations and occupations, and they are required to work one on one or to just be present to interact with the teens. The staff is responsible for raising the money to pay the rent and utilities and for all maintenance of the centre. Peter and his staff are impressed with the community support extended to them. People have dropped off everything from cookies to cash, and this all helps to keep the centre operating and lets the teens know that their community cares for them.

MORE ABLE THAN DISABLED CLUB

The club was founded in 1981 to meet the needs of all physically challenged persons in Campbellford/Seymour, Percy Township, the village of Hastings and the surrounding area. Doreen Sharpe was the primary motivator for the formation of this club and its purpose is to provide social interaction such as bowling, baseball, trips, fishing, and meals. Fund raising, such as draws and the sale of Nevada tickets, helps support the Venture Van used to provide special transportation.

Meetings are held monthly with guest speakers to raise awareness of issues facing the physically challenged. Speakers are also provided to other service clubs and schools for this purpose. The club is actively involved in transportation issues and in raising awareness of the need for ramps for those with special needs. Education is the focus of a weekly column in the local newspapers. Since 1991, the club has participated in the National Awareness Week to focus on the need for accessibility and also the lack of it in public buildings and stores locally. Elected officials and public figures have used wheelchairs and/or scooters to experience firsthand the lack of accessibility and have been astounded at the difficulties facing those with accessibility problems.

ENDNOTES

1   Information about the original Campbellford Hospital has been excerpted and/or transcribed directly from the following sources:
   Campbellford Memorial Hospital, Supplement to the Campbellford Herald, 1978.
   Campbellford Herald, April 20, 1983, Section 2, pg. 6.

Chapter   Eleven

The
$\mathcal{M}$ilitary

~ The Early Years ~

AFTER THE AMERICAN REVOLUTION

At the beginning of the nineteenth century, Britain was faced with two serious problems. First, the end of the American War of Independence and the Napoleonic Wars left her with a huge surplus army of foreign and Loyalist troops. Some fifty regiments had been raised in the colonies during or before those wars. As the colonies could not supply sufficient recruits, many of the rank and file came from Great Britain and Europe. A large number of loyal citizens were also displaced from the old Thirteen Colonies. Great Britain had no social system to provide for the large number of surplus military personnel and the displaced loyalists. She also needed to protect her remaining British North American colony from the expansionist policy of the new United States. An ideal solution to these two problems was the granting of free land, supplies, and food to all who agreed to settle in British North America. The one stipulation was that disbanded regiments must settle in designated areas and remain ready to serve under their old officers if called to duty. Civilians had more freedom but they could only select a new location from a short list of areas. The Royal Navy provided transportation and the promised supplies came from surplus military stock. Thus, Britain solved a surplus population problem, disposed of large stocks of military goods, and provided defense for the colony at a minimal cost. It has been estimated that seventy thousand civilians and twenty thousand soldiers came to British North America at this time.

THE EARLY MILITIA

Immediately after the war, a number of permanent or regular force regiments were raised in the colonies for home defense. While these regiments were well received by the settlers, again the bulk of the rank and file had to be recruited in Great Britain. The settlers were preoccupied with the work required to meet the requirements for possession of their free land grants. All these units were disbanded by 1802.

The Militia Act of 1793 required that every male inhabitant fit to bear arms had to enroll in the militia company in the area in which he lived. A regiment was to consist of no more than ten or less than eight companies, or more than one thousand men. These regiments were established on county lines, thus the 1st, 2nd, 3rd, etc., Northumberland Battalion of Infantry. If a county could not meet these requirements, it was allowed to establish either independent or flank companies. As a result, many independent companies of artillery and cavalry were formed. Some of these were almost private units, as they were completely equipped and paid for by the members of the company. Some of the uniforms worn were so garish and poorly designed that they were completely unfit for any real active service.

The Northumberland Militia Return or Roll Call for 1828 listed the personnel for the 2nd Regiment, 6th Company, located in Percy. As Seymour Township was only sparsely settled at this time, there was no closer local unit, so the men from Seymour Township enrolled in it. They were:

Erastus Blair	James Elliot	Isaac Platt
Isaac Blair	Joseph Errington	James Platt
John Blair	William Hall	Henry Robison
John Booth	George Hankeson	Joseph Robison
Barnabus Brunson	James Harris	Nicolas Spicer
Diar Brunson	Reuben Mallory	Samuel Stone
Augustus Criderman	Benj'n Merrels	Charles Tripp
James Criderman	Hiram Merrels	Ezra Tripp
Sam'l Cronk	Russel Merrels	Jonathan Tripp
Comfort Curtis	Burge Merriam	Tho's Tuck
Hiram Curtis	Jesse Merriam	Benj'n Vandal
John Curtis	Joseph Merriam	Phillip Waldron
Thos Curtis	Thomas Miles	James Warner
Sam'l Cronk	Philip Morran	John Wilkins
Corn's Dingman	Dan'l Morrow	Thos Wilson
Rich'd Dingman	John Naper	Dan'l Zufelt[1]
Jacob Dingman	Isaac Platt	
Jacob Dingman 2nd	Silas Parks	

LATER ARRIVALS

A second wave of immigration took place about the 1830s, comprised of unemployed individuals whose jobs had depended on the war effort, craftsmen displaced by the beginnings of the factory system, and discharged soldiers and sailors. This was in contrast to the Loyalists who were mainly dislocated land own-ers from the United States, former government personnel, and professionals. Again, the British government actively encouraged this migration by offering free land to military personnel, and by granting large tracts of land to land companies, who would help finance the migration of the displaced workers. The Campbell brothers and many other first settlers of the Seymour area came from this group. From this background it is easy to see that the early population of British North America would have strong military ties and a great desire to defend their homes.

THE REBELLION OF 1837

The first call for duty for the men of the Seymour area came as a result of the Rebellion of 1837. The Constitution Act of 1791 promised responsible government to the people, but in fact the members of the Executive Council were appointed for life and answerable to no one. Frustrated in their attempts to obtain some meas-ure of representation on the council, some members of the Legislative Council began to agitate for direct action. The political situation which developed closely paralleled that which had occurred in the old Thirteen Colonies in the 1770s. On one side were those supporting the Crown at all costs, and led by an elite group generally known as the Family Compact; on the other, were those demanding more representation in government. With both sides unwilling to compromise, conflict was inevitable. The reformers in Upper Canada were led by William Lyon Mackenzie, who had achieved some notoriety as the owner/editor of the Colonial Advocate, a reform newspaper, and as the member of the Legislative Council from York County. In Lower Canada, a similar situation existed, but it was complicated by racial tension, since the reformers were generally French and the Executive Council or 'Chateau Clique' were generally English. These reformers were led by Louis Joseph Papineau. In the fall of 1837, the reformers crossed over the line into open rebellion. In Upper Canada, the rebels were very poorly organized and equipped, while in Lower Canada the opposite was true.

The governor of the Provinces withdrew the entire British regular infantry and field artillery from Upper Canada to support the loyal forces gathering in Montreal. Expecting the local militia to put up little defense, Mackenzie began an extensive tour through Upper Canada, attempting to gather supporters to his cause. A "Provisional Government" was established on Navy Island in the Niagara River. When actual fighting broke out in Lower Canada, the rebels in Upper Canada began to act. The headquarters of the rebel forces was located at Montgomery's Tavern on Yonge Street in Toronto. On December 4, the rebels raised their flag and started their march down Yonge Street, intending to capture the City Hall with its store of military supplies. Met by a small armed group of loyal citizens and the Toronto Militia, the rebel force quickly retreated to the tavern, where reinforcements brought their numbers up to about a thousand men. Fewer than half that number were actually armed. When a force of five hundred militia from Toronto and the Gore District, under the command of Lt. Col. MacNab, attacked two days later, the rebels quickly scattered.

Simultaneous uprisings were to have occurred throughout the province. It appears that the Seymour area was primarily loyal to the Crown, as evidenced by the letter from C. C. Domvile, the military secretary, to Major General De Rottenberg, Toronto, November 28, 1838:

> "Colonel Campbell, who resides in Seymour ... stated positively, that the inhabitants of his township are loyal, and in Percy and the neighbouring country, half the bad feeling represented does not exist, – at Rawdon it certainly is bad. – Some discreet person should be sent to the latter place and its vicinity, to ascertain as accurately as possible the real state of that country."[2]

However, a small group of rebels from the area gathered at Stone's Tavern in Norham and raised their flag. The 5th Battalion of the Northumberland Militia (Percy Volunteers), under Col. David Campbell, Major Adam Meyers, and Capt. Matthew S. Cassan, Adjutant, was conducting training exercises at Percy Mills (Warkworth) when word reached them of the rebel gathering. The Volunteers immediately began the march of about a mile and a half to meet the rebels, who were under the command of Comfort Curtis. Curtis, it should be noted, was shown on the Muster Roll of 1828. Members on both sides knew each other well, as the population of this area was still relatively small. It was neighbour against neighbour, relative against relative, and could have resulted in civil war. Although armed only with clubs, farm implements and stones, the local rebels had a far different attitude than those in Toronto. Facing an armed, trained militia, they were not ready to back down. After a cold, wet march, the militiamen were in no mood to put up with the jeers and name calling of the rebels. Anger increased on both sides until it could no longer be contained. Col. Campbell had ordered that no shots were to be fired, and none were, perhaps due more to a sudden heavy downpour than to military discipline. About half of the militia broke ranks, and hand to hand fighting occurred, during which the militia hauled down the rebel flag. During the retreat ordered by Col. Campbell, the rebels counterattacked, recaptured and re-hung their flag. Both sides suffered some very serious broken bones, head injuries, and cuts and bruises. The Percy Volunteers were billeted in a nearby barn while the jubilant rebels staged an impromptu victory parade down the main street. The five local bars did a thriving business that night.

Campbell regained control of the militia, and his patience during the next few hours and following days prevented any further or more serious bloodshed. Curtis fled the scene, realizing that a warrant for his arrest would be on its way. He was carried to Kingston hidden in a hog crate, and crossed the St. Lawrence River to the United States. A year later, Curtis returned to Norham and the warrant was served. He was tried and acquitted.

The only other involvement that the Campbellford/Seymour area had with military affairs before the Fenian Raids was participation in garrisoning the military establishment at Penetanguishine from 1840 to 1843. The personnel for a battalion of incorporated militia was provided by the counties of Durham, Northumberland, Prince Edward, and Simcoe and the towns of Kingston and Perth. It is uncertain how many of them were from the Campbellford/Seymour area.

THE FENIAN RAIDS

Since the beginning of the nineteenth century, many Irish refugees had settled in the United States and Canada. Some were members of, or sympathizers with, the Fenian Brotherhood, an anti-British secret society dedicated to violence. By the middle of the 1860s, the Fenians had a plan to recruit a vast army from the Irish veterans of the recent American Civil War, capture Canada, and hold it ransom for a free Ireland. Canadians, seen as suffering under the yoke of British rule, would welcome the Fenians as liberators, and American politicians, seeking the Irish vote, would ignore Fenian liberation rhetoric. Their efforts were no secret. Arms and money were openly solicited. Ideas and plans were published in many newspapers. While there was a small vocal support in Canada, most Canadians rejected or feared the proposed Fenian invasion. The French-Canadians had no love of the Irish, the Protestants feared a Catholic invasion, and even many Catholics resented any activity that might increase friction between the two religious groups.

The militia were called out repeatedly to repel expected Fenian threats during 1865 and 1866. On St. Patrick's Day 1866, fourteen thousand militiamen turned out to face an expected invasion. The actual invasion, on May 31, 1866, was almost a disappointment. Instead of the expected thousands, about six hundred crossed the Niagara River from Buffalo to Fort Erie. They were met on June 2 by two militia battalions near Ridgeway and, after a confused melee, both sides retreated. The Fenians retraced their steps to Buffalo where they were interned by the American government.

The local Militia underwent special training in 1866. It is reported that Capt. Cassan drilled recruits on the ice at Meyersburg. Anyone who has laboured at mastering the intricacies of footwork on an ordinary dry surface must wonder at this. Captain G.F.A. Tice commanded a company of men from Campbellford on garrison duty in St. Catharines. The Campbellford Herald of Thursday, March 30, 1939 published the following list of the men who served under Captain Tice:

NO. 5 COMPANY 2nd PROVINCIAL BATTALION
FENIAN RAID, 1866

Captain	G.F.A. Tice	Henry Hill
Lieutenant	Hugh O'Neil	John House
Ensign	Henry Barwick	Wm. Knox, Jr.
Sergeants	Richard H. Bonnycastle	Wm. Knox
	Gilbert Dinwoodie	Adam Lever
	John Johnston	John McGrath
	Thomas Taylor	Thomas McQuaig
Corporals	John Bell	David Melville
	John Black	John Morrison
	Ernest Denmark	Benjamin Peeling
	John Wenman	Joseph Peeling
Bugler	Ezekiel Harris	Robert Peeling
Privates	Wm. Abernethy	Thomas Pope
	Maxwell Anderson	Thomas Rannie
	James Benor	Thomas Sergenson
	Charles Bonnycastle	Wm. Scott
	Henry Fraser	James Shillinglaw
	John Fraser	Robert Shillinglaw
	Wm. Fraser	James Simmons
	James Free	George Smith
	Wm. Greenwald	Peter Smith
	John Hannigan	

Other individuals served on detached duty as support troops for the British Regulars or other militia units. In 1898, the Herald noted that fifty men from Campbellford had participated in the Fenian Raid of 1870 and that those surviving were eligible to receive silver medals. Those who survived until 1898 included the following:

Maxwell Anderson	R. H. Bonnycastle	Wm. Greenwault
James Benor	E. Denmark	John Howes
Charles Bonnycastle	John Fraser	John W. Johnston

Thos. McQuigge	Wm. Scott	Thos. Taylor
John Morrison	Frank Shea	George Temple
Thos. Pope	Peter Smith	
Thos. Rannie	M. T. Stephens	

The local militia took no other part in this crisis. James Waters and Charles Bonnycastle were two local residents who were awarded land in Northern Ontario for their service in the Fenian raids.

REBELLION IN THE WEST

In spring 1869, the Government of Canada sent a party to the Red River Territory to survey and divide the land for future settlement. Much of this land was occupied by French-speaking Catholics and Metis, but the Government offered them no guarantees with respect to their land rights. Several deputations and petitions were made, but no response came from Ottawa. As a result, a provisional government was set up in Fort Garry (Winnipeg) under Louis Riel. The requests made by this provisional government, for the most part, were only that the Government of Canada extend to those living in the Red River Territory, the same rights that the citizens of the other provinces already enjoyed. Anyone in the Red River Territory who disagreed with the provisional government was arrested and charged with treason. One prisoner, Thomas Scott, formerly of Belleville, was very outspoken and disrespectful towards the provisional government, and Riel in particular. He was tried and sentenced to die for treason. Riel, using a pistol, carried out Scott's execution in public. This execution caused the Canadian government to send troops west to put down this rebellion.

An expeditionary force of about one thousand men was created, and about seven hundred were drawn from militia units across Canada. The Red River Muster Roll does not identify the units from which the Ontario Rifles were drawn. The expedition reached Fort Garry on August 24, 1870, only to discover that Riel and his associates had escaped to the United States. Order was quickly restored and a permanent garrison was established at Fort Garry. The British Regulars returned to their eastern posts and the militia remained for the winter.

Fifteen years later the same problems arose in the Saskatchewan Territory. To make matters worse, the buffalo herds on which the native people depended for food and trade, had been reduced in size and put off limits to the native people. Any pemmican produced was needed for the railroad construction crews. In addition, land was now being fenced off for cattle ranches and wheat farms. As he had in Manitoba, Riel set up a provisional government and sent demands to Ottawa. Again, Ottawa refused to negotiate in good faith. When a special force of mounted police was defeated at Duck Lake, military aid was quickly summoned. This time a force of over three thousand troops, nearly all Canadians, was called up to meet the rebellion.

A composite infantry unit was created from the militia regiments of the Ontario Midland Military District, in which Campbellford/Seymour was located. The Midland Provisional Battalion was under the command of Col. Williams from Cobourg. B Company was made up of the following men from the Campbellford area:

Captain	R H.Bonnycastle
First Lieutenant	John E. Govan
Second Lieutenant	A. Tomlinson
Colour–Sergeant	C. S. Strong
Sergeants	F. P. Strong
	Abram Fraser
Corporals	G. Batchelor
	Freeman Peeling
	E. Frederick
Bugler	Pte. George Dickson

Armstrong, G.	McDonald, D.	Potter, Charles
Begg, Robert	McGonegal, R.	Rannie, Charles
Bird, George	McGonagal, William	Rannie, Thomas
Clifton, R.	McKee, M.	Reynolds, Charles
Clute, G.	Metcalfe, William	Quackenbush, R.
Farnes, G.	Mills, W.	Shea, Frank
Fraser, Walter.	Mitchell, H.(E.)	Smith, G.
Frederick, Barnat	Morrison, George	Stroud, John
Giddy, W.	Nadoo, George	Thurston, C.
Hill, James	Nancarrow, Fred	Thurston, William
Hornbeck, George	O'Dell, George	Wood, Samuel
Jacobs, J.	Pope, Thomas	

On April 2, 1885, the men of B Company marched through the streets of Campbellford to the newly erected train station. They were proudly led by the town band. Most of the businesses, schools, and even the large mills had closed for the send-off. The parade route most likely began either in front of the Town Hall on Front Street North or Market Square, went south to Bridge Street, crossed the bridge over the Trent, and then went west along the old Hastings Road to the station on the northwest edge of town. It was lined by people waving flags and cheering heartily. The special train arrived from the west and the soldiers boarded, joining the troops from C Company (Lindsay), D Company (Millbrook-Manvers), and G Company (Peterborough). Puffing great clouds of smoke and steam, the engine drew the cars slowly out of the station, across the new bridge and on to Belleville. The trip took about two hours as the engine could only reach a top speed of between twenty to thirty miles per hour.

The following is from a letter sent to the Campbellford Herald by Capt. Bonnycastle.

"We arrived here (Kingston) about 3 P.M. and immediately went into barracks. We have eight companies and when drilled will make a fine battalion. Ever since our arrival we have been busy getting clothing, boots, uniforms, mufflers, mitts and all necessary requirements. Every company except the 40th have been presented with underclothing by their respective towns. Belleville men were presented with rubber blankets, but, as our company had to buy underclothing, it was quite a chore for me.

We expect to leave any minute and I feel assured not one but is ready and willing. No one knows how much he has to face-hardships of every kind-but no one grumbles. The families of men in Port Hope, Kingston and in most places are allowed so much while the men are away, the different councils doing their share. I wonder how our township will exert their loyal feeling during our departure."

Today (April 3rd) it is very cold, snowing all day. Our delay is caused by the railway being crowded with troops, one battalion from Montreal and one from Quebec. The batteries (artillery) have gone before us."

In May, at a Town meeting $344 was raised for 'comforts.' When the people of the township heard of this, a further, larger sum was raised.

Unlike the 1870 expedition, which had travelled in relative comfort by boat and train through the United States, these men were sent on a wholly Canadian route using the partially constructed Canadian Pacific Railway route. On April 5, the Eastern Contingent embarked on a special train for Renfrew via the Kingston and Renfrew Railway, where they changed to the CPR. Arriving at Dalton in northern Ontario, they began their first experience at crossing the 'gaps'. Fifty teams were waiting to convey them the next fifty miles in open sleighs. After fourteen hours in the bitter cold, they were glad to reach Camp Desolation and a huge log fire. After a short rest and breakfast, they began the next stage of the journey in construction flat cars. These were ordinary flat cars, which had four foot plank walls and seats added around the outside. There was also a row of seats down the middle but no heat. Some straw was laid on the floor but this provided little protection from the biting cold. After a chilling ride of one hundred and twenty-five miles, they arrived at the end of that section of track. The next day they began their first march, twenty-three miles across the ice of Lake Superior, in a blinding storm of sleet, snow, and rain. This progress by sleigh, railway car and foot continued until they reached Nipigon, where they boarded an emigrant train for Winnipeg, reaching there on April 14.

Immediately they were ordered to Qu'Appelle, a train ride of some nine hundred and fifty miles to the west. The contrast in the weather was extremely pleasant. Instead of cold, rain and snow, it was so mild that the settlers were preparing to put in their crops. After a short period of rest and the usual drill and exercises, the solders were ordered to Swift Current, which had been threatened by a small band of fifty natives. The first night, a typical spring storm struck – high winds with a mixture of rain, sleet, and snow. The sentries complained that they could not walk their beat in a straight line, as the wind blew them off course. At this point, the Battalion was broken up. E, F, G, and H Companies remained at Swift Current and the remainder moved north to the rebel headquarters at Batoche.

The march to, and the descent of, the Saskatchewan River was one of the longest and most difficult of any conducted during this engagement. The full details need a book in themselves. B and D Companies were assigned the task of holding the river crossing at Clark's Crossing, guarding both the supply lines and stores gathered there. Thus the Campbellford men missed the battle at Batoche on May 12. They rejoined their Battalion at Batoche on May 13. Subsequently they marched to Frog Lake via Prince Albert, Battlefield, and Fort Pitt. The Companies of the Battalion who had remained at Swift Current joined them there on June 18.

The return journey was much easier due to the summer weather, and the fact that more of the rail line had been completed. The Battalion left on July 4 and arrived at the Port Hope dock the evening of the nineteenth. After a welcome parade and review, B Company left for Campbellford and another hearty reception. The town band lead them from the station to a reviewing stand on the steps of the St. John's Methodist Church. After a speech by Reeve Bedford, they were each presented with a silver watch inscribed with their initials and NORTH WEST REBELLION 1885. They were then treated to a sumptuous supper. Their triumphant return was marred by the death of Col. Williams from illness during their trip home. He was the only member of the Battalion to die during the expedition. The Battalion received the Battle Honour 'North West Canada 1885,' the first awarded by the Canadian government.

THE BOER WAR

The nominal rolls of the Boer War show only one man from this area who took part. He was E. E. Mattries, a member of 'A' Field Battery RCA (Kingston), who came from Warkworth. There were others who had roots or family in this area. Three of these were Captain John D. Mackey, Wm. J. Doxsee, and W. J. Dickey who received recognition for their war service in the form of a gold chain and pendant presented to them by the employees of the Trent Valley Woolen Mills. Mackey and Doxsee had served in the Royal Canadian Regiment, and Fred Wood proudly displayed two large photographs of the regiment when they were entertained by royalty at Windsor Castle at the end of the war. The two men also received medals from the Duke of York and Cornwall at a ceremony in Toronto. Four others were mentioned in various resources as having served in the Boer War. They are C.W. Duncalfe, Joseph Dickinson, Fred Atkinson, and E. Roberts. Duncalfe and another soldier, Private F. Bradshaw, were wounded in action.

A mammoth victory parade was held on Thursday, March 1, 1900, to celebrate the news of the relief of the British at Ladysmith in South Africa. It culminated at the Victoria Skating and Curling Rink with speeches and festivities chaired by Reeve Charles Smith. On St. Patrick's Day, A.H. McKeel hoisted the Irish flag at his home to honour the heroes of the Irish brigade who were killed at the battle of Ladysmith. In the spring of 1900, the Campbellford Herald reported that the news of Pretoria's surrender to the British resulted in much celebration. Flags were prominently displayed on public buildings and private residences. The children were given a school holiday on May 31, 1900, to mark the event.

~ The Twentieth Century ~

WORLD WAR I — THE GREAT WAR

A significant number of reforms and improvements in the military were made after 1900 through the efforts of Militia Minister Fred Borden. One of these was the building or acquiring of armouries for a number of regiments. The Company in Campbellford benefitted, in that the Crown purchased the Ogilvie house at 34 Bridge Street West on July 20, 1914.

When Canada declared war against Germany on August 4th, 1914, a totally new experience faced the people of Canada. This time the whole country, both men and women, would be directly involved in the war effort. Women had served as nurses in both the Riel Rebellion and the Boer War, but they had never officially been part of the military. The Permanent Army Medical Corps immediately set up military hospitals, and the nurses became officers in the Canadian Army. This was a first for any army in the world.

With the enrolment of so many men in the armed forces, there was a shortage of labour on the home front. Women stepped in to fill the roles previously held by men. Not only did they serve overseas as nursing sisters and as drivers, they ran canteens and clubs, and freed men from office tasks. While women had worked in factories almost from the beginning of the industrial age, they had been, for the most part, confined to the production of cloth and clothing. Now women found employment in almost every kind of manufacturing plant, as Canadian factories were given large contracts to produce war material of all kinds. Offices employed large numbers of women.

During previous conflicts, volunteer work provided much scope for women, and it did so again. A Canadian Patriotic Fund was set up to collect money to help support soldiers' families. By the end of the war forty-seven million dollars had been collected across Canada. The IODE, Red Cross, Women's Institutes, and Khaki Leagues raised funds to help create nursing homes, hospitals, and sanitariums, and even helped build and stock a hospital ship. Every church and social organization became busy collecting scrap, knitting, and filling 'comfort' packages and ditty bags for those in the service.

If the Canadian government had sent existing regiments to serve overseas they would have, by the terms of the Imperial Defense Act, come under the authority of the Royal Army, with British officers replacing all the Canadian staff. In order to maintain some measure of Canadian control, new regiments were created. These were identified by a numerical designation only. Men from the Campbellford/Seymour area joined at least ten different Battalions – the 2nd, 21st, 39th, 77th, 139th, 155th, 235th, 247th, and 254th. Infantry Battalions and the 4th Machine Gun Battalion were raised in this area. Other men joined the various Corps of the Army, the new Royal Canadian Navy, or the fledgling Air Force, which at this time remained under the control of the Royal Flying Corps. In 1915, three local men joined the British Army Medical Corps, R. H. Bonnycastle, Richard Horkins, and Ernest Frederick. The local regiment, the 40th Northumberland Regiment, remained as a reserve unit for recruiting and training. The actual number of men who served is unknown but at least eighty paid the supreme sacrifice. Mayor W. J. Doxsee died at Ypres in 1915 while serving in the British Army Medical Corps.

From time to time, the Campbellford Herald printed letters from the front, either sent directly to the newspaper or to families. One from Private Bruce Elmhirst in November 1916, related the horrors of the war.

November 2, 1916

Dear Mr. Kingston:

We have started on another phase of trench life, and lest my former letter should be responsible for wrong impressions, all trenches are not alike. What I shall tell you will be plain, unvarnished facts, incidents that came within the range of my own personal observation and experience. And remember that I have not seen the worst, for we have been in no advance yet and this is but the first of November.

The first taste we had of the horrors of war was on a day when our signal officer took us up near the lines for observation purposes. We crossed a huge battlefield, acres in extent, so torn and honeycombed with bomb craters that there was scarcely a green thing growing. There were, however, some gruesome things to be found, relics of the savage battle waged here; rusted rifles, broken bits of equipment, water bottles, helmets, dead horses and mules, lying just where they were killed, with their pack saddles on. Boots attached to partly buried bodies protruding from the sides of shell holes, grisly, bony hands reaching up from the earth like talons, and up nearer the lines where we came under close shell-fire, were unburied men, mostly Germans, lying in shell holes, their flesh black, rotting, eaten away, flies crawling over them – horrible sights. The stench in places was sickening. A broken aeroplane and 'tank' were also stark reminders of earlier battle.

The next experience was on the day we went to the trenches. In the middle of the road up which we were proceeding, we came to a transport of six mules and four men lying in a mangled heap. Beside one mule lay what had been a man, his hands thrown above his head, his whole face blown away, leaving the remainder of his skull like a split nut with jagged edges and his body terribly mangled. A little further were three men piled in a heap of raw flesh and blood and torn uniforms, and one man with no visible mark lying by himself – all this the work of one shell.

Oh, we were plastered in mud and dirt by the time we reached the trenches. Traction in the 'hole' was non-existent and the effect of watching yourself and your fellows spluttering and falling and getting tangled in radio wires and equipment was positively sidesplitting.

I think it was the second day in, that the first disturbance occurred. The Germans had been shelling us pretty heavily; shaking the cavern and hurting our ears, even at the depths of our trenches. Two men were carried down from their observation posts, convulsed with shell shock. Our corporal, an old soldier of 24 years' experience in many lands, went up to see what was the matter and presently he too stumbled down the stairs, groaning, his breath coming in gasps, his arms pressed against his eyes as though to shut out the vision of the awful things he had witnessed – his nerves, for the moment, were completely gone. It seems that a shell had hit one man fairly, carrying away his head and when the corporal reached the place, the trunk was standing, partly buried in the earth, blood spouting from the veins standing up from his neck. They finally picked him up on a couple of shovels, carried him over the parapet and buried him, the corporal reading the prayers for the dead from a Roman Catholic prayer book. When he had nothing more to do to occupy his thoughts, the horror of it all overcame him.

Signal duty was a daily death knell. Signal men, sentries, and guides were appointed by the hour as crews, one by one, were felled by enemy fire. A young chap by the name of Griffiths is especially missed. He was always cheerful and was liked by everyone of us, trying to make the best of a bad situation. Poor Grifs! He was shot through the head and we dared not venture into the field to give him a proper burial.

Our last night in the trenches before being relieved is a night I shall never forget. It was like a hideous nightmare. Each one of us dearly hoped we might survive a few hours longer to reach safety. The dugouts and passages were crowded, full of wet, cold, exhausted men, some standing up the whole night long, others flopped down asleep in the mud, which had penetrated all of us and lay four to eight inches deep. Wounded men lay there too, impossible to take out, owing to the state of the trenches. In the passage to the entrance to our dugout, a man tossed through the weary night, his hand so badly shattered by shrapnel that it would have to be amputated. At the other end lay a man suffering through the agonies of 'trench feet', moaning and shivering, the tears running from his eyes for the awful pain – "like a toothache all through your feet," as someone said – the puffed, inflamed dogs bare, unable to endure anything touching them. It was nerve racking to go down those dark, cold, draughty, passages, to hear men groan and shiver, their teeth clicking like bones striking together, and on a lighting of a match to see them for a brief instant.

What wrings the heart most is the inability to give any aid. More than once during that sleepless night I was reminded of Dante's Inferno. We made up what oxo we had for the worst cases, but it was little enough. For most, there could be no relief from pain.

A letter from Capt. Richard Horkins to his mother, Joanna Mahoney Horkins, in October 1916, was a personal announcement of his death.

France

My Dearest Mother,

We are on the eve of a great battle and if this letter finds its destination it will convey the news that I am "Battled out, middle-peg." My last wish will be that you take it as a Spartan Mother that you are and be consoled to the Will of God. My duty to my country will have been served. but to you I owe much more. My only regret at this hour is my inopportunity to add to the comforts of your life and fulfill the obligations of a son to a mother. You will give my sincerest love to father, brothers and sisters and ask them to remember me in their prayers. As for you, dear mother, you will be in my dying thoughts.

Your affectionate son
Dick

From these, it is apparent how the soldiers tried to cope with the ugliness and horrors that surrounded them. Those that found no way to handle the stress usually either divorced themselves from any feelings or became 'shell shocked.'

The one letter that was dreaded was from either the Battalion commander or the War Office notifying the family of the death of their loved one. On September 12, 1918, the Campbellford Herald printed a letter of condolence received by Martin McArthur on the death of his son, Private Fred McArthur, who was killed in action on August 8, 1918:

France, August 14th, 1918

Dear Mr. McArthur:

You have doubtless received official word that your son, Pte. McArthur, No. 19238, was killed in action on August 8th.

I write to extend to you and his family our very deep and heart-felt sympathy in your great loss. "Mac," as he was lovingly known by us all, was a great favorite with everyone, and has proved himself a brave soldier many, many times.

I think the most encouraging words I can say are that he died bravely facing the enemy, and has added his full share of honor and glory to one of Canada's most glorious days in the field of battle.

Yours very sincerely,
R. F. SHEPPARD, LIEUT,
3rd Canadian Battalion

Even a letter from the Red Cross, telling of an injury, was welcome, as it meant that the soldier was alive and, for the time being at least, out of harm's way.

On November 11, 1918, at 5:00 AM, Matthias Erzberger, leader of the Catholic Center Party of Germany, signed surrender papers ending four years of war. In cities and villages around the world, the news was received with great relief and wild cheering. However, at Mons and along the front, the news was delayed. Word of the Armistice reached the Canadian Corps at 7:00 AM but it took two hours to spread the order that all shooting would stop at 11:00 AM. The Campbellford Herald carried the following report:

Campbellford Wild With Enthusiasm

"Early Monday morning all the flags of the town were in evidence and every boy and girl spontaneously gave vent to feelings of inexpressible joy at the downfall of the Hun.

Mayor Russell invited the townspeople to celebrate, proclaiming a half holiday. A thanksgiving service was held on the school grounds in which all denominations participated. The program was under the direction of the Ministerial Association. The choristers of the various churches led the singing of hymns with the town band accompanying. The Reverend A. R. Sanderson, President of the Ministerial Association presided. Mayor Russell in a few words reiterated the good news and expressed his pleasure as being privileged to call the people together on such an important occasion – 'the greatest in history, the downfall of autocracy and the end of the greatest tragedy the world has ever known'. Mr. C. L. Owen, Ex-M.P. spoke briefly on the armistice. Revs. Bilton, McIntosh, Clarke and Snyder also took part in the service. Several hymns of thanksgiving were heartily sung by the large crowd assembled. The children of the public school led in the singing of "O Canada." The war veterans were given a foremost place on the platform. At the conclusion of the service Mrs. Mary McArther (sic) was presented with an engraved silver plate by Mr. J. I. Adams, County Master, on behalf of the Northumberland County Orange Lodge, as testimony to the memory of her son, the late Hugh Neill McArther (sic), who paid the supreme sacrifice in 1917. The service closed with the National Anthem.

All day and evening the people thronged the streets "clad with happy faces and with holiday cheer." Boys and men, girls and ladies manifested their joy in many ways. The Kaiser and Crown Prince were burned in effigy and all applauded the act.

Next morning the debris was gathered up and the town resumed its normal state. Needless to say, the occasion was worthy of the celebration and there in no doubt every Canadian will always remember the day when Great Britain and her Allies emerged victorious from the greatest war of all time."

It was nearly a year before all the soldiers returned to their homes. The war had transformed much of daily life. Traction machines used to pull heavy war equipment and artillery were converted to farm use. The place of women in the community was clearly changed. The returning soldiers also brought with them many changes in attitude. The stress of the years of separation, horrendous battles and squalid trench life had a great impact. For many, the long desired homecoming was awkward. No one at home could really understand their experiences. What was important before the war and still was to those at home, had lost much of its value to the returning veterans. Peace and social reforms became their treasured goals.

The names of those who lost their lives in the Great War were inscribed on the Campbellford and Seymour War Memorial which was erected in 1926. The lists reads:

Abernethy, Mansel J.	Emlaw, Harold	McQuade, William
Anderson, Harry	Everleigh, Frank	Mills, James
Badgley, John Samuel	Free, Edgar	Nancarrow, Frederick
Bates, Albert	Hankinson, James	Nelson, Andrew Easton
Bateson, William Walter	Heath, David	Richardson, George
Bea, Arthur	Hicks, Samuel	Rutherford, Norman
Berry, Albert Edward	Horkins, Richard E. MB	Reynolds, James Arthur
Bigham, Willis	Hutchings, Alfred	Salter, Wm. J.
Brewer, Harry	Innes, Edward Angus	Savill, Charles
Campbell, Dugald	Johnston, Frank James	Scott, Andrew
Carruthers, Wm. J.	Johnston, William	Sharpe, Selborne
Coulter, James Everett	Lasher, Stewart	Simpson, Roy
Cowain, Richard O.	Lawes, Eric	Smith, Isaac
Crawford, Daniel	Lawrence, Albert	Smith, Joseph
Cropley, Samuel	Little, Robert Leslie	Stewart, Charles
Crowe, George Benjamin	Longmuir, George Edmond	Stewart, R. Ferris
Cutridge, Ernest Walter	Maddocks, Frank	Stickles, Alfred
Dolman, Garnet	Mailley, John	Stillman, Fred
Donald, Angus	Marriot, Harry	Varcoe, Roy
Doxsee, William J.	Mason, Bert	Weston, Edmund
Doxsee, George Ernest	Massie, James Reginald	Williams, Harry
Durran, George William	McArthur, Fred	Williams, Harry James
Ellis, Archibald Victor	McArthur, Hugh Neill	
Ellis, J. F. T.	McBride, James Campbell	

Lieutenant Robert Ferris Stewart, son of Mr. and Mrs. Jas. A. Stewart, Campbellford, died from wounds in France on April 12, 1917. He was a grandson of J.M. Ferris, former M.P.P., and a graduate of Campbellford High School, and a member of St. Andrew's Presbyterian Church. He received his military training at Kingston Military College.

Photo donated by Barbara Mann to Campbellford/Seymour Heritage Society Archives.

In addition, *A Century of Footprints* lists the following as also being killed in action in World War I:

Burnbrae	William A. Lamb
English Line	Albert Armitage
Hoard's	Murney Lemon

THE WAR MEMORIAL

Between August 1921 and June 1924, Campbellford Council considered the creation of a World War I memorial, such as a memorial park or a memorial hall. As early as 1922, the Campbellford and Bemersyde Chapters of the IODE had already begun to plan for a war memorial. In April 1923, a special War Memorial Committee, with representatives from Campbellford and Seymour, was appointed by Council to report on the progress made by the IODE with regard to a War Memorial. A Memorial Fund was set up and, after four years, the Committee was able to organize the erection of the Cenotaph on present-day Queen Street. It was designed by Alfred McKeel of Campbellford who also built the base and enclosure around the memorial. The forms for the construction of this, and many other area cenotaphs were manufactured in the local planing mill owned and operated by Charles Benor. The monument itself was built by the McCallum Company of Kingston. On it were inscribed the names of those who fell in World War I. The monument was unveiled on June 20, 1926 at a special service.

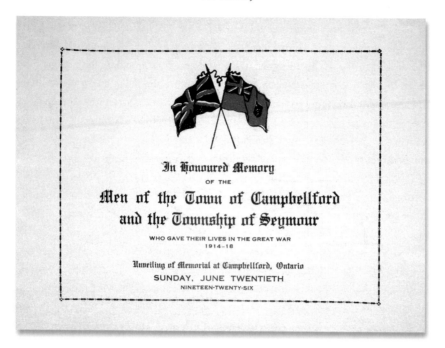

In Honoured Memory
OF THE
Men of the Town of Campbellford
and the Township of Seymour
WHO GAVE THEIR LIVES IN THE GREAT WAR
1914-18

Unveiling of Memorial at Campbellford, Ontario
SUNDAY, JUNE TWENTIETH
NINETEEN-TWENTY-SIX

Program from the unveiling of the War Memorial in Campbellford on June 20, 1926.
From the Campbellford/Seymour Heritage Society Archives.

In November 1932, the Council accepted transfer of the memorial from the IODE, with the mayor being authorized to execute a license with the federal authorities for the land on which the cenotaph stands.

Subsequently, the monument was reconstructed, a cement enclosure was placed around it, and electric lights were added for night-time viewing. In March 1939, A. H. McKeel posted a list of those who had served in the Fenian Raids, the Northwest Rebellion and the Boer War in the Campbellford Herald, and he subsequently asked that he be apprised of any additions to this list.

BETWEEN THE WARS

Following World War I, nearly everyone was tired of war and wanted nothing to do with the military. The Canadian military was significantly reduced in size. A small, dedicated group of men, known as the Northumberland Militia, met and trained at the new Armoury on Bridge Street. At that time there was a large, one storey, stone extension on the west side of the building which was used for drill and training during poor weather. The officers sometimes put their pay into a regimental fund to supply food and gasoline for training exercises, or even to pay some of the soldiers' wages. Due to government cutbacks, the Armoury was sold to the Town of Campbellford on November 8, 1920 for one dollar.

In 1936, two important events occurred. One was the dedication of the Vimy Ridge Memorial. France had permanently ceded a parcel of two hundred and fifty acres of land to Canada to recognize the Canadian effort in taking Vimy Ridge. The French Army had tried twice unsuccessfully to capture the hill at a cost of one hundred and thirty thousand dead and wounded. The Canadians, operating for the first time completely under their own command, succeeded in capturing extensive German trenches. The ensuing Canadian casualty rate was eleven thousand killed and wounded, and other Allied Commanders marvelled at the Canadian accomplishment.

The second occurrence of note in 1936 was the major reorganization of the Canadian Army. The 40th Northumberland Regiment, headquartered in Cobourg, was amalgamated with the 46th East Durham Regiment, headquartered in Port Hope. The new regiment was called The Midland Regiment and was based in Midland. The new name was chosen to honour the old Midland Battalion of the Rebellion of 1885, the Midland Military District in which these regiments were raised, as well as its new home. 10 Platoon, B Company of The Midland Regiment was located in Campbellford.

In the same years, Mussolini's invasion of Ethiopia, Hitler's repudiation of the Versailles agreement, and Japan's encroachment into mainland Asia were omens of impending war to those who were watching world events. Canadian political leaders, however, were slow to increase spending for the armed forces.

WORLD WAR II

The invasion of Poland by German forces on September 1, 1939, abruptly ended any further thought of appeasement, and the 'Peace in our time' negotiated at Munich a year previously came to an end. On September 3, Britain and France declared war on Germany and the Canadian Parliament followed suit on September 10. Mobilization of the 'Canadian Active Service Force' had already begun on September 1, and recruiting was in full swing. The country had just endured a ten-year depression and horrendous crop failures, and these hardships meant there was little difficulty in recruiting the first troops. There was not the same romantic rush to the 'Colours' as there had been in 1914, but a strong sense of loyalty and tradition still prevailed in the people of Seymour Township. Men joined the Royal Canadian Navy, all Branches and Corps of the Canadian Army, and the Royal Canadian Air Force. Initially many enlisted in the Midland Regiment, which was a reserve unit, but later transferred to the Hastings and Prince Edward Regiment when they found out it was a Foreign Service unit. Once again men appeared on parade clad in the uniforms their fathers had donned so proudly in 1914 and cast off so gratefully in 1918. As there was not enough available to fully outfit each soldier in the Reserve units, only pieces of uniforms were issued, giving each man something of a military nature to wear. By the end of October, all the men of the 1st Division were outfitted with the new uniform authorized in 1937. Their World War I rifles were not replaced until 1944.

In 1941, the Canadian Women's Army Corps was established and many women took this opportunity to take a more direct role in the war effort. They served in most of the places the men of the Canadian Army served – Canada, the United States, Britain, Italy, France, the Netherlands, and Germany. Not yet allowed to carry a rifle in the front lines, they served in support roles, officially or unofficially, performing almost every function in the modern army.

On the home front, efforts were similar to those during World War I. By late 1941, most people in the area were committed to a total war effort. Victory Bond campaigns were organized. School children collected bottles, cans, and even milk-weed pods, and contributed quarters for war saving stamps. Radio, unknown during the last war, was listened to carefully and the evening news thoroughly discussed with neighbours and fellow workers the next day. Again, the conscription question was not a serious issue in this area. After the entry of Japan into the war, rationing was introduced. With the establishment of Victory Gardens and a bit of 'over the fence' trading with their friends and relatives in the rural areas, most of the people of this region hardly noticed the rationing. Silk or nylon stockings, elastic, tires, and other rubber products and sugar presented the most difficulty. Although gas was also rationed, few people owned private pleasure cars and long distance travel was not common. Local travel was usually done on foot or by bicycle. The horse and buggy or wagon enjoyed a revival. Many farms still relied upon their teams for fieldwork and transporting produce to the railroad depot, cheese factories and the mills.

The Midland Regiment, also known as 'The Mad Midlands', was mobilized in the fall of 1940. After initial training, they were sent to New Brunswick, first to Sussex and then Saint John, and finally to Niagara-on-the-Lake. While there, fifty-two members were selected for service in Hong Kong where all became prisoners of war of the Japanese Imperial Army. Most of the remaining members of the regiment were moved to Prince Rupert, British Columbia, where they served for two years as infantry guard and coastal defense on the No. 1 Canadian Armoured Train. This train was the only one of its kind in Canada and its purpose was to protect the vital rail line to the harbour at Prince George from potential raids by Japanese troops landing from submarines. This harbour shipped out more war material to the Pacific than any other port on the whole western coast.

In December 1944, the Midland Regiment was sent to England and became part of the 14th Canadian Infantry Training Battalion. The regiment remained in England although some members were sent as replacements to units already serving in Europe. On returning home in 1945, B Company was transferred to Norwood and the Campbellford Armoury was sold by the town to the Legion on November 29 for one dollar.

The following lost their lives in World War II and their names are engraved on the Campbellford Cenotaph:

George Armstrong	James Farrell	Douglas Milne
Mac Atkinson	C. M. Coudy	Francis Oliver
John Baker	Willis Grieves	Gerald Rivard
W. F. H. Baker	Aylmer Haig	Arthur Rowe
Charles Bertrand	Raymond Hay	William Runions
Robert Blake	H. J. Herrold	Aubry Shapter
Charles Buschner	Eric Ingram	George Smith
Angus Donald	James B. Kerr	Harold Taylor
Eric Douglas	Arthur Lambert	L. A. Williams
Charles Dunn	Douglas McMullen	

In addition, *A Century of Footprints* indicates that Clifford Smith also paid the supreme sacrifice.

One local citizen, Tom Smith, has a remarkable story to tell of how he narrowly escaped death while fighting in France. In an oral history interview, conducted with Marilyn Scott of the Campbellford/Seymour Heritage Society on July 19, 1998, Tom related the following:

Arthur Milton Rowe served in the RCAF as a pilot and was killed in action in Egypt in 1942. Born in 1918, he was the son of Harold Rowe and Elizabeth Jane (Jennie) Roe.

Photo donated by Peter Hay to the Campbellford/Seymour Heritage Society Archives.

"....our battalion got into an ambush and the Black Watch was wiped out that day, for all intents and purposes. I was wounded on the hand. I had shrapnel and a gun shot wound on the hand, but got back safely and went to a tent hospital, which was run by the British. I stayed there and they bandaged it and in a day or so they said I had to go back to England for further treatment for this wounded hand. It turned out that the tendons were cut and the hand was broken. I went to a place called Bayeau, France, and there was a little airport there and we were going to fly back. There were about twenty-five wounded soldiers for this aircraft. We waited in the sun on this little airfield to go back to England when I happened to look at the jacket of my uniform and there was a slit in my uniform on the left breast over my heart. I opened up the pocket and I pulled out the little box, about 2" by 2" in which I carried the pills used to treat contaminated water.

One bottle of pills was just white powder, and there was a hole in the can where a bullet had gone through and the bullet was still there. It had missed my heart by a quarter of an inch and I was shocked. I showed it to the person next to me. I didn't know, naturally, who it was. Coming down the line of soldiers was a war correspondent who was talking to everyone as we waited to board the Dakota. When he came down to me, he asked where I came from and I said Campbellford, Ontario. He said that he used to catch 'lunge' down there. His name was Greg Clark, a reporter for the Toronto Star for many years who usually had a humourous vein but joined the war as a war correspondent. I told him about the bullet and showed him the powdered glass and how close it came.

He wrote it down and eventually a story appeared on the front page of the Star of how a Canadian soldier missed death by inches. I did not see the article but I still have the can and the bullet in a box at home and I often think how close things were."

In October 1945, the Government Information Service released the following statistics. Enlistment for the Campbellford area during the war totaled four hundred and sixteen men and women who served as follows:

Navy and Women's Reserve Navy Service	23
Army General Service	310
Canadian Women's Army Corps	4
Royal Canadian Air Force	76
Women's Division, RCAF	3

Unfortunately, the number of women who enlisted in the Royal Canadian Army Medical Corps Nursing Service was not listed. Returning veterans received many benefits that had not been available to their fathers in 1918. War Service Gratuities, Training Grants, and the Veteran's Land Act gave many the chance for a better life. However, there were problems. Returning soldiers often faced families that did not understand their difficulties in adjusting. There were more British war brides than in 1918 because Canadians had spent more time in England during this war, and while these women were generally accepted and treated with kindness, some met hostility and prejudice.

POST 1945

Since 1945, military activity in the Campbellford-Seymour area has been minimal. Local individuals have continued to enlist in the Canadian Armed Forces in a steady but small number. They have been found in many countries around the world supporting NATO and United Nations activities as well as contributing to their respective units.

During the Korean War of 1950–1953, nine local residents served with various Canadian military units in the combat zone. They were:

John Bell	Chuck Ingram	Bob Johnston
Wilmer Grieves	John Ingram	Charles Seaborn
Bev. Heenan	Poly Ingram	Arden Stephens

The people of Campbellford/Seymour have earned a positive reputation for the skill and devotion with which they served in the defense of their country.

CAMPBELLFORD CADET CORPS

The formation of Cadet Corps began in Canadian high schools in May 1909. The staff was selected from among the male schoolteachers. There were two corps: a junior corps for boys aged twelve to fourteen, and a senior corps for boys from aged fourteen to eighteen. With the establishment of the Strathcona Trust in 1910, free uniforms were available to most cadets. In 1931, the allowance for uniforms and junior corps was cancelled. World War II brought a huge increase in the cadet movement and the introduction of the first standard cadet uniform. In 1948, the Department of National Defense began to provide uniforms and equipment to the corps at no cost and the junior corps were disbanded.

During both World Wars, the military-type training intensified, and as the boys reached the age of majority, many left school to join the forces, providing the military with partially trained recruits. Once the need passed, the training concentrated more on citizenship, personal growth and self-discipline. In Campbellford, the local militia unit, the Midland Regiment, initially provided support and encouragement to the corps. Since 1954, the Hastings and Prince Edward Regiment has fulfilled this role and the group was known as the Hastings and Prince Edward Regiment, Royal Canadian Army Cadet Corps #2777. Throughout the existence of the Cadet Corps, an important function was participation in the annual Remembrance Day ceremonies.

During the 1950s, it was compulsory for all high school students, both male and female, to participate in the Cadet Corps. The Campbellford High School students formed a battalion. The boys were dressed in full army cadet uniform; the girls wore white blouses, navy skirts, and saddle shoes, with the exception of the girls in officer roles or those in the band, whose uniforms included jackets and hats. It was an annual event for the entire school to take part in 'a route march' through town. This involved the entire battalion marching from the high school to the train station on Alma Street. Following the march, the remainder of the events involved in the annual cadet inspection occurred on the lawn of the high school. This included a presentation by the band, displays of Bren gun assembly, and demonstrations of physical training, first aid skills, and wireless training. Awards were presented for accuracy in shooting, and many former students will recall target practice in the basement gym. Awards were also given to the male and female cadet who were deemed to be the best overall.

By 1965, the program was open to Grade 10 boys only, but in 1968, the corps was made voluntary for all grades. The Cadet Corps is officially sponsored by the local school board. The Cadet Corps flourished under the command of Major W.L. Rothwell from 1966 until his retirement in 1982. Major Rothwell was instrumental in making the corps a unit to be envied in dress and decor. The troupe enjoyed the winter bivouac outings and the summer camps at Ipperwash.

It was this initiation into military life that motivated many young men and women to seek careers in the military forces of Canada. Two local young men who illustrate this are brothers – Major G.J. (Greg) Forestell, retired, and Lieutenant-Colonel J.R. (Roy)Forestell, CD. After graduating from CDHS, Major G.J. Forestell entered College Militaire Royale in St. Jean, Quebec. After graduation, he entered the Armoured Corps, but reclassified into the Medical Corps after being injured. He held many positions in administration and retired after twenty-two years of service. He is now head of Information Services for Children's Hospital Of Eastern Ontario in Ottawa.

Lieutenant–Colonel J.R. Forestell, CD, has a wealth of experience in the Canadian military. He enrolled in the Canadian Forces in 1976 and upon completion of Armoured Officer training in the summer of 1977, he joined the Lord Strathcona's Horse Regiment (Royal Canadians) as the Ferret Scout Car Troop

Captain Scott Beamish conducting a winter exercise with some of the cadets of #2777 Royal Canadian army Cadets, ca. 1980s. The cadets are having their lunch of ready-to-eat meal packs, courtesy of the Canadian Army. They are involved in training for winter survival, and learn how to build shelters and deal with hypothermia. Left to right: Unknown, Unknown, Cadet Cormier, Unknown, Captain Beamish, Cadet David, Cadet Allen, Cadet Vickers, Cadet Bissonette, and Cadet Milligan.

Photo from the Campbellford/Seymour Heritage Society Archives, originally from the files of the Campbellford Herald.

Leader in C Squadron. During this initial tour he saw service in Australia, the Canadian Arctic and a peacekeeping tour in Cyprus. On promotion to Captain, he was posted to the position of Regular Support Officer to the Governor General's Horse Guard. He returned to regimental duty in January 1983 and over the following years completed a two-year exchange with the British Army on the Rhine, 17th/21st Lancers, completed the Canadian Forces Command and Staff College Course, and his second peacekeeping tour in Cyprus. Upon promotion to Major, he commanded Headquarters Squadron and then Reconnaissance Squadron. He was selected for staff college training and completed the Defense Services Staff College course in India in 1992 and was awarded the position of Chief Instructor at the Armoured School. On completion of French language training, he was posted to National Defence Headquarters, where he was the Senior Staff Officer in the Operations Centre and most recently the Strategic Plans Officer for Operation Abacus. He is now in command of The Queen's York Rangers (1st American Regiment) RCAC. These are only two examples of the impact of cadet training on the individual and on the community.

Colonel Forestell took command of The Queen's York Rangers on September 18, 1999 in the presence of His Royal Highness, Prince Andrew, the Duke of York, CVO, ADC, Colonel-in Chief.

Photo courtesy of Jim Forestell.

ENDNOTES

1   "Northumberland Militia Return, 1828" *Ontario Register*, Vol. 1, No. 4, October, 1968, pp. 237-238. The list has been put in alphabetical order but the archaic spelling has been maintained.

2   Betsy Dewar Boyce, *The Rebels of Hastings* (Toronto: University of Toronto Press, 1992), p. 148. Taken from the *Arthur Papers*, no. 516. Sir George Arthur was the last Lieutenant-Governor of Upper Canada.

$\mathcal{C}$ulture,
Entertainment
and the Arts

～ The Arts ～

EARLY ARTISTS OF
CAMPBELLFORD/SEYMOUR

Among the settlers in early times were many prominent painters. Several local women are worthy of mention. Lily Govan, 1856–1936, of Seymour West, studied abroad and painted portraits of several local residents. Annie Rowed, 1851–1920, was well known for her watercolour work, which included many local scenes and buildings. Louisa Sloggett Free, 1860–1957, also of Seymour West, produced both oil and watercolour scenes of local interest. Edith Brown Gay, 1873–1947, of Campbellford was probably the most productive painter of the time. Her distinctive style and use of colour in both landscape and still life are still treasured locally.

In 1834, the paintings of Henry William John Bonnycastle, 1813–1888, were shown at the Art Gallery in Toronto. He trained as a lawyer but never practised the profession. He married Eleanor Mary Susan Rowed and, on his death, was buried in the family plot on the farm on Concession 5. John Martin, 1846–1918, of Campbellford, was one of the most renowned artists of the area. He studied oil painting in England under Sir Thomas Webb.

CAMPBELLFORD ART CLUB

In 1953, a Lindsay artist, William A. Dennison, who painted colourful landscapes of the area, was asked to teach an art class in Campbellford. He taught in the basement of the library, where he gave instruction in oil painting and the use of colour. Some of the novice artists were George Palliser, Hilton Beatty, Dr. Charlotte Horner, Bessie Bland, Pat Garneau, Vera Newman, Francis DeCarrol, and Beth Taylor. Paavo Airola of Cobourg taught for the next two years, then left to work in Mexico. In 1956–58, the class was sponsored by the Night School in Campbellford High School and taught by Max Heinritz, a graduate of art colleges in Germany. He focused on basics, and stressed creativity and emotion, using oils. Max left for commissioned work in San Francisco.

In 1961, Peter Kolisnyk of Cobourg came with an excellent background, having won a number of awards in painting and sculpture. Peter taught not only oils but watercolour, charcoal, conte, inks, and mixed media. Working outside in good weather, the class depicted various scenes such as the Trent River, the Crowe River, Allan's Mills, the mills at Campbellford, Hastings, Warkworth, Century Village, and Kings Mill, apple blossoms at Huycke's orchard, fishing huts at Brighton, Campbellford from Candy Mountain, the fire hall, churches, barns, and Ferris Park. In inclement weather, the subjects were portraits, still life, flowers, and abstracts. Peter continued to instruct the local classes after he began teaching at York University.

The art club was formally organized March 4, 1966, and the following officers were elected: President – Vera Newman, Secretary – Barbara Greenly, Treasurer – Lillian Fox. In 1967, the executive was as follows: President – Vera Newman, Vice President – Ursula Kaufmann, Secretary – Margaret Macmillan, Treasurer – Lillian Fox, Social Convener – Grace Dunkley, Membership – Ruth Barnum.

A number of members joined the East Central Ontario Art Association which offered workshops in life drawing, etching, batik, silk-screening, and painting under the direction of teachers from the Ontario College of Art. It also hosted juried showings which brought recognition to several of the members. The Campbellford Legion provided a space for the group to paint for a number of years, as did the town council and the library.

Some of those holding office over the years were Pat Garneau, Ruth Barnum, Isobel Thompson, Vera Newman, June Bryons, Sara Johnson, Jim Harris, Lorna Harris, and Marjorie Boise. Members came from Warkworth, Havelock, Hastings, Trent River, Marmora, Madoc, and Codrington and included Debra Cryderman, Joyce Finch, Joan Joyce, Madeline Simpson, Jane Jones, Ava Chamberlain, Louise Simpson, Mayme Free, Merle Eidt, Tillie Bard, Nona Rutherford, Sandra Reich, Peggy Ballard, Lilian Bull, Clara Wilson, Dora Goodfellow, Ora Campbell, Helen Moire, and Cliff Dunn. During its quarter-century existence, the Campbellford Art Club provided on-going instruction, encouragement, satisfaction, and fellowship as well as an abundance of pictorial records and impressions of the area. Loyalist College was formed in 1967 and in 1970, art classes became a part of the Continuing Education program of that institution.

From 1993 to 1995, Cynthia and Frank Lowndes offered classes from the Townsend School of Art at 40 Front Street North, and area artists gave classes. Included in this group were Chuck Burns – watercolour, Sonja Cuming – watercolour, Margaret Forde – watercolour, Margaret Gall – paper tole, Dennis Gebhardt – gardening, Douglas Hall – woodcarving, Peter Hebner – watercolour wildlife, Tammy Laye – acrylics, Ron Leonard – oils, Lucy Manley – oils, Michel Proulx – photography, Carol Rand – folk art, Nora Roberts – oils, Janice Tanton – watercolour, Magda and Michael Wasilewski – watercolour and perspective drawing, Joy Thomas – children's art classes, and Margaret Macmillan – watercolour. Some of these courses are currently available through Loyalist College.

CAMPBELLFORD AND DISTRICT HORTICULTURAL SOCIETY

In 1974, initial efforts were made to form a horticultural society as a Campbellford Centennial project through the efforts of Dorothy Milne, Lorraine Capstick, and Amy Irwin. The Campbellford and District Horticultural Society was founded on December 7, 1975. The main objective of the club is to promote horticulture. Meetings are held monthly, with guest speakers making presentations on a variety of topics. Mini-shows are held and judged by Master Gardeners.

Each year a spring and fall plant sale and a pumpkin contest are held as fund raising projects. Currently, the Society is participating in the Hospital Auxiliary Christmas Bazaar and fifty percent of the proceeds from sales will be donated to the Auxiliary. Money is donated to the town for the beautification of local parks, and to the hospital, Heritage Society, and library for the improvement of their grounds. In 1998, a park bench was donated to Ferris Park in memory of Jim Trotter, Past President of the Campbellford Society, and also of the Ontario Horticultural Society. Members also maintain indoor plants in Campbellford nursing and retirement homes.

NORTHUMBERLAND ARTS AND CRAFTS INC.

The first Northumberland Arts and Crafts show was held at the Campbellford/Seymour Community Centre in July 1979 and was a very successful first effort. It was the result of much work and planning by a very dedicated group of artisans who were determined to introduce an annual event for the display and sale of their creative efforts. The decision was made to incorporate as a not-for-profit organization and to give the net proceeds of the shows to the community. The first directors of the corporation were: President – Jan Scheidt, Vice-President – Ken Hulsman, Mary Anne White, and Lillian Potten. Special guests at the opening of the first show were George Hees, Northumberland M. P., Wayne Rivers, Campbellford Councillor, and Helen Taylor, Miss Campbellford. There was much fanfare with bagpipes, a parade, and a dance after the show.

To raise funds to launch a second show, the organizers decided to sponsor the Mr. Campbellford contest. Hosted by Al Weaver and assisted by Glen Cochrane, the night proved to be extremely entertaining. The women offered their husbands as contestants and cajoled other local men to enter – twenty contestants in total. Judges were selected and the fun began. The contest was won by Jim Sheridan, who tripped down the aisle wearing his rhinestone tiara. He was almost undone by Gary Beaudoin who paraded on stage wearing his wife's leopard lounge wear. This wacky event provided sufficient funds to launch the Second Annual Arts and Crafts Show.

The second show, held in the summer of 1980, was even bigger and better than the first and featured for the first time, a quilt auction, a parade, an open-air concert and, thanks to the work of Jan Scheidt, a beer garden. The show moved its venue to the Curling Club in 1981 and remained there until 1996. A Christmas Show was added in 1981 and was held at the Masonic Temple for several years. The quilt auction was dropped in favour of a quilt show in 1984, and this has remained as a significant feature of the summer show. In 1997 the summer show moved back to the Campbellford/Seymour Community Centre in order to accommodate more vendors. Over seventy booths are now filled to capacity with the finest juried arts and crafts available.

Some of the past and present members of the group who deserve special mention are:

— Rose-Marie Bambrough-Kerr, who served as president for eight years;
— Isabel Ketcheson, who has been in charge of the quilt auctions and display;
— Daisy Pomeroy, a founding member;
— Evert Scheidt, who is always available to assist;
— Colleen Kozlowsky, who has acted as Treasurer for many years,
— Sue Wilkins, Susan Austring, and Thelma Johnston who did so much work in the beginning years;
— Jim Forestell, who has served as President for four years and has been re-elected for an additional two.

PHOTOGRAPHERS OF CAMPBELLFORD

1873	G. N. Simmons	1878–1902	John L. Richmond
1874	Henry C. Samo	1884	J. L. Conlon
1874	Fred J. Trost	1903	C. S. Gillespie
1876	George A. Bonter		

PHOTOGRAPHERS OF CAMPBELLFORD
(CONTINUED)

1903–1906	Turner's Photo Studio –	1903–1904 – M.N. Turner, Miss Bingham
		1906 – Nina Turner

1903–1925	F. C. Bonnycastle
1904–1907	Robert M. McGuire
1906	C. Frank
1908	Cecil Stark
1915–1940s	George F. Bailey
1950s	William W. Reid
1950s	Roy Smith
late 1950s to 1980s	John Coxwell
1990S	Michel Proulx

— Museums and Heritage Sites —

'HOME OF THE INDIANS'

Travelers along Grand Road might easily overlook a small shop tucked in at the end of a short laneway. Located at 204 Grand Road, it is home of one of the few museums devoted to the Indian Motorcycle. These motorcycles were manufactured in Springfield, Massachusetts from 1901 to 1953. Increased competition from rival manufacturers led to the end of their production, but they are now seen as a collector's item by biking enthusiasts, and have somewhat of a cult following.

Owner Charlie Mahoney has spent most of his life working with small engines, in particular, motorcycle engines. It was his father who instilled a love of motorcycles in Charlie, and he began tinkering about with them as a teenager. The simplicity of their design appeals to him. During his career, Charlie has restored and rebuilt Indian motorcycles for Indian enthusiasts from all across North America. His shop is often crowded with restored motorcycles, including a vintage 1916 model, and the last model built in 1953. Fortunately for Charlie Mahoney and other Indian afficionados, there is a large network which has kept original parts and accessories in circulation.

Charlie Mahoney and his Indian Motorcycle Museum have become an integral part of Campbellford's Canada Day celebrations. For years, the motorcycle exposition has been held in conjunction with the town's festivities. Indian buffs come from all over North America to put their bikes on display along the Trent Canal, across from Mahoney's Grand Road shop.

Hundreds of Indian Motorcyle enthusiasts assembled in July 1998, on Grand Road, opposite the Trent Canal, as part of the Canada Day festivities.

Photo courtesy of the Community Press.

MEMORIAL MILITARY MUSEUM

Harold Carlaw's Memorial Military Museum is situated at 230 Albert Lane. From Grand Road, some of the large military artifacts parked outside the museum can be seen. The museum is located on the same property as the auto body repair shop founded by Harold.

Harold was a mechanic from the age of sixteen, and was soon operating his own automotive repair business. Even as a teenager, he was interested in collecting wartime artifacts, searching for obsolete warplanes, and dismantling them for their parts. He retired from his business in 1981, and since then he has devoted his time and energy to collecting materials for the Memorial Military Museum. The museum has various artifacts dating back to the Boer War. The collection also includes restored aircraft, aircraft engines, and military vehicles from both World Wars, as well as more recent examples of military hardware. There is a large collection of old photos, documents, and artifacts relating to past conflicts. There is also a scale model of the ill-fated Avro Arrow on exhibit.

Carlaw's Memorial Military Museum hosts a steady stream of visitors, school children and adults alike. Harold Carlaw's goal for the museum is to instill knowledge of the past in today's youth and to promote local history.

Harold Carlaw demonstrates a vintage army motorcycle to three young history buffs.
Photo courtesy of Harold Carlaw.

CAMPBELLFORD/SEYMOUR
HERITAGE CENTRE

The Campbellford/Seymour Heritage Centre is located at 113 Front Street
North, in an old stone building just north of Market Street. It is the home of the
Campbellford/Seymour Heritage Society, whose mandate is to foster an aware-
ness of local history and pride in local heritage.

The building was constructed for Seymour Township in 1855 by John Longmans (Langman). It is built of quarried stone and local Canadian pine. The construction was done at a cost of £290 ($1450 approximately). At that time, the building had a vaulted ceiling and no partitions. It was the first, and for some time, the only public building in the area. It was an important meeting place for business and social activities; it was also used as a courthouse and a jail. When the local school burned down, the building was temporarily used as the school. When there were prisoners incarcerated, the children were given an unscheduled holiday. An annual ball was held which drew people from all over the area. This created a festive scene every New Year's, with the ladies in their best gowns, music by a local orchestra, and a bountiful midnight supper.

Campbellford was incorporated as a village in 1876, and at that time, the building was purchased for $600 from the township. Even though Campbellford owned the building, it was still shared with Seymour Township. The last court case that was held in the building was in 1914. For a period of time after 1918, it was vacant. In 1934, it became the headquarters for the Campbellford Public Utilities Commission (PUC). For this purpose, offices and partitions were installed. Finally, in 1988, when the PUC relocated to a larger facility, the use of the building was given to the Campbellford/Seymour Heritage Society by the town.

The Campbellford/Seymour Heritage Society held its inaugural meeting on January 20, 1983. Initially, monthly meetings were held in members' homes, at the town council chambers, and also at the Campbellford District High School library. The first meeting held at 113 Front Street North was on December 18, 1988. Due to its historical value, the building has been designated for preservation by the Local Architectural Conservation Advisory Committee (LACAC) through the local Town Council and the then Ministry of Culture and Communications of the Ontario government.

Today, the Heritage Centre serves as a repository to house both archives and artifacts. The archives collection contains photographs, postcards, documents, books, microfilm, microfiche, and newspaper clippings. There are also files and resources for use in historical and genealogical research. On the computer, the Centre can access CemSearch, a program with listings for cemeteries in Northumberland and adjoining counties.

In recent years, numerous special events and exhibits have been held at the Heritage Centre. The opening of the summer show has been the initial event of the Canada Day festivities for the area and has included such activities as skits, a military re-enactment, and a Victorian Tea. The Heritage Society hosts various walking tours of the town, noting the architectural styling and history of various buildings in Campbellford. There are also bus trips and visits to other heritage

Dressed in vintage costume, Margaret Macmillan, President of the Campbellford/Seymour Heritage Society, and her husband, Mayor Hector Macmillan, attend the Ontario Bicentennial celebrations at Christ Church in 1984.

Photo from the Campbellford/Seymour Heritage Society Archives.

sites. Another recurring activity is the antique evaluation clinic where qualified appraisers evaluate artifacts submitted by area residents. At regular meetings, the Society also hosts guest speakers, dealing with topics such as genealogy and archival research. Behind the Heritage Centre is a barn used to store large artifacts and implements not in use. It has unique shingle siding and a second floor.

The Centre is open to the public daily during the summer months when it is staffed by a student curator, and one day a week during the rest of the year when it is staffed by volunteers.

Theatres and Music Halls

THE CAMPBELLFORD MUSIC HALL COMPANY LIMITED

In 1875, the Campbellford Music Hall Company Limited was formed as a joint stock company, with Daniel Kennedy as President, Robert Dinwoodie as Secretary-Treasurer and George F. A. Tice, Stewart Cock, Ernest Denmark and Robert Cockburn as Directors. One hundred and sixty shares were made available at a cost of $25 per share. Forty-two shareholders signed the initial agreement. The first task was the construction of the Music Hall on the corner of Front and River Streets. In January 1875, a ball was held to celebrate the opening of the new hall. This was said to be the grandest ball ever held, with one hundred and twenty-five in attendance. Food was provided by D. Adams of the Campbellford Hotel. Music was performed by Professor Chalaupka's Quadrille Band. In 1892, there was a 'calico' ball at the Music Hall with between fifty and sixty couples in attendance. A few fellows from the Oddfellows' Band of Belleville supplied the music. This hall was also home to many live performances, both musical and dramatic. On April 4, 1893, the renowned poetess, Pauline Johnson, appeared at the Music Hall to lend support to fund raising for the Mechanics' Institute. The Globe newspaper of Toronto carried the following item on October 21, 1893:

> "This neat little hall furnishes accommodation for about 500 people and is furnished with a good stage and scenery. The lessees, Messrs. Geo. Horkins and Thos. Bowen, have given the citizens an opportunity to see some good entertainments this season and have a good many more in store for them during the winter." [1]

By the 1920s, the location was called the Opera House and provided a site for local amateur theatre groups to perform their productions.

REGENT THEATRE

This first theatre operated in the former Music Hall, now the Masonic Temple, at the corner of Front and River Streets. The theatre featured silent films, complete with an organ player for background. Florence Benor and Daisy Rowe Bland were two of the accompanists. The seating was graduated on wooden folding chairs. Because these movies were silent, words were dubbed in at the bottom of the screen. The picture was black and white. Admission was twenty-five cents in the evening, and usually the show was held on Saturday. Some patrons went every week because stories were often continued from one week to the next.

PRINCESS / HOLLYWOOD THEATRE

In February 1909, Messrs. Blue and Phillips opened a moving picture business on the west side of Front Street North. In August 1931, Joseph Hagerman of Belleville, who owned the business at that point, transferred the theatre to Abe Rappaport, a picture house operator of Toronto, on a ten year lease with an option to buy. Extensive renovations were undertaken and the theatre received a new name.

In November 1931, the first show was held in the newly renovated Hollywood Theatre, under the ownership of Abe Rappaport. A bright marquee and neon electric sign flashed messages at the entrance. The entrance hall, featuring a terrazzo floor, led to the interior which was raised from back to front to improve viewing of the screen. The walls were plastered in acoustic plaster to improve sound quality. The theatre was fireproofed and emergency exits made available. The lobby had two electric fireplaces, and, in front, a plaster pool with real water, fish, and a fountain on which coloured lights embedded in the walls cast flickering shadows. The show employed a ticket seller, a ticket taker, and uniformed ushers, who seated patrons with the aid of a flashlight. The theatre had padded seats and there were prizes at the door. Two shows ran each night and patrons could stay for the repeat performance, all for the low cost of twenty-five cents. Matinees on Saturday afternoon cost a nickel and were always packed with children. Foto Nite, which allowed amateur musicians or performers to display their talents, was held on Thursday evening. The chief operator was John Herd, with Ray Phillips as assistant. The Hollywood Theatre closed in the late 1940s.

ARON THEATRE

In 1946, the Aron Theatre, with three hundred and twenty seats, opened on Bridge Street East, complete with many improvements in structural design and quality of films. Colour was now the industry standard. The Aron continued to sponsor contests for local performers called Foto Nite. Community events, such as Remembrance Day services for the schools, and other civic events, were also held at the Aron. George Vice operated the theatre from 1963 until 1967. The new owners, Bill and Charlotte Moon, named the theatre the New Aron. Keeping a movie theatre operating in a small town has always posed a major challenge. It is difficult to satisfy both distributors and customers. The theatre continues to operate in the same location under the ownership of Paul and Lynn Imperial who took over in 1980. Movies are shown six nights a week. The theatre is also made available to community groups, such as Palliative Care, for fund raising purposes.

~ Dance Halls and Pavilions ~

EARLY DANCE HALLS AND LOCATIONS

A 1932 issue of the Campbellford Herald refers to a dance hall on Rear Street, operated by Elmer Jordan. The owner made application to extend his open hours for an extra half hour, but his request was denied by council.

Dancing was also held outside in the market area, near the site of Beamish's Carpet, during the summer months. It was common to have street dances on long holiday weekends, usually in conjunction with a carnival sponsored by one of the local service clubs.

EDGEWATER PARK PAVILION

In 1945, Wes Sweet started to build the dance hall just off Bridge Street West, behind the present King Auto, Radiator, and Tire. Live band music was provided, and, at one time, live broadcasts were carried over the Belleville and Peterborough radio stations. The pavilion was equipped with a special floating floor imported from Texas, and installed by an engineer who came for about a week, and ended up staying a month to supervise its placement. The floor had to have some give to it, but allow for safety precautions. The hall provided a large community facility, which was busy with regular dances, midnight frolics, wedding showers and Hallowe'en Shell Outs for the children. A television set was added to the facility. In 1950, Wes Sweet sold the business to Charles Wickens of St. Catharines, who continued to operate the dance hall for many years.

CORAL GABLES CASINO

On June 11, 1926, Coral Gables Casino at Trent River opened with a gala scene, under the ownership of Harold E. Burgis of Toronto. The Royal Varsity Five of Toronto provided the music. So large was the audience, that many were unable to gain admittance. No trace remains of this structure and the site is now government land.

WHITEHALL GARDENS DANCE HALL

This dance hall was built in 1925 by Jack Sedgewick who also ran a nearby hotel at Trent River. It had a variety of operators through the years, including Josephine Terry, George Johnson, the Cranham family, and the Watts family. Music was provided by five or six piece bands made up of local musicians, like Jack Grant and his Aces – Fred Dorie, Larry Brown, Ron and Grey Kemp, Reg Spalding and Doug Hutchinson. Others who entertained were Ray Peters, Arnold Bates, Ron and Bill Richardson and a group from Hastings which included Clifford Scriver and Lola McPherson.

Arn Bates and His Aristocrats. Front row, left to right, Bill Richardson, Ken Godden, Earl Godden, Jack Minicola. Back row, left to right, Dave Mitchell, Paul Minicola, Arnold Bates.

Photo donated to the Campbellford/Seymour Heritage Society Archives by Evelyn Godden.

Jitney dancing was popular – a couple paid a nickel to dance for five minutes, usually a waltz, mixed with a couple of fast numbers. Occasionally some prankster would dust the dance floor with itching powder, and couples would exit quickly to wash the irritant off their legs. Dances were held six nights a week during the summer months, with a midnight frolic on Sunday evening. In the winter, the floor was flooded and used as a skating rink.

In the early 1950s, Whitehall Gardens was purchased by Frank Openshaw of Toronto who converted the building to Openshaw's Marine. This business closed and in 1986 the building was bought by the Dart family, who demolished the structure in 1987.

CIRCUSES

From time to time, various travelling circuses came to town, much to the delight of the local citizens. The local paper usually reported on the quality of the shows and what follows is a sampling of those reports.

In 1874, the Great European Circus and Menagerie came to town. It included a mastodon exhibition in a Grand Street Pavilion, a grand street parade, and live exotic animals such as lions, hyenas, Bengal tigers, and tropical birds. Admission was fifty cents for adults, and twenty-five cents for children under ten.

On June 16, 1900, several thousand people came from about thirty miles around Campbellford to see the Lemen Brothers circus and menagerie. The circus elephant, 'Rajah' was claimed to be bigger than the renowned 'Jumbo'. The big show arrived in two special trains and set up on unoccupied land belonging to the Cummings estate near the train station. However, the Herald noted that "There was some disappointment with the attractions."

Frank Potts remembers the Ringling Brothers Circus coming to town in the early 1900s and setting up at the fairgrounds. How's Great London Circus attracted a large crowd on June 14, 1912. The Herald reported that "The show taken throughout was very creditable."

~ Music ~

INSTRUMENTAL MUSIC

In 1877, a citizen's band was formed in Campbellford, with James Dickson as leader. He remained in this role for nearly forty years, until 1915. In 1892, the band consisted of C. L. Owen, President, D. S. Archer, Vice-President, J. W. Hamly, Secretary-Treasurer, T. S. Tait, E. T. Morton, George A. Benor and George Horkins, Directors, with members W. Carey, John Rellis, Joseph Dolman, J. F. Smith, C. W. Smith, T. Bowen, James Mitchell, E. C. Hall, R. J. Wynn, John A. Irwin, R. A. Linton, and J. S. Turner. When J. T. Shunk became the conductor, in 1915, the group played Friday night open air concerts. The citizen's band eventually became, first, the 40th Regimental Band, and, later, the Northumberland Regimental Band. For many years, Campbellford provided the headquarters for this group, which was also well known throughout the district. R. T. Cowell was the leader, until he was replaced in 1925 by William Pearson, who was the organist-choir director at St. Andrew's Presbyterian Church. Concerts were performed at the local bandstand on the site of the former Post Office. On January 31, 1937, the Northumberland and Durham Regiments were disbanded and a new unit, the Midland Regiment, formed. At this time, a Midland Regimental Band was organized, and this band continued to serve the regiment until November 1938 when they decided that they did not wish to continue as a regimental band. Several towns within the two counties applied for the privilege of supplying a band to the regiment. At a meeting of the Midland Regiment in Cobourg in March 1939, the applications were considered. The Campbellford Band which had previously served as the regimental band for sixty years was selected.

Uniforms, consisting of a scarlet tunic with white piping, blue caps with red piping, and white belts, were purchased. The instruments belonging to the former regimental band were taken over by the new band. Instruments owned by the Corporation of the Town of Campbellford were donated to the band by the Town Council.

E. Dolman was the band leader for some time, until Don Bennett took over in 1946. Don was an experienced clarinet player and an accomplished keyboard musician. Rehearsals were held on Thursday nights in the front hall of the Legion. Council provided a yearly grant of $350. A junior band was also organized and Peter Battman became the assistant bandmaster. New uniforms and instruments were added as funds were raised through various performances.

The band was a prominent feature in Legion and Santa Claus Parades and played in many other nearby communities. In 1959, Peter Battman became the leader and later Bob Blakely, and J. M. Benor. The band was an integral part of community life for many years.

LOCAL MUSICIANS

Donna Bennett and Brian Finley

Donna Bennett was born in Campbellford on August 12, 1959, into the musical family of June Burgis Bennett and Don Bennett. June studied voice and sang in Emma Watson's Choralians Choir. She was also active at St. John's United Church, conducting the Junior Choir for fifteen years. Don Bennett, who served for several years as organist at St. John's, was famous for his musical talent, having played piano and clarinet in the Canadian Army Band, while arranging music for such greats as Wayne and Schuster. He also conducted the Campbellford Town Band. Francis DeCarrol inspired and directed Donna, casting her in leading roles during her teen years at Campbellford District High School.

Donna became interested in the operatic stage after attending a performance of Wagner's Die Walkiire at the Canadian Opera Company. She enrolled in the Faculty of Music, University of Toronto, earning a Bachelor of Music degree in 1982. Following further studies in New York, she earned a full scholarship to attend the Munich Hochschule in Germany, where she earned a Master's degree in voice while becoming fluent in German, Italian and French. She then attended the Opera

Campbellford Citizens Band, 1954. Bandmaster, D. D. Bennett. Front row, left to right: Paul Linton, Denny MacArthur, Bob Copperthwaite, Allan Nicholls, Jack Collette, David Rannie, John Johnson, Lyle Bland, Marshall Sills. Second row, left to right: Ernie Archer, Gerald Ferguson, Joe Clark, Ross Richardson, Don Bennett, Peter Battman, Ron Pierce, DonYoung, Joe Maddocks, Fred Dorie, Harold Pierce. Third row, left to right: Ron Barnum, Ruben Eason, Bob Cowell, Danny Frederick, Clarence Duncalfe, Jim Baker, Ev Steele.

Photo courtesy of Don Bennett.

School of the Royal College of Music in London, England, again as a full scholar-ship student. From there, her career blossomed throughout England and into Italy and Germany, and included several recordings, broadcasts and world premieres.

Brian was born in Montreal on September 16, 1960 and grew up in Los Angeles, Nairobi, and Calgary. From an early age, he was constantly playing the piano, composing, and arranging as well as acting and writing. He earned his ARCT from the Royal Conservatory of Toronto at the age of 17 with the mark of 91%. Following performances at the Banff Centre and the Victoria International Festival, he entered the Faculty of Music, University of Toronto in 1977 where he first met Donna. He earned both a Bachelor of Music (1982) and a Master of Music (1984) in Piano Performance. Over the next several years, he participated in no fewer than ten international piano competitions, including those in Washington, Lisbon, London, and Montreal. He was one of only three Canadians invited to participate in the Eighth International Tchaikovsky Piano Competition in Moscow, and was seen on Soviet television. He won the Third Prize in the AMSA International Piano Competition in Cincinnati, and the Gina Bachauer Award in 1989 which resulted in a debut with the Dallas Symphony.

In 1985, Donna and Brian were married and lived for over two years in

London, England. They per-formed together on several proj-ects throughout Europe, including appearances at Wigmore Hall, the Edinburgh Fringe Festival, and the London International Opera Festival. Meanwhile, they were also developing active concert careers in Canada. Now the par-ents of two sons, Donna and Brian concentrate their efforts closer to home, maintaining a busy schedule of concerts. In addition, they have made four commercial recordings, including

Donna Bennett and Brian Finley, 1998.

Photo courtesy of Donna Bennett and Brian Finley.

A Christmas of Love and Light, *Lullabies for Benjamin*, *Brian Finley at Wigmore Hall* and *Love's Old Sweet Songs*. Donna has performed with the Canadian Opera Company, Opera Mississauga, Tafelmusik, the Victoria Symphony, and Symphony London. Brian has appeared with several orchestras, including those in Dallas, Calgary, Windsor and Kingston. In addition, he has had some of his original compositions performed and/or broadcast internationally. Currently, he is the Artistic Director of the Brian Finley and Friends concert series which opened in Victoria Hall in Cobourg in 1991. Together, Donna and Brian direct the musical activities at St. John's United Church in Campbellford.

They are the co-founders of the *Westben Arts Festival Theatre* which is a not-for-profit community-based organization, committed to presenting top quality amateur theatre, a music school, and professional musical performances. They were awarded a Citizenship Award for the development of culture from the Campbellford Chamber of Commerce for 1997. Past projects include productions of *Jesus Christ Superstar* and *The Sound of Music*, both of which drew crowds of well over two thousand and involved casts and crews of over one hundred and fifty. Brian's *Requiem for a Millennium* was performed by a large community chorus and was recorded for broadcast on CFMX, and for a CD. *Westben* is now building its own facility – The Barn – on Donna's and Brian's farm, which will house a summer music festival scheduled to open on July 1 weekend, 2000. Eventually, a summer music school will be added to the facility.

Nancy Lynne Courtney

Nancy was born on November 10, 1954, at Campbellford Memorial Hospital to Bruce Sexsmith Elmhirst and Doris Irene Killingbeck. Nancy was the second of six children. The family farm where Nancy was raised is located in Seymour Township, Concession 7, Lot 5. Nancy's formal education started at S. S. #4, West's School, on Highway 30 North, and it continued at Hillcrest Public School and Campbellford District High School. Nancy studied piano and organ with Jean Archer and later with Rick Pritchard. She played the oboe in the school band, and was also involved as a performer in Gilbert and Sullivan theatrical productions at the high school. She was in the orchestra for the Pirates of Penzance, she sang the lead as Yum Yum in the Mikado, and provided piano accompaniment for Iolanthe. Through 1970–74, Nancy was the junior choir director and organist for Christ Church Anglican. She extended her pipe organ skills by continuing study with Don Anderson at Peterborough's St. John's Anglican Church. During her last year of high school, Nancy also taught piano and, among her students was Donna Bennett.

Nancy obtained her Honours Bachelor of Music degree from the University of Western Ontario in 1977, and received her Bachelor of Education degree from

Queen's University the following year. Nancy and husband, Eric Courtney, moved to Ottawa where Nancy taught private lessons in piano, music history, and theory for two years. After moving to Alberta, Nancy taught instrumental music to Grades 7, 8, and 9 at Okotoks Junior High and was also involved with the music program for senior students at Foothills Composite High School.

In 1987 the Courtneys returned to eastern Ontario, and Nancy finally secured a position at Hillcrest Public School. The small music room there is the place in which Nancy studied as a grade eight student. Despite the difficulty in securing consistent funding from the school board for a music program, the program introduced by Nancy was a success. Some of the musical instruments formerly used by the Campbellford Citizen's Band were moved to Hillcrest, and money was raised for maintenance and program administration. The PTA provided some financial help, and parents paid for necessary rentals.

Nancy believes that students can acquire musical skills with the right training. Their hard work pays off when they perform publicly at music festivals or other public events.

Johnny Douglas

Johnny Douglas is one of Canada's most successful and prolific songwriter/producers/artists. He has had over 150 songs recorded by such artists as Gregg Allman, The Jeff Healy Band, Ricky Van Shelton, Hemingway Corner, Junkhouse, Kim Stockwood, Sue Medley, Jim Witter, and many more. Twelve of his songs have placed in the Top Ten, including "Big Sky" by Epic recording artists "Hemingway Corner", which went to number one on The Record's Pop/Adult chart in September 1995. Johnny was a founding member of Hemingway Corner, whose well known hits include "Man On A Mission", "Love, Love, Love," and "Ride It Out." Of his top ten singles, Johnny produced or co-produced eight. Johnny won two SOCAN Songwriter of the Year awards in 1994 and 1995. He was voted Country Producer of the Year for 1995, and Top Country Songwriter for the same year for "Stolen Moments" recorded by Jim Witter. As a songwriter, he has been signed to EMI, Sony/ATV, and Still Working Music Publishing. He has had fifteen songs featured on movie soundtracks and two songs featured on the TV show "Party of Five." As a musician he has toured all across the U.S. and Canada.

Born in Campbellford, Johnny studied classical piano and music theory for eight years with Jean Archer. As with many others, his life changed with the Beatles' first appearance on Ed Sullivan. He worked the summer of his fourteenth year pumping gas for his father, Jack Douglas, at his Esso station on Bridge Street in Campbellford. His father matched what Johnny had saved and he bought a brand new set of drums. This, of course, was the beginning of the end. Rock and Roll took possession of our young hero's soul and he began playing with several friends in a band known variously as The Cymbol, Fang and the Frantic Bananas, and Your Mind's Eye. The band played everywhere in and around Campbellford, including the Masonic Temple, where they promoted their own shows, the Parish Hall, the new Community Centre, the Centennial Parade, the Riviera, numerous house parties, and just about anywhere anyone would let them. Around this time, Johnny began writing songs with friend and band-mate Peter Brennan, very much influenced by their heroes, the Beatles, and others of the day. Soon thereafter Johnny began playing guitar which would become his main instrument.

Leaving Campbellford in the fall of 1969, Johnny headed for California to pursue a career in music. The journey took him to San Francisco where the band he had joined recorded an album for CBS and toured with such well known acts as The Grateful Dead and Van Morrison. He then lived in Los Angeles for many years, recording for A&M Records with his own band and doing session work for many others. He also met and married his wife Catherine, who was born and raised in Baton Rouge, Louisiana. They moved to Toronto in 1981 when Johnny signed a deal as a solo artist with RCA Records, releasing two albums and touring extensively all across Canada. When their first daughter, Sarah was born in 1985, Johnny stopped touring and devoted himself to writing songs for, and producing, other acts.

In 1991, Johnny and family, now expanded to include new daughter Anna, moved to Nashville, Tennessee, where he signed a publishing deal with multinational giant Sony Music. In 1994, he found himself in another record deal, this time with Epic Records. But being back on the road touring again was getting old-hat and Johnny quit to return to Nashville to write and produce for others. He currently owns and operates his own recording studio in Brentwood, Tennessee, just outside of Nashville, where he makes his home with his wife Catherine and their daughters Sarah and Anna, and where he continues to write songs and make music. Johnny and family return to Campbellford every summer for a vacation to visit his mother, Fran, who makes her home on Doxsee Avenue.

Dave Noble

Dave was born in Toronto in June 1966 and attended Whiteoaks Public School and Lorne Park Secondary School. He played violin in several orchestras, including the Toronto Symphony Youth Orchestra and the Mississauga Symphony. He spent much of his time at the Royal Conservatory of Music in Toronto, where he was a scholarship winner in the Associate Diploma Program for Gifted Students. In addition to performing on violin, he plays several other instruments including piano and saxophone.

In 1985, Dave had to make a difficult choice between two loves: music and writing. He had always been a talented writer and opted to pursue a career in journalism. In 1989, Dave graduated from the School of Journalism at Carleton University and took a job as a newspaper editor in Nova Scotia. As a result of doing a story about a high school vocal jazz group, he decided to return to a musical career. He entered the Faculty of Education at the University of Toronto, and then earned a music degree studying jazz at Laurentian University where he met fiancee, Michelle Poutanen. She is a soprano vocalist and accomplished pianist.

Dave introduced jazz to CDHS in 1994. In 1997, the CDHS Vocal Jazz Ensemble won a silver standard at the Ontario Vocal Festival. The CDHS Senior Jazz Ensemble won the Quinte Rotary Festival's Stan Lynch Memorial Award as the most outstanding performers of the festival. Dave and Eric Lorenzen also produced "Little Shop of Horrors", the school's first musical in over a decade. The band produced its first compact disc, paying homage to the school's rural roots with its title "CDHS Jazz: 'til the cows come home". Dave was awarded the 1996 Civic Award for Arts and Culture, and he was also presented with a teaching excellence award from the Ontario Secondary School Teachers Federation. In May 1998, after qualifying in the Southern Ontario Musicfest competition, Dave directed his instrumental jazz ensemble to a gold standard in the Nationals in Vancouver, British Columbia. One of the CDHS students, Laurie Brown, was selected from thousands of students across Canada to join the national all-star jazz ensemble. At this same time in 1998, Dave and Eric Lorenzen were juggling their time to produce the ambitious and challenging production, "City of Angels". The dazzling show got rave reviews. Again in 1998, Dave was honoured with the Civic Award for Arts and Culture. More recently, he has been awarded the 1999 TV Ontario Teaching Excellence Award. The Jazz Band repeated its gold standard performance in 1999 and 2000.

Gerald Taylor

When Gerald Taylor accepted the job as organist for the Burnbrae Presbyterian Church in 1946, he never dreamed that he would be sitting behind the keyboard for fifty years. Gerald was honoured by the congregation in May 1997, for his years of service with the presentation of a plaque and a beautiful clock.

Gerald was asked by Roy Walker, the Clerk of the Session to take over the organist's duties at Burnbrae when the minister's wife, Mrs. Donald McKay, became ill. Gerald was only twenty at the time, and felt it was a large commitment. However, his mother was the choir leader and provided him with support and assistance. Gerald's father was also a member of the Burnbrae choir, but Gerald claimed that he 'couldn't carry a tune in a bucket'. He focused on piano and accordion from an early age, playing at many community functions, and at school festivals in the Stirling Theatre. He found these competitions, such as the Festival of Sacred Praise, a great learning experience. Gerald recalled heading north across the fields of his family's Concession 5, Rawdon Towship, farm to take lessons from Angus Todd, a school teacher who lived on Concession 6, just west of Wellman's Corners. Lessons were twenty-five cents each. He later took lessons from Marie Crosson and Sister Macrena in Campbellford.

Gerald also performed with several local bands, including Jack McCaughen's Trent Valley Ramblers, who played regularly on the Belleville radio station, and Pete Battman's Orchestra in Campbellford. Battman's group played regularly in Cobourg at Saturday night dances, and Gerald would often stop at the Burnbrae Church on his way home after midnight, and practice the organ until after two in the morning. The church was not heated all week, but the fires were started on Saturday to heat the church for Sunday services, so this was a time to practise in comfort.

Gerald has also played at over seventy-five weddings in the area and has been the organist at the Weaver Funeral Home for over twenty years. His four children share his love of music.

Spirit of the Hills:
— The Northumberland Hills —
Arts Association

Spirit of the Hills is an alliance of artists which was formed to promote the arts and cultural affairs in the municipality of Campbellford/Seymour and the surrounding area. On October 21, 1998, an initial meeting was held to discuss the feasibility of creating such an alliance and it was attended by the following interested citizens: Michel Proulx; Brenda Gabriel; Jim Forestell, President of Northumberland Arts and Crafts; Anne Linton, Secretary of Northumberland Arts and Crafts; Brian Finley and Donna Bennett, Westben Theatre Productions; Sharon Hamilton, Editor of The Link; Audrey Caryi; and Caroline Langill and Ursula Pflug, artists from Norwood.

The mandate of the group is to promote all forms of culture, such as the Performing Arts, Music, Literature, Visual Arts, Crafts, and Fashion Design. It presently operates with an acting Board of Directors, an Advisory Board, and several working committees, such as Public Art, Public Relations, Membership, and Ways and Means. During 2000, it will elect a permanent slate of officers. The acting Board of Directors consists of: Michel Proulx, Anne Linton, Ruth Stephens, Audrey Caryi, Joanne Carlen, Bob Leahy, and Alistair Grant.

The group is busy organizing and structuring a series of community based cultural events for the year 2000. An initial undertaking of the group has been to make an inventory of available public space where works of art can be exhibited and performances held. Other activities for the near future include officially introducing Spirit of the Hills to each of the local municipal councils, and to local business associations who may wish to display members' art in public and private spaces. The group also plans to organize, and/or participate in, several tours of artists' studios in the area. In addition, Spirit of the Hills will be involved in artistic displays at local events such as the Warkworth Maple Syrup Festival.

ENDNOTES

1   *The Saturday Globe*, Vol XLIX, No. 13622, pg. 2, col. 1.

Chapter Thirteen

⨯ports

*W*ritten documentation on the history and development of sports in

Campbellford/Seymour is quite sketchy outside of newspaper accounts.

Much of the information below was collected through interviews with

participants, organizations, and fans who witnessed these activities.

This account is not intended to be a definitive history of sports in the

area, as each activity could be a book in itself. Rather this is a sampling

of the events that occupied the leisure time of many local citizens.

BADMINTON

In 1955, the Campbellford Herald reported the existence of the Campbellford
Badminton Club, which operated in St. John's United Church auditorium on
Monday nights. Officers of the club included: President, Francis DeCarrol; Vice-
President, Don Baldwin; Secretary-Treasurer, Donna Carswell; Social Convenor,
Laura Atkinson; Games Convenors, Don Meyers, Ann Bennett, Jean Baldwin, and
Ken Kingston; Coaches, Fleming Hunter, and Don Meyers. In 1962, the executive
were: President, Carol Whitthun; Vice-President, Ron Simpkin; Secretary-
Treasurer, Ann Bennett; Social Convenor, Joyce Penhale, Assistant, Cathy Simpkin;
Games Convenor, Royden Elliott.

BOWLING

In late 1879, H. Huycke was reported to be building a small structure near his livery stables for 'lovers of the amusement of bowling.'

Large crowds attended the opening of Lockwood Lanes on Front Street
North in the fall of 1950. The owner was Vernon Lockwood, formerly of Picton.
Dignitaries who spoke on the occasion were Mayor, J.E. Ayrhart and Hon. William
A. Goodfellow, M.L.A. for Northumberland. Everett Phillips and Lloyd Taylor
were later owners, and the name was changed to Trent Valley Bowling Lanes. The

bowling alley, which is a five-pin facility, was soon bustling with league play in the evenings, and a youth league on Saturday morning. At first, the pins were removed and set up by 'pin' boys or girls who sat on the shelf above the pins and waited for the bowler to finish. Occasionally, these boys or girls dangled their legs within range of the ball and flying pins, and went home with a few bruises. Later, the pin setting system was automated.

Weekly bowling results have been posted regularly in the local newspapers, and from time to time there is news of local teams winning major tournaments. For example, on April 20, 1952, Lloyd's (Taylor) Sport Shop won the championship for the Campbellford Business Men's Alley Bowling League. The 1952 champions included Lloyd Taylor, Allan Taylor, Everett Phillips, Vernon Lockwood, George Rose, and Don Gentleman. Serving as spares were Dick Cairns, Bob Bennett, and Murray Locke.

Teams from the Campbellford Legion, both men and women, were very actively involved in bowling from the beginning. In 1964, 1966, and again in 1967, a team from the Legion Auxiliary, composed of Mary Reynolds, Wanda Tweedie, Mady Free, Dianne Ferrill, Irene Torrance, and Uerlen Lloyd won the Zone F2 Bowling Tournament. In one of these competitions, Tweedie and Reynolds won the High Doubles prize, with a score of 1362. The Legion Auxiliary also took top honours at the Provincial Bowling Tournament held in Ridgeway in April, 1967. In April 1975, Tom Smith and Gar Irwin were a doubles entry, representing the Canadian Legion Men's Bowling. They bowled in the Provincial Finals at Welland, Ontario, and each won a trophy clock for first place.

Bowling continues to be a popular sport, with one of the most active groups being the Golden Age Bowling League, consisting of seniors aged fifty-five and over. The present owner, Al Richardson, took over Trent Valley Bowling Lanes in 1978.

CRICKET

Cricket was originally played in the area currently occupied by the tennis courts and the lawn bowling green, and later at the fair grounds. Cricket was the sport favoured by the older settlers in the area, and played as part of the Victoria Day celebrations. Campbellford's opponents were usually from Warkworth, Stirling, and Brighton. From time to time, the local press reported on cricket activities. On June 14, 1883, Campbellford and Stirling played, with Campbellford winning by three wickets. Some of the players were Richard Bonnycastle, E. Nancarrow, Alexander Denmark, Thomas Tait, S. Abbott, R.V. Leslie, George Dickson, R. Whithead, J. Gow, and E. Rellis.[1] On July 1, 1883, a cricket team from Campbellford travelled to Picton and Napanee and won matches in both places.

In 1888, the executive of the Cricket Club was as follows: A. L. Colville, President; T.S. Tait, Secretary-Treasurer; R.H. Bonnycastle, Captain. An 1891 news report states that the Cricket Club was reorganizing for the coming season. The officers elected were: President, Edmond G. Burke; Vice President, James Dinwoodie; Secretary-Treasurer, Thomas Tait; and the Committee of Management, George Horkins, E. Platt, J. Ferris, A.L. Colville, and James A. Stewart.[2] In 1900, Thomas Tait was still secretary.

On July 27, 1900, Campbellford beat Brighton 199 to 50. The players were Daley, Platt, Tait, Blute, Fowlds, Kerr, and Picard. Tait, Blute, and Kerr were classified as doing the "good bowling." In September 1900, Campbellford beat Colborne 73 to 72. In 1901, the officers of the Cricket Club were as follows: Honorary President, A.A. Mulholland; Patron and Patroness, Dr. and Mrs. Macoun; President, W.C. Boddy; First Vice-President, Dr. Scherk; Second Vice-President, G.E. Burrows; Secretary-Treasurer, T.S. Tait; Committee of Management, J.C. Fowlds, D.E. Tait, R. Bonnycastle, Jr.; Membership, T.S. Tait, J.C. Fowlds.

Cricket declined in popularity about 1900, as evidenced by the decline in newspaper accounts.

CURLING

The Campbellford Curling Club was founded in 1886. That year, J.W. Dinwoodie built the first covered curling and skating rink. Subsequently, the club curled in the old Victoria Skating Rink on River Street, on two sheets of ice next to the skating ice. About 1912, the club moved to a facility on Ranney Street North behind the present library, which contained four natural ice rinks and a clubroom. The club continued in this location until it was leased as storage to Campbellford Cloth Company. In February 1943, the roof collapsed under heavy snow. During this period the Campbellford Curling Club was very active and boasted several Ontario championships. The local newspapers carried many articles about the achievements of local curlers.

In 1891, the officers of the club were: President, C.L. Owen; Vice-President, Robert Dinwoodie; Secretary-Treasurer, A.E. Jewett; Committee of Management, E.W. Gaudrie, G.W. Waters, Dr. Mallory; Representative Members, Dr. Macoun, J.W. Dinwoodie; Chaplin, Reverend D.J. Casey.[3]

The Campbellford Herald of February 18, 1897, reports that three rinks of Peterborough's best curlers played three Campbellford teams, with one of them defeating the visitors by twenty shots. The local team consisted of: Jas. Dickson, W.W. Thompson, R.A. Cumming, Dr. Macoun, R. Dinwoodie, T.S. Tait, R. Lowery, C.L. Owen, R. Boyes, D.H. Douglas, F.J. Smith and E.W. Gaudrie. When the play ended, the visitors were escorted to Mrs. Chester's restaurant and entertained at an oyster supper.

A Campbellford Herald advertisement on October 25, 1900, asked that all persons interested in curling attend a meeting at the St. Lawrence Hall on Monday at 8 PM for the purpose of reorganizing.

On February 27, 1902, two rinks played in Keene, with the first rink from Campbellford winning by nine points and the second rink losing by ten points. Players for the first rink were C.S. Gillespie, George Armstrong, Fred Smith, and Charles Smith, and players for the second rink were P. Corkery, James Blute, George A. Benor and T.S. Tait.

Some of the players in 1917 were: J.P. Archer, W. Wiggins, James Poulton Sr., Marshall West, Robert Dunk, Sam J. Moore, R.H. Cole, and Harry Denike. Campbellford Curlers won the district cup in Belleville in the winter of 1926. Two rinks were victorious. The rink skipped by S.J. Moore included J.P. Archer, W.S. Wiggins, and R.A. Dunk. The rink skipped by R.H. Cole included Joseph Poulton, M.H. West, and H.G. Denike.

Curling remained quite popular through the 1920s and 1930s, and Campbellford won the Ontario Curling Association District Cup in 1929. For many years after this, the local area did not have a separate curling facility.

Curling highlights from the winter of 1890–91.

From the Campbellford Weekly Herald, April 2, 1891.

CAMPBELLFO

CURLERS' CAREER.

NOTES OF THE WINTER'S PLAY.

The season has been a remarkably good one for this fine winter sport, and our curlers have made good use of the ice, and had a fairly successful season as regards matches and other matters. The club had presented to it three pairs of stones for competitors during the season. The president, Mr. C. L. Owen, gave a pair of Ballochmyles, Mr. J. S. Wilson, of Toronto, gave a pair of Grey Hones, and Mr. D. Kerr, of the St. Lawrence Hall, gave a pair of Ailsa Craig's with nickle plated handles. The Owen stones were won by R. Dinwoodie, the Wilson stones by E. W. Gaudrie, while the Kerr stone competition, which was among the junior members, was not finished. These are valuable additions to the club and were much appreciated by the members. There are now 25 pairs of curling stones valued at over $400. In matches the club played six, losing three and winning three as follows :—

Campbellford v. Belleville at Belleville—won			
"	"	" Campb'f'd—	lost
"	Keene	" Keene—	won
"	Peterboro	" Campb'f'd—	won
"	"	" Peterboro—	lost
"	Lakefield	" Lakefield —	lost

In the primary competition for the tankard, Campbellford was drawn against Lakefield and lost. In the competition for the Campbellford medal Keene defeated the home team.

PRESIDENT VS. VICE-PRESIDENT.

This game, which has been " on the cards" for some time, was played off on Good Friday. Mr. Owen, the president, not playing, was represented by Mr. Cumming. The score :

President.	Vice-President.
A. E. Jewett,	A. O'Connor,
M. Galvin,	T. Tait,
Dr. Macoun,	J. W. Dinwoodie,
W.Cumming,skip 16	E. W. Gaudrie, skip 4
R. Boyes,	D. J. Lynch,
R. Lowery,	H. McMechan,
D. Kerr,	Chas. Smith,
G.G.Eakins, skip 13	R. Dinwoodie, skip 4
—	—
29	8

The club had forty members this season, twenty of them being juniors, and several of these have done far better than was expected of them in one season.

The Curling Club was renewed in 1965 under the presidency of Harold Dunk. Initially, the club curled in Colborne because there was no facility with ice available, since the Davidson arena had been torn down in 1963. After the building of the Campbellford/Seymour Community Centre in 1967, limited ice time was available. Fund raising for a new curling facility began in 1975. In 1979, the Curling Club joined forces with the newly created Racquet Club, and the Campbellford and District Curling and Racquet Club was incorporated. In 1979, an application was submitted for a Wintario grant to build a new combined Club. The Meyers Sports Centre was built in 1980 on the fair grounds, funded fifty percent by Wintario, twenty-five percent by donations and fund raising, and twenty-five percent by a bank loan. It officially opened on November 30, 1980, with Russell Rowe, M.P.P. and George Hees, M.P., in attendance. The executive at that time was: President, Elizabeth Peever; Secretary, Irene Sparks; Treasurer, Donald Bennett; First Vice-President, Robert Bennett; Second Vice-President, William Machesney, and Third Vice-President, Mike Filip.

Substantial improvements were made to the racquet section of the club in 1986, necessitated by the growth in numbers from six in 1979, to one hundred and twenty in 1985 . Membership in curling was also on the rise, and total membership grew to 430 in 1992. The facility contains four curling rinks, two international calibre squash courts, regulation racquet ball and handball courts, a fitness centre, a kitchen, and banquet facilities. The Campbellford District Curling and Racquet Club is a registered not-for-profit organization and is run by volunteers.

Winners of the Dixie Lee Bonspiel, 1971.

Front, left to right: Casey Charles, Clare Ingram. Back, left to right: Hans Jehle, George Briggs — Dixie Lee manager, Michael Kaufmann.

Photo from the Campbellford/ Seymour Heritage Society Archives, originally from the files of the Campbellford Herald.

Curling activities include house league competitions for men, women, mixed teams, and senior men. Junior curlers and high school teams also use the facility. Special events have included the Fun Bonspiel, the Farmer's Spiel, the Lynn Forgrave Fun Spiel, the OPP Spiel, the Stedman's Ladies Spiel, the Campbellford Wholesale Mixed Spiel, the Masters Spiel, the Senior Mens Spiel, and the David Philp Memorial Wind Up Spiel.

Racquet activities include the friendly five racquet league for novice players, and the advanced house league for more experienced players. Special racquet events include the following squash tournaments – Campbellford Wholesale, Calcutta, Handicap, and Club Championship. Fund raising activities have included the Annual Beef Barbecue, the Touch of Country Decor and Sale, the Talent Auction, and the Wild Game Dinner.

Membership in the club has fluctuated, declining to as low as 330 in 1995. Currently, the Club is striving to recruit new members. Past Presidents of the club are:

1965–69	Harold Dunk	1984–85	Tom Thompson
1969–70	Roy MacLaren	1985–86	Rod Mockett
1970–71	Herman Sparks	1986–87	Dave MacDougal
1971–72	Earle Nelson	1987–88	Dave Burnham
1972–73	Gary Rowe	1988–89	Dave Foote
1973–74	Bill Oliver	1989–90	Dorothy MacDonald-Simons
1974–75	Barry Brown	1990–91	Ron Elmhirst
1975–76	Ray Sharp	1991–92	Peter Dooher
1976–77	Clare Moxley	1992–93	Mark Reid
1977–78	Don Meyers	1993–94	Rob Pope
1978–80	Charlie Godden	1994–95	Marie Forgrave
1980–81	Elizabeth Peever	1995–96	Al Ingram
1981–82	Bob Bennett	1996–97	Frank Lauzon
1982–83	Paul Philp	1997–98	George Thompson
1983–84	Mike Filip	1998–99	Jack Connor

CYCLING

In 1892, Campbellford Rovers Bicycle Club was very active. E.W. Burk and Fred Smith rode to Belleville in three hours and five minutes. In 1894, other members mentioned are: J.T. Benor, Irvine Frederick, E.W. Gaudrie, and W. Neill. In The Light of Other Days, the following story appears:

> "The time is Sept. 25, 1895. Seven bicycle riders undertake to run a competitive relay race against seven riders from Cobourg. They start simultaneously. E.W. Gaudrie, of the Campbellford team, goes as far as Bradley's

Corners when he passes the baton to George Horkins. His ride takes him to Morganston where Irvine Frederick is waiting. H. Bonnycastle meets him at Castleton and rides to Colborne. W. Neill takes the next shift meeting Jim Archer at Grafton and the latter rides into Cobourg. Fred Smith starts the run back. Fred Wood and C. L. Owen are the local timers. Campbellford wins by 16 minutes, the time being 2 hours and 26 minutes to the County Town and two hours and 23 minutes to return.

In the same year five bicycle riders from Campbellford and five from Peterborough competed in a 20-mile race at the local fair grounds. Four of the visiting riders finished 1, 2, 3, and 4. Three local bicyclists, E. W. Gaudrie, H. Bonnycastle and J.P. Archer finished the 20 miles, but Fred Smith and Pat Sarginson had to drop out." [4]

EQUESTRIAN ACTIVITIES

Harness Racing

In the 1880s and 1890s, there was horse-racing on the ice at Castiday's Bay just north of the Village of Campbellford at Crow(e) Bay further to the north. Ice racing was very popular and local horses competed with trotters and pacers from Peterborough, Belleville, and Brighton. W. A. Kingston reported: "In 1889, Campbellford and Seymour sportsmen displayed a marked penchant for horse racing. In the East Riding Show (green trot) there were four Campbellford entries, with Tosh Stephen's "Ina," Thos. Atkinson's "Gypsy Girl," J.W. Johnston's "Polly" and C.S. Gillespie's "Nora." In the 2:45 and in the running race J.N. Kent entered his "Bay Charlie" and his mare "Nell." [5]

From 1930 to 1970, harness racing took place on special holidays and at the annual fair at the Campbellford fair grounds Some of the owners and racers were: Henry Redcliffe, Ed Stanbury, Donald Johnston, Alex Stewart, Mr. McQuigge Mr. Thompson, Ted Atkinson, and Ron Isaac. It was discontinued for both economic and safety reasons. A fence should have been erected around the track and the cost was too prohibitive to consider. There were accidents reported, such as a horse breaking away from its sulky, knocking down a man, and narrowly missing a young child who had run into its path. Frank Potts can recall that his uncle Jim, who had an extremely loud voice, was in charge of keeping the spectators off the track at the fair. He would holler, without a megaphone, "the horses are coming, move back." Today, the track is used only as a training ground for harness racing.

Trail Riding

The Timbertrail Western Riders Club of Havelock has approximately one hundred members, with a large percentage from the Campbellford/Seymour area. The club has a judging show, which looks at riders' posture and the conformation of the horse, on the third Sunday of each month, June through September. This involves the showing of the following classes – Halter, English, Western, Pleasure, and Reining. There are also the speed events, with barrel racing, pole bending, flag races, and key hole. The general saddle horses are Quarter Horses, Thoroughbreds, Arabians, Apaloosas, Paints, and Pintos.

Several times between May and October, the group assembles in the Healey Falls area on a Friday night, with the horses tied for the night to picket lines. With an early Saturday morning start, the ride proceeds past Locks 15, 16, and 17, over to Bob Kelly's, which is across from the Lion's Club beach, over Candy Mountain, north across Concession 8 and 9 to the Healey Falls Road to Dick Lewis' farm and then back to Healey Falls. This trail ride attracts many out of area riders who trailer their horses to town to join with the group.

Riding lessons are also featured, with horses and saddles provided. As students progress, they participate in fairs, horse shows and some trail rides. Trophies are awarded for competition within the local club, and very skilled riders also compete outside. In March 1988, two Campbellford riders competed in the Toronto Quarterama Show, the largest horse show in Canada. Shelley Anderson rode her four-year-old mare, Healy Falls Morgan, to ninth place in the Youth Stake Race, seventh in Youth Pole Bending and fourth in Junior Pole Bending. Wayne Mack earned a sixth place ribbon in the Open Flag on his quarter horse gelding, Healy Falls Frosty. With classes containing as many as eighty horses, these wins were significant.

Sleigh rides are popular, with a single horse pulling a cutter or a team pulling large sleighs piled with hay bales as seats. At Wayne Mack's Quarter Horse and Charolais farm, there are winter trail rides which last about a half hour and are then followed by a pot luck around an open fire.

Each year the Chamber of Commerce Santa Claus Parade includes the Timbertrail Western Riders as a drawing card. Between forty and fifty riders and their horses are decked out in full regalia to trot through the streets of Campbellford, delighting thousands of residents and visitors.

FOOTBALL

Football appears to be an activity enjoyed by some local citizens around the turn of the century. This game was most likely the British form of rugby football. In the spring of 1900, about twenty-five football enthusiasts met at the St. Lawrence Hall to reorganize for the coming season. The officers of the football club were: President, Dr. McBride; Vice-Presidents, J.W. Cairns and J. McLaughlin; Captain, Norman Florin Hubble; Secretary-Treasurer, W.H. Harris.[6]

In 1906, the St. Andrew's 'Thistles' football club reorganized and the following were elected as officers: Honorary President, Rev. A.C. Reeves; President, J.P. Hume; Vice-Presidents, W.J. Armstrong and Robert Bell; Secretary, Gordon Cock; Treasurer, James Caskey; and Captain, R.M. McGuire.[7]

In more recent times, the Canadian style of football was adopted and usually played at the high school level. One of the local stars was Joe Brouwers, who attended CDHS in 1976–1980, a period of time when football was very popular. After graduating from high school, he attended Sir Wilfrid Laurier University where he played on the Varsity team for four years. He was drafted by the British Columbia Lions for the 1984–85 season, and then played for the Toronto Argonauts for the 1986 season. He returned to farming in Campbellford in 1988.

GOLF

In the summer of 1940, W. A. Hogle opened a golf course on the outskirts of Campbellford near the corner of Centre Street and Burnbrae Road, on the site of the Hogle Nursery previously owned by the Johnstons. William Hogle Sr. was the largest cabbage grower in Eastern Ontario. By 1942, the Nursery Golf Course had fifty members. The entire Hogle operation closed in 1950.

Currently, there are no golf courses in Seymour Township and local golfers use nearby courses in Percy and Brighton Townships.

HOCKEY

Arenas

In the beginning, ice hockey was played on frozen ponds, creeks, and any other available ice surface. An open rink in Gibson's field, later the site of Edgewater Park, was an excellent place for playing hockey. In 1886, J. W. Dinwoodie built the first covered curling and skating rink. In 1888 and 1892, references are also found to the St. Andrew's Rink. In 1898, the Victoria Rink was built on River Street at the present site of the Bell Telephone building. The building was the scene of a fire in 1901, and it collapsed under the weight of the snow the following year. In June 1902, the Campbellford Herald reported "that the Campbellford Skating, Curling, and Hockey Rink Company are liquidating all material of the wrecked building, the ground on which it stands, and the articles used in connection with running the rink are to be sold by auction."

Covert's Arena at Doxsee and Market Streets was built prior to 1916. It was a large igloo-shaped, metal-clad building, with little or no seating accommodation, and locally referred to as 'The Cedar Swamp' because of all the cedar posts supporting the roof. As well as being a skating rink, it was used as a cooper shop during the warmer seasons. In the summer of 1917, Walter Covert, the owner, advertised parking spaces for cars for fifteen cents, while the owners were shopping. In 1929, Archie

Meyers purchased this facility and renamed it the Meyers Arena. This building was used for hockey, skating, and curling. He operated it for two winters, until the depression forced its closure in 1931. He used it as a storage facility for Meyers Transport until it was demolished in 1942, and the tin was taken for salvage.

In 1929, the C. H. Davidson Arena was built on the current site of Sharpe's IGA Store. It was a large unheated metal structure with a seating capacity of 1800–2000, which was home to hockey and skating until 1963 when it was dismantled. The natural ice surface usually was available from January 1 to March 30. A large bank of snow, manually scraped from the ice and shoveled out a small window at the rear of the arena, would linger on long after the season's end. In 1950, the Town took over the management of the arena and the facility was renamed the Campbellford Community Centre. In an impressive ceremony at which an exhibition hockey game was played, the Campbellford-Peterborough Combines defeated the Toronto Talmac Team by a score of 9–3. Until the new Campbellford/Seymour Community Centre was erected in 1967, an open air arena was provided and hockey teams were required to rent ice in surrounding communities.

EARLY HISTORY OF HOCKEY IN CAMPBELLFORD/SEYMOUR

As early as 1899, Campbellford was part of the old Trent Valley Hockey League. In addition, there were other leagues operated by companies and even churches. Earlier hockey teams were made up of seven players – goal, defense pair, forward

One of the early hockey teams in Campbellford, ca. 1899. Front row, left to right: George Haig – goal, Ervin Frederick. Centre row, left to right: Jimmie Kerr, Billy Rockwell, Eddie Dunk. Back row, left to right: Bill Ferrill – Manager, Jim Blute, Tom Donald, J. P. Archer.

Photo donated by Mrs. George Haig and Eleanor Allan to the Campbellford/ Seymour Heritage Society Archives.

line, and a "rover." The rover apparently provided 'fresh legs' at forward or defense, as required. The pace, obviously, was considerably slower than today's games.

Hockey teams representing the firemen and the brass band played a pair of games in the Victoria Rink, with each team winning one game. Players for the firemen were: Charles Keir, goal; Ad McDonald, point; James Irwin, cover point, Charles Davidson, David Clazie, P. Sarginson, and Arthur Keir, forwards. The players for the bandsmen were: Mort Reynolds, goal; Walter Hill, point; J.D. Mackey, cover point; James Mitchell, Dave Mitchell, James Gibson, and George Green, forwards.

By 1910, local hockey was not only flourishing, but expanding rapidly. Teams playing in the "Town League" included the "Clerks' Team," "Trent Valley Woollen Mills" and "Campbellford Fire Company."

Charles Davidson, founder of Davidson's Motors, played goal and captained the Fire Company squad. Walter Blake skated for the Woollen Mill team. His son, Wilbert Blake, would be a future star player on the local scene. The Blake hockey tradition would continue on through his son, Tim, and a grandson, Zachary, four generations,

Clerks Hockey Team, Campbellford Town League, 1925–26.
Front row, left to right: H. D. Atkinson, Manager and sub.; R. E. Fox, goal; E. E. Labrash, right wing; S. A. Parsons, centre. Back row, left to right: S.F. Flint, right defence; T.H. Luckham, left defence; F.H. Wood, left wing; L.F. Blake, sub.; R.L. Bush, sub.

Photo from Campbellford/Seymour Heritage Society Archives.

Trent Valley Woollen Mills Hockey Club, Town League, 1914–15.
Front row, left to right:Walter Blake, right wing; Harold Henderson, centre. Middle row, left to right: C.Welsh, defence; G. Henderson, Manager; Bun Lott, rover and Captain; Ernie Bayes, goal. Back row, left to right: Chas. Holmes, defence; Jack Shaw, defence; Harry Denike, left wing.
Photo donated by W. Blake to the Campbellford/Seymour Heritage Society Archives.

spanning almost one hundred years.Young Zachary plays for the Campbellford Colts Novice team, which won the Ontario Championships in 1998–99.

A team of 1913–14 carried a logo on their sweaters representing the Eastern Power Company.This hydro-electric generating company predated the fledgling Hydro Electric Power Commission of Ontario. A "Hydro Hockey Team" was Campbellford League Champions in 1925–26. By this time, Ontario Hydro Commission had taken over most of the power generation and Eastern Power was no more.

Several young players identified in old team photos were well known residents such as: Dr. Ward Baker, M.D., T.B. Horkins, lawyer, Harry Denike, grocer, "Huck" MacArthur, electrician, J.P. Archer, insurance broker, Jim Baker, travel agent. L. Copperthwaite played for the "Outlaws" team in 1925, and a descendant of his, Al Copperthwaite, is caretaker at the present arena. Petherick's were Town League champions in 1939. Familiar farm boys in the line-up were the Watson brothers, Ray Thomson, Watson Murray, Ray Pollock, Harry Ewing, Ralph Turner, and Eric and Clare Ingram.

Campbellford had a girls' hockey team in 1920–21 and in 1921–22. They looked very chic in their sweaters and toques.

Campbellford High School Ladies/Hockey Team, 1920–21.

Left to right: Miss Armstrong, Captain; Helen Carnahan, Helen Wood, Evelyn Irwin, Norma Nadoo, and Helen Kerr.

Photo donated by Helen Wood to the Campbellford/Seymour Heritage Society Archives.

Five of the seven girls on the 1921–22 team have been identified as Thelma and Norma Nadoo, Grace Blue, Eleanor (Polly) Ferris Douglas, and Helen Wood. Equipment of 100 years ago bore little resemblance to hockey gear of today. Protection was minimal. The one-piece hockey sticks might wear out but they seldom broke. Straight skate blades were the fashion, and the boots to which they were attached had little support or protective padding. Tube skates would not make an appearance until the early 1930s.

The Campbellford Maroons were Trent Valley League Champions in the opening year of the C.H. Davidson Arena. This league, which probably played at Intermediate Level, may have been the oldest established league that played interlocking games with other towns. There were years when it did not operate. Two world wars interrupted play, and at other times, sufficient teams could not be fielded to make it viable. However, it spanned well over fifty years and provided many thrills for hockey fans. Notable performers on the Maroons team were T.B. Horkins, Buster Whitton and Huck MacArthur. Horkins, practising law in Toronto, would make the long trip down for games. A buzz would run through the crowd when he stepped on the ice. He was known to play with the same intensity that he exhibited when defending a client in court. Opposing players were often treated to some strong invective as Horkins skated backwards in front of their advance down the ice. Buster Whitton was fast and tricky and his exploits were remembered long after he hung up his skates. W. Blue also played for the Maroons. H.T. Scott, a local practitioner whose business was right beside the arena, was team chiropractor. Players did not have far to go after a game to get their joints sorted out.

Until it finally ceased operations in the late 1950s, Campbellford's Trent Valley League entry would provide entertainment and excitement for many fans. Teams used various names, such as Maroons, Sunocos, or Fords, and produced a number of championships. Owen Hendy charged along the boards, slashing, bashing, and bouncing off opposition players, in his headlong charge. Hendy was adept at whacking opponents knuckles with his stick. As he would confide to team mates: "If they can't hold the stick, they can't play the puck." After one particular game, he was searching the dressing room for his false teeth, only to find them in his mouth. He had forgotten to remove them before playing. Many remember the stick handling of Shillinglaw and O'Rourke as they 'dipsy-doodled' down the ice. Team mates of O'Rourke nick-named him "Circle." When he scored a goal, he would circle centre ice. Doug Free had great individual hockey talents, including speed and a hard and accurate shot. Along with Shillinglaw and O'Rourke, he would travel to Scotland to play following the team's championship year of 1946–47. A brother, Don Free, was a steady two-way player for many seasons.

Trent Valley League teams varied from time to time, but Marmora, Madoc, Stirling, Norwood and Tweed were the usual competitors along with Campbellford. Another feature was the rivalry that grew between Campbellford and Marmora over the years. Before the end of its operation, the league had expanded into two divisions, the new division made up of Quinte area teams. It would be difficult to single out any one team for particular merit. The 1929–30 Maroons were notable champions, as were the Sunocos of 1939–40, and the Fords of 1946–47. This post-war team was anchored by returning veterans of the latter (1939–40) squad – Blake, Robinson, Free and the ageless Hendy. Basil Robinson, an excellent centre and playmaker, would later be singled out for special honours, as would his team-mate, Blake, at right wing, who was selected Most Valuable Player in the twelve team league. Morley Maxwell was solid in goal and defense was handled by the addition of D. Free, J. Smith, D. Lambert, and R. Tanner. A story is told of one night when Doug Lambert was called on to take a crucial face-off. He had just broken his stick and skated over to snatch another one from the stick rack. In the excitement of the moment, Lambert never noticed, until he moved into the face-off circle, he had brought back a goalie stick! New legs on the forward line

Campbellford "Fords", Trent Valley League Champion, 1946–47, winners of the Bata Memorial Trophy.

Front row, left to right: B. Robinson, centre; O. Hendy, defence and Captain; Doug Free, defence; M. Maxwell, goal; A. Shillinglaw, right wing; Don Free, left wing; W. Blake, right wing. Middle row, left to right: H. J. Taylor, President; R. Hay, right wing; B. Peloquin, left wing; J. Smith, defence; D. Lambert, defence; R. Tanner, defence; Duke Savage, Manager-Coach. Back row, left to right: L. Taylor, Treasurer; Ken Kingston, Secretary; L. Shillinglaw, Vice-President; H. MacArthur, Director; G. Sinfield, Director; Terry Hendy, mascot.

Photo donated by Steve Thompson to the Campbellford/Seymour Heritage Society Archives.

included, R. Hay, A. Shillinglaw, and B. Peloquin. The team was good enough for another championship.

Some will argue that the 1952–53 entry in Trent Valley League was Campbellford's best. Certainly they were the best in the twelve-team league of that season, defeating Wellington for the championship. The roster had grown to fifteen players.

Blake was still providing offensive inspiration, but now as a playing coach. Free was skating as fast as ever and the big policeman, Archie Eadie, continued to patrol the blue line. Otherwise, it was a new and younger team. Some excerpts from the Herald of April 1, 1953 provide a little description:

> "Paced by the fast-skating kid line of Simpson, Wilson, and Jeffs"
>
> "Nelson – the classy net custodian"
>
> "Doug Free carrying the puck up ice almost at will"

"Defence players – Gino Pace, Jim Baker, and Al Taylor filling the gaps –
Pace skating miles to cover defensive territory"

"Jim Baker handy at breaking up Wellington thrusts"

"Vince Herrington again turning in a fine performance"

"Bill Cole hardworking little checker"

Other important cogs in this free-wheeling machine included D. Reid, defense,
G. Craig, wing, and Bergen Payne, centre. The Trent Valley League has been long
gone, but memories linger on. Wilbert Blake, who celebrated his eightieth birthday
in 1999, has a good memory. He recalls a time during the war when he was in the
Canadian Army in Holland. He has a medal given to him for playing on the champion team in the forces. Apparently they played during lulls in the fighting. Games
were played on open-air artificial ice surfaces and drew a throng of enthusiastic
Dutch fans. Undoubtedly, for them it was a welcome break from the grim realities
of the war. Whenever an aircraft approached, everyone would dive for cover.

By 1960, the Trent Valley League was history and a stimulating history it had
been for those who were fans of the local team. The natural ice was often rutted
and chipped long before the end of the game, and a haze of tobacco smoke hung
over the scene. Still the team played on with great enthusiasm and reckless aban-
don. They played for the love of the game and winning was the greatest reward.
There would be other Trent Valley Leagues to follow, but none with the storied
history of the original.

Minor Hockey

The Campbellford Minor Hockey Association (CMHA) was formed in 1958
by members of the Rotary, Legion and Kinsmen Clubs. They were joined by the
Lions Club in 1959. Representing these clubs were: Hector Macmillan, George
Bibby, Dante Pace, Ray McKinnon, Lloyd Bullen and Bill Rothwell. The purpose
of the Association was to promote and develop amateur hockey in Campbellford
and District for all players up to and including juvenile age. The affiliation with the
Ontario Minor Hockey Association (OMHA) would provide greater opportunity
for development and experience playing within a more structured format.

Minor hockey was not a new venture. Recognition should be given to the
individuals who preceded the formation of the CMHA for their commitment to
teaching and fostering the hockey skills of local youth. Harold Dunk, along with
Principal, Charlie Haig, organized Public School hockey in 1931. As teacher,
coach, and referee, Dunk left his mark. Many local lads, who were groomed at
public and high school levels, moved on to excel as adult hockey players.

In 1978–79, the Juvenile team made it to the Ontario finals. The following
year, the Pee Wee squad duplicated this achievement, while the Juveniles tri-

Trent Valley League Champions, 1952–1953.

Front row, left to right: Graham Craig, wing; Bill Cole, wing; Vincent Herrington, wing; "Ozzie" Nelson, goal; Doug Free, team captain and wing; Glen Wilson, wing; Wilbert Blake, centre and playing coach; Gino Pace, defence; Jack Free, trainer, holding Hon. W. A. Goodfellow Trophy for T.V. L. Northern Division Championship. Back row, left to right: Art Duncan, T.V.L. President, F. M. Rutherford, team manager; Doug Reid, defence; Alan Taylor, defence; Jim Baker, defence; Jim Jeffs, wing; Lorne Simpson, centre; Archie Eadie, defence; Bergen Payne, centre; Gerald Jeffs, team secretary; Dick Bridgeman, league secretary. In front: Eddie Collins, mascot, with Bata Trophy for League Championship.

Photo donated by Alec Rutherford to Campbellford/Seymour Heritage Society Archives.

Campbellford Atom All-Stars were the Trent Valley League champions and went on to become the Eastern Ontario Atom All-Star Championship in 1975. Front row, left to right: John Sharpe, Evan Loucks, Doug Watson, Bob Morrow, Robbie Ellis, Bruce Fry, Gord McMillan. Back row, left to right: Tom Thompson — coach, Jim Thompson, Stephen Battman, Jamie McIlmoyle, Paul Tillaart, Paul Copperthwaite, Peter Brown — manager.

Photo from the Campbellford/Seymour Heritage Society Archives, originally from the Campbellford Herald.

umphed as All-Ontario Champions. In 1980–81, they reached the finals and the following year repeated as Ontario Champions. The Bantam team advanced to the Ontario finals in the same year. The 1982–83 season saw the Atoms reach the finals.

Bennett's Home Furnishings Midget team were the heroes in 1983–84. Under coach Trevor Tinney, they had a remarkable record — winning ten consecutive games on their way to the championship. They did it the hard way, twice making comebacks in series where they trailed 2 games to 0. This team refused to quit. The line-up included: Jamie Pearson, Paul Kelly, Rob Stapley, Paul Nolan, Ryan Dewey, Kevin Doherty, Darren Meiklejohn, Kyle Craig, Alan Ingram, Tim Creasy, Randy Petherick, Eric Graham, Brian Watson, Steve Campbell, Scott Campbell, Rick Lemoire, Dean Spencer and Peter Locke.

By 1986, the Juveniles were again icing a strong team. For two consecutive years, they were Ontario Champions with triumphs in both 1986–87 and 1987–88. The latter championship series against Port Dover was particularly remarkable. The Campbellford Chrysler team won the first two games at home, but were thoroughly beaten by scores of 11–0 and 7–0 in the next two at Port Dover.

Even so, they were able to regroup and win the next game at Port Dover, returning home with a 3–2 lead in series games. Six hundred fans turned out, primed for a victory celebration, for the sixth game. Port Dover ruined the party, winning 6–3 to tie the series. So thoroughly did they dominate the game that some usually faithful fans decided against making the long trek to Port Dover for the seventh and final game. They missed a great game. Trailing 4–1 in the third period, the team put on a fine display of comeback hockey, scoring five times to win 6–4 and take the series.

For coach Tinney, it was another championship to add to his total. For the local Juveniles, it was four times as All-Ontario Champions in a span of eight years. Minor hockey continued to be a success story through the last decade of the twentieth century. In 1989–90, it was the Midgets again as Ontario Champions. A Pee Wee team reached the same plateau in 1992–93 and were followed by a Bantam team in 1993–94. The Midget entry was back for another Ontario Championship in 1994–95. Coach Jim Peeling praised this team as the "most disciplined team he had seen in a long time." In a comeback win against Mitchell in the final game, they overcame a three goal deficit to win 6–4. Goals by Carl Fernandez, John Van Allen, Mike Moore, Ian Pettey and Brad Petherick decided the issue – plus "superior goaltending by Summerfeldt."

The Novice Colts won the Provincial honours in 1997–98 and repeated the feat as champions of 1998–99. Coach Frank Toms is credited by many for the successive championships – both times won over Elmvale teams. The ability to instill discipline and to impart hockey skills made a difference. Members of this Graham Florists Novice squad included: Jamie McKelvie, Wesley Petherick, Sam McKeown, Andrew Craig, Zachary Blake, Brian Wood, Stuart Davis, Jesse Newton, Kirk Newton, Matthew Foster, Ryley Peters and Dylan Toms.

In sixteen of the twenty years from 1979 to 1999, teams from Campbellford and district have either won Ontario Championships or advanced to the final round. At the present time, CMHA manages teams at eight levels from Tykes, Novice, Atom, Pee Wee, Bantam, Midget, and Juvenile. They all carry the name Campbellford Colts. There is also currently a local Ontario Hockey Association team operating at Junior C level. They were preceded by two other teams which operated at the same level – The Campbellford GMC's and the Merchant Blues Two more teams, Bertrand Motors, and, more recently, Campbellford Clippers played at Intermediate C level. All had disbanded by 1985.

The success of the Campbellford Minor Hockey Association in developing players was demonstrated in a recent sports event. Cassandra Turner played for the Ontario Women's team in the 1999 Canada Games, where they won gold. A 1993 news clipping shows Cassandra being named as MVP Atom level, playing with a boy's team in her own age group.

Regrettably, there is not space to compliment all the winning teams, exceptional players, and the dedicated people who have coached, sponsored and promoted minor hockey. Some made significant contributions. George Bibby was one
of the founders of CMHA. His involvement spanned four decades and in this
period he served as President, Secretary Treasurer, Coach, and Referee. He
chaired the committee to build an open-air rink while the new arena was being
built and was also active in the latter building project. In 1983, he was recognized
by the Ontario Minor Hockey Association for his years of service as a recipient of
the Honour Award. In 1986, CMHA honoured three long-time supporters, Brian
Runions, Bill Mulholland, and Bruce Sharpe. Trophies were donated to minor
hockey in their names. The CMHA has a list of Life Members which contains the
names of those who have made exceptional contributions to Minor Hockey. Some
have served as President, others are acknowledged for their commitment to the
sports association.

Since its inception, the following have been approved for life membership:

Tim O'Ray	Brian Runions	Mike Cork
Art Larcombe	Joe Watson	Vince Doherty
George Bibby	Bruce Sharpe	Joe Barton
George McCleary	Dante Pace	Tony White
Claire Lisle	Bill Rothwell	Glen Craig
Arnold Drennan	Harold Douglas	Sharon Peeling
Bill Mulholland		

Sharon Peeling became the first woman to be selected as an Honorary Life
Member. She was cited for her outstanding contributions as Minor Hockey's
Ladies Auxiliary President.

Past Presidents in chronological order include:

Hector Macmillan	Bill Machesney
George Bibby	Ken Hulsman
Howard Wilson	George Bibby
George Bibby	Brian Runions
Dante Pace	Claire Lisle
Bruce Sharpe	George Bibby
Doug Stickwood	Ted Nicholas
Mike Cork	Larry Metcalfe
Harold Douglas	
Mike Cork	
Joe Barton	

The current President is Steve Thompson.

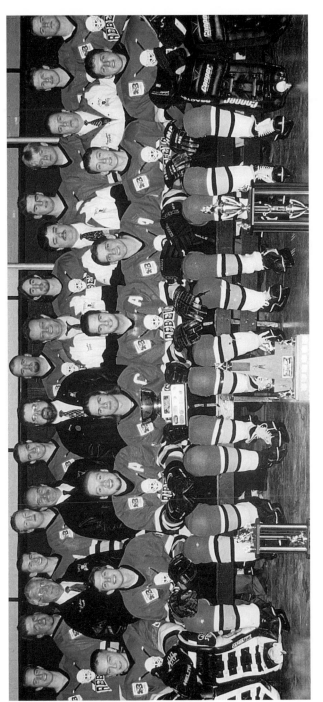

Campbellford Rebels, 1997–98.

Front row, left to right: Scott Metcalfe – Goal, Bryce Levesque, Ryan White, Kevin Larmer – Captain, Jim Hazelwood, Kevin Cork, Tony Goulah, Joe Larmer. Middle row, left to right: Tom Tanner – Coach, Ed Stapley – Coach, Trevor Tinney – General Manager, Larry Metcalfe – President, Jeff Fleming – Trainer, Mark Tanner – Executive. Back row, left to right: Travis Turner, Ian Pettey, Matt McCoy, John Quinlan, Cal Larmer, Mike Choinere, Mike Moore, Chris Taylor, Dennis McColl, Nick Myers, Jeff Petherick.

Photo courtesy of Larry Metcalfe.

Campbellford Rebels – Junior C

The idea of forming another Junior Hockey team evolved in 1991–92. Trevor Tinney and Larry Ellis appeared to be the prime movers of the venture. In 1992–93, the Rebels iced their first team in the Empire "B" Junior Hockey League, which was a seven-team loop originally, but currently consists of six teams. Competing teams are the Picton Pirates, Napanee Raiders, Ernestown Jets, North Frontenac Flyers and Colborne Black Hawks. From a last-place finish in their first two years, the Rebels fought their way into contention only to be eliminated by the Raiders the following two years. In 1996–97, they were able to beat the Raiders and went on to win the league championship. The Rebels would advance no further, defeated by the Lakefield Chiefs in the Ontario quarter-finals.

In 1997–98, they finished the regular season in second place, their best standing. Play-off wins over the Jets and Raiders brought a second successive league championship. The Rebels were the youngest franchised team in the league to ever capture two successive championships. Kevin Larmer was voted Most Valuable Player for the team and the league. Once again, they failed to advance past the Ontario quarter-finals, falling to the Little Britain Merchants. The 1998–99 Rebels would have their best ever regular season record. It was literally a two-team race. The Picton Pirates were overtaken by mid-season and by the end of the schedule, the Rebels were well in front of the pack. In one stretch, they went twenty-six games without a loss. Possibly it had been too easy. In a hard-fought play-off final against the Pirates, they were defeated four games to three.

LACROSSE

The earliest record of lacrosse dates to 1883 when Campbellford defeated a team from Peterborough in just over an hour, and Peterborough, in turn, defeated Campbellford in a second game in just six minutes. Apparently, a game lasted only until someone scored.

A twelve-man field lacrosse club was formed on April 26, 1900, at the St. Lawrence Hotel, Front Street. During the summer of 1899, some exhibition games had been played. On the newly formed club executive were: Honorary President, Rev. W.J. McCloskey of St. Mary's Parish; President, T.E. Bell; First Vice-President, Dr. McBride; Second Vice-President, Thomas Tait; Manager, H.B.R. Dryden; and Secretary/Treasurer, Pat J. Sarginson. Marmora, Madoc, Stirling, Havelock, Norwood, Hastings, and Campbellford participated in the Intermediate series of the Canadian Lacrosse Association. The 1903 team consisted of Manager and Coach, H.B.R. Dryden, and team members, H.M. Stevenson, Frank Shea, F. Pope, J.J. O'Sullivan, Leonard Shea, Harry Lowery,

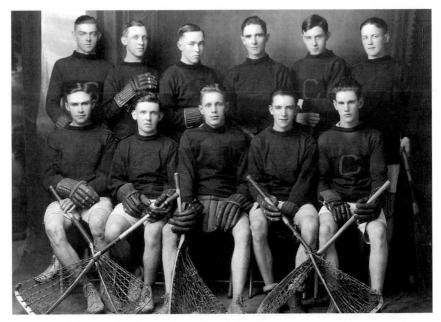

Campbellford Juvenile Lacrosse Team – 1922.

Front row, left to right: R. Copperthwaite, centre; F. A.White, outside home; C. Garrison, goal; C. Smith, second home; L. Bush, spare. Back row, left to right: J. Cowell, inside home; A.White, cover point; J. Archer, first home; V. Cochrane, point; H. MacArthur, first defence; P. Sanders, second defence.

Photo donated by Steve Thompson to Campbellford/Seymour Heritage Society Archives.

Dave Mitchell, Pat J. Sarginson, B. Gillespie, D. McCormick, J. Butler, Jim Kerr, Ed Saunders, Pat Shannon, and E. Crowe.

In spring, 1915, the Campbellford Social and Athletic Club entered a lacrosse team in the Ontario Amateur Lacrosse Association Intermediate Series, under the management of R. H. Cole. In August of that year, Campbellford defeated Tweed by a score of 6–2, to become Eastern Ontario champions.

Information about lacrosse in the 1920s and 1930s is somewhat sketchy, but one well-known event occurred when Father Phelan of St. Mary's Church was responsible for bringing the Montreal Shamrocks to Campbellford for a memorable exhibition game. Campbellford beat the Shamrocks 6–4 in overtime. Games at that time were played at the fair grounds, but there were no organized leagues. The local players at that time were Owen Hendy, Eddie Bush, Pat Kelly, Pat Shannon, T.B. Horkins, Frank and Tom Little, and a trio consisting of brothers Paul, Thomas, and Becky Jacks. Dick Cole was the manager of the 1920–21 Intermediate OALA team; Johnny Sutherland was manager of Junior Lacrosse

1920–21; Pat Kelly manager of the 1929–30 Intermediate OALA. The lack of facilities made play difficult as the players' dressing room was in Robertson's garage, which was the last house on Booth Street near the present high school field. In 1931, the Campbellford Maroon lacrosse team lost the league finals to Peterborough by a score of 4–3. Campbellford fielded the following team: goal, Sanders; point, Cochrane; cover point, Maybee; defence, MacArthur, L. Bush, D. Flint; centre, S. F. Flint; home, E. Bush, Whitton, F. Ingram, Hendy, Jacks; Subs, H. Ingram, Lambert.

Twelve man field lacrosse did not persist, and in the late 1930s six man Box Lacrosse was played at the Davidson arena. This lasted only a few years and eventually faded away. However, in 1970, Campbellford District High School fielded a lacrosse team, coached by Vic Conte and managed by Elvin Petherick. They were described in the yearbook as an enigma for winning the Stewart-Auburn All Ontario Consolation Trophy on May 24th, 1969 in Peterborough. The team included: Fred Tanner, Jim Johnston, Wayne Tuepah, David Giles, Larry Skinkle, Ted Jowett, Ken Garneau, Bob King, Gerald Free, Ken Wragg, Brian Bull, Allan Kerr, Marc Curle, Bill Bennett, Bob Jaques and Pete Brown.

LAWN BOWLING

Lawn Bowling originated in ancient Egypt, Greece, and Rome, migrated to England in the 1100s, to Canada in 1892, and ultimately to Campbellford in 1899. Campbellford has the distinction of being one of the oldest clubs in the area. A trophy won by Campbellford in 1899 was recently found by Helen Meyers, and is now on display at the club. The club house was placed on its present site, between the Rotary Trail and the Trent Canal, in 1919, after being drawn by horses from another unknown location. Very few records prior to 1935 are available. However, the Campbellford Herald reports the following officers for the 1927 season: President, J.P. Archer; Vice-President, Walter S. Wiggins; Secretary-Treasurer, George Nicol; Executive Committee, L.B. Glover, Dr. O.C. Watson, Dr. Haig, J.A. Stewart. An issue of the Campbellford Herald in spring 1938, lists the following officers for the Campbellford Lawn Bowling Club: President, Percy M. Locke; Vice-President, F.N. Brown; Secretary, J. P. Archer; Treasurer, J. D. Mills.

In 1939, an influx of ten couples raised the membership to sixty bowlers. In 1998, Beth Taylor, at age 94, was remarkable with her recollection of names of the members of the past. She recalls Mr. and Mrs. Pinky Smith, Ernest and Nettie Sloggett, Dr. Owen Watson, Charles and Ethel Palliser, Charlie Calver, Mr. Wragg of Warkworth, William Brady, and Honorary member Ross Douglas. Other early members were: Mr. and Mrs. Jack Linton, Wib and Thelma Kingston, Les Diamond, Mr. F.N. Brown, Mr. and Mrs. J. Archer, Mr. and Mrs. J.D. Mills, Mr.

and Mrs. Gregg, Lil Smith, Mr. and Mrs. Sayers, Doug Maybee, Mrs. Lillian Fox, Mr. and Mrs. Geo. Nicholls and Mr. and Mrs. Don Piercy. In 1939 the caretaker was a Mr. Mills and following him was Joe Poulton.

In 1940, a fireplace was installed to replace the old stove, and a bathroom soon replaced the outhouse. The old outhouse did have some class added to it by artist Beth Taylor. She would often hang oil paintings on the walls to brighten it up. In 1942, the executive was: Honorary President, J.F.R. Douglas; President, H.J. (Bert) Taylor; First Vice-President, W.A. Kingston; Second Vice-President, C.H. Calver; Secretary, J.P. Archer, Treasurer, J.D. Mills. The executive in 1945, as listed in the Campbellford Herald was as follows: Honorary President, J.F.R. Douglas; President, H.T. Scott; Vice-President, Lloyd Taylor; Secretary, J.P. Archer; and Treasurer, J.D. Mills. In 1948, a team of well known local business leaders played for the coveted Corbin Gold Trophy. The winning team: Lead, J.P. Archer; Second, J.L. Diamond; Vice, A.D. Bennett; and Skip, W.S. Wiggins.

In 1950, Mr. and Mrs. H. J. Taylor won the Ross Douglas trophy for local mixed doubles, edging out Mrs. and Mrs. Gordon Walroth in the finals by two shots. Mr. and Mrs. A. D. Bennett and Mr. and Mrs. Art Stinson were the other group winners.

An August 1965 newspaper picture features four bowlers, with a total of 178 years experience on the greens, whose ages added up to 343 years: A.J. Meyers, age 85; A.D. Bennett, age 78; J.P. Archer, age 89; and Joe Poulton, age 91. All but A.D. Bennett had bowled since the club's inception in 1919, with Bennett joining in 1925.

Campbellford had the distinction of having the 1964 Canadian Champion, from Toronto's Balmy Beach Club, add his name as a 1973 member. Stan Bond transferred to the Campbellford Club and generously acted as an instructor to any member requiring help.

In 1991, President Charlie Cook was instrumental in obtaining a government grant for club renovations. A comfortable front porch was added, electrical wiring upgraded, and a new roof installed. In 1995, the Campbellford Rotary Club, the Havelock Lions Club, and the Warkworth Legion assisted with the first stage of improving the overall facilities. This included the addition of benches and planting of trees. A longtime, energetic member, Peter Kurita, supported the expansion of the greens to international size, to enable Campbellford to host more tournaments and to provide local players with the experience of playing on international size greens. In 1997–98 the greens were extended to almost international size, with the club making a major effort in both raising the funds and assisting with the physical labour required. This project is still ongoing, with funding still required to complete this rather major undertaking.

Ernest Sloggett and his wife, Nettie Barnum, were long-time members of the Lawn Bowling Club. This photo, taken sometime in the 1970s shows Sloggett planning his shots.

Photo from the Campbellford/Seymour Heritage Society Archives, originally from the files of the Campbellford Herald.

Some past presidents of the Club include:

1940	Charles Palliser	1970s	Dr. Mansell Smith
1941	Bert Taylor		W. A. Kingston
1945	H. T. Scott	1987	Steve O'Henly
1952	Lloyd Taylor	1989	Charlie Cook
1953	Alf Burgis	1991	Bill McNeilly
1954	George Vice	1993	Cliff Richardson
1960	James McMullen	1995	Clare Moxley
		1997	Ula Boose

The Campbellford Lawn Bowling Club is in District 15 in the Ontario division, and this sector includes Kingston, Colborne, Madoc, Brighton, Kenron, Trenton, and Belleville. Each club has many district and in-house tournaments throughout the season. The tournament categories consist of both male and female, mixed, seniors, singles, pairs, triples and fours. There are several sponsored trophies awarded for tournament play, including:

— The Meyers Trophy, donated in 1924 for open competition. Campbellford won in 1955, 1976, 1977, 1978, 1981, 1990, 1991, 1995 and 1998.
— The Wiggins' Trophy, donated in 1924 by Walter Wiggins. This was for mixed competition and Campbellford won in 1978, 1979, 1981, 1986, 1996 and 1997.
— The Douglas Mixed trophy, donated in 1944 for Campbellford competition only. Two winning skips were Ernie Sloggett, 1944, and Bernice Adams, 1997.
— The George Free trophy, donated by George and Mayme Free for mixed open competition in 1975. Campbellford won this trophy in 1975, 1976, 1980, 1986 and 1990.
— The Bennett Trophy, donated in 1989 for Ladies competition. It was first won by skip Kathleen Jones in 1989, and Dorothy Roycroft skipped to victory in 1997. This trophy designation has been altered to a mixed status and winners were Bill Goacher and Verna Petherick in 1998.
— The Wib Kingston Memorial Trophy, donated by Thelma Kingston in 1993. Skip Norm Grisold and Kathy McNeilly won this trophy in 1993, and Skip Miriam Kurita and Clare Moxley in 1995.
— The Mallory Trophy, donated in 1994 by Helen Mallory in memory of her husband, Frank.

The Campbellford Legion, Forgrave Financial Services, Bennett's Home Furnishings, and the IDA. Drugstore all sponsor tournaments. The IDA Ladies Gala is one of the most popular tournaments.

Over the years Campbellford has entered teams in District Championships and many have gone on to play in the Provincials. Some of these recent players are as follows: 1997 Ladies Novice — Muriel Marsh, Irene Russell, and Sharon Osborne; Mens Novice — Jim Russell, Carl Dorge, and Bill Osborne; 1998 Senior Mens Singles — Peter Kurita; Senior Mens Doubles — Art Butcher and Peter Kurita. The 1998 Mens Novice team is another prime example of excellence on the Campbellford greens. Team members, Lead Baxter White, Vice Vic Clark, and Skip Carl Dorge participated in the District Playoffs round robin in Kingston on July 20 to gain entry to the Provincial Finals, also played at Kingston. There they defeated Port Elgin, Willowdale, and Milton but were defeated in the quarter finals by Simcoe, a young team which ultimately won the gold medal.

Bowling now takes place Monday, Wednesday and Thursday evenings, and Wednesday and Sunday afternoons. Participating in tournaments is not compulsory. The Monday evening game is followed with a social time, and this seems to be a time honoured tradition, just as the wind-down in late September had always closed with a pot luck supper. In 1994, the decision was made to have the dinners catered, making the evening more enjoyable for all members. Members volunteer their time for greens maintenance.

The club is always looking for new members. Traditionally lawn bowling has been looked at as a game for the elderly, but it can be enjoyed by all ages.

SKATING

In June 1968, Sally Alton and a group of interested people started the Campbellford Skating Club. They formed an association, joined the Canadian Figure Skating Association, and hired coaches from Peterborough and Belleville to teach local skaters. At times, membership in the Club has been as high as fifty skaters. Sally herself is a qualified skating judge and she arranged for other judges to be available for testing. Over the years, many colourful skating carnivals have also been presented. Carole and Jay Benor were active supporters, with Jay arranging the music for the events. Their daughter, Jayne, was the first skater from the local group to receive her gold dance medal. She went on to become a coach for the local club. The club continues to be active to the present day.

SNOWMOBILING

The Percy Boom River Rats is a local snowmobiling club, with Roger Ferguson of Hastings serving as President. They have two annual events, the Annual Fishing Derby and the Annual Poker Run, which are fund raising activities for local worthy causes. The club uses the trails of the Eastern Ontario Trails Association and other local trails.

SOFTBALL/BASEBALL

Most of the information about early baseball activities is taken from the 'Days of Yore' column of the Campbellford Herald. One of the earliest pieces of evidence about baseball in Campbellford/Seymour was a call for a meeting in 1886 at Mr. Mill's shop to organize a baseball team. In 1900, baseball was played at the fair grounds. On Dominion Day, 1901, a Campbellford team travelled by train to Hoard's Station where they suffered defeat. There is further evidence of other games around the same time period. A baseball match played at the fair grounds featured teams from the east and west sides of the river and the west won by a score of 36-13. Players on the East team were: O. Stimers, H.B.R. Dryden, R.

Bonnycastle, H. Shields, C. Armstrong, J. Brown, William Payne, and R. Foy. The west side players were: George Thomas, George Mills, T. Donald, S. J. Abernethy, A. Dibble, C. Walt, J.F. Maynard, F. Rendle, and W. Thomas. Teams from the Town and the Trent Valley Woollen Mills engaged in a baseball game at the fair grounds, with the Town winning 12–6. Players for the Town were: G. Eggleson, A. Armstrong, C. Davidson, R. Louch, T. Donald, R. Maynard, D. Clazie, F. McCoy, and G. Thomas. The mill team players were: S. J. Abernethy, W. W. Cumming, G. Henderson, W. Hill, R. Cumming, R. Reynolds, W. Dorie, A. Donald, and C. Williams. There was a Campbellford Baseball Club in the mid 1920s, with Charles Davidson as Manager, C.D. Daniels as Coach and R. Bell as Secretary/Treasurer. This Club won the Northumberland League in 1927.

There was a town softball league as early as 1926, consisting of St. Andrew's, the Clerks, the Outlaws, the Hydro, the Millionaires, and the Mill team which was later replaced by the Boxing Club team. That year the Clerks softball team defeated the Mill team to win the new Campbellford Cloth Company trophy. In 1927, the Clerks won the championship again, defeating the Hydro and the Millionaires in the playoffs. The 1927 team consisted of Messrs. Gay, Blute, Denike, Cook, Runions, Blake, Thomas, Atkinson, Maguire. Reeve Major J. M. Bygott presented the trophy to team captain, Jim Gay. Menie won the championship of the central district of the rural softball league, defeating Bethel. Team members were: Barney Eagleson, pitcher; S. Little, catcher; L. Shillinglaw, first base; L. Little, second base; J. Rannie, third base; A. Linn, short stop; J. Petherick, left field; R. Walker, centre field; and F. Little, right field. The Clerks Softball Team was the winner of the Glover Cup for Seymour and District in 1933. The executive of the Town Softball League in 1933 was: Honorary President, George H. Free; President, A. J. Meyers, Vice-President, A. G. Thompson; Secretary-Treasurer, Harold Dunk.

The Campbellford baseball team was honoured at the Clifton Tea Room in 1927 for winning the Sam Clarke trophy as champions of the Northumberland Baseball League. The team consisted of: Jack Cowell, captain, Thornton (Toey) Ibey, Charles Holmes, Frank DeCarrol, Malcolm Cook, Walter Badgley, Douglas Maybee, Earl Fox, Eric Coulter, Howard Davidson, Jack Nesbitt, Reverend C. D. Daniels, Perry Sanders, 'Bugs' Christie, Barney Eagleson, Ted Blute, and Manager, Charles H. Davidson. In 1937, the Seymour West softball team defeated Menie 12-11 to win the Glover trophy before a record crowd. Members of the winning team were: Atkinson, third base; McCulloch, centre field; McKenzie, first base; McCook, short stop; Wilks, catcher; Anderson, pitcher; Hooper, second base; Maycock, left field; and A. McKenzie, right field. The following year, this team defeated Petherick's 19–6 to retain the championship. The first night game held under the new lights on the high school diamond was played in 1947. In 1947, the

Clerk's Softball Team, champions of the Campbellford Town League and winners of the Glover Cup for Seymour and District, 1933. Front row, left to right: L. Holmes, pitcher; E. Bush, second base. Middle row, left to right: R. Upton, third base; O. Hendy, left field; Jack Phillips, mascot; H. Atkinson, left field; Ed Gillissie, first base. Back row, left to right: H. Denike, first base; H. Campney, short stop; D. Maybee, pitcher; H. MacArthur, catcher; B. Reynolds, right field; F. Spicer, short stop.

Photo donated by Steve Thompson to the Campbellford/Seymour heritage Society Archives.

Campbellford Legion team blanked the Brighton team. The local team consisted of: Ernie Hay, centre field; D. Robertson, short stop; Don Holmes, catcher; Ray Sanders, right field, P. O'Sullivan, first base, Ray Tanner, second base; W. Blake, left field; Bill Hay, third base; Howard Wilson, pitcher; and Tam Chadwick.

In 1950, Toronto Maple Leaf's star hockey goalie, Walter "Turk" Broda, brought his NHL softball team to town to play against a hand-picked local team at the high school diamond. The NHL team prevailed 14–11. The Campbellford team included: Bruce McComb, pitcher; E. Hoard, Mel McKeown, A. Taylor, P. O'Sullivan, Pat Doherty, G. Fralick, Ray Tanner, Ken Oddie, Charles Macoun, W. Blake, and V. Herrington.

In the 1950s, the Seymour Softball League, initially organized by Reverend Gordon Whitehorne, included teams from Burnbrae, English Line, Hoard's, Pethericks Corners, Rylstone, and Seymour West. The English Line team won the championship and the Herald Trophy in 1950, defeating Hoard's with the follow-

Hoard's Softball Team, mid 1950s. Left to right: Jack Rannie, Art Reid, Clayton Thompson, Gerald Heagle, Frank Potts, Jim Snarr, Carrol Sharpe, Harold Snarr, Harold Parr, Carl Snarr, Everett Parr, Ken Oddie, Doug Oddie. In front:, Doris Hoard — mascot.
Photo from the Campbellford/Seymour Heritage Society Archives.

ing lineup: Ken McMullen, pitcher; Ron Haig, catcher; Bob Bibby, first base; Ev Phillips, second base; Ray Grills, third base; Arden Haig, short stop; Don Pollock, left field; Bob Smith, centre field; and Bud Stephens, right field.

Rylstone was the champion of the Seymour League in 1951, under the strong pitching of Cam Meiklejohn. English Line won again in 1952. In 1953, Pethericks defeated Rylstone for the championship with the following lineup: Carlie Petherick, pitcher; Earl Petherick, catcher; Earl Fry, first base; John Petherick, second base; Ross Petherick, third base; Ron Barnum, short stop; Bill Petherick, right field; Frank Hancock, centre field; and Gerald Fry, left field.

In the fall of 1960, Petherick's team won the League championship again, defeating Hoard's in the final. The winning team members were: pitchers, Earl Fry and Carlie Petherick; catcher, Ralph Fry; other players, Gerald Brunton, Norman, Lyle, Eldon and Bill Petherick, Gerald Fry, Earl and Maurice Owens, Wayne Kerr, Jackie Watson, Duane Kerr; coach, John Petherick. Burnbrae won the championship in 1963, with Tom Holmes hurling a no-hitter in the fifth with his left arm in a cast due to an injury. The lineup of the winning team was: Gary Thomson, short stop; Bruce Ingram, right field; Ron Hart, third base; Tom Holmes, pitcher; Bill Linn, centre field; Les Little, catcher; Paul Keller, second base; Ron Twigg, first base; Harold Thain, left field; and John Oddie, spare. In 1965, the Hoard's team won the championship due to the pitching prowess of Howard Jeffs, with Lyle Couch catching. The team was honoured at a dinner at George's Restaurant on Centre Street, with League President Mel McKeown presiding. Barry Brown of the Seymour West team won the League's most valuable player award and was also the batting champion with an amazing .452 average. Gerald Brunton was named the League president for 1966.

On Friday, July 6, 1956, the Campbellford Lions were hosts to Havelock in a game at the local diamond. The story recounts Jim McComb pitching for five or six innings and Jackson taking over to finish the game. Gord Platt and Jason Field were the outstanding players both at bat and in the field. The largest crowd to date was in attendance.

By the early 1950s, the Campbellford Minor Softball Association organized baseball for many young people. A July 18, 1956, article in a local paper reported that the Campbellford Community Baseball League was formed to provide the opportunity for every boy to learn the basics. The focus was on Pee Wees, age 9–12, and Bantams, age 12–15. The Herald reported that in the summer of 1967, the following players comprised a new Campbellford Junior baseball team in town: Jim Peeling, Carl McComb, Bill Reid, Don Peeling, Gary Torrance, Terry O'Sullivan, Gary Stewart, Charles Mills, Fred Tanner, Dave Milne, Eugene Parcels. The sponsor of the team was Bruce Wallace. In July 1977, Campbellford Riviera won four straight in the Eastern Ontario Fastball League, sweeping a pair of doubleheaders from Brighton and Belleville. Don and Jim Burkitt each won two games.

The Campbellford/Seymour Recreation Department took over responsibility for running the town's minor softball program, until David and Diane Cleugh proposed forming a minor softball association in July 1991. By February 1992, the Campbellford Minor Softball Association was organized, with the following executive: President, David Cleugh; Vice President, Marlene Milne; Secretary, Debbie Petherick; and Treasurer, Diane Cleugh. The association depended on volunteers to assist with coaching and fund-raising. Players ranged from ages four to eighteen. The house league and rep league were divided into Mites, 8–9, Squirts, 10–11, Pee Wees, 11–13, Bantams, 14–16, and Midgets, 16–17. House league players play locally with other home town teams, while the rep league plays teams from other regions. The new association's aim was to strengthen Campbellford's softball program by working with Softball Ontario in developing the abilities of both players and their coaches. Funds were required, and an application for provincial funding assistance was approved. A pitching machine was one of the initial purchases.

On August 17–18, 1996, the CMSA hosted the Provincial Tournament. This was a prestigious first for Campbellford, as the Ontario Amateur Softball Association was celebrating its 75th year. Several clinics, including a national coaching certification program, brought thirty coaches from Oshawa to Napanee to the high school. The Association produces the "Inside Pitch" newsletter. It has also developed its own computerized registration system, and constructed two new diamonds at Hillcrest Public School. It has supported community initiatives, and has been established as a non-for-profit corporation under provincial law.

SWIMMING

In the early days, swimming was not an organized sport within the Campbellford area, but on Friday, August 1, 1929, there was a major swimming competition held as part of "Campbellford and Community Old Home Week." Several aquatic events were sponsored during the week, but the swim meet stands out in particular. In late afternoon, "The Big Swim" was held in the Trent River and Canal, with the main staging being opposite the present-day Riviera Inn. The swim was advertised as being open to the world. Cash prizes were offered: first prize, $500, second prize, $250, third prize, $125, fourth prize, $75, fifth prize, $50, and $100 to the first woman to finish the course. The course was a distance of three miles, in one-quarter mile laps. Seventy-five world renowned swimmers participated before ten to fifteen thousand spectators. Frank and Stanley Pritchard of Buffalo were two of the memorable contenders.

A marathon swim event was held on July 26, 1934, with fifteen entries in the boys' class. Cecil Lloyd won, covering the three miles in one hour, four minutes, and fifty-seven seconds. The other finishers were Leslie Wilks, Carl Nichols, Harry Rowe, Bill McEachern, and Don Nichols. The girls' event was won by Margaret McDonald of Hastings, who covered the one mile in twenty minutes and twenty-five seconds. The other girls who finished from among the eight entries were Etta May Downhill, Pauline Nesbitt, Margaret Ellis, Alice Tripp, and Grace Morrison.

In 1937, three Campbellford boys won an open one-mile swim at Hastings. Their placements were: first, Jack Tinney; second, Doug Nichols; and third, Joe Elliott.

TENNIS

The tennis courts have always been located adjacent to the Campbellford Lawn Bowling Club along the Trent Canal. One of the earliest references to a local tennis team comes from the Campbellford Herald in 1927. The officers of the Campbellford Tennis Club that year were: President, J. H. Bell; Vice-Presidents, Dr. H. B. Longmore and R.W. Scott; Secretary-Treasurer, N. Alex MacColl; Grounds Committee, Walter Henson, chairman, R.W. Scott, Harry Free; Games Committee, S.H. Neale, chairman, Lil Smith; Chairman of Membership, Hilton Beatty. Campbellford's tennis team won the Tummon Cup in Tweed on Friday,

Campbellford Tennis Club, 1928. Front row, left to right: Eleanor Ferris, Dorothy Linton, Harry Free, Lil Smith, Dr. H.B. Longmore, Hazel Scott, J.H. Bell, Evan Douglas. Middle row, left to right: Verna Weston, Josephine Longmore, Jessie Weston, Mrs. Don Douglas. Back row, left to right: Wilbert Kingston, Bob Scott, Hilton Beatty, Clifford S. Weston, Stanley H. Neale, Basil Linton.

Photo courtesy of Jim Crothers.

June 3, with the following players: Clifford Weston, Men's Singles; Wilbert Kingston and J.H. Bell, Captain, Men's Doubles; Jessie Weston and Harry B. Free, Josephine Longmore and Hilton Beatty, Mixed Doubles. That fall, the Club also won the Central Ontario Championship, defeating Peterborough, 5–2.

In 1933, the executive of the Club was: President, Dr. H.B. Longmore; Vice-President, Arthur Loucks; Secretary-Treasurer, J.R. Smith; Entertainment Committee, Lil Smith, Eleanor Ferris, Mrs. J.R. Smith, and Kate Free; Grounds Committee, Walter Henson and Harry Free; Membership Committee, Merwin Malcolm, Alex Little, and Elsie Connor. Helen Meyers recalls the following additional members in the 1930s: Ken Kingston, Lorne and Eric Scott, Alex Little, Don Bennett, Verna Weston, Jerene Malcolm Schulz, Vi Couch Maxwell, Mary Coxwell Bythell, Eleanor (Polly) Ferris, Grace Cairns Smythe, Lois Meyers Ross, Paul O'Sullivan, Lillian and Dr. Stu Stuart, Vi and Bob Anderson, Bob Linton, W. Peloquin, James Heptonstall, Art Orr, Hugh Nind, and Don and Helen Meyers. In December 1934, the tennis club was very active and a large circle of members had a wedding shower for Don and Helen Meyers at the Kingston residence. In the spring of 1937, the Campbellford Tennis Club held its annual meeting at the public library. The following officers were chosen: Honorary President, Dr. H.B. Longmore;

President, Dr. Hugh McLaren; Vice-President, Clifford Weston; Secretary-Treasurer, Hugh Nind; Committee Chairmen, Grounds, Ken Cairns; Membership, Hilton Beatty; Purchasing, Clifford Weston; Refreshments, Eleanor Ferris.

In 1942, Don Meyers was chosen president of the Campbellford Tennis Club, and other executive members included: Secretary-Treasurer, Hector Macmillan; Social Committee, Eleanor Ferris and Grace Cairns. In 1948, the executive consisted of: President, Don Henry; Secretary-Treasurer, David McEachern; Grounds Committee Chairman, Paul Bennett; Tournament Chairman, Wilbert Kingston.

The club became less active, and by 1952–53 the courts were covered in weeds. Larry Meyers, Ken Kingston, and Michael Holmes set about cleaning the courts and playing was reactivated. Belleville and Trenton were part of the Campbellford League and there was an association with Stirling and Point Anne in the Bay of Quinte Tennis League. In 1952, Larry Meyers and Barbara Smith were declared the best beginners at the Club, following their victory over Ron Pierce and Margaret Nelson. A Wednesday, July 11, 1956, tennis note in the Herald reports the Golden Jubilee Tennis Tournament. "It was a tremendous success in every way. Winner of the tournament was Mr. Cecil Dodwell and his fair haired daughter Donna."

In 1957, the executive of the Club included: Honorary Presidents, Harry B. Free and Clifford S. Weston; President, Ken Kingston; Vice-President, Paul J. Coughlan; Secretary-Treasurer, Peter Battman; Grounds Committee Chairman, Jack Stocker; High School and Junior Representative, Ronald Pierce; Social Convenors, Mr. and Mrs. Robert Anderson. Members of the team visited Point Anne in 1959 for friendly games. They included: Ladies and Girls – Vi Anderson, Margaret Bowey, Sandra Ness, Jacalyn Clarey, Maureen O'Sullivan, Jane Rutherford, Hazel Gillespie; Men and Boys – Harry Free, Robert Anderson, Ted Burley, Wally Rutherford, John Beatty, Ken Kingston, and Tony Shellam.

In 1962, Tony Shellam was re-elected president of the Club. The rest of the Executive included: Vice-President, Evan Meyers; Secretary, Kathy Daly; Treasurer, Ken Kingston. Honorary President was Harry B. Free. In the spring of 1963, close to fifty youngsters turned out at the tennis court for the opening class. In the winter of 1967–68, when Sally Alton moved to town, the Campbellford Club had an executive and a small membership consisting of Eldon Ibey, Ken Kingston, Robert and Violet Anderson, Mr. and Mrs. Trevor Clarke, Dave and Rick Whitfield and Neil, Mark, and Paul Burgess. At this time the club house had no running water, but there were strings of lights running the length of each court for night play. If a light was hit, a player would have to play the point over. The nets were stored in the club house and maintenance, including cutting the grass, was done by the members. In 1975/76 the club replaced the string lighting with four pole lights and then had plumbing installed in the club house a year later. Just one trophy can be found, a men's singles Kenneth G. Kingston Memorial Trophy presented to the Campbellford Tennis Club by the Campbellford Herald Publishing Co. Ltd in 1978.

In the summer of 1970, the Campbellford Tennis Club joined the Ontario Lawn and Tennis Association, and thus began the first years of league play. Sally Alton became the Campbellford Tennis Club and the Eastern Ontario Tennis representative. She advertised for players in all Campbellford schools and began teaching tennis to students in May through June. New members began joining the club, including Gerry and Bette Ireland, Jerry Boise, Doug Carswell and Eric Meyers. That year, the Campbellford Tennis Club joined the Lakeshore League which played May through September. An association with other clubs from Belleville, Trenton, Port Hope, Cobourg, Peterborough, and Brighton evolved. Each week there was one home game and one away game.

The Ontario League Tennis Association sent excellent coaches and Peter Dimmer provided day clinics to encourage young players. Through 1971–75, the OLTA helped to set up special programs and worked at reviving an interest in tennis. In 1973, the OLTA sent Jane O'Hara to Campbellford to teach tennis skills to school aged children and adults. In 1974, Brian Barker did the same. Both June and Brian were strong players and acted as club motivators. Sally Alton assisted these young people and hosted their stays. Because of this coaching, Campbellford

was able to send many young players to various OLTA tournaments hosted by the larger clubs in Peterborough, Kingston, and Belleville. The following young players developed: Ken Alton, Dave Boise, Ann Coughlan, Dan Ireland, Nancy Ireland, Lori Ireland, Dave Clark, Jeannie Kelly and Dave Field.

Jane O'Hara, left, of the Ontario Lawn Tennis Association, and Sally Alton, right, of the Campbellford Tennis Club became instructors for young tennis players in the 1970s.

Photo courtesy of Sally Alton.

Until 1990, Sally Alton provided coaching and lessons for all ages, May through June. The Lakeshore league flourished. Unfortunately, since that time, the Campbellford Tennis Club has declined in membership, although some individuals continue to play. Eric Meyers and others are trying to revive the club.

WRESTLING

During Old Home Week, 1956, live professional wrestling came to Campbellford. More than fifteen hundred enthusiastic spectators jammed into the Community Centre to watch the program. It was the largest crowd to ever assemble in the arena for a sporting event. New Zealand's Pat O'Connor won the main event, opposite Lord Athol Layton of Surrey, England. Abe Zvonkin, from Hamilton, Ontario was disqualified for hitting the referee, thereby losing the match to Gil Mains. The bout between winner Pat Flanagan of Toronto and Aldo Bogni of South America had the crowd on the edge of their seats. Later, the Rotary Club of Campbellford brought professional wrestling to Campbellford as a fund raising event. They worked with promoter Frank Tunney, who brought names like Whipper Billy Watson, Yukon Eric, Hardball Hannigan and the Midgets to town.

Wrestling is an extra-curricular activity at the Campbellford District High School. In 1957–58, Ken Thompson worked to create interest in wrestling and became the sport's first coach. Charlie (Chuck) Lynch was his successor in 1963, followed by Murray Fischer in 1973. The CDHS yearbooks highlight wrestling achievements such the wins in 1965, at both the Bay of Quinte and Central Ontario Championships and honours at the McLaughlin Invitational Meet in Oshawa. At the OFSSA finals, the team placed seventh out of 64 schools. Some of the local residents who were involved in wrestling included Joe Barton, Eric Meyers, Eric and Rudy Joss, Bill Stillman, Peter Oddie, Doug Gratton, Jim Connor, and Pete Dooher. In 1978, a marked increase in interest was noted, as the wrestling team had its best season in many years. They finished second in two meets and fifth in the Kawartha finals.

On December 19, 1985, three CDHS wrestlers, Glen Apars, Alex Yule, and Allan Ingram, won first place trophies for their performances at the General Vanier annual tournament in Oshawa. Larry Young took a second place award in his class. On March 5, 1986, the Herald reported that, at the Ontario wrestling finals at Brock University in St. Catharines, Glen Apars (141 pound class) and Alex Yule (heavyweight class) put on an excellent performance. Apars finished in the top 8 of 36, and Yule finished in the top 12 of 36. In 1987, at the COSSA championships held in Madoc, six members of the Campbellford team qualified to go on to the O.F.S.S.A. championships in Kitchener; they were Fred Clarke, Doug Jackson, Glen Apars, Larry Young, and Alex Yule. Other team members included Steve and

Bart Vickers, Mark Clark, Adrian Riley, and Tony Pearson. On February 13, 1991, at the Campbellford Invitational Novice Wrestling Tournament, Paul Derumaux finished first in the 90.5 pound, and Richard Lavoie first in the 104.5 pound divisions. Tyler Fischer also competed in the 97 pound, Pat Penny in the 185 pound, and Courtenay Cleverdon in the 104.5 divisions. At the Ontario Championships, Natalie Crosmaz-Brown won silver in 1996 and 1997 and gold in 1998.

～ Outstanding Local Athletes ～

K Y L E   P E T T E Y

Kyle Pettey was born September 24, 1983, at Kingston General Hospital, the son of Kathy and David Pettey who live on a farm at R. R. #1, Campbellford. When he was one and a half, Kyle was diagnosed with cerebral palsy. He attended Percy Centennial School in Warkworth. As a young teen, he began to compete in events for physically handicapped athletes. Since 1996, Kyle has won an impressive number of gold and silver medals for competing in various local and regional tournaments for disabled athletes. His main achievements have been in track and field, discus, and shot put. Regrettably, the complete list of these awards is too lengthy for inclusion in this book, but it is on record at the Campbellford/Seymour Heritage Society. Of special note is the fact that at the Seventh Annual Burlington Disabled Games in 1997, he was named Junior Athlete of the Meet.

On February 21, 1998, at the Annual Chamber of Commerce dinner, where the Civic Awards for 1997 were announced, Kyle was named "The Athlete of the Year." Chamber president Jim Rix noted that, "Kyle's determination to excel, coupled with his undeniable strength of character, has continuously impressed and inspired his family, friends and especially his track coach Tim Fillier. He is nothing short of

Kyle Pettey was presented with the "Unsung Hero Award" by Celia Southward, President of Cerebral Palsy Sports, at the Kitchener Year-end Awards Banquet in 1997.

Photo courtesy of Kathy Pettey.

phenomenal." The audience rose in unison to give Kyle a well-deserved standing ovation, and there was not a dry eye in the house.

Tim Fillier has been a role model for Kyle. Tim began grooming the young athlete in 1995, and has spent countless hours as his running coach. When Tim started coaching Kyle, he was still a student at Campbellford District High School, and it was during this time that he encouraged Kyle to become involved in shot put and discus. When Tim left for university, OPP Constable John K. Potts became Kyle's coach. He had experience as a discus and shot put competitor, and generously volunteered between twenty to thirty hours per week to bring Kyle to his current level of ability. He, along with Kyle's parents, require that Kyle maintain a good scholastic standing.

In 1998, Kyle suffered injuries to his back and wrist in a farm accident, and was in a body cast for three months. However, he went on to compete in several more tournaments, adding to his list of achievements and medals. At the Southwestern Regional Athletic and Boccia Meet, Kyle won the 'Unsung Hero Award', acknowledging his training disadvantages in a small rural community. In September 1998, Kyle earned his Scuba Diving Certificate at the Trenton Air Force Base pool.

Kyle attended the World Championship Trials in Ottawa on June 13–14, 1998. His invitation was extended because he had reached world standards in his specific events. This event is the first step in qualifying for the International Paralympic Games in Sydney, Australia in 2000. In the meantime, he has to continue to compete at international levels, such as the Sunshine Games in Miami. He continues to train at the CFB Trenton pool, and the Campbellford Curling and Racquet Club, and was chosen to attend a training camp at the University of Windsor, which afforded intense training sessions as well as the opportunity to study the national competition rules. Kyle qualified to attend the 1999 Australian Southern Cross Games for Commonwealth countries, where he won gold in discus and bronze in shot put. Through his achievements in 1998 and 1999, Kyle succeeded in qualifying for the Paralympic Games in Australia, but he must wait until a place opens for him on the team.

CASSANDRA (CASSIE) TURNER

Cassandra (Cassie) Turner was born May 20, 1981 in Campbellford Memorial Hospital to Byron and Gert Turner. She has excelled in every sport she has ever pursued, but hockey is her particular interest and part of family tradition. Her father was a minor hockey coach and manager. Her brother, Travis, plays with the Junior C Rebels in Campbellford's Empire "B" league. Brother Brad also played minor hockey for several years.

Cassie Turner, wearing the gold medal won by her championship team at the 1999 Canada Winter Games in Cornerbrook, Newfoundland.

Photo courtesy of the Turner family.

Cassie was a valuable member of the CDHS. Flames senior girls basketball team. She also played volleyball, soccer, and softball. In her grade ten year, Cassie won the Henry Forbes Award for Athlete of the Year. In 1997, the Chamber of Commerce "Athlete of the Year" award was presented to Cassie for her contribution to sports in this area. In April 1999, she won the hockey Defenceman Most Valuable Player Award as a member of the Scarborough Sting Senior Women's AAA and was also chosen for the All Star Team. On June 14, 1999, the Kevin Moon Award for hard work and dedication to sports and academics was presented to Cassie at CDHS.

Cassie is a first-rate defensive hockey player and was named to the 1999 Team Ontario midget girls team for the under seventeen-years-olds. She competed in the February 1999 Canada Winter Games in Cornerbrook, Newfoundland as the team's assistant captain. Cassie was chosen from among six hundred and fifty contenders for her position on this prestigious team. The team won Gold.

Cassie graduated from Campbellford District High School and was interested in continuing her academic studies in the Health Sciences field. She received offers from several universities, including Harvard, Brown, and Minnesota. These scholarship offers came as a result of her outstanding performance at the 1999 Winter Games and Cassie ultimately chose Brown University in Providence, Rhode Island, because of the high calibre hockey program at the school. Presently her sights are set on earning a spot on the 2002 Winter Olympic Games.

ENDNOTES

1 F. G. DeCarrol, ed. *Reflections: Campbellford Centennial Year — 1976* (Campbellford: np, [1976]),134.

2 *Campbellford Weekly Herald*, Thursday, April 2, 1891, pg. 3, col. 4.

3 *Campbellford Weekly Herald*, Thursday, April 2, 1891, pg. 3, col. 3.

4 W. A. Kingston, *The Light of Other Days* (Campbellford: W. A. Kingston, 1967), p. 96.

5 W. A. Kingston, *The Light of Other Days* (Campbellford: W. A. Kingston, 1967), p.94.

6 'Hereabouts in Days of Yore' in *Campbellford Herald*, 1975.

7 'Hereabouts in Days of Yore' in *Campbellford Herald*, April, 1975.

 isasters

— Tragedies of the Early Years —

One of the earliest disasters in Seymour Township is recorded on a small diamond-shaped slab of limestone at the Heritage Centre. This stone reveals a cross scraped into the limestone followed by the brief inscription, "Billy Bronson, 1781–1804, Lost in river." This marker was discovered in July 1979 in the Trent River at Crowe Bay by Austin Bennett, a summer cottager.

The Cobourg Star of July 16, 1840, reports that, "Thomas McIntosh, a lad about fifteen years, and only son of Captain McIntosh of the Township of Seymour, and late of the 92nd Regiment, lost his life on the 11th by the accidental discharge of his fowling piece."

In addition, the Cobourg Star of August 25, 1841 records, "A melancholy accident occurred lately in Seymour, when on the 14th of August, John Tice, Esq., eldest son of Lieutenant Tice of His Majesty's 7th Royal Fusiliers, drowned in Trout Creek while bathing. He was unfortunately subject to epileptic fits and fell and was suffocated."

From the Peterborough Despatch of April 13, 1848, we learn that, "Thomas Carr of Otonabee and two young men by the name of Quinn and Ford were drowned in the Trent River a little below Healey Falls. It appears that Mr. Carr who was engaged in the lumber trade was going down to Crowe Bay with a few men to collect some lumber lying there and, in running a small rapid, the boat upset and all were drowned. Mr. Carr was a highly respected man and has left a wife, and young family to lament his untimely loss. Quinn and Ford were single men." The Cobourg Star of April 19, 1848 further elaborates, "We deeply regret to find that Thomas Carr, George Ford and James Quinn of Colborne were drowned at Healey Falls in the River Trent on the 7th. They started from the foot of the slide in a skiff, intending to descend the rapid to Crow Bay where Mr. Carr had left some men employed at rafting time, but were not seen after they left the slide. The skiff came through, with a hole stove in it, and split from stem to stern but neither of the men were with it. It is supposed that they ran foul of a rock and stove their boat and were precipitated into the water. The distance is about a mile and a half, and the river exceedingly rough. Mr. Carr has left a family to mourn his loss."

The Christian Guardian, the newspaper of the Wesleyan Methodist Church, in the January 9, 1850 edition, reports, "A child of Michael Kelly of Healey Falls, age two, fell into a pot of boiling water Christmas morning and died the next morning."

Also from the Christian Guardian, June 29, 1853, "On the 14th, two men, named MacLennan and George Adams respectively, procured whisky from a tavern or store in the vicinity of Seymour Bridge in exchange for a ham. Both drank themselves into a state of insensibility and died of exposure."

The Canada Christian Advocate, the newspaper of the Episcopal Methodists, reported on August 17, 1853, "John Wellington Landon, son of Captain and Mrs. Landon, of Seymour East, was killed by lightning on the 8th in Mr. D. Allen's Store where he had taken shelter. His age was nearly nineteen years."

The Christian Guardian reports in the June 14, 1854 issue, "An inquest was held on the first in Michael Brophy's Tavern, Middle Falls, Seymour in view of the body of James McGrath, who was drowned along with Master Harvey Denmark, eldest son of Alexander W. Denmark, of Seymour on the night of the 22nd in the rapids where the River Trent enters Crow Bay. The verdict was accidental drowning."

The Peterborough Review of March 2, 1855, tells of another tragedy in Seymour Township. "A serious and fatal accident occurred on Thursday last at William Baker's Flour Mill in the Township of Seymour West by which three men were killed and others injured. The building parted, which let the joists out of their sockets and between 2,000 and 3,000 bushels of wheat fell upon those below and into the road. Unfortunately, there were some eight or ten men standing immediately under the wheat and, before they could escape, four were buried beneath it, three of whom smothered to death. The fourth, who was covered with the exception of his fingers, was rescued, but not until he was senseless. Three or four others were partially buried, some as deep as their waists and had to be dug out. Three men were killed: Robert Ramsay, miller, a single man; Jno. Landrigan, a single man from Asphodel; Jeremiah Curtain from Asphodel, who leaves a wife and four children to mourn his death.

The mill belongs to W. W. Meyers, Esq. and was considered to be a first class building and remarkably well and strongly built. We learn that Mr. Baker is repairing the mill by placing large iron bolts through it so as to prevent the recurrence of such a shocking tragedy."

A Century of Footprints relates the story of an 1856 tragedy at Healey Falls. "A group of excursionists were enjoying a boat trip on the Trent from Keene to Healey Falls. The Falls and the rapids were eagerly viewed by the holidayers, many of whom went to the foot of the slide on the stone-laden piers which separated the slide from the Falls. Among them was Miss Margaret Short from Otonabee. The stones were loose and also slippery from the spray, when near the foot of the slide, she slipped and fell upon the floating logs at the foot. Her weight carried her through the loose timber and she was swept down the swift current to certain death. John Londerville of Keene stripped off his coat and boots and sprang from the pier. In his unsuccessful attempt to rescue her, he was badly bruised and exhausted and would have perished had not Albert Chase run ahead down the path below the cliff in time to pull him out. It was a sad party that returned from Healey Falls. The old cemetery at Keene records the tragedy on a stone near her parents' graves, 'Margaret M. Short, drowned at Healey Falls, May 21st, 1856, aged 16 years.' John Londerville died at the early age of thirty-six, brought on from strain and exposure of his gallant deed." [1]

The Canadian Christian Advocate, in the August 31, 1859 issue relates, "John Renney, a farmer residing in the neighbourhood of Campbell's Ford, Seymour Township was murdered on the 19th by John Gibb. There had been much ill feeling between the two men for months"

The Campbellford Herald for 1876 records a number of tragic events. On the 11th of May, the Herald notes that the little son of Mrs. H. Locke died after being kicked by a horse. On June 1, the paper tells of Mrs. William Locke who died of poisoning by drinking Paris Green. In August, a two year old son of R. Stillman was drowned. On September 15th, the news is recorded of the drowning of Nelson Deline of Seymour in Crowe Lake.

On January 9, 1877, Samuel Dunk, age thirty-two, died suddenly at English Line. The following spring, his mother, the former Mary Locke, was found drowned in the nearby creek. It is reported that she was so despondent over the loss of her only son, that she took her own life. Subsequently, her husband married his daughter-in-law and raised a second family!

On November 30, 1888, Alexander Henderson rescued the fourteen year old daughter of James Alexander who had slipped and fallen into the raceway at the Smith Flour Mill. This water ran under a boardwalk and the two were swept under the walkway. Henderson succeeded in clinging to a piece of a rock shelf about eighty feet from where she fell in. His loud shouts attracted the attention of a crowd of men who had to raise the planks with crow bars to rescue the pair from their perilous position. [2]

~ Flooding ~

In the early years, prior to the building of control dams and the Trent Canal, flooding was a constant threat. On the twenty-sixth of March 1870, there was the beginning of a heavy snowstorm which lasted for seven days. Very suddenly, the weather turned exceptionally warm causing the snow to melt rapidly. A dam above Healey Falls could not stand the pressure of the high water and gave way. The river overflowed its banks and insecure buildings were swept away, including one mill at Middle Falls and two at Ranney Falls owned by R.C. Wilkins. For several days, everyone in town needed high rubber boots and travel on lower Front Street was only by boat!

~ Dangers in the Home ~ and Neighbourhood

In 1878, the five year old son of John Lee was severely burned by drinking a quantity of lye. Prompt attention saved his life. In the winter of 1900, an infant son of James Mack, age two, fell backwards into a pot of hot lye and suffered dreadful burns of which he died the next day. A tragic accident occurred at Petherick's School in 1906, when six year old Flossie Petherick, daughter of Daniel, received fatal burns when her clothing caught fire. Because there was no water available, the teacher had to run to the home of Mrs. John Simpson for assistance.

Methods of crossing the river took their toll in human and animal lives. In the spring and fall, it was common for teams and horse drawn vehicles travelling on the ice of the Trent River to break through the ice. Even the ferry was a problem as James Hay found out when he lost a valuable team in 1895, when they backed off the ferry when frightened by a dog. Runaway teams were always a hazard and many citizens lost their lives when tossed from a buggy or run down by out of control horses.

The story is told that, in 1893, Mrs. William Dunstan, a resident of Rear Street, was on her way to the country and left her two daughters in the care of her mother, Mrs. Gurry, on Centre Street. Mabel Dunstan, the elder ten year old daughter, and her aunt, who was only fourteen, went to the well. Mabel stepped on a loose board that covered the well and fell in. Her companion rushed to report what had happened. Mrs. Gurry dashed out, secured a rope to her waist, and instructed her daughter to hang onto it. Down she went into the depths of the well. Fortunately, the board which the little girl fell through had lodged against the sides of the well allowing the victim to hang on and keep her head above the water. Mrs. Gurry seized her and made her way up out of the well. When she was half way up, Fred Peake came along and offered some extra help. The little girl had fallen twenty feet of the thirty foot depth. She suffered bruises but was otherwise none the worse for her adventure. Mrs. Gurry, sixty years of age, showed presence of mind and courage in acting promptly to rescue her granddaughter.

In the spring of 1927, the youngest son of J. A. M. Thomson was badly scalded on the chest and face when he pulled a pail of boiling water off the table onto himself. In 1932, five year old Gordon Curle fell into a pan of boiling maple sap while trying to retrieve a mitten which had fallen into the sap pan. After his rescue, severe skin damage occurred when his clothing was removed. He required many skin grafts. Another tragedy occurred near Allan's Mills bridge on July 23, 1948, when Tommy Dutton was accidentally killed by a bullet from a 22 gauge shotgun. The sixteen year old boy was the only son of Thomas and Annie Dutton. The shooting was the result of careless operation of a firearm in the hands of a youth vacationing in the area. He had only recently been given the rifle by his father. Glen McAlpine, son of Carman and Rita was accidentally killed by a chunk of flying metal. He was helping to saw stove wood when the balance wheel of the sawing rig disintegrated. In 1957, George Seeney, age twenty-two was killed by a falling tree. In 1965, Larry Stephens, age four, and his brother, Ronald, age eight, narrowly escaped death or serious injury when they were buried in eight hundred bushels of grain which collapsed with the floor of the barn on the farm of Ross Stephens.

Weather Disturbances

Wind was also a natural enemy of the pioneers. On July 1, 1875, the belfry and bell of Christ Church were blown down in a heavy windstorm. During the summer of 1900, John Wood was knocked unconscious while cutting his lawn when lightning struck a nearby tree. In May 1912, Charles Bedford's chimney was struck by lightning, shocking his wife, while the same storm killed nine cows of the farm of George Anderson. In August of 1922, the home of W.F. Bailey in Seymour Township, just southwest of town, was struck by lightning. Although the residence did not burn, significant damage occurred. On August 6, 1926, the barn of Thomas Fry on Concession 11 was destroyed when struck by lightning. A quantity of hay and sixteen hogs were lost, but an automobile in an adjacent garage was saved. On June 28, 1933, the wooden silo of Thomas O'Rourke was blown down in a severe windstorm. In August of 1936, lightning struck the home of Mrs. Albert Stephens who was knocked from a chair. She was not injured but the chimney was shattered and a hole was torn in the roof. During the summer of 1938, Herbert Stillman lost a valuable team of horses when lightning struck them in a field. In August 1940, Arthur Sheridan at Healey Falls lost his barn and part of the contents in a lightning strike. As late as February of 1943, wind was a factor when about two-thirds of the roof covering the curling rink fell in a heavy windstorm. Hail was also a danger to crops and livestock. On July 4, 1947, the farmers of the Wilson Settlement in Seymour West lost many crops due to a heavy hailstorm. On the Ray Pettey farm, scores of young chickens were killed and the hail made the barnyard look like a snowy day in January. On September 5, 1944, a severe mid-night earthquake shook eastern Ontario with Cornwall receiving the brunt of the damage. This earthquake shook the Town of Campbellford. Dishes rattled in the cupboards and the doors of wardrobes were flung open. Electrical storms were also a concern for local residents. In the summer of 1950, Harry Grills lost eight cows and William Atkinson lost one during a violent storm. In October 1954, Hurricane Hazel swept through the area, wreaking havoc. Roofs were ripped off barns and transmission lines, television aerials and trees toppled. In the spring of 1955, lightning struck the party telephone line, tossing Mrs. Carman McAlpine of Stanwood across the room. The telephone was shattered and the injured party taken by ambulance to the hospital. In 1960, two cows were hit in the barn of Carlie Petherick but no fire ensued. In mid-June 1995, a violent storm swept through the local area, downing power lines, destroying property, and killing live-stock. Extensive damage occurred in the area of Codrington, but Campbellford did not escape the wrath as the roof was torn from Cheung's Restaurant and dropped on North Front Street.

⁓ Industrial Accidents ⁓

Industrial progress in Campbellford was not without its price. At Mr. Senior's mill, on April 23, 1889, Helen McKeel, a seventeen year old girl, was killed when her clothing caught in a revolving shaft. Fred Keir, son of Mr. and Mrs. George Keir, lost his life when he fell into a machine at William Keir's mill in July 1894.

A tragedy occurred at the Empire Cheese Factory in October 1900, when the cheesemaker, Charles W. Stephens, was accidentally shot and killed. His helper, Harold Rowe, was handing Stephens a gun to shoot a rat when the weapon dis-charged. In the spring of 1901, Charles Benor received a painful injury at his father's planing mill when his hand was mangled in two knives of a jointing machine. Three fingers were completely smashed and his left hand damaged for life. In the summer of 1915, Manson Dewey, son of Thomas, was accidentally killed at the Seymour Power Company Number 11 Plant when he became entan-gled in exposed gears while oiling a shaft. On March 21, 1919, John Costley lost three fingers when his left hand was crushed in a machine at the Northumberland Paper Mill. In the spring of 1951, Sid Seaborn received severe injuries when his hand caught in the carding machine at the Campbellford Cloth Company. On August 6, 1951, Christina Summers, widow of James Watson, was killed in a tragic accident at her son Harry's farm. In August 1963, Harry Stephens lost his right arm when it became entangled in a corn cutting machine on his farm.

Electrical accidents also posed many dangers. In the spring of 1933, Helen Bibby, the ten year old daughter of Sam Bibby, was playing on the roof of a shed on Sebastopol Street when she grasped a frayed 110 volt wire. Charles Collard and Doug Pickering who were nearby were able to disconnect the current and rescue the young girl who suffered burns to her hands. On September 28, 1922, Walter Sutton, who was in charge of the lift bridge, narrowly escaped electrocution when his left hand came into contact with a high voltage wire. He was knocked unconscious and all fingers on his hand severely burned. He had been cleaning up and preparing the bridge for painting. In the summer of 1942, Sam Flint and his brother Wally saved fellow Hydro employee Sid Hopping when he came in contact with a 550 volt line while working on a derrick sixty feet above the cement floor of Hydro's No. 10 Power House. He was knocked unconscious but the Flint brothers succeeded in rescuing him. On June 24, 1948, Cecil Stanley Buckles, a Hydro employee, was killed on duty during an electrical storm while working on a pole at Clark's Corners with fellow employee, Adam Yearwood. In January 1950, Donald Hogle, a local resident, was saved from electrocution on a 2300 volt line at Wellington by the action of Herbert McMann. Hogle suffered serious burns to his lungs and his left foot. He was revived by artificial respiration. Unfortunately, in 1960, Donald Hogle fell eighteen feet to the sidewalk when his spur failed to hold in a pole. On this occasion, he suffered a broken pelvis and wrist. In July 1958, another local resident, Arthur LaBrash, a twenty-seven year old Hydro lineman, died when the pole he was climbing near Oak Lake snapped and he came in contact with high voltage wires.

~ Contagious Diseases ~

In *The Light of Other Days*, it is recorded:

"that a pioneer community often was hit with a malady of a contagious nature which spread like wildfire. Hygienically, the community was lacking many amenities. The streets of the town were little better than barn yards with geese, fowl, pigs and cattle pasturing on the roads. Dead animals were often tossed into the river rather than being buried. Village

fathers had difficulty in enforcing the law in regard to the periodic cleaning of outdoor toilets. In summer, the water in the Trent River was unfit
for bathing. A pound was not established until the mid 1880s and even
then, it was virtually impossible for Mr. Stillman, the policeman to
enforce the by-law respecting same.

In 1887, within a three week period, twelve children under the age
of five died in a measles epidemic, according to death notices in the local
newspaper. In 1889, Campbellford was threatened with a serious outbreak of typhoid fever. People were warned to stay away from the town.
A number of children and adults perished with this illness." [3]

The incidence of death among children and females was particularly high.
Young women often died in childbirth, due to insufficient medical care and poor
hygiene and infectious diseases also took their toll. In the winter of 1901, a son of
the Sarginson family contacted smallpox. Quarantines were placed on both the
family and the attending physician, Dr. Montgomery, who was isolated in a room
in the residence of Robert Cleugh. Diphtheria was another dread disease which
was prominent in the fall and winter months. It had no cure and few effective
treatments. In one instance, five children from one household died of diphtheria
within a single week. Again, in 1915, typhoid struck the town and the Benor family had five deaths, within four months, three of which were definitely linked to
the disease. James and Matilda Benor and their son, Fred, apparently had been
infected by drinking from their well. On Easter Sunday, 1915, Helen E. Weston,
daughter of Fred Weston died from complications associated with typhoid. Vaccine
was supplied and the fee paid for the service was twenty-five cents. It was suggested that the cause of the outbreak was the unhealthy condition of the river and
that the water supply should be brought from Crowe Bay.

On December 27, 1919, diphtheria claimed the life of eleven year old Harry
Jacobs. The Spanish Flu, brought back from Europe after World War I, claimed
many victims in 1919. No sulpha drugs or penicillin were available. Minnie Maud
Cleugh, the mother of Aylmer Petherick, succumbed to this disease. Joseph, son
of the late Charles and Mrs. Hannah Stephens who had served in the Great War,
died of the 'flu at the time of his discharge in 1919. An isolation hospital was set
up at the fair grounds. In February 1939, an epidemic of scarlet fever forced the
closure of schools and cancelled midget and juvenile hockey games, preventing the
Campbellford teams from advancing to the next level in the playoffs. In the early
1950s, polio was prevalent in Ontario and it was with great relief that Dr. Salk's
vaccine came into common use.

⌒ Danger in the Water ⌒

The proximity to the river poses constant danger for young and old. What follows is a sampling of some of the tragedies and near-tragedies that occurred over the years. On March 1, 1882, William Doxsee, age seven, drowned when he fell from a bridge near Menie Cheese Factory into the creek. The Campbellford Herald of March 12, 1910 tells a tale of a near disaster which was prevented by the brave actions of a local man. "Max Varcoe, the eight year old son of William Varcoe, slipped into the river and the current was taking him under the ice when he was rescued by a neighbour boy, James Jacobs, age fourteen." I.T. Frederick, who lived on Grand Road near the aqueduct, had spotted the Varcoe boy in trouble in the frigid March waters. Young Jacobs attention was called to the boy's plight and being a strong swimmer, he entered the numbing water and managed to pull the other lad to safety. Mr. Frederick was so impressed that he called the matter to the attention of the Royal Humane Society which recognized James Jacobs with a medal for his act of bravery. On April 10, 1910, Thomas James Dunk, age twenty-seven, the son of Mr. and Mrs. William Albert Dunk drowned in Crowe Bay.

The building of the Trent Canal was also hazardous work. Mr. Little, a powder man on the job, died in 1911 when a charge misfired. During the spring of 1915, Lottie and May Scott were rescued by Andrew Ibey, Frank Milne, Roy Simpson and Walter Scott when their canoe upset in the Trent River opposite the fair grounds. In the fall of 1917, John Garneau rescued Mrs. A. H. McKeel from drowning. Her husband rewarded Garneau with a gold watch. On July 20, 1918, nine year old Donald McGaw Frederick, son of M. H. Frederick drowned on the east side of the river. Henry Redden rescued a seven year old girl from the river in 1919 when she toppled off the Queen Street Piers while playing with a group of children. In 1925 James Blue and his sons, William of Campbellford and Edison of Philadelphia, suffered burns when gasoline exploded in a motor boat which they were operating on the canal. In July 1932, Robert Simpson Scott, the nine year old son of Mr. and Mrs. Walter Scott, drowned when he rode his bicycle into the Trent Canal. On March 23, 1937, Bud Runions rescued the four year old daughter of H. Gladstone when she tumbled off the corewall into the frigid water. On June 21, 1943, Donald Huble, age 20, drowned at the Black Bridge. Harry Field and Bill Oliver made a valiant effort to save the non-swimmer but to no avail.

In the summer of 1952, a thirty-two foot pleasure craft, the Lady Minto, owned by E. N. Nourse of Toronto sank in Bradley Bay after it strayed from the channel and struck an underwater object. A passing aircraft from Trenton Air Base assisted in attracting other boats to the rescue. None of the four occupants was injured. In the summer of 1953, the body of Alta Stewart of Trent River was found floating by Joanetta Baker and Fred Long. In the fall of the same year, Harry Smith, the lockmaster at Healey Falls and a World War I amputee, was tragically killed when the vehicle in which he was riding left the West River Road by Sutton's Locks just north of town and careened into the Trent Canal. In the summer of 1962, Howard Donald, five year old son of John Donald, was able to save three year old Brent Bell, son of Graydon, from the deep waters of Trout Creek. On June 19, 1960, Doug Ellis and Earl Wood rescued Paul Irwin and Ricky McNutt from the river. Their bravery was recognized in 1963 with a Carnegie Medal. In 1965, Tom Seguire saved his brother, James, from drowning. Clarence Duncalfe and Charles James Brooker drowned in the lock south of town when their car failed to stop for the opening of the swing bridge.

In June 1984, Murray Ferrill, an employee of Parks Canada was on duty at Lock 8 at Percy Reach when a terrified father reported that his son had fallen in. Ferrill jumped over the railing into the water twenty-four feet below. He succeeded in grasping nine year old Jeff Chow of Toronto and bringing him to safety. In December 1996, eleven year old Charmaine McLean saved a ten year old boy from drowning when he fell through the ice on the Trent River at Green Acres. A second boy was able to successfully remove himself from danger. Charmaine extended her coat sleeve to the child while her cousin ran for adult assistance. Her father and a friend returned with a hose with which they were able to pull both Charmaine and the victim to safety. Charmaine admitted that she was frightened but a film shown to her class by the OPP had given her the correct approach to attempt.

On February 20, 1999, three local teens were honoured for saving the life of an eight year old girl in June 1998. Andrew Towns, Adam Macmillan and Scott McKelvie had been riding mountain bikes when they witnessed the young girl fall into the swollen river on the east side of Ferris Park. Macmillan and McKelvie quickly jumped into the water and swam to the area where the girl was last seen. Towns ran along the top of the falls and dove into the water. Macmillan succeeded in locating the young girl and with Towns help was able to pull her to shore and take her to a nearby house for help. The youngster suffered a broken arm in the mishap but would surely have been lost had these young men not acted promptly.

⁓ Danger on the Train Tracks ⁓

The coming of the railway in 1879 introduced new dangers. On May 31, 1892, a freight train jumped the rails and several cars piled up at the farm of William Stephens on Concession 4, Lot 16. Brakeman Robert Purdy of Port Hope was buried in oats and died in the wreckage. The derailment was blamed on an obstruction placed on the tracks and the railway offered a reward for information. During the spring of 1912, Garnet Cassan, a brakeman on the Grand Trunk Railway, lost four toes when he slipped and his foot was run over by the wheels of a moving train in the yard at Lindsay. In the summer of 1912, James Hutcheon was struck by a train two miles east of town. He was walking on the tracks, a dangerous route for someone who had lost his hearing.

In July 1928, a tragic accident took the life of Muriel (Keeler), wife of James Jacobs, and her son, Lloyd, age seven. Mrs. Jacobs, along with Lloyd and two other children, Helen and Stewart Donald, had been crossing the high CNR bridge when they heard the sound of an approaching train. Mrs. Jacobs urged the Donald children to run while she frantically tried to carry her son to safety. The mother and child fell thirty feet to the highway below and their injuries were so critical that both died. The other two children managed to scamper to safety beyond the bridge. Three daughters, Barbara, Phyllis and Jean, and James Jacobs, the father, were left to mourn their sad loss.

The railway crossing on Centre Street was the scene of a disastrous accident at the end of August 1950. The entire family of Ken Milne was wiped out when their car was hit by the train. John Kenneth Milne, his wife, the former Doris Pauline Ingram, daughters, Faye Jean, age 10, and Betty Marie, age 8, perished in the crash, as well as Mrs. Milne's mother, Nora Jane Petherick Ingram. In the winter of 1956, Joseph Maddocks was badly mangled at the Gair Company Plant on the site of the old pulp mill when he fell between two shunting box cars. His injuries were severe and his left arm and leg and his right foot and ankle had to be amputated. During the 1960s, Mike Walmsley averted a major derailment in Campbellford. An earlier derailment in Trenton caused trains on the main CNR line to be re-routed through Campbellford. Mike was fishing from the train trestle in Trout Creek and heard the noise of a rail splitting due to the increased use of the track. If another train had gone over the trestle, the train could have derailed and landed in the creek. Mike reported the problem to Charlie Redden, the station master, who put the semaphore signal up to stop the next train. Walmsley received a letter of appreciation from the CNR for his quick action.

～ Danger in the Air ～

On October 24, 1956, a plane crash on Concession 10, Lot 11, Seymour Township, took the lives of two Campbellford residents. George Stafford, age 30, owner and pilot of the plane, and Gary Stapley, age 17, his passenger, died as a result of the crash. George Stafford, who was killed instantly, was an experienced pilot, having served overseas in World War II as an air gunner. He was instrumental in establishing the small private airstrip on Highway 30. Gary Stapley, who died later in Peterborough Civic Hospital, was to have taken his pilot's test the next day. His father, Doug, had already bought him an aircraft. There were no witnesses to the crash. The wreckage was spotted in a field about one hundred yards off the roadway by Graydon Bell, a school bus driver who promptly summoned help.

～ Chronological List of ～ Significant Fires

1874	Ely and Young's Cabinet Factory and the Wallace Block were destroyed.
April 9, 1875	This major conflagration started in a combined grocery store owned by S. and B.C. Johns at the corner of Front and Bridge Streets. Two large hotels, the Phoenix, operated by Bluton and Brickley, and the Campbellford Hotel, operated by D. Adams, as well as seven other buildings which housed Head and Marshum's Harness Shop, E. McNulty's Dry Goods, John Whitton's Butcher Shop, Crook's Watch and Clock Shop, McCarthy's Shoe Shop, J.C. Mathieson Grocery, the offices of Dr. Pettigrew and R. Cockburn and a Jewellery and Fancy Shop were destroyed. Even the timbers of the wooden bridge caught on fire. The fire was followed by floods which filled the cellars. All loose material was swept downstream.
May 22, 1875	The residence of Daniel O'Sullivan on Concession 12, Lot 6 was destroyed by fire.
1875	The barns and sheds of James West were lost to fire when struck by lightning.
1876	Campbellford Cloth Company and other mills on the same site were destroyed.
June 18, 1878	The east side woollen mill, owned by Morice and Company of Montreal and the Fogg Warehouse suffered fire loss along with the stables for the Queen's Hotel and the Victoria Hotel. The fire started in the picking room. The fire brigade was able to save Dickson's Foundry and the stone house across the road.

1882	The barn and stables of Jasper Locke on Concession 6, Lot 18 burned to the ground.
1885	The old grist mill recently purchased by Charles Smith was lost to fire.
1889	The combined public and high school building was reduced to rubble after a fire erupted in a register. Staff and students were hastily and safely evacuated.
Fall 1891	The old Dinwoodie saw mill north of Campbellford was destroyed by fire. The building had been leased to Henry Redden who used it to manufacture cheese boxes.
Nov. 2, 1891	The Post Office and General Store operated by Amos Hubble at Stanwood was lost in a fire.
Mar. 21, 1892	The residence of George Johns of Seymour East burned.
July 21, 1894	The flour mill at Meyersburg owned by the Sills Brothers was destroyed by fire.
Aug. 1895	The moulding department in the Whyte's Foundry suffered fire damage.
Dec. 25, 1899	The first St. Mary's Roman Catholic Church burned to the ground on Christmas morning.
1900	The barn, outbuildings, grain, and farm implements of Thomas Rowe on Concession 12 were lost in a fire.
Nov. 16, 1900	The Wallace Block at the corner of Bridge and Front Streets was destroyed by fire.
Winter 1900	O. A. Eaton's Tannery, later the site of Anderson's Dairy, burned.
Feb. 6, 1901	Fire damaged the Victoria Skating and Curling Rink on River Street.
1904	A chimney fire at the old Dominion Hotel building at the corner of Bridge and Rear Streets caused limited damage to some scorched clothes.
Winter 1909	The residence of Mr. Innes, formerly the old Beattie farm, was destroyed by fire.
Aug. 22, 1912	The residence of R. B. Meiklejohn of Seymour East was burned but most furniture was removed.

Feb. 1916   Fire damaged the main building at the paper mill.

Oct. 11, 1917   Northumberland Paper and Electric Company suffered fire loss.

1917   A spectacular fire occurred at the Munitions Factory on Alma Street

Nov. 1920   Barns owned by James White and John Gorman were lost. Both fires were caused by sparks from threshing machines. The contents of the barns, including the threshing machines, were completely destroyed.

Summer 1925   The hay barn and outbuildings of Thomas W. Stephens, about one mile west of Campbellford, containing the season's crop were lost. Neighbours managed to save most of the livestock and farm implements.

1926   During an electrical storm, the barn of Thomas Fry on Concession 11 of Seymour was struck by lightning and burned to the ground. Losses included a quantity of hay and ten hogs.

Summer 1926   A house beside the Salvation Army Citadel, owned by T.J. Horkins and occupied by Mrs. Rountree and family, was destroyed. All escaped injury.

May 29, 1927   The residence of Edgar Stollery on Concession 3 was destroyed. Mrs. Stollery and neighbour, Leo Fry, were injured when trying to save articles from the fire.

Feb. 3, 1930   A second major fire occurred in the Wallace Block.

April 23, 1932   The Gair Pulp Mill near Ranney Falls and the Ibey residence were demolished when a mountain of seven thousand cords of logs went up in flames, supposedly from sparks from the kiln.

1933   A frame house on Maple Street owned by Richard and Albert Parcels was lost in a fire.

1933   The general store at Hoard's Station owned by Reg Parks was destroyed by fire.

August 1936   A grass fire on the McKenzie farm on River Road West was extinguished by Hydro employees and neighbouring farmers.

Aug. 6, 1936   A grass fire on government owned land at Healey Falls threatened the home and cottages of Mrs. George Dunham.

Gair Pulp Mill fire, April 23, 1932.
Photo courtesy of Harry Cubitt.

Aug. 13, 1936   The barn of Robert C. Ketcheson of Menie was lost along with the year's crop of hay and grain and livestock.

Nov. 1936   The rear of T. L. Diamond's Real Estate Office was damaged by fire. Barber Anderson went right on cutting hair in the front of the building as firemen battled the fire.

Nov. 1936   The barn of Herbert Tinney on Concession 2 was destroyed by fire.

Winter 1937   The residence of Joseph Kelleher southwest of town was lost to fire. It had been one of the first brick houses constructed in Seymour Township. Mr. Kelleher suffered burns trying to save the furniture and the family dog but all were lost.

Winter 1937   The barn and contents of William M. Stephens just east of town were destroyed. The livestock and the family home were saved.

Mar. 18, 1937   The Bank of Montreal on the northwest corner of Front and Bridge Streets suffered fire damage. Aber-Knit Company and D.J. Lynch's Law Office were damaged. William Elphick, a resident on the third storey, was trapped and had to be rescued.

April 3, 1937   The Kerr Block, on the east side of Front Street North, housing several businesses and upstairs apartments, suffered heavy fire damage.

Spring 1938   A spectacular gasoline explosion occurred while Earl Craighead, the deliveryman for the oil company, was replenishing the tanks at Cassan's Service Station. Earl was able to remove the truck but the blast wrecked the pumps and damaged the garage.

Aug. 29, 1938   The barn of Mr. and Mrs. Carleton Rowe was struck by lightning during a severe thunderstorm. Mr. and Mrs. Rowe and family escaped, even though he was stunned. Two cows were also knocked down. The whole interior of the barn went up in flames.

Aug. 1940   Prompt action by the local Fire Department quelled what could have been a serious outbreak at the home of Mrs. Charles Black on Ranney Street.

July 15, 1941   Trent Dehydrated Products Plant was burned.

Winter 1942   The residence of Mrs. J. Asseltine, an elderly lady who lived just off Naseby Street, was lost in a fire.

July 25, 1942   Prince of Wales Cheese Factory on Concession 7, built in 1889 by James Shillinglaw, was destroyed by fire.

Aug. 13, 1942   Gravlin Bale Shoe Factory suffered fire damage.

May 1943   The barn, drive shed and stock of Raymond Free of Seymour West were lost in a fire.

March 6, 1944   A.D. Bennett Furniture Store was damaged by fire.

May 14, 1948   The barn of Fred Kelleher, situated south of town near Bradley Bay, was destroyed in a fire which burned a quantity of hay, farm implements and eighteen veal calves.

July 4, 1948   A spectacular fire consumed the barn and contents on the farm of John Isaac Free.

April 1949   Fire damaged the pulp mill.

Spring 1950	A duplex on Doxsee Avenue occupied by the families of William Heenan and Bill McCrory suffered damage from a fire originating in an oil burner. Lorraine McCrory showed great presence of mind in getting her younger siblings out safely.
Spring 1950	The James Milne residence on Concession 11 was lost in a fire. Mr. and Mrs. Milne were attending a funeral but their daughter, Ruth, was able to get the other children out safely.
Summer 1950	The residence of Jack Meier on the West River Road was considerably damaged by fire.
Fall 1950	Allan's Grist and Lumber Mill on the Crowe River was destroyed by fire.
Jan. 14, 1951	Craig Beattie's Feed Mill was destroyed by fire.
Spring 1951	The residence of Don McArthur just off the West River Road suffered fire damage.
	The tenant house owned by Charles Johns on Concession 4 was destroyed by fire. A young couple and two infant children were left homeless.
	The Rosser house at the Gair Company on the site of the old pulp mill burned.
Summer 1951	The barn and hen house of Eugene Mahoney of Seymour West were lost in a fire.
Dec. 19, 1951	McArthur Meat Market, Birks Drug Store and other west businesses and apartments were damaged by fire, leaving several families homeless. A disaster relief committee was established to assist the fire victims.
Feb. 12, 1952	The Swiss Cheese Factory, formerly Woodlands, suffered fire damage.
Mar. 1952	A plane swooping low over a burning building drew the attention of Arden Haig to a fire in the pigpen of Donald J. Stephens. Losses included seven sows, one boar, a tractor and some choice lumber.

June 1952   Reg Seymour's barn and its contents were demolished in a fire which also took the life of his Finnish hired man. The Seymours were attending the graduation of their daughter, Marion.

Jan. 8, 1953   The old Keir Mill, Walter Jones' Farm Equipment, and the Free Methodist Church were lost to fire. The heat from the fire was so intense that it melted the windows in the Jones residence across the road.

Spring 1953   The residence of Willis Stephens, occupied by the Cecil Bedell family, was damaged when a gas lamp caused a flash fire. Clifford and Beverly Bedell received burns when they threw the lamp out a window.

Nov. 4, 1953   The barn of Robert Irwin as well as some machinery owned by Carl Owens was lost to fire.

Apr. 4, 1954   The Wallace Block at the southeast corner of Front and Bridge Streets which included the A.D. Bennett Store, Gibson's Stationery, a hair dressing shop, Stanbury's Restaurant and upper apartments were damaged. Laurie Nesbitt was able to rescue Pete Bennett's father from this blaze.

Apr. 1955   Spring grass fires on Candy Mountain were an annual occurrence. On this occasion, the chicken house and small barn of Harold Jones on Portage Street were also destroyed.

May 1, 1955   Keith Bailey's cottage on Bradley Bay, adjacent to the locks and Potts' Resort, was lost to fire.

Winter 1956   The farm house of Wellington Wood of the Stanwood area was burned to the ground, leaving the parents and six little girls homeless.

July 1958   Damage in the range of $25,000 resulted from a fire in Bennett's Warehouse behind the Campbellford Herald Office.

Winter 1960   The Bateson family home in the Wilson Settlement was destroyed by fire during a blinding snowstorm. Bill Bateson escaped but his wife and four children perished.

Feb. 15, 1960   Fire damaged the Trent Wire Products building at Weldrest Cleaners on Bridge Street West. The business manufactured wire hangers.

Summer 1960   The Canal Concrete Products Limited on the West River Road suffered fire damage.

1961   The bodies of Clarence and Audrey Rowe were found in the charred ruins of the family barn on Concession 12. Both had been shot. A third sibling, Cecil, died the next day of a self-inflicted gunshot from a 12-gauge shotgun.

Sept. 1, 1962   The farm house of Albert Petherick and Albert Tinney on Concession 10, near Petherick's Corners, was lost in a fire which left only the kitchen.

Winter 1965   The residence of Leonard Maybee, about one mile north of town on the East River Road, was lost to fire. The parents and eight children were left homeless.

Winter 1966   Seven businesses on Front Street including Scheidt's Gift Shop, Frank's Food Market, Pace's Health and Beauty, Bruce Wallace's Men's Wear and the T. Eaton Company Order Office were burned. The Moonlight Café was badly damaged and the Lew and Stan Shelly Jr. families were left homeless. This blaze jumped two fire walls and finally stopped at a third. Fourteen below zero temperatures and a false roof hampered the firemen's efforts. The Town's new pumper was used for the second time since its purchase.

March 6, 1966   Bridge Street Public School was reduced to rubble. Bob Wickens had a bad scare when his breathing tube became disconnected from his air pack. He made it out safely on his own.

May 19, 1967   The barn on the farm occupied by Ted Simpson was lost to fire.

Aug. 1971   An old frame building, once used as a cottage on the property of T.J. Horkins on the west side of the Crowe River near the weir dam, burned to the ground.

May 24, 1975   An early morning fire destroyed the Healey Falls home of Harold and Mabel Brunton. The couple perished in the fire.

Apr. 5, 1980   Spontaneous combustion ignited silage at Steve Sanders' farm. This was the first use of the new Seymour Township pumper.

Campbellford Public School on Bridge Street was destroyed by fire on March 6, 1966.

Photo donated by Isobel Clark to Campbellford/Seymour Heritage Society Archives.

Feb. 21, 1986   A fire at the Linton Block at the northeast corner of Bridge and Front Streets destroyed eight businesses and left seventeen people homeless. Businesses included the Salvation Army Thrift Store, Joan's Stationery and Gifts, Wayne Buck's Law Office, His and Hers Beauty Salon, Doro Fashions, Campbellford Travel, Thornton Waters Financial Services and, ironically, the source of the blaze, Clean Sweep Chimney Services. More than fifty fire fighters were on site. The damage was two million dollars. An older lady climbed out a second storey window and was standing, frozen with terror, on a ledge over Manse Shaw's Pool Room. She was rescued by Bob Wickens who brought her safely down a ladder.

ENDNOTES

1 *A Century of Footprints* (Campbellford.: Campbellford/Seymour Agricultural Society, 1967), p. 77.
2 All excerpts were taken from the following indexes:

Cobourg Star, 1831–1849 – Births, Marriages, Deaths. Transcribed by Percy L. Climo, Cobourg, 1980 (Peterborough: New Horizons Committee, Kawartha Branch, Ontario Genealogical Society, 1985), various pages.

Cobourg Star, 1831–1849 – Births, Marriages, Deaths: Supplement. Transcribed by William Amell, Peterborough, 1985 (Peterborough: New Horizons Committee, Kawartha Branch, Ontario Genealogical Society, 1985), various pages.

Peterborough Newspapers, 1837–1856: Gazette, 1845, Despatch, 1846–56 – Births, Marriages, Deaths. Transcribed by William D. Amell, Peterborough, 1982 (Peterborough: Kawartha BMD Books, 1987), various pages.

Peterborough Review, 1854–1868 – Births, Marriages, Deaths (Peterborough: Kawartha BMD Books, no date), various pages.

Donald A. McKenzie, *Death Notices From The Canada Christian Advocate, 1858–1872* (Lambertville, NJ: Hunterdon House, 1992), various pages.

Donald A. McKenzie, *Death Notices From The Christian Guardian, 1836–1850* (Lambertville, NJ: Hunterdon House, 1982), various pages.

Donald A. McKenzie, *Death Notices from the Christian Guardian, 1851–1869* (Lambertville, NJ: Hunterdon House, 1984), various pages.

Donald A. McKenzie, *More Notices from Methodist Papers, 1830–1857* (Lambertville, NJ: Hunterdon House, 1986), various pages.
3 W. A. Kingston, *The Light of Other Days: A History of Campbellford and Seymour Prior to 1900* (Campbellford: W. A. Kingston, 1967), p. 158.

$\mathcal{P}$eople

The following brief accounts describe the lives of some of the citizens

of Campbellford / Seymour. They were randomly chosen from accounts

submitted to the Heritage Society for inclusion in this book. Some

made their mark on the local community, and some made an impact

on the larger Canadian community. All are examples of ordinary

people doing extraordinary things.

ROY BARNUM

Roy Barnum was born in Seymour Township in 1910, son of Fred and Cora Barnum, whose farm was located on Concession 9 of Seymour East at Rylstone. Fred Barnum was the local postmaster, and their home was used for the collection of mail before it went to the Burnbrae Post Office for pick up and delivery. Roy remembers a wonderful family life. His parents often read to him and his siblings, and Roy could read before starting elementary school. He remembers playing in the sawdust at Allan's Mills, and buying Orange Crush for five cents, making it last longer by punching a hole in the cap. He recalls tuning in to KDKA, Pittsburgh, Pennsylvania, with his first radio, made by Harold Spencer. Roy remembers that he held the red flag at the Bonarlaw Station, where the CPR trains arrived from Ottawa and Montreal. He recollects heaving wagon loads of cheese from the Rylstone Cheese Factory on to the trains at the Springbrook Station. He used to attend the silent movies at the present Masonic Temple each Saturday for only five cents.

Roy had two sisters, Evelyn and Helen, and one brother, Don. Roy completed his elementary education in Rawdon Township at the Union School, and entered Campbellford High School at age twelve. While he was in high school, he boarded with his grandparents, Mr. and Mrs. John Meiklejohn on Oliver Road. At that time, there were only four homes on Oliver Road – all built by Roy's grandfather. Roy was a member of the Cadet Squad and was championship winner three separate times in track and field. By age sixteen, Roy had completed fourth form and part of fifth.

After high school, while helping in his family's sugar bush, he was approached by pharmacist Fred Wood to apprentice at his drug store. Roy had always been interested in pharmacy and this was an offer he could not refuse. Having completed his fifth year of high school, he apprenticed with Fred Wood for two years, and then enrolled at the University of Toronto, graduating with a degree in Pharmacy in 1932. He was the youngest graduate in the class. In Toronto, Roy met his future wife, Ruth Stewart, a nurse at Wellesley Hospital, whom he married in 1932. They have a son Robert (Bob), now retired from the RCMP and living in Kingston.

Roy worked in Toronto until 1941, when he and Ruth made the decision to return to Campbellford and purchase Wood's Drug Store. Located at 4 Front Street South, the store was in an ideal location because all town residents had to pass it when they went pick up their mail at the Post Office, which was down the street. Barnum's Drug Store closed in 1975.

In June 1998, at the high school's seventy-fifth reunion, Roy was among the oldest graduates. He remembers starting his first year at the old high school in 1922 but moving to the new location around Easter in 1923. Roy was honoured by the University of Toronto with a sixty-five year medal, being one of the two survivors from his University of Toronto pharmacy class of one hundred and two students.

JOHN ERNEST BIRKS

John Ernest Birks, a native of Trenton, Ontario, won the John Ross Robertson Gold Medal from the Ontario College of Pharmacy on graduation in 1911. He worked in Toronto and Orillia before coming to Campbellford in 1920 when he purchased the business operated by James W. Cairns. This was on the west side of the river, at the southwest corner of Tice and George Streets. This building was owned by Irvine Frederick who rented the two upper floors to the government for offices during the building of the Trent Canal. In August 1923, Birks purchased the building from Frederick and began renovations to make the two upper floors into living quarters. Each floor contained a modern apartment.

He operated a very successful drug store over the years, serving both urban and rural customers. In those days, prescriptions were relatively rare, as doctors provided medications to their patients. The bulk of the sales were from veterinary supplies, patent medicines, basic cosmetics, school supplies, fishing tackle, and candy. Birks died of a heart attack while delivering medicine to a rural customer, on December 12, 1944 at age fifty-six.

WILLIAM (BILL) BOYD

Bill was born in Campbellford in 1898. His parents, Mathew Boyd and Rose Anne Redden, had a homestead just north of Campbellford, not far from the present community centre. Although Bill did not stay in the area for too long, he was still a local idol. Some remember him as a very bright individual, one who sought excitement. Before leaving town in 1914, Bill worked on the construction of the Trent Canal.

His first stop was Regina, Saskatchewan, where he joined the Royal North West Mounted Police, the forerunner of the Royal Canadian Mounted Police. Bill was chosen to pose in police uniform on horseback at Lake Louise for a Canadian Pacific Railway postcard. Bill was also chosen to escort the Duke of Connaught when he visited the Canadian west.

In 1917, Bill resigned from the Mounted Police and joined the Royal Flying Corps, becoming both a flying instructor and a fighter pilot. To the delight of the townsfolk, on a summer day in 1917, Bill Boyd landed the first aircraft ever flown over the area at the Campbellford/Seymour Fair Grounds. It was a Curtis JN-4 Trainer aircraft , the Canadian Jenny. He flew a number of missions over the western front in World War I, and was credited with downing two enemy aircraft. Unfortunately he was shot down himself, but survived almost unscathed. He remained with the Flying Corps until 1921.

His next career was with the Ontario Provincial Police where he rose to the rank of inspector. World War II interrupted this assignment and Bill rejoined the Air Force as a squadron leader. At the end of the conflict, he returned to the OPP as the inspector of guns and explosives. He remained with the OPP until retirement in 1960, having completed forty years of service.

Bill Boyd and his 'Jennie' at the fair grounds in the summer of 1917.

Photo from the Campbellford/Seymour Heritage Society Archives.

Bill was married twice. His first wife, Anne Elizabeth, predeceased him, and he later married his second wife, Marion. Bill had four sons, Bill Jr., Victor, Thomas, and Bruce. Bill had the honour of pinning flight wings on his son, Victor, when he graduated from bombing and gunnery school. Victor was killed in action over Malta. Bill passed away on December 18, 1984. at age eighty-six at Sunnybrook Medical Centre, where he had resided for several years. He was buried in South River, Ontario, his residence after many years with the OPP.

BILL BRUINS

Bill Bruins was born in Apeldoorn, the Netherlands. In 1958, at the age of nineteen, he followed two brothers to Canada, leaving behind a brother, two sisters, and his parents. Bill joined one brother in Vancouver, British Columbia, to start his first job making wigs. In the early 1960s, Bill enrolled at the Reformed Bible Institute in Michigan, where he met Dorothy Zwart of Carrying Place, Ontario, whom he married in 1965. The decision of his brother-in-law to join the OPP encouraged Bill to consider police work as a career. In 1967, Bill was accepted by the OPP and posted to Listowel for seven years. He transferred to Campbellford OPP in 1974, where he served for the next twenty-four years, the last seven as the detachment's Community Service Officer. When he arrived, there were only five officers on the Campbellford Town Police Force, with Sammy Baird as the Chief. There were also eight OPP officers covering the outlying areas. In 1975, the OPP became the official police force for the town as well as the outlaying areas, and Chief Baird and three officers joined the OPP. The highlight of Bill's career was working with the grade five and grade six students in the elementary school system. At this level, he made presentations on safety, including bus safety, and assisted the teachers with the Values, Influences and Peers Program. He also conducted lectures and seminars at the Campbellford District High School.

Bill Bruins, at his retirement from the OPP, on February 27, 1998.
Photo courtesy of Bill Bruins.

Bill and Dorothy have three children: Kelvin, married and living in Cobourg; Mike, who recently completed a university degree; and James, who is completing paramedic studies. On February 27, 1998, Bill retired, after thirty-one years of public service. He plans to stay in the Campbellford area where he pursues several hobbies including gardening and tapping his own maple trees. He remains committed to helping with a youth drop-in centre called The Fishing Hole. This is a project to which Bill and other volunteers have devoted six years of planning and development.

HAROLD N. CARR

Harold Carr came to town to purchase Trent Valley Creameries on Doxsee Avenue from Stanley Southworth. When the Campbellford Rotary Club was formed in 1928, he was among the charter members, and, in 1930–1931, became the third president of the town's oldest service club.

After serving a term on Town Council, he was elected Mayor. While serving in this office, Northumberland Riding Liberals were seeking a local candidate to back the new party leader, Mitchell F. Hepburn, and Harold Carr was selected. On Tuesday, June 19, 1934, he was elected to the Ontario Legislature to represent Northumberland in the same election which saw Mitch Hepburn sweep the ruling premier, George Henry, and his Conservatives, out of office. An election in 1937 saw Carr returned for a second term. World War II caused the 1942 provincial election to be deferred, and the unexpectedly long term of office proved to be demanding for Carr and his colleagues. During his tenure at Queen's Park, paving was begun on Highway 30 from Campbellford to Brighton, and Campbellford also secured a profitable contract with Ontario Hydro for the sale of excess electricity generated by the town-owned power plant near Crowe Bay. With considerable reluctance, Carr informed a disappointed Premier Hepburn in October 1942, that he would not seek re-election whenever the date was announced. The Liberals also lost the riding to the Conservatives represented by Brighton Township farmer, William A. Goodfellow. Harold Carr was the last Liberal member to represent Northumberland in the provincial legislature in Toronto and the only resident of Campbellford to serve as a MLA or MPP in recent times.

After his retirement from public service, Harold Carr disposed of his interest in Trent Valley Creameries and operated the Frosty Lockers, later purchased by H.J. (Bert) Taylor. Harold Carr passed away in Toronto on Wednesday, February 20, 1974, in his eighty-seventh year.

JOHN FRASER ROSS DOUGLAS

J. F. Ross Douglas was born November 3, 1898, near Warkworth, the son of John H. and Clara Douglas. John H. served as Liberal MP for East Northumberland.

Ross completed his high school education in Campbellford and graduated from the University of Toronto in 1926. He attended Osgoode Hall, graduating in 1929. He returned to Campbellford and, in 1932, purchased the law practice of George A. Payne. He was an all-round sports fan and an avid lawn bowler.

In September 1937, after attending a local dance, he was taken ill, and ten days later, was diagnosed as suffering from infantile paralysis. The disease paralyzed both his legs and affected some internal organs. From September 1937 until April 1938, he lay in a Toronto hospital, attached to a Bradford Frame, a steel and canvas stretcher, with both legs in splints. He was so encouraged by appeals from his clients from Campbellford, that he became determined to resume his law practice. He returned to Campbellford in time for the opening of the Masonic Temple in 1938. For some time, with the help of a personal-care assistant, he used crutches along with heavy metal leg braces. Ross found this very inconvenient and decided instead to use a portable wheel chair. Once more he could be somewhat independent.

In 1946, Ross married Eleanor Pauline (Polly) Ferris. They resided on Front Street North where he continued to practice law and serve as an active member of the community. Ross passed away on September 2, 1977, and Eleanor on December 7, 1991.

H A R R Y   B .   F R E E

Harry Free was born in 1889 at Maplewood Farm on Concession 7, Lots 3 and 4, property that had been in the Free family for three generations. His full name was Abraham Henry Beattie Free, but he preferred Harry. Harry attended West's School and later Campbellford High School, graduating in 1907. In 1909, he passed a correspondence course in stationary engineering.

In 1912, Harry enrolled at Queens University in Kingston, but his studies were interrupted by World War I. His whole class of would-be engineers enlisted, and by February 1915, he was with the Canadian Engineers' contingent of the British Expeditionary Force in France. Some of his letters home were printed in the Campbellford Herald. Early ones are optimistic, but then the horror sets in. Harry tells his family: "even then I would not write of what we see. Surely the men that return from the war will be changed. I know I am. Sights that would make me sick at home are a matter of pure indifference now." After almost three years of fighting in the trenches, and winning the Distinguished Conduct Medal, Harry transferred to the Royal Flying Corps. He trained as a pilot in Scotland, then came home to teach other Canadians how to fly at Mohawk and Rathbun airports near Deseronto.

At the end of the war, Harry returned to the family farm. His father died in 1921, leaving Harry with responsibility for the farm, but flying was in his blood. He completed his studies at Queens, graduating in 1928 with an Engineering degree.

That same year, he was hired by the newly-formed Kingston Flying Club as its first flying instructor. Thousands attended the opening of Kingston's new airport in 1929. Harry personally ferried the club's brand new De Haviland Gypsy Moth aircraft from Toronto to Kingston, and that same day took first place in a thirty mile air race.

For the next ten years, Harry taught flying three days a week, then flew back to his farm for three days, landing his old "Jenny," the popular name for the Curtis JN-4 biplane, in a suitable pasture. When the children attending West's School heard his plane arriving, they rushed outside to see him fly overhead, much to the teacher's dismay. Harry pared down the farm operation, getting rid of the animals that needed daily care. He also found time to give the occasional talk on flying to the local Rotary Club. The Kingston Flying Club survived the Depression, and by 1939, Harry had trained more than a hundred young pilots, many of whom joined the Royal Canadian Air Force and flew in World War II.

In 1942, Harry retired to the family farm. Harry worked actively with the Department of Veterans' Affairs, helping veterans get benefits for their service. In 1969, Harry was honoured by friends at a surprise 80th birthday party. Among the guests was Gordon MacGregor, a Battle of Britain hero and former President of Air Canada, whom Harry had taught to fly. Harry died in Campbellford Hospital on August 21, 1973, at the age of eighty-three.

ANNIE GREENLY

Annie Greenly was born on October 9, 1899, at McCutcheon's Landing, to Andrew and Annie Wight. Annie had nine siblings, Mary Logan, Agnes Nazar, Laura Goodfellow, Francis, Bill, Tom, Norm, Mel and Charlie. When Annie was a baby, the Wight family moved to Trent River, where her father owned and operated a fishing tackle store. Annie later worked in the store and also did fishing tackle demonstrations at Eaton's Department Store in Toronto.

After her husband, Earl Greenly, died in 1969, Annie moved to Campbellford. Annie is still very adventuresome and proved this point when, on her 100th birthday, she had the courage to go for a ride on Ray Foster's Honda Gold Wing motorcycle. She rode twice around the parking lot at the Forrest Dennis Senior's Building where her birthday party was being held. She was dubbed a "Biker Babe" by Mayor Cathy Redden. More than 300 people attended her birthday party in October 9, 1999, and MPP Doug Galt brought greetings from Lt. Governor Hilary Weston and Premier Mike Harris. Since Annie had formerly lived in the Havelock area, Bob Watson, Deputy Reeve of Belmont, Havelock, and Methuen, was on hand to add his congratulations. Northumberland MP Christine Stewart also sent greetings. Annie was an honoured guest at the municipal levy to celebrate the arrival of 2000.

Annie remains active today by playing cards several times each week, and she still attends some functions of the Havelock Legion Auxiliary. Annie is a Life Member of the Trent River Women's Institute. She also joins in some of the activities at Multicare Lodge where she has resided since April 1999.

B A R B A R A   M A U D E   G R E E N L Y

Barbara was born in Brancaster, Norfolk, England, in 1908. Her father, Edward George Puddephatt was the chief gardener at Lord Leicester's estate in Leicestershire, and her mother, Lily May, was a teacher. Barbara arrived in Canada in 1914 on her sixth birthday, along with her mother, two maids, and three younger brothers. The family was joining her father, who had preceded them by a few months. The threat of war motivated their move from England.

Edward became a hired hand in Morganston at Ernest Davidson's farm. The family grew, with the addition of five more children. Barbara attended school in Morganston, and later at Pine Grove School, when the family moved to Cramahe Hill. From age nine, during summer vacations, Barbara worked as a domestic in various homes. Because she was the eldest in the family, she also had responsibility for many chores at home. Eventually she moved to Toronto where she worked at Langley's Cleaners and Dyers. On April 16, 1930, Barbara married Gordon Greenly at Simpson Avenue United Church. They had one daughter, Gayle, and helped to raise eight other children. She also worked at the Bata Shoe factory, and sold dew worms, to assist with family finances.

In 1952, Barbara started a new career as an artist. She studied with artist Paavo Airola in Campbellford. The Carlton Card Company was the first to commission a series of four paintings after viewing and buying some of her previous work. Barbara has sold and given away hundreds of paintings and her home still looks like an art gallery. Her proudest moment was when she was chosen out of three thousand artists to hang her painting, "Woods in Autumn", in Toronto's New City Hall. She was also asked to exhibit a painting at the Ontario Pavilion at Expo '67 in Montreal.

On April 12, 1980, the Greenlys celebrated their Golden Wedding Anniversary. Six years later on December 18, 1986, Gordon passed away. Barbara continues to live in her own home with Community Care assistance. On September 6, 1998, a large party was held to honour Barbara on her 90th birthday. She received many cards, gifts and plaques from friends and family. The press was there to note the occasion, but she made make their job easier by writing her own newspaper account of the proceedings.

FLORENCE HEADRICK

Florence was born in Skye Glen, N.S., on February 13, 1938. At age sixteen, following the death of her father, Florence moved to Glace Bay where she finished high school. Following graduation, she began her nursing career at Glace Bay General Hospital. In January 1959, she transferred to Inverness Memorial Hospital. In August 1959, Florence moved to Ontario, marrying Aubrey Headrick in November of that year. When the young couple moved to Campbellford, Aubrey, also born in Nova Scotia, joined the staff at Campbellford District High School. They had five children and Florence was a stay-at-home mom until 1972 when she started nursing part time at Campbellford Memorial Hospital. She spent twenty-nine years at the hospital. In 1988, she began her involvement with medical missionary work, when she went to Haiti with the Evangelical Medical Aid Society. She worked as a nurse practitioner and dispensed medications in places from Ecuador to the Ukraine. This work was entirely voluntary and was undertaken on her vacation time.

Florence was recognized by the Rotary Club of Campbellford, for her work in helping to deliver health care to people in underdeveloped countries. In 1992, she was the first non-Rotarian to receive the Paul Harris Award in appreciation for the substantial contribution to the Rotary organization's humanitarian and educational programs. The Chamber of Commerce honoured Florence in 1996 by naming her the Citizen of the Year. In March 1997, she was also presented with a Citation for Good Citizenship by the IODE for fulfilling the association's mission to improve the quality of life for children, youth, and those in need. Florence has conducted a drug abuse prevention program for local schools, in partnership with the Ontario Provincial Police and Campbellford Memorial Hospital. As a consequence, the OPP successfully nominated her for the Solicitor General's Award. The community feted Florence at her retirement party at the Seahorse Banquet Hall on November 9, 1996.

T. J. HORKINS

Thomas J. Horkins (1855–1942) was a prominent businessman in Campbellford for many years and something of a local character as well. As late as the 1930s, he was still operating a general store at a location adjacent to Dooher's Bakery on Bridge Street East. As recollected by many local citizens, the store was a bit of an 'Aladdin's cave,' containing a vast variety goods. Rural customers could buy fence wire and horse collars, housewives could buy biscuits and kerosene, and school children could always get scribblers and writing pads that were somewhat dog-eared but inexpensive. John Lisle tells the following story about the Horkins store in a letter to one of T. J.'s granddaughters:

"Across the street from Horkins', another popular Irishman ran a grocery store. There, one morning, two men were discussing Horkins' store and its vast and varied inventory of goods. One chap argued that Horkins could produce almost anything you asked for. A $5 bet was the result of this argument and George O'Sullivan, the grocer, held the stakes. Crossing Bridge Street, the two men walked into the T. Horkins store and asked for the agreed-upon item to purchase. Tommy looked thoughtful for a moment, excused himself and scrambled down to the cellar below. He was back shortly, puffing and panting, as he delivered the requested goods – a church pulpit."

It is also reported that T. J. kept his own coffin at the back of the store and paid a local lad three cents to dust it on his way home from school. The store was quite a successful business and, through it, T. J. was able to acquire other properties, both in town and in the rural areas. Credit was always available at the store, but failure to pay often resulted in foreclosure. T. J. also built a resort hotel near Crowe Bridge but it was not successful; the property was passed on to one of his sons after his death.

The Horkins family at their Crowe Bridge cottage in the early 1940s. Front row, left to right: Joanna Mahoney Horkins, granddaughter, Mary Jo Horkins (Wormell), Thomas J. Horkins. Back: Thomas B. Horkins, their son and father of Mary Jo.

Photo courtesy of Mary Jo Wormell and Barbara Samson-Willis.

T. J. was a short, stocky man with unlimited energy, who served on town council and on the Fair Board. He was proud of his Irish heritage. He was the son of Luke Horkins (1814–1896) and Mary Ann Ryan (1826–1915). Luke had come to Canada in the early 1840s and settled briefly in Kingston before moving to Emily Township, Peterborough County, where he worked briefly as a school master. In 1850, he married Mary Ann Ryan, the daughter of Patrick Ryan (1792–1851) and Elizabeth Dwyer (1804–1880?), both of whom were Peter Robinson settlers. The Horkins moved to Campbellford in the 1850s, but it is thought that Luke may have operated an inn or liquor store in Warkworth before opening a general store in Campbellford. T. J. was the second child and first son born to Luke and Mary Ann. He married Joanna Mahoney (1866–1949) in 1889 in Norwood. Joanna was the daughter of Bartholomew Mahoney and Honora Walsh of Norwood.

The couple had seven children: Dr. Richard Horkins, (1889–1916); George Francis Horkins, (1890–1957); William Bernard Horkins, (1892–1952); Monica Mary Horkins Kelly, (1896–1978); Beatrice Barbara Horkins Cook Cooney, 1897–?); Dr. Harold A. Horkins, (1902–1959); and Thomas Bartholomew Horkins, (1907–1960). T. J. and Joanna valued education for their children, and T. J. bought houses in Toronto to accommodate his children while attending post-secondary school. Both girls became teachers, Richard and Harold became doctors, while William and Thomas became lawyers. Of the children, Thomas, or T. B., is perhaps the best known locally because of his hockey prowess. Even after he was practising law in Toronto, he would take the train home and arrive in time to join the local team for at least two periods of play, much to the delight of his loyal fans.

The Horkins were staunch Roman Catholics and strong supporters of St. Mary's Church. Many family members are buried in St. Mary's Cemetery. When T. J. died in 1949, he left an estate of almost $39,000 which included twenty-five different real estate properties in Campbellford, Seymour Township, Percy Township, Marmora Township, and the City of Toronto.

FRANKLIN (FRANK) LINTON

Frank Linton was born on November 17, 1911, in the family home at the corner of Napier and Queen Streets. His parents were Robert A. Linton (1869–1939) and Agnes Sloan. His grandparents, Robert Linton (1836–1923) and Mary Oliver (1848–1928), first settled in Meyersburg, and established a blacksmith and carriage shop. This business was eventually moved to Queen Street in Campbellford to a site which later became the Harris Feed Store. Frank's grandparents lived in the large stone house at 51 Front Street North, which was more recently owned by Bud Davidson and later, became a business establishment.

Frank attended school in the former parish hall on Doxsee Avenue, with teachers Eva Dunn and Mabel Funnell Thomas. After graduating from high school, Frank was sent to Pickering College in Newmarket. When he returned to Campbellford, about 1929, he and his sister Aileen opened a ladies wear business on Front Street. To supplement his income, Frank became a "stringer" for the Peterborough Examiner, The Toronto Star, The Ottawa Farm Journal, MacLean's Building Reports, and the Daily Commercial News. This required that Frank attend board meetings for the various cheese factories, the cheese board, and several other organizations, as well as council and school board meetings. Frank, now dubbed "Scoop," became quite knowledgeable about community events.

In 1939, Frank joined the 2nd Midland Regiment, serving in Peterborough at the CABC 32 Training Centre as an orderly room clerk, and he advanced to the rank of Corporal. Following the war, Frank went to work for the Prudential Insurance Company where he remained for the next thirty-four years. During this time, Frank was briefly involved in municipal politics, serving as a councillor in 1956-1958. In the 1980s, Frank returned to council and served as Chairman of Finance, and subsequently Reeve. Following the death of Hector Macmillan, Frank completed the term as Mayor in 1991–92.

For many years, Frank was a member of the Campbellford Memorial Hospital Board, where he acted as Secretary for several years, and as Chairman in 1973-76. Until his death in February 1998, Frank was active with the Multicare Board and the Rotary Club of Campbellford. He also served on the Citizen's Advisory Committee for Warkworth Penitentiary.

Frank loved railroads and his basement housed a model train complex. His elaborate model train layout and accessories were donated to the Town to be reconstructed at the Resource Centre, by the Campbellford/Seymour Model Railroad Club. The Club hopes to replicate the track layout of the Grand Junction Railway in the Campbellford area.

Frank and his wife, Georgina Ruth Louise (Joy) Riendeau, had four children: Arthur, retired and living in Campbellford, Paul, in Burlington; David, in Campbellford; and Anne, in Témiscaming, P.Q.

WALTER LOWE

For many years, Walter Lowe (1881–1979) was a familiar figure in Campbellford. His cheery greeting and smiling face were hard to resist, as he sold tickets to raise thousands of dollars for every service club and organization in town. Walter was a valued member of the Campbellford Fire Brigade for forty-two years. Upon his retirement from employment with the Trent Canal, he began a long career of volunteerism. He had a great love of music and played the cornet in the Campbellford

Walter Lowe, attired in his Legion regalia and wearing his military medals, ca. 1960s.

Photo from the Campbellford/Seymour Heritage Society Archives, originally from the files of the Campbellford Herald.

Citizen's Band. He was a veteran of World War I and annually played the Last Post and Reveille for the November 11 Remembrance Day Service. Over the years, he also played the same two selections at countless funerals for veterans.

GEORGE LUCY

George Lucy was born in London, England, on October 26, 1892. In 1906, he emigrated to the Eastern Townships of Quebec where he lived for several years and learned the printing trade. He worked for five years as foreman in a printing plant in Cooksville, Quebec, before he trained in Philadelphia as a qualified lino-type operator. This was followed by employment with the Montreal Star and the

Hartland, New Brunswick, Observer. In 1917, George was married in Dryden, Ontario to Ethel E. Richardson. By 1921, George was in Campbellford, where he had secured a position as a printer with the Campbellford Herald. The Town was so busy that there were no accommodations available for his wife and family, so he sent them to her parents' home in North Bay while he stayed in a boarding place for eight weeks. Eventually, the family was reunited and grew to include two sons, Douglas and Gordon, and two daughters, Clara and Marion.

George had great musical talent, both instrumental and vocal. He was an accomplished tenor soloist with St. John's United Church Choir, and performed in many local talent events. As well, George was an excellent cornet player and served over thirty years with the Northumberland Regimental Band. After he retired in 1966, he organized and directed a senior citizen's choir which was very popular at local functions.

George was employed with The Campbellford Herald for forty-five years. For much of that time, he wrote a column called 'Heard on the Street Corner' under the pen name, "The Herald Robin." The popular column included items of local interest.

George was an early member of the Campbellford Oddfellows Lodge, from which he received a fifty year jewel. He loved to fish and ice skate and often dressed in costume for skating carnivals. George lived to celebrate his ninetieth birthday with family and friends in 1982. He passed away in 1988.

HECTOR MACMILLAN

Hector Macmillan was born in Campbellford to Peter Macmillan and Edith Pennington. After attending Campbellford Public School and High School, he joined the RCAF in 1941 as a wireless air gunner. Hector flew Coastal Command attached to the RAF with the rank of Sergeant. On his return home, he was the first World War II veteran to join Branch 103 of the Canadian Legion. After the war, he bought the family egg and poultry business which he operated until 1950. At that time, he opened the first IGA Store in the area, followed soon after by a second store in Brighton. Hector married Margaret Steele and they had two daughters, Jill and Sandra, and a son, Hector. In 1966, he went into the car business, opening the Chrysler and Jeep Dealership which he operated until the late 1960s. During the 1950s and 1960s, he also served as Chairman of both the elementary and high school boards. In the 1960s, he followed his father's example, serving as a member of Town Council. He also joined the Rotary Club and served as President in 1961.

In 1971, the family left the community and bought the former McClung Hardware Store in Trenton, operating it as a Pro Hardware Store until 1973. Hector then moved on to become General Manager of Counterweight Canada at corporate headquarters in Toronto. In 1980, the family returned to Campbellford where he opened a food and gas business, known as Macmillan's Top-Valu. Upon returning to his home town, Hector renewed his interest in local affairs and, in 1982, was elected Mayor for a three year term. He was acclaimed in 1985 for a second term and re-elected in 1988 for a third term. In 1988, Hector sold Top-Valu to the Cheung family.

Throughout his municipal career, Hector took great pride in the local community. He was a charter member of the Campbellford/Seymour Heritage Society, and took pride in the beautification of Old Mill Park. During his term, the Blue Box Recycling Program was introduced. He often spoke to school classes about municipal affairs and the duties of a mayor. Hector passed away suddenly on January 10, 1990. The funeral was held in St. Andrew's Presbyterian Church where he had been a life-long member.

PETER HALL MACMILLAN

Peter Hall Macmillan was born at Torrisdale Hall, Kintyre, Argyllshire, Scotland in 1883, the youngest son of Hector and Agnes Macmillan. He emigrated to Canada in 1912 and settled in Campbellford. In World War I, he enlisted in the Argyll and Sutherland Highlanders and was sent overseas. In 1917, he was invalided home to a hospital in Kingston after developing pneumonia while on duty in the trenches. In the a hospital, he met a young nurse, Edith Pennington from Campbellford, and upon his discharge, they were married and returned to town. After farming on the English Line and later on Church Street North, he began an egg grading station, setting up this business on Bridge Street East where the Aron Theatre now stands. In 1940, the business became known as P.H. Macmillan and Son when his son, Hector, became a partner.

P. H. Macmillan, a community-minded man, was a member of the Town Council of Campbellford for twenty-five years, filling every position except that of Mayor, an office to which he never aspired. He died in 1971 at the age of eighty-seven.

JOHN MACOUN

John Macoun was born in County Down, Ireland, in 1831. He left Ireland for Canada in 1850 with his mother and elder brother, and settled in Seymour Township one month after his nineteenth birthday. After an initial start as a laborer on various township farms, including one purchased by his mother, and a short time spent clerking in a Campbellford store, he eventually bought his own piece of land with a view to clearing it for farming. But after six years of hard work, he quit farming to become a teacher, in spite of having left school at age thirteen. Macoun had a remarkable degree of self-confidence. He studied an English

Grammar text for three days, then walked forty-three miles in winter to talk to the County Inspector, who arranged for him to board and train at a local school. After three weeks of concentrated learning, Macoun returned home in triumph with his teaching certificate. Macoun's first teaching position was in Brighton. In 1860, he took a position at Number 1 School in Belleville. Two years later he married Ellen Terrill of Wooler, and they had three daughters and two sons. In 1869, he was offered the post as Chair of Natural History at Albert College, Belleville.

Ever since boyhood, John had avidly pursued botany as a hobby, and used all his spare time to increase his knowledge, and to reinforce field observation by intense theoretical study. He had already done some local exploring in summer vacations, including a trek to the source of the Trent River, and took his first trip west into Lake Superior. In July 1872, Macoun set off on what would be the greatest adventure of his life. He planned to see the prairies by going as far west as Manitoba. However, on the lake steamer between Collingwood and Owen Sound, he chanced to meet Sandford Fleming, the CPR's Engineer-in-Chief, who was on his way to make a personal survey of railway's route west. Macoun was asked by Fleming to join the expedition as official botanist, and as a result ended up seeing, not just the prairies, but the whole west – Winnipeg, Edmonton, north to Fort McLeod, through the Rockies and down the Fraser River – ending up in Victoria, after many hair-raising experiences, some seventeen months later.

Macoun undertook four more expeditions: in 1875, into the Peace River area of Alberta; in 1879, along the North and South Saskatchewan Rivers; in 1880, into the southern region of Saskatchewan; and in 1881, through the lake and river systems of Manitoba. After each expedition, Macoun wrote lengthy reports for the Canadian government, in which he advanced some fairly revolutionary theories about the farming potential of the southern parts of the prairies west of Calgary. While earlier explorers had considered these regions to be part of the American desert, and therefore unfit for settlement and agriculture, Macoun was extremely enthusiastic about their farming potential.

In 1881, he was asked to give his views at a meeting with Jim Hill, an American railway magnate and member of the four man CPR Executive Committee. By this time Macoun's reputation, both as botanist and explorer, was international; his lectures were attended by prominent politicians and businessmen, and his word carried a great deal of weight. Hill wanted the CPR to take a southern route across the Prairies and through the Rockies, not the longer northern route already surveyed, but needed settlers along that route to make the railroad pay for itself, by hauling in goods and taking out farm produce. Macoun's testimony helped Hill's case, which means that the breathtaking rail journey through Kicking Horse Pass owes its existence in part to an Irish immigrant from Seymour Township.

In 1882, at the age of fifty-one, John Macoun left Belleville to take up residence in Ottawa. He already had a permanent position with the government, and now became active at the highest levels of scientific endeavor. He became one of twenty members of the new Royal Society of Canada, and started work on the first complete catalogue of Canadian plants. He continued to travel into regions like the Gaspe and Nova Scotia, Cape Breton and Sable Island, back west as far as the railway went, to England and Ireland, and to Vancouver Island. Over the years, he extended his studies to ornithology, and in 1899, began a Catalogue of Canadian Birds. In 1903, he spent his first summer in thirty years at home, remaining in Ottawa while one of his sons went exploring in his place.

Between 1904 and 1911, when he suffered a slight stroke, he continued travelling and working on studies of such varied subjects as bird and marine life, seaweeds, trees, and seedless plants. In 1912, he and his wife resettled in Sidney, B.C. and he restricted his work to trips around Vancouver Island itself and some of the neighboring islands. The death of his son, James, in January 1920 was a great blow, and he died as a result of heart failure the following July.

John Macoun rose from almost entirely self-taught beginnings to became Canada's foremost botanist, had some fifty species of plants, mosses and lichens named after him, made several incredible explorations of the Canadian west, and had a major influence on the final choice of the CPR's route through the Rockies.

ELIZABETH SCOTT MATHESON

Elizabeth Scott was born in 1866 in the stone one-room cottage owned by Alexander Donald, her grandfather, postmaster for the Burnbrae Post Office. James and Jeannette Donald Scott raised a family of eleven children here until they moved to Onion Creek, Manitoba, in 1878. Everyone was always urging Elizabeth Scott onward. First, it was her brother Tom, who encouraged her to give up an apprenticeship as a seamstress and study teaching. She did this at age seventeen, and went to teach at the Marchmont Home for Homeless Children in Belleville. After only a month she was told: "You're a square peg in a round hole, Lizzie." Ellen Bilbrough, who financed the home, paid for her to attend the Women's Medical College in Kingston, but at the end of her first year, in 1887, Elizabeth could not afford to continue.

In 1892, she married John Grace Matheson. He had been a somewhat wild youth, but after his marriage, he settled down and became a missionary for the Anglican Church at Onion Lake. The area included two Cree Indian Reserves, Sekaskooch and Makoo. Matheson traded furs, taught religion to the Indians, and mastered the Cree language. Elizabeth ran the mission school. One day, an old Indian came to the mission and asked Elizabeth to amputate his badly infected foot. Elizabeth could not do it, so he had his son do it, and he survived. The incident prompted John Matheson to urge Elizabeth to return to her medical studies. A doctor was needed at the mission and it would have to be Elizabeth.

She enrolled for her second year at Manitoba Medical College in 1895. That same year she gave birth to her third child. Since she was the only female student in the course, she chose to continue her studies at the Ontario Medical College for Women in Toronto, Ontario. She graduated in 1898 as Doctor of Medicine, becoming the first woman doctor in the west.

When she returned to the mission, she set up a clinic. Many times she would cross the prairie fields by horse and carriage to call on ailing patients on the reserves. The Cree people came to call her Mu-ske-kes-qua – Cree for Medicine Woman. However, the medical profession did not willingly acknowledge her credentials, and she was constantly recalled for re-examinations, while male doctors were allowed to quietly continue their medical practices without re-qualifying.

A serious epidemic of smallpox in 1901 put her skill as a doctor to the test. Her tireless efforts were finally officially recognized and she was appointed the government doctor for the Indian people. In 1918, she was appointed assistant medical inspector to the Winnipeg Public Schools, a position she held until she retired in 1941, at the age of seventy-five. In 1935, Dr. Matheson paid a visit to her relatives in Seymour Township.

Elizabeth Scott Matheson had nine children. The Matheson Mission home was also open to many foster children. This much loved wife, doctor, and mother lived until 1957 when she was ninety-one. The story of her long and illustrious career is told in the book, *The Doctor Rode Sidesaddle*, by Ruth Matheson Buck.

ARCHIE JOHN MEYERS

Archie John Meyers was born on a farm near Listowel on July 13, 1880. He went to school in the Town of Listowel and played hockey for the Listowel Intermediate team which won the Ontario championship in 1898. He attended McGill University and, in 1902, married Hilda Kennedy. She, along with their first born child, died of tuberculosis in 1906. At this time, Archie was working in the drafting department of the Locomotive and Machine Company in Pittsburgh, Pennsylvania, and he eventually took charge of the department. In 1908, he married Hilda's sister, Winnifred Lenora Kennedy, and they had two children, Donald Homer, born April 12, 1913, and Lois Gwendolyn born April 7, 1916.

From 1908 to 1918, Archie was in charge of the drafting department for the construction of the steel cantilever bridge which crossed the St. Lawrence River between Quebec City and Point Levis, providing both rail and road transport. The family then moved to Peterborough where they resided at the home of Archie's father, John Wenger Meyers. Archie designed and supervised the construction of the cement grain storage elevators of the Peterborough Cereal Company Limited, which was owned and operated by his father. At this time, the Peterborough Cereal Company acquired control of a flour and feed mill in Campbellford, and Archie became general manager of the Campbellford subsidiary. He purchased a large brick house at 93 Frank Street, Campbellford, and moved his family there in 1919. The mill operated successfully until 1926 when the grain and produce market crashed and caused the company to declare bankruptcy.

Archie Meyers was elected to Town Council in Campbellford in 1920, and was elected Mayor from 1921 to 1926. During this time, he supervised the installation of water mains, sewers and cement sidewalks. In 1926, he opened a garage and service station. He purchased a 1927 Willys Knight stake truck and started hauling between the Campbellford Cloth Company Ltd. and its parent company, the Toronto Carpet Company in Toronto. This was the beginning of his trucking company. He also purchased a small bakeshop in Campbellford and expanded it to serve an area within approximately twenty miles. As the roads were generally not cleared of snow in the winter, he adapted three Model T Ford trucks for snow-ploughing. Two of these were used to deliver bakery products, and the third was sold to a local doctor to replace his horse-drawn sleigh. In 1927, he was elected to the Public Utilities Commission and he served until his retirement from public life in 1958. During these years, he worked with the manager, Percy Denyes, to ensure the efficient and economical operation of the local power plant.

In 1929, he purchased the old Covert Arena, renamed it the Meyers Arena, and sponsored the junior hockey team. His son, who was still attending high school, took charge of this operation in off-school hours and on weekends. After two winters, the depression peaked and his son graduated, forcing the closing of the arena. When the former music hall and silent movie theatre on Front Street South closed and the building was purchased by the Masonic Lodge, Archie used his engineering skill to redesign and rebuild the condemned structure with a steel self-supporting framework, new foundation, basement and second storey. It served the town for many years as the only recreation and meeting hall, as well as providing excellent accommodation for the three Masonic Lodges.

In 1931, he designed and built the first school bus to serve the new Campbellford High School. It replaced the CNR special train which had transported about forty students from Keene and Hastings to Campbellford daily. The bus was driven by his son, Don, and, because of its solid oak, square construction, was called the Meyers Egg Crate. The students composed songs and poems about it which they rendered during the hour long journey to and from Keene. The same year, A. J. Meyers purchased two small two-ton trucks and Meyers Transport was a reality. These trucks travelled to Toronto on alternate days taking written purchase orders from Campbellford merchants to Toronto each day, phoning them to the wholesale supply houses, and picking up the shipments the same day.

In 1946, A. J. Meyers joined a small group of businessmen who planned to build a thirty-bed hospital in Campbellford. A. J. became chairman of the Building Committee. Money for the project was hard to raise, and it was 1948 before there seemed any hope that financing could be secured. The Committee felt that the public would respond with greater support if they could see some activity on the site. In February of that year, a contract for the foundation and concrete floor was given to W. Spencer and Sons for $9,600.

By the winter of 1949–50, this work was completed and the ground floor closed in, but sufficient funds were still not available to complete the structure. A. J. designed, and had built in the Meyers Transport repair shop and garage, a six-foot long box stove made of two oil drums welded together. This was used for the next two winters to keep the frost from damaging the partially completed hospital building. The stove burned four-foot long hand-split hardwood cut from a woodlot near Allan's Mills in which Archie had part interest. The wood was trucked to the hospital by Meyers Transport and the stove burned twenty-four hours a day during the winter, with A. J. Meyers assuming all costs. In 1950, Archie's wife, Winnifred, died suddenly, and he tried to overcome his grief and loneliness by working for the hospital.

During the next two years, Archie also kept busy building one of the first houseboats to ply the Trent River System. It was a life long dream come true when the twenty-six foot long boat, made of cedar and aluminum and powered with a twenty-five horsepower outboard motor, was launched in 1952. He kept it at his son's cottage between Hastings and Trent River, slept aboard most summers and hosted weekend trips. In the fall, Archie and three of his old friends, Dr. O. C. Watson, Glen Thompson, and Lou Glover, used the boat for duck hunting. He personally maintained and operated this boat for fifteen years. It was then moved to a waterfront lot near Trent River Village, where it was converted to a small cottage for Archie's granddaughter, and her two small children.

In 1952, additional funds became available from the Provincial Government to incorporate into the Campbellford Memorial Hospital a ward for the care of chronic patients. In November, the Building Committee entered into a contract with Spencers to complete the building. At the official opening in August 1953, Archie was presented with the key to the building. At the annual meeting in 1954, the Hospital Board paid tribute to A. J. Meyers for his untiring efforts in his eight-year tenure as Chairman of the Building Committee, for his donation of several properties on Oliver Road, and his financial contributions. He was also made an

Honorary Chairman of the Board for life. At a Civic Reception and Banquet in 1958, Archie was presented with a gold watch to recognize his lifelong service to the Town of Campbellford.

After his retirement, Archie maintained his interest in lawn bowling, and, in 1965, he skipped a team to win the Corbin Bowling Tournament in Belleville, securing one of the most sought after trophies in Ontario. He continued to drive until he was ninety and everyone respected his right to double park in front of the poolroom on Front Street while he went in to get the morning paper. Archie passed away quietly in November 1973 in his beloved hospital.

PAUL GERARD O'SULLIVAN

Known locally as 'O'Mally,' Paul was born in Campbellford on July 3, 1918, to George O'Sullivan and Mary Nathan. The family included Francis (Frank), Margaret, and Joseph (Father Joe), former pastor of St. Jerome's Parish in Warkworth. Paul's grandparents, Cornelius and Mary O'Sullivan, sailed from County Cork to Canada as very young children in 1852, and their Irish Catholic heritage is a significant part of the family's life. On March 17, 1999, green balloons decorated the exterior of the O'Sullivan residence at 76 Booth Street North, the Irish music could be heard blaring away, the dinner table was set with green serviettes, an Irish stew was simmering on the stove, ladies were wearing green corsages on their green blouses, green Irish decorative pieces were all over the house, and Paul was resplendent in his green shirt, tie and sweater. St. Patrick and Paul's ancestors would have been proud.

Paul attended St. Mary's School and Campbellford High School, until his graduation from Grade 13 in 1937. Two of Paul's earliest memories are the building of the High School and the installation of the sewers on Booth Street in 1925. As a teenager, he worked in his father's grocery store at 48 Bridge Street East, telephone number 188, and went to the family cottage at Crowe Bridge in the summer. He played hockey, tennis, golf, and softball, went to the movies, starred in High School musicals, such as Sunbonnet Sue opposite Pauline Rutherford, and chummed around with his many friends, Lloyd Richardson, Jim Kerr, Ken Kingston, Bob Linton and Abe Robertson.

While still attending high school, Paul began working at the Bank of Montreal at the north-east corner of Front and Bridge Streets on March 15, 1937. Three days later, faulty wiring caused the bank building to burn down and it was relocated temporarily to the opposite corner at 3 Front Street South, present location of The Top Drawer, until it was rebuilt on its former location. Paul was transferred to the bank branch in Lindsay in 1940, living in a boarding house on Sussex Street. He joined the Air Force in 1941, and was posted to Rockcliffe near Ottawa as a guard for hangers, aircraft, and technical buildings. He went on to Initial Training School at the Eglinton Hunt Club where he qualified as a pilot. He was then transferred to London, Ontario, for an eight week Elementary Flying school course. He went on to Aylmer, Ontario, to Flying School for a three-month training course for flying Harvards. His first night solo was harrowing, when he found himself totally lost over Lake Erie. When he did find land again, he could sight no identifying terrain. He received his wings on his birthday in 1942.

Paul went to Quebec Airways at Arnprior for an instructor's course. Private flying schools had been conscripted by the RCAF for basic training, and Paul became the Flight Commander over sixteen trainees, some being accomplished bush pilots. It was during this period that Paul was labeled 'O'Mally' by an American cohort, and the name stuck. In 1943, Paul became a Flight Lieutenant and was transferred to Trois Rivières where he met Suzanne Gauthier whom he married on October 9, of that year. Paul and Suzanne (Sue) came back to Campbellford in 1945, to the family home on Booth Street where they still live. After the war, the Bank of Montreal offered him a job, but Excelsior Insurance offered him a more lucrative salary. Paul worked for the Excelsior Insurance from 1945–48 and then opened his own agency in general insurance. He took a three year correspondence course from Queen's University, Kingston, earning his Chartered Life Underwriters' Certificate. In 1949, he also opened a real estate business which he sold on in 1988.

Paul and Sue have lived a busy life in Campbellford. They have always been active in St. Mary's Catholic Church, supportive of community endeavors and have proudly raised their family to be fine and productive citizens. They have four daughters, Maureen, Joanne, Erin, and Nicole, and one son, Terry. Paul has been very active with the Rotary club and was President in 1960. He received the prestigious Paul Harris Fellowship Award in July 1988 in recognition of his exemplary Rotary service. He served as the Campbellford Memorial Hospital Treasurer for seven years and is a Life Member of the Hospital Association.

FRANK AND DORIS POTTS

Doris Margaret Rannie Potts was born on September 19, 1913 at the family farm "Fogorig," in Seymour Township. Her parents, Ed Rannie and Charlotte Jane Donald, also raised two other children, Oscar Alexander (1907–1977), and Florence Sophia Chatten, born in 1923. The Rannie family settled in Canada when Doris' great grandfather, a farmer and blacksmith, arrived from Scotland to farm near Menie in 1842. Doris attended Masson's School, S.S. #7 Seymour. After graduating from Campbellford High School, she went to Peterborough Normal School in 1932–33. She taught in area schools for thirty-eight years and continued to take summer courses. After qualifying as a librarian, she established the school library at Hillcrest Public School. Doris retired from teaching in July 1973. She was proud of having served as President of the Northumberland and Durham chapter of the Women Teachers' Federation of Ontario during 1970–71.

Doris met Francis John Potts in 1931. Frank was born on April 5, 1914, at Concession 1, Lot 7, Seymour Township, to John Wesley Potts (1868–1955) and Ida May Forrest (1877–1951). Frank had four sisters. His great grandfather, George Potts, came to Canada from Kent County, England in 1837 with his wife Rebecca, and settled on the top of the sand hill known as Potts Island in the Percy Reach/Bradley Bay area of the Trent. George Potts' first intention was to build a hotel on the sand hill, and when this did not materialize, he moved to the American mid-west and started a ranch. Unfortunately, before the family could join him, he was robbed of his cattle money and murdered. Frank attended English Line School and Campbellford High School. Through his father's guidance, Frank became quite proficient in swimming, handling a canoe, and the use of fire arms. Trapping, fishing, frogging and guiding became his first career, which, during the Depression, furnished Frank with a respectable living.

Doris and Frank were married in 1940. They rented an apartment on Queen Street while Frank worked in the woollen mill. They were separated while Frank was in the army during the World War II. Doris continued to teach, and shortly after his return, they purchased a home and the general store in Menie in 1946. Frank managed the store, acted as secretary-treasurer for both the Burnbrae School and the Menie Cheese Factory, and worked in the office at the Community Livestock Auction at Hoard's Station for twenty years. They owned and operated the general store until 1965.

In 1986, Doris received the Volunteer Service Award from the Ontario Ministry of Citizenship and Culture, in recognition of her work in support of the Seymour East Women's Institute and the Campbellford Horticultural Society. In 1987, the Local Architectural Conservation Advisory Committee gave Frank and Doris a certificate of thanks for their contribution to heritage conservation, as evidenced by the preservation of the historic features of their general store. In 1996, they were given the Ontario Heritage Foundation Award for their contribution to local heritage conservation, having been nominated by both the Town of Campbellford and Seymour Township. Doris and Frank are founding members of the Campbellford/Seymour Heritage Society, and have actively preserved family histories and local heritage. They have been members of Hoard's United Church since shortly after their marriage, with Doris serving as choir leader and pianist for many years, as well as an elder. Frank has been steward, elder, trustee, and cemetery board member. In 1993, the Potts moved to town to settle at 40 Grand Road, making it easier to carry on their volunteer efforts.

GEORGE STEPHEN POTTS

George Stephen Potts, generally known to district residents as 'Uncle George', was born on Potts Island, near Percy Boom in Brighton Township on April 8, 1866. He was the son of Stephen J. Potts and Harriet Stollery. George had several brothers and sisters: Eliza, James William, Phoebe, John Wesley, Charles, and Angelina Jane. George did not begin his formal education until he was ten years old. The Potts children were taken to and from school in Murray Township by their father to protect them from attacks by roaming wolves and bears.

George enjoyed nicknaming the people who lived on English Line. There was Plough Point Ned, Crummy Bill, Red Bill, Little Ned, Old Billy and Humpy Dick. George was a local character and story teller. One story is of him and Crummy Bill out hunting, when George decided to light up his pipe, not realizing that some gunpowder had leaked out into his pocket mixing with his tobacco. As soon as the lighted match reached the bowl of the pipe he said, "I never saw a brighter flash of lightning" as the bowl disappeared and his eyebrows were scorched off. Crummy Bill rolled on the ground laughing at this spectacle. Another time he was fined for not paying for two sweat pads, felt pads placed under a horse collar, that he had obtained in Warkworth. He travelled by boat to Meyersburg, and then walked the remaining four miles. Meeting the dealer at the hotel, George asked him if he remembered two ninety pound bags of potatoes having been delivered with no pay. Apologies resulted and he was invited to stay for dinner.

In 1905, George married Caroline (Dolly) Adams when he was thirty-nine. His proposal words were: "I don't think there is anybody that would suit me any better." They were married for thirty-two years, living in a house that he had bought from William Diamond on Concession 1, Lot 12, Seymour Township. George also welcomed Caroline's brother, Jim Adams, and her sister, Eliza Brown, into his home as part of the family. After Caroline's death, George married her cousin, Lida, but unfortunately her ill health and subsequent death resulted in a very short marriage. After Lida's passing, Harry Sanders moved into George's home. This too was not for a long time period, as George's house caught fire and all was lost. George then moved in with his sister, Mrs. Peter Stephens, her son, Alex, and his wife, Irene.

Much of George's early life was spent on the Trent River. He hunted, fished, trapped, did log drives, and guided, while living in a cabin on Hickory Island. There is an interesting story told by George to family and friends. One cold autumn morning at about daylight, he heard two shots and then someone calling for help. He got into his skiff and rowed toward the calls. Some distance down the shore of the island, he found an overturned canoe and a duck hunter in the water. The hunter's arm was over the end of the canoe, with a twelve gauge double barrel shotgun in hand. George hauled the virtually drowned individual into his skiff and

George Potts, as photographed by F. C. Bonnycastle, sometime in the 1920s.

Photo courtesy of Frank and Doris Potts.

headed back to his cabin. The survivor was Stewart Cock, son of Robert Cock, whose property is now a portion of Ferris Park. A reward was offered to George for saving Stewart's life but George would not accept any payment. When Stewart still insisted on a reward, George said the only thing that he would consider was acceptance of Stewart's shotgun when he was finished with it. This was a British-made Greener and considered quite valuable. Agreement was reached. When Stewart Cock died, the shotgun was willed to George. He later gave it to his nephew Frank Potts who in turn passed it on to a younger family member.

Uncle George died at the age of one hundred and two in October 1968. He had enjoyed a grand birthday that year with congratulations flowing in from far and near. The nattily dressed George said that he felt in better health at one hundred and two than he did at one hundred.

CATHERINE CLEMENT REDDEN

On July 28, 1950, Catherine (Cathy) Down was born at Belleville General Hospital to Wesley Clement Down and Margaret Louise Barrie, who lived Concession 4, Lot 27, Brighton Township. Cathy's childhood home was a farm purchased from Wesley's grandmother, Mary Anne Down, born in Shiloh, Cramahe Township in 1868. Mary Anne Down and her husband, John Wesley Down, born 1850, farmed this property which was settled by Richard Down, born 1790, the first of the Down family to immigrate to Canada from England in the early 1800s. Cathy's father, Wesley Down, born in 1919 to Elizabeth Clement and John Arthur Down, was raised on the adjacent farm. Cathy's mother, Margaret (1922–1970), was born and raised on a farm near Galt, now Cambridge. Margaret's parents, William Carrick and Agnes King, were descendants of early Scottish settlers.

Cathy was the first of eight children: Patricia, Jean, Nancy, David, Sandra, Louise, and Richard. Cathy attended Stone, Holland and Orland schools in

Brighton Township, and East Northumberland Secondary School in Brighton. In her elementary school years, Cathy recalls fishing in the creek, herding the cows for milking, having picnics on Vinegar Hill, which was the site of the original Richard Down homestead, walking a mile and a half on a narrow gravel road to school, and being able to go to town on a Saturday if the chores were done. The 4-H club played a major part in Cathy's life. She achieved provincial honours (12 clubs), became a 4-H leader, and President of the Junior Farmers of Northumberland County in 1973–4. In history class, she developed an early love for political debate. Cathy began to sing competitively at age four and won the Rotary Award Scholarship Senior Vocal prize in Belleville in 1975. In high school, she enjoyed the marching bands and musicals. Her first part in a musical production was in "Where is the Mayor?"

After graduating from Peterborough Teacher's College in 1970, she began teaching at Kent School, where Principal Bert Whitfield became a strong influence. He gave her the incentive to continue her education through the summer months at both Queen's and Trent Universities. At Kent School she taught grades three and six, and was also the music teacher for ukulele, recorder, voice, and choir.

Cathy and Brian Carswell Redden were married July 21, 1973. Brian was born at 246 Grand Road, Campbellford, to Inez and C.L. Redden. C.L. is well remembered as being associated with the CNR, where he was a station agent. Cathy and Brian have two sons, both born in Campbellford. Andrew William Redden, born on November 1, 1976, is now a legislative assistant at Queen's Park. Ian Thomas Redden was born on April 5, 1978, and has joined the family business, working on the Internet Service. In 1988, Cathy became involved in the family business, working on the Advertising Channel. In the fall of 1988, during Hector Macmillan's term as Mayor of Campbellford, Cathy was acclaimed to Town Council. She remained on Council until 1991 when she ran for Mayor against Charles Ibey and Bert Rogers, defeating both. In 1994 she again defeated Charles Ibey, and in 1997 she defeated Don Pollock for Mayor of the amalgamated Municipality of Campbellford/ Seymour.

The Church has always played an important role in Cathy's life. From 1970 to 1980, she was in the choir at St. John's United Church, and participated in solo, duet, and quartet performances. She taught Sunday School, and is a past president and life member of the United Church Women. She was a member of the Warkworth Festival singers for three years, and later she took on several roles in musical productions directed by Brian Finley.

Since 1976, she has been associated with the Campbellford/Seymour Agricultural Society. In 1984, she became involved with the Lake Ontario Regional Library Board and served as the Ontario Bi-Centennial chairperson for

Campbellford/Seymour. The New Year's Day Levee was introduced that year, with Jack Parsons as the first Town Crier, and the Levee has since become a tradition. In 1986, Cathy was a founding member of the Women's Network. She also helped form the Hillcrest Parent's Group, which raised funds for equipment and school supplies, and lobbied for the establishment of crossing guards.

During Cathy's term of office, many changes have occurred. When she was chair of the Canada Day celebrations in 1989, a major fire broke out in a building at the corner of Bridge Street and Grand Road, just across from where the celebrations were taking place. Cathy and others initiated a collection for the victims. This was the beginning of the Fire and Emergency Fund, which is still active today. In 1992, the new Campbellford/Seymour logo was introduced and the lights were installed under the bridge. Road work and major infrastructure were completed on primary arteries. The library addition and interior renovations were completed, the Multicare Lodge was built, several new businesses, such as No Frills and Tim Horton's were introduced, and a new Canadian Tire Store was built. A draft of a Strategic and Official Plan, incorporating Campbellford, Seymour, Percy and Hastings, was completed. Cathy credits her staff and Councils for much of the above.

RUSSELL ROWE

Russell Rowe was born in 1914 to Harold and Jennie Rowe, who farmed in Seymour Township. He attended elementary school at Stanwood and then boarded in Town to attend Campbellford High School. Following graduation, he attended Peterborough Teacher's College and began teaching at Rylstone School in 1934. He went on to teach in Hamilton but after only seven years, decided to change careers and began selling real estate. When World War II broke out, Russell joined the RCAF in 1941. He became a pilot instructor at Caledonia and achieved the rank of Flight Officer. During the war, Russell's brother, Arthur, was killed overseas. After the war, he became a bond salesman with Harrison and Company for three years. He was transferred from the Hamilton-Waterloo region to eastern Ontario and made Campbellford his temporary headquarters. In 1955, Russell moved to Cobourg. He and his wife, Marjorie McKeown, had six children. During this time, Russell was employed as an investment consultant and stock broker.

In 1963, Russell was elected as the Conservative member for Northumberland in the Ontario Legislature. He continued to hold this seat through four subsequent elections under Premiers John Robarts and William Davis. In 1971, he became Deputy Speaker of the Legislative Assembly and served as Speaker of the House from 1974 to 1978. Colleagues remarked on how Russell brought dignity and prestige to the Speaker's position. During his tenure, he represented Ontario at official functions all over the world. He also served on Standing and Select

Committees on Colleges and Universities, and Economic and Cultural
Nationalism. Despite his busy schedule, he always tried to be responsive to the
individual problems and needs of his constituents. In 1982, Russell retired from
political life, and a gala testimonial dinner held in Port Hope in his honour was a
sell out. The Rowe family suffered further losses in 1975, when Howard, Russell's
brother, was killed in a plane crash while fighting a forest fire in British Columbia.
His sister, Mabel, and her husband, Harold Brunton, lost their lives in a tragic
house fire on the evening after the funeral of his mother, Jennie. Russell passed
away in Cobourg in September 1994.

KEN SISLEY

After forty-five years of delivering mail to the two hundred and thirty
Seymour Township customers on R.R. #5, Ken Sisley retired in March 1990. He
was presented with a plaque from Canada Post commemorating his years of service. As well as delivering the mail, Ken sometimes went beyond the call of duty, to
free horses caught in fencing, or to check elderly customers who were not picking
up their mail. People used to wait by their mailboxes regularly to chat with him,
though it became more infrequent in later years as new people moved into the area.

Ken began his postal career, after returning from war-time duty in September
1944, delivering mail to the route's one hundred and twenty customers in a 1939
Dodge coupe for $100 a month. Before that he had worked on various area
farms, but an injured leg forced him to find a less strenuous job. He also worked
part-time as a nursing orderly at Campbellford Memorial Hospital and at a photo
and gift shop.

MORLEY TANNER

Morley Tanner was born in 1918 in Rawdon Township to Thomas James
Tanner and Margaret Jane Ray. Morley spent his early life there, along with five
siblings. In April 1935, he came to Campbellford to make butter and cheese at the
Trent Valley Butter and Cheese Company owned by Grant Anderson. He met and
married Madge Huble in 1939. Morley worked for a short time for Meyers
Transport and also for Horsman Beverages while Morley Horsman was serving
overseas during World War II. For the next twenty-five years, he operated a car
business. From 1960 to 1975, Morley worked in the investment business.

In 1962, Morley was elected Mayor of Campbellford, an office which he held
until 1974, thus becoming the longest serving mayor. During his tenure, many
changes and improvements occurred. The new bridge was built, as well as the
sewage treatment plant, the water filtration plant, the extension to the
Campbellford Memorial Hospital, the Warkworth Penitentiary, the Community

Centre, the swimming pool, the Senior Citizen's Apartments, the new Post Office, the conversion of the Town Hall, and the moving of the Boy Scout building to Kennedy Park. In 1970, he served on a national commission on taxation.

Morley purchased the Hillsdale Nursing Home which he operated for several years. He then began building houses and factories, totaling over one hundred homes and three plants. No government assistance was involved in any of these building ventures. Fifty-six homes were constructed on the site known as Parkview Estates. Morley and Madge have two sons, Fred and Tom, and six grandchildren. In 1996, he was named Shriner of the Year for the Kawartha area.

BETTY THAIN / KATHERINE ELIZABETH CURLE

Katherine Elizabeth Curle was the food columnist for the Campbellford Herald and other newspapers in Lakefield, Cobourg, Port Hope, and Warkworth from 1975 until the middle of the 1990s. She is the daughter of Allan Curle and the late Ella Cock Curle of R.R. #1, Campbellford. Her lively homespun columns on food preparation and delivery were always informative and fun. She credits her interest in cooking to living on a farm and learning basic culinary techniques from her mother, a superb cook and baker. Katherine, writing under the name Betty Thain, also shared her enthusiasm for cooking through evening courses and day workshops and for a time ran a catering business. In 1987 and 1989, the Campbellford Herald published two cookbooks entitled Cooking with Betty in response to requests from her readers. At present, Katherine, a graduate of Trent University, is employed at Lady Eaton College at that institution where she assists with housing accommodation for residence and off-campus students.

DR. JACK EDWARD TRIMBLE

Jack Trimble was born in Toronto on October 9, 1917, to James Duncan Trimble and Beatrix Mary Johnson. Jack and his two brothers, Fred and Duncan, grew up on Hillsdale Avenue, Toronto, attended Davisville Public School and later North Toronto Collegiate. Following high school, Jack enrolled at the University of Guelph to study veterinary medicine, graduating in 1940. He then moved to Campbellford, where he met Helen McGee, whom he married November 8, 1941. They remained here for a year and then moved to Calgary, where Jack became a meat inspector with Burns Meat Packers. Their first child, Jim, was born in Calgary on March 22, 1943. The family returned to Campbellford, where daughter Judy was born on December 30, 1947.

Jack's first medical office was on Front Street, behind the Morgan's Garage office. Later, he moved it to the basement of his home at 34 Booth Street. His final move was to 84 Bridge Street East, and he often had Don Graham assist him. Jack was the only veterinarian in the area, with both large and small animal practice.

There are many stories about Jack and his animals. Frank Potts tells of Jack going to a farm to attend to a cow. The farmer was not present, so Jack just carried on with his job. When the animal had been taken care of, Jack noticed a lonely pig in his sty, found some paint, crawled into the sty and painted eye glasses on the pig's face. He was just leaving his calling card.

Cy Johnson, Jack's neighbour on Steelcrest Road, told of watching Jack rescue a frog. Jack was gardening, and came across a snake with a frog stuck sideways in its mouth. The snake was having no luck turning the frog so that it could be swallowed. Jack picked up a stick, whacked the snake who immediately spit out the frog. The frog was so grateful that it literally followed Jack around the garden for the rest of the day.

A similar thing happened with a heifer which had not been eating or drinking, and appeared to be failing. When Jack was called, he reached down the heifer's throat, and pulled out an old rubber boot heel. The heifer would not leave Jack's side, and kept nudging him as if it was saying "thanks."

Jack had a 'friend,' Gramps, who went with him on his calls. People would see Gramps appear from nowhere, and wonder what was up. It turned out that Gramps, who was a groundhog, reserved a space next to the car engine, and when they reached their destination he would just pop out, wait for Jack to do his job, and then hop back into his allotted space to ride back home with his friend, Jack.

Jack and Helen (McGee) Trimble, ca. 1980.
Photo courtesy of Judy Barton.

Cy also tells of Jack being in Yellowstone National Park camping with his family. Jack had put the Coleman cooler under the car, went swimming and came back to see a bear walking away with the cooler. Jack ranted and raved at the bear, his arms flailing, frightening the bear so that it dropped the cooler and ran toward Jack. Jack was terrified, but the bear could not catch him because it kept sliding in "something". Finally, it just ran off into the woods.

Jack had a wonderful sense of humour, and loved to have fun, but was totally dedicated to his profession. Bill Scott speaks of Jack in a different vein. Bill's father, W.F. Scott owned Valley View Farm on Highway 30. Jack was often at the farm, to do blood testing on the cattle. These cattle were frequently shipped to the U.S. and to Puerto Rico, and to ensure safe delivery, Jack would go along as their "cow sitter" on the trip. He would usually stay with the cattle for a week to guarantee their health.

Jack retired in 1977 and there was a large retirement party at the Campbellford Arena. Jack, and his wife Helen, stood in the reception line for hours greeting the well wishers. After the dinner, speeches, and dancing came the highlight of the evening. Dressed in Jack's overalls and hat, Howard Sheppard, MPP for Northumberland, sat back in a motorized golf cart driven by Alex Rutherford. The cart was a surprise gift from the area farmers as a thank you for all that Jack had done for them over the years. Jack and Helen later bought a property in Dunedin, Florida, and they spent their time equally between Campbellford and Dunedin. Jack had good retirement years and passed away on July 8, 1989.

LILLIAN POTTEN-TURNER

Lillian was born and grew up in North Toronto. She attended Northern Technical and Commerce School and then married Sgt. Leonard Potten. Len served overseas in World War II, and when he returned, they settled in Hastings where he was Chief of Police. They moved back to the Toronto area, where Len was head of Crime Prevention for the Metro Police Force, and Lillian was a Supervisor of Accounts Payable at Oshawa Wholesale. Over the years they had five children, Catherine, Charles, Len, Carol and Joan. In 1972, when retirement approached for Len, they bought a home in Seymour Township. Unfortunately, Len passed away prior to retirement. Lillian decided to remain in the Campbellford area and opened the first H&R Block franchise. During the time she owned and operated the franchise, Lillian married Arthur Turner, a retired Metro Toronto policeman who had grown up in Hastings.

Lillian is active in support of the Library, Northumberland Arts and Crafts, Campbellford Memorial Hospital, Ferris Park, and the Heritage Society. She was the first female president of the Campbellford Chamber of Commerce in 1982–83. She received the "Service above Self Award" from the Rotary Club in 1992, in recognition of her financial support for the Boston Marathon. On April

26, 1993, Lillian became the first female member of the Rotary Club. She was elected as a Director of the Rotary Club for 1999–2000.

Lillian co-chaired the "Elephant Day" celebrations in recognition of the centennial of the opening of the Campbellford bridge built in 1877. When the bridge originally was opened, an elephant was ridden over the structure to ensure that it was safe for travel. Lillian found that she would not recommend riding on one of these great and surprisingly hairy creatures while wearing shorts.

Lillian entered politics in 1988, first as councillor, and then as Deputy Reeve from 1994 until 1997. During her political life, Lillian has worked on every Tourism Committee and she promotes Campbellford wherever and whenever she has the opportunity. The thirty-foot tall, lighted, Two Dollar Coin that is a prominent fixture in Old Mill Park, was Lillian's idea.

Lillian has owned and operated The Top Drawer clothing store at 3 Front Street South for the past fourteen years. In 1996, Lillian received the "Person of the Year" award for unselfish community service from the Chamber of Commerce. In 1997, the Chamber gave Lillian the "Citizen of the Year" award for her service to the community. On Canada Day in 1997, Lillian was presented with the "Canada Day" award from the citizens of Campbellford.

HELEN ATKINSON WRIGHT

Helen Atkinson Wright was born in 1909, the eldest child of William Atkinson and Bessie Campbell of Norwood, both of whom were teachers. The Atkinson family traces its roots in Canada to 1832, when English naval officer, Thomas Atkinson, arrived with his family and began farming on land overlooking Crowe Bay. That property is still owned by descendants of the Atkinson family today.

Her father's devotion to teaching influenced Helen, and, after graduating from Campbellford High School in 1929, she attended Peterborough Normal School. Her first teaching position was in Ottawa, but adventure called, and she applied for a position in Black River Township near Matheson, northwest of Kirkland Lake, where she taught for two years. The Wright family, with whom she boarded, introduced her to their eldest son when he came home for a visit and there was an immediate attraction. William Wright was a bachelor teacher on a CPR railway school car, operating out of Fort William, northwest to Kenora.

The idea of a travelling school in a railway coach was conceived by J. B. McDougall, school inspector for Northern Ontario in the 1920s. While travelling in the northern part of the province, he noted that there were no facilities to educate the children of track workers who were so vital to the safe operation of the railway. He saw that the work crews who did major repairs were living in old railway coaches and he envisioned education being delivered in a similar fashion. His idea of a better quality coach fitted up as a schoolroom with desks, blackboards and libraries in half the coach, and tiny living quarters in the other half was accepted by the CNR. The first school coach went out on the CNR line north of Capreol in 1926 and was so successful that the CPR fitted one out for a north-

Helen Atkinson Wright and her husband, William Wright, in front of their railway school car, ca. 1955.

Photo courtesy of Shirley Little.

western Ontario route in 1928. William Wright was the applicant chosen for the position of teacher. He loved the challenge of the north and, in Helen, saw a potential wife with the qualities which would enable her to cope with the demands of an unusual life style. They married in August of 1933. Helen assisted him by teaching children with special needs and with language difficulties.

The railways were so pleased with the response to the venture that five more cars followed on different lines. The Wright car was transferred in 1939 to the Chapleau subdivision where it served children at six different stops. Pupils were from many different backgrounds – First Nations, French-Canadian, Italian, and Finnish – and got a basic education in grades one to eight. Six to eight pupils at a stop got a week of intensive teaching followed by five weeks of assigned home-work. The Department of Education paid for the teachers and the school supplies, and the railway provided and maintained the school cars and was also responsible for moving them. The co-operation and support over the years was remarkable and the appreciation from the families was heart-warming. Helen and Will formed many enduring friendships over the thirty-seven years they spent on the rails and raised four children of their own. It was no life for sissies, and the teachers and their wives on the seven school cars made a life-time commitment, both to the task and to each other.

CPR School Car #2, in which the Wrights worked and lived, was phased out in 1967 but found a place in a railway museum at St. Constant in the province of Quebec. Helen and Will left their home on wheels for a solid stone bungalow in Bobcaygeon where they enjoyed life in a fixed location until Helen's death in 1990 and Will's death in 1999. Their daughter, Shirley Wright, was a pupil in the school car operated by her parents, and after completing grade eight, she came to live with Atkinson relatives in Campbellford so that she could attend Campbellford High School. She married Bill Little of Seymour West in 1953 and raised six children in Seymour Township.

MARY MARGARET WEST

Mary Margaret West was the great-granddaughter of William West, a native of County Antrim, Ireland, and Elizabeth Gilpin, who settled on Concession 6, Lot 6, Seymour Township prior to 1857. Her grandparents were Samuel West and Martha Emily Gothard. Her father, Charles William (Carl), was born on the family homestead, married Helen M. Douglas, and became an outstanding engineer who worked on both the Trent Canal and the St. Lawrence Seaway.

Carl and his wife moved to Thorold and Mary Margaret was born there on August 15, 1925. After graduating from Osgoode Law School in Toronto, she joined Ontario Hydro in 1951 as a corporate lawyer. During her tenure with

Ontario Hydro, she held the positions of Associate Solicitor, Associate Solicitor of Projects and Contracts, Senior Solicitor, and Associate General Council of Corporate Affairs. Mary Margaret, the last of the West family to bear the name, died on May 17, 1986. Her ashes are buried in the small West's Corners Cemetery located at Concession 7, Lot 5, where her forebears are also interred. Her will provided for the continuing maintenance of that cemetery.

The Campbellford area has benefitted significantly from the bequests in her will. She left $800,000 to St. John's United Church, Campbellford District High School, and the Campbellford Public Library. She also bequeathed the family sterling silver tea service to the Seymour West Women's Institute. Her farm estate, the original Gilpin land at Concession 7, Lot 5, where she often walked while on holiday, was left to the protection of the Nature Conservancy of Canada and the Lower Trent Region Conservation Authority. The farm, which has no buildings, is presently a sanctuary for wildlife and home to many species of trees, shrubs, and herbaceous plants.

Chapter   Sixteen

Vignettes

This chapter is a collection of stories from and about some members of the

Campbellford/Seymour community. None of them fitted smoothly into the

previous chapters, but it was felt that they were too interesting to overlook.

Most surfaced while this book was in preparation, either through research

done by members of the Campbellford/Seymour Heritage Society, or

through contributions of local citizens. Some were edited, but some

were left as written by the contributors. Some of them are poignant,

some are humourous, but all of them shed some light on what life

was like in the community in bygone days.

Why a little town read the Riot Act

By EARL MCRAE
Star staff writer CAMPBELLFORD

The precise moment of The Making of Sammy Baird is a source of great controversy here.

Some tell you it was when he took out his six gun and fired the shot into the air.

Others tell you it was when he bamboozled the town mob by hustllng the prisoners out the front door instead of the back.

Most say it was at two minutes after four in the afternoon when the first call came into the jailhouse.

Since majority rules in a just society, the story shall begin at two minutes after four last Saturday afternoon.

Now, Campbellford itself is a river town of 3,600 persons about 30 miles east of Peterborough. There's a chocolate factory and there's a rug factory and they employ most of the townsfolk.

That's during the week.

A Town Without Pity

Sammy Baird is police chief of Campbellford — and a Big Man there since he stood off an angry mob and caused the Riot Act to be read to avoid violence at the jailhouse. But he's also abused by many people — like the one who covered the town's population sign he's holding with obscenities.

There are still the weekends to contend with.

The womenfolk troop downtown to Pace's Fruit Market and the Sharpe Market. Their men drop in front of television sets with a bottle of beer and watch whatsever on. The oldtimers slump on the curb outside Shaw's Billiard Hall and talk about the way it once was. The kids pack Trent Valley Bowling Lanes or the Quick Lunch Café or they roar around town in daddy's car.

Mainly, they roar up and down Front St. because of the dingy red brick building jammed between the Esso gas station and the barber-shop. It's the town jail. It houses the person of Samuel Baird.

He's the town police chief. He chain smokes, has a smalltown haircut of shaved back and sides and when he lifts an arm to scratch his head, the seams of his uniform strain. He's very tough. He's the scourge of all town punks.

Never learn

But punks never learn, so they drag at 80 miles an hour past Sammy Baird's jailhouse on the weekends hoping he'll chase them.

He does – and last Saturday, he caught two of them.

"Call came in about two minutes after four from some people about this truck roaring around town in a dangerous manner," said Baird, 36, who's been chief here for 13 years.

Baird jumped In his cruiser and chased the truck, bringing it to a halt up Front St. There were two kids in the truck. Baird told ————, 21, he may be charged with dangerous driving.

A kid jumped out the passenger side and yelled at Baird: "One of these days I'm gonna mow all you cop bastards down." ————, 19, was arrested for causing a disturbance and drinking liquor under age.

Baird told ———— to beat it. He'd get a summons later. He took ———— down to the cells and locked him up. Then, Sammy spoke to witnesses and charged ———— with careless driving.

It was now about 6:30 and Sammy ran home to change his clothes for his evening job at the Aron Theatre. He's an usher.

Constable Leonard Thompson came on duty. At 7:30 ————'s parents came down to the stationhouse and the kid was released on his own recognizance. Thompson left the station at 8:30 to patrol the town.

He was cruising along when this white convertible passed him. Somebody in the back seat screamed "hey wop" at Thompson.

He chased them into the parking lot of the Sharpe Market where their car screeched to a halt and five of them jumped over the sides and strode over to Thompson's car. He rolled his window up and locked the door.

One kid looked at Thompson and said: "Oh sorry, I thought you were Baird."

"We're gonna get Sam tonight," one of the punks threatened. "We're gonna slit his guts from here to here and spill them all over the street."

The punks sauntered back to their car and left rubber.

Thompson sat there and wondered if they were the same punks who painted all the town's population signs last month with obscenities about Sammy.

Thompson roared over to the Aron Theatre where Sam was ushering people in to see Gentle Giant starring Dennis Weaver.

Sammy told Thompson he'd seen the punks too. They'd driven by shouting obscenities and threats at him. Thompson left on patrol. The punks parked across the street from the theatre and made fun of Sammy being an usher.

Sammy picked up the phone in the lobby and called Thompson at the station. The kids saw him doing it and drove off.

Constable Ernest Stacey of OPP was called up and he and Thompson drove to the theatre. They told Sammy there was a gang of youths up at the Sharpe market parking lot breaking bottles and blocking traffic. Sammy ran home and strapped on his gun belt.

The three cops went to the station and phoned colleagues from Hastings, Peterborough and Brighton. Soon, there were 12 cops at the station. It was 10:15 p.m. The posse jumped into four cars and headed up Front St. to the parking lot

They saw 200 people in the lot pushing and shoving.

Baird and his men arrested three persons. Two for causing a disturbance and one for obstructing police. ——— ——— and ———, 20, were charged with causing a disturbance. ———, 21, for obstruction.

The three were taken down to the jailhouse while the rest of the mob was told to "move along." It did. Right down to the jailhouse.

———, ——— and ——— were thrown into two cells with sagging cots and scribblings on the wall.

200 strong
Meanwhile down Front St. came the mob, 200 strong. Young and old, male and female.

The angry townsfolk tramped down an alley and formed at the back of the jail where they shook their fists and yelled:

"We're coming in to get you Baird. Your blood's gonna flow tonight. Let those three guys out Baird, we're warning ya."

Baird and Thompson did nothing. They thought the mob would go away. It grew bigger and louder. It got so bad, the cops figured they'd better get the prisoners to another jail.

Baird had an OPP cruiser pull up at the back door on pretence the inmates would be coming out the back. The back doors of the cruiser were opened. The mob pressed in. Baird hustled the prisoners out the front door and into another cruiser for the trip to the county jail in Cobourg.

Suddenly, the mob broke into a howl when a police car honked its horn and nudged through for the back door of the station. In the back seat was a guy known as the toughest kid in town. Built like an oak tree and weighing about as much too.

He came out swinging his fists and caught a cop on the jaw dropping him to the ground where someone kicked him in the face. That did it. The crowd went crazy. It surged in on the police car punching and kicking.

Sammy Baird did what he felt he had to do. He took out his .38 and fired a slug into the air.

"Get back," he barked over the din. "Hold it where you are." It worked because the mob froze and quietened.

———, 23, was charged with drunkeness.

In his cell he grabbed the bars and yelled: "C'mon in and get me, get me, outta here." The horde went nuts again and oozed up to the back door.

Charged

——————————— was arrested and charged with assaulting a police officer. He was thrown in the jug too.

Sammy Baird locked the doors of the jailhouse and phoned Ev Steele, the town justice of the peace who also sells cars. Ev ran over, mounted the back steps of the jail and read the Riot Act. After the reading of the Riot Act, you've got 30 minutes to clear out or be charged.

The mob screamed so loud Ev Steele could hardly be heard – until he said the last words: . . . may be sentenced to life imprisonment."

The people shut up then – but they didn't move until there was one minute to go.

At 1:30 a.m. everybody was gone and all was quiet at the back of Sammy Baird's jailhouse.

Baird says 32 of the demonstrators will be charged with causing a disturbance.

But, the incident won't be forgotten and already people in high places are beginning to wonder what has turned Campbellford into a Town without Pity.

The Ontario Police Commission had someone down recently investigating the efficiency of the three-man force. But, OPC chairman Percy Milligan says the investigation was not sparked through any long-running dissatisfaction with the force. "Council requested it and we have conducted a study as how the force can be improved. We do this all the time

Does council, then, feel there's some sweeping up to do?

"I have no time to talk," shouted Mayor Morley Tanner throwing his hands into the air. "The quieter we keep this whole thing, the better. We're gonna have people down here from Ottawa if we aren't careful."

Says one member of the town police commission, who asked to remain anonymous: "Sam has been chief 13 years here and a constable for four years before that.

"He's too close to many of the people here to do the job a chief should do."

But, then he says: "Maybe this thing the other night though will change the feelings of a lot of people. Where else are we gonna get a guy who will stand up to the mob like Sammy did. It was his finest hour."

— *Toronto Daily Star, Sat., April 20, 1968, p.11*
— *names have been deleted to protect the identity of those involved.*
Reprinted with permission —— Toronto Star Syndicate

CRAIG BEATTIE AND HIS "JENNY"

by Margaret Crothers

Craig Beattie (1905–1998) was raised by Dick and Jen McKelvie, and from an early age was interested in learning to fly. His parents would not allow him to take flying lessons because they were concerned for his safety. So when he was in his twenties he went to Leavens Brothers in Belleville and took four flying lessons. Eight lessons were considered the minimum to qualify. He then bought an old "Jenny" from Leavens Brothers. The "Jenny" was a First World War training plane, which had a 42-foot wing span and was powered by an 85 horsepower V8 water-cooled engine. It required a complete overhaul before becoming airworthy. It was dismantled and moved to the ground floor of a vacant hotel on Front Street in Campbellford, now occupied by the Riverview Restaurant. Craig was the lead mechanic and his assistants were Eric Scott, Bill McKelvie, and Bill Nelson.

All fabric covering was removed, one wing spar was replaced, and new covers were made of high grade factory cotton. The covers for the four wings were sewn in the form of large socks, on an electric sewing machine loaned by local tailor, J. A. Frederick. After the new fabric was in place, several coats of banana oil, coloured with aluminum powder, were applied to tighten the fabric, giving it a rigid structure. When the overhaul was completed, the sections of the aircraft were trucked to Mohawk Field near Deseronto where they were re-assembled. The last test before an actual flight was to determine if the plane was "tail heavy" or "light" with the controls centralized. Craig piloted the plane along the ground on the four mile runway at half throttle and determined what adjustment should be made to the angle of the stabilizer. He ran about two miles on the ground at half throttle and, suddenly, to everyone's consternation, he rose some fifty feet into the air, now making his first combined solo and test flight. He made it down in one piece, but the aircraft was badly damaged.

Craig was a natural inventive mechanic and was employed repairing aircraft in North Bay and Montreal during World War II.

WHO WAS BLAKER?

by John Lisle

Who was Blaker? Did he ever exist? These are questions that have been asked many times before now. In all probability, they will never be answered. The legend, though not the man, was alive in the 1920s and still repeated into the 1930s and 1940s. When it started is unclear, as is its authenticity.

Blaker was a man of mystery. His usual haunts were the semi-wilderness areas in the northern part of Seymour Township – as old timers would phrase it, that part of the township "north of the forks." This defines the area enclosed by the Trent and Crowe Rivers, which, flowing southeast and southwest, came together north of Campbellford. It was an apt expression at a time when there was little else existing on which to pin a location. Blaker, reportedly, would be seen on road or trail, but when contact with travellers appeared imminent, he would fade away and disappear into the heavy bush that covered most of the countryside. The packsack that he always shouldered was equally mysterious. It was local lore – the story embellished and enhanced with each succeeding generation. In the rocky terrain down river from Crowe Bridge, there is a cave. Here, the story went, was where Blaker hid his treasure. The entrance was low and forbidding. There is no evidence that anyone ever fully explored the cave, although a few amateur spelunkers did venture in a short distance before turning back. The great rock slabs that formed the ceiling pressed down from above, forcing explorers to their hands and knees – for some a claustrophobic experience. Signs on the floor indicated other inhabitants. The chance of meeting a skunk or a porcupine in such close quarters was not a pleasant thought. Blaker must have been desperate for private lodgings if he holed up in this cave!

Still, there was evidence that to some folk, it was more than a myth. Down river, a short distance from the cave entrance, a pit had been dug at some time, in an effort to intercept the course of the cave. It was about ten feet deep and must have been a laborious dig through layers of rock and earth. The excavation had been abandoned without contacting the subterranean passage. Blaker's secret, if he had one, remains undiscovered.

As with many legends handed down through the years, different versions of the same story have surfaced. In one of them, it is claimed that Blaker was a prospector who discovered gold or silver. An Indian assisted him in working the mine and was kept blindfolded when entering or leaving the area of the dig in order to keep the location secret. There is also the disparity in his name. Was it Blaker, or, as some remember, Bleeker? On one fact, all would agree. He was, and will remain, a man of mystery.

THE STRONG AND SILENT SMITH

by John Lisle

Dan Brown was our local blacksmith. He readily fit the stereotype of the "strong and silent smith". Many yarns were exchanged at Dan's forge as farmers waited for horses to be shod or a plough point renewed. The following story may have had its origin here, though it is doubtful it received any further promotion from the reticent blacksmith.

Dan owned a 1928 Whippet auto which he drove slowly and carefully when he made the occasional trip to Campbellford, accompanied by Mrs. Brown. Automobiles had come late to his life – he would never acquire the same comfort zone behind the wheel that came naturally with his horse and buggy. Mrs. Brown would sit stiffly at his side, clutching her basket of eggs, to be used as barter for produce, her shoulder pressed against her door. There was little conversation unless initiated by Dan. He disliked any distraction from the task of driving the machine.

On one such occasion, as they cruised cautiously down the side road between Stanwood and Crowe Bridge, Mrs. Brown fell out of the car. The door had not been properly latched. At that moment, Dan had been absorbed in the process of meeting and passing an oncoming vehicle. The Whippet lurched onto the shoulder of the road as he swung it well clear of the other auto. A slight tilt and sway, the door swung open and Mrs. Brown dropped quietly on the grassy fringe. Dan turned the wheel to the left, bringing his car back on track, the door closed again. If there was any outcry of alarm, Dan did not hear it. He was a bit deaf. Concentrating solely on his driving, he drove on unaware of the absence of his wife. About five miles on down the road, in the area of Petherick's Corners, Dan passed some comment. With no response forthcoming, even when repeated, he stole a quick glance to his right. He was alone.

Since Dan was not noted for unnecessary or frivolous conversation, there's no way of knowing what his thoughts were at the moment of his shocking discovery. He did turn and retrace his route, possibly a bit speedier than usual. He no doubt was greatly relieved to find Mrs. Brown perched on a roadside stump and none the worse for wear. The eggs did not escape so easily.

Dan Brown's shop was located on the Concession 13 just east of the store and cheese factory at Stanwood. He probably started his trade there around the turn of the century. Records indicate a busy smithy – not only in shoeing horses, but in the repair of farm tools and equipment. The repairing of wagon and buggy wheels and replacement of sleigh runners was also much in demand. Brown would continue to ply his trade on into the 1940s supplying a valuable service to the community. The blacksmith shop, built in 1899, managed to survive earlier small fires, usually started from the forge. It did not escape the one of 1942 which burned the building to the ground.

CAMPBELLFORD —
AS SEEN BY CIS STUDENTS

From essays by Gary Raine, Tammy Shank, and Ron Stanbury
Students at Campbellford Centre for individual Studies
37 Margaret Street, Campbellford, Ontario
December 11, 1998

As you approach the town of Campbellford, you will be intrigued by its scenic beauty. Nestled in the Trent Valley, the town is surrounded by tree-covered hills. The advantageous site lies mid-way between the cities of Belleville and Peterborough, with good highways to both.

The Trent River flows through the centre of the town and this attracts our many local businesses and out-of-town visitors. The Trent-Severn Waterway, above and below the town, provides not only beauty but also power from several dams along its course. Within a six mile radius of Campbellford are numerous summer resorts, providing abundant fishing opportunities for both local and visiting fishermen. These, of course, produce important revenue for the ardent entrepreneur and for the workforce of the area.

Deer, foxes, wolves and rabbits seem to like the area, as do partridges, wild turkeys and pheasants. Because of the generous supply of bodies of water, ducks and geese nest here and provide fine hunting in the fall. Bird-watchers will never be disappointed at the variety and numbers of both common and rare birds who find the Campbellford area to their liking.

This part of Ontario has fine farmland so, in addition to the crops, we see dairy cattle, beef cattle and sheep in the fields. Behind the scenes are successful pig and chicken farms. Some enterprising farmers are venturing into ostrich, rhea and elk farming. Excellent market gardens provide produce for local groceries and farmers' markets. In season, we have maple syrup operations, strawberry and raspberry pick-your-own locations and Christmas tree farms.

Though Campbellford, like many other towns on important waterways, believed, at its inception 150 years ago, that its industrial future lay in its river traffic, we find today that the future lies in a happy combination of relaxed country life and access to major traffic arteries. The Campbellford of the future will attract industries which want to give their employees the benefits of fresh air, clear lakes and a slower pace. At the same time, those employers and their employees will need to know that their products and their cultural lives are within easy reach of major metropolitan areas. Investors and entrepreneurs will see that Campbellford can do all of this. The town can also offer a pleasant and productive location for those who operate their own business from home. Computers and cell phones allow for instant and effective communication despite distances from major markets.

At the end of their working lives, Campbellford residents will be happy to stay in the area. They will be joined by an increasing number of retirees from other areas. Campbellford will provide extended home-care and retirement communities for the elderly. This will provide valuable employment opportunities for the young people and encourage them to stay in our town. This happy mix of generations will provide a stable environment for all Campbellford residents, from the very young to the very old. Healthy life-styles, now and in the future, require a clean and beautiful location with opportunities for both work and leisure. Our

Campbellford, as we see it growing in the next millennium, will be the ideal choice for full, happy and productive lives.

A CAMPBELLFORD LYRIC

by Carole Jenkins

A most beautiful place for hearts to reside
Is in the Campbellford countryside,
Where streams and rivers course and flow
Making lush green fields to thrive and grow
Through vales and hills they weave and wend
Till they reach the Lake, their journey's end.

Many people who come to seek solace and rest
Can only be glad they've accomplished their quest
For the scenery delights the most jaded eye
Like the Ferris Park range, reaching up to the sky,
Or the Trent Waterway, rippling all through town
Resembling a sprite in her shimmering gown.

Oh, this land is so bless'd with cows, sheep and farms,
Mother Nature's endowed us with so many charms
And one of the most remarkable features
Is the abundance of life in the form of wild creatures,
Like turkeys and deer and ducks, beaver and otter
And the myriad fish that inhabit the water.

Be thankful, my friends, for such precious bounty,
For Northumberland is a most splendid County
And the joy of life spent in this Eden-like clime
Is reflected in Campbellford faces that shine
In the glow of the knowledge of what they have got
In this idyllic Campbellford-Camelot.

THE CHRISTMAS LIGHT LADY

by Marilyn Scott

Betty Ellis has come to be known as "the Christmas light lady" of the community of Campbellford/Seymour, where she is a municipal councillor. She lives twelve kilometres north of Campbellford on Concession 13, in a modest home on a half-hectare lot severed from the family farm some years ago. What began with a simple string of lights on the fence in 1975 has grown into a major display of illuminated Christmas motifs. The number of lights in 1999 was between 15,000 and 18,000. The lights are on timers and are on between 5:00 PM and 11:00 PM, from late November until early January. The display contains many different Christmas themes – elves, candles, reindeer, stars, snowmen, candy canes. There is a nativity scene, and of course, old St. Nick. The two-metre lighted wire outline of a school bus on the front lawn, with her name emblazoned across it in red mini-lights, is Betty's favourite, because she is the owner-operator of a school bus. She also uses the bus to drive busloads of local seniors to visit the display. She invites visitors into her home, which is crowded with Christmas decorations. Community support helps keep Betty's light show in operation. Her Hydro bill is enormous, about $2000 for the six weeks over last Christmas, and the display uses one 200 amp service. Annually, visitors donate enough change to pay her Christmas hydro bill.

THE SLIPPERY SLOPE

by Gwen Dubay

In early times, when people died, their bodies were prepared for burial by close relatives or neighbours. However, there were firms which assisted the family with their funeral arrangements. One of these was the Ely and Irwin undertaking business which operated in Campbellford in the early part of the century. Wes Sweet told a tale from the period following World War I about Bill Irwin, the undertaker. According to Wes, he went one cold, snowy evening with Bill in the horse and cutter to pick up a body at Healey Falls. Bill decided to take a short cut across the fields. The trip went well and they were on the way back to town with the body of an elderly lady wrapped in a sheet. They were coming up a long hill on the west River Road when the runners caught in a fence. The horses began to panic and it took both men to calm them. Meanwhile, the body escaped and went sliding down the hill! Both men then left the horses and chased after the deceased, running and falling on the slippery crust. Finally, they caught the body, wrapped the sheet back around it and got themselves and the deceased back in the sled. Not surprisingly, Wes informed Bill that he was not available to assist again with any undertaking trips.

LIFE ON PUFF BALL INN ROAD

by Bernice Free Nakashima

Our mother died when we were young, so we had more freedom than some children but also more work. We fed the threshers, stooked oats, hauled hay, drove the young cattle from our farm to Edmund Brown's to pasture, and gathered sap at our maple sugar bush. We built forts in the hay mow and ran across the rafters in the barn. We were able to walk the top rails of the line fences. We helped draw in wood and pile it for our winter's supply. When we were home alone, we would climb to the top of our windmill, knowing that was one place we were forbidden to go when Dad was there! We picked stones and used them to build up a lane through the swamp. We went "mud-catting" at night and would come home with a five gallon pail full of fish. We used an old scow and the Teasdale's motor to boat to an island behind McCulloch's farm. We strung up a rope from a tree which hung out over the water. We spent as many hours away from our chores as we could, perfecting our jumps and dives. Thirty years later, our rope is still a favourite spot for the local children to play.

Early in the spring, we helped our neighbours, Cecil and Ray McCulloch drive their cattle back to Slaughter Island where they pastured for the summer. It was a great adventure to herd the cattle into the water and watch the men in canoes direct the animals to the island shore. When Ron McMillan and Dad were using the island for their cattle's pasture, a bull didn't survive the swim. Its throat was cut and the carcass was floated back across the river for a trip to the butcher shop! Great excitement!

On Hallowe'en night, we had to really work for our candies as we often bicycled around the concessions to collect our treats. As we didn't have real costumes, Gerald, Allan, Arthur, Leslie and James would dress as girls and Carolyn and I would dress as boys. Our neighbour, Ray McCulloch, always pretended he didn't know who we were and we always blew out the candle in his jack-o-lantern!

We enjoyed going back to Joss's Cheese Factory for fresh curd, salty and sometimes warm. We often bicycled down to Puff Ball Inn to fish or down to Neil's for a swim. The "cottagers" would roar up and down our concession road all summer, leaving big clouds of dust. We could only imagine how different their lives might be in the cities.

Once I was in tears because my only dress, a hand-me-down, was too long for me to wear to the School Christmas Concert. I still remember standing in my leotards while my six siblings waited in their winter boots and coats while Dad took galloping stitches around the hem of the dress! He told me later it was exactly the same length as Linda Ellis's dress and I was so pleased!

I remember going to my first movie in town when I was about fourteen…and I thought it was a wonderful thing!

We were fortunate to have our neighbours, the Doherty's, to give us rides to and from town when we were older … and Ray and Kathleen McCulloch would take us into Campbellford for Sunday School at the Presbyterian Church.

GHOST STORIES

based on stories by Frank Potts

During the first quarter of the twentieth century, ghost stories were part of rural folklore and no doubt were told for centuries before that. Some of the ghostly tales of the past, and even of the present, tell of doors opening and closing with nobody near, objects flying across rooms for no apparent reason and noises in the night with no explanation. The art of story telling as family entertainment is rapidly being lost, and the printed word cannot have the colour of the good old verbal experience. What follows is an attempt to capture, in his own words, some of the stories that Frank Potts recalls being repeated at family gatherings over the years.

"One of the superstitions held by some relatives of mine was not to seat thirteen people at a table for a meal. I suppose this was somehow related to the last supper of Jesus and the twelve apostles. Fear of the number thirteen is called triskaidekaphobia, so they say.

An episode leading up to my first ghostly experience took place before I was old enough to remember. A neighbour of my parents who lived about two miles down the road decided to come for a visit one night and his walk took him past an abandoned house which was reported to be haunted. Looking toward the house he saw an unearthly figure moving along at the same speed he was travelling. Not having any desire to keep company with a ghost he increased his pace to faster than he thought possible and arrived at my parents' home exhausted and had to be taken home by horse and buggy, not wanting to walk past that house in the dark again. Many years later I had been at an uncle's place playing King Pedro one night and was walking past this same old house on my way home when I thought about the neighbour's experience. I looked toward the house and there was the figure moving along with me. When I stopped it would stop, when I backed up so would the ghost. I had never heard of a ghost doing physical harm to a human and, in spite of the tingling at the back of my neck, decided to confront whatever it was. I began slowly making my way through the snow directly toward this apparition and finally came close enough to see that it appeared to be headless and maybe shrouded. Up to this point every word of this experience is true but I am unable to disclose my conversation with the ghost because it turned out to be a very old clothes line pole!

Cemeteries quite often were associated with ghost stories. One night I was returning home after calling on the girl who later became my wife, when in the light beam of the old Essex sedan I could see something white moving among the tombstones in the English Line Cemetery. I turned the car so the object could be seen more clearly and it was a Holstein calf that had wandered into the graveyard.

My great uncle, William Potts, had a small cabin on a poplar ridge east of Potts Island where he stayed while trapping in the area. A few hundred yards to the west was a large Indian burial ground, possibly used by the Point Peninsular Indians some three or four thousand years ago. One night after supper, Uncle Billy, made a fire outside the cabin and sat down beside it to relax and plan the next day's activities. After a time, when the flames had died down to a pleasant glow, a very large Indian, in full chieftain's regalia appeared on the opposite side of the fire. "Good nighty" said Uncle William, his usual greeting after the supper hour. At that instant, the Indian disappeared without a sound, leaving no evidence of having been there. This experience was very real to Uncle Billy.

Then there was "Gracie," a ghost that for many years haunted a house in a nearby village until the house burned. It was thought that would be the last of Gracie. A local bachelor purchased the property and proceeded to build a house on the old foundation. When he would arrive at the partly completed house in the morning, he would find light bulbs loose and some burned out so he began to wonder if Gracie had decided to occupy the new dwelling. He went inside the house one night and was standing in the dark hallway when a loud tapping started on the wall in front of him. Gradually, it came closer and he backed away. Suddenly, he was struck on the chest by something and fell backwards over a pile of lumber. I don't recall hearing the cause of the burned out bulbs or if Gracie ever returned. Most of the excitement was caused by the bachelor's dog approaching him in the dark and wagging his tail against the wall, causing the tapping sound. It was the dog jumping up and putting his paws against the man's chest that caused the fall over the lumber.

Two local boys were staying in a log cabin along the Trent where a man was reported to have died from a shotgun blast to the head, supposedly self inflicted. Just before daylight one morning, the boys were awakened by a strange rattling sound inside the cabin, and when their eyes became adjusted to the light, they could see a tin can rolling over the rough boards on the floor, first one way then back again. Eventually they discovered a weasel in the can trying to get a meal from what was left of the pork and beans.

A survey crew decided to stay in a building in the northern part of the township, and during the night, the whole building seemed to shudder. After a few times the men decided to investigate, thinking perhaps a bear or porcupine might be under the building but there was nothing to be seen. Next morning, a bullet hole was found in one of the walls, and later in the day, the crew heard from neighbours that a man had been murdered in that cabin some time before. They wondered if the ghost of the murdered man had returned.

A sister of mine died at the age of two, long before I was born. I don't recall having heard what illness she had, but a doctor called, and after examination and treatment, assured my parents she would be fine. A short time later, Dad and Mother were sitting at a table in the next room when they heard three distinct raps on the table. They then entered the little girl's room, only to find that she had died.

While I was still in Canada during World War II, I had a dream that I was trying to rescue my nephew, Douglas McMullen, who was in Europe with the RCAF, from a shallow well with fast running water. I was unable to reach him as he passed by in the water. Shortly after this dream, we received notice that Doug had been shot down and killed while on a mission over France at almost exactly the time I had the dream Coincidence? ESP? Who knows!

Sometimes weird things show up in the darkness. My dad was coming home through the woods one dark night after helping a neighbour to cut wood, when he saw what appeared to be glowing eyes of a very large animal. Being armed with an axe and not much afraid of anything, he decided to investigate and found the "eyes" to be Foxfire, a phosphorescent light emitted by wood in certain stages of decay.

A friend of mine, F.C. Bonnycastle, and I were coming out of marshland after duck hunting, when a light which looked like a full moon, was drifting over the marsh. F.C. had seen this before and said it was caused by a luminous marsh gas, perhaps methane.

There is a classic ghost story about a farmhouse in Seymour West that became haunted during the early 1930s. It even made the headlines in the Campbellford Herald, with an artist's conception of the ghost made from the description given to him by people who thought they had seen it. It looked like a striped pillow flying through the air. Several young people gathered at the house one night, in hopes of seeing this strange phenomenon. About midnight they were sitting in a darkened room when one of the windows began to rattle and a fierce looking horned creature with flashing eyes appeared outside the window. This was a bit much for the crowd and they disappeared very quickly, with one fellow in his haste almost cutting his throat on a clothesline. Another was in such a hurry that he didn't take time to get his car; he just ran. They fell over each other trying to make a quick exit from that weird place. The explanation of this phenomenon was later revealed. Two brothers who lived nearby had recently killed a beef and dressed it out. They then spent considerable time fastening a pole to the skinned head of the animal and arranging a candle or flashlight inside. They proceeded to lift the horned head to the window. It was rumoured later that the 'ghost' was invented to discourage anyone from buying the place because the tenant feared eviction if the farm was sold."

THE BLUE DRESS

by Margaret Crothers

I had taken my dogs for a walk out to the mail box and was returning to the old farm house. It was broad daylight and the sun was shining and a stiff breeze blowing. It was October 25, 1997. As I rounded a curve in my lane, I could see our maple syrup evaporator behind the house and standing beside it was a girl in an old fashioned blue dress with long sleeves, the hem touching the ground, and on her head she had a blue sunbonnet shading her face. The wind blew her skirts out behind her and she was holding her sunbonnet on with her hand. I was sure it was my granddaughter Kathryn, as she loves to dress up. I called out to her but she did not answer; the wind must have blown my words away. I lost sight of her as the road turned again. I walked around to the back of the house to see her but no one was there, only an old silver fence post standing beside the evaporator, glinting in the sunlight. Then I realized my granddaughter was not at the farm that day, and her old-fashioned dress was brown, not blue. Was the girl an apparition from another era revisiting her ancestral home?

THE GRANDFATHER CLOCK

based on the memoirs of Barbara Greenly and on an account as told to Marilyn Scott in an oral history interview

Gordon Greenly had a beautiful butternut tree in his wood lot, but it became necessary to cut it down. After drying the logs, he sawed them in his own saw mill, and then sent them to be planed and sized, and sanded. He sent for a Sir Wilfrid Laurier pattern and works from the Murray Clock company and hired a craftsman, Gord Hughson, to build a handsome grandfather clock. The completed clock was given as a gift to Gordon and Barbara Greenly on their fiftieth wedding anniversary by their family.

Gordon passed away on the afternoon of December 18, 1986. His funeral service was held at Hoard's United Church, just down the road from where he had lived for many years. When the family left home for the service, the grandfather clock was operating perfectly. After the funeral service, when the family returned home, they noticed that the grandfather clock had stopped. It was determined that the clock had stopped at the exact time that the hearse, carrying Gordon's remains, had passed the family home on the way to the church. The clock could not be set in motion.

Several years passed, and efforts to start the clock were unsuccessful. In 1990, Barbara's niece decided to pray over the clock, and miraculously, the pendulum started to swing, but the Westminster chimes remained silent.

Before he passed away, Gordon's wife Barbara had painted his portrait. The painting had never been framed and hung. She finally decided to complete the task, and hung the portrait on the wall not far from the grandfather clock. Immediately, the chimes rang out and the clock started to work as it had when Gordon was alive.

OUR PERCY REACH GHOST

by Marilyn Scott

We had been in our new home for just a few short weeks, when one very quiet night we were surprised by an unexpected guest.

Picture an open concept house with a kitchen entrance on the east side and living room fireplace on the west. Hardwood flooring is laid from one end to the other. My husband and I were on the lower level, directly under the fireplace area. This house has seven exits, and, being new to the area, we had checked and locked all doors for the night. Suddenly we heard footsteps entering from the east and then seemingly disappearing out the west side, right through the fireplace. My husband ran upstairs to see who was in the house. He checked everywhere, and then checked all of the doors. Every door was securely locked. No one was in the house.

Two weeks later the identical scenario occurred. This was not a frightening experience. Where we are situated is where some of Seymour's first settlers lived. We decided that one of the settlers was just walking through what was once a path along the river at Percy Reach. We felt quite fortunate to have our very own ghost visiting. I was happy that I had not been on my own, because I am sure that without a witness, I would have been told that it was the wind or at least my imagination.

Our visitor has never returned.

A HOMING DOG

by Barbara Fox Pechkovsky

"Dog finds his Way Home, 130 miles, 11 days late". This was a heading in the Toronto Daily Star in September 1960. "Smokey, a six year old German shepherd, turned up at his former owner's house after 11 days and over 200 km. through strange country." Tom and Donna Fox had sent him to Donna's sister to live on a farm near Maple, now the site of Canada's Wonderland. They felt that he would be happier on a farm where he could have free run rather than be tied up in Campbellford.

It was dark when he left his birthplace for the first time. The next day, at his new home, Smokey slipped his collar and disappeared. Efforts to find him failed. Eleven days later when Tom's Dad, Bob, stepped out of his truck at his workplace on Alma Street, there was Smokey to greet him with prolonged cries. He was thin, exhausted and had cracked and bleeding paws. He had a broken rope around his neck, evidently acquired from a second escape in a strange home. He recovered from his injuries and remained the rest of his life with his family in Campbellford.

SATURDAY NIGHT WAS SPECIAL

by Barbara Fox Pechkovsky

In the Forties going to town on Saturday night was special, at least for me. Although I grew up in town I loved spending part of my vacation with my Aunt and Uncle on the farm, and on Saturday night we went to town.

Preparations for the highlight of the week began early. For some farming wives, many of whom did not drive, this might have been the only time of the week to meet old friends, particularly those from the other side of the river. Plans for the night were laid out by conversations over party line telephone, which often had eavesdroppers. Private conversation or other business such as exchanging dress patterns, plants or recipes was kept for a visit in the car on Saturday night.

Work stopped a bit earlier on Saturday afternoon. The chores, such as milking, were done as early as the cows could be milked without upsetting their routine. At the house the warm water reservoir on the cook stove was refilled as quickly as it was depleted so that all the Saturday night bath water had some warmth to it. The rain water was collected in the cistern. If it hadn't rained for some time, it was important to conserve the water and to ignore the musty odour.

Now fresh and clean, we had a quick meal and headed for town, hoping to be early enough to have a good parking spot on Front Street, the best being in the middle, between Selrites, now Stedman's, and Long's on either side of the street. Parked at this vantage point one could see the hordes of people crowding the streets and meet those one knew, mostly everybody. Private visits were carried out in the car for the women or outside the shops. The men often conversed near or in the billiard hall, a place women were never seen, or they sat outside on the seats provided to watch the world go by or discuss current issues. The local barbershops were also favourite places to find out the latest news.

Almost every Saturday, raffle tickets were on sale for some good cause and one local character was particularly good at cornering everyone to buy one. The Salvation Army Band added its rousing gospel sounds to the evening. They interspersed their music with sermons and scripture from their spot on the northwest corner of Front and Bridge Streets.

At this time Campbellford was proudly 'dry,' so there were no bars or stores selling alcoholic beverages. The stores did a rousing business and even the doctors' offices were open for business as I recall. What made Long's a very special stop, especially on a hot evening, was their very wonderful ice cream cones, sodas, milkshakes, and huge menu of sundaes. It was a "must" place to go to celebrate any special occasion. It was my hope to order the three scoop banana split when the occasion was really a celebration.

These evenings always flew by too quickly. We returned to the farm with the trunk loaded with the week's purchases of groceries, pig feed, our stomachs full of ice cream, and best of all, our heads spinning with the excitement of Saturday Night in Campbellford.

TRACING BRITISH EMIGRANT CHILDREN

by Ann Rowe

This article presents an examination of the practice of sending to Canada young emigrant children from the British Isles. My expertise in this field is limited to sharing my personal experiences and frustrations as I sought information about my mother's roots. In 1968, after the birth of my second child, I became interested in my family's origins. My curiosity stemmed from my inability to complete the family tree chart in the centre of a baby book which had been received as a gift.

My initial efforts proved fairly fruitless as both my parents were deceased by this time. My two older sisters and my one brother could offer little of value, since they did not seem to know much more than I did. There was a collection of old pictures, but unfortunately, no one seemed to know who they were. My mother's obituary contained some clues which stated that she was born in Woodford, England, daughter of Mr. and Mrs. Arthur Langley, and was survived by one sister in Canada and two brothers in England. The family speculated that some of the pictures were her relatives.

The most promising source of information seemed to be my mother's older sister who was past seventy years of age at the time and living in Frankford. There seemed to be some initial reluctance to talk about their early life. After several visits, I finally learned that the two girls had been sent to Canada as children, presumably because their parents had died. The elder of their brothers had also been in Canada but he later returned to England. My aunt offered to loan me a personal item which she had retained – her mother's catechism book which was inscribed "Emily Jane Fletcher," my maternal grandmother's maiden name. In addition, she tearfully identified one of my pictures, a tiny young woman in a Salvation Army uniform, as her mother. She had a different pose of the same lady without her bonnet. Her collection also included a wedding portrait of her brothers' weddings and also pictures of their families as young children. Nevertheless, the most surprising was yet to come. The last picture was a slender balding middle-aged man whom Aunt Margaret calmly told me was her father. But how could this be? I had been led to believe that the girls had been orphaned long before they were sent to Canada. She carefully explained what little she knew – a tale of sadness, separation and hardship. Emily Jane and her family were of the Anglican faith as the catechism book supported. Her parents did not approve of her husband and, therefore, the young couple avoided contact with them. Although they were married in the Woodford Parish Church of England and their children were subsequently baptized there, Emily Jane became involved with the Salvation Army. When she later became ill and died, her parents refused to help with the children because they disapproved of both her husband and her religion. Because their father could not care for them, the children were placed in an orphanage, first the girls and soon after, the boys.

In addition to this startling new information, my aunt produced a packet of letters which revealed that the younger brother had been prevented from emigrating to Canada because he suffered from chronic bronchial asthma and was therefore considered unsuitable for farm labour. However, despite this serious disability, he was considered able to be conscripted into the Royal Navy for service. One letter was even from the old Granny wishing that things had worked out differently and trying to keep some ties open by naming other family members who were still alive. These letters provided an opening to probe further into my aunt's early memories. In a series of visits, I learned that the two girls came to Canada at the ages of eight and ten. Their brother, Arthur, had come earlier.

This was the first time that I heard the name, Dr. Barnardo. Aunt Margaret explained proudly that my mother and herself were sent to Canada by the Barnardo Home. From the Peterborough Home, they went to the home of Mr. and Mrs. Bill White of Uxbridge. At this time, they were within a very few miles of their brother, Arthur, but did not realize it. The Whites eventually had a baby and the girls were sent to Midland to Mr. and Mrs. William Hope, an uncle of Mrs. White. The Hopes took excellent care of the girls, both graduated from high school, and they received extra benefits such as piano lessons. Margaret was sent to Peterborough Teacher's College in 1916–17 by John and Emma Armstrong who lived across the road from the Hopes. She then went to teach at Detlor in North Hastings where she met and married Uncle Fred Miller in 1918. They celebrated their sixtieth wedding anniversary in 1978. He died soon afterward, but she lived until October 1990, when she died at age ninety-two.

My mother, Jennie, was sent to Ontario Business College in Belleville. Following her graduation, she went to work for a Mrs. Cook in Campbellford, where she met and married, in 1919, George David Boyd.

Arthur, the elder brother, lived with a family named Flagg at Newcastle. He married an Uxbridge Township girl named Mildred Musselmann in 1916. During World War I, Arthur joined the Canadian Army and served in England with the 116th Battalion. At this time, he established a contact with his maternal grandparents and also with his father, who was still alive. He returned to Canada at the end of the war. His wife, Mildred, died of tuberculosis in 1921. His second marriage in 1922 was followed by the birth of two sons and a daughter by 1925. Arthur's greatest desire was to return to England, which he did, along with his wife and children. They resided in an area that was levelled during the Blitz of World War II and no further contact ever occurred.

James William, the younger brother, joined the Royal Navy at the age of fifteen and was required to stay in for twelve years after his eighteenth birthday. His letters tell of his bitter attitude toward his father for giving the children over to the Barnardo Home. Despite his lack of regard for the Navy, he had incredibly interesting experiences in Gibraltar, Africa, the Red Sea and three years in China. He tells of finally serving his time, then being recalled when World War II broke out. In 1940, he missed the connection to his ship. The ship went down with great loss of life. From 1941-43, he served off the coast of Newfoundland, off Boston and Iceland, and in the Orkney Islands. Finally, his unit assisted in the demobilizing of Germany. His last correspondence was in 1949. No contact has yet been established with his three daughters, although I am still hoping.

My aunt was also able to provide sufficient personal data on her brothers and sister that I could request a search of the English parish records for official documents to support her recollections. I spent considerable time and money on these, but they proved invaluable in extending the generations back even further.

Armed with this personal information, I began an intensive reading program to learn more of the background which led to the emigration of young men and women to Canada. Several books were just coming onto the market. One of the most revealing of these was Kenneth Bagnell's excellent resource, *The Little Immigrants*. Another extremely useful source was Gail Corbett's, *Barnardo Children in Canada*. As Bagnell enunciates, "This is the story of a special group of children — over 80,000 of them. Some of them became our mothers and fathers; all became the parents of much of our history." As I learned of the terrible hardships suffered by many of these young children, I was thankful that my family was as lucky as they were.

Although Barnardo himself died following an illness in 1905, parties continued to be sent out under the organization until 1914 when threats of war broke the emigration cycle. Former Barnardo boys and girls responded to the war cry and went to the front to serve. Corbett places this number at eleven thousand Barnardo protegees who enrolled in the Great War with over half of these coming from Canada. Some family ties were re-united as soldiers in England visited their former homes or contacted the London office for information. We know that one of these was my uncle, Arthur, who visited his father and maternal grandparents. Between 1916 and 1919, emigration to Canada ceased. Then, says Corbett, "burdened with volumes of new orphans, Barnardo's sent out its first post-war party." This continued for a short time, but, by 1925, changes in the Canadian school leaving age to sixteen years virtually stopped the sending of young children. The practice dwindled with the last Barnardo emigrant to Canada arriving on July 8, 1939. At that time, Bagnell tells us that it was estimated that three in every two hundred Canadians were Barnardo boys or girls or their descendants. An after-care section operated in Toronto until 1963 when the Canadian office closed its doors and all records were sent back to England.

In the late 1970s and early 1980s, there was a great interest in the practice of sending young children to Canada. Several books were published and a photographic exhibit travelled throughout the country. The Hastings County Museum featured this display and it gave me the next possible lead in my research. Large display boards showed pictures of actual Barnardo children before and after they came into care. Many local residents eagerly scanned the faces for hints of their heritage. Although I did not find my own family, an address was posted to which interested parties could write for family information. This photographic display proved to be so popular in the Belleville area that an annual reunion for Barnardo children and descendants is now held each autumn at the Hastings County Museum.

I subsequently sent a letter to the After-Care Section and received an astounding reply. Not only did the letter spell out explicitly why my mother and family came into care, but also enumerated all family members , maternal and paternal, including their occupation and place of residence, who could not or would not assist in caring for these children. Information also included the actual dates of custody, the name and date of the ships on which they sailed to Canada, and subsequent enquiries from their father and grandmother with regard to their welfare. Obviously their files are very thorough. It was a sad tale of alcoholism and abuse. I debated long and hard about sharing this information with my aunt. After discussion with her two daughters, we decided that she would want to know what I had uncovered. If you are not willing to receive unwelcome news, I would suggest that you not pursue this line of investigation.

Barnardos continues to operate homes and projects to children in need of care. Financial support comes from donations and local authorities without government assistance. The After-Care Section is responsible for the maintenance of all Barnardo ledgers, as well as those from Annie MacPherson's homes. These records are an invaluable resource for Barnardo descendants in search of their roots. While Barnardo children formed the great majority of childhood emigrants, at the height of the movement, over twenty-five philanthropic institutions were involved in similar programs. As late as 1958, nine agencies were still involved in childhood emigration schemes to some extent. It was not until January 1982 that it became a legal requirement for any volunteer association to get the consent of the Secretary of State before sending a child abroad. It remains to be seen what the final analysis may reveal. There is no doubt that there was deception, exploitation and abuse. While the best interests of the child were loudly proclaimed, the increasing volume of evidence seems to indicate that the reality was otherwise.

In 1998 and 1999, I had the opportunity to attend gatherings of Barnardo descendants held in Peterborough. A concerted effort is underway by this organization to share their wealth of information with surviving children and their families. I was able to request copies of the pictures in their files which I had not asked for previously. These have since arrived with copies of further information not sent previously. Few of the original Barnardo children survive but many second and third generation descendants are able to access this wealth of family information.

Author's Note:
While conducting research, I found a reference in the Campbellford Herald of 1901 to the arrival by train in Campbellford of three little girls from the Orphans' Home. They were to live with a Miss Kerr, a Mrs. Chase, and a Mrs. Wiggins for a three year trial period before final steps for adoption would be taken.

THE ALLANS' JOURNAL AND THE MILL

by John Lisle

About 1840, or possibly earlier, when young David Allan first explored this particular area. In another ten years, it would be part of Seymour Township. At that time, it was mostly forest and bush, broken here and there by cleared land of the early pioneers. Here, in the northeast corner of the township, Allan found what he was looking for – a place to build a mill.

Curiously, little is known of this man whose activities would have such an impact on a developing community. The 1871 census records a birth date of 1817, and that he was a mill owner. He had previously worked a farm in the Burnbrae area. He was possibly related, perhaps a son, to Captain Thomas Allan whose estate of 1,000 acres was in the same area. They were both active members of the Burnbrae Presbyterian Church, and are buried in the same section of the cemetery there.

Undoubtedly David Allan had experience with the water-powered grist mills. He also had the nature to accept the challenge of this new venture. The young Scot was still in his early twenties. The Crowe River bore little resemblance to the burns of his native Scotland, but he could see the river's potential as a source of water power. No doubt he explored its course, or enough of the waterway to satisfy his concern on whether it could provide a constant supply to drive his mill. While he tramped through the bush and virgin forest, he would recognize the wealth of timber readily accessible to the river. So natural, also, to visualize rafts of saw logs moving down river to the future sawmill.

First a grist mill – a growing community needed it. Farmland was expanding rapidly, and there was grain to grind. David Allan chose his mill site carefully. Upstream, the river broadened into what is now known as Rylstone Lake. Downstream, the river quickened as it narrowed and dropped down a rapids. Here he would build his dam. Previously, a ford had existed in this area, a short distance upstream from the proposed mill and dam. The Crowe was shallow at this point, probably quite passable for the horse-drawn vehicles of the era, except for the time of spring runoff. Now, before proceeding with a dam, Allan would build a wooden bridge to connect the 13th concession road which crossed the river here. With the bridge in place, the dam, down river from it, could be completed. Work on the mill foundations was already in progress. Across the river from the mill site, a rock shelf provided a secure location to anchor the northwest end of the dam. Here, too, the control works of the dam would be located – squared timber stop logs that could be inserted or removed as river levels dictated. Seldom would these operations be required, except, possibly, during high spring runoff periods. On the mill side of the river, the dam was keyed to a ridge of rock that rose at that point.

The mill site was well chosen. The rocky ridge that thrust up here, and extended over halfway across the river, turned the stream toward the opposite shore and its main channel. The ridge provided a good base on which to build a dam. It is assumed that the foundation walls of the mill were poured before construction of the dam continued. In the wall facing upriver, a rectangular opening was formed. A heavy steel water gate was installed to cover the opening on the upstream side. Particular attention was given to this detail. It must be strong enough to withstand the pressure the river would exert against it. It must move freely up and down when manipulated. Opening and closing the gate was the key to energizing the waterwheel or shutting it down. Inside the foundation walls, a sluiceway or "flume" was designed. This would form a conduit that carried surging water through an open water gate to spin the waterwheel. Then, energy spent, it would exit down a rock-strewn tail race to merge again with the river.

The ponderous waterwheel was eased down and positioned in the sluiceway. There, its vertically aligned fins in the horizontally mounted wheel would catch the full impact of unleashed water power. Its thick vertical shaft was ready to be harnessed with the wooden-cogged ring gear that would propel its power via more gears, belts and pulleys to the machinery of the mill. There was much to be done before that could happen. Probably some of the workmen continued with the construction of the mill and the intricate installations of the machinery that would be required. Special skills were needed to place the heavy millstones to precise tolerances for satisfactory performance. Other workmen turned their attention to completing the dam.

It would be arduous work, manual labour for the most part, as they inched their way across the irregular contours of the rock ridge, clearing the rubble and razing a thick wall of concrete and stone, keyed to the bedrock below. The river sent probing fingers against their emerging barrier. A berm of earth and rock served as coffer dam to keep the river at bay in low areas where it sought to encroach. Timing was all-important. Dam building was seasonal work, dependent on the mood of the river. Knowing the fury it could unleash, particularly in the springtime, they worked long and hard through the summer months when the Crowe was most docile. Reaching the end of the rock ridge, they were faced with deeper water and the main channel, which hugged the far shore. It was time to divert the river. A new channel was dredged through the shallow water and swampy vegetation on the mill side of the stream. An opening had been left in the dam at that point. About eight feet wide, it would eventually be closed with stop logs. The end purpose of this opening was as an emergency measure. If a breakdown should occur that required rapid lowering of the water level, the stop logs could be lifted to facilitate repairs. For now it would be used to siphon off some of the river flow. With much of the stream diverted away from the normal course, the dam builders were able to push their project on across to the opposite shore. The stop logs could now be dropped in place, effectively throttling the river.

The Crowe River had been trapped to be harnessed for industry. River levels below the dam were probably drastically reduced for a while before the river mustered enough volume to creep over the top of this unnatural barrier. Probably some flow was maintained though, as the pioneers were well aware of the abundance of fish in this stream.

One particular feature of the Allan dam is worth noting. It did not cross the river directly by the shortest route. For over half of its course, the dam was placed on the ridge of rock that stretched out from the mill side of the river, as previously described. Where the ridge dropped away into deeper water, the dam turned and angled upstream to its terminus at the opposite shore. The reason for this indirect route is open to conjecture. Building along the ridge required less material and easier working conditions than could be expected in deeper water. It also provided a more stable base on which to key the dam. A more likely reason is its effect on water flow. By designing the dam with the end opposite the mill farther upstream, more water would be diverted toward the mill and waterwheel. A sawmill was soon to be built. Log drives would be coming down river. The dam design would also help to swing the logs toward the mill and its waiting saw.

Upstream from David Allan's new dam, as far as Callahan's Rapids, a new landscape was forming. Creeping over low banks, the Crowe swept outward, seeking new boundaries, creating a small lake where once it meandered through a jungle of cattails and bulrushes. In time it would be named Rylstone Lake. Loggers had been busily harvesting the wealth of timber that stood in the path of rising water. Piles of pine and cedar logs were secure and ready for the trip down river when the time was right. The litter of tree branches, wood chips, and bark left in the wake of the loggers disappeared along with the stumps of hewn trees beneath the surface of the new lake. For David Allan there must have been a sense of relief mingled with the satisfaction he felt. The sometimes tempestuous river was now in his grip and under control.

Sometime between 1846 and 1848, the grist mill was completed. The stage was set, one day, for a scene possibly similar to this projection:

> David Allan steps over to a large iron wheel that crowns the shaft projecting from watery depths below. He leans over the wheel, grasps the spokes, throws weight and muscle into turning it — and raising the water gate. The pressure of water against the gate initially restrains its opening. Then, as the water begins to surge under the rising gate, it exerts upward pressure and the iron wheel turns more freely. A torrent of water charges along the sluiceway to hurl its mass against the paddles of the waterwheel. The wheel responds. Steadily it picks up revolutions, spinning faster and faster. Allan steps over to a long lever and eases it forward. A friction clutch in the machinery below the floor closes, harnessing the waterwheel's energy. Pulleys creak into action; belts flap and strain. The mill pulses as it comes to life.
>
> There are many local people here today to experience first-hand this momentous occasion. They stand in awe, hearing, feeling the power newly generated. They watch as grain is poured into the hopper and disappears to be crushed between the whirling millstones and returns again

to a waiting bag. It is a significant moment in the history of the young rural community and its value to be appreciated for generations to come.

David Allan wasted little time before turning to his second project. The sawmill was up and running sometime between 1850 and 1854. Attached in an "L" configuration to the grist mill at one end, the opposite end facing upstream extended out over the water of the mill pond. From this placid backwater, logs could be winched directly from the water to log carriage and the waiting saw. The sawmill was soon to become the busiest part of the Allan's Mills operation.

It was a time of rapid expansion. Seymour township formed its first council in 1850 and David Allan was a member of that council. As roads were extended and improved into the northern part of the township, settlers poured in to take up the land. Sawn lumber was in great demand for the many buildings being erected. As the only saw and planing mill in the area, Allan had a constant demand for his product.

A great deal had been accomplished over the span of ten years. A bridge had been built, a grist/saw mill erected and in operation. An access road, driven through the bush, connected the mill to the township road where it turned off the bridge and ran past the Allan house. Land had been cleared for a small farm operation as well.

A record of the mill activities still exists today. It is the property of the McKeown family – handed down to Reg McKeown through his mother, Grace Allan.

The Allan journal, which has survived the 144 years since its first entry in 1854 provides a fascinating window on these pioneer times. The daily entries, penned in fine flowing script, tell a story of a flourishing business in cash, credit, goods, and barter. A business so varied in its scope, that many people within, and outside the community would be involved directly, or indirectly, in its operation. Early entries indicate extensive activity in logging and the river drives. It appears that Allan is provisioning a logging shanty somewhere upriver. There are numerous entries of food staples – barrels of pork and flour, potatoes, butter, and sugar, plus all the incidentals required for food preparation, including utensils.

Each customer in the journal is given, and retains, the same account number for further transactions. Currency, until the 1860s, is in pounds sterling. The penmanship of the first few years is obviously that of a scholar. The census of 1871 records a Henry Allan – "Clerk." He is one year younger than David Allan. It is possible that he wrote the early entries and was probably related to the miller.

A "rafting account," while indicative of preparation culminating in the river drive, sometimes uses terminology that was applicable in that era, but unfamiliar today. There is mention of "binding cribs in the forest and of running crib boards from forest to river." These would be the rafts of logs. Another entry is for 200 oars, row locks, and 1500 pickets. It was customary to form rafts of logs for the river drive. Tall straight trees were felled on skids made from smaller trees. A chalk line was run along the sides and the "scorers" then stood on the log and cut up to the line with their 3 1\2 foot axes. Rolling the log, they would repeat the scoring on top and bottom. The final squaring was done by the broad axe men. It was a task that required both skill and endurance. The squared logs were called "boards" after squaring. Several of them laid out to form a base – more stacked on top to form a "crib." Lashed together, they formed a raft.

River drivers then rowed the raft down river to the mill. Usually in the spring when the water levels would be high. A journal entry states a price for the saw logs – two shillings, ninepence (60 to 70 cents) each. Another entry reads: "65,000 feet of boards – rafting at twenty-six pounds" (approximately $130.00).

Also in the "rafting account," an entry of "Board for men making flouts"? Listed along with transversers, lashing poles, and a large number of oars, one can only conclude it is part of the equipment required to make up and transport a log crib down river.

The Allan house, which fronted on the river, close to the bridge that now spanned it, was quite spacious. Several of the mill and farm workers boarded there. An outside staircase provided a separate access to their tiny second floor rooms.

For a time, it was also the local Rylstone Post Office. The record shows frequent charges for postage. Apparently, for several years, David Allan must have operated a store on the premises – a very general store, judging from the items charged to customers. This may have had its start as a service to loggers who could not conveniently get to town. One entry reads, "One half gallon whiskey – 1 shilling, 7 pence. "There are two entries for "fiddle strings" to Peter Smith. Tobacco was a regular item charged to local workmen. Boots and mitts also show up frequently. Barter was a popular medium in completing transactions. Many of the goods purchased from Allan were subsequently paid for by work performed for the miller. Sometimes, farm produce was used to clear the bill. Beef, pork, grain and field peas often appeared in the ledger to settle accounts, as well as livestock – cattle and pigs mostly.

Wages then, as now, varied as to the work performed. A farm hand could expect about $12.00 per month. In contrast, it is recorded that, for thirty-seven days on the river, a man was paid nine and a half pounds. By the dollar standard, this works out to be approximately forty-five dollars. Better than one dollar a day! Of course, the man performing chores on Allan's farm would have his meals included and considerably less hazardous work than working on river drives.

The miller had broad legal authority regarding the river. Saw and grist mills were springing up all over Upper Canada to service emerging pioneer communities. To protect his own interests, it was essential that he had control over the waterway that powered his mill. He controlled the water levels and had free access to the shoreline – necessary when driving logs.

During the earlier years of operation, it appears that the sawmill soon surged ahead of the grist mill in activity. The record shows thousands of saw logs coming down the river. Demand for sawn lumber was constant.

It was in this period of feverish activity that David Allan realized the need for another man to operate the mill. A son had been born in 1852. James would succeed him sometime in the future. For the present, David was hard pressed as he strove to look after the post office, the store, his little farm and the operation of the saw and grist mills. He found his man in John Lisle, an immigrant from Newcastle, England, who had experience from working in mills there, and more recently, at Canniff's Mills near Belleville. Sometime in the early 1860s, he took over the operation of the Allan Mills, a post he would occupy for the next twenty years or more, until young James came of age.

By the end of the century, the journal entries were in a different hand, probably that of young James Allan. Near the end of the century, there were notations that another Allan had joined the work force. "Willie working for John Meiklejohn." "Willie had started work at the Marmora Mill." This would be James' son, W.T. Allan, who would carry on the business in the twentieth century.

An August 1901 entry records that "Willie paid L. Meiklejohn by bicycle $12.00." Another is quite interesting to speculate about, "Willie gone to work at mine today." Stories speak of a mine that Allans worked for a while. It was supposedly located on the Crossen farm, which was situated directly across the river from Allans' place. To add weight to this speculation, a later journal entry records the purchase of blasting powder and fuses.

Many of the pioneers who march page by page through Allan's book are in a way known to the descendants of these early settlers. Known by the stories handed down from fathers in the 1930s and 1940s. Some of these were colorful characters known for various eccentricities. Some of these early pioneers were entrepreneurs or leaders, skilled in particular trades or professions.

The Allans were leaders in trade and commerce. Most people in the area were affected or involved by the various operations of the mill. Activities were numerous.

One set of millstones turned out the grist for livestock feed. Another set ground flour, both pastry and bread. Bran and cornmeal were produced. In other parts of the rambling building, lumber was sawed, a planing mill dressed boards and another machine turned out tongue and groove lumber. A shingle mill converted blocks of cedar into roofing shingles. A notation in 1907 suggests the arrival of another piece of machinery. Freight costs of $22.44 were paid for hauling a waterwheel from the station at Bonarlaw. This second waterwheel would bring something radically new and until now unknown in the neighborhood. It would spin the turbine to generate electricity. The Allan buildings were the first to receive this new form of light and power. Several nearby cottages and farm houses were soon to follow and enjoy the luxury provided by electric current. No doubt it was a decided improvement over the coal oil lamps it replaced, but hardly comparable to the steady sixty-cycle power of today.

Sometimes the lights would become quite dim when there was insufficient water to spin the wheel to the required revolutions. This was particularly noticeable when the mill was in full operation and the bulk of the water was diverted to the waterwheel that powered the machinery. Still, the rest of the neighborhood felt a touch of envy at those lucky ones who were spared the monotony of daily fueling of oil lamps and polishing globes. Hydro was still in its infancy. There were no set standards of wiring codes yet. Power routes from Allan's generator took the path of least resistance. Poles were used when necessary, but trees and fence posts were also utilized to deliver the power. The furthest power service was supplied to John Lisle's farm house which was about a half mile from the mill. That distance must have been close to the limit of the generator's potential.

From the 1860s and on into the next century, one item was produced in the sawmill with great regularity – stone boats. More likely, at prices ranging from $1.25 to $1.50, it was only the planks that were sawn with the customer assembling the finished product. Even so, from the number tallied in the book, it would appear that every farmer in this part of Seymour was equipped with a stone boat.

James Allan was a precise bookkeeper. His entries provide an interesting comparison to prices of today. Around the turn of the century, a bag of potatoes was worth forty cents, Bread was worth ten cents a loaf, ten dozen eggs at fifteen cents a dozen cost $1.50, butter was twenty cents a pound, cheese sold for ten cents a pound and maple syrup brought $1.00 per gallon. In 1891, W. Hoard ploughing with a horse for three and a half days at one dollar per day earned $3.25. An 1892 entry reads, "John Lisle by one hundred and twenty-eight pounds of beef at five cents per pound, $6.40. "Good bookkeeping was certainly necessary. Goods changed hands sometimes by cash, sometimes by barter and sometimes a combination of both. A day's work might also be part of the equation. An entry of 1899 reads, "Bought of T. Horkins – single buggy – $65.00 to be paid in wood (maple) at $2.75 or $3.00. "A later entry indicates payment – "twenty-two cords of wood at $3.00." In 1900, Allan exchanged two calves for bobsleighs with W. Crossen – $12.00. In January 1901, "bought of J. Diamond, one cutter to be paid as follows, fourteen dollars in wood this winter – (if there is sleighing), thirteen dollars in cash, August 1901, thirteen dollars in cash, August 1902." The clause in the deal, "if there is sleighing" is worth a chuckle. It was probably inserted in case of difficulty getting the wood from the bush. Or was it that he didn't require the cutter if there was a lack of snow!

An entry of 1900 states, "Paid to D. Akins for plough bought last spring – $8.00." It was a kinder world in which to do business. There was no pressure for quick payment, a handshake was as honored as a promissory note and interest was usually omitted except for sizeable loans. In 1901, there is a barter transaction which is negotiated comfortably for all involved. "Bought of W. J. Meiklejohn, a young colt for twenty-seven dollars and let William Crossen have it to pay for the cow I bought from him."An earlier entry had read, "Bought of William Crossen, one cow to be paid July 1, without interest." In the only entry of its kind, a yoke of oxen is bought of David Allan in 1853. Price – twelve pounds, five shillings. By the mid-sixties, the dollar was the standard of currency.

The Allan farm was small – a few fields and barn between the house and the mill. Yet they seemed very active in raising, selling and butchering pigs as well as keeping a herd of milch cows. There are numerous notations such as the 1903 entry, "took the young sow to J. H. Lisle," or "red sow to W. S. McKeown." The black sow, the spotted sow – they all got a trip to various places – where there was a boar available to perform the service. Subsequent entries would record litters of pigs born and, still later, sales of hogs or days spent killing and butchering. Sometimes several days running would be spent at the latter activity, suggesting a lot of salt pork in barrel. A 1901 entry reads "Sold 46 lbs. of head cheese." Obviously all the pork was not for home consumption. In 1895 the journal records: "Sold seven pigs @ $4.25 per hundred (1,060 lbs.) $43.00."

Over the first sixty years or more of operation, the gristmill charge for grinding (or cracking) appears to remain the same – 6 cents per bag. Many paid for the cracking by working for the miller or in produce. The mill also sold chop at slightly over $1.00 per hundredweight.

Everyone, it seemed, farmer or not, kept a pig or two for the barrel – even Johnson the Stanwood cheese maker and Dan Brown, the blacksmith. The latter individual receives a considerable amount of ink in the journal. He is called on often to install buggy and wagon tires, for shoeing horses and forging new plow points.

Ben Redden is on record as the thresher of those times. Many of the area farmers who did frequent business with the Allans still have roots in the community today. The Meiklejohns - W.J., Chester and Sanford, Rutherfords – Richard, George, Robert and Harold. Jim Forde, his brother Charles, Jim McAlpine, and the Lawrences – C.D. and Kent, John Lain, and D. Petherick – the list goes on. Wallace Hubbel was usually available when there was wood to cut. His skills with an axe were well-known. There is also recorded, "Payment to Hubbel for his work in the mine ($13.00)." More stimulus for speculation on the Allan mine!

It appears that David Allan was responsible for the upkeep of the local township road. The record shows that he hired men and teams to perform road maintenance and received payment in turn from Seymour Township. In 1896, extensive dam repairs are indicated. The Allan's were able to provide work (which went on from July to September) for eight men with teams and sixteen laborers. Payment was in cash, barter, chop and lumber.

An entry of 1895 reads, "Bought of church an organ. Gave a horse @ $45.00. One note ($40.00) payable at 5% – 1897." This was probably the organ from the old Rylstone church which closed in 1893.

The year 1900 was an election year. Recorded in the journal "Received of Dominion Government – pay for election held Nov. 7 in Stanwood schoolhouse – $12.00. Paid Jas. E. Johnson for schoolhouse – $4.00. Paid R.D. Rutherford for poll clerk $2.25. Paid Jas. Allan for D.R.O. – $5.75."

In other elections held throughout the years, James Allan appears repeatedly as the District Returning Officer. He also appears to be quite involved in the operation of Stanwood Cheese Factory and regularly pays a D. Riley for hauling cheese to Campbellford.

Obviously the Allan family were devout church-going people. Continuous support for the church at Rylstone and also the one at Burnbrae is indicated. There are frequent donations to Rev. R.H. Warden "special collections from Rylstone church." Mission donations list the China Famine Fund, Japanese Famine Fund, and Russian Famine Relief. Also regularly assisted are the "Sailor Mission" and "Church Schemes." The "Toronto Poor," "Sick Children's Hospital" and "Toronto General Hospital" also were recipients of donations.

Apparently it was customary (for those who could afford it) to pay a fee for a church pew. An early entry in the book reads, "To church sittings – two pounds, five shillings." This is for three of the family, including David Allan. Another entry indicates payment for Widow Watson's seat – 1854.

By the year 1888, James Allan had taken over ownership of the mill. In 1902, he records a barn-raising bee. In 1904, there are major renovations to the house. It is raised, cellar enlarged, plumbing installed. The improvements are extensive – inside and out. James Allan crams a page of the journal to itemize all building materials and furnishings purchased. There are payments to Benor scattered at random but more frequent after the turn of the century. An entry of 1903: "Paid Benor for 80 cogs @ 5 cents – $4.00."

Possibly Benor is a carpenter or millwright. The cogs are handmade of wood. They are to replace worn ones on the huge wooden gear of the drive wheel. As the years pass, more and more are required. The time would come, on into the twentieth century, when Will Allan would find it difficult to replace these cogs. The artisans who fashioned them are gone, along with a dying trade.

James Allan bought considerable produce, groceries and clothing mostly, from the general store of D. Bell of Belleview. This location also known at other times as Big Springs and the Diamond would eventually become Bonarlaw, named after Andrew Bonar Law a British parliamentarian of the time. An invoice from Bell's store is dated 1905.

Leafing through this journal that James Allan has so meticulously maintained, provides answers and provokes new questions. Early entries list a large number of "Mares Insured – one pound, five shillings." On the same pages are "Mares leap – 10 pence?" There were probably a lot of horses used in the logging activity. Concern for keeping them healthy and in working trim is indicated by the tonic that was prescribed in the journal:

> "For horses: Six lbs. flour of Sulphur, Six lbs. Epsom salts, Two pounds Bicarbonate of Soda, Two lbs. Saltpeter – A heaping tablespoon twice a day in grain."

Entries from 1901 to 1911 record large quantities of flour purchased from F. J. Smith, Campbellford and also from Meiklejohn/Russel. A sample of these orders:

"100 bags Beaver Patent @ 2.60 ea., 40 bags Smith best @ 2.50 ea. 1700 Beaver Patent @ 2.50 cents ea., 800 Smiths Bests @ 2.70 cents ea."

These entries remain a puzzle. Why is a business that grinds flour buying it in quantity? Whatever the answer may be, the journal does not reveal it. Early in 1997, 88 years later, something turned up that may be connected to Allan's flour trade. Thirty-eight printers blocks were presented to Campbellford

Labels advertising flour products, produced from the printer blocks for Allans Mills Flour.

Printer blocks from the Campbellford/ Seymour Heritage Society Artifacts collection.

Heritage Society. Reportedly, they had been found during the demolition of a building. Possibly in the Campbellford area? No further information is available at this time. The metal stampings, which measure 3 3/4" by 2" are mounted on hardwood blocks. Each one bears a different logo and advertises seven-pound bags of pastry flour. They carry the name of W.T. Allan – Allan Mills – Bonarlaw.

Will Allan, son of James, was gradually taking over the business by 1910. He obviously intended to move into a large production and sale of pastry flour judging from the extent of this promotion. Allan Rutherford, one of the few local residents who can relate to that era, recalls that Will Allan did produce pastry flour for a while. He believes that the venture petered out due in some extent to difficulty in procuring sufficient quantities of the particular type of wheat required. It was probably James' idea to start with – he was inclined to new undertakings and ventures. It is likely that after Will took over the mill in 1915, he eventually discontinued the flour milling activity. Will Allan's main interest and pleasure was in sawing logs into lumber.

The June 1913 journal reads: "Rylstone P.O. closed May 13/1913. Mailed to the P.O. inspecter, the P.O. supplies and stamps – $39.00." David Allan had previously opened the above Post Office in his house, supposedly in 1865, possibly sooner, as the journal record would suggest. He was postmaster until his death in 1892, at which time the duties were accepted by James Allan. The Allans had maintained the post duty at Allan's Mills for 48 years or more before its closure, brought on by the first rural mail delivery which commenced later in 1913. That section of the Crowe River known as Rylstone Lake probably derived its name from the previous post office at Allan's.

An entry of 1915 reads: "Sold to W.T. Allan (son) mill and land – 86 acres more or less – North lot 25 in 12th Conc. Seymour. Also south part of lot 25 in 13th conc. Up to high water mark for the sum of $3,000.00 dollars."

The journal continues on but is no longer involved in the running of the mill. James Allan has moved to Booth Street in Campbellford and purchased Mrs. Susan Meiklejohn's house. He continues to record all his transactions in great detail. In 1918, he bought – "of D. Douglas a Ford car – $612.00. Paid license – $10.00 – 4 gal. gas $1.50." All expenses incurred while owning the auto are scrupulously detailed, even to gasoline purchased.

He is also into raising silver fox. In 1926, the journal shows purchase of one pair of two year-old fox for $1,100.00 and one pair of pups for $700. The breeding and rearing of silver fox for the pelts was, for a while a popular and profitable occupation. There are loans noted in the ledger – mortgages bought and sold – James Allan remains active – never really retires from the business world. An entry of 1929 records "the sale of Crossen farm to W. Haggarty for $2,600." This farm is directly across from the Allan house and the bridge. It is where the mysterious mine was located, as noted earlier, and was, apparently, owned by the Allans.

The last entry, in 1929, notes "two pair of silver foxes – $1500.00. Boarded by W. T . Allan." There are still many unused pages in the book, but James Allan had run his race. A monument in Rylstone Cemetery records, "James Allan, 1852–1929." Another monument in Burnbrae Cemetery bears the name "David Allan, 1817–1892." A fitting inscription might well read, "A man with a vision." He was still a young man when he first surveyed the Crowe River and recognized its potential. He had realized his dream, and passed the fruits of his labours on to his descendants. The mill he built was a boon to the pioneer community. It would continue to service the area for another sixty years after his death. It provided work for numerous local lads and influenced the lives of many people. His grandson, Will, would carry on the tradition deep into the twentieth century, nursing along the aging machinery, but still busily sawing lumber and cracking the grain brought in by local farmers. Will, the last owner of Allan's Mills, would own and operate the mill from 1916 until its fiery death in 1950. It could be correctly expressed that he stood tall in the community, in both a literal and figurative sense. An old school photo of Will reveals a lad head and shoulders above his schoolmates. In manhood, he stood well over six feet, a long lean framework of bone and sinew. Like his father and grandfather, he was a quietly, dominant force in the neighbourhood, and a well respected one. Annie, his genial wife, was as short as Will was tall, the disparity particularly apparent when they stood together. At those times, he always appeared to stoop a little as if to compensate for the height differential. A strong, lantern-jawed face, a visage that brooked no nonsense, he was sometimes a bit intimidating to the lads who laboured under his firm hand. Will Allan was a serious man on the job, a no nonsense boss. His attitude was well-warranted. Many hazards lurked around the mill machinery. Safety standards were unheard of. Workmen's Compensation was still in the future. Common sense and discretion were essential tools to staying healthy. To my knowledge, Will Allan never was personally involved in a serious industrial accident over many years of mill operation.

Many of the local lads worked occasionally at the mill, usually helping in the lumber sawing part of the operation. Some memories from another era of Allan's Mills in the 1940s: The road to the mill wound through the woods in a down river direction before turning right to its destination. Along the way, it passed tall piles of fresh-cut lumber, carefully stacked to dry in the summer sun. The approach to the mill was a large semi-circle at the centre of which a tall stoop projected from the grist mill. It had been built to accommodate unloading from high wagons in pioneer days and, for the lower vehicles now in use, it was an upward lift to unload. Sometimes there would be a lineup of vehicles waiting, trucks, cars pulling trailers, wagons, buggies, democrats, all manner of conveyances. No one seemed to fret over delay. This was a popular meeting place, a chance to talk and gossip, to pick up any fresh community news.

To the right of the grist mill, and attached to it was the saw mill, a place of noisy activity. A skidway stuck out from its open side, piled high with logs. A string of stove pipes, suspended on poles, led from the saw mill to an ever-growing mountain of sawdust. Though it was constantly being hauled away to serve as live-stock bedding and cover for ice houses, it never seemed to get any smaller. Like a huge inverted ice cream cone, it dominated a low area in front of the mill. The road looped around it before swinging back to rejoin itself near the entrance. The miller stood on the tall dock waiting to receive the bags of grain and to roll them into the mill on his two-wheeled trolley. A tall man in chop-dusted overalls, and a peaked 'railway' cap, eyebrows powdered in floury dust. A cigarette dangled from his lips. Will Allan was a chain smoker, lighting another from the butt of the one just finished. Eighty to one hundred cigarettes a day were consumed. Actually, he wore them more than he smoked them. Lean and sinewy, he slung the bags onto his trolley and wheeled them inside to the hopper. Here, on the milling floor, the ear was assaulted with a medley of sounds. The floor resonated with the thump of heavy machinery. Inside an enclosed chute, that rose from floor to ceiling, little buckets clattered as they moved in an endless cycle. They scooped up the freshly ground "chop" and carried it to waiting bags. The shrill of a saw in a nearby room came from the shingle making machine. Here blocks of wood were being sawn into cedar shingles.

Through memories dulled by time, certain features stand out. On one wall was the long work bench where Will Allan also maintained his account book. It was his own ledger. The one quoted from in this history retired with his father, James. A tale is told of one day when Will sat at the bench labouring over journal entries. The river was heavily populated with black water snakes. The mill, with all its nooks and crannies became, in time, a favoured habitat for many of these black snakes. They especially liked the attic area right above the grist mill where they could bask in the sunlight that filtered through dusty windows. The many mice that also enjoyed mill lodgings were, in turn, enjoyed by the black snakes, a sup-plement to their normal water-based prey. The miller's concentration on his fig-ures was suddenly shattered in startling fashion. One of the resident black snakes slipped off an overhead beam and landed on his open book!

Beside the bench stood a safe, a square solid object that seemed out of place with all the spare parts and mill accessories scattered about. More tools and equip-ment decorated rough-boarded walls. A short corridor led from the grist mill to the saw mill. Here, through an opening in the floor projected the shaft, topped by the iron wheel that operated the water gate. Dark waters swirled in the depths below, seeking passage through the opened gate.

Entering the saw mill, the first machine encountered was the edger saw. It performed the last operation in lumber production, trimming away any 'wane' edges on boards that had just been sawn. Beyond it, the big lumber saw dominated the scene. Above it, suspended from an overhead beam, there was a wire mesh screen set in a wooden frame. It hung between the sawyer and the saw. Its purpose was to deflect any splinters of wood or knots that might break away in the sawing process and be hurled in the direction of the sawyer. There were several holes and patched areas in the screening, mute evidence of "near misses." Beside the saw and running the length of the building was the track that carried the log carriage to and from the saw. In another area, there were piles of boards recently smoothed out by the nearby planer and tongue and groove lumber turned out by the shaper.

This riverside portion of the mill also contained the generator/turbine. When the rest of the mill was shut down and silent, its measured beat could still be heard, a giant heart beat, muted but powerful, sounding out a rhythmic "crump, crump, crump." Unlike the waterwheel that powered the mill, the one that drove the generator ran continuously.

As mid-century approached, Allan's Mills was still doing a thriving business in both grist and saw mill trade, Though now a man in his sixties, W.T. Allan seemed hardly to have lost a step to time. The mill too was aging. Its rough plank floors now worn smooth by booted feet, countless footsteps in the traffic of a hundred years. Harder now to replace failing machinery parts, the manufacturers of the original running gear no longer were in operation. Allan was able to overcome these maintenance difficulties although sometimes it required "shopping around" to places where similar type mills still existed. The ancient plant still functioned reliably, it was not a mechanical failure that shut it down suddenly, so finally.

The autumn months of 1950 were warm and dry in this area. Fall ploughing was in progress, farmers hopeful that fall rains would soon arrive to soften the sun-baked soil. At the mill, a busy day was in progress, a skidway of logs being steadily converted to lumber. The workers were glad of the breeze that sprang up from the west that afternoon. It made working conditions a bit more comfortable.

There are various opinions on what initiated the disaster about to happen. Could it have been one of Will Allan's cigarette butts? Possibly, but unlikely. He was a careful man, deliberate in his ways. The butt that he used to light the following cigarette was always carefully mashed before being discarded. Was it a build up of sawdust in the blower pit, heated by friction against belt or pulley and finally bursting into flames?

The electric motor that drove the blower is also a likely suspect. Working hard in the dusty confines of the pit, it may have started arcing, producing the flash that reached flammable material so close at hand. Whatever the cause of the ignition, the resulting fire was an almost spontaneous reaction. Allan was midway through a cut, hand steady on the control lever, as he propelled log and carriage against the saw. Attention concentrated on the sawing operation, he still caught, in his vision, the puff of smoke that suddenly rose from below. Immediate action was reflex, automatically controlled by years of experience in other crises. Reverse the log carriage, shut down the saw. A call for help sent employees running for buckets while Will scrambled into the pit in a desperate effort to quench the fire before it gained a foothold. It was already too late. Everything in the mill was tinder dry after a long hot summer and fall. In a cramped crawl space, under the saw mill floor, the fire continued its relentless march. Floor boards were pried up to gain better access, and the hurriedly-assembled bucket brigade was delivering water as fast as they could dip it from the Crowe. More local folk kept arriving to join the human chain as news quickly spread. It was all to no avail. The demon that raged in the bowels of the old plant would not be denied. Gaining strength every minute, it fed on the bone-dry planking of the floor and burst through. Spreading across the remaining floor, the conflagration found new fuel in shavings of the planing mill and the stack of planed lumber. The fire fighters were pushed back reeling from the fury of the blaze. Nothing left to do now but try to retrieve any equipment and material still within approachable reach. The flames raced up the walls and attacked the roof. An ominous pillar of cloud rose over the Crowe River, shot with darting flame and a cascade of fiery sparks. The breeze, which had afforded pleasant relief to sweaty workmen such a short while ago, was now an ally of fire. Airborne sparks, pushed by the westerly wind, rained down on the bridge a good three hundred yards upriver. This they could save, and volunteers were dispatched to wet down the planking as it started to smoulder. First built by the Allans and last to crumble into ashes was the grist mill.

In the final act of the drama, last scene before the curtain closes, the safe which had squatted so solidly and securely on the milling floor, tilted slightly, then dropped through to the tail race below. In the maelstrom then raging, no one noticed its quiet exit. Little was left but stark concrete walls as evening shadows crept in. A few logs still smouldered on the burnt-out skidway and within the stone and concrete foundations, glowing coals, the ashes of the mill. Amid the rubble, resting in the mill race, lay the waterwheel which had driven the mill for over one hundred years. A statistician would enjoy calculating the revolutions it had made in all those years! Its tilted shaft rising from the riverbed, appeared to be pointing an accusing finger skyward.

Sombre thoughts must have occupied Will Allan's mind as he stood there staring at the glowing embers. It was the end of an era that had spanned three generations, starting with the vision of David Allan. It was a tragedy the neighbourhood could sense – the mill had been an integral part of the community for so long. True, its value was gradually diminishing, eclipsed by more modern and efficient machines and changing market conditions. It had almost run its race. Another fifteen years, possibly before it would have shut down. There were no Allan sons to step in and continue the tradition. What a wonderful treasure to our heritage, if it had survived. A working pioneer mill, unchanged, one of the very few that remain. It was not to be.

Will Allan did not quit. There was still custom sawing to be done. The grist mill was gone but sawmill facilities could be put together and this he proceeded to do, setting it up in one of the barn buildings near the house. No water wheel now to drive his equipment. His power source, a tractor. At this location, Allan continued to saw logs for several more years. It was not through necessity that he continued his trade. Bethlehem Steel was considering an iron mine on his property and had already paid him for the mining rights. How "ironic" that the metal the Allans had searched for earlier some distance away on the Crossen farm would be discovered almost on their doorstep! No – Will Allan kept on sawing because it was something he enjoyed doing and did well.

In the wake of the fire, the river, no longer restricted by man-made barriers, swept through the wreckage, scouring the site of the mill, returning it gradually to nature. A new dam would eventually span the river, some twenty years hence. Anchored to the shoreline about fifty feet above where the old dam terminated at the mill, it would follow a straight course across the river. Consideration was given to locating the far end further upstream as well. The engineers concluded that the best place to tie it to the shore was at the same point that David Allan had chosen for his pioneer dam more than one hundred and thirty years ago. Previous to the construction of the new dam, escaping water had reduced water levels significantly. This created an opportunity to retrieve many logs from the river bottom, waterlogged but in "mint" condition. Relics from the river drives of over a century ago.

Nature and the river have not yet managed to reclaim the mill site, to obliterate what was once the scene of so much activity and industry. Slowly, steadily, though, they are erasing the past. The causeway leading to the mill is still intact, a ridged mound discernible beneath crawling vines of snake berry, thickets of berry brambles and the up thrusting growth of elms, willow and prickly ash. The vast and towering sawdust pile is gone, vanished into the soil to stimulate new growth in an encroaching jungle of green life. Constantly harassed and undermined by the river, some skeletons of the foundation walls stand, defiantly erect, while other parts have collapsed into the chortling stream below. The waterwheel has survived, a short stem of its shaft poking through the rock rubble that clogs the mill race. Nearby, the watergate, trapped in the same debris, has resisted the erosion of time, its heavy iron casting impervious to corrosion. The Allan safe, which came to rest in the tail race after the fire, has moved. Raging waters of the 1997 spring run-off somehow managed to pluck it from there and carry it down river for another hundred yards or so. It lies in the shallows, rusting sides still tightly gripped in steel bands. A heavy black object, incongruously obvious in an unnatural setting, and already home to many crustacean creatures that thrive in this part of the Crowe River.

The river rolls on, oblivious of the aspirations and ambitions of man. It is the same river that David Allan trapped to drive his mill and still serenely following its same course. Bethlehem Steel abandoned their proposed open mine pit. It would have involved a costly diversion of the river. The Crowe flows on, as it has since well before the dinosaurs roamed the land.

I look across the river. The dancing waters of the tail race sparkle in the afternoon sun. Sometimes, in the quiet of the night, beyond the voice of the restless river, I imagine another sound, remote and muffled, but steady with the rhythm of a heart beat. A ghost of the past — the Allan's Mills waterwheel.

Author's Note:

John Lisle, as previously noted, managed the Allan Mill during its earlier years of operation. It was quite natural that he would gravitate to that line of work upon his arrival in 1855. Ample experience in the milling trade had already been acquired before emigration to Upper Canada. The pioneer Lisle homestead was conveniently close to the mill. It was a good place to settle down, do a little farming, operate the mill and raise a family. As a great grandson of this pioneer, I've discovered interesting parallels in our life history.

John Lisle Sr. was born in Northumberland County, England in 1825. He was wed in 1854. John Lisle, author of this article, was born in Northumberland County, Ontario in 1925. He married in 1954. One hundred years separates two of the most important dates in both our lives.

SCHOOL DAY MEMORIES OF STANWOOD, S.S. # 9

by Madeline Simpson

My first memories of school, date back to when I was a beginner. I was six, and so, I sat at a double desk with my oldest sister. My teacher was Miss Daisy Sparkes, whom I addressed as "ma'am". She was English, and had complete control of her classroom, without use of threats or strap. One glance from her steely blue eyes, and the unlucky person caught in a misdemeanor, wanted to sink through the floor and out of sight. She was an excellent teacher, and my model for a future career.

Usually, my siblings and I walked through the fields to school, when the weather was dry enough in the spring, summer and fall. It was a short-cut, and we often sighted bluebirds that nested in the hollow fence-posts or in the stump fence. We were fascinated by the baby killdeer, that ran along the path on their little pink legs, looking like wind-up toys; while their mother tried to distract us with her appealing cries. In haying time, it was always easy to locate the meadowlark's nest, for Dad always carefully cut a wide circle around the nest, so as not to disturb the inhabitants. Sometimes, we stopped at a well, for a refreshing drink of spring water, or to chat with a kindly, elderly neighbour lady, while she watered their cattle. I can still see her in my mind's eye, wearing her ankle-length black skirt, long-sleeved blouse, brimmed hat and her welcoming smile.

Even in winter we traveled the fields, for there, the wind didn't pile up drifts, as it did on the road. My eldest sister led the way and broke the trail, while the rest of us followed behind her, including cousins and neighbouring children. Sometimes, we might stop briefly, to exclaim over the rabbit tracks in the snow covering the wheat field. The multiplicity of tracks made us speculate that the rabbits were having a party.

As we started for school on a cold morning, we often carried in our mittened hands, a warm wrapped dish of food, which Mom had prepared and put in the oven, while she attended to farm chores and breakfast. This not only warmed our hands on our walk to school, but also provided us with a warm lunch at noon. At 11:30, a nod from the teacher, gave us permission to place our warm food dish on top of the box stove to heat. The appetizing aroma was delicious to the senses, and we felt sorry for those who had only cold sandwiches for lunch.

We were allowed to leave the school grounds at recess and noon-hour. In the warmer weather, the girls could be found just across the road, on rail fence teeter-totters we fashioned ourselves. Older children were more likely to be playing ball in the back school yard. In June, noon-hours might be spent wading in the brook which ran through the woods on the neighbouring property, while the boys played tag or hide and seek.

In winter, at recesses, those who had sleds, could squeeze in a few rides down the hilly road, just opposite the school. At noon-hour, a run down the same hill would take you to the foot of a much steeper hilly road that wound about in a S-curve. Sleds were pulled to the school each morning, and shared with the less fortunate. Bob-sleds were very popular, for they could accommodate many riders. The driver lay "belly-whacker" down at the front. Then the riders piled on, either belly down or sitting. If upright, they placed their legs and arms around the person in front for security. The last rider got the sled started with a good push, and then jumped on at the last minute; and they were off for an exciting and swift ride. Single sleds, being lighter, sometimes went farther than the bob-sleds. When the bell rang, the loiterers, still on the hill, could rush to get on a sled that would take them almost to the school hill. A short run uphill to the school would get you there panting, but on time. As I look back on it now, I think how lenient our teacher was, to allow us this pleasure. When snow melted on the roads, there were still banks of snow on the "steeps," where precipitous banks led down to a swamp. This was an ideal place to fashion slides, and many a child sat on a wet bottom the rest of the day.

Miss Sparkes' Christmas concerts were the highlight of the year in our community. Much preparation went into this event, starting in November. Each school day, after the last recess, practice for a play began. Parts were allotted to even the poorest and shyest. I still remember those plays, "Christmas at the Manor House" with an English setting; "The Christmas Story" with a cast of the entire school population. Older children were taught how to make angel wings, shepherd's crooks etc. One Christmas, all the Mother Goose characters appeared on stage. I recall one parent who walked 5 miles or more, with her children to see the concert, the one delight of her meager life. Many years later, when I taught at S.S. #9, it was my pleasure to try to produce concerts that were comparable to Miss Sparkes'.

I remember my next teacher, who was red-haired, young and pretty. A sand table was her first acquisition and I remember pleasant hours spent around it, fashioning land and water shapes we had learned about in geography. Scrapbooks, too, were a part of learning, and buckets of flour paste were used to fill these books with pictures.

So, the years passed and soon I had finished Senior IV (grade 8), since the means to pay for a boarding place in Campbellford (there were no buses except from Hastings) were not available, I took a Continuation Course in public school, which covered 1st and 2nd Form (Gr. 9–10) of High School. A classmate and I were practically self-taught, as our teacher seemed to be pre-occupied with his other eight classes. Fortunately, I was able to go to High School for the remainder of my education. (Form II–V)

When I began my career as an elementary school teacher, the example and the precepts set by Miss Sparkes were my guide.

PIERRE BERTON AND A LOCAL POLITICAL BATTLE

Based on an account by Joanne Simpkin

While touring the Trent-Severn Waterway on a houseboat with his family in 1961, Pierre Berton became involved in some of the local political intrigue. As he

travelled along the waterway, he wrote descriptions of his progress for the Toronto
Star and the arrival of his houseboat was much anticipated along the way. After
being somewhat overwhelmed by the public attention along the route, Berton and
his family were looking for some peace and quiet, but inadvertently became
embroiled in Campbellford politics. In his book, My Times: Living with History,
1947–1995, he writes:

> The kids were getting irritated by all this public fuss. "Can't we find a
> quiet spot where we can have a skinny dip without being bothered?" they
> asked. I found a small, isolated cove where, in the calm waters, we briefly
> disported ourselves. I knew it couldn't last because I'd been receiving
> messages from the mayor of Campbellford about welcoming us with a
> brass band. And sure enough, as we splashed about, a group of
> Campbellfordians popped out of the bushes and, in spite of their good
> suits, waded knee-deep out to the houseboat. There they identified them-
> selves as members of the Campbellford Chamber of Commerce. Would
> we be their guests for lunch when we arrived? We cheerfully agreed, only
> to find ourselves in the centre of a local political battle. The next day the
> mayor himself and the city treasurer were lying in wait for us. Would we
> be his guests at dinner? the mayor asked.
>
> "But we've already agreed to lunch," I told him. The mayor looked
> mystified; the city treasurer looked perturbed. They asked for descrip-
> tions of our erstwhile hosts, like police demanding descriptions of a
> criminal gang. I gave them, and the mayor said darkly that he would have
> to look into the matter. An hour later he returned. "It's a political trick,"
> he said. "The Chamber of Commerce is run by Conservatives. They're
> trying to shut out us Liberals. Why, did you know that not a single coun-
> cil member has been asked to that lunch? They've been plotting behind
> my back to steal you before we could get you into town." I felt as if I'd
> stumbled into a scene from Leacock's Sunshine Sketches.
>
> Sure enough, lurking two full locks before Campbellford were the
> leader of the chamber, complete with fast cars to spirit us all away. The
> lunch was refreshingly free of politics, but enough, finally, was enough.
> We wanted to get away from all of it." [1]

The report by the Campbellford Herald in July, 1961, about the visit of the
Berton family casts a slightly different light on the event. The following is a transcript of the story:

Campbellford Products Presented To Columnist

CAMPBELLFORD (ENS) Score of people turned out here to welcome Toronto newspaper Columnist Pierre Berton and his family when they stopped off for a two-and a-half hour visit on Wednesday.

The family were guests of the Chamber of Commerce, and lunched at the Riviera Inn informally with George Nicholls, president of the Campbellford chamber and Mrs. Nicholls, and Campbellford photographer William Reid and Mrs. Reid.

The Chamber was notified In advance of Mr. Berton's visit, and was asked not to plan any formal civic reception. This has been discouraged throughout the tour

EXPRESS INTEREST

The houseboat used by the Bertons was met at Lock 14 above Campbellford.

The family expressed interest in a new tourist park which they passed on the way to the Locks and were taken to the park operated by D. A. Burgis where they enjoyed a swim before lunch.

Following the luncheon, George Nicholls presented Mr. Berton with a 10-pound cheddar cheese, a product of Seymour Township, and presented the children with quarter pound chocolate bars, made in the town.

COMMENDS CHAMBER

Mr. Berton commended the chamber for the efficient and informal way in which the visit was conducted, and said that as a boat operator on the system, he was pleased to see a new tourist information sign erected by the chamber near the town dock.

He said there was a distinct need for such information signs and directories. He made use of the free telephone provided by the Chamber to phone for provisions for his boat.

The tour, down the Trent waterway which started at Georgian Bay, ends Friday at Trenton. The Bertons will return to Toronto along the north shore of Lake Ontario.

Pierre Berton had a particular impact on the life of one local citizen, Joanne Jacobs Simpkin. Joanne had graduated from high school and was about to enter teachers' college. She was fortunate enough to travel with the Bertons on their houseboat between Lock 14 and town, during which she and Pierre had a lengthy conversation about the importance of a university education. Joanne feels that this conversation made a real difference in her life.

Pierre Berton and Joanne Jacobs Simpkins, on board the Berton houseboat as it travelled from Lock 14 to town in 1961.

Photo courtesy of Joanne Jacobs Simpkins

She did attend teachers' college, and went on to teach in Scarborough, but she quickly enrolled in a part-time studies program at Queen's University in Kingston and eventually graduated. She says that she will always be grateful for the "much appreciated gesture and learning experience" which she shared with Berton.

ENDNOTES

1 Pierre Berton, *My Times: Living with History, 1947–1995* (Toronto: Doubleday Canada Limited, 1995), pp. 213–214. Quoted with permission from Pierre Berton.

General References

Texts

Angus, James T. *A Respectable Ditch: A History of the Trent-Severn Waterway*, 1833–1920. Kingston and Montreal: McGill-Queen's University Press, 1988.

Brown, Lorraine. *The Trent-Severn Waterway: An Environmental Exploration*. Peterborough: Friends of the Trent-Severn Waterway, 1994.

A Century of Footprints. Campbellford: Campbellford/Seymour Agricultural Society, 1967.

DeCarrol, F. G. B ed. *Reflections: Campbellford Centennial Year – 1976*. Campbellford: np, [1976]

Ferris, K. B. and McGregor, J. F. "A Brief History of the Town of Campbellford," *Souvenir of Campbellford Golden Jubilee*, 1906–1956. Campbellford: np, 1956.

Guillet, Edwin, C. *Valley of the Trent*. Toronto: Champlain Society for the Government of Ontario, 1957.

History of Campbellford. Campbellford: Classes of 1939–1940, Campbellford District High School, 1940.

Illustrated Historical Atlas of the Counties of Northumberland and Durham, Ont. Toronto: H. Belden & Co., 1878.

Kingston, W. A. *The Light of Other Days: A History of Campbellford and Seymour Prior to 1900*. Campbellford: W. A. Kingston, 1967.

Walking/Driving Tours of Campbellford/Seymour. Campbellford: Campbellford/Seymour Heritage Society, 1984–1999.

Wilson, T. J. *Campbellford's Story*. Warkworth: Warkworth Journal, 1956.

Newspapers

Campbellford Herald. Campbellford: December, 1973-December, 1996. Available at Archives of Ontario on microfilm, N120, reel #1–10, N 558, reel #1–38. Reels #1–10 also available at Campbellford/Seymour Heritage Centre.

Community Press. Stirling: April, 1985- present.

The Campbellford Courier. Marmora: September, 1985–present.

Maps

Energy, Mines, and Resources Canada. *Campbellford 31C/5*, edition 5. Ottawa: Canada Centre for Mapping, Department of Energy, Mines, and Resources, 1994.

Ministry of Agriculture, *Province of Ontario. Fire Insurance Plan, Campbellford, Ont.*, June 1900, revised to May 1911. Prepared by Chas. E. Goad, Civil Engineer. Montreal and Toronto, Canada and London, England. Toronto: Ministry of Agriculture, Province of Ontario, 1900, 1911.

Compiled Plan of the Town of Campbellford in the Township of Seymour in the County of North. Made by Fraser Aylesworth, Ontario Land Surveyor. Madoc, Ont., Feb. 27, 1927.

Archival Resources

Archives of Ontario, Toronto.

National Archives, Ottawa

Northumberland Land Registry Office, Cobourg

Campbellford/Seymour Heritage Centre

Chapter References

Chapter 1   Beginnings

Texts

Allans' Journal, property of the McKeown family, handed down to Reg McKeown by his mother, Grace Allan.

Bean, David. *Landform Survey of Ferris Provincial Park*. Lindsay: Lindsay Forest Office, Department of Lands and Forests, 1972.

Bus Tour of Seymour East. Campbellford: Campbellford/Seymour Heritage Society, July, 1989.

Chapman, L. J. and Putnam, D. F. *The Physiography of Southern Ontario*, 2nd ed. Published for the Ontario Research Foundation, Toronto: U. of Toronto Press, 1966.

Driving Tour of Seymour East. Campbellford: Campbellford/Seymour Heritage Society, August, 1995.

Hall, Susan L. and Jones, Roger. *Northumberland County Environmentally Sensitive Areas Study, 1976*. Peterborough: Department of Biology, Trent University, 1976.

Krueger, Ralph and Raymond Corder. *Canada: A New Geography (Revised)*. Toronto: Holt, Rinehart and Winston of Canada, Ltd., 1974

North on 30: Trent River and Healey Falls. Campbellford: Campbellford/Seymour Heritage Society, August, 1997.

Rogers, Glenda. *Natural Areas Summary for the Municipality of Campbellford/Seymour*. Campbellford: Lower Trent Conservation Authority, 1998.

Seymour Township By-Law, May 31, 1875.

Maps

Plan of Emilyville, laid out for Robert C.Wilkins, Esq. On part of Lots number 8 and 9 in the 5th Concession and a part of Lot number 9 in the 6th Concession of the Township of/ Seymour. L. Benson, P. L. Surveyor, Belleville, June 25, 1852.

Contributors

Margaret Macmillan	Early history of Campbellford/Seymour
John Lisle	Stanwood, Allan's Mills
Ann Rowe	Districts and Hamlets
Margaret Dart and Joan West	History of Trent River
Dorothy Thomson	History of Rylstone
Doris and Frank Potts	History of Menie
Marilyn Bucholtz	Early history/geography of Seymour Township

Archival Materials — Campbellford/Seymour Heritage Society
Polmont Orange Lodge Ledger
Campbell Family History Files

Archival Materials — National Archives of Canada
National Archives of Canada, RG31, Statistics Canada. *1851 Census, Canada West, Northumberland County, Seymour Township, Part 1*. Microfilm C11739.

Archival Materials — Archives of Ontario

Archives of Ontario. *Campbellford Herald*. Campbellford: Jan. 15, 1880–Mar. 15, 1883. Microfilm N120, reel # 3.

Archives of Ontario. *Computerized Land Records Index*, alphabetical listing by name of township, Microfiche, #057 and by surname, Microfiche #001-053.

Archives of Ontario, RG 1 — A — IV, Crown Land and Resources, Schedules and Land Rolls, Vol. 31. *Return of Lands sold and located in the Township of Seymour in the Newcastle District from the year 1823 to the 1st March 1832*, pp.1–18. Microfilm, MS400, reel 11.

Archives of Ontario, Records of the Office of the Registrar of Ontario, RG80-8-0-71, Vol. E, *Northumberland County Register of Deaths, 1881*, p. 171, #12700, David Campbell, microfilm, MS835, reel #28.

Archives of Ontario, GS ONT. 1-1109, Surrogate Court, Northumberland and Durham, Cobourg, *Will #1640, David Campbell*.

Chapter 2   The River Valley

Texts

Cristall, Ferne et al. *The Percy Portage*. Peterborough: Trent University Press, 1973.

Walking Tour. Campbellford: Campbellford / Seymour Heritage Society, June 26, 1994.

Contributors

John Lisle	Allan Mill
Morley and Madge Tanner	Campbellford Pulp Mill
Larry Healey	Northumberland Paper and Electric Company
Campbellford / Seymour Chamber of Commerce	Various Resort Brochures
Frank and Doris Potts	Various cottages / resorts on Percy Reach
Eleanor Brown and Margaret Dart	Various cottages / resorts in Trent River area
Dennis Little	Various cottages / resorts in Lake Seymour and Crowe Bay
Kelly Pender	Crowe Valley Conservation Authority
Marcia Keller	Keller Vacation Properties
Don Keller	Fisherman's Paradise / Camp Eagle Eye
Jacqui and Raymond Whyte	Parkside Cottages
Dan and Linda Heidt	Percy Boom Haven / Jake's Cottages
James Jackson and Morag Gow	Percy Boom Lodge
Nan Sayers and Bill Le Suer	Puffball Inn
Kay Smith and Madeleine Montrose	Trent House Hotel
Kathy Herrold	Villa Trent
Carol Roebuck and Dorothy Douglas	Ferris Park
Jim Kelleher	Lower Trent Conservation Authority

Archival Resources — Campbellford / Seymour Heritage Society

River Valley Vertical Files

Chapter 3   Agriculture

Texts

A Fair Share: A History of Agricultural Societies and Fairs in Ontario, 1792–1992. Toronto: Ontario
 Association of Agricultural Societies, 1992.

Macoun, John. *Autobiography of John Macoun, Canadian Explorer and Naturalist, 1931–1920.* Ottawa:
 Ottawa Field-Naturalists' Club, 1979.

Contributors

Lloyd Anderson	Horses
Curle Family	Maple Syrup Industry
Carolyn Donald	4-H Clubs
Bob Eley	1999 Campbellford Fair
Ruth Haig	Junior Farmers' Association
JohnLisle	Ayrshires
Ruby McCulloch	4-H Clubs
Art Nelson	Holsteins, Jerseys, Campbellford/Seymour Agricultural Fair/Board
Cindy Nelson	Campbellford/Seymour Agricultural Fair/Board
Don Pollock	Cheese Industry
Ann Rowe	Rowe Family
Alison Wagner	Campbellford Fair/Board

Archival Materials — Campbellford/Seymour Heritage Society

Brae Cheese Factory Ledgers, 1873–1909. Donated by Lorna and Ken Oddie, Campbellford.

Annual Programs of Campbellford/Seymour Agricultural Society Fairs. Campbellford/Seymour
 Agricultural Society.

Agriculture Vertical Files

Chapter 4   Business, Commerce and the Professions

Contributors

Don Frederick, Murray Johnston, Lawrence Craighead, John Lisle	Memory Lane
Frank Potts	Banking
Lilian Brode	Accounting Profession
Neil Burgess	Lawyers
Ann Rowe	Barbers
Dick Beattie	Beattie Mill
Don Bennett	Bennett's Furniture
Art Bertrand, Wayne Bertrand	Bertrand Motors
Tom and Bev Burgis	Burgis Hardware
Debbie Fox	Farmer's Market
Bob Eley, Bob Murison, Harold Carlaw, Phil Sheaff	Canadian Flight Equipment
Wayne Gunter, Steve McCarthy	Canadian Tire
Bob Eley	Clarion Boats
Uerlen Lloyd	Clifton Tea Room/Chateau Restaurant
Chuck Davidson	Davidson Motors

Mario Milano	Dart Cup
Alice Donald	Donald Plumbing
Peter and Chris Dooher	Dooher's Bakery
Annabelle Ellis	Ellis Delivery
Barbara Pechkovsky	Fox Fuels
Ann Rowe	Hotels
Laurie Nesbitt, Carole and Wayne Bertrand	Horsman's Beverages
Jack and Irene Torrance	Jack's Place
Gwen Dubay	Jacobs Plumbing
Francis Long	Long's Restaurant
Margaret Macmillan	Macmillan's I.G.A.
Barbara Pechkovsky, Neil McKeel	McKeel Companies
Anne Craig	Palliser's
David Carlaw, Jim Jones	Replicar
Dennis Little	Stapley/Little Machine Shop
Wilfred Turner	Turner's
Jeff Weaver	Weaver Funeral Home
Anne Linton, Wayne Bertrand, Elzo Eisinga	Weldrest/Classic Cleaners
Rod and Mary Lynn Williams	William's Auction
Gary Wood	Cook's/World's Finest Chocolate

Archival Materials — Campbellford/Seymour Heritage Society
Business History Vertical File
Campbellford/Seymour Oral History Files

Chapter 5   Municipal Affairs and Services

Texts
Water-Works of Canada, compiled by Leo G. Denis, BSc. Ottawa: Commission of Conservation, 1909.

Contributors

Bill Petherick	Seymour Council Lists
Donna Wilson	Campbellford/Seymour Library
Bill Bruins, Marilyn Scott	O.P.P.
Gwen Dubay, Bob Wickens, Laurie Nesbitt	Campbellford/Seymour Fire Department
Jack and Nancy Parsons	Town Crier
David Wheeler	Post Office
Ann Rowe	P.U.C.

Archival Materials — Municipality of Campbellford/Seymour
Minute Books of Town of Campbellford and Township of Seymour Councils, January 21, 1850–present.
Bylaw Books, Town of Campbellford and Township of Seymour, January 21, 1950–present

Archival Materials — Campbellford/Seymour Heritage Society
Municipal Vertical Files

Chapter 6   Schools

Texts

Boland, Edgar. *From the Pioneers to the Seventies: A History of the Diocese of Peterborough, 1882–1975*, 1st ed. Peterborough: Maxwell Review, 1976.

Campbellford High School 1923–1973. Campbellford: Campbellford Herald, 1973.

The Heritage Years, compiled by the Stirling Historical Book Committee and the New Horizons Committee. Stirling: Stirling Book Committee, 1984.

A Backward Glance: A History of Rawdon Township, compiled by Young Canada Works 1238-RK-2. Madoc: Madoc Review Ltd, nd.

Tweedmuir History, curator Dorothy Thomson. Campbellford: Rylstone Women's Institute, 1947–present

Tweedmuir History, curator Ruth Haig. Campbellford: Seymour East Women's Institute, 1947–present.

Tweedmuir History, curator Grace Wynn. Campbellford: Seymour West Women's Institute, 1947–present.

Tweedmuir History, curator Joan West. Campbellford: Trent River Women's Institute, 1947–present.

Newspapers

Peterborough Examiner, Monday, October 15, 1923.

Maps

Campbellford Sanitary System for Public and High School, Plan of School Grounds. Scale: 20' = 1." James, Loudon, and Hertzberg Ltd., Consulting Engineers, Toronto. C-81–4 — July 4, 1917; C-81–3 — July 27, 1917; C-81–2 — July 27, 1917; C-81–2 — July 27, 1917.

Contributors

Margaret Crothers, Barbara Samson-Willis	History of Campbellford Schools, Campbellford High School
Laurie Johnson	Campbellford High School
Diane Cancilla	Centre for Independent Studies
Bert Whitfield, Donalda Runions	Kent Public School
George McCleary	Hillcrest Public School
Vera Newman	Home and School Association
Gladys Petherick	S.S. #2 — Pethericks
Carolyn Free Donald, Bernice Free Nakishima, Ruby McCulloch, Kay Frederick	S.S. #3 — Connelly's
Grace Wynn, Kevin Curle	S.S. #4 — West's
Doris Potts, Ruth Haig	S.S. #5 — English Line
Marion Smith, Grace Wynn	S.S. #6 — Meyersburg
Doris Smith	S.S. #7 — Masson's
John Lisle, Madeline Simpson	S.S. #9 — Stanwood
Margaret Dart, Joan West	S.S. #10 — Trent River
Doris Potts, Shirley Twigg	S.S. #11 — Burnbrae
Grace Wynn	S.S. #12 — Fleming's/Percy/Seymour Union School

Archival Materials — Campbellford/Seymour Heritage Society

Schools Vertical File

Chapter 7   Churches and Cemeteries

Texts

Boland, Edgar. *From the Pioneers to the Seventies: A History of the Diocese of Peterborough, 1882–1975*, 1st ed. Peterborough: Maxwell Review, 1976.

Campbellford Baptist Church: A Brief History. Campbellford: Campbellford Baptist Church, 1996.

Centenary of Presbyterianism, 1836-1936: St. Andrew's Church, Campbellford, Ontario, An Historic Sketch, compiled by W. J. Harold Dunk. Campbellford: Presbyterian Church of Canada, 1936.

Centennial of Canadian Methodism, published by direction of the General Conference. Toronto: William Briggs, 1891.

Cornish, George H. *Cyclopaedia of Methodism in Canada: Historical, Educational, and Statistical Information Dating from the Beginnings of the Work in the Several Provinces of the Dominion of Canada and Extending to the Annual Conferences of 1880. Vol. I, Beginnings to 1874*; Vol II, 1881–1903. Toronto: Methodist Book and Publishing House, 1903.

Collins, Robert. *The Holy War of Sally Ann: The Salvation Army in Canada*. Saskatoon: Western Producer Prairie Books, 1984.

The Methodist Yearbook: Recognition Volume. Toronto: William Briggs, 1917.

Muir, Elizabeth Gillan. *Petticoats in the Pulpit: The Story of Early Nineteenth-Century Methodist Women Preacher in Upper Canada*. Toronto: United Church Publishing House, 1991.

Reflection — Renewal — Rebirth: A Century of Fellowship; Tabernacle United Church, English Line 100th Anniversary, 1890–1990, compiled by the Centennial Committee of Tabernacle United Church. Campbellford: Tabernacle United Church, 1990.

A Short History of Anglican Witness — Seymour Township and Campbellford, 1835–1979, compiled by Hilda and Frank Bonnycastle. Campbellford: Christ Church, Campbellford, 1979.

A Short History of Anglican Witness — Seymour Township and Campbellford, 1835–1994, compiled by Hilda and Frank Bonnycastle, updated by Ethel Higginson. Campbellford: Christ Church, Campbellford, 1994.

St. Andrew's Church, Campbellford, Ont. — 1858–1908, compiled by Rev. A. C. Reeves. Campbellford: St. Andrew's Presbyterian Church, 1908.

The Story of Rylstone Church: Souvenir Booklet, 1968, compiled by Rev. Grant Meiklejohn, ed. by Winnie Jones. Stirling: Rylestone United Church, 1968.

The Story of Springbrook United Church, 1882–1957: 75th Anniversary Souvenir Booklet, compiled by the 75th Anniversary Committee. Stirling: Springbrook United Church, 1957.

Contributors

Dave and Joan Lane	Christ Church
Doris Maki	Anglican Church Women
Fran Douglas, Margaret Macmillan, Elva Kerr	St. Andrew's Presbyterian Church
Ann Rowe	Early Methodist Congregations
Doris Potts, Norma Thompson	Hoard's United Church
Carole Benor	St. John's United Church
Donalda Graham	St. John's United Church Women
John Lisle, Dorothy Thomson, Mabel Brunton	Stanwood United Church
Ruth Haig	Tabernacle United Church
Margaret Dart	Trent River United Church
Gladys Petherick	Zion United Church

Pat Bendl, Father C. Hickson	St. Mary's Catholic Church
Pamela Goudreault	St. Mary's Catholic Women's League
Rev. R. K. Campbell	Glad Tidings Pentecostal Church
Marion and David Smallwood	Campbellford Baptist Church
Wilf Turner	Jehovah's Witnesses
Margaret Anne Rowan	Church of Jesus Christ of Latter Day Saints
Ann Rowe	Cemeteries

Archival Materials — Campbellford/Seymour Heritage Society
Churches Vertical File

Chapter 8   Organizations

Texts

Ambrose, Linda M. *For Home and Country: the Centennial History of the Women's Institutes in Ontario.*
     Guelph: Federated Women's Institutes of Ontario, 1996.

Contributors

Steve Grills	Kinsmen Club
Anne Locke, Donalda Runions	Kinettes
Eric Holmden	Lions Club
Bev Scott	Lioness Club
Bob Scott	Rotary Club
Joy Herrington, Jack Bell, Elwood Irwin, Doug Robertson	Campbellford Royal Canadian Legion and Auxiliary
Marie Locke, Shirley Simpson	Campbellford and Bemersyde IODE
Dorothy Thomson	Rylstone Women's Institute
Ruth Haig, Doris Potts	Seymour East Women's Institute
Grace Wynn, Eileen Rutherford	Seymour West Women's Institute
Margaret Dart, Joan West	Trent River Women's Institute
Doug Carswell	Masonic Lodges
Marguerite Burgis	Easterm Star
Carl Free, Ralph Kerr	Loyal Orange Lodge
Jack and Irene Torrance, Audrey Johnston	Oddfellows and Rebekahs
Vivian Smallwood	Guiding
Doug Carswell	Scouting
Gordon Thompson	CDHS Environmental Club
Betty Taylor, Carol Roebuck, Bob Scott	Friends of Ferris Park
Joyce Stephens	Campbellford Senior Citizens Club

Archival Materials — Archives of Ontario

Archives of Ontario. F878, *Inventory of the Papers of the Loyal Orange Association of British America.*
     Loyal Orange Lodge No. 526, Seymour Township, Ontario, July 1993.

Archival Materials — Campbellford/Seymour Heritage Society

Organizations Vertical File

Chapter 9   Communications and Transportation

Texts

Hansen, Keith. *Last Trains from Lindsay*. Roseneath: Sandy Flats Publications, 1997.

Hopkins, J. Castell. *Encyclopedic Canada*. Vol. 5. Brantford and Toronto: Bradley-Garretson Co. Ltd., 1896.

Schroeder's Antiques Price Guide. Paducah, Kentucky: Schroeder's Publishing Company, 1996.

Maps

Canadian National Railways, Central Region Southern Ontario District, Campbellford Subdivision, Belleville Division. Division Engineer's Office, Belleville, Ont., August 15, 1940. File 1020-Ca.37, Jan. 18, 1946. A. V. Johnston, Acting division Engineer.

National Archives of Canada. National Map Collection, #156709. *Proposed Deviation of Part of the Grand Junction Section of the Midland Railway Company of Canada: Campbellford*. J. G. Macklin, Engineer.

Contributors

Marilyn Scott	The Despatch
Rolly Ethier	The Courier
John Campbell	The Campbellford Herald
Alan Coxwell	Community Press
Margaret Crothers, Carolyn Donald	Post Cards
Marilyn Scott, Goldie Loucks, Helen Wood,	Telephone
Vera Newman, Gert Heffernan, Donna Carswell	
Katherine Cochrane	CKOL Radio
Bob Eley	Television and the Internet
Ann Rowe	Roads
Margaret Crothers, Barbara Samson-Willis	Railways
Brian Redden, Marilyn Scott	Charlie Redden
Fred Ames	Ames Coach Lines
Elizabeth Free Loukes	Air Connection

Archival Materials — Bell Telephone Company of Canada

Bell Telephone Company of Official Telephone Directory, District of Eastern Ontario. Montreal: Bell Telephone Company of Canada, 1900, pg.44-5.

Archival Materials — Campbellford/Seymour Heritage Society

Campbellford Despatch, 5 issues, dated February 23, 1899, September 12, 1901, November 3, 1904, July 5, 1906, November 14, 1912.

Communications and Transportation Vertical File

Post Card Collection

Oral History Collection: Interview with Brian Redden

Chapter 10   Health and Social Services

Texts

Access-Ability, Newsletters of Haliburton, Northumberland and Victoria Access Centre

Campbellford Memorial Hospital Annual Reports

Campbellford Memorial Hospital Foundation Annual Reports

Children's Aid Society of Northumberland 100th Anniversary Flyer

CMH Communicator

Newpapers

Campbellford Memorial Hospital, Supplement to the Campbellford Herald, 1978.

Contributors

Frank Linton	Campbellford Memorial Hospital
Marlene Bailey	Memories of Campbellford Memorial Hospital
Margaret Crothers, Don Bennett, Gwen Dubay	Ambulance/Emergency Service
Marilyn Scott	Hospital Auxiliary
Margaret Crothers, Wendy Warner	Campbellford Memorial Hospital Foundation
Margaret Crothers, Jim Bryson	Hospital Volunteers
Ann Rowe	Dentists/Doctors
Margaret Crothers	Multicare Lodge
Margaret Crothers	Self-Care Accommodation
Margaret Crothers	Retirement and Nursing Homes
Marjory Oke	Public Health Unit
Gene Duplessis	Wellness Centre
Diana Rutherford, Leona White	Palliative Care
Carolyn Lee	Access
Margaret Crothers	VON
Thea Dunk	Block Parents
Mary Cook	Campbellford and District Association for Community Living
Barbara Samson-Willis	Children's Aid Society
Fran Douglas	Cancer Society
Barbara Samson-Willis	Community Resource Centre
Don Bennett, Doris Thompson	Food Bank
Bill Bruins, Peter and Mary Panabaker, Marilyn Scott	Fishing Hole

Archival Resources — Campbellford/Seymour Heritage Society

Health and Social Services Vertical Files

Chapter 11   The Military

Texts

Boyce, Betsy Dewar, *The Rebels of Hastings*. Toronto: University of Toronto Press, 1992.

Gray, William. *Soldiers of the King*. New York: Stoddart, 1995.

Marteinson, J., et al. *We Stand On Guard*. Montreal: Ovale Publ, 1992.

Morris, D. A. *The Canadian Militia*. Erin: Boston Mills Press, 1983.

Morton, Desmond. *A Military History of Canada*. Edmonton: Hurtig, 1985.

Nicholson, G. W. L. *Canada's Nursing Sisters*. Toronto: A. M. Habbert Ltd., 1975.

"Northumberland Militia Return, 1828" *Ontario Register*, vol. 1, No. 4, October, 1968

Stewart, C. H. *The Concise Lineages of the Canadian Army*, 1955–Date, Rev. Toronto: Stewart, C. H., 1972.

Withrow, W. H. *A Popular History of the Dominion of Canada*. Toronto: William Briggs, 1884.

Contributors

Marilyn Scott	Tom Smith Interview
Neil Smith	Military History of Campbellford
Neil McKeel	Cenotaph

Archival Resources — Campbellford/Seymour Heritage Society

Military Vertical File

Legion pamphlet on initiation of the Cenotaph.

Archival Resources-Hastings and Prince Edward Regimental Museum

Files and other materials relating to participation of Campbellford area citizens in war efforts between 1828 and present day.

Chapter 12   Culture, Entertainment, and the Arts

Newspapers

The Saturday Globe, Vol XLIX, No. 13622.

Contributors

Margaret Macmillan	Early Artists
Jean Tilney	Horticulture
Anne Linton	Northumberland Arts and Crafts
Ann Rowe	Photographers
James Jones	Museums
Charlie Mahoney	Home of the Indians
Harold Carlaw	Memorial Military Museum
Margaret Macmillan	Heritage Centre
Ann Rowe	Theatres and Music Halls
Ann Rowe, Austin and Violet Dunk	Dance Halls and Pavilions
Ann Rowe, Don Bennett	Instrumental Music
Marilyn Scott	Local Musicians
Fran Douglas	Johnny Douglas

Archival Resources — Campbellford/Seymour Heritage Society

Culture, Arts, and Entertainment Vertical Files

Chapter 13   Sports

Contributors

Ann Rowe	Badminton
Marilyn Scott	Bowling
John Lisle	Cricket
Marilyn Scott, Barbara Samson-Willis	Curling
Ann Rowe	Cycling
Marilyn Scott, Shelley Anderson	Equestrian Activities
Jim Crothers, Nancy Brouwers	Football
Ann Rowe	Golf
John Lisle, Wilbert Blake	Hockey
Marilyn Scott, Ann Rowe	Arenas

Marilyn Scott	Lacrosse
Marilyn Scott, Helen Meyers, Beth Taylor	Lawn Bowling
Margaret Crothers	Snowmobiling
John Lisle, Ann Rowe, Barbara Samson-Willis	Baseball
Ann Rowe, Barbara Samson-Willis	Swimming
Sally Alton, Marilyn Scott	Tennis
Marilyn Scott	Wrestling
Sally Alton	Skating
Marilyn Scott	Kyle Pettey
Marilyn Scott	Cassie Turner

Archival Resources — Campbellford/Seymour Heritage Society
Sports Vertical Files

Chapter 14   Disasters

Texts

Cobourg Star, 1831–1849 — Births, Marriages, Deaths. Transcribed by Percy L. Climo, Cobourg, 1980. Peterborough: New Horizons Committee, Kawartha Branch, Ontario Genealogical Society, 1985, various pages.

Cobourg Star, 1831–1849 — Births, Marriages, Deaths: Supplement. Transcribed by William Amell, Peterborough, 1985. Peterborough: New Horizons Committee, Kawartha Branch, Ontario Genealogical Society, 1985, various pages.

Peterborough Newspapers, 1837–1856: Gazette, 1845, Despatch, 1846–56 — Births, Marriages, Deaths. Transcribed by William D. Amell, Peterborough, 1982. Peterborough: Kawartha BMD Books, 1987, various pages.

Peterborough Review, 1854–1868 — Births, Marriages, Deaths. Peterborough: Kawartha BMD Books, no date, various pages.

Donald A. McKenzie. *Death Notices From The Canada Christian Advocate, 1858–1872*. Lambertville, NJ: Hunterdon House, 1992, various pages.

Donald A. McKenzie. *Death Notices From The Christian Guardian, 1836–1850*. Lambertville, NJ: Hunterdon House, 1982, various pages.

Donald A. McKenzie, *Death Notices from the Christian Guardian, 1851–1869*. Lambertville, NJ: Hunterdon House, 1984, various pages.

Archival Resources — Campbellford/Seymour Heritage Society
Disasters Vertical Files

Chapter 15   People

Texts

Buck, Ruth Matheson. *The Doctor Rode Sidesaddle*. Toronto: McClelland, 1974

Macoun, John. *Autobiography of John Macoun, Canadian Explorer and Naturalist, 1931–1920*. Ottawa: Ottawa Field-Naturalists' Club, 1979.

Contributors

Marilyn Scott, Roy Barnum	Roy Barnum
Donna Carswell	John Ernest Birks

Marilyn Scott	Bill Boyd
Marilyn Scott, Bill Bruins	Bill Bruins
Angela Travers	Harold Carr
Marilyn Scott, Fran Douglas	J. F. Ross Douglas
Bob Eley, Margaret Crothers	Harry Free
Marilyn Scott, Annie Greenly	Annie Greenly
Marilyn Scott, Barbara Greenly	Barbara Greenly
Marilyn Scott, Florence Headrick	Florence Headrick
Marilyn Scott, Art Linton, Barbara Samson-Willis	Frank Linton
Margaret Macmillan	Walter Lowe
Ann Rowe	George Lucy
Heritage Centre Files	Hector Macmillan
Margaret Macmillan	Peter Macmillan
Bob Eley	John Macoun
Doris Potts, Margaret	Elizabeth Scott Matheson
Marilyn Scott	Archie Meyers
Paul and Sue O'Sullivan, Marilyn Scott	Paul O'Sullivan
Frank and Doris Potts, Marilyn Scott	Frank and Doris Potts
Frank Potts, Marilyn Scott	George Potts
Cathy Redden, Marilyn Scott	Cathy Redden
Ann Rowe	Russell Rowe
Margaret Crothers, Barbara Samson-Willis	Ken Sisley
Morley Tanner, Gwen Dubay, Ann Rowe	Morley Tanner
Katherine Curle, Margaret Crothers	Betty Thain
Marilyn Scott, Judy Barton, Cy Johnson	Jack Trimble
Lillian Turner, Marilyn Scott	Lillian Potten-Turner
Shirley Little	Helen Atkinson Wright
Margaret Crothers	Mary Margaret West

Archival Resources — Campbellford/Seymour Heritage Society
Family History Files
Oral History Files

Chapter 16   Vignettes

Texts

Bagnall, Kenneth. *The Little Immigrants: The Orphans who Came to Canada.* Toronto: Macmillan, 1983.
Berton, Pierre. *My Times: Living with History, 1947–1995.* Toronto: Doubleday Canada Limited, 1995.
Corbett, Gail H. *Barnardo Children.* Peterborough: Woodland Publishing, 1981

Contributors

Margaret Crothers	Craig Beattie and his 'Jenny'
Marilyn Scott	Christmas Light Lady
Gwen Dubay	Slippery Slope
Joanne Simpkin	Pierre Berton and the Local Political Battle

Archival Resources — Campbellford/Seymour Heritage Society
Family History Files
Oral History Files

$\mathcal{I}$ndex